The Routledge Companion to Photography Theory

With newly commissioned essays by some of the leading writers on photography today, this companion tackles some of the most pressing questions about photography theory's direction, relevance, and purpose.

This book shows how digital technologies and global dissemination have radically advanced the pluralism of photographic meaning and fundamentally transformed photography theory. Having assimilated the histories of semiotic analysis and post-structural theory, critiques of representation continue to move away from the notion of original and copy and towards materiality, process, and the interdisciplinary. The implications of what it means to 'see' an image is now understood to encompass not only the optical, but the conceptual, ethical, and haptic experience of encountering an image. The 'fractal' is now used to theorize the new condition of photography as an algorithmic medium and leads us to reposition our relationship to photographs and lend nuances to what essentially underlies any photography theory—that is, the relationship of the image to the real world and how we conceive what that means.

Diverse in its scope and themes, *The Routledge Companion to Photography Theory* is an indispensable collection of essays and interviews for students, researchers, and teachers. The volume also features extensive images, including beautiful colour plates of key photographs.

Mark Durden is an artist, writer, and academic. He has written extensively on contemporary art and photography. Recent books include *Fifty Key Writers on Photography* (2012) and *Photography Today* (2014). With Ian Brown and David Campbell, Durden regularly exhibits as part of the artist group Common Culture. With Campbell, he also recently co-curated a number of substantial exhibitions on art and comedy: *Double Act* (Bluecoat, Liverpool, and the MAC, Belfast, in 2016) and *The Laughable Enigma of Ordinary Life* (Arquipélago, centro de artes contemporâneas, São Miguel, in 2017). Durden is currently Professor of Photography and Director of the European Centre for Documentary Research at the University of South Wales, UK.

Jane Tormey is an Honorary Fellow of Loughborough University. Her writing focuses on the exchange of ideas between art practice and other disciplines, the conflict between aesthetics and political content, and the ways in which aesthetic traditions can be disturbed by and through photographic/filmic practices. Published work includes: "The Ghost in the Image" in Boelderl and Leisch-Kiesl (eds.), *Die Zukunft gehört den Phantomen* (transcript, 2018); *Photographic Realism: Late Twentieth-Century Aesthetics* (2013) and *Cities and Photography* (2012). She is co-editor of *Art, Politics and the Pamphleteer* (forthcoming 2020) and the book series *Radical Aesthetics–Radical Art*.

The Routledge Companion to Photography Theory

Edited by
Mark Durden and Jane Tormey

Routledge
Taylor & Francis Group
LONDON AND NEW YORK

First published 2020 by Routledge
2 Park Square, Milton Park, Abingdon, Oxon OX14 4RN
605 Third Avenue, New York, NY 10017

First issued in paperback 2021

Routledge is an imprint of the Taylor & Francis Group, an informa business

Publisher's Note
The publisher has gone to great lengths to ensure the quality of this reprint but points out that some imperfections in the original copies may be apparent.

British Library Cataloguing in Publication Data
A catalogue record for this book is available from the British Library

Library of Congress Cataloging in Publication Data
Names: Durden, Mark, editor. | Tormey, Jane, editor.
Title: The Routledge companion to photography theory / edited by Mark Durden and Jane Tormey.
Description: New York : Routledge, 2020. | Includes bibliographical references and index
Identifiers: LCCN 2019025081 (print) | LCCN 2019025082 (ebook) |
ISBN 9781138845770 (hbk) | ISBN 9781315727998 (ebk)
Subjects: LCSH: Photography–Philosophy.
Classification: LCC TR183 .R68 2020 (print) | LCC TR183 (ebook) |
DDC 770.1–dc23
LC record available at https://lccn.loc.gov/2019025081
LC ebook record available at https://lccn.loc.gov/2019025082

ISBN 13: 978-1-03-208536-4 (pbk)
ISBN 13: 978-1-138-84577-0 (hbk)

Typeset in Bembo
by Swales & Willis, Exeter, Devon, UK

Contents

Figures

Plates

Contributors

Ariella Azoulay is Professor of Comparative Literature and Modern Culture and Media, Brown University, US. Her publications include: *From Palestine to Israel: A Photographic Record of Destruction and State Formation, 1947–1950* (Pluto Press, 2011); *Civil Imagination: The Political Ontology of Photography* (Verso, 2012); and *The Civil Contract of Photography* (Zone Books, 2008).

Malcolm Barnard is Senior Lecturer in visual culture at Loughborough University. His interests lie in the theories and philosophies of art and design, especially in the areas of fashion, photography, and graphic design.

David Bate is Professor of Photography at the University of Westminster, London, UK. His publications include *Photography: Key Concepts* (Bloomsbury, 2016), *Art Photography* (Tate, 2015), *Photography and Surrealism: Sexuality, Colonialism and Social Dissent* (I.B. Tauris, 2004), the artwork photobook *Zone* (Artwords, 2012), and *Notes on Otherness* (forthcoming, 2019). He is a founding co-editor of *Photographies* (Routledge journal).

Jill Bennett is a Laureate Fellow at the University of New South Wales, author of *Empathic Vision* and *Practical Aesthetics* and founder of *The Big Anxiety*, a festival of mental health. Her multidisciplinary lab uses immersive media to visualize human experience.

Elspeth H. Brown is Associate Professor at the University of Toronto and the Director of the LGBTQ Oral History Digital Collaboratory. She is the author of *Sexual Capital: A Queer History of Modeling, 1909–1983* (Duke University Press, forthcoming) and *The Corporate Eye: Photography and the Rationalization of American Commercial Culture, 1884–1929* (Johns Hopkins, 2005).

Victor Burgin is an artist and writer. He is Professor Emeritus of History of Consciousness at the University of California, Santa Cruz, and Emeritus Millard Chair of Fine Art at Goldsmiths College, University of London. Burgin's more recent theory books include *Parallel Texts: Interviews and Interventions about Art* (2011), *Situational Aesthetics* (2009), and *The Remembered Film* (2004).

David Campany is a writer and curator. He teaches at the University of Westminster.

Justin Carville teaches Historical and Theoretical Studies in Photography at the Institute of Art, Design and Technology, Dun Laoghaire. He is the author of *Photography and Ireland*

(Reaktion, 2011) and is currently working on a book tentatively titled *The Ungovernable Eye: Photography, Ethnography and Race.*

Gerry Coulter (1959–2016) was the founder and editor of the *International Journal of Baudrillard Studies* (*IJBS*) and for more than a decade contributed significantly to the development of the field of Baudrillard Studies. Gerry's primary contribution was twofold. First, he enabled scholarship by others in Baudrillard Studies through three initiatives: the foundation and editing of *IJBS* from January 2004; the online publication of a concordance—*The Baudrillard Index* (2007)—covering almost all of Baudrillard's books published in English; and his last book—*From Achilles to Zarathustra* (2016)—a resource that lists and explains the theorists, artists, intellectuals and others that Baudrillard refers to in most of his books. Second, through his own scholarship in Baudrillard Studies, with two books—*Jean Baudrillard: From the Ocean to the Desert, or the Poetics of Radicality* (2012) and *Art After the Avant-Garde: Baudrillard's Challenge* (2014)—and numerous articles such as the one in this *Companion*, Gerry leaves a legacy of innumerable insights, challenges, opportunities, and directions for future progress in the international and multidisciplinary field of Baudrillard Studies. (Bio written by Richard G. Smith, Editor of the *International Journal of Baudrillard Studies*.)

Todd Cronan is Associate Professor of Art History at Emory University. He is the author of *Against Affective Formalism: Matisse, Bergson, Modernism* (2013) and articles on "previsualization," chance photography, Brecht, Rodchenko, Max Ernst, R. M. Schindler, Richard Neutra, Merleau-Ponty, Santayana, Simmel, and Valéry. He is a founder and editor-in-chief of *nonsite.org*

Mika Elo is Professor in Artistic Research at the University of the Arts Helsinki. His research interests include theory of photographic media and philosophical media theory. He is participating in discussions in these areas in the capacity of curator, artist and researcher.

Ruthie Ginsburg is a fellow researcher at Minerva Humanities Center, Tel Aviv University. Her research, combining political philosophy and critical visual exploration, concentrates on photography and visual practices of human rights organizations working in the Occupied Territories.

Martin Hand is Associate Professor of Sociology at Queen's University, Kingston, Canada. His publications include *Ubiquitous Photography* (2012), *Making Digital Cultures* (2008), *The Design of Everyday Life* (co-authored, 2007), plus articles and essays about visual culture, digitization, technology and consumption.

Robert Hariman is Professor of Rhetoric and Public Culture in the Department of Communication Studies at Northwestern University. His book publications include *Political Style: The Artistry of Power* and two volumes co-authored with John Louis Lucaites, *No Caption Needed: Iconic Photographs, Public Culture, and Liberal Democracy* and *The Public Image: Photography and Civic Spectatorship.*

Thomas Keenan is Director of the Human Rights Project and Associate Professor of Comparative Literature, Bard College, NY. His publications include *Mengele's Skull: The Advent of a Forensic Aesthetics* (with Eyal Weizman, 2012), *New Media, Old Media* (co-edited with

Wendy Chun, 2005), and *Fables of Responsibility: Aberrations and Predicaments in Ethics and Politics* (1997).

John Louis Lucaites is the Samuel L. Becker Distinguished Professor in the Department of Communication Studies at the University of Iowa and the Provost Professor of Rhetoric Emeritus in the Department of English at Indiana University. His publications include *Crafting Equality: America's Anglo-African Word* (with Celeste Michelle Condit) and two books co-authored with Robert Hariman on the relationship between photography and public culture.

Andrea Noble (1968–2017) was associate director and a founding member of the Centre for Advanced Photography Studies at Durham University, where she made field-defining contributions to Latin American studies, photography, and visual culture studies. Andrea's first three books, *Mexican National Cinema* (2005), *Photography and Memory in Mexico: Icons of Revolution* (2010), and *Tina Modotti: Image, Texture, Photography* (2000), revealed how visuality shaped Mexican modernity. Her co-edited volumes, *Photography: Theoretical Snapshots* and *Phototextualities: Intersections of Photography and Narrative*, as well as her countless essays, advanced new paradigms for cross-disciplinary visual analysis. In her most recent work, a book on *Tears in Mexico* and a co-edited volume on the *Cold War Camera*, Andrea shed new light on the shaping of politicized emotional communities and the visual mediation of the global cold war. In her research, mentorship, community collaborations, and, most of all, friendships, she inspired colleagues, artists, and students to explore questions. (Bio written by Thy Phu, 2019.)

Daniel Palmer is a Professor and Associate Dean of Research in the School of Art at RMIT University, Melbourne. His latest book is *Photography and Collaboration: From Conceptual Art to Crowdsourcing* (Bloomsbury, 2017).

Thy Phu is Associate Professor at Western University in Canada. She is the author of two books: *Picturing Model Citizens: Civility in Asian American Visual Culture* is published by Temple University Press, and *Feeling Photography* is a collection of essays co-edited with Elspeth Brown.

Sandra Plummer is Senior Lecturer of Critical and Contextual Studies in Contemporary Art Practice at Duncan of Jordanstone College of Art and Design (DJCAD), University of Dundee. Her PhD examined contemporary photography through the philosophy of Deleuze. She has published her research in *Photographies*, *Photoworks*, *Source*, *Rhizomes*, *Textile*, and *Philosophy of Photography*.

Paula Rabinowitz, Professor Emerita of English at the University of Minnesota, serves as Editor-in-Chief of the *Oxford Research Encyclopedia of Literature*. Her publications include *American Pulp: How Paperbacks Brought Modernism to Main Street* (Princeton University Press, 2014), *They Must Be Represented: The Politics of Documentary* (Verso, 1994) and *Black & White & Noir: America's Pulp Modernism* (Columbia University Press, 2002).

John Roberts is Professor of Art & Aesthetics at the University of Wolverhampton, and the author of a number books including: *The Necessity of Errors* (Verso, 2010), *Photography and Its Violations* (Columbia University Press, 2014), *Revolutionary Time and the Avant-Garde* (Verso,

2015), *Thoughts on an Index Not Freely Given* (Zero Books, 2016) and *The Reasoning of Unreason: Universalism, Capitalism and Disenlightenment* (Bloomsbury, 2018).

Molly Rogers is a writer and independent scholar. She is author of *Delia's Tears: Race, Science and Photography in Nineteenth-Century America* (New Haven and London: Yale, 2010).

Nancy Ann Roth is an independent researcher who has translated three of Flusser's books from German to English: *Into the Universe of Technical Images* (2011b), *Does Writing Have a Future?* (2011a) and *Gestures* (2014b). She is based in Cornwall, UK.

Daniel Rubinstein is a Reader in Philosophy and the Image at Central Saint Martins, University of the Arts, London. His book *Fragmentation of the Photographic Image in Digital Culture* will examine the radically fractal nature of images with a specific link to desire and memory (Routledge, forthcoming). He is the founding editor of the journal *Philosophy of Photography*.

Ashley Scarlett is Assistant Professor in the School of Critical and Creative Studies at the Alberta College of Art and Design. Her research explores aestheticizations of the digital, with recent publications appearing in *Parallax* and *Digital Culture & Society*.

Conohar Scott is a lecturer in photographic theory and a practising artist at the University of Lincoln. Conohar's research interests include exploring the representation of industrial pollution in photography and the application of art as a tool for advancing environmental advocacy and participatory democracy.

Shep Steiner is Assistant Professor of Contemporary Art at the University of Manitoba. His most recent text on photography is "Mirror on the Wall: Photography, Logos, and the Problem of Writing in Ken Lum," *Asian Diasporic Visual Cultures and the Americas*, vol. 2, no. 3 (fall 2016).

Hilde Van Gelder is Professor of Modern and Contemporary Art History and Head of Art History at the KU Leuven. She is co-director of the Lieven Gevaert Research Centre for Photography, Art and Visual Culture and editor of the Lieven Gevaert Series (Leuven University Press) and *Image [&] Narrative* (Open Humanities Press).

Jeff Wall is an influential Canadian artist, known particularly for his back-lit photographic tableaux, which are presented in galleries at a scale that demands physical engagement. Following the aesthetic reductions of conceptualism, Wall embraced the pictorial and fictional possibilities of photography. His exhibition profile is extensive and international.

Kathrin Yacavone is Assistant Professor in French at the University of Nottingham. Her research focuses on modern French literature, thought, and visual culture; literary theory and cultural studies; and the history and theory of photography. She is the author of *Benjamin, Barthes and the Singularity of Photography* (2012) and editor of *Photography in Contemporary French and Francophone Cultures* (2014).

Marta Zarzycka is a researcher studying user experience for a tech company in Austin, Texas, and was formerly an Assistant Professor at Utrecht University, the Netherlands. Her book *Gendered Tropes in War Photography: Mothers, Mourners, Soldiers* was published by Routledge in 2016.

Introduction

Mark Durden and Jane Tormey

Any account of photography today comes up with what Joanna Zylinska has aptly referred to as the "mathematical sublime"—the hundreds of millions of photos uploaded to Facebook every day, the billions of photographs on Instagram, the trillions of pictures that have been taken so far (Zylinska 2017: 19). In light of photography's ubiquity and the fact it is now embedded in our day-to-day lives, what aspects of thinking about photography have been neglected? How has thinking about photography changed? As Thy Phu, Elspeth Brown, and Andrea Noble argue in the first essay in this book, it is only recently that the specific impact of feeling on the study of photography has received serious attention. The importance of such discussions is how they reveal the ways in which responses to photography that entail emotions are still social and cultural. Emotions are not simply 'inner' or individual, but are shaped by the prevailing dominant cultural norms in which individuals find themselves. For Susie Linfield, for the last forty years critical judgment has had a negative relation to photography, or, as Robert Hariman and John Lucaites point out, what has been excluded is how it "articulates civil society, the public sphere, democratic citizenship, human rights, and other institutions and ideas that define modernity." So we can also speak of a shift in attitude and understanding of photography, away from negation and towards an exploration of how it can "better serve progressive ideals" (Hariman and Lucaites).

In 2001, Geoffrey Batchen asked whether the history of photography can leave behind the primacy of the photograph's "taking" and confront the complex trajectory of its construction as a system of representation: "Can we at last abandon our investment in originary moments and dare to articulate instead the temporal and ontological convolutions that make photography the strange and fascinating phenomenon that it is" (Batchen 2001: 106). In talking about the manner in which photography is habitually considered, his statement implies an impasse in how we theorize photography. In James Elkins' *Photography Theory* (2006), contributors hovered around the impact of digitalization on the nature and specificity of the medium. As early as 2008, Robin Kelsey and Blake Stimson suggested that discussions of the particular nature of photographic indexicality were exhausted and that photography, owing to its availability via cell phone and social networks, had begun to turn toward its capacity "to remap the interstices of everyday affiliation" (Kelsey and Stimson 2008: xxiii). If photography no longer retains its special status as a discrete medium, what then is the purpose of photography theory? That question assumes the value of essentialness and an ontology that distances itself from the complexities of reality. Certainly, what emerges from this collection of essays, which differs from the assumptions of essentialness, is the embedded nature of the photograph in everyday events and its social commentary.

This book presents critical approaches to photography theory with regard to current debates, controversies, and questions, as well as consideration of photography theory's direction, relevance, and purpose. We asked contributors to consider how questions about photography have shifted in response to cultural theories and philosophies more generally and as a consequence, for example, of digitalization. Although the book is structured in three sections, Aesthetics, Politics, and Theories, it was notable how interdependent these aspects were. For example, nearly all contributors talk about relationships between photography and politics in some way or other. Meaningfully categorizing these essays as being principally about theory, or about aesthetics or politics, presents problems, as one can only approach the complex and mutable forms of 'photography' from multiple perspectives. The difficulty is best illustrated in Gerry Coulter's celebration of Jean Baudrillard's photographs, which are testament to his thinking about the relationship of subject to object and the world. In placing his essay in "Aesthetics," we recognize an emphasis in this volume on the intriguing relationship between theory and practice on many levels. Similarly, or conversely, we place Kathrin Yacavone's expansion of Roland Barthes' immersion in the relationship between the image and writing, and his increasing concern with 'affect' as a necessary consideration of aesthetics in practice, in the "Theories" section. Thus, this interdependence underlines our assumption that practices *theorize* rather than merely illustrate theories.

Rather than summarizing each and every chapter, this introduction uses essay content as a prompt for reflection on the significant aspects of theories, and the condition and direction of contemporary photographic practices. Authors' names in brackets indicate the source of comment and/or the essays in which further discussion can be found. While dealing with different ways in which different uses of photography have been framed in terms of concepts and ideas, in recognition of the origin of the word theory in the Greek *theoria*, which means "beholding" or "viewing," this book also contains essays that address the ways in which photographs have been beheld and viewed. The "Aesthetics" section encompasses a range of interdisciplinary perspectives on practices, in all sorts of contexts, such as the psychological and cognitive aspects of viewing and remembering (Bennett). There is little discussion of form in the single image (Wall and Campany), whereas the book frequently discusses social practices (Bennett, Ginsburg, Keenan, Durden) or work in series (Plummer, Steiner, Tormey) and uses of photography in social media and public culture (Hariman and Lucaites, Hand and Scarlett). David Bate's discussion of Jacques Rancière's ideas is helpful in explaining the direction of this first section: Rancière's return to the earlier term *aesthesis*, which predates preoccupations with beauty or the sublime, introduces a broader framework within which to locate the sensory experience of photographic images (Bate). In the "Theories" section, we sought to include different perspectives from which to view practice in order to review how visual strategies used in practice can be seen to characterize or reflect developments in philosophical discussion. Some contributions in the "Theories" section provide an exegesis of philosophical attitudes to photography (Barnard, Roberts) and do not relate much to the practice of photography, whereas others are very much concerned with the subtleties of authorship (Palmer) or the development of new philosophies emerging from the practice of photography itself (Rubinstein, Elo).

Essays underline the changing nature of the photographic apparatus and the physical and conceptual expansion in our relationships to/with photographs since the development of digital technologies and their impact on communication. The term 'apparatus' is used here to introduce an understanding of the photographic as an expanded system of relations that reaches beyond the material device of a camera to encompass, for example, algorithmic systems and the political implications of the production and dissemination of imagery. Having assimilated the histories of semiotic analysis and post-structural theory, critiques of representation continue to move away from the notion of original and copy and towards materiality, process, and the interdisciplinary. These appear in different guises throughout the book: civil imagination, non-representational theory, neuropsychology. Photographic representations are value-ridden and as such can be framed in the light of different theories and viewed in very different ways. In Jacques Derrida's terms, representations of reality are already structured and determined by existing cultural and institutional frames (Derrida 1981, 26); in Gilles Deleuze's terms, the limits of representation are extended by integrating "the depth of difference in itself" (Deleuze 1994, 262). Rather than a means of comparison for measuring resemblance to something, difference recognizes the particularity of individual things; Deleuze's theory of difference encourages a focus on the singular experience. A thread running through the book across the many perspectives suggests that the dominance of visual representation is giving way to a rethinking in terms of the context and production of engaging with the image. The implications of what it means to 'see' an image are now understood to encompass not only the optical, but the conceptual, ethical, and haptic experience of encountering an image. Significantly, the remit for 'photography theory' is extended and less insular.

Digital expansions

It is clear that the old representational model of photography is inadequate to take account of photography in terms of its digital expansion, which has shifted focus away from photography's essentialness and privileging of "the private moment over the public, the origin over the journey, the aesthetic over the social" (Batchen 2001: 105–6). Digital media and their expanding perspectives force a rethinking of photography's "temporal and ontological convolutions" in order to negotiate photography's everyday social status and our neglect of "the *making* of photographs" (Batchen 2001: 105–6; our emphasis). Countering the premise of momentary capture, digital photography generates the continuous transformation of reality via infinitely proliferating code. Online communication provides the possibility of simultaneous distribution and access to global public networks. It has the potential to invite immediate multidirectional communication, and social media platforms offer an infinite process of exchange without necessarily an end product. By extension, images, and how we are able to interact with them, become central to how we frame the world, so much so that our interface with the digital image engenders a different level of relationship to time and space, and thereby our subjectivity. Hand and Scarlett discuss how digital personalized photography, particularly via smartphone and social media, has reconfigured the temporality of the image and the possibilities of temporal experience. The photographic moment has become "the 'incessant' visual communication of 'moments' (e.g. Snapchat)." As it "takes place (almost) all the time it intervenes in the routines and rhythms of everyday life" (Hand and Scarlett).

In this world of online image exchange, both the uses *for* the photograph and the viewer's experience *of* the photograph are potentially extended and prolonged by means of participation and addition. The 'fractal', which theorizes the new condition of photography as an algorithmic medium, is upheld as a more accurate way of accounting for the dispersal of photography and how photography functions today (Rubinstein, Elo). Where the window on the world model is allied with passivity, fractal photography can be seen as an active seizing "through algorithmic processing." In practical terms, 'tagging' embodies the discontinuous logics of digital processing and the networked afterlife of images (Elo). Tagging in digital networks has led to the shift from snapshot culture, made of fixed digital documents, to what Elo refers to as "tagshot culture," dynamic data objects. The notion of fractal photography challenges long-held views about our thinking about photography by rejecting "its reliance on universal totalities that are unable to account for the fragmented, discontinuous, non-binary, and multi-gendered realities of contemporary life" (Rubinstein).

The kind of transformation of reality afforded by digital technologies has provoked alternative views to the representational discourses that have dominated photography theory. A nonrepresentational view emphasizes the *active* properties of digital photography and its capacity to construct experience, distinct from the visual aspects of the still and passive image. As a consequence of its different material structures, photographs no longer merely picture the *visible* manifestations of power structures, and any critique of photographic representation must now account for the mechanisms of production that are *not* visible. Nonrepresentational discourse asserts the non-visible over the dominance of vision and its correlative notion that reality is out there somewhere to be revealed and made visible. The aesthetics of digital processing and the fractal image is one of immersive immateriality, so that the 'self-sufficient' image is unraveled entirely: content, function, and meaning are merged in processes of construction and distribution that cannot be equated with rational representation (Rubinstein). Reconceptions of photography as a result of digital processes and computation open up possibilities of participatory communication, as in pressing the 'like' button. Rubinstein argues for the "political potential of the digital image," which can construct experience and includes the institutions and processes that govern the use of the image.

Discussions of digital technologies have emphasized the digital image's condition of multiplicity that embodies "instantaneity and simultaneity" in a potentially constant process of ongoing network exchange (Rubinstein et al. 2013: 9–11). In a counterargument, the dispersal and movement and traffic in images are not new to digital culture, which could be said to merely speed up a process that was already integral to photography. For example, Molly Roger's text shows us the movement and traffic in a nineteenth-century image portrait, and Paula Rabinowitz shows how the image of the atomic bomb mushroom cloud was appropriated and used by all sections of the media to such an extent that it became "an icon of desire and love" and "central to acculturating citizens to mass destruction in the postwar years" (Rabinowitz). But, besides the reach and speed of dispersal, and as a result of its production and dissemination, the digital image has assumed an expansive social function. No longer limited by human vision or the possibilities of visual representation, digital technology has dispersed the experience of photography (Elo) and fundamentally shifted its role. The photographic event is part of an extensive physical and virtual network, encompassing a mesh of technologies and social interactions—an "assemblage," to draw upon Deleuze and Guattari's term (2004: 3–28). As photography becomes an instrumental component of human space and exchange, digital distributions of photography significantly change our apprehension and contribute to a form of democratized knowledge created through searching and participation by which viewers can become authors (Palmer). No longer occurring in isolation, but shared and consumed by communities, the viewing of images on the computer screen is an act of reaction and duration; *experience* of the image in relation to time is governed by this continuous creation of networks of sense and meaning contributed by participant spectators (Keenan).

We highlight the significance of digital image production here in two respects: a photograph potentially transformed by online digital intervention can be understood as generating a prolonged process of production and meaning, rather than a definitive record; the process of producing (*making*) photographs, which is complex and dependent on context and the circumstances of all involved in that production, gives emphasis to the social over the aesthetic.

Temporal expansions

Derrida's concern with temporality (Barnard) provides a philosophical grounding for the topical theorizing of the 'fractal' (Rubinstein, Elo) and for a consideration of photography that privileges the *making* of photographs over the *taking* (Batchen 2001). Derrida's reframing of perception establishes a fundamental premise that underlines much contemporary discussion of photography—that the photograph does not start or finish in the instant: "In perception there are already operations of selection, of exposure time, of filtering, of development: the psychic apparatus functions also *like*, or *as*, an apparatus of inscription and the photographic archive" (Derrida 2010: 15; original emphasis). Any perception, whether of an image or the world, takes time and is not of one instant, but "duration" (Derrida 2010: 10–2). Perception of an image is a complex, dynamic process of looking back, via memory perhaps, and projecting forward, anticipating possibilities. The process of photography extends, in advance of pressing the shutter, and proceeds through subsequent display, interpretation, and use of the image; it is a "photographic event" and *active* (Derrida 1998). Derrida's description of perception as a "psychic apparatus" and of the "photographic event" as happening when it is thought of or looked at, rather than as a definitive moment or object (document), extends our relation to the image (digital or otherwise). His challenge to spatial and temporal logic in many of his references to the photograph anticipates later discussions of the online digital image, which places its apprehension beyond the visual (Rubinstein et al. 2013: 8–10). The digital image in particular, and its prolonged process of production and meaning, has duration and is not of an instant or a definitive record. The process of *making* an image online accentuates the dependence on circumstance and social production, which extends far beyond what is visible. Digital screen images can be seen as more fleeting and ephemeral, or as more virtually immersive than physically separate. Adding another dimension to the photograph's materiality, viewing images on screen is not a tactile experience as there is no edge or tangible threshold that is characteristic of viewing an image framed or on paper—as an object. But, at the same time, our engagement with the touch screen is now a physical act as we use our fingers and thumbs to swipe, enlarge, reduce, send, and delete images. However it is described, the nature of its materiality and of the physical sensation in apprehending the digital image is different; it is a "photographic event."

Where Derrida contributes a repositioning of how we approach our understanding of representation and the complexity and uncertainty involved in our apprehension, Deleuze and Félix Guattari have moved us toward a re-engagement with sensation and affect. And as affect does not 'mean' any *thing*, we are forced to ask—what is happening? Affects are events of duration that are more about experience than signification and representation. What this brings to our thinking about photography is a concern for experience itself, beyond an understanding of signs, a questioning of these signs and what moves against or confuses these signs. The nonlinear structure of Deleuze and Guattari's *A Thousand Plateaus* demonstrates an alternative approach that does not strive for interpretation of some underlying reality or grounding principle. The focus on possibility and imagining over fact is indicative of a way of thinking that has contributed to a fundamental change in attitude to the way images are used, and in reading and sensorily encountering images (Tormey, Phu, Brown, and Noble). Rather than the compulsion to generalize experience into something that can be universally shared, and rather than a transcendent (self-sufficient) image that aims to explain or translate experience, the insistence on difference extends the apprehension of images. As eventful space, an image provokes thought and experience of qualitative differences that extend over time, so that thinking about a photograph encompasses all that is brought to mind and all that can be imagined about it. Deleuze's thinking challenges the reductive structure of model and copy, of cause and *effect*, and of subjectivity. Sarah Pickering's *Public Order* series, as discussed by Sandra Plummer, can be seen to present "simulacral-phantasms," in accord with the Deleuzian concept of the simulacrum, which destabilizes and throws into disarray the distinction between model and copy (Plummer). In recording realms of artifice and simulation, Pickering's photographs are documents that undermine representation and expose photography's role in the construction of socio-economic stereotypes. Photography's relationship to the model can be seen as destabilized by drawing attention to readymade constructed worlds, the streets and buildings of a fake town, used for training the police, military forces, and emergency services. What is happening in Pickering's photography echoes a theme that runs through many essays in this book—that of rupturing the assumptions associated with, or the conditions for, what we believe the referent to be.

Countering a concern for establishing identity via resemblance, Deleuze gives emphasis to difference as a positive attribute, rather than being assumed to be negative. It is an approach that undermines the whole premise of truth and falsity and disassembles the notion of simulacra. If what is central is to determine 'true identity', then falsity and simulacra are a problem. If, on the other hand, the focus is the potential of difference, then this concern is undermined. By privileging the different qualities over the common characteristics, it develops what is understood as representation. For Deleuze, the simulacrum is not a resemblance or mere copy, but is itself—a new thing; the real is not lost, as Baudrillard suggests, but is becoming other (Plummer). This is easier to understand if we think in terms of events and creative processes, rather than definitive (original) things. Meanings emerge from processes of copying and imagining, as well as from material substance; any one *thing* is its expectation, what happens to it, and its future possibilities. In this way, the changing condition of experience is understood as a non-fixed state of 'becoming' rather than identity, just as encounters with a photograph can be seen in terms of process and are not fixed. Not limited to a notion of the photographic instant, photography is determined by what it *does*, rather than what it is. Translating this approach to images is complicated by the photograph, which is assumed to 'copy' the real world. We know images are just one facet of the world: not copies, but extensions of its properties and possibilities—not anything other than themselves.

François Laruelle provides an updated metaphor for the photograph: "A photo is more than a window or an opening, it is an infinite open, an unlimited universe from vision to the pure state, with neither mirror nor window" (Laruelle 2011: 107). His conception of "non-photography," more than questioning photography's relation to the real, emphasizes the distance between the photograph and the objects depicted. Aligning the photograph with a fractal system, irreducible to representation, he rejects what we generally associate with photography—concerns with the real and the social world—and positions all photographs as "absolute fictions" in the sense that they are ideologically blank or incapable of any reality, agency or influence (Laruelle 2011: 74). Seemingly at odds with our assumptions, this discussion perhaps points to self-perpetuating preoccupations for photography theory that rely on received notions of representation: the degree to which photography reliably informs us of the real world; the manner in which photography is culturally embedded; the tension between an active and constructive representation and one that merely replicates. In his attempt to divorce philosophy as a science from ideology and the interpretations of the humanities, Laruelle separates photography from its subjective operations of analysis or social engagement. Laruelle's non-photography can be seen as an illustration of his thinking: in rejecting photography's representational alliance with the world, he explains a philosophical liberation from what we assume to be subject to the "historic and causal trajectories" that predetermine our thinking (Roberts). Laruelle's non-photography forces a fundamental shift in thinking about our relationship to objects—away from a position that assumes that we, as subjects, constitute the world and are separate from the objects in it.

Just as Deleuze and Guattari's consideration of life beyond the limits of the human subject has contributed to subsequent developments in 'post-human' thinking, John Roberts suggests that Laruelle's philosophy can be seen to share a rethinking of the object and of representation with that of speculative realism. As a brief philosophical movement, speculative realism included a diversity of positions that attempted to disrupt what is thought of as realism and encompassed object-oriented ontology as a key line of thought, "a bluntly *realist* philosophy," which "holds that the external world exists independently of human awareness" (Harman 2018a: 10; original emphasis). As an example, Graham Harman asserts that, as the real object is autonomous, it cannot be wholly discovered and is always eluding us. In a relation with the object (he includes artworks), the spectator and the object are combined, the sensual qualities fuse with the object—it is a new object of which the spectator becomes part. Harman rejects the formalist assumption that "the autonomous art object must be devoid of human ingredients or participants" (Harman 2018b: 119). Art is "essentially *theatrical*, a compound object made up of the (usually) physical work plus the spectator" (Harman 2018b: 119; original emphasis). Harman is also useful for recognizing what Baudrillard's ideas share with object-oriented theories. Baudrillard draws attention to "the specific relation between the sensual object and the beholder," which he terms "seduction" (Harman 2016: 129–30). The notion of seduction by the object effects a reversal of a subject-centered conception of the world with that of the object, which explains his consistent fascination with the photograph whereby "it is the object which thinks us." Where the photograph has been understood to confirm our relationship to objects by representing them *for* the subject (photographer), Baudrillard describes the photographic act as a duel in which the subject (photographer) might "disappear as a subject" and be defined by the object (Baudrillard 1999: 145–52).

Such attempts to achieve a "fundamental re-correlation of subject and object" are significant for thinking about photography, as they question whether our understanding of reality is distorted by our immersion in it—rather than our distance/separation from it (Roberts). The complex relationships between visual appearance and knowledge, and the contradictions inherent in our immersion in the world that we view and our interpretations of it, are heightened via photography. Questioning the division between appearance and reality upsets an aesthetic that is bound by photography's singular access to the world outside and what it signifies for us. An ocular representational worldview understands it through pictures, which reduce the world in standardized forms of replication: "image/model, subject/object, figure/ground" (Rubinstein). Seen as the means to realize reality, photography and its aesthetics derive from the premise of revelation—of what is there, but not seen, until that moment of 'capture'.

Photography can either be seen to mediate the world for us or it can be seen as "absolute fiction." If photographs are, as Laruelle asserts, incapable of any reality, agency or influence, what does this separation from photography's social engagement with the world bring to a consideration of how we look at the real world or social documentary photography? Where does this disruption of representational order leave us with regard to 'picturing' the real world?

Documentary expansions

Abstract theories may lead us to reposition our relationship to photographs (Laruelle, Derrida, Deleuze) and lend nuances to what essentially underlies any photography theory—that is, the relationship of the image to the real world and how we conceive what that means. Consideration of this relationship returns us to persistent points of conflict with regard to photographic practice: one being attitudes to the document and/or art, and the other the capacity of the image for political efficacy and/or the advantages over language. The dialogue around aesthetics and photography between David Campany and Jeff Wall serves to introduce fundamental distinctions between 'art' and the photographic specialism of 'documentary'. Here, their exchange is insightful about the limits of the "essayistic" documentary model, which involves "too much subservience to the motif or subject matter." Studying photography in the context of fine art, Wall did not have to engage with the "institutional network of journalism," and it is against this that one understands the importance and centrality of the single image in Wall's work, which characterizes uses of photography that distance the "picture" from its subject matter. With this kind of artistic fabrication in mind, the contentious suggestion is made that the mnemonic dimension is no longer appropriate in considering such art photography (Campany).

Allied to this, Victor Burgin's interview with Hilde Van Gelder brings to the fore arguments concerning the relationship between language and the notion of 'pure visuality', and the relationship between art and politics more specifically. Burgin's stance is consistently critical of art with pretensions to be effectively political, and even more so of practices that assume a semblance of criticality and superficially engage with politics. He raises problems with the way in which the artists' turn to documentary in the past quarter century does not depart from conventional media forms but merely calls upon the "same general knowledge and interpretative capabilities I deploy when I read a newspaper." He states, for example, that documenting people at work does not "'take on' the issue of the globalisation of the labour force" and can only illustrate it: "I find something profoundly distasteful in the spectacle of workers having a last increment of value extracted from them by 'political artists' parading their moral narcissism in pursuit of their careers." He argues that, if they do no more than recycle what is already available in mass media, they provide nothing and their work will "remain irrelevant *as art*." Burgin sees instead that the critical power of an artistic practice is to work against "the consensual categories and descriptions" (citing Rancière) of mainstream media, providing an occasion for "the critical speech of others to emerge."

This view contrasts with the legacy of Allan Sekula, which continues to influence the political field of photography and offers an alternative practice to *either* the "pure visuality" of picture *or* the transparent evidence of document. Sekula's emphasis on a political understanding over notions of humanism—or art—contrasts with Burgin's assertion that art cannot be politically effective. For Burgin, Benjamin Buchloh's term "critical realism," which he used to describe Sekula's work, is inaccurate and a contradiction in terms. But, taking different directions with regard to the use of photography, Burgin and Sekula each reiterate

Bertolt Brecht's observation regarding the limitations in photographing complex political operations, such as a factory. Each have contributed to changes in the assumptions of photographic practice and the contrasting positions between art and documentary: a suspicion of the "self-sufficient" image (Sekula) that uses political content for aesthetic purpose (Burgin); an understanding that subjective reality (psychic or ideological) must always be part of any 'objective' reality (Burgin); the significance of context in the choice of subject matter and in the understanding of the viewer's construction of meaning (Sekula). Burgin identifies the functional role of photography and the use or misuse of its capacity to provide a semblance of the real world as the central issue. His questioning of the possibility of effective documentary in order to make political adjustment signals the significance of the context for that documentation. One could say that the level of criticality is dependent on the manner in which the image refers to the social and political implications of any complex situation. One could also say that Sekula demonstrated this throughout his work: that the photograph is dependent on the conditions in which it is read and the assumptions of its context. Reviewing Sekula's fascination with the possibility of "instrumental images" without rhetorical structure, Thomas Keenan introduces the perspective of the performative nature of photography, as an event that requires a number of procedures. Further consideration of Sekula's "manifestation of interest," that all images communicate a point of view, lends another way to understand the digital photograph as agent, as its technologies incorporate the necessity of a reading mediated by circumstance (Keenan).

There is an undoubted tension in photography theory here. On one hand we have those like Rubinstein who, insisting that representation needs to be subject to critique, oppose the "privileged" documentary model with the notion of fractal photography. Then we have an approach such as Keenan's, coming from a concern for the politics of human rights, which re-evaluates the documentary mode and advocates a forensic sensibility to indicate the commitment to evidence and testimony. Keenan draws upon the idea of a "counter-forensics," a term used by Sekula in an essay on Susan Meiselas's work in Kurdistan. The manner of documentation used in the *Kurdistan* project encompasses seemingly 'objective' observations of its subjects and their circumstance, alongside a collective archive made by those same subjects. It shows how photography can be used as both an instrument of surveillance by an oppressor state and as a way of challenging that same imperial power: "the exhumation and identification of the anonymised ('disappeared') bodies of the oppressor state's victims becomes the key to a process of political resistance and mourning" (Keenan). For Keenan, counter-forensics redeploys a different notion of humanism that engages photographic archives not only as sites of abstract equivalence, but also as sites for political struggle. Hariman and Lucaites also offer a positive view of the productive and democratic potentialities of photography in which their model is realist and the photography itself is documentary, but the site of display and its social impact become important. They discuss how the photograph is positioned within the temporary exhibition and the ways in which photography now constitutes a variant of Andre Malraux's "Museum without Walls," as evinced by the attention to exhibitions of photographs in public spaces and their political possibilities in terms of their community uses (see also Tormey).

Held up as a problem for documentary by Sekula, humanism is conceived in terms of the way in which documentary entails a celebration of an abstract humanity, "the dignity of the passive victim." Mark Durden addresses the ways in which this humanist model is tested in many contemporary practices that expand the documentary form, by being "responsive to the disruptive and 'deviant' force of the referent." Countering the appraisal of "passive victim" or the self-sufficiency of the singular moment, there is a reorientation towards the subject in the photograph, as with Meiselas's work. Photographers are adopting strategies that confuse our familiar expectation of the document as reliable witness by, for example, the introduction of elements of fiction, or by deploying a conceptual framework of systems photography, an archival logic, such as we see with Joachim Schmid's appropriated images showing women photographed by a serial killer and Luca Santese and Arianna Arcara's appropriations of found photographs, which speak of the racialized history of Detroit. Here "the aesthetic is integral to their politics" (Durden). A critical target for Shep Steiner, in his playful reading of Max Becher and Andrea Robbins' work, is the trigger analogy of the moment, allied with modernist photography and John Szarkowski. Becher and Robbins present a critique of religious conservatism and the American narratives derived from western genre films and television—a kind of "investigative journalism" (Steiner). Their archive mode is one of slow cataloguing—a concern with often volatile subject matter in which stereotypes are disrupted with insistent photographic acts of repetition.

The possibility of art photography being a form of "investigative journalism" perhaps depends on the degree to which the photographic 'reality' makes the context and circumstance visible. Insisting on one model or the other as being better or worse relies on upholding the essentialness of the medium, rather than the differential, and perpetuates a reductive conception of photography (Hariman and Lucaites). In 2019, the distinction between "art world documentary" and "other documentary work" (Burgin) is not perhaps so clear, or useful. Artists, such as Walid Raad (Lebanon), Emily Jacir (Palestine), Ravi Agarwal (India), Yto Barrada (Morocco), Ursula Biemann and Alfredo Jaar (in Africa), do not dissociate themselves from the ethical responsibilities associated with journalism. The encounter with their subject matter is not second hand, and they conduct their own investigations or work alongside other researchers. The notion of politics being integral to the aesthetic can be seen in the counter-forensics promoted by Forensic Architecture.

Ariella Azoulay has argued against practices having to distinguish between being political or aesthetic and proposes a framework for discussing photographs that regards them as made up of "complex actions that exist simultaneously in several dimensions." Judgments of images as being one or the other assume that the aesthetic or the political are attributes of the image, and that it can be "devoid of stylistic components," which it is not. Rather that reducing what is seen in the image "to the photographer's intention," the image should enable us "as spectators to re-position ourselves" and "let us be engaged with its happening, its victims, our fellow citizens" (Azoulay 2010: 242–57).

Political expansions

As can be seen in Ruthie Ginsburg's case study, any 'reality' has many facets, so that photographs showing the "care-giving" activity of the non-governmental organization Physicians for Human Rights, Israel, not only expose victims' suffering to the public, but also violate the rights of those represented (Ginsburg). Here it can be seen that the image is both constructed by the reality depicted and contributes to the construction of that reality. Much more than a simple depiction, other factors than its referential functions are essential to a photograph's meaning and effect. Tormey's examination of photography projects that attempt to represent complex political situations, such as war and atrocity, considers Judith Butler's argument that the circumstances that determine the image—the 'frame'—necessitate more attention. Butler asks: "which reality is it that is represented? And how does the frame circumscribe what will be called reality?" (2009: 85). If the photograph not only *depicts* an event, but *augments* that event by means of its subsequent dissemination and display, then that display becomes part of its production; it potentially changes how the reality of the event is understood.

Discussed from an ethical point of view, the photograph's presence, besides the mechanical framing by the camera, looks back to the intentions or circumstances of its making and forwards to its continuing production of meaning through processes of dissemination. So, for example, in giving political attention to how photographs circulate or "migrate," war photography has to be reviewed in light of its dispersal and the attention paid to screens and the context of display (Tormey, Zarzycka). Zarzycka discusses the "digital volatility" of image migration that has changed the conditions of spectatorship. A disregard for specific context can develop in the process of images' dispersal and mediation, to the extent that their significance can be transgressed and distorted. Azoulay's "civil imagination" forces us to think of photography 'beyond representation' in ethical terms and besides the presence of the camera, which is always implied. In these terms, the visual encounter is always anticipated, "regardless of whether an image is produced or preserved" (Phu, Brown, and Noble). On another level, the "civil contract" must include more than a passing acknowledgment of the individual person in a photograph. As much as photographs are now dispersed, "decontextualized and recontextualized" (Hariman and Lucaites), there is still need to work on their "historical contingency" and to give ethical consideration to the individual (Rogers, Zarzycka). Rogers rethinks the term 'atrocity photograph' in relation to an image in which the atrocity-event, although not visible in the picture, played a part in its production—an 1861 commercial studio portrait of Cynthia Ann Parker cradling her young daughter, taken shortly after she was forcibly 'recaptured' by Texas Rangers from the Comanche. Rogers extends discussion beyond a photograph of Parker as cypher for the Pease River Massacre, or for mother and child. Giving us narratives connected to the photograph, re-animating and repositioning it to tell of the violence that underlies it, Rogers demonstrates Parker's specific history as different and, in this respect, bereft of sentimentality.

For Azoulay, the photograph has been overly identified with the photographer. Instead, what is important is the way in which photography presents traces of an event. What went before and after the photograph was taken becomes central, who is photographed, and how we receive those depictions. For Azoulay, historical work aslant to the dominant histories, such as that of Rogers, signals an expanded field of research that has opened up a political dimension. If one takes Azoulay's reorientation of photography to a civil contract, it is a phenomenological approach that considers the photograph as a product of exchange. Conceiving of the political implications of the photograph as a product of exchange is underlined by online digital production, which facilitates access to those social processes in which the image is embedded—the 'frame'. Such conceptions of the embedded alliance of photographic depiction, with the conditions and responsibilities associated with its production, can be seen in extreme contrast to Laruelle's abstract discussion of photography. Where the image has been used for the certainty of witness and evidence, it is now part of a system of 'opening' that is in a continuous process of exchange—a different sort of 'window'.

Aesthetic expansions

Many of the practices that are discussed in this volume directly engage with ethical implications and require a different sort of reading (Durden, Steiner, Tormey). Significantly, ethical content can be seen to drive much of the development in photographic practices by means of their strategic structure and the treatment of subject matters, to the extent that the direction of criteria in which politics and ethical concerns predominate reconfigures the parameters of 'aesthetics'.

Debates that focus on the relationship between art and politics anticipate Rancière's observations about the dissident voice that aligns art with politics—in Burgin's terms, "offering an alternative to the media"—and the (aesthetic) ways that give form to reality by refiguring that reality in ways that do not conform to the "'normal' order of things" (Rancière 2010: 35). As photography has become a complex mesh of practices, theories such as Rancière's broaden the perspective with which to think about photography. Rancière's theories help to "loosen the essentialist definitions of 'photography'" and identify different discursive directions; they introduce or validate a different emphasis for looking at practice (Bate). Ignoring traditional divisions, such as what constitutes high or low art, and art or documentary photography, Rancière addresses different modes of practice and mixes up questions of value. His 'regimes' problematize the more traditional categories of aesthetics as he configures them differently and in relation to their functions and how art operates, rather than its subject matter (Bate). His premise of 'dissensus' promotes the possibility of art (and the use of photographs) to reconfigure normative processes and consensual understanding. Bate's examination of Rancière's discussion of 'dissensus' and the 'political' functions of photography that work through "their aesthetic operations" helps us to reposition a photography aesthetic that engages with the social and political.

As parameters for aesthetic operations change, so does the aesthetic 'object'. In this non-essentialist engagement, practices are increasingly presented as 'projects' rather than 'objects', and, in consequence, besides visual documents, multifaceted projects can include collated archives and scientific interpretations (see Misrach in Scott). Such documentations are not simplistic. Relinquishing the primacy of "the private moment" (Batchen 2001), they often use strategies that minimize authorial voice by presenting the artist's work democratically alongside content made by the 'subjects', as in Meiselas's *Kurdistan*, or by collaborating with people from other disciplines. For example, photographers, working with activist and autonomous groups such as citizen scientists, can potentially bring about an awareness of environmental ethics (Scott). Describing authorship as having been in a constant process of decentering since the birth of the medium, Daniel Palmer reiterates Vilém Flusser's observation that photographers "are effectively enslaved to the dictates of its program" (Palmer). Authorship, Palmer argues, necessarily responds to its technical developments, of greater automatism and intelligence. He discusses ways in which artists working with found photographs, such as Patrick Pound, and the selfie's ultimate severance from meaningfully composed individualized accounts of the world acknowledge the decentered status of the creative photographer. Todd Cronan offers a valuable reworking of assumptions about aesthetics and authorship associated with modernist conceptions of photography. Reconsidering the assumptions behind Minor White's theory of "pre-visualization," which was "anything but an account of inner intention being projected onto external matter," he argues that White believed the photographer needed to "become something like a super-audience to oneself." Exploring ideas about photography at the same time that the minimalists declared the artist and work less important than the viewer's encounter with the artwork, White's ideas resonate with a contemporary democratization of authorship.

One could say that photographic practice has taken an ethical and discursive turn over an affective one. Alternatively, Phu, Brown, and Noble's historical and theoretical overview of the relationship between emotions and photography establishes how the 'affective turn' has influenced photography studies and the impact of photographic performance; the simultaneous properties of the photograph can present material fact, psychical fiction, and ideological perspective. Championing an alternative to a reductionist view that excludes materiality and emotion and considers language and rationality the only way to conceptualize the world,

Phu, Brown, and Noble advocate a broader framework in which the sensory experience of photography can be responded to: we need "to grasp more fully the role of images in constructing emotions, in a process that illuminates the importance of racialized, gendered, and sexualized subjects in establishing normalized expressions." From another perspective, Jill Bennett explores the ways in which certain forms of digital photography, as sensory experience, are highly cognitively compatible with human memory, a "neurophenomenology." As she argues, the relationship between visual memory and real-world events is not simply reduplicative. Memory is distortive rather than reduplicative, and the referent is unstable and subject to continuous remaking. The continuous photo-documentation of everyday life by small wearable automatic cameras is not formed out of intentional awareness, and it is this that makes them closer to memory.

Theoretical models are often not only challenged by photography, but inadequate to it. In their different ways, Barthes and Flusser explain photography as a beyond to language. Responding to newly available material through posthumous publications, Yacavone's appraisal of Barthes' later writing tells us of his insistence on an increasing preoccupation with the distinction between word and image. With their use of photographs "as first and foremost affective and emotional vehicles," she shows the continuities between the phenomenology of Barthes' second book, *Michelet*, and what was to be his last, *Camera Lucida*. Both evidence an attempt to replace language by the photographic image and suggest that Barthes' structuralist analysis of the medium, although important and influential, was "a kind of intellectual detour." Barthes' impassioned approach to photography in *Camera Lucida* offers "the first sustained, if incomplete, attempt to think, feelingly, about photography" (Phu, Brown, and Noble). Nancy Ann Roth discusses Flusser's "way out of language" through technical images. His preoccupation with technical images involves a distinction between writing and photography in which the latter is part of a "magical," nonlinear relation to knowledge. Visually grounded consciousness is described as "magical" in that it allows for the possibility of events repeating themselves or reversing order, whereas writing sustains a logical and linear "historical" conception of time. For Flusser, in the pre-industrial age, the tool was a function of the person; in the industrial age, the person was a function of the machine; and now, with the photograph, we have a new relation in which the apparatus and the person mutually complete one another. For Baudrillard, photographs demonstrate the way the object demands attention; his preoccupation with the capacity of the photograph and the relationship "between concepts and images" (Coulter) can be seen as a way of visualizing his theories. He enjoyed photographs because something always remains that is inexplicable, defies logic and continues to acquire meaning and assert a life of its own; their "unseizable enigma" returns us to the "object's own magic" (Baudrillard 1997: 28).

The many different lines of thought included in this volume indicate the expansion in perspectives that inform what is understood as photography, but do not establish any one direction for photography theory. The fact that there is no easy way to sum up this content is significant; the purpose of photography theory must be, then, to examine and exploit photography's interdependence with other disciplines. However, despite the frequent interdependent address to theories and practices, there are clearly tensions between different premises for developing discussion, between a concern for the aesthetic object and the values accorded to the possibilities of visual representation. There are distinctions between those more interested in photography's relationship to reality and its representation, and those who advocate non-representational alternatives, which are explored in more abstract terms. For those whose prime interest is the uses of photography, whether the focus is with the implications of the photograph as a document, or the event of photography, or who is represented (Azoulay), the concern is with the social and political and the potential of photography as a medium to witness events and situations (Keenan, Scott).

Contributors discussing the potential of the medium, of "what might be" or "what could be" or "what might have been" (Campany), suggest approaches other than the rational and ocular viewing of photography. Theories, such as 'non-representation', can be interpreted as offering a reductive view of the photographic document, focused as they are to counter "universal totalities" and documents that claim to accurately represent the world. In aiming to think beyond outmoded forms, the model of representation that photography appears to be allied with—referent and representation, model and copy—is associated with older models of documentation that are assumed to be 'essentialist' and fixed, and are thus thought to be problematic. The properties of photography, in appearing to simulate reality, were founded on its ontological origin. The transformation from analogue to digital therefore has provoked the opportunity to question the cultural assumptions that arose from that ontological status. Whether, in consequence, a new ontology emerges is dependent on whether the particular qualities of dispersal, embedded in the social, are thought to be available exclusively through the digital process of production (thereby, its 'essence'). It does appear that the photography community has not yet exhausted its pre-occupation with the nature of photography as a medium. Photography may not be able to relinquish its ontological heritage, but is no longer predominantly to be seen as a singular medium—as a physical object.

Having provided an aesthetic account of photography, and having established its medium-specific status and independence from 'art', it is significant that, towards the end of the twentieth century, photography contributed to the critique of representation and celebrated the liberation of fictional constructions resulting from conceptualization. Photography practices moved away from the primacy of the photographer's individual perspective, singular meaning, and definitive portrayal. 'Post photography' and 'post conceptualism', art subsumed photography, and photography facilitated the developing function of art to engage with the social and the political. Having asserted its status as an autonomous art form, photography continues to both follow and dictate the expectations of 'art' in many ways. As such, photography is a "fluctuating constellation of different devices, material cultural practices and representational forms" (Frosh 2019: 118). In practice, photography is more akin to the post-structural conception of 'apparatus' or the generic term 'writing' (Bate). Continuing Tagg's claim that there is no such thing as photography in and of itself, a post-medium, non-essentializing discourse considers photographs as they circulate. Dependent on the institutions and agents that define it, photography's description as "a flickering across a field of institutional spaces" (Tagg 1988: 63) is remodelled by Azoulay. Greater understanding of the equivocal nature of the photographic document has established an aesthetic that attempts to expose the extended frame of circumstance and institution. This insistence on framing can be seen in the frequency of series (Robbins and Becher) and in the documentation of peripheral content in addition to central subject matter.

Ideas of non-representation can be seen as an attack on the capacity of photography to provide account for the real. Peter Osborne describes what is imagined to be the loss of the real, which has accompanied the digital, as an anxiety. Exploring the role of photography in contemporary art and aligning it with Deleuze's philosophy of difference, he usefully argues that the significant change for photography (and its ontology) is less to do with the technological form and more with its expanded reach and use, its expanded cultural function and sensibility. The shift is one of greater intensification and ease of flow or circulation. Whereas the ontology of the photograph was modelled on its still form as an object, what is an additional photographic characteristic now is its "distributive unity," which is not dependent on its particular technological form. The manner of distribution—of "distributive difference"—and how we use and cognitively relate to photographic documentations of our lives is extended by the additional properties of the digital medium (Osborne 2013: 122–3). Although the digital image is championed as being particularly mutable, any photographic reproduction initiates traffic in images, a traffic that undermines the photograph being thought of as a fixed medium or thing, or reducible to any one meaning (Rabinowitz, Rogers). With the ubiquity and ceaseless dispersal afforded by digital production, the digital image may signal a break from literal reference, but it cannot deny its content and reference to the real world—it need not be seen at odds with representation. Asserting practice *and* theory "as actively possessing appearances," Roberts negotiates the apparent conflict of Laruelle's theory of photographs as abstractions with their status as representations of the real world. He concludes that photography is a process of abstraction, but, as "a specific set of social determinations," photographs are also "contentful" and can provide a "socially discursive account." He reconciles the conflict by asserting that photographs, rather than mimetic replications that 'act for' naturalistic appearance, are closer to "a form of staged production" and, thereby, an active process.

As photography evolves in response to the many perspectives applied, the different conceptual frameworks used to deny or describe what 'realism' might be are unlikely to be reconciled. The fundamental shift that comes with the digital production process is twofold: with the process of ever-greater distribution via digital traffic, photography's capacity has gained social status, and the nature of our experiencing the image is phenomenologically different. The frame that mediates the photographer and what is photographed is now understood as extended by its relation to societal and cultural structures. Photography's access to the real, its 'realism', is remapped with regard to the "interstices of everyday affiliation," "civil imagination," and the understanding of the image as not confined to an image-object. As forms of popular photography are now more closely entangled in our lives and tied to the social realm (Hand and Scarlett), there is the sense of a new realism here, as photography affects and determines how we engage with the world. More than the literal image or singular picture, realism is understood as multidimensional—dissensual, conceptual, mnemonic, visceral, durational—and incorporates the spectator's encounter and responsibility and the cause and effect of histories (see Rogers). Hariman and Lucaites propose that, after the twentieth-century critique advanced a reductive conception of realism, "what is needed is a reinvigorated realism that requires a stronger conception of the photographic imagination."

The generic term 'photography', which has perpetuated a form of essentialism determined by its specific technology, now accommodates an increasing range of practices and disciplines (Bate). When the photographic document was assumed to be indisputable evidence, arguments concerning its capacity to enable interpretation or to form argument were inhibited by an inevitable comparison with the capacity of language to provide comprehensive understanding. If, on the other hand, it is understood that both language and image provide only fragmentary perspectives, then the image can be seen to contribute a further qualitative frame to an understanding of reality. Photographs are neither wholly transparently evidential nor emotionally obscure; they are both factual and have psychical reality (Burgin). They can be described in contradictory ways as their attributes are both literal and 'unsayable' and can refer to the world poetically, politically, and discursively (Tormey 2013). Understanding that the photograph is not distinct or transparent but mobile and malleable tends to make our response more questioning and redirect our understanding of the potential of meaning to be one of process. Images move between past, present, and future; they can be reused in different contexts or revised through memory or used to speculate futures (Rabinowitz). The assumptions of networked processes undermine the certitude of facts, and of the singular image (Bate). Practices have utilized fiction, as in the works of Jeff Wall or Walid Raad, and documentary works are more performative than descriptive (Steiner). Incorporating a number of interpretations of J.L Austin's utterance (Steiner, Phu, Brown, and Noble), conceptions of the photograph as performative in the way that they construct, incite, and insinuate, reconfigure the relations of subject and object in fundamental ways of comprehension.

Contemporary photographic practices, born out of an expanding technology and its processes of dissemination, form part of an "infinite open" and assume a conceptual sophistication and technological authority that influence art in general, toward manifestations of ethical responsibility. In the twenty-first century, understanding the photograph in terms of individual psychology has been supplemented by not only the structural dynamics of the photograph's construction, but recognition of a responsibility for the ongoing construction of meaning and consequence. The visual document undoubtedly retains its useful capacity to provoke affective response, provide counter-forensic testimony and form argument. Rather than photography aesthetics having surpassed itself and reached an end (Coulter), it is evident that what is expected of photographs has changed direction and gathered momentum. It is an expectation that asserts agency and 'reindividuation', in contrast to the historic celebration of forms of abstract humanism, as in Steichen's *Family of Man* (Keenan). Rather than reaching an impasse, the photographic aesthetic has developed and adjusted the relationship between the private and public, the origin and process, and the aesthetic and the social (Batchen 2001). The site of the aesthetic is dispersed along with the varied conditions in which it can be framed (Bate). Practices that have responded to the breakdown of essentialist definitions, the social mobility of digital images, the durational systems of production, the assertion of ethics and a reawakening of feeling each contribute to its expansion. Practices and theories move toward a focus on the event of photography and on what it *does* in practice. Deleuze invites consideration of materiality, affective intensities, and attention to the particularity and changing condition of experience. Where Rancière's advocacy of the political emerges from his thesis that dissensus and aesthetics have a common motivation, Azoulay's argument forces attention away from the intention of the author to the responsibility of the spectator. She challenges us to "unlearn" photography, to "disengage from many 'formative' debates that shaped the discipline" (Azoulay and Carville.)

Digital technologies and global dissemination have advanced the pluralism of photographic meaning—untethered from a naïve realist premise and reproducible across multiple media platforms, photography is not one 'thing'. In response, photography theory has radically pluralized. It is an expanded interdisciplinary field of theorizing photography we are encountering, a breadth beyond the boundaries of singular containing discourses.

References

Azoulay, A. (2010) "Getting Rid of the Distinction between the Aesthetic and the Political," *Theory, Culture & Society*, 27 (7–8), pp. 239–62.

Batchen, G. (2001) *Each Wild Idea: Writing, Photography, History*, Cambridge, Mass.: MIT Press. The essay 'Taking and Making' in *Each Wild Idea* (2001) is a revised version of (1991) "Creative Actuality: The Photography of Max Dupain," *Art Monthly Australia*, no. 45, November, pp. 2–5, in which he begins a discussion of "notions of intention, authorship, and value" and "how the making of photographs is always caught up in the complex entanglements of their own history.".

Baudrillard, J. (1997) "The Art of Disappearance," in Zurbrugg, N. (ed.) *Jean Baudrillard: Art & Artefact*, London: Sage, pp. 28–31.
Baudrillard, J. (1999) *Photographies 1985–1998*, ed. Wiebel, P. Ostfildern: Hatje-Cantz Publishers.
Butler, J. (2009) "Torture and the Ethics of Photography: Thinking with Sontag," in Butler, J., *Frames of War, When is Life Grievable?* London; New York: Verso, pp. 63–100.
Deleuze, G. (1994) *Difference and Repetition*, trans. Paul Patton, London: The Athlone Press.
Deleuze, G. and Guattari, F. (2004) *A Thousand Plateaus*, trans. Brian Massumi, London: Continuum.
Derrida, J. (1981) *Positions [1971]*, trans. Alan Bass, Chicago: University of Chicago Press.
Derrida, J. (1998) *Right of Inspection ["droit De Regard," 1985]*, trans. David Wills, New York: The Monacelli Press, pp. n.p.
Derrida, J. (2010) *Copy, Archive, Signature: A Conversation on Photography [2000]*, trans. Jeff Fort, Stanford, California: Stanford University Press.
Elkins, J. (2006) *Photography Theory*, Abingdon; New York: Routledge.
"Forensic Architecture Investigations," www.forensic-architecture.org [Accessed 4th October 2017].
Frosh, P. (2019) *The Poetics of Digital Media*, Cambridge: Polity Press.
Harman, G. (2016) "Object-oriented Seduction: Baudrillard Reconsidered," in Brouwer, J., Spuybroek, L. and van Tuinen, S. (eds.), *The War of Appearances: Transparency, Opacity, Radiance*, Rotterdam: V2_Publishing, pp. 128–43.
Harman, G. (2018a) *Object-Oriented Ontology: A New Theory of Everything*, London: Pelican.
Harman, G. (2018b) *Speculative Realism: An Introduction*, Cambridge: Polity Press.
Kelsey, R. and Stimson, B. (2008) *The Meaning of Photography*, New Haven; London: Yale University Press.
Laruelle, F. (2011) *The Concept of Non-Photography, Trans. Robin Mackay*, Falmouth: Urbanomic, New York: Sequence Press.
Osborne, P. (2013) *Anywhere or Not at All*, London; New York: Verso.
Rancière, J. (2010) *Dissensus: On Politics and Aesthetics [various Essays from 2000]*, trans. Steven Corcoran, London; New York: Continuum.
Rubinstein, D., Golding, J., and Fisher, A. (2013) *On the Verge of Photography: Imaging beyond Representation*, Birmingham: Article Press.
Tagg, J. (1988) *The Burden of Representation: Essays on Photographies and Histories*, Basingstoke; New York: Palgrave Macmillan.
Tormey, J. (2013) *Photographic Realism: Late Twentieth Century Aesthetics*, Manchester; New York: Manchester University Press.
Zylinska, J. (2017) *Nonhuman Photography*, Cambridge, Mass.: MIT Press.

Part I
Aesthetics

1

Feeling in photography, the affective turn, and the history of emotions

Thy Phu, Elspeth H. Brown, and Andrea Noble

What does it mean to feel photography? Since photography's inception in 1839, critics and spectators have intuited our manifold ways of feeling photography. However, until recently, the impact of feeling on the study of photography has received less serious attention. Consider, for example, the category of 'desire'. Although desire is a key term in photography studies, the field chiefly acknowledges rather than interrogates the appeal of the camera and the images that it produces. Notably, Geoffrey Batchen's influential work counters conventional histories, which credit Louis Daguerre with the invention of photography, by demonstrating that the desire for photography was so pervasive that no one inventor can be credited with this technological invention (Batchen 1997). Well after its invention, the desire for photography persists. When it comes to the black diaspora in the US, desire lies at the core of Frederick Douglass's faith in "pictures and progress" (Wallis and Smith 2012). That pictures were a record of progress into the ranks of humanity for those who had been brutally dehumanized made photography valuable—and desirable—as a political resource for emancipated slaves. In the twentieth century, desire erupts most forcefully and eloquently in the work of Roland Barthes, for whom the concept anchors a personal, subjective, and highly emotional approach to photography (Barthes 1981). Desire, then, has been a crucial way for scholars to grapple with the powerful connection that individuals and communities have with photography. Curiously, these conversations have unfolded without full recognition of desire as an affective category, even though the work of psychoanalytic theorists, from Sigmund Freud on, has decisively shaped desire in this way. Instead, the tenor of most discussions about what it means to feel photography accords with what cultural historian Barbara Rosenwein describes as "unfocused" emotions talk (Rosenwein 2006). In short, feeling tends to arise in a loosely thematic and largely descriptive way, rather than as a mode of analysis. However, this "emotions talk" has acquired increasing focus, particularly with *Feeling Photography* and continuing with numerous publications (Brown and Phu 2014; Phu and Brown 2018). Taken together, these recent works have grappled with the implications of a shift—described as the "affective turn" (Clough and Halley 2007)—for criticism in photography studies, by drawing on a number of disciplines for insights into what affect, emotions, and feelings might mean for the analysis of images. Our own research contributes to this affective turn by considering how theories of affect, feeling, and emotions might enrich our understanding of photographs.

This chapter offers a review of recent work that brings together photography and affect, emotion, and feeling. After a brief discussion of how photography scholars have taken up these terms, we identify fruitful new directions concerning photography, emotion, and the sonic; affect's role in constituting the optical unconscious; and the idea of 'presence' as a site of abundance that indexes affective histories within the photograph. A second section takes up the role of emotion as an analytic within historical studies, while demonstrating the possibilities for photography studies. What would an image-based approach to the history of emotions look like? We sketch a 'messy' answer to this question in our third section, which provides a brief, comparative history of tears and their photographic significance.

Focusing emotions talk

There is no scholarly consensus concerning the meaning of the theoretical terms affect, feeling and emotion; rather, preference for one term over another reveals disciplinary allegiances more than anything else. Still, it is helpful to consider, briefly, the ways these terms have been taken up by photography scholars. In humanities discourse influenced by work in the life sciences, affects are pre-cognitive, corporeal states of being that are eventually manifested in the body as emotions and in the mind as feelings. Freud, for example, considered 'affect' as a generalized concept for all those embodied processes—including desires—that, when they reach the conscious mind, can be understood on the one hand as feelings or, on the other hand, as physiologically charged emotions (Tompkins 1962–1963). Brian Massumi's work on affect, influenced by Gilles Deleuze, emphasizes intensity, a somatic and non-cognitive event that resists narrative or structured mapping. In this approach, 'affect' exists apart from feeling or even the "unclaimed experience" of trauma (Caruth 1996), both of which can be understood as social and cultural discourses that emerge in relationship to personal or collective history. Whereas most affect theory focuses on the individual, some sociologists (Hardt 1999; Ahmed 2004b) understand affect as emotions in circulation as a form of currency that moves between individuals. This understanding of affect as central to how modern capitalism builds economic value has been influential in work that examines the relationship between photography and political economy (Brown 2009, 2019). As discussed below, however, historians of emotion (Leys 2011) and others dispute the transhistorical assumptions undergirding this work, which often describes a set of basic affects independent of history and culture. Feelings, as a keyword, has emerged in photography studies through the influence of queer and feminist scholarship (Sedgwick 2003), work on public feelings (Cvetkovich 2007), and critics who have helped politicize negative affects (Munoz 1999; Dolan 2005; Berlant 2007; Stewart 2007).

Feeling Photography drew from these insights to focus 'emotions talk' in two key ways: first, by drawing attention to an incipient theory of feeling in the history of photography and, second, by developing feeling as an analytic for engaging with photography. When it comes to the history of photography, we can see the incipience of feeling across a broad range of photographic genres. In emotions studies, scientific photographs recorded facial expressions—and, as it turns out, produced these very expressions by both stimulating and simulating the emotions that they sought to objectively record. Lavishly illustrated studies by Guillaume Duchenne (1990), Jean-Martin Charcot, and Charles Darwin (1979), among others, not only profoundly influenced how we perceive and comprehend feelings, but also became foundational to affect theory generally. Documentary photographers from the nineteenth century to the present day often seek to elicit sympathy through the production of images, which they circulated for the purpose of producing sympathetic communities who they hoped would be moved to act. This faith persists to the present day, and is renewed in work by Sharon Sliwinski (2011) and Wendy Kozol (2014), among others, that calls for a community of sympathetic spectators who would be inspired to act ethically. Yet, this process of producing feeling communities surprisingly overlaps with that of commercial photographs, especially when it comes to print advertising and the fashion industry, in which the circulation of images fuels a desirous marketplace (Wissinger 2007; Brown 2009). In the digital age, the exchange of photographs over social media offers an instantaneous and simultaneous shorthand for expressing a spectrum of emotions, from grief to joy, and everything in between.

For their part, critics have evinced strong feelings about the significance of photography. As noted above, the emergence of photography was a desirous event, as evident in the widespread fervor that anticipated and greeted the invention of the camera. For a generation of modernists, starting with John Szarkowski in the 1960s, the project of legitimizing photography as a field of study entailed, variously, a passionate embrace of some images, namely those that were formalist (and emotionally restrained), and dismissal of others, such as pictorialism, for its decorative, and seemingly excessive emotional style. Similarly, the field of photography studies developed under the sway of a Marxist commitment to ideology critique along straight and austere lines. In particular, the task of "thinking photography" (Burgin 1982) sought, though ultimately unsuccessfully, to eschew feeling altogether. That these critics felt strongly about photography could hardly be doubted. Strangely, what was even stronger was their unvoiced yet palpable distrust of feeling as excessive and therefore antithetical to photography criticism. Even Susan Sontag (1977), who was fascinated by photography, was ambivalent about images because the feelings they evoked were, as she put it, "messy" and not conducive to the ethical action that she advocated when it came to redressing violence. The muchness of feeling in response to photography seemed to be a problem stemming from photography's inherently abundant quality (Edwards 2012). It was not until Roland Barthes' *Camera Lucida* that feeling would be unequivocally embraced. So impassioned is Barthes' approach to images that this landmark book is now—though it wasn't always—seen as offering the first sustained, if incomplete, attempt to think, feelingly, about photography.

Feeling, then, is more than just a theme in photography studies or a description of responses to images. Feeling is an analytic tool for thinking and interpreting photography in new ways. This approach enables us to grasp more fully the role of images in constructing emotions, in a process that illuminates the importance of racialized, gendered, and sexualized subjects in establishing normalized expressions. Emotions studies, such as the one conducted by Guillaume Duchenne, drew their subjects from among the destitute and mad, who were vulnerable and socially powerless groups. As noted above, state surveillance refined methods for identification, in response to the anxiety that racialized bodies especially occasioned, for their ostensible interchangeability and capacity to evade detection (Cho 2009). A focus on feeling in photography helps elucidate the process by which visual conventions are established and entrenched, and the political purposes that this process serves. Abject bodies have been the vehicles through which we have been taught how, when, and for whom to feel (Sheehan 2014).

Given the political importance of attending to context, in *Feeling Photography* we privileged feeling instead of affect as a way of avoiding the problematic ahistorical assumptions of affect theory. The term 'feeling' also has the advantage of underscoring tactility, to draw attention to a broader range of sensory experiences of photography, which encompass not just the optic but also the haptic. However, a focus on feeling in photography is challenging precisely because the ephemeral nature of feelings makes them difficult to archive. At the same time that scientists seek to register the nuances of emotional expression in controversial projects such as Paul Ekman's facial action coding system, critics are pondering, as we explain more fully below, what it might mean that some feelings, particularly traumatic ones, are unphotographable and unarchivable.

Alongside the publication of *Feeling Photography* in 2014, new work has emerged that continues to shape the relationship between photography and affect. The remarkable book *Image Matters* (Campt 2012), for example, builds on Fred Moten's (2002) earlier work on photography's sonic and affective dimensions in understanding the impact of *Jet* magazine's publication of a 1955 photograph of African American teenager Emmett Till's destroyed face, on view in an open casket. Tina Campt takes up Moten's emphasis on the photograph's sonic potentiality to consider the role of sound in the affective work of family photographs among Europe's black diaspora, drawn from the Dyche Photography Studio, a commercial studio that photographed black and Asian communities in Birmingham, England, for much of the twentieth century. In this shift from Moten's singular image to the serial of the Dyche archive, Campt offers both an intervention into archival theory and a new way of reading photography and feeling, as encompassing a broad range of sensory experiences that includes haptic, optic, and sonic dimensions.

Another new direction within photography and affect concerns what disappears from the visual field through the work of affect. What can and cannot be seen within the photographic field, and how are sites of what Walter Benjamin called the optical unconscious enabled through feeling? A fascinating study has explored what lies at the "edge of sight" in a volume exploring US photography (Smith 2013). Ariella Azoulay's work even goes so far as to insist on "the event of photography," as a temporally unfixed series of encounters that unfold despite the absence or irrevocable loss of an image (2012). This concept of the event of photography not only radically transforms how we understand photography—that which does not require an image—but also lays bare the importance of desire as the impetus that drives this event. In *The Afterimage of Empire: Photography in Nineteenth-Century India*, Zahid R. Chaudhary (2012) pursues this question in relation to affect, aesthetic form, and colonial photography. Aesthetic form, he argues, is the process through which we make sense of the world, including the feelings that emerge in response to external stimuli, and filters what can be seen, touched, or felt, and as such it is where politics enters the scene of sense-making. Chaudhary pursues this argument in relationship to several eyewitness accounts of famine in nineteenth-century India, showing how Christian sympathy emerges as a 'civilizational affect'. That is, Christian sympathy, when it came to the famine's visual record, operates as a complex affective shuttle, shifting between feeling and not-feeling, between emotional response and anesthesia. Famine photographs engendered a capacity for suffering within the Christian viewer, while at the same time enabling the persistent deferral of any action to alleviate that suffering.

In making his argument about the political work of aesthetic forms in filtering information about the world, Chaudhary works with Benjamin's notion of the 'optical unconscious' in order to explain how photography shows more than we could possibly see as well as something beyond the horizon of sight. Benjamin's concept of the optical unconscious and photography is taken up most extensively in the work of Smith and Sliwinski (2017). As an example of what a focus on affect and seeing/not seeing in photography can offer, consider Laura Wexler's analysis of Barthes' political unconscious, which appears in Smith and Sliwinski's volume (2017). As is well known, Barthes did not reproduce the Winter Garden photograph in *Camera Lucida* because, he argues, the image could not possibly have the same affective force for the reader as it does for him, the writer. Yet Wexler shows how Barthes' insistence on the presence of his mother in the Winter Garden photograph enables another type of filtering function. This filter disappears the other figure in that image, namely her older brother Philippe Binger (Barthes' uncle), whose surname connects the family to Barthes' grandfather, Louis-Gustave Binger, a famous French military officer, governor of the French colony of the Ivory Coast, and eventually the Directeur des Affaires d'Afrique for the French colonial government in Africa. In other words, the Winter Garden photograph indexes French colonialism through the figure of Barthes' Binger, but Barthes' affective investment in the trace of his mother has functioned as a cognitive shield against the French colonial history in Africa—not only for Barthes, but also for photography scholars. Though there can be little doubt that Barthes felt keenly about photography, this new work reminds us of the necessity to historicize this feeling.

Another new direction within photograph and affect concerns the idea of 'presence' as a site of abundance that indexes affective histories within the photograph's making. Drawing on the work of historian Eelco Runia (2006), Andrea Noble (2010) emphasizes the need to consider photography's invocation of presence. Situated within the contemporary turn to memory, remembrance, and trauma, Runia argues for metonymy, the trope of 'presence in absence', as a more appropriate tool than 'metaphor' with which to grasp how the past continues to inhabit the present. Presence is embedded within the photograph, a trace of the very materiality of the image; it is an inscription of lived experience for those in front of the camera, as well as the person behind it, and reminds us that, no matter how asymmetrical the power relations between those on either side of the camera are, the subject is never passive. Presence as the site of affect within photography enables scholars, for example, to destabilize monolithic notions of the gaze.

New work on domestic images and their significance for challenging assumptions about intimacy also offers an exciting way of organizing personal and political relationships. In addition to Wexler's study of Barthes' disavowal of his family connections to a colonial history and Tina Campt's research on family photography within Europe's black diaspora, Nicole R. Fleetwood (2015) also explores the political intimacies of family photography. Fleetwood shows how vernacular photography, taken from *within* the walls of the US prison system, circulates between the incarcerated and their loved ones outside prison, building circuits of attachment in the process and gendering the emotional labor of maintaining bonds of intimacy that institutional violence, in the form of the prison industrial complex, unleashes on the most vulnerable families, who are often (in the United States at least) poor and black. Indeed, new work on family photography has challenged conventional understandings of family, the bonds of love and even hatred that tie members together—and produce the images that both record and create these bonds (Phu, Brown, and Dewan 2017). Similarly, anthropological projects on "return", which entail repatriating ethnographic photographs that were taken in a context of violation, provide intriguing new frameworks for rethinking family intimacy.

Historicizing the emotions in photography

Thus far, we have examined the affective turn in terms of affect theory and its implications for photography studies. We now consider the 'affective turn' in historical studies, and its significance for photographic analysis. When it comes to historical studies, the affective turn has happened, for the most part, in isolation from debates in affect theory. Look at any number of the books or articles by historians devoted to the emotions and one finds 'affective' employed as an adjective, but rarely are those debates explicitly invoked, which is why, instead of affect, emotion is a keyword here (a term that *Feeling Photography* invoked, even though the book singled out feeling for the reasons outlined above).

Historians understand the emotions to be at the heart of human and historical life; as practices—a term to which we will return below—fear, love, hate, and so on, are "something people experience and something they do" (Scheer 2012). Historians tend to use the term emotion to denote a phenomenon that emerges at the interface of the mind and body in an agent who is, in turn, situated within and shaped by a specific socio-cultural environment. Where 'affect theory' establishes a linear understanding of 'emotional' processes, with affect as the body's response to stimuli that takes place at a pre-cognitive (but not pre-social) level that then gives rise to semiotically mediated emotion, we are more persuaded by those approaches that seek to emphasize the circuitous ways in which affect and emotion shade into one another (Ngai 2005; Leys 2011). While acknowledging this terminological hinterland, we are more drawn to critics who favor feeling (Cvetkovich 2012), not just because of its tactile dimensions noted above, but also because of its conceptually productive imprecision and ambiguity.

Historical approaches to the emotions pivot on the fact that, although the capacity to experience emotions might be universal, they are neither uniformly expressed nor aroused by the same conditions the world over or indeed across time. That is to say, emotions are not simply 'inner', or individual. Instead, because they are communicated through language, gesture, ritual, images, and so forth, emotions are shaped by the dominant cultural norms that prevail in the context in which individuals find themselves. Thus, by extension, modes of emotional expression are not fixed, but vary over time, and across and within cultures. Here is the chief difference and conceptual advantage offered by the history of emotions approach, which emphasizes cultural context, continuity, and change. In contrast, affect studies adopts a problematically ahistorical approach.

Three terms in particular have acquired currency to describe elements of this historicized phenomenon: "emotionology," "emotional regimes," and "emotional communities." Peter and Carol Stearns coined the first term to refer to the collective emotional standards of a given society or identifiable groups within it that determine emotional expression (Stearns and Stearns 1985). The second is William Reddy's concept of an "emotional regime" (Reddy 2001) that signals the emotional normative order that is enforced by any enduring political regime. The medievalist Barbara Rosenwein invented the third term to denote the way in which in any given society there can be multiple, overlapping "emotional communities," contending that, as individuals move between them, they may adapt their emotional style accordingly (Rosenwein 2002).

Though nuanced by epistemological and historical distinctions—for Rosenwein, for example, "regime" is a modern concept that does not lend itself to early historical periods—all three historians emphasize the way in which emotions are shaped by and themselves shape human interactions, and they are centrally concerned with how societies and communities cohere. As Ute Frevert has demonstrated, emotional dispositions and styles—such as those that clustered around notions of honor in nineteenth-century Europe and, indeed, beyond—fall in and out of history as evinced in practices such as dueling (Frevert 2011). Insofar as they move us, emotions motivate human action: what we feel for another (fear, love, sympathy, etc.) and what we ourselves feel (afraid, ashamed, annoyed, etc.) determine our behavior and actions towards them, and theirs towards us. In short, emotions have a social function; studying not only what they do, but also "how they work" (Katz 1999), can contribute in significant ways to our understanding of what motivates people and groups to do the things they do.

Nevertheless, as historians have grappled with the study of the emotions in the past, arguably there has been an overemphasis on the role of text-based modes of representation in the construction of emotional standards, regimes, or communities. Take, for instance, Reddy's other important contribution to theory of the emotions, "emotives." Drawing on Austin's speech act theory, for Reddy, "emotives" are items of discourse that are simultaneously descriptive and performative, that both express emotional experience and construct it. Significantly, Reddy illustrates his concept through a series of language-based instances, where, for example, the utterance "I love you" is an emotive that serves to intensify the feeling for the beloved. (Can a visual artifact such as a photograph equally be considered an emotive?) The insistence on language-based models has had two consequences. On the one hand, as Monique Scheer has argued, historians have tended to reinforce a mind/body, inner/outer split, where instead we need to work with "the mutual embeddedness of minds, bodies, and social relations in order to historicize the body and its contributions to the learned experience of emotion" (Scheer 2012). Drawing on Bourdieu's notion of practice theory, Scheer advocates an approach to the emotions as a form of practice that is always embodied, where methodologically, "a history of emotions inspired by practice theory entails thinking harder about what people are doing, and to working out the specific situatedness of these doings. It means trying to get a look at bodies and artifacts of the past" (Scheer 2012: 217).

This brings us to the second consequence of an overly text-based approach to the emotions: it can exclude other cultural forms, which can restrict the utility of historical approaches to the emotions to the field of photography and visual studies more broadly. Margrit Pernau and Inke Rajamani address this dilemma from the perspective of conceptual history, where an

> exclusive focus on language does not capture the richness of expressions of emotion nor even a society's knowledge of emotions: concepts of emotion are developed not only in texts, but in pictures, in sounds, in the way space is organized, and in how people move.
>
> *(Pernau and Rajamani 2016: 47)*

Although the history of emotions has yet to engage in serious discussion of images, this approach nevertheless offers a new direction that would enrich photography studies. What would an image-based approach to the history of emotions look like, and how might this advance photography studies? In the following section, we gesture towards a comparative, though brief, history of tears and their photographic significance as a way of modeling a visual history of the emotions. If the overview of tears we provide below seems messy, this is because the contexts we touch on are deliberately broad, dispersed, and varied in subjects and sites. Given the messiness of feelings, it is also necessary to capture a history that is likewise messy. The methodology that we experiment with here draws on attempts to develop mess as an analytic for historical inquiry (Manalansan 2014). Rather than construing mess as an epistemological problem, Martin Manalansan contends that we should consider mess on its own terms. Tears—as a marker of the messiness of feelings, and as an index of what can and cannot be seen—strike us as a productive starting point for a new visual history of the emotions. Here, we gesture towards this new visual history.

Weeping and its visual histories

In Mexico, tears are political, though they may not be obviously seen as such. Notably, during the 1968 Mexican Olympic Games, a distinct set of images characterized the host nation's vexed emotions in response to the student movement, which gathered momentum in the run-up to the inauguration of the games scheduled for October 12 and culminated in the violence of the Plaza de las Tres Culturas Tlatelolco on the night of October 2. The visual memory of Mexico 1968 comes charged with struggles for civil rights and social justice and relied on the presence of the global media. Three years before the Games, President Gustavo Diaz Ordaz (1964–1970) had remarked, "all the eyes of the world would be on Mexico in 1968 and that he hoped Mexicans would respond to their responsibilities in providing a warm and dignified reception for all visitors" (González de Bustamante 2013). Before the eyes of the world were trained on Mexico, his regime made sure to crush the student movement on October 2, when the military opened fire on a peaceful demonstration, gunning down a still unknown number of students and bystanders.

One image in particular stands out, for all that it has now largely been overlooked—that of a teary-eyed young man, Felipe 'Tibio' Muñoz, the winner of the host nation's first gold medal for 200-meter breast stroke on October 22. Following his trainer's strategy, the 17-year-old had held back on the first length to then come through on the second, touching down ahead of the Soviet, Vladimir Kosinksy, and the North American, Brian Job. When the swimmer stepped up to the podium beside his rivals, as the three nations' flags were raised and the Mexican national anthem struck up, the floodgates opened, to put it colloquially. The tears streamed down Muñoz's cheeks as he attempted to wipe them away. Similarly, in a press conference later, Muñoz was inconsolable, with the press noting that, "he cried like a child from the excitement" (*lloraba como un niño por la emoción*; Camarena 1968).

Far from mocking his tears as unmanly, commentators celebrated and shared in Muñoz's emotional display of joy and pride in his victory. Of course, it is not unusual to see a male athlete break down in tears. As bastions of "idealized heterosexual masculinity" (MacArthur and Shields 2015), the sports field and stadium are acknowledged places of sanctioned male weeping, sites of emotional refuge for athletes and spectators alike. Under the extravagant headline "¡Apoteósico! ¡Dramático!" (Amazing! Dramatic!), the daily newspaper *Ovaciones* rejoiced in the triumph of the young man from the Mexican middle class—and his class affiliation is significant—who "went wild, let his feelings go to the point of spilling tears when the gold medal was hung across his chest." Nor was Muñoz alone in breaking down emotionally. The same newspaper goes on:

> That moment, for which we have no words to describe, was the greatest that not just Mexico, but the Olympics, have seen. Amazing! Dramatic! Hysterical! *Unforgettable*! The national anthem was sung by ten thousand souls, moved to their core, struggling to get the notes of the adored national anthem from their aroused throats.[1]

We have italicized the adjective 'unforgettable' because Muñoz's performance was to some degree forgettable. As stated at the outset of this section, the tearful Olympic gold medalist is not the figure who comes to mind when we think of the Mexican Olympics, either in Mexico or beyond, his triumph largely superseded by two acts of protest that occupy a more prominent position in the cultural memory of the long 1960s. Nevertheless, in the cold war context of the time, the triumph of the Mexican swimmer over representatives of the two superpowers was not lost on journalists of the pro-government press, particularly in light of the previous months' student unrest. *El Universal* reported that the swimmer was from the Isaac Ochoterena School, where, three months previously, "the spark of student unrest had been ignited" (Ibid). In the politically charged, competitive spirit of the age, the same newspaper noted that the fact that the rivals came from the two countries that, "according to various versions, could have been the instigators or beneficiaries of said conflict, cannot help but be symbolic."

In fact, Felipe Muñoz's extravagant tears open onto the largely untold story of Mexico 1968: a narrative of those sectors of society that opposed the student movement and supported the authoritarian government crackdown on it. As Eric Zolov has argued, if it is to move beyond a dichotomy of a "heroic" left and a "traitorous" right, the "historiography of the Global Sixties must move beyond the internal debates and practices of the left to examine the debates and practices on the right as well" (Zolov 2013: 359). In report after report, the Felipe Muñoz triumph plays out against the backdrop of global conflict, both symbolic and real—the safe return of the Apollo spacecraft, the search for peace in Southeast Asia—at the same time as it constructs an image of a pristine national youth that is encapsulated in the cartoon "clean youth" (El Universal 1968). Such a story is triggered by a set of photographic images of the medal ceremony that, through their widespread dissemination in the press at the time, represent a form of 'emotive', communicating and intensifying a feeling of national pride that stands in contrast to that of the shame of the student massacre. Excavating this story might evoke mixed feelings in the researcher, but it is one that needs to be told.

Whereas, in Mexico, the state deploys the visual display of tears to conjure national emotions, in diasporic Vietnamese communities, the public enactment of tears, as captured in photography, serves as a lamentation for the loss of nationhood. Take, for example, another vision of 1968, this time from southern Vietnam: a lovely young woman, her hair in artful dishevelment, weeps into her hands, which cling to her beloved's dog tags (Figure 1.1). Shadows edge the back of her head, while warm natural light illuminates her clasped hands and teary face. This striking portrait appears at the center of *Viet Nam in Flames*, a photobook commissioned and published by the government of Vietnam, which was produced by the civilian photographer Nguyễn Mạnh Đan in collaboration with Nguyễn Ngọc Hạnh, a colonel in the Army of the Republic of Vietnam.

The photograph's narrative of grief is complicated by the story that Nguyễn Ngọc Hạnh tells of its making. In an undated interview, the photographer recounts that he was moved to take this picture after encountering the gruesome scene of a massacre at Củ Chi (Huynh 2011). He recounts coming upon a woman who searched frantically among a half dozen decapitated bodies for evidence that would confirm her husband's death. After helping, he tried to photograph her, but was unsuccessful because she was too distraught. Ironically, what made this scene photo-worthy—its outpouring of emotion—also rendered it unphotographable. Shortly afterward, his 11-year-old daughter found another grieving young woman, named Tâm, whose lover had been taken prisoner after his plane was shot down.

There is more to this remarkable story, however. It was the photographer who teased out the model's cascading hair; his own daughter read love letters that the woman's beloved had written, while, in the background, his friend, who was a skilled musician, played the sad songs so often aired on Saigon radio stations. Against this lachrymose backdrop, Tâm's tears spilled forth, tears that are a proxy for the other woman, whose paroxysms of grief could not be pictured. This tale of the making of the photograph underscores the earnest effort that went into these performances, to get the historical detail just right, to make the experience of reenactment 'true'. For the same reason, Nguyễn Ngọc Hạnh's overwrought photographs are easily dismissed, particularly by the Vietnamese state, as contrived reenactments.

However, disparaging the photograph as staged misses the point. After all, its staginess is not just self-conscious but also part (albeit controversially) of the convention of war photography. This staging is also significant because it reveals the performative function of tears insofar as they are a social ritual (Ebersole 2000). For this reason, whether they were authentic or inauthentic, induced or spontaneous, matters less than the fact that they are to be seen and recognized. In this sense, the proxy image better captures the nature of weeping than

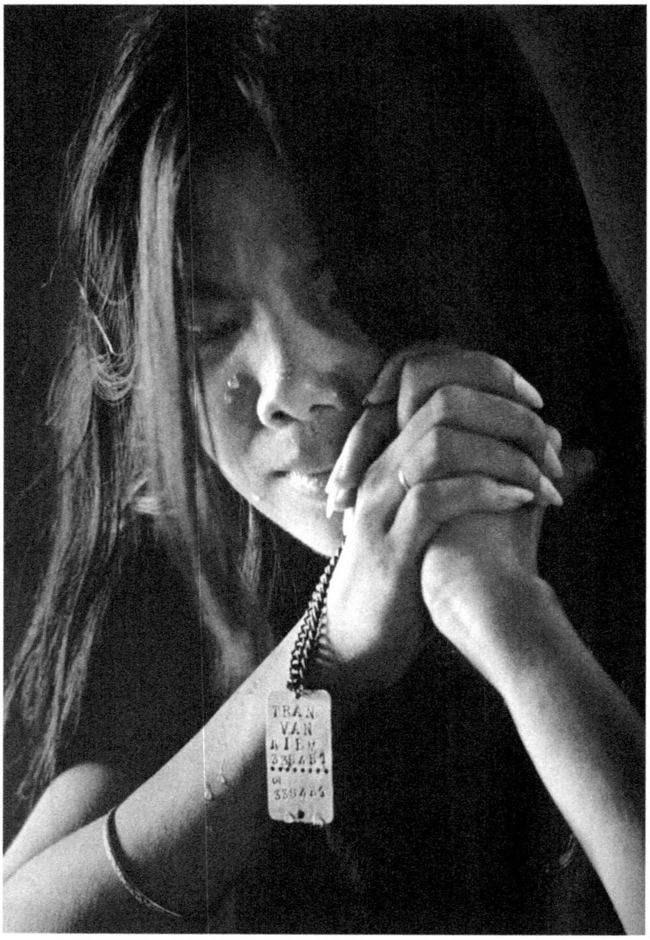

Figure 1.1 Nguyễn Ngọc Hạnh, *Tiếc thương* (1965). Courtesy Lich Thanh Tran

the photograph that Nguyễn Ngọc Hạnh had originally wanted to take. This image we see is a public engagement with grief, one that requires others to be on hand as active participants, and not simply as passive spectators in this performance of weeping. In this manner, the viewers of this photograph might likewise be called upon to observe—and participate—in the act of weeping. This may be why Nguyễn Ngọc Hạnh preempted his critics when he insisted the young woman's tears were real (*nước mắt thật*)—not just for her but for those who enacted this collective ritual, whether at the moment of its making, or during its subsequent circulation within the diasporic Vietnamese community, many decades after the book's publication.

To understand the significance of tears we need to consider the adjacent image (Figure 1.2), which features a soldier—perhaps this weeping woman's beloved or at least a proxy for him—whose face is shown in extreme close-up, either moist with sweat or, more likely, drenched by rain. This is a photograph that evokes weeping. It does so, however, without tears, by means of a kind of pathetic fallacy. The woman's tears, a proxy for the paroxysm of grief that could not be represented, are in turn a proxy for those that are shown yet withheld on the man's face. By juxtaposing the moistness of a man's stolidly composed face beside that of a tearful woman's face, the photo-book unmistakably genders weeping. Women shed the tears that men may not, indeed that men dare not, perhaps because doing so might expose a weakness unbecoming in soldiers, who were expected to fight bravely and heroically. What is striking is that, in representations of weeping, it is rare to show tears. Instead, weeping is suggested through gestures, such as a downturned gaze, crinkled eyes, a covered face.

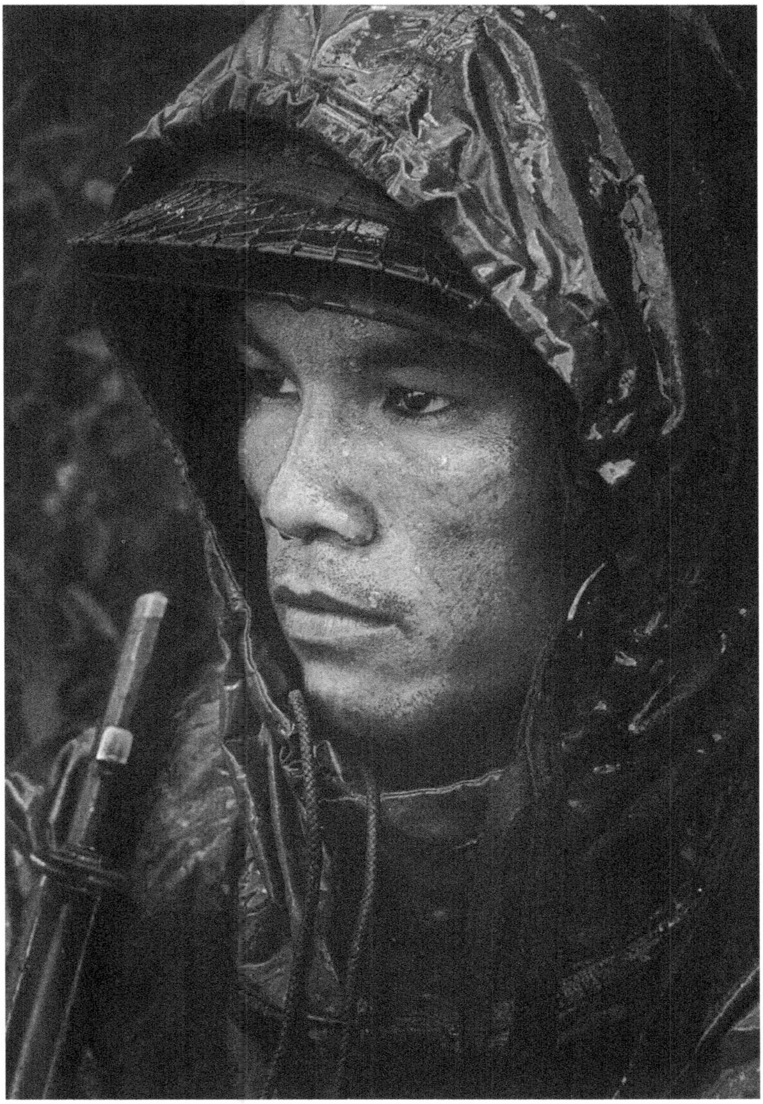

Figure 1.2 Nguyễn Ngọc Hạnh, *Stoic Soldier* (1965). Courtesy Lich Thanh Tran

For all that they are only suggested, these tears of sorrow presage the coming loss of nation, as a pivotal part of the Vietnamese diaspora's story, which has for decades held at its core an attachment to such scenes of lamentation. Since the fall of Saigon on April 30, 1975, the diasporic Vietnamese community has marked its profound and inconsolable sorrow over the loss of nationhood with 'Black April' commemorations, pageants in which refugees, who are now retirees resettled in far-flung ethnic enclaves in Canada, Australia, the United States, and elsewhere, don their old uniforms, reenact the story of their struggle and flight, and display the photographs that attest to their suffering and survival. In San Jose, California, where Nguyễn Ngộc Hạnh eventually moved after his release from a communist reeducation camp in Viet Nam, photographs from *Viet Nam in Flames* are often exhibited as an important part of Black April events. Taken many decades earlier, these photographs are not just a record of what has been: their melancholic mood seems to presage the devastating loss that was then still to come. In what amounts to a form of nostalgia that is as much prospective as it is retrospective (Boym 2001), Nguyễn Ngọc Hạnh recounts this particular scene of ritual weeping with remarkable clarity, many years after the photograph was printed, when he had become a prominent member of this diasporic community. In his remembrance of the scene, the photograph's sorrow becomes a figure for the diaspora's collective lament. A close look at *Viet Nam in Flames* suggests, then, how the figure of tears might function as recognition of proleptic loss. The melodrama of *Viet Nam in Flames* offers an idiom for remembrance of the war for a generation of the diaspora whose collective memories are organized in equal parts grief and survival. Here, tears bring together a community not for national ends, but rather in the absence of nationhood.

Tears are also a crucial means of bringing together a wholly different community, consisting of transitioning individuals and their families, with completely different effects. Over the past several years, the Transpartners Oral History Project, headed by Elspeth Brown, has interviewed dozens of people, mostly women, whose partners have transitioned from female to male. In an unusual move, the focus is on partners, not the person who transitioned (although, in two cases, the partner has also since transitioned). In these interviews, narrators are asked about visibility, queer community, affective labor, surgeries and hormones, sex lives, name changes, and parenting. The interviews are confidential: narrators are assured anonymity, as the contents of these interviews are deeply private and personal. In many situations, the couple is stealth, which is to say that the trans person is not 'out' as trans, and the interview could potentially violate their privacy. Tears and photography shadow the interview, erupting at unexpected moments: narrators describe crying, or their partners' crying, in private and public settings, from grief, frustration, or joy. But these tears cannot be represented. What makes these unseen, and thus unphotographed, tears a topic of photography studies?

In *Civil Imagination*, Ariella Azoulay pushes us to think photography beyond representation (Azoulay 2012). Photography, she argues, is a matter of relations and effects and exists whether or not a camera is on the scene; the event of photography, she argues, exists long after the photographic event. In this way, Azoulay encourages us to think how the camera is always potentially in view, creating a modern culture shaped by what she refers to as the "photographic situation" (Azoulay 2012: 22). Transition is a photographic situation. The camera is always implied, and often in view, as the transformation of the body from one sex to another demands documentation. Trans men in transition document the transformation of their bodies through photography and video, posting images of their bodies one month, two months, and so on, on T, or testosterone. This photographic documentation is shared with others on YouTube, blogs, Facebook, and other social media platforms, and those considering transition follow these photographic events as visual roadmaps of gender affirmation.

These photographic endeavors co-produce what Tina Campt has called subjects in becoming: forms of identification, subjectivity, and belonging that are in the process of formation (Campt 2012: 16–17). Partners engage in this photographic documentation; they are often, but not always, the photographers.

But photography cannot document tears, at least here. Narrators describe their tears in relationship to transition, as well as (with some frequency) crying in the interview itself. In some cases, the regulation of tears functions as part of the partner's affective labor, their gift to their transitioning partner. Anna, a young university student, described how she and her partner Mika had been fine while waiting for his top surgery, but, once in the hospital, she lost composure, irrationally afraid that he might not make it through the routine surgery.

> I managed to hold it together, because I said "I love you. You'll be fine," kissed him on the lips [and] they wheeled him down the hallway. I went the opposite direction, held my breath the whole way down the hallway, and promptly burst into tears as they closed the door behind me. Making sure that he didn't know that I was in tears was … my only goal … so that he would be okay.
>
> *(Brown and Anna 2012)*

Here, Anna performs emotional labor for her partner by shielding him from her tears, making sure to cry behind closed doors. Her regulation of tears is part of what Jane Ward has described as "gender labor" (Ward 2010: 237): "the affective and bodily efforts invested in giving gender to others, or actively suspending self-focus in the service of helping others achieve the varied forms of gender recognition they long for." At the same time, however, Anna's narrative reads photographically: we see the disappearing gurney, see her collapse in tears behind closed doors. Anna's gender work thus unfolds amidst a photographic situation; though the camera is not present, Anna comports herself as though it were, in anticipation of a visual encounter regardless of whether an image is produced or preserved.

In Azoulay's view, photography's ontology is a "certain form of human being-with-others in which the camera or the photograph are implicated" (Azoulay 2012: 13, 18). Family photography, as a genre, documents the "being-with-others" of the domestic sphere. These photographs record what Catherine Zuromskis has called "aspirational fictions" that allow us to record ourselves and our histories as we would like to remember them (Zuromskis 2013: 33). As Pierre Bourdieu (1996) and others have argued, such photographs rarely, if ever, record tears: their function is to render these aspirational fictions of happiness and belonging as fact, through what Barthes has called the photograph's "that-has-been" indexicality. Tears in a family photograph would most definitely puncture domesticity's aspirational fiction. Hence, we have another site where photography fails to represent tears. In the case of transition, however, temporality itself poses a problem. Gender transition is itself an aspirational enterprise, a process of corporeal self-making that unfolds in real time. In this sense, family photographs of the "that-has-been" body, the pre-transition body, pose substantial ontological and representational challenges within the trans family. If photographs record the "that-has-been," and the body is in the process of becoming the "that-will-be," how do partners negotiate family photography in the midst of transition?

When partners in this project are asked about the role of family snaps within their homes, their responses range widely: some partners weave in photos of the old self, whereas others remove them. Kara had been with her partner Ethan for seven years before his transition about a year before our interview. She described how their family photographs are "getting slowly removed and tucked away" (Brown and Kara 2013). "Actually," she says, "this week

I took another photograph out of our living room and put it upstairs in the closet." Both partners have been removing the photos. For Ethan, a key motivation is that these images represent him as female. Kara understood this de-photographing as part of the process of transition: "I knew intellectually that there would be a moment where we're not going to keep photographs of a stranger in our home." But she looked forward to making new aspirational fictions when Ethan's body caught up to his gender identity: "we've got new adventures to go on and there will be new photographs and that's cool." Partner intimacy, so resistant to the documentation of tears, can sometimes evade photography itself. Partners in transition, though perhaps evading the "event" of photography within the home, nonetheless remain in dialogue with the photographic event: the camera is a powerful form of "commotion and communion," regardless of the photograph itself (Azoulay 2012: 15).

In bringing together these diverse scenes of weeping, we do not intend to impose a false sense of unity between them, but rather we acknowledge their disconnection. Though this unorthodox approach might seem unruly and even chaotic, we think it is an apt and necessary way to point to new directions in the affective turn. Feelings, after all, are messy. Historicizing the emotions, in this case the pleasures and sorrows of tears, offers insights into the ways that photography shows—and fails to show—a full spectrum of feelings as they circulate between public and private spheres, the cultural work that these feelings make possible and foreclose, and above all the histories of which they are a part.

Acknowledgments

We gratefully acknowledge the Social Sciences and Humanities Research Council of Canada for supporting our research. This chapter is dedicated to the memory of Andrea Noble, who taught us so much about feeling and friendship.

Note

1 Source details are not available for this extract. This part of the chapter was written by Andrea Noble, who died in 2017. Brown and Phu are not specialists in her area and do not have access to her notes.

References

Ahmed, S. (2004a) "Affective Economies," *Social Text*, 22 (2), pp. 117–139.
Ahmed, S. (2004b) *The Cultural Politics of Emotion*, London: Routledge.
Azoulay, A. (2012) *Civil Imagination: A Political Ontology of Photography*, London: Verso.
Barthes, R. (1981) *Camera Lucida: Reflections on Photography*, trans. R. Howard. New York: Hill and Wang.
Batchen, G. (1997) *Burning with Desire: the Conception of Photography*, Cambridge: MIT Press.
Berlant, L. (2007) *Cruel Optimism*, Durham: Duke University Press.
Bourdieu, P. (1996) *Photography: A Middle-Brow Art*, Stanford: Stanford University Press.
Boym, S. (2001) *The Future of Nostalgia*, New York: Basic Books.
Brown, E. (2009) "De Meyer at *Vogue*: Commercializing Queer Affect in WWI-era Fashion Photography," *Photography and Culture*, 2 (3), pp. 253–275.
Brown, E. and Anna (2012) "Anna," interview #0025.
Brown, E. and Kara (2013) "Interview with "Kara": Interview # 0029.
Brown, E. (2019) *Work! A Queer History of Modeling*, Durham: Duke University Press.
Brown, E. and Phu, T. (eds.) (2014) *Feeling Photography*, Durham: Duke University Press.
Burgin, V. (1982) *Thinking Photography*, London: Palgrave Macmillan.
Camarena, A. (1968) "Lloraba como un niño de la emoción," *Esto*, p. 17.

Campt, T. (2012) *Image Matters: Archive, Photography, and the African Diaspora in Europe*, Durham: Duke University Press.
Caruth, C. (1996) *Unclaimed Experience: Trauma, Narrative, History*, Baltimore: Johns Hopkins Press.
Chaudhary, K. (2012) *Afterimage of Empire: Photography and Nineteenth-Century India*, Minneapolis: University of Minnesota Press.
Cho, L. (2009) "Citizenship and the Bonds of Affect: The Passport Photograph," *Photography and Culture*, 2 (3), pp. 275–287.
Clough, P. and Halley, J. (eds.) (2007) *The Affective Turn: Theorizing the Social*, Durham, NC: Duke University Press.
Cvetkovich, A. (2007) "Public Feelings," *South Atlantic Quarterly*, 106 (3), pp. 459–468.
Cvetkovich, A. (2012) *Depression: A Public Feeling*, Durham: Duke University Press.
Darwin, C. (1979) *The Expression of Emotions in Humans and Animals*, New York: St. Martin's Press.
Dolan, J. (2005) *Utopia in Performance: Finding Hope at the Theatre*, Ann Arbor: University of Michigan Press.
Duchenne, G.-B. (1990) *The Mechanism of Human Facial Expression*, trans. R. Cuthbertson (ed.) Cambridge: Cambridge University Press.
Ebersole, G. (2000) "The Function of Ritual Weeping Revisited: Affective Discourse and Moral Discourse," *History of Religions*, 39 (3), pp. 211–246.
Edwards, E. (2012) "Objects of Affect: Photography Beyond the Image," *Annual Review of Anthropology*, 41, pp. 221–234.
El Universal (1968) "Juventud Limpia," p. 6. [online]. Available at: http://archivo.eluniversal.com.mx/estilos/19376.html [Accessed October 26, 2016].
Fleetwood, N. (2015) "Posing in Prison: Family Photographs, Emotional Labor, and Carceral Intimacy," *Public Culture*, 27 (3), pp. 487–511.
Frevert, U. (2011) *Emotions in History: Lost and Found*, Budapest and New York: Central University Press.
González de Bustamante, C. (2013) *Muy Buenas Noches: Mexico, Television, and the Cold War*, Lincoln: University of Nebraska Press, pp. 236–237.
Hardt, M. (1999) "Affective Labor," *Boundary 2*, 26 (2), pp. 89–100.
Huynh, D. (2011) "Nhiếp ảnh gia Nguyễn Ngọc Hạnh và những tác phẩm một thời vang bóng," *Người Việt*, [online] Available at: http://saigonecho.info/main/doisong/danhnhan/23694-nhip-nh-gia-nguyn-ngc-hnh-va-nhng-tac-phm-mt-thi-vang-bong.html [Accessed April 27, 2016].
Katz, J. (1999) *How Emotions Work*, Chicago: University of Chicago Press.
Kozol, W. (2014) *Distant Wars Visible: The Ambivalence of Witnessing*, Minneapolis: University of Minneapolis Press.
Leys, R. (2011) "The Turn to Affect," *Critical Inquiry*, 37, pp. 434–472.
MacArthur, H. and Shields, S. (2015) "There's No Crying in Baseball, or Is There? Male Athletes, Tears, and Masculinity in North America," *Emotion Review*, 7 (1), pp. 39–46.
Manalansan, M. (2014) "The 'Stuff' of Archives: Mess, Migration, and Queer Lives," *Radical History Review*, 12, pp. 94–107.
Moten, F. (2002) "Black 'Mo'nin'," in: D. Eng and D. Kazangian (eds.) *Loss: The Politics of Mourning*, Berkeley: University of California Press, 63, pp. 59–76.
Munoz, J. (1999) *Disidentifications: Queers of Color and the Performance of Politics*, Minneapolis: University of Minnesota Press.
Ngai, S. (2005) *Ugly Feelings*, Cambridge: Harvard University Press.
Noble, A. (2010) "*Photography and Memory in Mexico*: *Icons of Revolution*," Manchester: Manchester University Press.
Pernau, M. and Rajamani, I. (2016) "Emotional Translations: Conceptual History Beyond Language," *History and Theory*, 55 (1), pp. 46–65.
Phu, T. and Brown, E. (2018) "The Cultural Politics of Aspiration: Family Photography's Mixed Feelings," *Journal of Visual Culture*, 17 (2), pp. 152–165.
Phu, T., Brown, E., and Dewan, D. (2017) "The Family Camera Network." *Photography and Culture*, 10 (2), pp. 147–163.
Reddy, W. (2001) *The Navigation of Feeling: A Framework for the History of Emotions*, Cambridge: Cambridge University Press.
Rosenwein, B. (2002) "Worrying about Emotions in History," *The American Historical Review*, 107 (3), pp. 821–845.
Rosenwein, B. (2006) *Emotional Communities in the Early Middle Ages*, Ithaca: Cornell University Press.

Runia, E. (2006) "Presence," *History and Theory*, 45, pp. 1–29.
Scheer, M. (2012) "Are Emotions a Kind of Practice? (And Is That What Makes Them Have a History?) A Bourdeauian Approach to Understanding Emotions," *History and Theory*, 51 (2), pp. 193–220.
Sedgwick, Eve Kosofsky (2003) *Touching Feeling: Affect, Pedagogy, Performativity*, Durham: Duke University Press.
Sheehan, T. (2014) "Looking Pleasant, Feeling White: The Social Politics of the Photographic Smile," in: E. Brown and T. Phu (eds.) *Feeling Photography*, Durham: Duke University Press, pp. 127–157.
Sliwinski, S. (2011) *Human Rights in Camera*, Chicago: University of Chicago Press.
Smith, S. (2013) *At the Edge of Sight: Photography and the Unseen*, Durham: Duke University Press.
Smith, S. and Sliwinski, S. (eds.) (2017) *Optical Unconscious*, Durham: Duke University Press.
Sontag, S. (1977) *On Photography*, New York: Farrar, Strauss and Giroux.
Stearns, P. and Stearns, C. (1985) "Emotionology: Clarifying the History of Emotions and Emotional Standards," *The American Historical Review*, 90 (4), pp. 813–836.
Stewart, K. (2007) *Ordinary Affects*, Durham, NC: Duke University Press.
Tompkins, S. (1962–1963) *Affect imagery consciousness: The Negative Affects*, Volumes. I and II. New York: Springer.
Wallis, M. and Smith, S. (2012) *Pictures and Progress: Early Photography and the Making of African American Identity*, Durham: Duke University Press.
Ward, J. (2010) "Gender Labor: Transmen, Femmes, and the Collective Work of Transgression," *Sexualities*, 13 (2), pp. 236–254.
Wexler, L. (2017) "The Purloined Image," in: S. Smith and S. Sliwinski (eds.) *Optical Unconscious*, Durham: Duke University Press, pp. 264–280.
Wissinger, E. (2007) "Modelling a Way of Life: Immaterial and Affective Labor in the Fashion Modeling Industry," *Ephemera: Theory And Politics In Organization*, 7 (1), pp. 250–269.
Zolov, E. (2013) "Introduction: Latin America in the Global Sixties," *The Americas*, 70 (3), pp. 349–362.
Zuromskis, C. (2013) *Snapshot Photography: The Lives of Images*, Cambridge: MIT Press.

2

Jacques Rancière

Aesthetics and photography

David Bate

In dozens of books, lectures and interviews, the French philosopher Jacques Rancière has made a significant contribution to recent discussions of contemporary art. Given that photography has now joined the list of fine arts, albeit as a somewhat junior and more recent member, we also need to ask: what is the relation between photography and aesthetic discourse? Why? Because so far photography has had a rather awkward relation to aesthetics. While art photography is part of these discussions in contemporary art and philosophy, 'photography' is nevertheless an apparatus that is active across many other spheres of cultural practice too. Some of these uses have little or no relation to art. How, then, might Rancière's work be of use to those interested in photography as a wider cultural practice rather than as simply a component of contemporary art and art criticism? This chapter aims to consider this issue: the wider relation of photography to aesthetics in the work of Rancière.

Rancière's work is unusual in that it belongs to a thread of radical French intellectual thought that began in the 1960s and is distanced from the usual traditions of aesthetic discourse in classical philosophy. However, Rancière was also, for many years (from 1969 to 2000), a professor of philosophy at the University of Paris VIII (Saint Denis, Vincennes) in France. Since he retired in 2000 (though he is still an honorary professor), his lectures, books, essays and interviews have become prolific. Artists, art historians, critics and theorists alike have read his work with great interest, which is not only due to his polymath interests in art, across the whole gamut of contemporary practices (e.g. cinema, literature, music, painting, performance, theatre, video and photography), but also because of the conceptual framework, language and questions that he has brought to these fields of cultural activity. Writing after postmodernism, Rancière is clearly less interested in 'medium specificity', as his writings eschew traditional notions and values attributed to each of them. No doubt important here is the fact that, although Rancière broke with the radical French thought of his formative time, he has not lost the general perspective on culture that such theories advanced. These theories were centred in the political philosophy of Louis Althusser, whose once influential key writings on ideology, such as "Ideological State Apparatuses" (Althusser 1971), dominated certain forms of political and cultural theory and had informed film studies and photography theory too. Although Rancière rejected the political thesis of Althusser, Rancière's theoretical work remains committed to considering the ideological (or 'political') functions of photography through their aesthetic operations. This much, at least, is adopted from Althusser, in the examination of how the body is affected by the regimes of representation into which it is constantly being inducted. This is very different from a conventional aesthetic discourse, with its notions of 'beauty' and 'truth', through which photography is usually examined, tested and evaluated as a 'fine art'. Rancière also constantly expresses a clear interest in the historical and material conditions of artworks too. He often refers to their context, alongside the issues of performance, exhibition space and thus the "modes of perception and regimes of emotion, categories that identify them, thought patterns that categorize and interpret them" (Rancière 2013: x). In this way, Rancière marks himself out from philosophers of aesthetics and shows that political philosophy can contribute to the development of critical aesthetics, rather than adopting, as some others do, the position of a philosophical *ideologue*.

So, this chapter poses two further questions: first, what does philosophy—or, more specifically, what can aesthetics—have to say about photography today; and second, what contribution do Jacques Rancière's recent writings make to the understanding of photography? I will start with the first question, because the issue of what philosophy has contributed to debates about photography gets in the way of aesthetics, as it is developed in Rancière's work.

It should be stressed at the outset that Jacques Rancière's work, rooted in philosophical and aesthetic theories, has arguments and discussions that can often remain abstract and pitched at a rather general level. These abstractions can create some difficulties, precisely because they do not aim or claim to address the simple empirical categories of photographic practice familiar in everyday discourse. In fact, the accumulation of those social and historical categories might be said to be precisely one of the very obstacles to rethinking what 'photography' is or does today. In this sense, Rancière's work makes photography appear as something slightly unfamiliar within his framework of categories. For example, Rancière often refers to 'art' or the 'arts', but uses these terms in numerous ways, which can be confusing. 'Art' is not necessarily something only to be found within a museum or art gallery, but also in cinema, music and many other cultural practices, as ways of 'doing things'. By definition, these other practices include a variety of different types of photography. Rancière's general conception of 'art' as ways of making and doing things is broad, and this is already one of Rancière's contributions towards rethinking aesthetics, asking *where* aesthetic questions and problems can be found. We have become far too accustomed to think that art is only what *appears* within the discourse of art and its related practices of art criticism and history. What also distinguishes Rancière's work from other philosophers is that he develops his work in dialogue with (rather than ignoring) work already developed in art and photography theory. The aim of the following argument is not to go over and explain all the categories that he uses, but to consider the ways in which Rancière's work might be introduced to help us reconceptualize photography, perhaps even to rethink photography theory. This involves first putting into context the question of aesthetics and philosophy, before engaging with Rancière's contribution to the debates and the issue of photographic aesthetics.

Aesthetics and philosophy

Aesthetics, as a branch of philosophy, is usually linked to the tradition of the fine arts, although that was not the aim of its original founder. Aesthetics as a discipline is generally attributed to Alexander Gottlieb Baumgarten and his book *Aesthetica*, published in 1750–58, which is widely regarded as the beginning of aesthetics as a distinct discipline (Barasch 2000: 2). Baumgarten's aim in instituting aesthetics had been to deal with what philosophy had until that point tended to ignore: the experience of the human body. Baumgarten's work set out to develop, explore and understand the "domain of sensual cognition" (Barasch 2000: 2) and drew on the Greek term *aisthesis*, which designates experience, as the sensations that affect human perception and the corporeal body. (Rancière revived the use of this Greek word as the title of his 2013 book *Aisthesis*.) However, Baumgarten's 'aesthetics' quickly became synonymous with the development of an art criticism and theory. Art became the realm that was designated as dealing with these affective states, beyond the pure logic of 'rationality'. As this new field of 'aesthetic' enquiry became increasingly rarefied, with the narrow scope of its objects and its focus on 'beauty'—a discourse that culminated in European romanticism—it lost its more open-mined aim of sense experience in the wider cultural sense. For its eighteenth-century purveyors, the 'aesthete' became a 'man of sensibility' whose values were a matter of 'taste'. Firmly located in aristocratic power-based structures, and especially in England, aesthetics developed into a defensive discourse on a corrective 'social taste' based on the value-judgements of the 'aesthete', these persons of special taste (Williams 1983: 32). Even the very influential concepts of the 'beautiful and sublime' introduced by Edmund Burke, the English conservative, eventually became a somewhat limited binary opposition for anyone wishing to pursue a more broadly expansive field of aesthetic enquiry into human experience (Burke 2008 [1759]). Traditional aesthetics had little to say about the bad new things such as photography and cinema.

Likewise, in parallel to the development of aesthetics, the role of philosophy in the study of photography has not been very developed or useful either. The aim of classical philosophy, in the end, is to do *philosophy*, not photography, which is merely a newly acquired object in its gaze. In philosophy, photography becomes an object of its philosophical discourse. As the old saying goes, 'water' is not the same thing to a fish, a fisherman or a meteorologist. Similarly, photography is not the same thing to a photographer, an art critic or a philosopher. In philosophy, photography is not the same object as it is to a photographer. We may note that even the French philosopher Jacques Derrida, who wanted to get out of philosophy by deconstructing it (and the metaphysics of presence in philosophy) and argued philosophically to do so, once argued that this was nigh on impossible to do (Derrida 1981). So, when philosophy or its agents (philosophers) speak about photography, it is as a concept broadly conceived as useful to philosophy, not photographic practice. Philosophy subjugates photography to the aims of philosophy, as an object to deal with philosophical questions such as the 'essence of being', 'truth', 'realism' and 'ontology', or other such apparently immutable and foundational values. In short, photography becomes an object *for* philosophical speculation. Although there is obviously nothing wrong with this activity, such philosophical practice has made little contribution to the understanding of photography, either as a general cultural practice, or as its myriad of different usages and varieties of purpose. Nor has it, because these are not its concerns, dealt with the concerns of the parties involved in its practice and meaning, or indeed the values involved in the social institutions that produce and distribute photographic images or the people who use and consume them. The vicissitudes of contemporary photography and its ideologies show little regard for philosophical notions of truth, even in news photography, let alone the abstract logic and niceties of its rigour. We might say that, although the abstract notion of 'truth', for example, has philosophical value, it is not at all clear how this question on truth can have any real impact on understanding practical photographic discourse.

Photography theory, with its interdisciplinary framework (sociology, semiotics, psychology and cultural theory), has already developed such discussions and answers in response to specific problems and questions over many decades. That philosophers have often tended to repeat these same theoretical problems as though they are new questions (which, of course, they may be in philosophy), without apparently realizing that they have already been addressed elsewhere, is baffling. In this respect, there has been a problem with the questions philosophy has asked in its recent discourses, because philosophical speculations on photography have tended to ignore these existing discourses of photographic theory (Walden 2010). An example here is the recurring, fundamental question posed about photography concerning its 'identity': *what is photography?* This question, already asked many times in many different ways and places, always tends to presuppose a *singular* answer: 'photography is *this*' *or* 'photography is *that*'.

Many such discussions turn this question on photography into the matter of its *singularity*. Photography thus becomes, in its theoretical-philosophical conception, a singular 'essence' situated in one or another of the many cliché ideas of photography. The essence of photography is (a) in the 'instant', as seen in the everyday practices of snapshot photography, which (b) always tell 'the truth' about (c) 'reality'; or the essence of photography is (d) in 'manipulation', through 'tricks' and deceit, as with 'creative' computer manipulations; or, more abstractly, photography *is* (e) the 'freezing of time' or (f) the 'capturing' of a moment. Others popular notions emphasize (g) the importance of the horizon line and frame or (h) deep focus as *the* valued essence of photography. Some modernists may also claim that photography has (i) a technological essence, which is usually based on the falling of light on a (analogue) chemical base. There are updates to this model from techno-modernists who argue that these old theoretical formulations of photography have simply disappeared and are reformulated (j) as invisible metadata. Alternatively, it may be argued that (k) the 'photographic' is straightforwardly continued by the newer technical base of light falling on a sensor, registered as computerized signals and composed of pixels and metadata—thus configured as a new abstract computer code.

In the many versions of these 'essences', photography is fundamentally *realistic* and 'truthful' or, conversely, always *manipulative* and 'false'. Photography may thus be an art, or not, depending on whether it is 'objective', or not, and thus completely flawed, or conversely raised to the dignity of an art as a result. All these sets of propositions, 'chaotic conceptions', in their formulation of what photography is end in the reduction of the complexity of photographic practices down into an abstract singular *essence*. Philosophers, just as much as everyone else, have fallen into this linguistic trap, perhaps unintentionally set by the early pioneering figures in 'photography', who coined the term *photography* in their attempt to create a name for these diverse practices, then needing something to unite them. We are left, precisely, with the impression that photography is a singular entity. This common-sense notion of photography as a singular medium, repeated in recent philosophers' work, returns our thinking to zero (Walden 2010). To repeat these old arguments about the identity of photography is to make the same mistakes, treading over old ground with little new light and even less heat than they ever had before. Yet, paraded as 'new' theories of photography, these 'philosophical' ideas have also implicitly constituted photography as an aesthetic form.

Photography theory, at least in its late twentieth-century, pre-amnesia mode, came up with a radical solution to the problem of defining 'photography': to recognize that what we call photography is *not* a singular thing, and thus cannot be defined as such. We find this argument appearing in different places, formulated differently in different disciplines: in sociology and anthropology, for example, it was recognized that photography had a variety of different uses and values, but it was also to be found within the theoretical arguments developed in the new growth of communication studies emergent in the 1960s. It could be found in the theories of the Italian semiotician Umberto Eco, who aimed to elaborate the various specific, distinctive photographic codes alongside the non-photographic codes at work in a photographic image (Eco 1982). Any photograph, Eco argued, is a complex combination of diverse codes, such that any photograph can be organized in a variety of ways, depending upon the particular codes deployed in it. In Eco's work, one of these codes was called 'aesthetic' (as a component of stylistic codes), but it was one to which the other codes of photography could not be reduced, at least not within a semiotic framework (Eco 1982: 38). The theoretical conclusions were clear: there was no unified 'language' of photography; there would only be, at best, 'dialects' speaking in different tongues. Genres could be conceived as larger units of meaning, organized by particular combinations and arrangements of codes. The theoretical definition of 'photography' would be closer to what we call 'writing', an abstract term that designates a practice which involves all kinds of functions and purposes, languages, dialects, lexicons, verbs, adjectives, nouns, phonetics, phonemes, discourses, grammars and institutions.

The discursive field of photography

The lack of singularity in what we are still obliged to call 'photography', for want of a better term, was usefully summarized in John Tagg's encapsulating phrase: "Photography as such has no identity" (Tagg 1988: 63). This statement can be grasped even more tangibly at an institutional and discursive level. The different institutional practices that mobilize photographic technologies do so in ways that are very often contradictory or are used for different aims. Military and police photographs, for instance, are radically different in their aim, form and purpose in political and judicial discourses from the function of glossy advertising photographs, whose aim is to sell luxury goods and products to consumers. The highly crafted Photoshop fantasies that place commodities and their ideal users within dream-like fantasy or fairy tale existences have little to do with the ontological certainties of the medium required by the command of military and police photography. During World War Two, the new military use of aerial photographs demanded specialized training to make them legible, such that photograph 'interpreters' were employed to pore over the aerial photographs for signs of troops, weapons and hidden military installations. Equally, when the medical photograph of a traumatized body is made, it has a completely different function and status to fashion photographs, whose purpose is to eroticize or embellish parts of the body, through the gaps and styling of the clothing. Do all these differences seem obvious? So, when a philosopher attempts, as an intellectual discourse, to claim that photographs are ontologically certain (or, conversely, uncertain) objects, we are right to ask: of what photograph do you speak? How can a single example justify a universal claim about photography? 'Photography' has so many different functions and uses that its singular definition does not exist.

Instead, we have to say that these are *discursive fields* of photographic practice, which should replace the certitude of the singular, and which require more specific social and historically materialist accounts of these practices. Such an account would thus seek to situate the detailed specificities of use and functions of photography within this larger framework, a framework that might be able to grasp what we should call, no matter how inelegantly, our contemporary *photographies*?

Some may, however, insist that, despite all the various 'surface' differences between innumerable photographic practices (e.g. fashion, documentary, advertising, military, art, social network feeds, tourism, agitprop, etc.), 'photography' is in fact unified by one thing: the specific characteristics of it as a *medium*. Here, again, the proposition of the 'medium' attempts to sneak through the back door of technology the definition of 'photography' as a unified entity, as an apparatus with an inherent set of singular characteristics. Photography, as such, turns out to be some kind of a persistent 'myth'.

The term 'myth' here is used in the sense that Roland Barthes had once proposed it, as borrowed from Claude Lévi-Strauss (Barthes 1973). As a concept, 'myth' was introduced to understand the process by which historical material—that is, culture and cultural meanings—is turned into natural material, as 'nature', which thus puts it beyond any critique (Barthes 1973). At the same time, this myth of the 'nature of photography' also serves to further legitimate its existence. So, what we call 'photography' (as the sum of a variety of different cameras, pictures, forms and institutional uses) is given its imaginary unity in the nominalist function of its very name. Myths are maintained as long as a common belief in them exists, no matter how historically contingent the belief is. People may one day look back at our culture and wonder how on earth we could have ever believed photography existed! Indeed, we may suspect that one of the reasons for the very persistence of 'photography' as a categorical term today is precisely because it is at a time when the belief in its singularity as a 'medium' is under threat from all sides, permeated by computational and other social-technological values. Perhaps there is a vague intuition here, in the idea that 'photography' is already the residue of an older, categorical defence of the photographic image, renewed and deployed as a weapon against its very abolition in the uncertainties of a 'post-medium' age. I say all this not to demean, diminish or dismiss the significance of the categorical use of the terms 'photography', 'photographic image', or even 'aesthetics' and 'philosophy', but to outline problems and issues that beset anyone wishing to pursue the relations between them. Just as the term 'photography' creates a problem with the notion of its singularity, so too do the terms of philosophical speculation upon it and the accompanying but separate field of aesthetics.

If the aesthetics of photography is to be developed as a particular field of enquiry, then we need a broader framework in which the sensory experience and its affect on the body of photographic images can be located. We need a conceptual framework for aesthetics. We can already see some attempts to generate these sorts of framework within the historical debates of photography. These historical debates about the definition of photography in the nineteenth and twentieth centuries can be seen as precisely a struggle between different versions of the aesthetic, argued as essentialist myths concerning photography: about what it should, could or would ideally *be*. Nineteenth-century debates, subsequent to the notion of the photographic image as a 'copying' device for nature, were developed as a series of polemics about its aesthetic characteristics and most fully characterized and articulated in the debates of Pictorialism. The pictorialists argued that photography should maintain a certain affinity and expressive continuity with the sensibilities of European painting and its traditions, although they differed in how photography should do this, and it is possible to see a number of deviations within this field. The early twentieth century brought two new aesthetic ideals, which fought each other: modernism and the avant-garde. Modernism held that there was a specific characteristic to photography as a medium, located in its purity as a 'straight' (and thus 'unmanipulated') picture. The beauty of photography was in its honesty, a value defined by purity in its process, and as a 'purely visual' practice. Avant-garde photography wanted to smash up those traditional aesthetic values of beauty and purity and did so by intervening *within* them, including on the photographic image/object. Sometimes this meant literally tearing up a picture or disrupting its precious 'visuality' by adding written text, noise, smell or other disruptive materials. Modernism and avant-garde were both aesthetic discourses overlaid by a third 'aesthetic' programme, one that did not want to present itself as such. This was social documentary and photographic realism. Documentary photography (and other commensurate documentary practices—film, writing and theatre) was instituted by existing older literary forms of narrative and its motifs (description, action and tragedy) being taken up and presented in a newer, predominantly visual, form.[1] In the 1980s, postmodernist practices recognized the fracturing of these three overlapping aesthetic discourses so that modernism, avant-garde and realism were rejected in all their endless 'seriousness'. After this, all these old aesthetic formations have found themselves being exploited, used for a multitude of purpose for which they had not been intended. Now mixed and 'mashed up' into the publicity industries of advertising, fashion, music and popular consumer cultures, the attempts to return to the older categories remains a constant project, albeit overlaid by the sense of déjà vu. It is precisely dissatisfaction with these categories that Jacques Rancière brings into the scene of art and aesthetics:

> I do not think that the notions of modernity and the avant-garde have been very enlightening when it comes to thinking about the new forms of art that have emerged since the last century or the relations between aesthetics and politics.
>
> *(Rancière 2004: 20)*

Yet this argument already risks getting ahead of itself, as Jacques Rancière's contribution towards the discussion of art has been to shatter its internal coherence from another perspective.

The three regimes

Rancière's work on aesthetics offers a different conceptual framework in which photography can be addressed not as a singular form, but as forms of identification within what Rancière calls the "three regimes of images" (Rancière 2004: 20). Rancière's use of the term 'regime' is worth paying attention to as this term operates as part of the conceptual framework that he uses to situate arguments about modernity, art and the specific cultural practices that manifest them, including still and moving photographic images. We can already see in this framework the rethinking of the cultural sphere in which arts and media practices are conceptualized.

Within this framework, 'photography' needs no longer to be a mythic singular entity segregated from art, nor to be reduced to one or more of its social or empirical functions (e.g. the promotion of reality or fantasy in documentary or advertising, etc.). Instead, 'photography' can be a summary term, recognized as without essence, but defined as a totality of different practices, with no singular purpose. The functions of these different *photographies* in their contributions to cultural practices may be grasped in quite specific ways, *differently*.

In his book *The Politics of Aesthetics*, Jacques Rancière outlines three "major regimes of identification," as distinct conceptual categories. These are: the *ethical* regime of images, the *representative* regime and the *aesthetic* regime (Rancière 2004: 20). The representative regime is probably the most familiar of the three, given the general concept of 'representation' is already so familiar, if not dominant, in studies of photography.[2] The traditional aim of representation is *mimesis*, to "produce specific entities called imitations" (Rancière 2004: 21). The representative regime is harnessed towards establishing forms of normativity in the world, although it is not its necessary aim. That is to say, mimesis (or imitation) is the standard instrument and procedure by which communities, cultures and societies define themselves *as* themselves. This nuance to the logic that the representative function is not necessarily 'normative' is important, because the representative function is not a matter of any particular form, 'medium' or even ideology (e.g. in literature, photography, cinema, music), but the collective effect of them as disparate elements contributing towards the representative regime. So, for example, all the genres of photography inherited from painting—notably, landscape, portraiture, pictorial scenes (historical tableaux as news photography) and still life—typically belong to this long history of practices that aim to demonstrate the appearance of society to and as itself. Such a function of representation is not restricted to what today we crudely call the 'mass media' or 'art', as the representative function might well overlap into and across these arenas in complex ways.

It is worth noting that an attempt to develop an analysis of this 'representative' function in theoretical studies of the photographic image is exactly what Roland Barthes had identified in his various essays on photography, such as the 1964 "Rhetoric of the Image" (Barthes 1977), through to even his last work, *Camera Lucida* (Barthes 1980). In fact, Rancière refers to Barthes' last essay precisely because of its engagement with the division between the "sayable" and "visible" in the representative regime (Rancière 2007: 9–11). Just as Rancière drew on Aristotle's *Poetics*, so too did Roland Barthes for his "Rhetoric of the Image" essay, linking the concept of *image* (via its linguistic root in *imitari*) to *imitation* as representation. Barthes sought to analyse the operations of photographic mimesis in the representative operations at work in an advertising image for French pasta. Barthes outlines the mechanics of classical rhetoric and its figures (e.g. metaphor, metonymy, puns) busy at work in the communicative logic of the modern advertising image, just as much as they already were in classical paintings. His essay aims not only to deconstruct the supposed 'innocence' of an advertising image, but also to show the complexity of codes at work in a photographic image. It was quickly pointed out that such rhetorical figures of representation are active in other forms of photographic image, as well as in advertising: documentary, photojournalism and art, only differently (Burgin 1982). Such semiotic analyses aimed to 'deconstruct' the hallowed social distinctions held about different photographic practices, not to diminish one or another of them, but, as indicated at the time, so that we may construe their semiotic differences *differently*. Although we are all too used to separating art and media (and now the newer categorical distinction of 'social media') as separate entities, these categories can be brought out using Rancière's conceptual framework, as part of the representative regime (and the conflicts that lie within it).

This new framework of regimes also enables us to address an oft felt 'unease' within critical debates when 'commercial or industrial' photography is discussed uneasily as art or as a 'creative practice'. Here there is often a reluctance to assign artistic merit or *any* critical aesthetic value to commercial fields of photographic practice. In this sense, 'art' or 'artistic' are used as terms of value, but only assigned to a commercial practice when and where it has been *authorized* as such by their presence within the art institution. Hence the tautological functional definition of art that what is 'art' is defined by the network of museums, galleries, magazines, criticism and art market discourse that name things as such, reserved for objects identified as 'artworks'. Commercial photography is often conceived as 'creative' or 'artistic' by those who work within the field, who sometimes feel that such definitions generally exclude the aesthetic merits of their practice. Similarly with the multifarious industrial and social uses of photography, which are not usually—only with rare exceptions—included in art institutions. (One might argue that photography galleries were set up to circumvent this problem, only to find that they now perpetuate the problem with these contradictions.) However, commercial images, in general, would tend to fall within what Rancière calls the *ethical regime* of images. Here:

> 'art' is not identified as such but is subsumed under the question of images. As a specific type of entity, images are the object of a twofold question: the question of their origin

> (and consequently their truth content) and the question of their end or purpose, the uses they are put to and the effects they result in. The question of images of the divine and the right to produce such images or the ban placed on them falls within this regime, as well as the question of the status and signification of the images produced.
>
> *(Rancière 2004: 20–21)*

We might note that the ethical regime of images can cover a broad spectrum of public images—news, journalism and documentary pictures, through to fashion and advertising—and the ethical limits of all these images, for example in their relation to religious images or political discourse. Such a broad spectrum of image is included because the *ethical regime* is a Platonic category that is concerned with the way an image affects communities and the individuals who receive it. However, as Rancière points out, this is not to reduce ethics to the notion of politics, because politics, as 'the political', is seen as a sum of operations at work across all three regimes. This brings us to the third and perhaps most complex conception, Rancière's *aesthetic regime.*

The aesthetic regime is what is identified as art, though not as it was in the eighteenth and nineteenth centuries—that is, as categories of taste or specific 'sensibilities'. For Rancière, the aesthetic is "something" that will occasionally interfere with the mimetic conventions of the representative regime. This interference or distinction, Rancière argues, must be a "pure instance of suspension, a moment when form is experienced for itself. Moreover, it is the moment of the formation and education of a specific type of humanity" (Rancière 2004: 24).

Rancière goes on to trace glimpses of the aesthetic regime within traditional aesthetics theories—in Kant's historically unknowing 'genius', in Schiller's 'aesthetic state' and Schelling's definition of art as the identification between a conscious and unconscious process—or, in literature, in Marcel Proust's unwilled novel and the later surrealist 'automatism' of image production or the cinematic operation of scenes in Robert Bresson's films (Rancière 2004: 23). However, these local (European) examples do little to elaborate the problematic of the aesthetic regime as he sees it.

At the heart of the aesthetic regime in Rancière's thought, the 'aesthetic' is something that interferes within the representative regime's conventions. In fact, we may usefully relate these two regimes, aesthetic and representative, more or less directly to Rancière's political couplet, the categories of *consensus* and *dissensus.* In this distinction, the representative regime is linked to the consensual dimensions of society, whereas the function of the aesthetic regime of image correlates to the dissensual sense, which interrupts the representative regime's conventions of sense. However, the category of dissensus is not to be equated with the call for yet another new 'avant-garde', simply to update the old avant-garde's strategies of 'shock' and 'anti-aesthetic' practice. This is because, first, an art that already announces itself as dissensual in a nostalgic form is unlikely to have much effect, but also because the dissensual is defined as a kind of rupture or conflict that may come from *within* the representational regime: "Dissensus is a conflict between a sensory presentation and a way of making sense of it, or between several sensory and/or 'bodies'" (Rancière 2010: 139). Clearly, the photographic image, so central in the everyday workings of consensual society, would be highly susceptible to these conflicts in the representative regime and its sensory affects that Rancière calls aesthetic. We should note here that the aesthetic regime of the image is not entirely or simply identical with the history of art, as some have assumed, or with the types of object collected in art museums, which are meant to represent these instances. (An idea of which many are likely to be unconvinced.)

We are not to assume that the given narratives of art history are identical to specific histories of modernity, especially given that these narratives of art history are so often mutable and changing. Rancière is indeed sceptical about modernity within art and the confusion in its histories, even claiming that the history of art makes attempts to conceal the aesthetic regime within its own institutional narratives. "It traces, in order either to exalt or deplore it, a simple line of transition or rupture between the old and the new, the representative and the non-representative or the anti-representative" (Rancière 2004: 24).

Now we may see why or how images that emerge to serve the function of the representative or ethical regime, as located within the sphere of commercial images, may well actually contribute to the aesthetic regime too. Certain pictures, images or projects in these fields, such as fashion, editorial photography and magazine essays—and, to update the references, even Snapchat images (or other social media image platforms)—may well have an affect within their relation to the aesthetic regime, by creating a dissensual effect from within the representative/ethical regimes. Such unexpected consequences may not even be intended by the author of the work, or necessarily be recognized by them or the art institution. All this is why the dissensual effect of the aesthetic regime is not to be *simply* or exclusively identified with the art establishment or its opposites. However, in general, Rancière does tend to draw the dissensual definition of politics together with art in a relation of direct equivalence: "artworks can produce effects of dissensus precisely because they neither give lessons nor have any destination" (Rancière 2010: 140).[3] Rancière offers an account that can at least *acknowledge* and *recognize* the sense perceptions of aesthetic pleasure and excited disruption of image experiences, which are not already defined as 'art'. On the other hand, it also shows that what is considered to be art may not necessarily have any 'dissensual' aesthetic effect, at least not now, and in fact may only further reinforce the existing representative regime, giving it yet more life and vitality. These new conceptions of the aesthetic, representative and ethical regimes work together to loosen the essentialist definitions of 'photography' from their jaded roots. This is because the aesthetic, ethical and representative issues of a practice are not (any longer) founded in the technical properties of a medium.

Aesthetics and its relation to the representative regime belong to the 'ethos', the community of individuals that constitutes any society. Thus, aesthetics is not reducible to singular concepts of the medium, or to any specific institutional affiliations of photographers as artists or as 'truth seekers', and so on. These are also the reasons why Rancière, unlike many other philosophers around today, rejects a singular general global concept of Western art or aesthetics. So, how, if such 'ground clearing' leaves us rudderless and without direction or just dizzy from the vertigo of these new vocabularies, should we return to the object of this essay—no matter now how imaginary—'photography'? How can we account for photography in the aesthetic regime today?

Aesthetic regime

For Rancière, aesthetics, or aisthesis as he later refers to it, is the 'aesthetic regime' whose function "delegitimizes the representative age's well-ordered plots and in turn grants legitimacy to the pathos of knowledge" (Rancière 2009a: 61). What examples might be chosen to make such a statement clearer or more 'obvious'? Rancière's essays and remarks on photography are somewhat scattered and dispersed across his writing, although his contribution to the aesthetic debates of photography is just as clearly introduced through his views on literature or cinema.

Speaking of his relation to cinema, Rancière says that it is one of a *cinéphilie*, as born of a love of cinema. This passion, he remarks, "lacks discrimination" (Rancière 2014: 2), which results in a mixing up of taste and values. This mixing creates a certain disruption in established views, breaking some of the usual boundaries in cinema studies between good and bad films, categories that are often treated as a difference between 'high' and 'low' culture. Cinema is divided between films that are regarded as 'serious' works, as 'the worship of art' (Rancière cites his displeasure at having to view Sergei Eisenstein's *The General Line*, 1929) and thus to be studied, in contrast to those movies made precisely to be 'enjoyed', works of 'entertainment' (Rancière cites Anthony Mann's popular western, *Winchester 73*, 1950; Rancière 2014: 2). Introducing his essays on film in *The Intervals of Cinema*, Rancière argues that cinephilia, and not only his own (we could call this 'cultural cinephilia'), tends to circumvent these distinctions and, in effect, begins to also question the values of the aesthetics of all art, and the modernist purity that had once governed it:

> Cinephilia questioned the categories of artistic modernism not by deriding high art but by restoring a closer and less obvious linkage between the types of art, the emotions of the narrative, and by discovering the splendour that the most commonplace objects could acquire on a lighted screen in a dark auditorium: a hand lifting a curtain or fumbling with a door handle, a head leaning out of a window, a fire or car headlights in the night, drinking glasses glittering on a bar … it introduced us to a positive understanding, in no way ironic or disillusioned, of the impurity of art.
>
> *(Rancière 2014: 3)*

Rancière beautifully lists those fragmentary scenes in cinema—metonymical images—that draw the spectator into their own imaginary, beyond the filmic diegesis and the narrative plot of a movie. The 'emotions of the film' that belong ostensibly to the representative regime are interrupted, overlaid and overlapped by these other scenes that linger in the viewer's imagination. Yet the productivity of these metonymical images—which are usually transitional scenes in film, from one moment of plot to another—also impacts on our expectations of artistic modernism outside the cinema. In effect, the enjoyment of cinema in this general sense of discrete aesthetic pleasures, which can also operate across all photographies, is what belongs to the *aesthetic* regime of the image. (It is an argument that builds on "The Third Meaning" in Roland Barthes's essay of the same name; Barthes 1977.) These operations can serve, Rancière argues, as a disruption—a dissensus—both within the representative regime, of which they are also part, and also as a critique of artistic modernism itself. We may note that these small types of fragmentary scene in cinema, or elements from them, have their equivalents—despite the differences—within still photography too. The small detail that is just one component of the picture—which can attract the viewer's eye to be absorbed into it, for example, within an advertising image—can offer an enjoyment that is extant to the totalized scenario, whose general aim and function is to situate the publicity product within the representative/ethical regime. It is from these metonymical signifiers that the mixings of aesthetic value in art and perceptive enjoyments across images in the wider visual culture operate as both within, *beyond* and against the rationalist reasoning of the representative regime. Rancière's categories enable us to open up these instances in scenes to scrutiny and offer the possibility to rethink the values and relations of different images. Thus, here is the lesson showing why the categorical singularity of photography in philosophical traditions of aesthetics is problematic today. If 'photography' is not a singular entity, then the categorical aesthetics that it generates are not a singular or 'pure' thing either. This is precisely the problematic that Ranciere's account enables us to address, even though Rancière sometimes does not appear to visit this himself in his writings on photography.

Aisthesis

In a recent essay on photography by Rancière called "The Majesty of the Moment" (2013), he comes quite close to sounding like a classical photography historian. His argument is centred on the nineteenth-century aesthetic debates of photographic 'Pictorialism' and, eventually, the transition to photographic "modernism" at the beginning of the twentieth century. For this story, Rancière pours over photographic history books such as Helmut Gernsheim's *Creative Photography: Aesthetic Trends* (Gernsheim 1962). Gernsheim's pioneering books on photography published in the twentieth century, often co-authored with his wife, Alison Gernsheim, not only collated materials and research work that attest to these narratives and the great figures (*sic*) within these histories of photography, but also formed them, the actual narratives themselves.

After trekking through the now familiar nineteenth-century aesthetics debates in photographic Pictorialism (e.g. photography *as* painting, and the 'painterly' values of European art in their effect on the photographer's ideas about 'art'), Rancière ends up at the door of the American aesthete, photographer and critic Alfred Stieglitz. Stieglitz's position is pivotal in the history of art and photography, because he imported the new twentieth-century modernist currency in art (painting, sculpture, drawing) from Europe and initiated the new fine art photography discourse via his New York-based *Camera Work* magazine in the early 1900s. Famously, the very last issue of *Camera Work*, in June 1917, included a portfolio of Paul Strand's photographs, which are endorsed by Alfred Stieglitz as the birth of a brand new *straight* aesthetic of photography. This new 'American' photography was 'direct' and 'objective', as Strand himself put it, in his own immodest essay on his work in the same magazine (Strand 1997: 780). Strand's work was presented, it is subsequently assumed—the notion is taken up by Rancière—as the very announcement of the death of Pictorialism (a death claimed all too prematurely in my view). In this account, Rancière comes suspiciously close to the existing normative accounts of the emergence of modernism in art photography, a narrative that repeated in education and endless books on the history of photography, ever since Gernsheim or Beaumont Newhall (Newhall 1964). So, having introduced a conceptual framework of regimes, aiming to disrupt the location and conception of aesthetics in culture, Rancière appears to retreat back into an existing narrative of established views of 'fine art photography' as art and its history in a turn towards the singularity of photographic aesthetics. Why? This traditional narrative on photographic art surely seems at odds with his disruptive interest in *mixing things up*.

Rancière turns to this historical moment when the aesthetics of photography is said to turn because his interest is not so much to repeat it as a mythical event—the chronological determinism of nineteenth-century Pictorialism rejected for a new twentieth-century modernism and the 'straight' photograph, and so on—but in order to reconsider the terms in which this transition is understood. What defines this transitional moment for Rancière is not the inevitability of a technological form finding its true voice, that is, the emergence of a modernist voice of photographic sharpness and *objective* focus over the painterly *fuzzographic* forms of Pictorialism. No, Rancière takes a different tack and rejects this traditional explanation. The modern vision is not so much pitched against the old ways of doing things, he argues, but is in the fact that it is this straightness that really enables the camera to register the marks of modern civilization on the human body. As Rancière elegiacally puts it in the last sentence of his essay:

> The objectivity of photography is the regime of thought, perception and sensation that makes the love of pure forms coincide with the apprehension of the inexhaustible historicity found at every street corner, in every skin fold, and at every moment of time.
>
> *(Rancière 2013: 224)*

We should take this term 'objectivity' with a pinch of salt (as a figure of speech) in his writings; it is not so much a realist thesis for photography as it is a mark or coda for the photographic "affirmation of 'straightness'" (Rancière 2013: 223). It was, he argues, this form of photography that had the capacity to register the new ways human beings bear the wear and tear of the industrialized habitat, to show its novel stains on the body (if not on the actual metonymical soul) of the human being. This is not a 'refusal' of Pictorialism, but rather its modification:

> 'Straightness' only defines an artistic process if these long hands of the artist-model and these deformed feet are taken to condense the conquest and suffering of a civilization that has sparked the limbs of individuals according to their occupations, routes and rhythms, as it has raised sky-scrapers in cities, and mixed clouds of smoke from trains and steamers with the clouds in the sky.
>
> *(Rancière 2013: 223)*

Perhaps even today, when we look at the photographs from that issue of *Camera Work* and Paul Strand's portfolio in particular, it is easy still to be struck by the awkwardness at work in them. It is not simply a question of whether the human figures are no longer 'pictorialist' and photographed 'straight', because the portfolio is far more uneven than this. The street portraits of figures are not entirely regular; dark angular lines, rarely horizontal, vie in the pictures with the expressive features of faces, figures and clothes, which all look to be worn through the brutality of life. In one picture, the figure looks blurrily out past the camera. These anonymous human figures fit into the photographic frames uncomfortably; their awkwardness is precisely what constitutes the dissensual interruption of these images. We can see something operating outside or beyond the representative framework of these images, as in Strand's famous photograph of a white picket fence, that iconic marker of domestic territory and space, which appears as somewhat saturated, solid and sharp, yet shabby in its flimsy off-white tones and the dark sombre building structures in the background of the image. These novel rhetorical forms of Strand's 'aesthetic' images are not unified (as is often claimed about them), but varied, not yet worn out by their endless repetition within the representative regime. Yet, it is as though something remains at work in these images to make them feel distinct, still now, something that is feasibly the "pathos of knowledge," which Rancière refers to as characteristic of the aesthetic regime (Rancière 2009a: 61).

In a sense, perhaps we find here also the limits of aesthetic-philosophical propositions. By indicating the details of the aesthetic regime in operation, these detailed instances risk being taken as 'general ideals', as a universal ideal that can be 'applied', like a manifesto strategy, to anything else at hand. But this is not the case. Consider again, in the late 1940s, after fascism in Europe, whether the interest in this straightness as an objectivity of photography is tenable as a dissensual form in the manner that it was in 1917, and the answer is likely to be very different. The painful disillusion that followed from what military industrialization had done to human bodies in the two world wars (the mass destruction of cities and their civilian populations and the development of concentration camps) on one hand, and what the representative value of 'objectivity' (in propaganda) had done to the photographic regime on the other, is a quite different set of conditions for any proposition about aesthetics and the effects of 'photographic' truth today. This is one lesson of Rancière's work in *Aisthesis*: it is always set within the conditions of a framework of regimes and thus not pure—that is, as an autonomous aesthetic that exists by itself. The value of Rancière's tripartite schema of the aesthetic, representative and ethical regimes is plain to see. There is no fixed formal or essential programme for aesthetic intervention or effect, without ethical and representative regimes also being included, negotiated and drawn into the account of aesthetics.

Today, with the technical evaporation of 'photography' into computer code, the question remains: what kinds of project would now contribute to an aesthetic regime? When social media platforms or websites urge image activity by suggesting that their users are artists, making radical revolution by uploading images, is this doing no more than supplying the representative regime with its new crowd-sourced imitations of life? Is the camera phone image and the *selfie* the de facto ubiquitous form of which the modern *ethos* of the species is made manifest as a (unethical?) regime of images? Where is the "pathos of knowledge" that Rancière speaks of and seeks as constitutive of the aesthetic regime across the different practices of photographies existent today? It should be clear by now that, to reiterate, there is no essence to be derived from the aesthetic regime, no technical 'medium' or form, no essential characteristics, no structural certainty or uncertainty of form and content that can define its existence. While there is no reason why, for example, computer algorithms cannot be used to serve human interest in aesthetics (artists are indeed already at work on this), neither are there any guarantees that these will lead to any function outside the representative regime. Although we know the photographic image is *de*coded and recoded when it is assimilated to computer and internet matrix screens—what we still, perhaps quaintly, call a 'social network'—the horizon of aesthetic expectations derived from these visual experiences is yet to be addressed. Primarily sensorial, experienced as playful and ephemeral, our relations to photographic images are now mostly framed by a set of conditions radically different from the traditional art gallery. Images are made present directly on transient screens, and often seen in transient locations that can be public spaces (rural, suburban, urban) or private places (bathroom, domestic kitchen, bedroom, lounge, washroom, etc.), which creates a very different representative environment. It is an environment that defies even any specific location of culture in which an aesthetic experience of dissensual interruption might be possible. And what of the ethical regime, the values of which find their voice in images said to be beyond speech. We live now in computerized societies where the contemporary mutative practices of 'advertorials', 'edutainment' and other mutative practices invent new modes of living through merging, confusing and hybridizing older value systems and distinctions. These and the so-called new fields of computer stimulation are what constitute the challenge for contemporary aesthetic thought. A challenge for criticism, for our faculties of reception and our ability to perceive the new contradictions they may awaken within us. As Rancière puts it: "Aesthetics is the thought of the new disorder" (Rancière 2009b: 12). In this way, aesthetics is not something to be separated from the computerization of the world. If Rancière's work shows us anything, it is that these new image regimes and the antagonisms between them of representation, ethics and aesthetics are the very site of our new questions of aesthetics. These are the places where struggles about 'how we must live' today in our different communities are to be fought out. They are, thus, also where those who wish to pursue 'photography' must now look to see why, how, where, when and what images are dispersed across them.

Notes

1 'Postmodernism' was the name given to the shattering of the rivalries between these three, modernism, realism and avant-garde, as they all collapsed under the weight of their own ideological contradictions, aided and abetted by the subsequent growth of globalism and expansion after the invention, impact and intervention of the internet.

2 Readers already familiar may see an affinity between the regime in Rancière's work and the same term used by Michel Foucault in his work *The Order of Things*: the episteme or 'regime of truth' (1980). However, these are quite distinct and different in Rancière, and are not linked to specific historical periods and conceptual shifts in episteme, as Foucault aimed to outline.
3 It is worth noting that Rancière draws extensively on the work ofSchillerFriedrich (1967) *On the Aesthetic Education of Man*.

References

Althusser, L. (1971) *Lenin and Philosophy*, New York: Monthly Review Press.
Barasch, M. (2000) *Theories of Art 2: From Winckelmann to Baudelaire*, London: Routledge.
Barthes, R. (1973) *Mythologies*, London: Paladin/Granada.
Barthes, R. (1977) *Image-Music-Text*, London: Fontana Press.
Barthes, R. (1980) *Camera Lucida*, London: Fontana Press.
Baumgarten, A. (1750–58) *Aesthetica*, Frankfurt: Oder.
Burgin, V. (1982) "Photographic Practice and Art Theory," in V. Burgin (ed.) *Thinking Photography*, Basingstoke: Macmillan, 39–83.
Burke, E. (2008)[1759] *Philosophical Enquiry into the Origins of Our Ideas of the Sublime and Beautiful*, Oxford: Oxford PaperbacksOxfoPO.
Derrida, J. (1981) *Positions*, Chicago: University of Chicago Press.
Eco, U. (1982) "Critique of the Image," in V. Burgin (ed.) *Thinking Photography*, Basingstoke: Macmillan, 32–38.
Foucault, M. (1980) *The Order of Things: An Archaeology of the Human Sciences*, London: Tavistock.
Gernsheim, H. (1962) *Creative Photography: Aesthetic Trends*, London: Faber & Faber.
Newhall, B. (1964) *The History of Photography: From 1839 to the Present Day*, London: Secker &Warburg.
Rancière, J. (2004) *The Politics of Aesthetics*, London: Continuum.
Rancière, J. (2007) *The Future of the Image*, London: Verso.
Rancière, J. (2009a) *The Aesthetic Unconscious*, Cambridge: Polity Press.
Rancière, J. (2009b) *Aesthetics and Its Discontents*, Cambridge: Polity Press.
Rancière, J. (2010) *Dissensus: On Politics and Aesthetics*, London: Continuum.
Rancière, J. (2013) *Aisthesis: Scenes from the Aesthetic Regime of Art*, London: Verso.
Rancière, J. (2014) *The Intervals of Cinema*, London: Verso.
Schiller, F. (1967) *On the Aesthetic Education of Man*, Oxford: Oxford University Press.
Strand, P. (1997) "Photography," in A. Stieglitz (ed.) *Camera Work*, London: Taschen, 780–781.
Tagg, J. (1988) *The Burden of Representation*, Basingstoke: Macmillan.
Walden, S. (2010) *Photography and Philosophy: Essays on the Pencil of Nature*, Chichester: Blackwell.
Williams, R. (1983) *Keywords: A Vocabulary of Culture and Society*, London: Fontana Press.

3

Ambiguity, accident, audience

Minor White's photographic theory

Todd Cronan

> The unpredictable is never overcome, but it is accepted as a working condition by the artist which he must seek to overcome or fail to do anything.
>
> *(Minor White 1958a: February 7, 1952)*

> When you show a photograph to a person, what he gets from it, or brings to it is the only really discernible fact in the case. His response may be wrong, insane, stupid, irrelevant, irresponsible, ignorant, but nevertheless, for him, his response is a fact. ... Only you are wrong in assuming that he will respond as he is supposed to do, and for making pictures which can be misunderstood.
>
> *(Minor White 1963: 15)*

Previsualization and its enemies

In a brief and trenchant statement of intent, Robert Frank declared in 1958 that his photographs were "not planned or composed in advance and I do not anticipate that the onlooker will share my viewpoint" (1958: 115).[1] Every word of this was directed against a dominant line of modernist thinking in photography. Frank was taking a position against the Stieglitz–Weston–Adams tradition of "previsualization," a mode of practice that was being consolidated and canonized in the pages of Minor White's *Aperture*, which he edited from 1952 until his death in 1976. White summarized the previsual approach in 1951:

> Printing is a materialization of an image latent in the photographer's mind from the moment of seeing. The negative is but a step towards the original statement. Mr. Adams uses the term 'previsualization' to mean the mental image of the print the photographer has while looking at the original subject. Thus when he previsualizes, he looks at the scene but sees in his mind's eye a print of it. Printing from a previsualized negative is to get out of it the content remembered to have been inserted. ... 'previsualization' is a discipline. When a man can do it, he has become one with his camera.
>
> *(White 1951: 549)*

If White associated the technical aspects of previsualization with Adams (he wrote the above while teaching alongside Adams at the California School of Fine Arts), he associated the Zen-like merger with his medium—becoming "one with his camera"—with his mentor Edward Weston. When White saw, he saw like a camera: "I have made enough pictures so that now I see like a lens focused on a piece of film, act like a negative projected on a piece of sensitized paper, talk like a picture on a wall" (1980: 307).[2] White went so far as to describe the combined technical/mental act of previsualization as occurring "without thought, and without communicating." "I was not trying to do anything," he reflected (1980: 309).

Like Frank, Garry Winogrand overtly opposed the previsual tradition when he famously observed, "I photograph to find out what something will look like photographed." "I don't have anything to say in any picture. My only interest in photography is to see what something looks like as a photograph. I have no preconceptions" (1972: 1). White and Winogrand shared the sentiment that they had nothing to say, but their sense of the noncommunicative was starkly different. The whole point of previsualization was to insist that one should "find out" what something looked like photographed *before* one took the shot. From White's perspective, Winogrand's thousands of printed and (many, many more) unprinted negatives were the necessary 'background' for a previsualized photograph; for Winogrand, there was no moment when visualization could or should turn into automaticity. The challenge for Winogrand was something like the opposite of previsualization, that is, to hold off the moment of consummation, to delay the process of development, until he had "virtually no memory of the act of taking an individual photograph" (1988: 50). Then again, previsualization similarly functioned for White as a tool to detach himself from "being too intimate" with life; the "camera image," he affirmed, "automatically provides aesthetic distance" from the immediacy of life (1958a: 1948–1949).[3]

John Cage, who was close with Weston in the 1930s (his wife from 1935 to 1945, Xenia Kashevaroff, was Weston's former lover), followed Winogrand in refuting the previsual paradigm. "You see, I don't hear music when I write it. I write in order to hear something I haven't yet heard … The notation is about something that is not familiar" (2003: 62–63). Cage identified previsualization with a narcissistic involvement with self-portraiture, regardless of the actual subject matter. "Edward Weston told me photographers photograph themselves no matter what their cameras are focused on," Cage wrote. Against this approach, Cage cited the work of Robert Mahon, who, "Using chance operations … found a way to let each photograph photograph itself" (1983: 159). Confirming Cage's suspicion, White stressed the centrality of projection in his practice: "The photographer projects himself into everything he sees, identifying himself with everything in order to know it and feel it better" (1966a: 166). Writing in *Memorable Fancies* in 1953, White declared, "the foundations of my thought [are …] anthropomorphism—man seeing himself in everything. *And seeing himself better than he can when looking at his own image*" (1958a: April 11, 1953; original emphasis).[4] Not only is a photograph a self-portrait, but a photograph serves the purpose of self-portraiture when the self is not present at all. But it wasn't just that *his* thoughts rested on anthropomorphism: *all* thought did. White concluded that, "Suggestibility is part of the foundations of human nature. Most of our lives depend on suggestibility, the arts especially" (1966b: 174). The human being lives in a mimetic relationship with the things of the world. In other words, Cage grasped something essential about the previsual approach. At the basis of White's photographic theory was the idea that humans see humans in everything. This was essential because the "pathetic fallacy" was the basis upon which the vast, seemingly infinite array of responses to works of art would find its *only* common ground (but it was enough) (1956: 40). White put it this way: "The importance is this: if people are suggested to everybody, there is a common basis for experiencing the print that works for both photographer and the spectator" (1952: 67). It was also upon this "common basis" that White founded his account of photographic agency. Because suggestibility was at the "foundations" of human nature, the photographer had to become an expert in how it functioned; the practice of equivalence (as he described his practice) was the only way to "deal with human suggestibility in a conscious and responsible way" (1966b: 174).

Even those artists most closely associated with White, such as Harry Callahan, Aaron Siskind, and Frederick Sommer, attempted to distance themselves from the previsual approach. A.D. Coleman asked Callahan about it in a 1971 interview: "Do you previsualize at all?" By the 1970s, the reader was well prepared for the answer:

> No, I think previsualization is *in* pictures, but I don't think of it in the terms that Adams and the others do. I understand what it means to them, but it doesn't mean anything to me. In fact, I like those little accidents. … I sort of believe it's untrue. I mean, are they previsualizing a masterpiece, or a perfect print, or what? If I knew every picture I made was going to be a real picture, maybe I could go along with that, but I can't.
>
> *(1972: 4)*

Callahan's denial is perhaps more complex than it first appears. Callahan clearly rejects the *technical* side of previsualization, the approach identified with Adams. But he seems to assent, in part, to the stronger position White took, that—with the proper mental attitude—the world made itself available to a photographic order. Moreover, nothing could be closer to White's attitude than Callahan's affinity for recording "little accidents." As I will show, previsualization was most properly suited to the recording of a special mode of accident, to the creation of what White called "Found Photographs."

Well before Frank, Winogrand, Cage, and Callahan registered their dissatisfaction with the previsual approach (even if their target was the technical aspects of the project), anti-visualization was codified by Callahan's predecessor, László Moholy-Nagy, who recruited Callahan to teach at the Institute of Design in Chicago. Moholy-Nagy declared in 1929—at the same moment the principles of previsualization were publicized by Weston (they would debate the matter in Carmel several years later)—"*Even with a right understanding for the material, speed and distance of thinking are not adequate for foreseeing all the possibilities of [photographic] development*" (1980: 241; original emphasis). There simply was no level of technique or habit of seeing that could get ahead of the photographic mechanism. The medium outran the agent. In a sense, photographic theory has not progressed much further than Moholy-Nagy's skepticism. No matter the photographer's skills, one could not foresee all of the outcomes of what the camera produced. The camera's built-in indifference to human agency—it recorded any- and everything that appeared before the lens—has historically served to undermine the agent using the device. Or, at least, it has served to undermine any agent who claimed they could foresee, previsualize, what their camera recorded.

In his homespun takedown of previsualizers, Lee Friedlander thematized the problem of mechanical indifference:

> I only wanted Uncle Vern standing by his new car (a Hudson) on a clear day. I got him and the car. I also got a bit of Aunt Mary's laundry and Beau Jack, the dog, peeing on a fence, and a row of potted tuberous begonias on the porch and seventy-eight trees and a million pebbles in the driveway and more. It's a generous medium, photography.
>
> *(1996: 103)*

In a sense, the generosity of the medium could be construed as a weapon against those photographers who really wanted their Uncle Verns, but who refused to accept their Aunt Marys, Beau Jacks, and the millions of pebbles. Then again, Friedlander's whole notion of going out with your camera "and the pictures are staring at you" replays White's basic sense of "accidents" that seem to be "staring at me" in those "intuitive instants when pictures are isolated out of the chaos of non-pictures" (1956: 40). White described his whole "found" practice as one where the "object tries to understand you" (1958a: January 19, 1957). Friedlander similarly spoke—in the aptly titled *Self Portrait*—of the moment when "Witness is borne and puzzles come together at the photographic moment which is very simple and complete." Like White, Friedlander calls this revelatory moment "a mysterious intersection of chance and attention" (1970: n.p.).

If one wants to find a true refusal of the previsual claim, refusal at the level of technique and attitude, one would have to look at the theory and practice of Marcel Duchamp and his legion of admirers. Duchamp's claims in "The Creative Act" of 1957 laid the groundwork for a multitude of avant-garde attacks on previsualization, most of them centered on the ontology of the "index."[5] Like White, Duchamp envisioned the artist as someone who has all but fused with his medium, to become something of a medium himself. For this artist, Duchamp says, "we must then deny him the state of consciousness on the esthetic plane about what he is doing or why he is doing it." Duchamp describes the artist's "creative act" as one where the "artist goes from intention to realization through a chain of totally subjective reactions" (1973: 139). The most crucial step in Duchamp's argument, one with prodigious consequences for what comes after, is his commitment to separating intent and realization. Part of the point of previsualization for White was to discard this false division.[6] To "act like a negative" was to insist on the identity of intent and execution. Previsualization, despite what its critics insisted, was anything but an account of inner intention being projected onto external matter. Rather, it was Duchamp who enforced this distinction in order to build his audience aesthetic upon it—more precisely: to build his audience aesthetic on the ruins of artistic intentionality. The barrier Duchamp saw (or raised) between intent and realization was identical to the one opened up between work and audience (the difference between artistic intent and the "verdict" of "posterity"; 139). White would certainly agree that his works could only be judged after the fact by the spectator. Then again, as I will show, it was *the* guiding premise of the *Aperture* enterprise to train photographers to take an audience-based approach to their own work (see Cronan 2014b). In White's words, the aim was "to learn to look at his own photographs as if they were made by some other photographer" (2012c: 320). White provided all manner of practical advice to achieve this condition. Above all, he advised "*gathering responses*" to one's pictures in order to learn how "to predict responses" (2012c: 320; original emphasis). This was *not* what Duchamp was suggesting. Like Moholy-Nagy, Duchamp insisted that there was an insuperable barrier between what an artist wanted to say and what they were saying (a point White will make at length, but use for something like the opposite conclusion). For Duchamp, the work always outran the artist. Everything hinged on the putative gap that opened up in the movement from "intention to realization," what he called the "difference between what he intended to realize and did realize." When the artist emerged from his trance, the "result," says Duchamp, is "a difference between the intention and its realization, a difference which the artist is not aware of" (1973: 139). Duchamp turned this gap into an ontology—a fact, not a challenge—and into an opportunity to rid the work of the artist. The work of art was a bundle of artistic failures—the "unexpressed but intended" combined with "the unintentionally expressed"—for which the remaining stuff ("*à l'état brut*") lent itself to spectator's creative work. Exploring this unintentional terrain was the foundation stone upon which the spectator performed their "creative act" on equal terms with the artist (but it could really only serve to undermine the artist, as Duchamp intended).

In hindsight, the most striking fact about Minor White's career is that he dedicated his career to exploring the features and limits of what he called "Creative Audience." White pursued his vision of creative audience in his teaching and in an extraordinary sequence of seven unpublished book manuscripts contained in the White archive at Princeton University Art Museum, including *Cameras Are for Seeing* (1952), *Fundamentals of Style in Photography and the Elements of Reading Photographs* (1953), *Canons of Camerawork* (1963), *Consciousness in Photography and the Creative Audience* (1969), *Photography for Consciousness (The Expressive Photographer)* (1971), *Creative Audience* (1972), the *Visualization Manual* of 1972, as well as numerous articles on the subject for lay audiences and for professionals in the pages of *Aperture* and similar journals over twenty years. The import of White's theoretical project has never been clearer or more salient than today. No artist or theorist that I am aware of explored the problems and questions of audience response further than White did throughout his career. Moreover, he was exploring these questions at the precise moment when not only Duchamp, but also his progeny among the minimalists, declared the artist and the work "less important" than the "space, light, and the viewer's field of vision" (Morris 1994: 17). When Duchamp's "Creative Act" was published in *Aspen* magazine in 1967, it appeared alongside Roland Barthes' seminal account of the "Death of the Author," which hinged on the turn from the self-important work (of the "Author-God") to the reader's individuated textual pleasures. The latter, of course, became the ground upon which Barthes articulated his massively influential account of photography in *Camera Lucida*, driven by a vision of audience experience predicated on the viewer's "addition" to the work, the *punctum*—the "accident which pricks me"—which was unintended by the photographer (1981: 55, 27).[7] Without rehearsing Barthes' infamous claims, it is important to see the proximity, and crucial difference, between Barthes' vision of the "the birth of the reader," who is summoned by "the death of the Author," and White's vision of reader response (1967: n.p.). Barthes affirmed those artists who committed authorial suicide, "the author [that] enters his own death," so they could pass the text (not the work) on to reader for their own creative purposes. White's sense that he was "not a photographer" and that "something does die in me when a picture is born" was also the condition for his vision of the "creative audience" (1980: 309). But White's point was the opposite of Duchamp's/Barthes': to become an audience to oneself was the condition for the birth of the artist. When the artist died to himself, he was in the position to see for himself what he was really saying, and also to understand what everything else was saying (the world became a work of art). Once the photographer reached the point where the "object tries to understand you," then things as we know them die and objects come to life (1958a: January 19, 1957). And, if the photographer has to die to make a picture, so too does the world have to enter into decay to come to life. The latter is the condition for his commitment to abstraction, to photographing "cracked paint, peeled bark, oil slicks on the pavement, the jaguars in the asphalt jungle" (1956: 42). In White's formulation (writing of the crash of a porcelain bowl, but it holds for the destructive transformation of anything, including himself), "The death of the bowl was the birth of an object" (1980: 307).

Most recently, Robin Kelsey has deployed Jacques Lacan's notion of the gaze—run through an utterly orthodox version of the (willing) death of the author/(traumatic) birth of the reader position—to interpret the work of White's friend and colleague Frederick Sommer. Sommer's notorious photographs of chicken parts, Kelsey writes, projected a "subversive force" for White and Adams by virtue of his "lamination of prodigious technique to abject subject matter" (2015: 239). Mobilizing all the technical virtuosity of previsualization, Sommer reverses its enculturating significance—naturalizing the arbitrariness of the sign—in order to expose the "material basis—a baseness—for a naming that must forever be deferred" (2015: 242). Sommer's inclusion of senselessness at the heart of a seamless photographic performance disables the "social and natural dimensions of the sign … together" (2015: 242). In Kelsey's telling, intentional significance is undermined by its proximity to and indistinguishability from the accidental. Sommer is able to "dispel the distinction between conventional message and accidental inclusion" (2015: 246). Kelsey's conclusion crucially introduces the viewer into the equation. Writing of the great Arizona landscapes, Kelsey observes,

> As the viewer stands before a visual field empty of interest but saturated with signs of optical attention, she or he becomes, by default, the element that stands out. … Through this failure [to offer something to see,] the viewer loses command of the visual field and is drawn willy-nilly into the picture.
>
> *(2015: 246)*

The viewer is drawn, that is, into a traumatic experience of the "arbitrariness of signification." (The final step, not exactly taken here by Kelsey, would be coming to terms with arbitrariness as the condition for creative response.)

Like many similar arguments (whether Duchamp, Barthes, Krauss, or Lacan is the cited authority), the author seems unpersuaded by their own account of signification. If language is indeed arbitrary, from what purified condition, however temporary or contingent, could that fact be recognized, *displayed* to another? What vision of the artist (or art historian) is it that imagines transparent access to arbitrariness? What else is this but the naturalization of—the ideal command over—the condition of arbitrariness?[8] Although Kelsey's targets here are Weston and Adams, he glosses right over White. Kelsey reprints a 1962 dialogue between Adams and White about Sommer's work. Adams was clearly repulsed by most of it, and White thinks Sommer's efforts to "make us face up to the reality of death" were too limited (2015: 239). Against both Adams and Sommer, White reflects that neither conceived of the "totality of endlessness" (2015: 239). Adams's positivism about life, Sommer's about the nature of the sign (at least in Kelsey's telling), put an end to the challenge of photographic communication. White aimed to confront endlessness, to come to terms with accident, over the course of a lifetime.

Ambiguity

Among his most concise statements as a photographic theorist, White's 1957 "The Ambiguous Expressive/Creative Photograph" editorial for *Aperture* opens with a critique of "informational pictures," which he identifies with documentary photography (1957a: 3). White thought the documentarian "blind as a bat to what his medium actually does … He is as deluded as a lunatic" (1958a: September 15, 1953). Deluded because he believed there was "one" meaning the viewer could extract from the photograph, and that meaning put the viewer "face-to-face" with the referent. White's exemplary instance of ambiguous photography is the work of Sommer, whose work could not identified with its referent, but rather through the indirect route of "implications." The latter, he reflected, are "notoriously open to a variety of interpretations," adding that these interpretations are "notoriously private." White takes the reader (fast) to the heart of a kind of skeptical inquiry, seemingly reaching

Duchamp's point about the absolute break between intent and realization. And yet it was White's aim in virtually every piece of writing to clear the seemingly impenetrable wall between artist and audience by passing straight through it. Whereas it would seem that "interpreting photographs can only lead *away* from the photographer's intentions, actually the effectiveness of the expressive/creative photograph grows out of what each viewer gets by and for himself." What could this possibly mean? How could it be that what the viewer gets "for himself" leads *toward* the photographer's intentions, rather than away?

At this point, White shifts gears toward the subject of dreaming. Sommer's photographs function for viewers "like a kind of daydream" (White 1957a: 3). And, like a dream, one can "puzzle out an understanding" of the picture according to one's "own nature." These "readings," due to their "personal intuitive" nature, should be left "unpublished." White insists on the addition of "text" next to Sommer's photographs to enforce the point that photographs are "always more ambiguous than specific," that is, not one to one with the referent. Because so many viewers and photographers falsely imagine their photographs "communicate," White exacerbates the ambiguous dimension by forcing the viewer to construe photographs outside the context of direct reference. For White, the inclusion of poetic text dislodged the referential function, and at the same time it reestablished the author's intention. As he noted in his *Memorable Fancies*, "Any fine photograph is open to numerous interpretations; an expanded title or short story would guide the spectator to the intended meaning" (1958a: July 24, 1947).[9]

White goes on to deflate a consensus view of photographic communication. The basic mistake is to imagine "if one of our photographs mean 'x' to us, it can only mean 'x' to everyone" (White 1957a: 3).To those with a documentary instinct, the practice of reading photographs will come as a necessary and therapeutic shock. The barest survey of audience response will show that "others … think it means 'y' or 'z' or any other letter of any other alphabet" (3). The whole point of the editorial is to show that "photographs do not communicate," and yet the alternative to communication is not privacy but evocation. Because photographers are unaware of the fact their photographs evoke far more than they communicate, "we can hardly be expected to have the faintest idea how to go about evoking" (1957a: 3). In other words, White's point in the editorial is about the correct terms to construe photographic intentionality, even if it is under the pressures of knowing that audiences dream up things in front of pictures that are *seemingly impossible* to predict. I say seemingly, because White was committed from first to last to a mode of photography and pedagogy that took up the challenge of predictably photographing the "unseen and unseeable" (1958b: 53). This the point of his otherwise turgid claim that, "To find out how others *dream* our photographs is a start." Start to what? Find out how viewers dream, then make them dream how you want them to. How people dream, of course, is "unpredictable," but, he added (in a related context), "not entirely so. It's unpredictable, nevertheless this is the approach used by the creative photographers" (2012a: 148). Even though one has "no assurance that others will feel" what one wants them to feel, the "knowledge that one may frequently fumble in trying [to communicate evocatively] is only a challenge" (1966a: 167).

In the conclusion to the editorial, White stresses the point that photographers are inevitably going to encounter viewers "more knowledgeable … than the photographer" (1957a: 3). Those viewers will "find more in a photograph than the cameraman himself." Indeed, these viewers can "read in it things the like of which the photographer never dreamed." If the photographer has "never dreamed" what the viewer sees, then it was imperative for them to dream harder. It is the "wise" photographer not to be "offended" by other people's dreams; the photographer must become the master of dreamwork, so that the viewers' dreams become the photographer's own.

In a brilliant unpublished study of 1952 entitled *Cameras Are for Seeing*, White elaborated on the seemingly perverse claim that the photographer should "find out how others *dream* our photographs." The point was a simple one about heightened awareness of what one's photographs mean. Because the photographer was so immersed in his artistic process, he needed to step outside himself to see what he was saying. The following passage describes the special *kind* of meaning available to the photographer once they have given up the idea that their intentions communicate in some one-to-one fashion.

> To make equivalents for other people, the photographer has to find out how they respond to his photographs. ... He has to discover as exactly as possible how closely their feelings match his own ... About the most he can expect is the same channel, the same area or level of feeling ... Checking reactions of the viewer frequently and elaborately is more necessary in photography than in other media because the ever-present literal subject in the photograph always gives something to everybody and unless the photographer checks carefully that something may be altogether different than what he blithely takes for granted. It takes a well-trained photographer to get his feeling A1 to happen at all like AX in another person. So far as the photograph as a source of experience goes, the concept of the equivalent gives the photographer a mechanism whereby he can control the photograph. It is the statement he wants to make.
>
> *(1952: 79–80)*

What is at stake for White is a conception of art wherein the artist must come to terms with the sheer, seemingly imponderable depths of division between artist and beholder. What kind of art can be responsibly made under those conditions? Notice that White was not willing to cede an ounce of "control" over the photograph under the conditions of open-endedness. The photographer goes to work with a newfound awareness of the limits of precise communication, but with the now widened field of working in the "same channel, the same area or level of feeling" as the viewer (White 1952: 79).

There is a moment in every White text where he seems to revel in burying the photographer under the weight of skeptical isolation, as though artist and viewer were stranded in themselves. From the depths of isolation, the achievement of communication is all the more extraordinary. As he explained in an important unpublished study of the *Fundamentals of Style in Photography and the Elements of Reading Photographs* of 1953,

> There are so many interpretations, and everyone has his own associations with objects, and the photographer can not predict what all those associations can be. *The difficulty of deciding which interpretation is the 'right' one, or the one intended by the photographer is largely solved by accepting the possibility of many meanings.*
>
> *(c. 1953: 209; original emphasis)*

Rather than chasing down *all* the associations of every conceivable viewer, White asks artists to exchange "one" meaning with "many." But saying that something could mean more than one thing presented no challenge to the question of intentionality or control. Paradoxically, White insisted that taking ownership of the most extravagant forms of response was the *only* way to recover something like the fullness of artistic intentionality.

Whether it was photographer or audience, White insisted there was a "right" meaning, but that meaning was the most capacious. This is what White crucially calls "The Main Meaning." Here is White:

> colored, warped, twisted by the personality (unique, of course) of the beholder. Consequently there are as many "meanings" as there are beholders. For each of these, he alone has *the* meaning. Frankly it is pointless to talk of *the* meaning. On the contrary it is entirely valid to talk of the *main* meaning.
>
> A group of people looking at a picture, while they will not reach identical reactions will experience similar ones … will come closer to the same feeling than they are able to indicate in words.
>
> In pictures, contrary to target practice, where a miss is as good as a mile, any response in the direction of the target is a bull's eye.
>
> *(c. 1953: 248)*

A response was not a direct hit, not an extraction of some artist's "message," as the (cardboard) model of intentionality attacked by Duchamp/Barthes and their followers suggests, but rather seeing along with the artist, and in a sense seeing the world together as though for the first time.

In a key *Aperture* essay from 1962 on "Varieties of Responses to Photographs: Exercises in the Prediction of Other People's Responses," White laid his cards on the table about the role of audience response. He noted that, from the "hundreds of responses to scores of pictures," he had begun to see "how predictable is the spectrum of human responses."[10] The photographer must come to terms with what was truly predictable (the "main meaning"), and what was not (a specific one). In the clearest terms, White states that the "goal is a photographer who can consciously know more about the communicative-evocative power of his own photograph than any collective audience can show him" (2012c: 323). To become something like a super-audience to oneself, to take full responsibility for what one's works mean, to fully intend oneself to another, was White's project, and arguably the project of *Aperture* at large.

Built into the whole notion of creative audience was a core distinction between a response and what he called a "reaction." Reactions were "*accidental, uncontrolled and unmanageable, more or less compulsive, happening that took place during the event of looking*"[11] (1968: 45; original emphasis). White remorselessly critiqued the idea of viewers reading photographs as nothing but a "mirror of themselves" (1957b: 56). To the untrained, "Looking at a photograph they will hear themselves talk, and hear nothing of what the photograph says or what the photographer is trying to say" (1957b: 56). White (along with Walter Chappell) asked readers to "board the train of associations" into the "wild blue yonder on no more than a single feather" and then, later, begin the process of sorting out the "irrelevant associations" in order to "isolate those associations which … seem to pertain to the photograph" (2012: 236–37).

For White, the art of evocation, the ambiguous photograph, was the only viable terrain for artistic exploration. White referred to Alfred Stieglitz's *Equivalents* to describe the crucial difference, as he saw it, between documentary *and* self-expression, on one side, and art, on the other. Although Stieglitz thought he was making "materialized … feelings about a person" with his clouds, they were in fact "equivalent to his own experience with unseen and unseeable spirit itself" (1958b: 53).[12] Photography, he insisted, "must" give access to "other worldliness" if it is to achieve an "art medium" (1958b: 53). Equivalence, as he saw it, was the common denominator of *all art*, the "perennial trend, as old as man in art" (1966b: 172). Writing in *Memorable Fancies*, he reflected on what he called the "secret of the ambivalent, the ambiguousness of photography," concluding that "ambivalence is the heart of photography" (1958a: May 29, 1956). Which is to say, the secret heart of art itself.

Another, more obvious, way to describe the ambiguous photograph is to simply call it "abstract," although White preferred the terms "extraction" or "isolation" (1966b: 173). White frequently affirmed his connection with other abstract photographers at the time who were exploring similar terrain, including Sommer, Callahan, Aaron Siskind, and Wynn Bullock. For White, the defining feature of an ambiguous/abstract photograph was its "paradoxical" relation to the referent, at once bound and free. The aim was for the "photographer to free himself from the tyranny of the visual facts upon which his camera is utterly dependent" (1958b: 53). An abstract photograph could loosen up the referent so the photograph could become an independent reality, freeing up the capacity for audience response. As the "degree of metamorphosis increases, the original object has less and less bearing … and the mental image within the spectator becomes increasingly the only possible source of experience" (1958b: 54). According to White, the photograph at this point splits in two, the "physical photography and a mental image," which were "somewhat dissimilar." The mental image, he explained, depended "largely on what the spectator brings to the photograph." It's important to see the work being done here by the words "somewhat" and "largely." At no point is there any actual break between referent, photographer and response. Here is White's most succinct way of describing the proper photographer–photograph–spectator relation:

> When the link to the original subject is broken or stretched thin, the spectator is left to his own associations. To date the photographer attempting to work … in this private world of other people's mental images, can do little more than hope to channel the spectator's associations with a title. Still this intangible and almost unknowable climate of the spectator's mental image must be the future artist photographer's field of communication.
>
> *(1958b: 54–55)*

Whether pessimistic or optimistic about the capacity to "channel" the spectator's understanding, it is clear that White saw no alternative to this broad evocative approach. In some strong sense, *Aperture* was where the "future artist" went to explore this new, "almost unknowable" (the wording is key) "field of communication" (1958b: 54–55).

Accident

In the same issue of *Aperture* where "The Ambiguous Expressive/Creative Photograph" appeared, White offered concrete reflections on the type of photographic practice associated with the ambiguous work. White's study of "Peeled Paint, Cameras and Happenstance" was reprinted from the London journal *Photography* under the title "Happenstance and How it Involves the Photographer." Here, White affirmed the "intuitive instants" where "pictures" are "isolated out of the chaos of non-pictures" (1956: 40).[13] Pictures exist in the world for those able to see them. He saw "accidents" of "weathered concrete" and "knotholes" "staring" at him. And though he described himself as the "willing victim of the pathetic fallacy," there is strong sense in which he does not think it is a fallacy at all. "Mountains are ominous, clouds remind me of friends or enemies, the grain in a sleet-slashed pine board" is "more eloquent" (he means it literally) than a "person who has tried to confide in me over dinner or a dozen cocktails" (1956: 40–41).

White suspects that the whole project of seeing the faces in the "cracked paint, peeled bark, oil slicks on the pavement, the jaguars in the asphalt jungle" risks being construed as nothing but a "morbid" obsession driven by a "psychological compulsion" (1956: 42). Yet again, White courts solipsism, a kind of morbid self-interest as the condition one must arrive at and then find one's way out of. Indeed he was obsessed with the "visual changes wrought by disintegration." Far from decline, the path that ran from new to old is filled with the scribblings of a hidden language. White offered one of his more cogent pictures of his mystical attitude:

> A wall, for instance, from the time the last coat of paint is applied until it collapses of natural causes, is little short of a blackboard upon which happenstance does the writing. The chemical components of the paint, the types of wood beneath, the rhythm of the seasons, all work together according to the laws of physics, thermodynamics, chemistry, wet and dry. And out of these utterly logical metamorphoses, chance writes the hieroglyphics in its own four-dimensional logic.
>
> *(1956: 42)*

White insisted that the messages written on the cracking wall were categorically unrelated to the material agent of the writing, they documented nothing. The words on the wall "do not have to be a statement of decay any more than a word written on a black-board must pertain to black-boards or chalk" (1956: 42). The documentarian, the social photographer, as he sees it, categorically fails to distinguish message from referent.

White compares the decay of manmade objects to writing on a blackboard, whereas the erosion of natural objects—an approach he inherited from Weston—suggests a sculptor making a carving (1956: 43).[14] At this point, White seems to sum up his position on chance photography: "Chance reveals new forms: the photographer is the one that must be intuitive enough, imaginative enough, clever beyond all reason, to recognize those forms which will have meaning for human beings" (1956: 44). But it is a ruse. White is actually uninterested in the isolation of pictures from the chaos that already meant something to humans. More like the opposite: he is committed to photographing forms that bear "no possible significance to human beings." The true artist-photographer "strains every effort to see what angels see." Angels can read all of the signs written on the earth, living and dead; for them everything is a script to be read.[15] It is the task of the artist-photographer to bend "his camera out of shape to make it report what angels see." He means this literally: the photographer must attempt to produce a kind of angel's--view reportage. Resorting to "every subterfuge of sign and symbol that chance throws in his way," he must dislocate the effect of reality, to show us that he "sees like an angel" (1956: 45).

White draws all of his themes together in a powerful concluding statement. Returning to his opening question, about why he prefers older to newer buildings, he explains:

> the older a building gets, the further removed it is from the hand of the architect or builder. And the further it gets from them, the more the imprint of their personality fades. As age creeps on and chance takes over, the photographer can find things that were never intended by the originators. (I am speaking here of course of Occidental builders; Japanese builders, for instance, built with predictions of weathering drawn into the plans.) Finally, the building is more like the photographer than the builder.
>
> *(1956: 73)*

Through use and weathering, the building progressively loses its connection to the architect's intention. To the degree the structure loses connection with its maker, it becomes *White's* work and not the architect's. As the pressures of time temper the architect's hand, the changes set the work free for the photographer's hand. The problem with Japanese architects, on this account, was that time is written into their projects from the beginning, which makes their intentions increasingly adhere to their structures over time, and forecloses the photographer's capacity to make it over to his own intent.

Over and over, White pondered whether his accidental photographs could be described as intentional under any label (did he have a "moral right" to call his photographs "his own")? If he was only taking what "chance and accident give him," then was the "photograph really his?" (1956: 73) Here again, White's notion of previsualization made "possession a little more secure" (1959: 6). The photographer had to be "present to see it," as the scene "would not exist" without his attentive look. To see the "ulterior meaning" of a thing, to see the world whole, as "an angel might predict," was the *only* viable condition for ownership (6). White offered a beautiful analogy for the kind of intentionality chance photography provided: "If a fisherman can claim his catch, a photographer can claim his found photographs."[16] To see as an angel was the ability to take an accident and "turn [it] to purposes which are not accidental" (1956: 73). To these "way-out-beyond-knowing" photographers—the photographer as recording angel, or, more mundane, the photographer who truly knows "what they are doing"—"the accident is no accident." The "accidental," for the photographer who has studied in depth the vastness of human nature, "is reduced to purpose." At this point, the "claim to ownership is utterly solid" (1956: 73).

Approaching the *punctum*: White at the limits of communication

White's position evolved constantly. His late writings stress his skeptical view with special intensity. Writing in the *New York Times* in 1972, Minor White saw the communicative potential of photography to be almost zero. According to White, "the photographer is the last to know what his photographs really communicate" (1972). For White, photographs communicate loud and clear, but *what* they communicate bore little resemblance to what the photographer aimed to communicate or thought that they said. Until the end, White maintained a powerful vision of photographic communication, only now it seemed as if everything in his account seemed to refute the idea the photographer can get anything across at all. "Everyone else knows more about the various levels in his image than he does," White remarked. Speaking of self-portraits, he noted that, even though we are "not very good at reading pictures of ourselves," it turned out "our neighbors and enemies are experts! So ask them." Enemies know us better than we ourselves. Photographs are full of meaning, but the photographer cannot access it. White immersed himself in this kind of radicalized skeptical psychology. Meaning was everywhere, except for the expressing agent. The title of the article well reflects the aims of his late work at large: "Exercises to Meet and Deflate Your Ego By."

White goes on to describe the psychological blockages that prevent the photographer from knowing what they are saying so clearly to others. The photographer was unable to know his photographs because he was so "blinded by his projection of what he wanted to see at exposure and, most unbelievable of all, continues to see in the photograph!" (1972). If the photographer was blinded by projection, and this blindness continued after they are shown the failures of their previsualization, then what exactly was the point of photography?

Like Duchamp, White established a keenly skeptical framework for photography. "We may set out to" do something with our photographs; "We may aim to show" something by them, but these aims are perpetually thwarted by the impersonal medium. Whatever we "set out to" do, the "camera records" what it wants to (1972). The psychological blockages between photographer and viewer were so enormous and so seemingly constitutive that White concluded that, "photographer and viewer see only what they want to see in a photograph [so] any communication that takes place is entirely accidental." If one was condemned to only see oneself, then agents seemed to be trapped in a kind of blind narcissistic universe. And yet, "communication" persisted. We are left to wonder: communication of what to whom? Is there such a thing as accidental communication? If communication was condemned to sheer accident and we always only saw ourselves, then what was the point of the "exercises" to "reduce, erode, and deflate" the ego? Then again, nothing about this task of deflation suggested a kind of Barthesian suicide, only an attempt to get a certain kind of subjectivity out of the way. Compare this, for instance, with the thematics of erosion considered earlier; here, White contends subjective erosion plays an equally central role. Like the eroded world of chance "reduced to purpose," here White hints at an inverted world of full communicative exchange when the ego reaches its lowest point. Thus, in the last sentence, he offered that, with enough practice, "some day" his "wise Self" might "dominate and direct" his camera (to see the *self* from an angel's perspective; 1972).

A few months earlier, in the *New York Times*, White took an even more skeptical line toward communication in an article on "The Secret of Looking" (1971: 31–32). Dropping the whole notion of *making* photographs—they "constitute only a minor part" of "photographic creativity"—he argued that, "Viewers and how they respond to photographs are the major part." White offered two key factors behind his counterintuitive decision to focus on response at the expense of production. Because very few students aimed to be professional photographers, and there were "more applicants than there are jobs for," why not direct education toward the jobs they *will* be asked to perform, "as an audience" for pictures. The second, more strictly sceptical, condition is what we might call the "ubiquity of images" thesis, the "uncritical ingestion of millions of images every year." "Millions of students exposed to countless photographic images all their lives" cannot "cope" with the output (1974: 8).[17] The result of this dual condition—lack of jobs plus image surplus—is a shift in the role of pedagogical enterprises from the production to consumption of images (1971: 32).

The point of photographic education now is to show that the "viewer can be as creative as the photographer" (1971: 32). This raises the question of how the photographer or photographs matter to this educational program at all. If the viewer is as creative as the photographer, why not drop photographer and photographs altogether? White touches this point, but recoils from it, noting that the "same kind of creativity arises in making psychic contact with the livingness of a tree ... as arises in making similar contact with the livingness of the same tree seen in a photograph." It is "similar" contact, not the same. Rather than drop the photograph and commune with the tree, White suggested that a "'creative audience' arises" when a "group comes together to share with each other" their "journey" through "any image." The central difference between a tree and an image is that only the latter bears intent (presuming the students are not angels who can "read" the writing of trees). And yet the question of meaning seems to be suspended at this point when he comes to define a response as "making efforts to *communicate* the experience [of an image] lucidly." It appears he is making an argument for the independent cogency of a response in its independence from the work, but quickly adds that the point of the exercise is to give access to the "blockades that prevent" one from "seeing anything ... deeply." By "blending" all the responses they will inevitably arrive at an "understanding of the image," which was impossible "by themselves." As he notes at the time, one has to remove the barriers that "color response," such as "prejudice" and "pet compulsion." If a reaction has "no bearing on the photograph," then a response, however "personal," is still on the path to "understanding" (1968: 44).

As I have tried to show, White offered one of the most explicit, thorough, and consistent accounts of audience response ever conceived. Although White drew every conceivable psychological-skeptical conclusion from this audience-based analysis, and although he affirmed the seemingly ontological divide between photographer and audience, this skeptical orientation was driven by the effort to *overcome* the incorrigible privacy of reaction for the corrigibility of response. To fully intend one's work—to take ownership of the least detail, to own the most extravagant response—was the condition for the possibility of unprecedented forms of expressive communication. Nothing less was demanded of the photographer. As White insisted, "whatever goes on" in a photograph must be "seen and felt and has, since made, been subject to close scrutiny. It is intended. *It is intended that whatever connotations*" a pictorial element has "*for the spectator should be linked in the spectator's mind to the figure*" (c. 1953, 181; original emphasis).

White's notion of full intentionality was only conceivable in light of his dogged, indeed implacable, sense of the barriers in the way of communication. In a sense, every aspect of White's project pointed toward a fully Bartheisan sense of privacy, of every photograph being inevitably reducible to the spectator's *punctum*. But what is so striking about White's project is how close he gets to this affective vision of photography, but resists the seemingly inevitable consequences with a kind of moral aversion. In a sense, White's *Memorable Fancies*—where (sometimes graphic) autobiographical notes collide with photographic theory—turns over and over again around the difference between response and reaction. The features of "pain and anguish" in his work are "plain enough," he records. But whether it is a "lad or a lassie with china blue eyes I am troubled over," that, he insists, "should have no bearing" (1958a: "1948–1949"). "Wish for intercourse? Who doesn't? Also a feeling of being alone expressed? Who isn't alone?" (1958a: February 16, 1947). This appears directly after the note that "the camera injects a bit of objectivity." No moment of privacy on closer examination is as private as it seems, it is a shared feature of human experience. And, as I have been arguing, the whole process of audience response, and of making oneself an audience of one's own pictures, was to "jolt the photographer out of the vacuum of his own self-love" (2012c: 321). The process was "ego-battering, but only in such a way can any photographer earn the full, not partial, psychological, or inner ownership that emigrates from his camera" (2012c: 323). Maybe White put the matter best in a very early formulation from the *Memorable Fancies*: "A definition of Great Art: If a man makes something that can be loved for its own sake and not its associations he makes great art" (1958a: 1934).

Acknowledgments

The Publishers would like to thank Princeton University Art Museum for the use of the epigraphs in this chapter. Princeton University Art Museum holds the Minor White Archive.

Notes

1 Frank added, "However, I feel that if my photograph leaves an image on [the onlooker's] mind—something has been accomplished" (1958: 115). Compare this with White's view that he didn't "give a damn whether [his photography] is art, beauty, truth, or trivia so long as it causes a feeling of what the world means in the spectator" (1958a: September 15, 1953).

2 White observed that, "When I look at anything I see only a photograph. … Camera transformations are my familiarity" (2012b: 212).
3 Writing in *Aperture*, White reflected, "Because *of* the camera the symbols of his inner growth are automatically public symbols as well" (2012b: 211).
4 White's unpublished daybook, *Memorable Fancies*, has no consistent pagination, just dating by entry. It is a heavily worked-over document with innumerable revisions, redactions, inserts, etc. The only secure identifier for any of the variants is to list the date after 1958.
5 Among the more influential accounts—drawing together Duchamp, Lacan, and Barthes—is Rosalind E. Krauss, "Notes on the Index: Part 1" and "Notes on the Index: Part 2," (1985).
6 These matters are brilliantly considered in light of G.E.M. Anscombe's theory of intention and Garry Winogrand's photography in Walter Benn Michaels, "'I Do What Happens': Anscombe and Winogrand," (2016a) and Michaels, "Anscombe and Winogrand, Danto and Mapplethorpe," (2016b).
7 There is at least one important alternative to the affective, private sense of *punctum* (as I am using it here); see Fried, "Barthes's *Punctum*" (2005).
8 These issues are explored at length in Cronan (2013).
9 Here, as elsewhere, my sense of White's project, centered on the question of intentionality, diverges in part from Hershberger's (2015). See, above all, the section entitled "The Beholder" (2015: 5–7).
10 Compare this with Hershberger's sense of the "predictably *un*predictable … outcome in interpreting photographs and sequences" (2015: 6).
11 White's colleague Ralph Hattersley attacked "reactive" criticism in the pages of *Aperture*. Under the heading "IRRELEVANT MEMORIES," he offered a half-joking description of the problem: "Something in a picture you are analyzing reminds you strongly of an event in your life completely unrelated to the picture at hand, thus stirring up inappropriate thought patterns and emotions. Your judgment becomes badly warped. Example: in a picture of a dog, the settee on which the dog sits is like the one in your Aunt Jane's funereal living room. Your rejection and condemnation of the picture is in reality a subconscious revenge on this awful aunt for her treatment of you as a child. A very difficult trap to avoid" (1963: 106).
12 It appears that White is referring to Stieglitz's own sense that the *Equivalents* were not about "subject matter," that there were no "special privileges," no particular bodies involved in making them.
13 For a broader historical sense of White's approach to chance photography see Cronan (2014a).
14 White pauses to interpolate, "Photographs themselves are subject to erosion," and "many a fantastic alteration can be found" on them. As the inevitable process of "deterioration proceeds, chance ultimately writes a palimpsest on every one" (1956: 44).
15 This is what White meant when he observed "The metamorphosis of anything is constantly going on … a manifestation of complex forces at work—so complex we call it a fact of chance" (1958a: December 25, 1955). Chance was what humans called the complexities at work that passed beyond the human capacity for knowledge. It was a higher order, one *potentially* available to a talented visionary.
16 Metaphors like this are largely drawn from the work and writings of P.H. Emerson. For a brilliant analysis of issues related to the ones raised here, see Palermo (2007).
17 Here White writes of the necessity for a photographer's "revising his images until some degree of communication is achieved (not necessarily 100%)." The photographer takes up "audience feedback" as the "seed for the photographer's next creative work" (1974: 11).

References

Barthes, R. (1967) "The Death of the Author," *Aspen*, 5-6, Fall/ Winter, n.p.
Barthes, R. (1981) *Camera Lucida: Reflections on Photography*, trans. Richard Howard, New York: Hill and Wang.
Cage, J. (1983) *X: Writings '79-'82*, Hanover, NH: Wesleyan University Press.
Cage, J. (2003) *Conversing with Cage*, 2nd ed., ed. Richard Kostelanetz, New York and London: Routledge.
Callahan, H. (1972) Interview with A.D. Coleman, *The New York Photographer*, 4, January, pp. 3–6, 11.

Cronan, T. (2013) *Against Affective Formalism: Matisse, Bergson, Modernism*, Minneapolis, MN: University of Minnesota Press.
Cronan, T. (2014a) "Photography: Chance" in *Encyclopedia of Aesthetics*, 2nd ed., ed. Michael Kelly, vol. 5, Oxford and New York: Oxford University Press, pp. 148–151.
Cronan, T. (2014b) "Review of Aperture Magazine Anthology—The Minor White Years, 1952-1976, ed. Peter C. Bunnell," *History of Photography*, vol. 38, no. 2, pp. 204–206.
Duchamp, M. (1973) "The Creative Act" in *The Writings of Marcel Duchamp*, eds. Michel Sanouillet and Elmer Peterson, New York: Da Capo, pp. 138–140.
Frank, R. (1958) "A Statement" in *U.S. Camera Annual*, ed. Tom Maloney, New York: U.S. Camera Publishing, p. 115.
Fried, M. (2005) "Barthes's *Punctum*," *Critical Inquiry*, vol. 31, no. 3, Spring, pp. 539–574.
Friedlander, L. (1970) *Lee Friedlander: Self Portrait*, New York: Museum of Modern Art.
Friedlander, L. (1996) "An Excess of Fact" in *The Desert Seen*, New York: DAP, p. 103–106
Hattersley, R. (1963) "Notions on the Criticism of Visual Photography," *Aperture*, vol. 10, no. 3, pp. 91–112.
Hershberger, A.E. (2015) *The Time Between: The Sequences of Minor White*, San Francisco, CA: First Edition.
Kelsey, R. (2015) "Frederick Sommer Decomposes Our Nature" in *Photography and the Art of Chance*, Cambridge, MA: Harvard University Press, pp. 214–248.
Krauss, R.E. (1985) "Notes on the Index: Part 1" and "Notes on the Index: Part 2" in *The Originality of the Avant-garde and Other Modernist Myths*, Cambridge, MA: MIT Press, pp. 196–220.
Michaels, W.B. (2016a) "'I Do What Happens': Anscombe and Winogrand," *Nonsite.org* 19, May 3, 2016, http://nonsite.org/article/i-do-what-happens. [Accessed May 18, 2017].
Michaels, W.B. (2016b) "Anscombe and Winogrand, Danto and Mapplethorpe", *Nonsite.org* 20, Oct. 26, 2016, http://nonsite.org/article/anscombe-and-winogrand-danto-and-mapplethorpe. Accessed May 10, 2017.
Moholy-Nagy, L. (1980) "The Future of the Photographic Process" in *Photography: Essays and Images*, ed. Beaumont Newhall, New York: Museum of Modern Art, p. 241.
Morris, R. (1994) "Notes on Sculpture, Part 2" in *Continuous Project Altered Daily: The Writings of Robert Morris*, Cambridge, MA: MIT Press, pp. 11–22.
Palermo, C. (2007) "The World in the Ground Glass: Transformations in P.H. Emerson's Photography," *The Art Bulletin*, vol. 89, no. 1, March, pp. 130–147.
White, M. (1951) "How Concepts Differ For Two Cameras," *American Photography*, vol. 45, no. 9, September, pp. 546–551.
White, M. (1952) *Cameras are for Seeing*, unpublished bound manuscript, Minor White Archives, Princeton University Art Museum.
White, M. (c. 1953) *Fundamentals of Style in Photography and the Elements of Reading Photographs*, unpublished bound manuscript, Minor White Archives, Princeton University Art Museum.
White, M. (1956) "Happenstance and How it Involves the Photographer," *Photography*, vol. 11, pp. 40–45, 73.
White, M. (1957a) "The Ambiguous Expressive/Creative Photograph," *Aperture*, vol. 5, no. 1, pp. 3.
White, M. (1957b) "An Experiment in 'Reading' Photographs," *Aperture*, vol. 5, no. 2, pp. 51–75.
White, M. (1958a) *Memorable Fancies*, unpublished bound manuscript, Minor White Archives, Princeton University Art Museum.
White, M. (1958b) "On the Strength of a Mirage," *Art in America*, vol. 46, Spring, pp. 52–55.
White, M. (1959) "Minor White," *Camera*, vol. 38, no. 8, August, pp. 5–6.
White, M. (1963) *Canons of Camerawork*, unpublished bound manuscript, Minor White Archives, Princeton University Art Museum.
White, M. (1966a) "The Camera Mind and Eye" [1952] in *Photographers on Photography: A Critical Anthology*, ed. Nathan Lyons, Englewood Cliffs, NJ: Prentice-Hall, pp. 163–168.
White, M. (1966b) "Equivalence: The Perennial Trend" [1963] in *Photographers on Photography*, ed. Nathan Lyons, Englewood Cliffs, NJ: Prentice-Hall, pp. 168–175.
White, M. (1968) "Extended Perception Through Photography and Suggestion" in *Ways of Growth*, eds. Herbert Otto and John Mann, New York: Grossman, pp. 34–48.
White, M. (1971) "The Secret of Looking," *New York Times*, November 21, pp. 31–32.
White, M. (1972) "Exercises to Meet and Deflate Your Ego By," *New York Times*, September 3, p. D15.
White, M. (1974) "Photographers' Audience: A Preliminary Report of Some Research at M.I.T.," *Exposure*, vol. 12, no. 1, pp. 8–11.

White, M. (1980) "Found Photographs" [1957] in *Photography: Essays and Images*, ed. Beaumont Newhall, New York: Museum of Modern Art, pp. 307–309.
White, M. (2012a) "Criticism" [1953], in *Aperture Magazine Anthology—The Minor White Years, 1952–1976*, ed. Peter C. Bunnell, New York: Aperture, pp. 141–150.
White, M. (as "Myron Martin") (2012b) "Of People and For People" [1956] in *Aperture Magazine Anthology—The Minor White Years, 1952-1976*, ed. Peter C. Bunnell, New York: Aperture, pp. 205–213.
White, M. (2012c) "Varieties of Responses to Photographs: Exercises in the Prediction of Other People's Responses" in *Aperture Magazine Anthology—The Minor White Years, 1952-1976*, ed. Peter C. Bunnell, New York: Aperture, pp. 320–343.
White, M. and W. Chappell (2012) "Some Methods for Experiencing Photographs" [1957] in *Aperture Magazine Anthology—The Minor White Years, 1952-1976*, ed. Peter C. Bunnell, New York: Aperture, pp. 224–240.
Winogrand, G. (1972) "Monkeys Make the Problem More Difficult: A Collective Interview," *Image*, vol. 15, no. 2, pp. 1–14.
Winogrand, G. (1988) "Interview," *Modern Photography*, no. 52, June, p. 50.

4

Testing humanism

The transactions of contemporary documentary photography[1]

Mark Durden

Ariella Azoulay describes photography's referent as "deviant, jarring and devoid of any standard within the paradigm of modern art" (Azoulay 2015: 58). In defining what she refers to as a "political ontology of photography," Azoulay overhauls a dominant conceptualization of photography, drawn from the power of artistic discourse, that "negate[s] the presence of the photographed subjects who look out from the photographs as well … as the testimony borne by their presence there" (Azoulay 2015: 53).

The implications of this reorientation towards the subject in the photograph will frame my discussion of four contemporary documentary works. Documentary is being used here to include appropriationist strategies that are distanced and detached from the event of the photograph, motivated in part by absences and gaps in information about the appropriated photographs' source, as well as the more familiar and long-standing mode of documentary in which photography becomes a means of making connection with people. My first two examples break with the social transaction that documentary entails and are especially responsive to the disruptive and "deviant" force of the referent. Both accent the spectatorship of photographs as they involve not the production of new images, but the appropriation of old images. Both test the humanist model of documentary by retrieving images that are connected to the violent negation of its subjects: Joachim Schmid's book of portrait photographs assumed to be taken by a serial killer and a book presenting scanned copies of mostly rotten and degraded photographs found on the streets of Detroit, by Arianna Arcara and Luca Santese. The next two projects serve as counterpoints to the first examples. Dave Jordano's photographs of people in Detroit hold faith in the value of the aesthetically determined photograph as a register of an essentially empathic relation with those pictured. Bearing some affinities with the illustrational and storytelling mandate of journalism, Laia Abril explores the possibilities of the form of the photobook to edit together a range of material—oral testimonies, family photos and stills from home movies, photographs taken by Abril, facsimile letters and documents—in order to bring us painfully, intimately close to a family's tragedy, creating a memorial portrait to a young woman who died as a result of an eating disorder.

Joachim Schmid's book *L.A. Women* (2011; produced with the self-publishing platform Blurb) presents more than 140 color portraits of mostly black women, often grainy, diffused photographs, and also including some that appear to be stills from videos (see Figure 4.1).

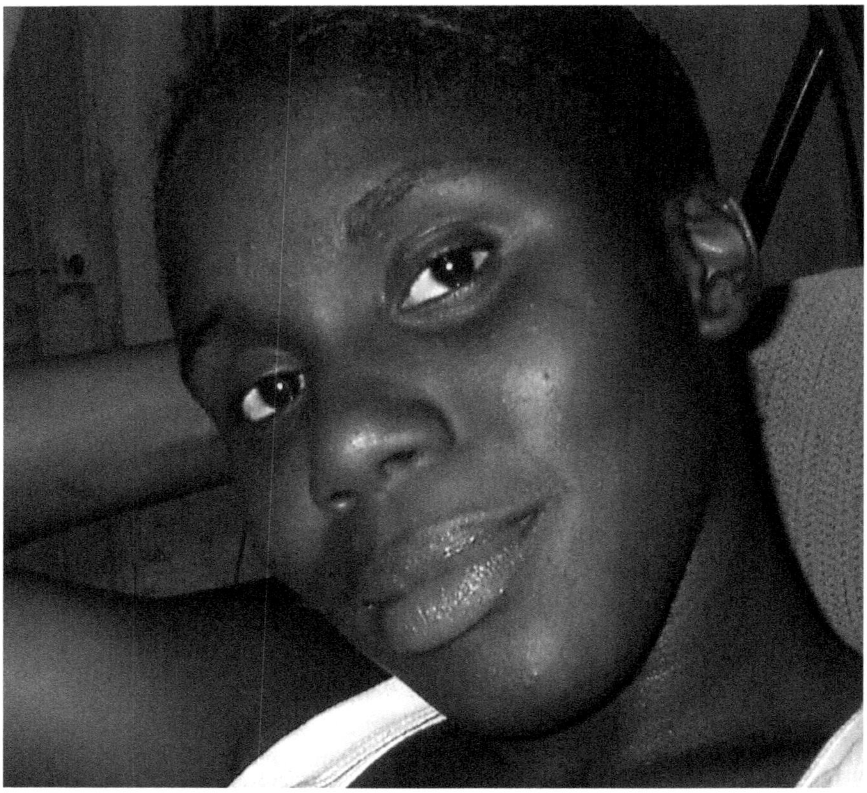

Figure 4.1 Joachim Schmid, from *L.A. Women* (2011). Courtesy the artist

Most women are smiling, happy, complicit in the act of being photographed. Some are photographed in the passenger seats of cars. Some of the women appear to be asleep. Schmid gives us a short introductory text to the photographs, explaining where they were found and reflecting on the particular gruesome circumstances in which they were probably taken:

> In December 2010, the Los Angeles Police Department released one hundred and eighty photographs that were found in the possession of a serial murder suspect. All of them are photographs of women. These women may or may not be residents of Los Angeles, they may or may not be prostitutes (as were the women in the investigation). They may or may not be murder victims. We don't know. We don't even know whether the arrested suspect took these photographs himself. Without knowing where the photographs come from, most of them wouldn't be worth a second glance; for you and me, that is. Of course this is different for friends and family of the women depicted. And it is certainly different for the person who took these pictures. From the testimony of one surviving victim we know that the woman was first photographed, then shot, and then raped before she was dumped in the street. Most of the women were clearly alive when the photos were taken; some are smiling, some are posing. Some appear to

> be asleep, they may or may not be sleeping the big sleep. Some of them may have been shot soon after or just before the photographer shot the picture. We don't know. It is actually the fact that we don't know anything—apart from the context where these photographs come from—that makes them so eerie. We want to know more but the pictures don't tell us. We look at them and they look at us. That's all there is.
>
> *(Schmid 2011: n.p.)*

There is a reliance on the evidential value of the photographs, but they tell us little. A macabre and gruesome history of photography is opened up here. Looking at eyes that looked at their killer, we voyeuristically usurp a relation that is in our imaginary outside a humane and ethical mode of looking. They both invite and disrupt the documentary eye-to-eye appeal. One might even suggest they are anti-portraits in this respect: they fail the photographic transaction. They might look like snapshots, but they are about the annihilation or an erasure of their subject—an erasure that goes beyond the assumed murderous activities of the photographer, but points to the wider erasure and invisibility of those people pictured. They function as evidence of neglect, lack of care, and institutional racism. The photographs were found at the home of Lonnie Franklin Jr., tried and sentenced to death in August 2016 after being convicted of killing nine women and one teenage girl. Detectives, however, believe him to have killed many more. He was nicknamed the "Grim Sleeper" because of a suspected gap in his killings between 1988 and 2002. But it is feared he never really "slept." As reported in the *LA Times*:

> Many of the women were initially listed as Jane Does. The deaths drew little, if any, media attention. Police kept the slayings quiet despite suspicions that a serial killer was stalking black women—a decision that led to outrage and condemnation from many who attribute Franklin's longevity as a killer to police indifference.
>
> *(2016)*

Both the humanist tradition and association of documentary are ruptured by such appropriationist work. In contrast, one should think of James Agee's declaration towards his impoverished tenant farmer subjects in the documentary book *Let Us Now Praise Famous Men*: "I looked them in the eyes with full and open respect" (Agee 1941: 29). Agee's desire for connection was countered by Walker Evans' accompanying portraits that register the tension behind the social difference underlying their production, marked and evident through their aesthetic and beauty, which, as Agee reminds us, is the result of class privilege.

There are echoes too of Roland Barthes' fascination with a portrait photo of Jerome, Napoleon's younger brother, that starts his quest for photography's ontology in *Camera Lucida*: "I am looking at eyes that looked at the Emperor" (Barthes 1982: 3). Napoleon died before the invention of photography, so no photograph of him exists. But, in contrast to Barthes' lyrical meditation, Schmid gives us an unpoetic and blunt closing description of his encounter with the obduracy and silence of the photographs in *L.A. Women*: "We look at them and they look at us. That is all there is." But they are not looking at us, of course. We are (possibly) looking at eyes that looked at their killer. We imaginatively enter into a transaction that remains unfathomable, no traces of the murderous intentions of the one who takes the picture in terms of how those photographed respond; instead, these are mostly portraits showing women smiling to camera. Without an awareness of their context, they suggest a happy and convivial exchange with the photographer, the intimacy of family photographs. This is their horror. There is also another way of seeing this in relation to

Camera Lucida: Barthes' remarks about the temporal "Punctum" of Alexander Gardner's photograph of Lewis Payne in prison before he is hanged—"*He is dead and he is going to die*"—are now played out before every one of Schmid's appropriated portraits, with the gruesome twist that the photographer is their possible killer, and the portrait taken, a "trophy" image (Barthes 1982: 95; original emphasis). Schmid's practice involves a kind of rogue history of photography, attentive to and fascinated with image uses that are ordinarily not seen and valued within its dominant narratives: in this case, the dark realm of serial killer photography.

Thierry de Duve's (2008) essay "Art in the Face of Radical Evil," on the exhibitions (at the 1997 photography festival in Arles and at New York's MoMA in the same year) of photographic portraits of victims of the Cambodian genocide, has particular relevance in relation to Schmid's *L.A. Women*. Some 6,000 negatives were found in 1979 when the Vietnamese liberated S-21, a former school in the borough of Tuol Sleng in Phnom Penh, which Pol Pot had turned into a torture center and extermination camp. Every man, woman, and child entering S-21 was photographed before being killed. The photographer was not the killer, but simply part of "a deranged genocidal bureaucracy" (de Duve 2008: 15). According to an interview he gave on the occasion of the Arles festival, the photographer, Nhem Ein, said he had no choice: it was either that or be killed. Trained and appointed as photographer in chief by the Khmer Rouge and working with a staff of five, he took up to 600 photographs a day of people he knew were innocent and had been sentenced to death. Unease over their status meant the curator of these photographs in Arles refused to grant Nhem Ein the title of artist or the photographs the status of art and had "gone out of his way to de-aestheticize the installation as much as possible" (de Duve 2008: 18). Their inclusion in the exhibition was political, not aesthetic—"to remind us that two million people, out of a population of seven million, had been massacred [in Cambodia] and that nobody moved" (de Duve 2008: 4).

De Duve initially views "the expressions of the human condition emanating" from these photographs "as being attributed to the photographer's own sensitivity to the humanness of humankind" and his "empathy with his models" (de Duve 2008: 9). But this is not so. The photographer is never solely responsible for what is in the frame. In later recognizing that the rapport is with the subjects in the photographs and not the photos themselves as objects of study, de Duve notes the fact that, "our aesthetic interest in photography is shot through with feelings, emotions, and projections of sympathy or antipathy that address the *people* in the photos beyond the photos themselves" (de Duve 2008: 12–13).

The curator labeling them as non-art fails to register the "new aesthetic" these photographs have "forced us to open, that of *genocidal images*" (de Duve 2008: 15). Quoting Dionys Mascolo in response to Robert Anselm's account of his life in Dachau concentration camp—"The attack against the species is the work of the species. The SS is not different from us"—de Duve suggests that, "Perhaps humanism's greatest philosophical inconsistency is to presume that inhuman behavior excludes some humans from humanity" (de Duve 2008: 15). The genocidal images become "a crucial test case" for art's universal address, and, at the end of his essay, de Duve suggests that calling the photographs by the name of art becomes one way "of making sure that the people in the photos are restored to their humanity" (de Duve 2008: 23).

Schmid's intervention is direct and succinct and creates a book that unsettles our ethical values at the core of the documentary exchange and the humanist model underpinning it. With so many looks to camera that appear to be compliant and happy, the portraits are distinct from those discussed by de Duve. Before the S-21 photographs, he writes how their individuality had to be recovered from:

> some little detail that told something specific, not about their lives or personalities, but about their present ordeal, the material conditions of detention, the fear on their faces or the disarming abandonment in their eyes at the very moment of the snapshot.
>
> *(de Duve 2008: 22)*

De Duve points out that, although "Nhem Ein did not execute his victims, they were dead already to his eyes, in as much as they are not spoken to and will soon be disposed of" (de Duve 2008: 23). As a result, the "responsibility of addressing them is imperatively transferred to the viewer of the photographs" (de Duve 2008: 23). The same is true before Schmid's *L. A. Women*—we take on the responsibility of what it means to address those photographed and the circumstances in which they were pictured. Most do not give us signs of their pending death, and this is their extraordinary power: that we cannot read the horror of their situation of being before their suspected murderer. They are also not aesthetic in the ways in which de Duve encounters and experiences the genocidal images—these are low-resolution, low-grade, amateur photographs in which we encounter their base-line documentary functionality in recording an encounter between photographer and subject.

Like Schmid's *L.A. Women*, the large landscape-format book *Found Photos in Detroit* (2012), by Arianna Arcara and Luca Santese, unsettles the humanist optic often seen as integral to documentary photography (see Plate 1 and Figure 4.2). The book presents scanned copies of "[P]olaroids, letters, prints of photographic evidence, police documents, mugshots and family albums" found on the streets of Detroit (Arcara and Santese 2012: n.p.). In accordance with the forensic material presented inside, the book's cover has the appearance of a file of evidence—plain brown with a white sticky label bearing the matter-of-fact title. The book contains explosive and dramatic material: documents of crashed cars, crime scenes, dead bodies, blood, guns and bullets, burnt-out buildings, and Polaroid portraits of predominantly African American subjects that we identify as mug shots. Violence is the overriding note here, not just through the crime scene documents, but also in the language of the typed and handwritten letters containing death threats that are also included among the photographs. An integral element of our experience of these photographs is the degraded condition many of them are in. There is a knowing interplay between the state of destruction documented and the ruin of the photographs themselves—especially in the documents of the interiors of burnt-out homes, in which their evidence of destruction has the same aesthetic as degraded photographs. This makes us aware of the corollary between harm to the image and harm to the subjects portrayed, horrifically evident in the last of the fire-ruin documents, in which fragments of a burnt body are just discernible amidst a burnt-out interior.

Found Photos in Detroit negotiates a gap and distance, to do with when and where the pictures were taken and their information, an absence that has to be negotiated, but ultimately confirms a view of a dangerous, nightmare Detroit. It involves an act of retrieval of something that was not meant to be seen, was left to be destroyed by the elements. Schmid's portraits were already visible; they were not hidden. His intervention pulls them away from their public use by the police, missing people awaiting identification. Instead, he accents a perverse and morbid fascination with such portraits, all charged by the horror of the context in which they were found and the assumption that we look at eyes that are looking at

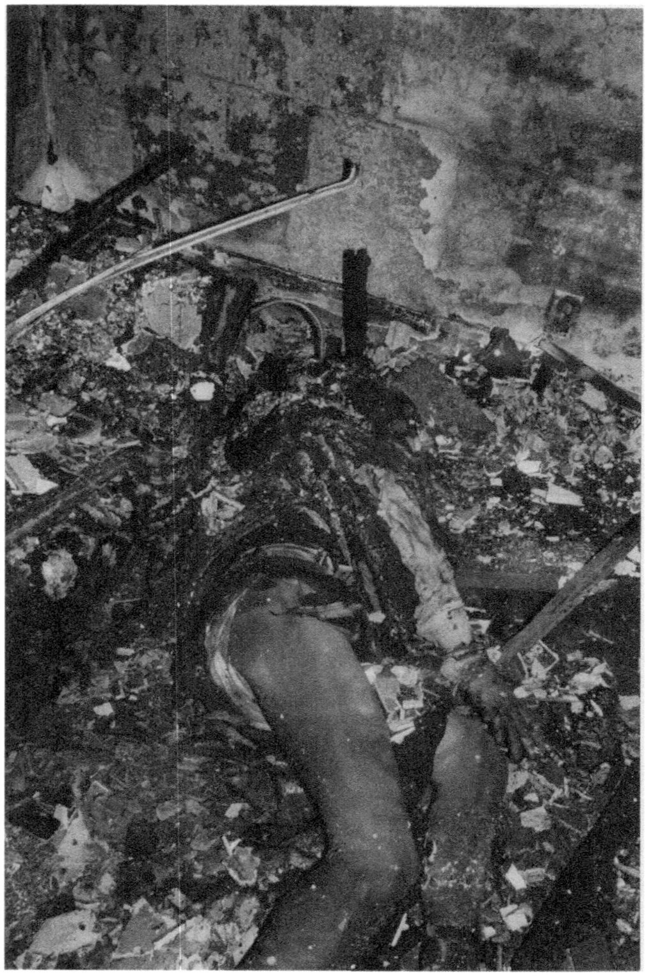

Figure 4.2 Arianna Arcara and Luca Santese, from *Found Photos in Detroit* (2012). Courtesy the artists

the person who will murder them, as well as the ghoulish potential that those who appear asleep may be drugged or dead.

Arcara and Santese's book begins with Polaroids whose images are lost as they were once stuck together and now pulled apart, establishing a recurring motif about the destruction and erasure of images and a clear relationship to the status of the predominantly black American subjects photographed. There are some family album photographs, but the majority appear to be police photographs. Putting snapshots among these other pictures levels everything—the relationship between subject and photographer is very different in the family album portrait, often reciprocal and intimate.

Found Photos in Detroit calls attention to the instability and volatility of its found photographic material: the latter's physical condition acts violently, extending the ruin of a former glorious city to the image and (metaphorically) the bodies of those pictured. Schmid too is appropriating volatile, evidential material, connected with a police investigation, opening up another history of photography, linked to the photographer's assumed murderous activity and the way in which so many photographs fail to register it.

Although its collection of pictures is very different, Arcara and Santese's book bears a relationship to Yves Marchand and Romain Meffre's lavish 2010 book of large-format color photographs, *The Ruins of Detroit*. Marchand and Meffre's photographs of the abandoned offices of the Highland Park Police Station, which closed in 2001, provide a record of the place where we assume Arcara and Santese were able to gather much of their sensitive, forensic photographic material. One of Marchand and Meffre's photographs of the interior of the police station includes a huge pile of photographs in the foreground, which the caption informs us are "Polaroids dating from the 1970s."

Marchand and Meffre's *The Ruins of Detroit* forms part of what Dora Apel has termed a "deindustrial sublime," their absorption with "the romanticized horror and beauty of grand and 'fabulous' ruins" marking a "decadent consciousness that aestheticizes its own decline" (Apel 2015: 99). Their aesthetic vision sees the ruins of Detroit as akin to the "remnants of the passing of a great Empire," not the consequences of racism, the ravages of capitalism and political neglect (Marchand and Meffre 2010: n.p.). In relation to Marchand and Meffre's photographs of the abandoned police station, Apel notes how the scope of underfunding in police investigations was revealed in 2009, "when prosecutors in Detroit discovered more than eleven thousand boxes of potential evidence in rape cases left completely unprocessed" (Apel 2015: 81). The case, she says, "rivals the 11,000 unsolved city homicides, dating back to 1960, reported in Charlie LeDuf's *Detroit: An American Autopsy*" (Apel 2015: 81–2). Arcara and Santese gather evidence showing us this neglect; this is the political imperative underlining their project. Their found photographs evidence lives that have been negated, destroyed like the pictures themselves. But the collection, preservation, and sorting of these pictures ultimately feeds an aesthetic of the ruin, collapsed into the cruel, voyeuristic captivation with the degraded spectacle of the damaged lives of others.

One group of photographs, each picture blown up so it fills a page, shows an African American boy, his shirt off, facing and then turning away from the camera; lighting and context change, suggesting that the portraits are taken at two different times. The poses and gestures repeat and suggest that this is a document of him showing how he has been beaten, abused. We are aware of his fragility and vulnerability. These pictures have survived intact; undamaged, they nevertheless evidence damage and also open up a space of pathos and empathy in relation to this child, colliding with the effect of so many of the other appropriated photographs in which the subjects remain abject and others in which attachment and identification are sundered.

In the last pages of *Found Photos in Detroit* there is a preoccupation with the pictorial effects of the degraded surfaces of photographs: full-page spreads of enlarged photographs in which the emulsion has washed off to form abstract patterns of colorful liquid stains. Such enlargements do not bring us closer, but underscore the severance and gap this project negotiates. The book ends with two exterior urban winter snow scenes, the blankness and emptiness of the pictures animated by the way the surfaces of the pictures are rutted and scored by rivulets created by running water, but now clogged up with the dirt and grit of the street. Just as architectural ruins are often shown being taken over by nature, so nature can be seen taking over these photographs—an accent that distracts from the fact these are specific cultural images. There is nothing natural about their abandonment and neglect. *Found Photos in Detroit* signals its detachment and lack of humanity through fixation with the material state of the photographs. Much as it entails a rescue and salvaging of pictures that otherwise would have remained forgotten and left to rot, it revels in the aesthetics of decay and ruin and the vicarious thrill of its documents taken from a violent, murderous reality.

In his 1936 essay "Narrate or Describe?" Georg Lukács made a distinction between "observer" and "participant" in realist fiction that still has particular relevance for thinking documentary today, despite the fact that photographic visuality is, in his discussion of literature, a problem. Lukács contrasts descriptions of horse races by Zola and Tolstoy. With Zola, "every possible detail at a race is described precisely, colorfully and with sensuous vitality" (Lukács 1978: 110). But, for all its virtuosity, "the description is mere filler in the novel" (Lukács 1978: 110), whereas Tolstoy's account of Vronsky's ride and fall "is no mere tableau" but "thoroughly integrated into the total action of the novel" (Lukács 1978: 111). Whereas, in Zola, the race is "*described* from the point of view of an observer, in Tolstoy it is *narrated* from the standpoint of a participant" (Lukács 1978: 111; original emphasis). Documentary photography can very easily be just about observation and spectatorship, even though so much of its motivation is about trying to elicit engagement and involvement with those represented. Documentary is always about negotiating distance and gaps, between the event, the photographer, and spectator. Only, with appropriationist strategies, this gap is more evident: we are more conscious of what is missing, what is left out. Yet the danger of the alternative model is a faith that the silent, still photograph can open up a point of meaningful human connection.

Lukács believed that, "modern realism has lost its capacity to depict the dynamics of life" (Lukács 1978: 147). The "poetic level of life decays" under capitalism, and he felt descriptive literature was intensifying this decay (Lukács 1978: 27). For Lukács, "A character's physical appearance possesses poetic vitality only when a factor in his rapport with other men" (Lukács 1978: 138–9). The problem with the "descriptive method" is that it involves "a passive capitulation" to the consequences of "fully-fledged capitalism," which entails a dehumanizing reduction of the individual "into a soulless appurtenance of the capitalist system" (Lukács 1978: 146).

The question of rapport, the "poetic vitality" integral to the realist fiction championed by Lukács, is central to the documentary work of Dave Jordano: his pictures show us a dynamic and resilient humanity in the face of the destructive reality of capitalism manifest in the neglect and destruction of Detroit. His photographs show, as the title of his book puts it, *Detroit: Unbroken Down* (2015). The portraits of people and places in Detroit present us with an important political counterpoint to "ruin-porn"—a term coined in relation to the tourism of the city (Apel 2015: 20). Jordano's work is, as he has said, "a reaction to all the negative press that I felt Detroit has endured over the past few years" and involves a concern with what he refers to as "the human condition, the heart of what a city is all about, the people left to cope with harsh realities of a post-industrial town that has fallen on the hardest of times" (Pollock n.d.: n.p.). His portraits are respectful, people are complicit and appear at ease in posing to have their picture taken. With a communitarian aspect to many of the photographs, the accent is on world-building and world-making.

Jordano grew up in Detroit in the time of the auto industry, returning in 2010, after 30 years' absence, and has said, "perhaps there was something of my earliest days here to rediscover" (Pollock n.d.: n.p.). He shows us how people live their lives, despite the bad situation. Posed, his pictures are not static but are often responsive to gestures and expressions on the part of his subjects. The people photographed are compliant to the ritual and ceremony of having their photograph taken but they are not passive. A number of pictures involve an act of showing: the portrait of a young black male, who reveals the Detroit tattoo running down his forearm, or the youth before his car that has been made into a memorial to his mother. Such display speaks about place and belonging, attachments and connections. Jordano's pictures are also abundant in signs of creativity and productivity within these abandoned, blighted sites, testament to how people survive, form allegiances and bonds, how they have reclaimed and re-used spaces.

Jordano focuses on the "more economically distressed neighborhoods of the city" (Barr, Zukin, and Bey 2015: 19). In response to the question of his own privilege and agency in relation to those he pictures and the documentary tradition of visualizing various forms of victimhood, he says:

> I don't think of myself as someone who is privileged in the sense that I am living a better life from the subjects I photograph, simply because I might have more money or come from a different social class. Money and status are not pre-requisites for compassion. I've never placed myself above anyone I've photographed and I would never think that my skin colour or background would in any way impact the relationship I would forge with the people I meet.
>
> *(Barr, Zukin, and Bey 2015: 20)*

A rapport and ease with those pictured comes across in his photographs. While, as he says,

> most of the people I've photographed are poor and financially struggling … they problem solve by finding solutions to deal with their daily lives and work towards those means to achieve their goals. This is what I find so inspiring in the people I've met in Detroit and I try to relate to those emotions and feelings in the work I do.
>
> *(Barr, Zukin, and Bey 2015: 20)*

Premised on the principle that, "if you give respect you'll get it back," his photographs are celebratory of people's lives and lifestyles (Barr, Zukin, and Bey 2015: 20).

In his depiction of two women with their young children in a play area on a makeshift stage on an empty lot, the inclusion of his own shadow interlinking with the scene serves as a little sign of desired connection and echo of the communitarian message broadcast by the large red lettering across the mural on the wall in the background: "DETROIT UNITED—THE RISE OF OUR PEOPLE." In *Stacey and Carlitha, Jason's Memorial Site, Southwest Side, Detroit* (2012), Jordano's photograph becomes an act of commemoration, a tribute to the dead, and testimony to the resilience of the surviving family members (see Plate 2). It shows a woman with her arms wrapped protectively and affectionately around the shoulders of a young girl. They are standing beside a portrait of a man, identified in the painting as Mosco, and a small shrine with flowers and candles and the figure of the Virgin Mary. The improvised memorial marks the spot where the man was murdered. Stacey is the murdered man's sister, and Carlitha his daughter, who she is bringing up as her own, as the girl's mother left her and her father when she was 4 years old.

In *Mo, the Birdman of Detroit*, a man stands in front of the small doorway to a makeshift structure attached to his house, looking up to the heavens, his head illuminated by a diagonal of sunlight (see Plate 3). Pigeons line the roofs of his home and are all over the ground before him. The tableau celebrates and underscores his passion. Notes to the photograph inform us he has loved pigeons since his childhood in Iraq and has attached pigeon coops to his house and put them around his yard. The woman seated in the shade of the doorway beside him is his tenant and works as a prostitute.

The Darkness in the Light, made as he was working on *Detroit Unbroken Down*, and referred to as its "caveat," is an ongoing series of portraits of women working as prostitutes to feed their drug addiction. With an under-resourced and minimalized police presence, "their free reign of the neighborhoods seemed as casual and familiar as the local postman" (Jordano, n. d.). The women stand and hold a casual pose for the camera, which often represents them in full figure and against a variety of settings and in different seasons (see Figure 4.3). The act of picturing proceeds from an attempt to resurrect a care and feeling denied them in life.

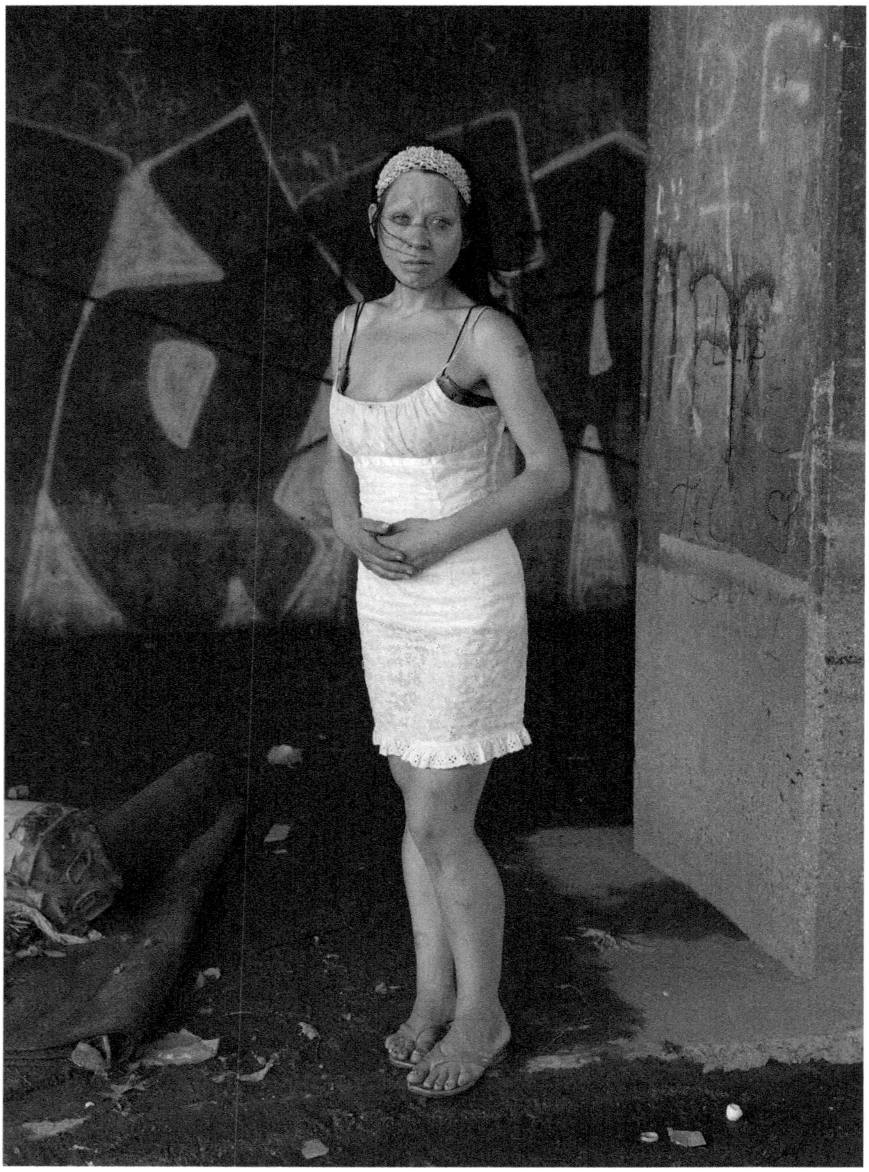

Figure 4.3 Dave Jordano, *Melanie, Detroit* (2011). Courtesy the artist

Jordano has spoken of intending to create an ambiguity in who they might be, "alternate possibilities of identity," inviting us to see them as "a relative or friend, a sister or a loved one" (Jordano, n.d.).

Jordano's respectful approach affects how those depicted present themselves to camera—his pictures are rare in documentary because they do not appear to bear traces of a conflict or anxiety over the social differences between photographer and subject. The photographs' very aesthetic is integral to the lives of his subjects, their way of being, and way of world-making, and in resistance to the dominant narratives of ruin and despair and breakdown. Although typical of the documentary transaction in which one class looks at another, it is the generosity in their making and how this is reflected in the ease with which his subjects appear to address the camera that make them unusual and distinctive.

My final example, *The Epilogue*, a photobook by the Spanish photographer Laia Abril (2014), through visual and textual fragments creates a memorial portrait of a young woman, Mary Cameron "Cammy" Robinson, who died from her third heart attack caused by her bulimia in 2005, aged 26. Having initially trained as a journalist and then worked for Oliviero Toscani's *COLORS* magazine as photographer and photo editor (for nearly five years), Abril has said how her projects are about "telling the most uncomfortable, hidden, stigmatized, and misunderstood stories. I often find myself trying to photograph invisible issues, aspects recurrently connected to mental states, mental illness, prejudices, and taboos" (Colberg 2018b).

As the title implies, this book is something that comes after, after a life and in response to a family and friends still grieving and hurting over the loss of a loved one. The book seeks a truth and honesty in terms of the focus on the tragedy and trauma of a family's daughter's illness and death and the "collateral damage" created by what happened to her. Quotes taken from interviews with her family and friends, her therapist, and her boyfriend's mother (her boyfriend declined to be part of the book) create a powerful multi-vocal account of Cammy's life and the impact her eating disorder and death have had upon them. The book also includes facsimile copies of private family letters, as well as reproductions of family photographs and stills from family videos, extracts from medical records, her newspaper obituary, her birth and death certificates, and pages from her teenage diary (see Figure 4.4). It is a tribute to an exceptional life of the daughter of a typical white middle-class American family and also a testimony to the family's openness and willingness to let another young woman into their lives and allow her to tell the story of their daughter.

The book is not judgmental or interpretative. Apart from the inclusion of her own photographs—including portraits of the family and their homes, interiors, ornaments, and objects—Abril assembles her documentary from statements taken from the interviews she has recorded and personal material and documents that the family made available. The presentation and simulation of a number of handwritten letters in the book serve as interruptive inserts among the pages—although facsimiles, having been printed on matte paper, their touch and texture are different to the pages in the book. There is a difference between the pictured artifact and the physical letter that we have to fold out to read. The first letter from the son to his parents expresses his love to them for all they have done for him and how he cried in thinking how hard every Mother's and Father's Day must be for them. Touching and reading such private letters "patheticize[s]" (Barthes 1979: 25) our relation to everything else in the book. Such writing is not literary, it is ordinary, vernacular, as are the transcriptions of the speaking voices in the interviews. The book accents non-digital modes of communication, handwritten and tactile modes of address such as the letters. There is one mobile phone image, but it is photographed to include the object of the phone, bearing an image (taken by Cammy's therapist) showing the lift where Cammy had her second heart attack.

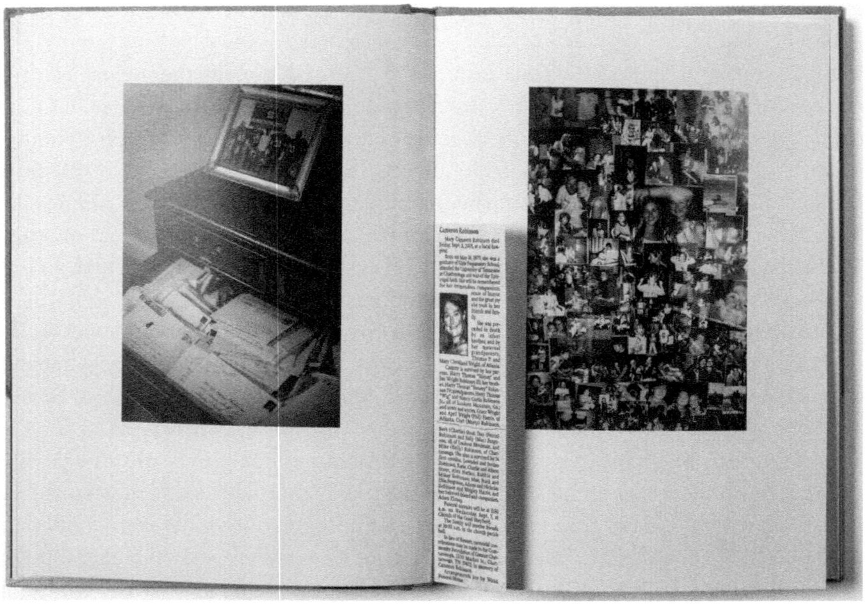

Figure 4.4 Laia Abril, from *The Epilogue* (2014). Courtesy the artist

Abril's own photographs include portraits of the family and friends, their home, as well as objects, including an answering machine kept by Cammy's cousin because it preserves a recording of her voice. Some of them are evidential, like so much material gathered in the book. But others introduce a lyrical and poetical sensibility: there are some mournful pictures of the family house—for example, the book begins by showing us its gray clapboard façade, and a later image isolates a rain-spattered terrace. A leafy sunny picture showing the family's former house where Cammy spent her childhood and teenage years centers upon a wooden sign bearing the street names "RED RIDING HOOD TR" and "CINDERELLA RD," fairy tale allusions that, in the book, now strike a discordant note. A photograph showing grass teeming with "ladybugs" is connected with the release of two thousand of them to honour Cammy's memory by her best friend Ashley and her mum. Cammy had been associated with the insect since she was a child, and, as her best friend says, "It's very funny we will be having a bad or good day, and when you need her there will be a ladybug at your shoulder! No matter what you believe that is our way to know she is there!" (Abril 2014: n.p.).

Selected family album photographs of Cammy and video stills, appearing to be sequenced in chronological order, gain intensity and heightened interest when read in terms of our knowledge of the consequences of the life they picture. With one of the first family photographs included, of the mother and Cammy as a baby, the mother's image is lost to light leaking onto the film—an accident that becomes portentous of the tragic separation and loss that are to come (see Figure 4.5). In one family portrait, we are conscious of the way it appears to evidence Cammy's hyperactivity; in another showing her with friends she is the only one not smiling. Pictures register the shifts in appearance as her weight changes: in one of her later and last photographs, showing her in the arms

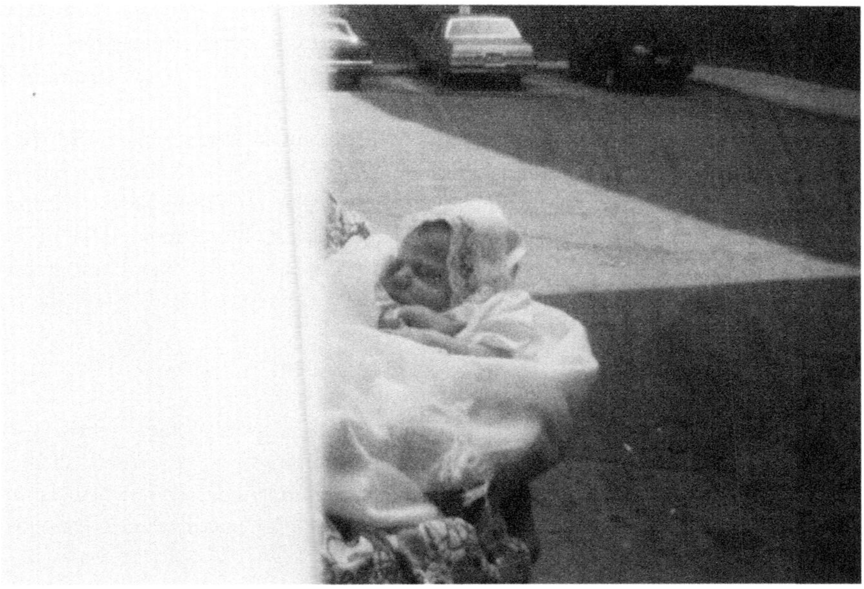

Figure 4.5 Laia Abril, from *The Epilogue* (2014). Courtesy the artist

of her boyfriend, someone is pointing their finger at her too-thin exposed torso. Just before this, a snapshot of her larking about with her boyfriend carries an unintentional, painful allusion to her illness: with his hand pushing a frothy substance into her face, it also looks like she is vomiting. These photographs are supplemented throughout the book with edited transcripts from the interviews. Presented as an assemblage of short, fragmentary statements by different family members and friends, many build up a further succession of portraits, some of them creating prose equivalents of family photographs. Wejun, Cammy's father, says:

> Jan and I were fixing dinner, Cammy and Adam were sitting at the table playing, and drinking red wine and having the best time [...] Tommy and Kristen were watching TV across the room and I thought: "God, it's not going to get better than this." It was just wonderful.
>
> *(Abril 2014: n.p.)*

In one of the later transcripts, the mother says: "The girl we thought we knew was not. To be perfectly honest I don't think I ever knew Cammy" (Abril 2014: n.p.). The disclosure is important as it offsets the potential sentimentality of a project such as this. No matter how much her family and friends love her, they never really know her. The quote also rebounds on the documentary project as a whole, the assumption that we can really get close. Her brother is given the final words in the book—his anger on being woken to be told Cammy was in hospital: "My first thought was: 'Right, here we fucking go again. This is like the fifth time this happens'"; then, when driving,

> we're crossing a bridge to the hospital [and] there is a little garden you can see from there; and I felt like I saw Cammy in that garden; it was not like a thing in my imagination. I felt like I'd seen her spirit, I saw her with my eyes, it was just something that I really felt.
> *(Abril 2014: n.p.)*

A photograph showing what we assume might be the highway bridge, lined with American flags and with a figure running across it, follows. The clouds are clearing, and there is a patch of blue. The overhead traffic light is on green. A following page containing the death certificate, bearing the cause of death as cardiac arrest, blunt and matter of fact, jars with the intimacies of the transcripts of voices and the poetics of Abril's photographs. The last picture of the book shows a small leafy tree before a white clapboard house, the top part of the image dissolved in light.

The Norwegian writer Karl Ove Knausgaard has said that:

> If … you want to write about life, simplification is a great danger, which you must constantly guard against. You do that by going as close as you can where all the broad sweeps, all the higher-level generalisations, no longer apply and are nowhere apparent.
> *(Knausgaard and Ekelund 2014: 18)*

This is crucial to *The Epilogue*. For Knausgaard, in life, "simplification and generalisation are necessary, they constitute the framework for the everyday and for life with others, the absence of which would make everything chaotic and confusing" (Knausgaard and Ekelund 2014: 18). But, in literature, "it is precisely the breaches we look for … it appears in crises, when someone dies, when someone falls in love, when all the rules, all the limits are lifted in one fell swoop" (Knausgaard and Ekelund 2014: 18). Documentary tends to home in on crisis moments in the lives of others, and all my examples represent crises—but all avoid containing those events with familiar platitudes and generalizations.

The Epilogue adheres to a documentary mode of gathering and ordering material that registers the devastating effects of an eating disorder upon family and friends. The book communicates the anger, guilt, grief, and despair of those left to pick up the pieces and, at the same time, the incredible resilience and love that are shown. For all the damage and destruction unleashed by their daughter's illness and death, the family bond and ties are still very much in evidence and strong, and this is something that is brought out from the book's very beginning with the son's love letter to his parents and Abril's portraits of them with their grandchild. Life and love continue, regardless.

While following the journalistic premise to "pry intimately" in to the lives of others, and not without journalistic strategies of storytelling, it opens out a powerful empathic space (Agee 1941: 7). At the same time, a quest for the truth about what happened, a point of understanding, is never fulfilled. For all the strategies deployed to bring us close, to elicit identification and connection, we cannot in the end know its subject—a lack visualized in the montage on the back and front of the book, in which two formal school portraits of Cammy's face, from different ages, are covered over by a rectangular block of blue. One can read *The Epilogue* in terms of the inequalities and damaging effects of a culture predicated on impossible feminine image ideals, all the pressure that this puts on young women. America has the highest rates of eating disorders, and this is an important reason Abril chose the country. All this is integral to how we are invited to read the content, anchor the work in broader themes. However, what is remarkable and distinctive about this approach to documentary is how it brings us close by creating a portrait out of the intimacies of the traces and memories that remain.

Schmid and Arcara and Santese test the humanist values and expectations we bring to photographs. Both acts of appropriation are in the face of oblivion, and the photographs are charged and made exceptional by their violent context. The effect is to reorient the photographs to the viewer, put the moral responsibility towards those depicted onto us. The wretched images of Arcara and Santese visualize and spectacularize those who are seen without humanity or dignity, extensions of the ruin aesthetic associated with Detroit and disturbingly played out through the retrieved damaged photographs that bear evidential traces of lives destroyed by violence. Schmid's are awkward because those photographed appear compliant in being photographed; their look does not appear to disclose the assumed reality. Their humanness unsettles us, because of the barbarity associated with the person who took their pictures and the eyes we imaginatively see them through.

According to Bill Nichols, "Documentary directs us to the world of brute reality even as it also seeks to interpret it" (Nichols 1991: 110). Documentaries present an argument about the historical world. What is distinctive about my first two examples is how the act of appropriation and re-presentation of material is bereft of a sense of an argument. Both signal a documentary degree zero, in which we have to deal with the implications of the evidential material that is presented to us. The effect is to shatter the familiar expectations of the documentary form. Dave Jordano's photographs offer lyrical and beautiful affirmations of the humanity of those represented, pictures showing acts of collectivity and creativity, of world-building in the face of the ruins of disastrous economic neglect. The aesthetic of these pictures is integral to their politics. Jordano is the most authorially present as a documentary maker, and his photographs are more typically documentary, motivated to show us a real that counters a dominant cultural stereotype of Detroit in terms of the ruin. Laia Abril's remarkable book deploys a range of evidential material to bring home the traumatic and devastating impact of a young woman's eating disorder. Through assembling visual and textual documentary fragments, threaded through with the lyricism of some of her own photographs, she builds up through multiple subjective accounts a vivid portrait of the life of a young woman and her struggles with a terrible illness. It is a documentary shaped and determined by the oral testimonies of those who loved and knew Cammy and the visual documents and traces she has left behind. In many respects, the book extends and expands the documentary form. It can be seen to deploy elements within all three of my former examples, but maintains a faith in a humanist ideal, even though the life it recounts is one in which intimate and close relations have been tested to the limit.

Note

1 Earlier versions of this essay were presented as papers at Glasgow School of Art in February 2017 and at the Maison Française d'Oxford in January 2018.

References

Abril, L. (2014) *The Epilogue*, Stockport: Dewi Lewis.

Agee, J. (1941) *Let Us Now Praise Famous Men*, New York: Houghton Mifflin.

Apel, D. (2015) *Beautiful Terrible Ruins: Detroit and the Anxiety of Decline*, New Brunswick,New Jersey, and London: Rutgers University Press.

Arcara, A. and Santese, L. (2012) *Found Photos in Detroit*, Pianello Val Tidone: Cesura.

Azoulay, A. (2015) *Civil Imagination: A Political Ontology of Photography*, London: Verso.

Barr, N. W., Zukin, S., and Bey, D. (2015) *Detroit Unbroken Down*, Brooklyn, New York: Powerhouse Books.

Barthes, R. (1979) "The Photographic Message," in *Image-Music-Text*, selected and translated by S. Heath, Glasgow: Fontana/Collins, pp. 15–31.

Barthes, R. (1982) *Camera Lucida*, London: Jonathan Cape.
Colberg, J. (2018b) "A Conversation with Laia Abril." https://cphmag.com/conv-abril/ [Accessed February 14, 2018].
de Duve, T. (2008) "Art in the Face of Radical Evil," *October* 125 Summer, pp. 3–23.
Jordano, D. (2015) *Detroit: Unbroken Down*, New York: PowerHouse Books. https://davejordano.com/detroit-unbroken-down [Accessed January 10, 2017].
Jordano, D. (n.d.) *The Darkness in the Light*, https://davejordano.com/detroit-unbroken-down/detroit-darkness-in-the-light-1 [Accessed January 10, 2017].
Knausgaard, K. O. and Ekelund, F. (2014) *Home and Away*, London: Harvill Seker.
LA Times. (2016) "The 'Grim Sleeper' is Sentenced to Death for String of Murders," www.latimes.com/local/lanow/la-me-grim-sleeper-sentencing-20160810-snap-story.html [Accessed December 9, 2017].
Lukács, G. (1978) "Narrate or Describe?" in *Writer and Critic*, edited and translated by A. Kahn, London: Merlin Press, pp. 110–148.
Marchand, Y. and Meffre, R. (2010) *The Ruins of Detroit*. Göttingen: Steidl. www.marchandmeffre.com/detroit [Accessed December 12, 2017].
Nichols, B. (1991) *Representing Reality*, Bloomington and Indianapolis: Indiana University Press.
Pollock, D. (n.d.) "Dave Jordano: Unbroken Down" www.urbanautica.com/interview/dave-jordano-detroit-unbroken-down/280 [Accessed January 10, 2017].
Schmid, J. (2011) *L.A. Women*, San Francisco CA: Blurb.

5

Jeff Wall speaks with David Campany[1]

Jeff Wall and David Campany

Introduction, Mark Durden

Jeff Wall's commitment to the single image from the latter part of the 1970s distinguishes him from many other photographers whose work was, as David Campany puts it, "serial, sequential, typological or in suites of some kind." The dialogue that follows illuminates Wall's practice and motivations—reflecting upon his shift of photography away from journalistic and essayistic uses and showing how he broke with a subservience to the motif or the subject, what he refers to as "photography's instinctive commitment to subject matter." Painting becomes an important point of reference because it is less devoted to a single subject. There is a different relation to the medium in painting: painters had a much more "assured relation to their art form," and it is this he looked towards in his relationship to photography. Because of their dependence on subject matter, photographers could only have a short burst of accomplishment.

Wall remains engaged with the richness and complexity of everyday life but does not go out hunting with a camera like Garry Winogrand or Robert Frank. Observed events are instead re-staged. With Wall's tableaux, there is a gap between "the noticing and the making of a picture derived from it," and this brings his practice closer to painting, because it does not have access to the instantaneous and involves a translation of events and things. Henri Cartier-Bresson tried to counter the way things escape us, "by being so quick that the loss of experience would not occur." This commitment to capturing the fleeting and momentary can become "too sentimental"—and, for Campany and Wall, photography only became open to artistic exploration when that "mnemonic burden was lifted." Wall therefore refers to the tense of his staged tableaux as being "what continually is," and this brings his photography closer to painting and sculpture, which, as he says, "have the ability to keep things happening perpetually. Painting and sculpture are in the present tense."

Jeff Wall speaks with David Campany

DAVID CAMPANY (DC): It's probably not possible but let's try to talk specifically about photography and your relation to it. Many of the great photographers of the past came in to their own particular relation to the medium and more or less stuck with it, maybe peaking early and staying with that approach. From the beginning your relation to photography seems to have been much more complex, less certain perhaps, and the strength of your work has emerged from this.

JEFF WALL (JW): Yes, I guess at the beginning I was kind of testy with photography, or at least unsatisfied about a lot of things, and that made it seem like I had some kind of issue with the medium itself, but it wasn't the case. It was really just my way of trying to find a handle on this huge medium. I think it's a very elusive medium, don't you?

DC: I do. Was that feeling of being outside photography coloured by what other people were doing with it?

JW: I just felt confronted with it in some way. Slowly over a period I moved toward it and found myself really fascinated by it. But at the same time, I was dissatisfied with what you just described. I noticed at some early point that many famous photographers who one admired did have a period when they seemed to accomplish their best work and then after that it didn't seem to be the case any more. I remember that worried me right from the beginning.

DC: Many of them achieved their best work before the age you arrived at when you decided photography was really the thing for you.

JW: I was coming from an angle that was so much informed by the other arts that it couldn't help but have an effect. And I feel there is a different relation between the medium and the artist in painting. The painters I admired never had a short burst of accomplishment followed by something else. They kept developing different ways of painting that went on for decades and I always felt they had a much more powerful or assured relation to their art form.

DC: Does that mean there was no such thing in photography as 'mature work', the way a painter might arrive at mature work after a long, long period?

JW: It could be. I have never thought of it that way. But also, a painter could arrive at something very quickly, very young, and sustain it or change it, evolve. Maybe one counter-example is Cezanne (if we're talking about the best artists) because he seemed to have been doing quite inferior painting for a stretch and then when he stopped doing that and came into his own he sustained that for a period of time. But even he's a bit of an exception. If you take other artists from the same period like Seurat or Manet you don't see that. You see early work that's very accomplished and then it just keeps going and changes and gets more mature. So, painters seemed able to have a more sovereign relation to their medium, and I wanted something like that. I wouldn't have wanted to accomplish something over ten years and then not be able to match it. Maybe time will tell us that I'm in that boat anyway, but I don't want to be in that boat, obviously.

DC: Already we're drifting from photography but let's go with it. I guess the other parallel with painting that strikes me as very stark in your work is the commitment to the single image which is there from when you begin making your lightbox transparencies in the latter part of the 1970s. I can think of very few artists or photographers who were making such singular images at that time. Singular pictures with a capital 'P'. Everything seemed to be serial, sequential, typological or in suites of some kind, which was an inheritance either of Pop and Conceptualism or art reportage modelled on the photo-essay. Even today there are comparatively few who are willing or able to work in a very singular way. Where does that come from?

JW: I think it comes from the same source. One of the issues or conditions with photography as it was practised was the idea that the single picture wasn't adequate: one had to delve into something and report on it in an essayistic sort of way. I thought there was too much subservience to the motif or subject matter in that. The practice was driven by the availability of significant subject matter and once that subject matter was somehow done, then what? A lot of photographers made their work in relation to a specific situation. Maybe Walker Evans is a good example, because it was the Depression era in America that allowed him to do what he did and he did it perfectly, and that was certainly enough. But that wasn't the position I wanted to be in, and I think it has to do with photography's instinctive commitment to subject matter, as if the subject matter is what's important. Such photographs, no matter how good they are, are devoted to the revealing of the subject matter. But that's not what modern painting is about. Modern painting is about making paintings, and therefore about finding the occasion or motifs that will make that possible. There's no important artist whose work is devoted to a single subject or to the meaningfulness of the subject. Subjects can be important and timely but they don't have that relation to the picture. So maybe that's something that I insisted on for my own practice. That's why some people say "Oh yes, it's borrowing from painting," which it probably is in that sense, but photography is perfectly capable of including that.

DC: It may be that the presentation of any photograph in the space of art makes it more about photography than, let's say, an image presented in the space of journalism. It becomes more about photography simply because the space of art draws attention to form. That's partly what art does to all photographs. When Walker Evans described his work as 'documentary style' it seemed to lead many to look to the images themselves for small but significant differences from documentary photographs. But it's more to do with the use, or suspension of use, of the photograph in art.

JW: Yes, Evans' pictures do look like documentary photographs, and in many cases they are documentary photographs, but they're done better than other documentary photographs are done in terms of picture making and maybe that's also what he meant by 'documentary style'. It seems he was fated to have a particular relation to a particular range of subjects. When the opportunities for those subjects seemed to have passed, his career really changed gear. On the other hand, he was very aware of just what we've been talking about, that there should be a suspension of this engagement with the subject matter to allow an engagement with representation. He was perfectly aware of it, yet he was still subject to it, it seems. That's what's so perplexing about Evans.

DC: He was a maker of extraordinary single images, more than enough to be a great museum artist, but he was also very committed to editing, to exploring how images represent by playing them off each other in a highly reflexive way. That's what he did so well in his books and his work at *Fortune* magazine

JW: His individual images are first rate but he wasn't that interested in them being experienced that way.

DC: Do you think they could only have been made that way, with that attitude? It strikes me that many of the greatest photographs made between the 1920s and the 1960s (photography's high modern period, I guess) came out of that hybrid circumstance in which art and its emphasis on representation was there in the minds of those photographers but was not the sole or primary concern.

JW: Yes, probably.

DC: Evans knows a lot about art, he follows it. But he's not necessarily caught up in the 'canon', not before the 1960s anyway. Evans' precursor Atget is the supreme example of this, pursuing his work at a significant remove from art and making the most of those fluid, hybrid circumstances. A certain hybridity was open to you but in a different way, from within art. You were from the start very much an artist making photographs yet knowing there was this relation to other forms of photography outside art.

JW: I think I had it much easier, because the field changed shape so much since the end of Evans' period. Around 1970 when I began to really get interested in photography, Evans was still around, teaching at Yale, and I guess I could have gone to Yale and studied photography and got in his class. It never occurred to me. But, by that time, the idea that one had to be a photographer by being in the institutions that sustained photography—essentially journalism—was over. I wouldn't have even thought about practising photography the way Evans did—getting a job in photography and then maybe trying to make a creative statement within that situation. It seemed totally unnecessary. Great work got made that way but there was this place called fine art that was absolutely open to anyone working in any way by that point. So it was much easier to move right to the centre of the problem without ever having to engage with that institutional network of journalism and so on in order to even get your photographs seen. My generation never had to do that. There were still photographers working in that way, as itinerants on the road, writing their *Leaves of Grass*-poetic journalism. Some of it was very good, like Garry Winogrand, Robert Frank, and Lee Friedlander, but a lot of it was really tired. When I saw Frank's *The Americans* in the early 60s, I thought it was great. I thought a lot about it and found that I definitely didn't want to do anything like that. Evans and Frank had done it in ways that seemed perfect. It seemed unnecessary to even try to do that, to imitate the journalist-writer.

DC: The more I look at your early works, like *Picture for Women* (1979) or *The Destroyed Room* (1978), the subject matter seems to be photography, as a means of making things visible. Maybe there are some ideological questions about the inextricable relation between photographic seeing understood both phenomenologically and socially. These pictures are at least partly about gender, power, and looking as inscribed in photographic representation at the time. But as time passes those relations change but what remains in those images is a fascination with photography.

JW: Yes, that's true, especially in those two pictures, which are statements about their own practice. That was something derived from those times and from the other art forms.

DC: Partly because of your interest in the history of images, when I read either your writing or the writing about your work the photography you make tends to come across as a series of immaculate and highly calculated gestures or thoroughly worked-out positions. When I look at your photographs, I just don't think that way. I can think that way and I'm interested in the rich mix that comes out of a sort of art historical mediation of your work. But I imagine there is a whole other set of concerns, fascinations, and pleasures that are in play that don't often manifest in that writing and way of thinking. Does that ring true?

JW: Yes, for the most part, and it's partly my own doing. For some reason—and there is no really clear reason—I started writing around the time I started making photographs and the reception for the writing was quite good; so, then I got asked to write something else. And so on. I found I had this 'career' as a writer, which I didn't really want and wasn't really that interested in. It just happened. But it was exciting to think things through and writing was an obvious form for that, so I just did it. It created an atmosphere in which some people who were perhaps more interested in writing found my written things more interesting than my pictures. That certainly coloured some of the reception of my photography, especially earlier.

DC: It's a way of thinking about the work that misses something essential in the practice of actually doing it and making it.

JW: My writing has almost always been about something other than my own work. When I wrote something, I had some sort of analysis to make, usually of another artist's work. I just went through thinking out loud about that person's art. That's valid, but I don't think it resembles the way I make my pictures. The only way it resembles it is that I have written only when someone has asked me to do so. That's a bit like suddenly having an intuition about a subject that might lead you to make something of it in a photograph. I like the spontaneity in that. I've never written anything of my own volition, I've only done it through the suggestions coming from other people. Just as I might be walking down the street and I see something that suggests a picture.

DC: How do your pictures change from the suggestion to their final form?

JW: Well, I'm sitting here looking at my two photographs of a stone basin in Rome. They didn't change because I shot them in about ten seconds. So they are not good examples. But if I work on something for an extended period, the resulting, finished picture never looks the way I thought it might when I started out. But, to partly contradict myself, there is often something there at the beginning, something unthought-about and therefore very spontaneous that remains throughout. That thing, whatever it is, must be part of the original suggestion for the picture. In a picture like *Basin in Rome*, the original thing is there from the first instant and is captured an instant later and the work suddenly stops.

DC: Those two photographs come closest to that whole way of thinking and practising photography that wanted to collapse the immediacy of the perception into the image itself, which really crystallizes as a picture-making idea with Henri Cartier-Bresson. Making photographs never happens in quite that way, but the spirit they're after or the idea they perpetuate is that there is a real intimacy between happening to notice something and photographing it. You've made pictures a little bit like that but most of the time you have introduced a gap, or made very apparent the gap between the noticing and the making of a picture derived from it. That's the kind of work with which you are most associated. Can we explore that gap a little? It must be a source of aesthetic possibility and also pleasure, for you and the audience. That gap is inherent in painting because it has little access to the instantaneous. I look at Goya or Menzel and I sense they have seen something—maybe a play of light on a wall, a relation between bodies—they have noticed it and tried to see if it will make an interesting translation into painting or a starting point for one.

JW: I think that's right and it's inherently fascinating. In life we do experience the way things escape us. Most experiences are not recorded. Cartier-Bresson's type of photography tried to cure that in a way, if you think of it as something that needs to be cured, by being so quick that the loss of experience would not occur. Barthes wrote about that too—the "that has been" aspect. That is poignant and it is an essential part of photography, that desire to not lose something fleeting that seems valuable, and to capture it in a picture. But that creates an obstacle, too. The picture is like an arrow flying into the motif.

DC: That's a very Barthes-like phrase!

JW: Yes, it's as if capturing the motif is all that counts. But if it's going to be art then it has to be a good picture regardless of the motif. If the commitment is to capturing the fleeting motif, that can become too sentimental. I think that aspect of Barthes's thinking about photography *is* very sentimental and in the end I'm not convinced it is even very engaged with the aesthetic aspect of the medium. It's essential, but not a complete account of photography.

DC: I would agree but I sense Barthes knew that. He seemed to dislike any hint of art in photography and felt that what was essential about the medium was quite outside of art. But as you say what Barthes thought was essential is not the whole story.

JW: I think it's also a residue of an avant-garde idea, that to be interested in 'Art' is a pompous folly. But that idea hasn't held up very well.

DC: The domination of the "that has been" in the understanding of photography has its roots in the crisis of mnemonics. There was a desire to invest photography with the power to solve the problems of modern memory and record (even though it also made it worse, as everyone from Kracauer to Debord to Sontag pointed out). As the twentieth century progressed that burden or potential lifted from photography when other media were obliged to carry it, if it was carried at all. By television, mainly. I see Barthes as making a last attempt to hang on to that mnemonic function. Perhaps that's what he was mourning. My intuition is that it was only when that mnemonic burden was lifted a little that photography became newly open to artistic exploration and photography began to "matter as art as never before" as Michael Fried has put it. Photography came to its current position in art by moving beyond the grip of the "that has been," but it couldn't really have happened until it did.

JW: That conception of the medium is not a problem for journalism, or for other practical uses of photography. It's only limited for art.

DC: One of your important paths was to introduce preparation and collaboration—"staging." This can suspend many things, not least the documentary claim and the tense associated with. There are many kinds of images that may qualify as tableaux but the tense of the staged tableau in particular is "what might be" or "what could be" or "what might have been."

JW: Or "what continually is." The other arts have the ability to keep things happening perpetually. Painting and sculpture are in the present tense. It is part of what pictures are, and photography can have it too, to some significant extent, I think.

DC: Do you think photography's relation to artifice is unresolved?

JW: Yes. It should be unresolved. If it was resolved, it probably wouldn't be interesting any more. But that relationship exists in all the other arts, it is not peculiar to photography. I wasn't primarily interested in what distinguished photography from the other arts. That question seemed to be pretty much exhausted by the time I got into it. It was central from around 1920 and most of the interesting discussion was to do with the fact that if photography was art it would have to be an art unlike all the other arts. Well yes, that's true, but it is nevertheless a limited aspect of the phenomenon. How could photography not have kinships with the other depictive arts? And artifice will always be a part of that because we can't have art without artifice.

DC: When I look at your work I see relations to all kinds of other arts, but I also see an unwavering commitment to the medium of photography, not necessarily defined in a particular way.

JW: I love photography and always have. For me it is something very easy to be devoted to and I enjoy it immensely. I'm glad you see it because I feel it very strongly.

DC: Is it possible to separate the experience of a picture from its medium? Is it possible to say "that's a good picture" irrespective and prior to the medium in which it is made? I know you are interested in 'first impressions' and the idea of those impressions being spontaneous and maybe uninformed by whatever preconceptions we have about the medium in question. For me, many of your works dramatize a certain tension on this point, between wanting to see each one as a picture and wanting to see it as a photograph.

JW: I guess we're talking about the tableau as outlined by Jean-François Chevrier. That is, as a special kind of image, one that immediately strikes you as having salient aesthetic qualities. When we see such a picture we enjoy it in a very pronounced way. But you are never unaware that you are looking at the outcome of a specific medium—a painting, or a photograph or a drawing. The spontaneous excitement or enjoyment we experience is set off by the treatment of a medium such that it results in this particular result, this picture.

DC: But it strikes me that there is a lot at stake in this not knowing whether you are responding to a picture as a picture or a picture as a photograph (or a painting or a drawing). Precisely what is at stake is going to be different in each and every encounter but I think a great deal always hangs on this. Does the medium modify our assessment of the pictorial achievement? Can we assess pictorial achievement outside a recognition of the medium? I really don't know but I feel that not knowing very distinctly when I look at your work. So many photographers want to imitate painting (usually Hopper, Vermeer, or Chardin) and they model their compositions on them but they always disappoint.

JW: Maybe that's because they are usually bad imitations and hence inferior pictures.

DC: You don't think that for whatever reason we prefer different kinds of picture in different kinds of media?

JW: I think it's more to do with quality. If someone did in photography what you always thought was something that only worked in painting, you'd respond to it being great and you would be convinced. It's always about whether an individual can make something happen.

DC: Let's talk now about how your pictures come about, how one day you are not really thinking about this or that, and then suddenly you are. I presume you don't go out 'hunting' like Frank of Friedlander but in your own way you are equally engaged with the complexity and richness of everyday life.

JW: I'm always hunting, I just don't always have a camera.

DC: Sure, it doesn't matter whether you have a camera or not. The question is to do with the emphasis placed on, or the amount of time spent looking at and thinking about everyday life, which is your abiding source, if not subject.

JW: I don't go walking around *as if* I had a camera, but I'm always paying attention to every opportunity that comes my way, and you never know what it might be. I'm always trying to find something, without knowing what it is.

DC: What's your relation to the transparency mounted in the lightbox now? Is it the same as it ever was?

JW: At the moment, I'm not making any new works in lightboxes. I have wanted to move into a different medium for some time, just like when I began making black and white prints. I would like the lightbox to be one of the forms in which I work, not necessarily the primary one. So, for seven or eight years I've been working on alternate colour possibilities, and this has coincided with the great increase in the quality of inkjet colour printing. I started my picture *After* Spring Snow *by Yukio Mishima* (2000–2005) nine years ago and it turned into the first inkjet print I did. I originally thought it would be a lightbox but it wasn't viable in that medium, and so it became a kind of prototype for working with opaque colour prints. So now I'm making inkjets, as well as traditional black and white photos, and lightboxes.

DC: Personally, I always experienced a tension in the lightbox presentation. On the one hand, it was attractive because any light source is attractive and that made the picture significant in a different way. On the other, I have found it hard to look at and a little unsettling in ways that have precluded me really concentrating on the images. You started making them at a time when few people thought a single photograph could be significant, so the lightbox helped in that regard. And also those early works were very much about visibility, illumination, certain conditions of seeing explored in a deliberately agitational way, playing in a Brechtian vein on an unsettling of the spectator. But as your work progressed it seemed you wanted a more engrossed spectator and that agitational quality was counterproductive. Again, I stress that's a personal response.

JW: I agree with you. That dissonance attracted me at the beginning, in the 1970s, when dissonance as such seemed necessary, a necessary way to put 'art' or at least the conventional way of identifying art, in question. I think I pushed hard at that for quite some time. But, on the other hand, that probably led to me making pictures where the backlighting wasn't the most appropriate choice, and the image turned out to be too bright, too prepossessing.

DC: It's surely part of your influence that today people are prepared to take single photographs seriously, in a way that they weren't in the 1970s or even 1980s. The lightbox seemed to be necessary to help make that case.

JW: I would like to think that that's not the case, that if opaque prints had been good enough back then and I'd used them they would have done it, but I'll never know.

DC: I guess there are things you can do pictorially with an opaque print that you can't do on a lightbox. Expanses of shadow never look good and I have noticed you avoided them, presumably for this reason. You made up for it by having so many areas of near darkness in your black and white work.

JW: Yes, the opaque print is obviously much better for darks. Of course, they are not as vivid as a transparency, but they don't need to be. Overall, an opaque picture is more gentle than a transparency.

DC: Beyond the printing, is your work itself becoming more gentle?

JW: I've been accused of that.

DC: It's not an accusation.

JW: I feel that depiction itself is a gentle, affectionate art form, regardless of the subject. Enjoying depiction seems to me to be an expression of affection for the existence of things overall.

DC: Maybe it's just mature work now.

JW: Well I like the fact that when I was younger my work wasn't very mature. At 28 I wouldn't have wanted to be mature. At that time there were followers of the classic photographers—I've taught people like that—and they were old before their time. I wouldn't have wanted that.

DC: Picture making is always a challenge so I imagine you are trying to solve different kinds of pictorial problem.

JW: That's partly true. Fifteen or twenty years ago I was doing quite a lot of pictures with figures seen rather close up and I wanted to do something else. So, I deliberately did differently structured pictures, often ones in which the main motif was further from the camera. But, overall, my main concern is to avoid repetition of pictorial solutions. I'd rather repeat a theme than a composition.

DC: There has been a degree of change in the people in your photographs, a change in what they're doing and how you have depicted them. I think of a lot of the earlier photographs being not exactly confrontational or frontal but often with a very purposive attitude or gesture, even if that gesture performs a certain ambiguity. I'm thinking of a picture such as *Mimic* (1982). In some of your more recent work, such as *'Intersection'* (2009), I wouldn't even call them gestures. It's a street picture, very beautiful I think, where the bodies of the walking figures don't tell me they have been posed by anything other than the arrest of the shutter.

JW: I'm glad you like that one. It is a 'street photograph' by the way, in the classical sense. Shot in two minutes.

DC: But then in *Siphoning* (2009), a picture of a man siphoning gas out of a car, I do see some similarities with your earlier work.

JW: I see that too. I wanted to explore again those feelings you get when you're in the close presence of a depicted figure. In *Men Waiting* (2006), the figures are quite far from the camera; that opens the space up. I liked that but I felt I wanted to get closer to figures again, the way you see in older pictures like *Mimic*.

DC: There are no gestures here the way there might have been in earlier work.

JW: Well twenty, twenty-five years ago I was interested in the idea of *gestus*, the gesture that could have some sort of identifiable significance. But in my photograph of the guys carrying the engine [*Men Move an Engine Block* (2008)], there's gesture there because they're doing something, moving their bodies, but it's not the same kind of gesture.

DC: Yes, there is no gesture there in the sense that a gesture is a significant image or sign before you have photographed it.

JW: Yes, I'm less interested in gesture the way I was but I could imagine getting interested in it again because it's a rich and fascinating field. That notion of '*figura*' is still really fascinating and I got a lot out of it for a long time. But you know, no matter how wonderful it is—at a certain point you're tired of it. I did get very tired of that kind of figuration and so I tried to do something else. And to me that new thing was a kind of neo-realism.

DC: Neo-realism as it evolved out of post-war Italian cinema has a spirit that is close to what you've called 'near documentary'—using whatever means to get situations you depict to look and feel as close to how they might have looked and felt had you'd seen them yourself.

JW: It's the 'documentary style' par excellence and is in some ways more challenging and complex than simply taking documentary photographs. The *results* are not better, just different. There was something mannerist about what I used to do and I liked that. I think that mannerism is significant, meaningful, and artistically rich. I wouldn't mind finding a way to recover that again.

DC: Maybe *gestus* in the way we are thinking about it was one way of reconciling the stillness of photography with a meaningful depiction of the living body.

JW: Yes, but it's a disturbing way. That's what's so interesting about it. It's also completely unacceptable to a lot of people, especially among those devoted to photography.

DC: And if people can't find the aesthetic courage to credit you with that?

JW: They have other standards and those standards may be perfectly valid. But they're not the only standards. That clash is good and fascinating and I wouldn't want to let go of it. That style of mannered gesture and improbable presence—that's also part of what photography is. If it works it can be great. If it doesn't it can be particularly terrible.

DC: It can be artistically objectionable.

JW: If you are a classical street photographer you cannot fall below a certain level because the medium and the subject matter won't allow you to. It's too established. If you go into the street and you are reasonably competent, the worst you can be is boring, not outright bad. The photos won't be artistically objectionable.

DC: By the same token you can't reach above a certain level either?

JW: It's more of a narrow range but great things can be done, as we know, so there is no limit to how good the results can be, but at the bottom level you are protected. With mannered artifice, you can get to real depths. The approach is much more risky. But it makes it fascinating because it's so against the grain that when it works it can be really fantastic.

DC: I have noticed that in staged art photography in general that there seems to be a preference for depicting certain kinds of situation or psychological state. Alienation is too broad but it would include anxiety, melancholy, fragmentation, indecision, nervousness, or something fraught. Obviously much of this photography has been interested in the depiction of daily life, and for most of us that's how daily life is. However, a range of theorists has described the nature of the medium in similar terms: anxious, melancholy, fragmented, indecisive, nervous, fraught. It's as if photographers have found a fit between human depiction and the character of the medium. Do you think there is something in this?

JW: That's interesting. If you go back before the beginning of modern art, whenever that might be, things were different. In a portrait of a duke by van Dyke, for example, everything seems untroubled. The duke has no doubts, he's confident in who he is and why, and in that sense it's pre-modern. The person depicted doesn't appear to have any inner dynamic, any inner uncertainty. It's an official view of the upper class, the dominant class. Modern art is not about that. It's about uncertainty and change. It's Hamlet. It doesn't always have to appear in the same psychological register. It could be anger or even weird levity. My work *Man in the Street* (1995), of the almost smiling guy with the bloody nose, is a little like that. But I don't think the method favours any particular situation or mood. For example, a new picture, *Figures on a Sidewalk* (2008), shows a woman walking past us and she does not seem to express anything anxious or troubled (see Plate 4). I was impressed by what might be her serenity.

DC: Serenity is very elusive in the world, especially so for photographers, because as soon as the photographer is noticed it evaporates. So this image is doubly strange. An elusive state 'caught' on camera. It could only have been staged but that makes it all the more miraculous because nothing about her betrays the presence of the very close camera. It's as if you or we are as invisible as she is.

JW: She was not unaware of being photographed but she seemed so detached from being photographed. She just did what I asked her to do, which was simply to walk by the camera without looking at it.

DC: If only we could ignore photographers we could achieve serenity! It reminds me of some of the pictures in Bill Brandt's book *A Night in London* (1938). Many of them could only have been staged but Brandt managed to capture behaviour that seems quite indifferent to his presence. The camera is close, right there in the scene, so there's nothing really voyeuristic about it. But the photographer's presence feels totally spectral, as if a ghost is observing it all. Compared to *Mimic*, which is superficially similar to *Figures on a Sidewalk*, there is no performance for the camera and no drama at all, only the drama of representation.

JW: It would be interesting to see those two hanging together in the same room, because they are structurally similar.

DC: I think of street photography as the only genre specific to photography. The others are shared with or borrowed from the other arts. At least it's the one that could make the best claim to being unique.

JW: That maybe has a lot to do with the nature of streets but maybe what's unique is not the street itself but the way it excites the hunter-mentality of many photographers. But, the hunter-photographer can hunt anywhere.

DC: Can I ask you about one of your pictures of a space that is not a street? It's titled *Ossuary Headstone* (2007).

JW: An ossuary is the place where they place bones from old individual graves when they need the space again. It's a common pit. That headstone marks the opening. Below is a cavern, which in this case I think has been sealed because it's full. I made it in Sicily when I was there trying to make some landscapes. I found it by accident, and love all those beautiful colours and so just shot it very quickly (see Plate 5).

DC: Did the shroud of Saint Veronica carved on the headstone have anything to do with it too? It's something of a metaphor or analogy for the medium. An indexical trace of Christ left in sweat on cloth that also reads as a recognisable image of him.

JW: I've been trying to make pictures of places. *Concrete Ball* (2003), *Fortified Door* (2007). They've worked out well so I do them when I can. *Still Creek, Vancouver, Winter* (2003) was taken where I made a picture called *The Drain* back in 1989. I really liked the location so I went back and shot it just as a place. These pictures are not really landscapes even. They're just little places.

DC: I'm not sure where it formally started but I think I noticed in your *Catalogue Raisonné* a declaring of your images as either 'Cinematographic' or 'Documentary'. The first term signals that the picture is made through preparation and collaboration. The second signals that the scene or situation was shot 'straight'. So, if a picture such as *Clipped Branches, East Cordova St., Vancouver* (1999) is labelled 'Documentary', we know you didn't clip the branches and they are where the title says they are.

JW: I categorized the pictures for that book.

DC: Maybe it forces too hard a distinction between artifice on one side and its absence on the other. Many documentary pictures, yours and other people's, have a feeling of theatre about them anyway, perhaps because photography theatricalizes the world, simply by representing it. That's one reason. The other has to do with an unnecessary giving away of the game, or drawing attention to the wrong properties of your pictures.

JW: I noticed that people were getting totally wrapped up in questions of whether I'd arranged things or not and to what degree. For example, they would ask if I put all those things in the suitcase in *Rain-filled Suitcase* (2001), and after a while I thought that all that was becoming a distraction.

DC: If one picture is staged, it raises the possibility that they all might be.

JW: Right. But it doesn't help people to experience anything. People who in my opinion ought to be enjoying the experience of the picture were getting waylaid by the idea that they had to decipher its making. So, I thought I'd cut that out by just using these two categories, very rough and ready. All they mean is that I worked on that picture in one or the other way. I thought it would clear things up but in some ways I think it created more confusion, weirdly enough, because then people want to know what a documentary photograph actually means.

DC: You have been making photographs for a long time now and you have quite a defined oeuvre, in the sense that there are your 'works' and there is nothing else. It's a very fixed body of work with no ragged edges. There are photographers and photographic artists for whom a catalogue raisonné would be quite impossible, their production being so widely dispersed. Defining the oeuvre of Cartier-Bresson, or Evans, or Frank, or Weegee would be nearly impossible. Maybe they themselves or posterity chooses a core of images for which they are known, but the outer edges are pretty undefined.

JW: That catalogue raisonné was defined as dealing with my main work from 1978 on and so what I'd done before was excluded. Nothing of the earlier work was included in the exhibition, either. So, including, say, early photographic pieces from the 1960s seemed irrelevant. I have no interest in that work and I doubt anyone else would, either.

DC: Within that body of work there is room for all kinds of anomalies. I know you never really rule out any particular way of working but there is a centre to what you do and there are peripheral things. You've made a couple of works with your mobile phone. You've made a public sculpture in Rotterdam. You've done a sort of performance. I'm intrigued by an elliptical narrative you made about a decade ago.

JW: Yes, I have branched out in my own timid way. *A Partial Account (of events taking place between the hours of 9:35 a.m. and 3:22 p.m., Tuesday, 21 January 1997)* is a bit of an anomaly—multiple images in a kind of sequence. I would love to do something similar again; I've tried but I couldn't discover an event that could carry it. It's an interesting way to work and it's very hard to do well. The two-frame work *Man in the Street* was a sort of compressed version of that idea. They are related in that each sequence can be read either way. You can't tell when it starts and when it ends. You can read them left to right, or right to left. *A Partial Account* came about because I was commissioned to do a mural in tapestry for a courtroom in Holland. So, you see, I've also made a tapestry! It was for two long walls, facing each other across a courtroom, so I had to do it in that long rectangle. The sequence of images was to suggest or intimate an event but to lack enough information to permit anyone to define or characterize the event and the nature of the participation by any of the people you see in the pictures. It was to relate to the incompleteness of evidence or testimony in trials. Once I'd completed the tapestry, I felt that it could also be interesting as a pair of lightboxes.

DC: You've had large retrospective shows in the last few years [2004–2006]. Did they prompt you to re-evaluate things?

JW: The problem with those shows is that there is always so much to do beforehand, then the openings, then all the people, so it becomes a bit of a blur. Then you leave town and you don't really see the shows, not in any leisurely way. Instead of a chance to look back, it's all happening in the present again. Anyway, I prefer to look ahead. My constant re-evaluation is through a more personal activity of judging my pictures, older and recent, repeatedly, comparing them as to their quality, and being as strict about that as I can be. I do it while I'm working on something new, comparing it with other things for different reasons, or else I just do it because I feel I have to and that somehow that energy will help me with the next picture.

DC: But coming back to where we started, if your relation to the medium is always churning, always shifting, there is no final settling of accounts.

JW: There's no final account, but there is definitely an account being kept.

Note

1 First published as the booklet *Jeff Wall Speaks with David Campany*, Fundación Telefónica/La Fábrica Editorial, Madrid, 2009.

6

Deleuze and the simulacrum

Simulation and semblance in *Public Order*

Sandra Plummer

Conventionally understood as a copy (or a facsimile of a copy), *simulacrum* is a Latin term denoting an image, likeness, or semblance. This definition of the concept has obvious application to a medium that was characterised by its capacity to generate "nearly fac-simile copies" including "a multitude of minute details which add the truth and reality of the representation" (Talbot 1844). Yet the philosophical complexity of the simulacrum is belied by readings that disregard the particular nature of its representation. The philosopher Daniel W. Smith asserts that simulacrum derives from "the Latin *simulare* (to copy, represent, feign)" (Smith 1997: x). The simulacrum pertains to a specific type of copy—the false copy that produces a semblance of reality. This chapter will consider the concept of the simulacrum with particular reference to the philosophy of Gilles Deleuze. In Deleuze, the simulacrum embraces the complexity of distinct forms of Platonic mimesis. Deleuze proposes that the philosophical origin of the concept occurs in Plato's *Sophist* where the simulacrum is posited as a "phantasma" in distinction to a true likeness.

Gilles Deleuze (1925–1995) was one of the most important French philosophers of the twentieth century. Deleuze was part of a generation of thinkers (alongside his contemporaries Jacques Derrida and Michel Foucault) who came to prominence in the late 1960s and whose work has been labelled as post-structuralist.[1] Whereas Deleuze's early writing often focuses on the history of philosophy, his later work (including his collaborations with Felix Guattari) demonstrates increasing engagement with politics, psychoanalysis, science and literature. Deleuze's influence on the arts has been considerable. His writing has engendered new thought on the philosophy of film (*Cinema 1*, 2005 [1983] and *Cinema 2*, 2005 [1985]) and on painting (*Francis Bacon: The Logic of Sensation*, 2003 [1981]). Deleuze's contribution to photography, however, is less clear. This chapter will consider Deleuze's concept of the simulacrum and its pertinence to contemporary photography. In the first section, I will focus on Deleuze's account of the simulacrum derived from his close reading of the concept's Platonic origin. Plato's dialogue will be analysed in light of Deleuze's reading. I take the simulacrum to be that which purports to be a true copy of the model it appears to resemble, but which is actually a false likeness. The distinction between truth and simulation is central. I will propose that the concept of the simulacrum has particular resonance with photography's capacity to produce a copy of the real. Moreover, it is when photography engages with the simulacral (transcending its status as a truthful, technologically generated medium) that we observe its true potential. The second section of this chapter will comprise an analysis of Sarah Pickering's *Public Order* series (2002–2005), which explicitly challenges the conception of photography as a purveyor of truth. I will begin, however, by briefly considering theorisations of the simulacrum and its relation to photography.

Photography and the simulacrum

The photograph's relation to the simulacrum is twofold. On the one hand, the concept of the simulacrum may be seen as antithetical to photography's historical alignment with truth, the evidentiary and the objective documentation of *what has been*.[2] On the other hand, simulation has always been at the heart of the medium. Although the simulacral nature of photography has received comparatively less attention from scholars, it is evident from as early as 1840 in what has been described as the first staged photograph—Hippolyte Bayard's *Self Portrait as a Drowned Man*. The disregard of photography's simulacral capacity (in favour of its truthfulness) has wider relevance to art history. Michael Camille has argued that the simulacrum has been repressed in art history because "it subverts the cherished dichotomy of model and copy, original and reproduction, image and likeness" (1996: 31). The simulacrum is *not* a reliable copy; rather, it destabilises copying by throwing into disarray the distinction between the model and copy. The simulacrum overthrows the foundational notion of the model as primary in art and challenges the idea of representation.

Philosophically, the simulacrum possesses the capacity to undermine the structure of model and copy that has persisted since Plato. Smith attributes the origin of the philosophical re-emergence of the concept to Pierre Klossowski (Smith in Klossowski 1997). The simulacrum recurs in French philosophy from the 1960s through writers such as Klossowski, Deleuze and Foucault. The concept was also explored by Derrida in *Dissemination* (1981) with direct reference to Plato, before gaining further recognition in Baudrillard's theorisations of simulation and the hyperreal. Camille examines philosophical, literary (including Guy Debord and Philip K. Dick) and artistic developments, drawing particular attention to photography's "challenge to 'auratic' art" (1996: 34).[3] The conceptual resonances between aura and simulacrum are supplemented by Klossowski's contribution to the translation of Benjamin's "Work of Art" essay.[4] Benjamin's account of the decline of aura is constructed within a reflection on the experience of modernity and the historical development of photography concerned with the "presence of the original," the copy and authenticity (1999 [1936]: 214).

In "Reinventing the Medium," Rosalind Krauss reads Benjamin's essay in relation to the convergence of art and photography whereby the latter's "perfect instance of a multiple-without-an-original" and "structural status as copy" engendered ontological collapse (1999: 290). Krauss insists that photography not only enables the reproduction of works of art, it undermines the concept of the "original" through which artworks are constituted. In "A Note on Photography and the Simulacral" (1984), Krauss considers the photograph's status as copy in relation to the simulacrum, and with reference to her own translation of Deleuze's "Plato and the Simulacrum" (1983). Krauss insists that photography performs a *deconstructive* mechanism that challenges the differences between "the original and the copy, the first idea and its slavish imitators" (1984: 59). Photography deconstructs art by enabling the production of a false copy that undermines "the whole system of model and copy, original and fake, first- and second-degree replication" (1984: 63). Photography's mediation *as* duplication problematises the ontological existence of the artwork as an "original." Moreover,

Krauss reads photography as "the image that is resemblant only by mechanical circumstance and not by internal, essential connection to the model" (1984: 63). This insistence on photography's simulacral replication of the model's *external* appearance will be seen to have particular pertinence to Deleuze's reading of Plato.

"Plato and the simulacrum"

> Stranger: When we say that he deceives with that semblance we spoke of and that his art is a practice of deception, shall we be saying that, as the effect of his art, our mind thinks what is false?
>
> *(Plato, 1935)*[5]

> [S]imulacra are precisely demonic images, stripped of resemblance. Or rather, in contrast to *icônes*, they have externalised resemblance and live on difference instead. If they produce an external effect of resemblance, this takes the form of an illusion.
>
> *(Deleuze 2004a: 155)*

Deleuze's most sustained account of the simulacrum was published as an appendix to *Logique du sens* in 1969.[6] Translated as "The Simulacrum and Ancient Philosophy," the appendix comprises two sections: "Plato and the Simulacrum" and "Lucretius and the Simulacrum." Although drawing on a number of Platonic dialogues, including the *Statesman* and the *Phaedrus*, it is Plato's *Sophist* that is most pertinent as it is the origin of the Platonic idea of the simulacrum. In *Difference and Repetition*, where Deleuze also discusses the simulacrum, he asserts that "The whole of Platonism … is dominated by the idea of drawing a difference between 'the thing itself' and the simulacra" (2004a: 80). Smith reiterates the point that Plato's goal was to select or "*faire le difference* (literally, to 'make the difference') between true and false images" (2006: 91). For Deleuze, however, the task is to transform the type of differentiation that occurs within the Platonic account of the simulacrum; his reformulation of the concept as possessing a positive—internal—difference from the original can be read as an overturning of Plato's philosophy.

Deleuze begins his "Plato and the Simulacrum" essay by posing the question, "what does it mean 'to reverse Platonism'?" This question is initially attributed to Nietzsche, who saw the reversal of Platonism as the task of philosophy. Deleuze, however, also traces the desire to abolish the Platonic "world of essences" and "the world of appearances" to Kant and Hegel (2004b: 291). Deleuze's concern here is not restricted to the denunciation of essences and appearances. He moves from essence (intelligible, Idea) and appearance (sensible, image) to an investigation of the particular question of the distinction between copies and simulacra (2004b: 294). In this Deleuzian exegesis, copies are secondary possessors that are well founded because they resemble that which they copy (2004b: 294). Conversely, simulacra are false pretenders that dissimulate. Deleuze's analysis comprises a discussion of contrasting forms of resemblance (in the distinction between internal and external resemblance). Simplistically, the distinction is between good copies and bad copies, or between copies-icons and simulacra-phantasms. Whereas the former resembles the Idea of the original, the latter produces only a deceitful external resemblance. Deleuze insists that the reversal of Platonism must be achieved through a revelation of its motivation: Platonism can only be reversed by being tracked down, "the way Plato tracks down the Sophist" (2004b: 291).

The *Sophist* is a late Platonic dialogue that follows an attempt to define the sophistic charlatan philosopher. The opening sections of the text make clear the intention of the dialogue—to "begin by studying the sophist" and to "try to bring his nature to light" (*S* 218b). The goal of the dialogue then is to distinguish and define the sophist. The *Sophist* begins with Theodorus introducing the Stranger from Elea to Socrates. Hearing that the stranger is from the school of Parmenides and Zeno, Socrates assumes that he may be an exponent of sophistry. Sophists were viewed as false philosophers who sought verbal victory over others, yet with little regard for the truth. It is in this sense that sophistry is viewed as an "art of controversy" (*S* 232e) and as "a practice of deception" (Cornford 1935: 190). The *Sophist* is of relevance to the concept of the simulacrum because it is in the course of the dialogue that we discover the nature of authentic and inauthentic practices of philosophy and of true and false representation. Sophistry, according to Francis Macdonald Cornford, is "the false counterfeit of philosophy … and has its being in the world of *eidola* that is neither real nor totally unreal" (1935: 173). In searching for the paradoxical figure that is the "true sophist," Plato examines the relation between reality and appearance and proposes clear distinctions between the copy and the simulacrum.

The Platonic method of division provides the means through which the sophist will be defined. As Cornford notes, the dialectic is used to separate things that are "alike" and "the Division is a downward process from that genus to the definition of a species" (1935: 183–4). Following the Platonic method, "the species [sophist] is to be defined by systematically dividing the genus that is taken to include it" (1935: 170). If the sophist is to be found, then he must be sought in sophistic practices. Plato's dialogue begins with the genus arts, which is divided into the *acquisitive* (in the sense of acquiring that which already exists) and the *productive*, and into further subdivisions within these categories. Later divisions explore the acquisitive arts through the two subdivisions of "arts by capture" and "by exchange." The sophist is initially placed in the former category of "arts by capture" under "hunting" (*S* 231d), but is subsequently examined under the latter category of acquisition "by exchange," where he is deemed a peddler of "wisdom" (charging fees for his "knowledge"). In Division VI, the sophist is discerned to use the art of persuasion—seeking to deceive others with false knowledge. The *Sophist's* seventh and final division explores the genus of the *productive* arts. It is within this genus, via an exploration of real and unreal (images) that the sophist will be found.

Returning to the question of photography, we could surmise that it is an *acquisitive* art, not simply because of its immediate linguistic correlations with hunting (*snapshot*, for example, derives from a hunting term), but by virtue of its action—to "capture" or *take* images. Writing on resemblance, Deleuze views photography as a process "which captures relations of light" (2003 [1981]: 80). Photography is also, however, a *productive* and creative art that transforms reality. Though dismissive of photography's capacity to function as art, Deleuze concedes that the "photograph 'creates' the person or the landscape" (2003 [1981]: 64). Deleuze's assessment of photography is that it functions as the simulacrum rather than the true copy: "the most significant thing about the photograph is that it forces upon us the 'truth' of implausible and doctored images" (2003 [1981]: 64). Deleuze also compares photographs with the actions of Lucretius's simulacrum (2003 [1981]: 64).

The final division of image-making in the *Sophist* is where we encounter the distinction between the *copy* and the *simulacrum*. The first category of image-making is "the making of likenesses (*eikastikê*)" the perfect copy that "conforms to the proportions of the original" (*S* 235d). The Stranger in the dialogue insists that the "first kind of image," which is "like the original, may fairly be called a likeness (*eikon*)" (*S* 236a). The second kind of image, however, produces only an *appearance* of a likeness. The Stranger indicates that the second form of image is something that appears to resemble the original, that "seems to be a likeness, but is not really so" (*S* 236b). The first type of image is a true resemblance; the second type belongs to the art of "semblance (*phantasma*)" (*S* 236b). This distinction between true and false copies forms the basis of Deleuze's analysis of the simulacrum.

Whereas Plato's dialogue on image-making distinguishes between "likenesses" and "semblances," Deleuze's distinction is between "two sorts of images"—*copies* and *simulacra* (2004b: 294). Deleuze's "copy" corresponds to what is described by the Stranger in the *Sophist* as "likenesses" or *eikastiké*. *Copies* are "secondary possessors" that are "well-founded pretenders," as they are "guaranteed by resemblance" (2004b: 294). Deleuze's simulacrum corresponds to the second form of Plato's division of image-making—the "semblance" or *phantasma*. Simulacra, according to Deleuze, are "false pretenders, built upon a dissimilarity" (2004b: 294). The term "simulacra" here is understood as the Latin translation of the Greek *phantasma*. Perhaps in acknowledgement of Plato's Greek (*eikon* and *phantasma*), Deleuze also construes the "copies" and "simulacra" as "copies-icons" and "simulacra-phantasms." Deleuze insists that the *resemblance* of the copies-icons to their original confers upon them the status of "good images" (2004b: 294). These well-founded claimants are "endowed with resemblance" in contrast to the dissimilarity of the unfounded pretenders (2004b: 294).

The origin of Plato's concern to distinguish the validity of rival claimants arises within the context of Plato's Greek *polis*. Plato's sophist thrives within an agonistic society as a self-appointed philosopher. In contrast to the state-appointed wise man deemed to be in possession of wisdom, the philosopher in the cities of Greece was categorised as one who seeks wisdom "but does not possess it" (Smith 2006: 92–3). This is the context wherein the problem of resemblance and authenticity arises. Deleuze notes that the problem of rival claimants also occurs in Plato's the *Statesman* and the *Phaedrus*. The purpose of Plato's dialectic, according to Deleuze, is not to discern a species but to "select lineages: to distinguish pretenders; to distinguish the pure from the impure, the authentic from the inauthentic" (2004b: 292). Deleuze is critical of the Platonic system of selection, which he views in terms of descending degrees of hierarchical ranks of participants down to "the one who is himself a mirage and simulacrum" (2004b: 293).

Plato's account of difference operates within a transcendent hierarchy premised on failure to resemble the Idea. The Idea is created in response to the problem of judgement. The Idea, then, becomes a "criterion" for judging between the authentic and counterfeit claimants: "Only the Idea," writes Smith, is "'the thing itself', only the Idea is 'self-identical'" (2006: 96). As Smith notes, "the claimant will be well-founded only to the degree that it *resembles* or imitates the foundation" (2006: 96). The question of lineage and resemblance to the Idea (or foundation) was central to Plato's task to establish the difference between the just claimant (the good copy) and the pretender (the simulacrum). The claim of pretension from the unfounded claimant corresponds to the simulacrum's claim to the Idea. As a philosopher of immanence, Deleuze is opposed to a Platonic judgement that places the transcendent Idea at the top of a hierarchy of resemblance. Deleuze unpacks the structure of copy and simulacrum and frees the latter from its position at the bottom of a Platonic chain of similitude. Rather than being defined in relation to lack, Deleuze's simulacrum possesses difference as a positive attribute.

Possessing internal distinction from the model, Deleuze's simulacrum can be seen as an affirmation of difference and as a reversal of Plato's transcendent structure. Deleuze's account overthrows the hierarchy of similitude within which difference and the simulacrum are established. The Deleuzian simulacrum moves in the direction of difference rather than sameness—a difference that is not secondary to, or preceded by, a superior identity but is a difference *in itself*. In Deleuze's definition, the simulacrum, far from resembling the Idea, is always becoming other. The difference between the simulacrum and the copy is no longer a question of *degree*, but is rather a "difference in nature" (2004b: 295). Deleuze's simulacrum may possess a resemblance to the original but this is merely external. There is internal difference; the simulacrum does not pass through the Idea. The (good) copy, on the other hand, possesses a form of internal resemblance that bears a relation to the Idea of the thing that it copies—the "internal essence" (Deleuze 2004b: 294). The Deleuzian simulacrum escapes the repressive Platonic depths and rises to the surface, unencumbered by the hierarchical distinction between essence and appearance, model and copy.

How might photography function in relation to Plato's division of image-making? The photograph can be seen as the copy of a thing that is itself a copy of the original Idea (or form). This relation recalls the discussion of representation in Plato's *Republic*, where "art" is conceived as distantly removed from the truth. Plato's division of the productive arts distinguishes a trio of "makers": God as the producer of the Form/Idea, the craftsman who reproduces it, and the artist who produces an "appearance" of the craftsman's copy. The artist is placed at the bottom of the trio as someone who produces a representation far removed from reality. The artist copies the carpenter's rendering without understanding the original "Idea." Plato suggests that, in the example of the bed, the painter is only capable of rendering an appearance of a copy, and from a particular viewpoint. Two-dimensional media possess particular challenges in their restricted capacity to represent reality. Reflecting on the *Republic*, Patton asserts that the painter can only "represent the bed as seen from a certain angle" (1994: 148). This limitation is equally true for photography. In the *Republic*, all art is categorised as mimetic appearance-making.

In the *Sophist*, however, a distinction emerges between "two forms of imitation": the true *likeness* "conforms to the proportions of the original in all three dimensions" (*S* 235d), whereas the *semblance* (the simulacrum, or bad copy) enacts a deviation from the original it purports to resemble. The simulacrum is analogous to a large artwork where the sculptor or painter distorts the "true proportions" in accordance with the perspective of the viewer (*S* 235d–236). In the case of a classical sculpture, this "correction" of the true proportion is made to ensure that the lower parts of the sculpture—that are closer to the viewer—do not look out of proportion with the (more distant) upper parts when viewed from below. The dialogue concludes that such distorted works are not likenesses but *semblances*, or, in Deleuze's terminology—simulacra. Although the photograph comprises a two-dimensional imitation, it is also *potentially* a "good copy" in its capacity to "reproduce the true proportions" of the original (*S* 235e).

The simulacrum in photography: Sarah Pickering's *Public Order*

Questions of similitude and authenticity have been a recurring feature in the work of Sarah Pickering, a British artist who predominantly works with photography. Pickering became increasingly interested in the work of Jeff Wall, Thomas Demand and Cindy Sherman as a graduate student at the Royal College of Art in the early 2000s. She was acutely conscious of how "fine art photographers" were "making something in front of the camera" (Pickering 2015). Pickering was also influenced by Baudrillard's account of simulation where reality is replaced by "signs of the real."[7] Contemporary photography that engages the Deleuzian simulacrum (where there is an intentional internal difference from the Idea of the original) highlights the conceptual role of the artist in *making* "copies" of reality in a manner that exceeds the mimetic and functional aspects of the medium.[8]

In *Public Order, Fire Scene* and *Incident*, Pickering can be seen to challenge the nature of photography's existence as a documentary and indexical medium.[9] But her work still functions as a document of staged scenes and is still indexical in this respect. The unreality and artifice entailed in these series may recall constructed photography consisting of events or tableaux staged for the camera (as in the work of Wall and Demand). However, Pickering's subjects are not created in order to be photographed. Moreover, the work exists at the level of the documentary in combination with 'real' spaces. It is the virtual nature of these—paradoxically real—environments that is the source of the fictive in Pickering's work. The streets and interiors in *Public Order, Fire Scene* and *Incident* have been constructed as simulated spaces for training UK police, military forces and emergency services. These sites are more than props or backdrops though: they are the stages on which simulation training occurs in a convincingly real way. Pickering witnessed training exercises where new recruits were subjected to verbal abuse and even had petrol bombs thrown at them.[10] A different kind of reality exists in *Fire Scene*, where the interiors are also a site of investigation enabling forensic analysis training of actual burnt buildings. The knowledge that these spaces are in fact simulated environments problematises the works' apparent documentary nature. *Public Order, Fire Scene* and *Incident* reproduce the surface appearance of 'reality' in a manner that resembles the original. However, the work does not reproduce the Idea (or "internal essence") of its model. In what follows, the focus will largely be on Pickering's *Public Order* series and its relation to the Deleuzian simulacrum.

Public Order largely comprises exterior shots of a place called Denton. This much is evident from the iconic London Transport sign at the entrance to the station (see Figure 6.1). But all is not as it seems. Denton is not a borough in London but a site used for the purposes of riot training. Pickering's "Denton" consists of several UK police force training sites. This fictional Denton stretches from Gravesend to Hounslow, from Greater Manchester to the Midlands, and was photographed over a period of three years, from 2002 to 2005. Denton sounds like a real place, and there are several villages and towns called Denton in England and in the United States. Denton is also the fictional setting for the *Rocky Horror Picture Show* and the village in the British TV series *Touch of Frost*, based on the *Frost* novels by R. D. Wingfield. Similarly, this photographed Denton is a fictional construction akin to a film set.

Denton Underground Station appears to depict an empty suburban street. The photograph is dominated by the station entrance in the foreground and an adjacent street receding into the background. Ubiquitous street furniture such as lampposts and CCTV cameras, as well as the lines painted on the tarmacked road, compound the impression of an everyday scene. The neutral skyline, combined with the dominant grey of the concrete construction, recalls the topographical photography of the Bechers. Details such as the painted doors and window surrounds (in addition to the bright colours of the London Transport roundel; see colour plates and book cover) provide convincing props, but a closer look at the street on the left reveals 'houses' that consist only of brick facades. The initial impression of an everyday street scene belies the truth of this simulated construction.

Lola Court comprises the rear view of a modern housing development. The scene consists of concrete-block houses and a similarly coloured grey fence. The compositional space evokes claustrophobia and suggests a sinister presence. The unease inherent in the picture is heightened by scorched areas that trace a violent or traumatic event.[11]Traversing through the open gate, it is possible to enter the shadowy interior of the doorway. Yet these apparently real houses have no homely interior and evoke only the uncanny. They are empty shells, entirely devoid of furniture, curtains or any trace of residents. *Lola Court* recalls the

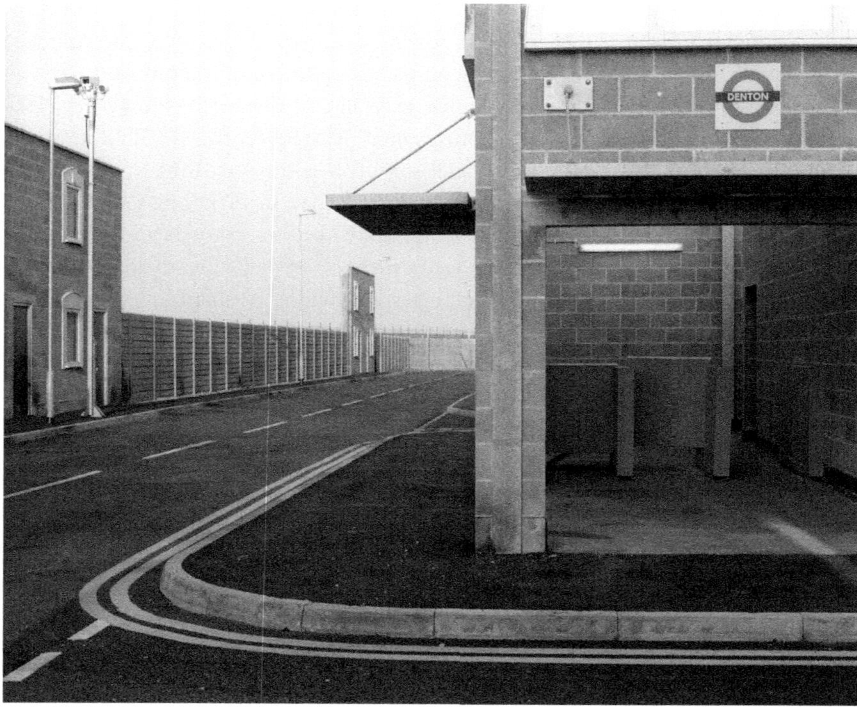

Figure 6.1 Sarah Pickering, *Denton Underground Station* (2003), from *Public Order* series. Courtesy the artist

simulacral home constructed inside Tate Britain by the artist Michael Landy (*Semi-detached*, 2004), where the familiar-looking exterior masked the domestic void inside. The buildings in *Lola Court* echo Deleuze's simulacrum—externally resembling (a real house) but possessing internal difference from the Idea. By depicting the external semblance rather than the interior reality, *Lola Court* produces a paradoxically 'truthful' repetition of the false original. This "good copy" of a simulacrum problematises the Platonic distinctions between original, copy and simulacrum.

Public Order pictures everything we would expect to see in a suburban area. *Front Garden, School Road* includes a landscaped area of shrubs and trees adjacent to a bus shelter; *Farrance Street* shows the back of an Indian restaurant and takeaway. Whereas the concrete-block buildings are in Gravesend, the houses fronted by London bricks (some of which are brightly painted) and the majority of the shops are located in Hounslow. Occasionally there are signs of the real purpose: charred buildings, discarded shopping trolleys, bricks and tyres evidence the aftermath of a staged riot. *High Street* contains an extant barricade; *River Way* includes two smashed-up cars. *Victoria Road* has extensively scorched buildings, including the burned face of a male figure on an advertising poster accompanied by the text "Allure." This self-referential element—the photograph within the photograph, or *mis-en-abyme*—recalls Walker Evans's *Torn Movie Poster* (1931) and highlights further the degree of construction within the image. The solitary model looks directly out at the viewer while conveying the glamorous appeal of Chanel's *eau de toilette pour homme*. The 'allure' has long faded, however, both in this poster and in its neglected environment. The advert is not only ironic, but knowing; it operates as a simulacrum within the simulacral environment (where it was used to authenticate a simulated space). When re-photographed, the advert prompts reflection on the documentary and indexical aspects of photography. The poster is doubly indexical in its photographic tracing of the figure and in its subsequent physical recording of fire damage sustained during simulation training. Framed within *Victoria Road*, the poster becomes a re-presentation that serves to undermine its original representational function.

Job Centre, Transport Lane (see Figure 6.2) depicts the area at the back of a train station. The dominant greys in the photograph are punctuated by the amber hue of the stationary train and the bright yellow of the employment service logo and delivery truck. The train appears to be destined for Glasgow Central. Marooned in a make-believe town, this scene recalls the surreal juxtaposition of Breton's locomotive abandoned for many years in a forest (*L'Amour Fou*). This example of Breton's "convulsive beauty" is particularly pertinent to photography. Krauss sees Breton's image of a stationary train—of "something that should be in motion but has been stopped"—as "intrinsically photographic" (1986: 112). Detached from "the continuum of its natural existence," the train is turned "into a sign of a reality it no longer possesses" (1986: 112). For Krauss, "the still photograph of this stilled train" is a "representation of an object already constituted as a representation" (1986: 112). Similarly, the found object of the stationary train in *Public Order* is an intrinsic part of an environment

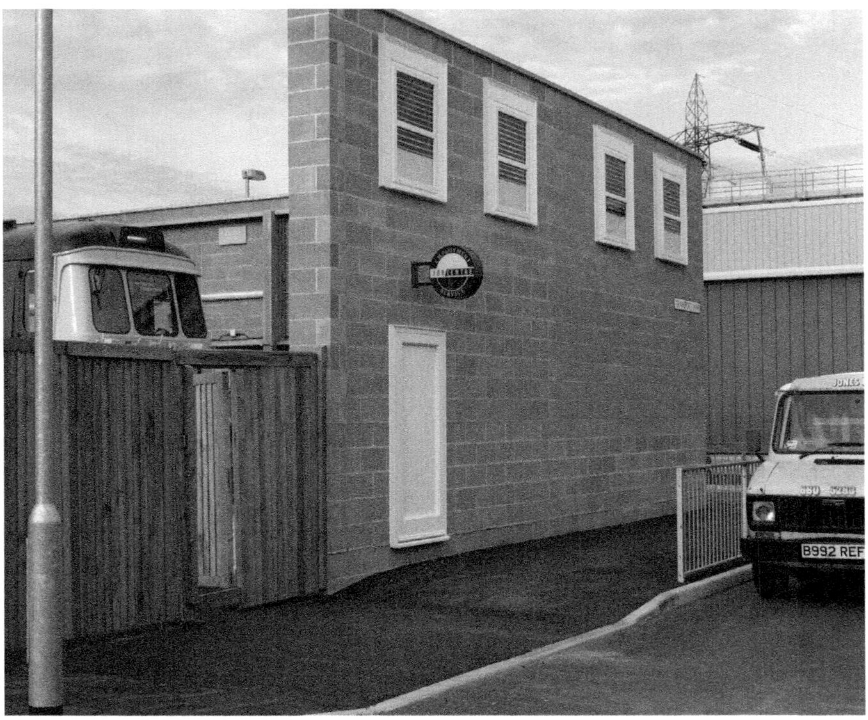

Figure 6.2 Sarah Pickering, *Job Centre, Transport Lane* (2004), from *Public Order* series. Courtesy the artist

that is *already* representational. Denton is an image of an image, and *Public Order* is a copy of an image without an original. The fake town is already a simulacrum that produces a semblance of the outward appearance of a—supposedly real—town without origin. *Public Order* is not simply a copy of a copy at a 'third remove' from reality: it duplicates a 'model' that has no foundation. In re-presenting the town photographically, *Public Order* diverges from Denton's real purpose or Idea.

Public Order also provokes reflection on the reality behind the simulacral nature of Denton. Alongside the seemingly innocuous artificial constructions, reside signs of the real. The inclusion of the job centre is of particular significance. Pickering observes that class stereotypes proliferate throughout the training grounds of the police, military and emergency services (2015). *Public Order* training spaces are devised as stereotypical, run-down working-class towns. These simulated environments are purposefully designed as similar to places where public order is deemed necessary. It would seem that such dystopic spaces are where disorder occurs. The unloved housing developments, unprepossessing fast-food outlets (including a burger joint and a Tandoori restaurant) and the dated Flicks nightclub—in addition to the employment agency—all reveal something of the bias inherent in their construction. One of the training sites has its own football pitch; another contains the exterior facade of a dreary pub. The decisions behind the design of these carefully crafted environs suggest an institutional gaze that encompasses socio-economic criminal profiling. The designers' impetus to create riot-training spaces in areas of suburban neglect and urban decline—as well as high unemployment—conveys a considerable degree of class prejudice. The notion that such a town would require a Foucauldian "disciplinary method" is further highlighted by the CCTV cameras that are also omnipresent in many British cities. However, in this fabricated scenario, the CCTV cameras are actually real—they exist in conjunction with a panopticon viewing tower enabling those in authority to oversee the riot training. The virtual, insidious institutional gaze behind the design of the space is accompanied by the actual gaze of senior police officers in a central control room.

There are disturbingly real elements then behind these constructed sets. The interior scenes of the Greater Manchester Police unit photographs—despite lacking some of the degree of detail of the other sites—are real in other ways. *Guards/Violent Man* depicts the training area for dealing with a violent person. Beneath the painted "violent man" sign is the storage unit for the props for the "re-enactment" (including shelves of black riot-proof helmets with protective visors). Pickering is intent on showing us behind the veil of these simulacral spaces. She ensures that the artifice is revealed—sometimes by selecting a scene or camera angle that reveals the theatrical components. By reflexively pointing to the fake construction, such photographs engage with the simulacrum only in order to destroy its illusionary power. *Semi-detached* also reveals its constructed reality (see Plate 6). Two concrete-block houses comprise a single building; positioned in the centre of the photograph, they are in perfect alignment with a lamppost that bifurcates them. Whereas the painted green door on the left maintains the illusion offered by the frontal view, the open doorway on the right reveals the real green landscape behind it. This open door (which Pickering encountered in situ) is a void in the image—a gap in the field of representation that reveals the 'real': the 'no man's land' that lies beyond the secure perimeter fence of this military zone. The open door in *Semi-detached* is a rupture in the constructed surface of the image, a wound in the image *as* picture. The visibility of the real landscape (of the Thames estuary) behind the facade reveals the construction of the house *as* an image. *Semi-detached* then functions by means of external *resemblance* to the original, but it clearly diverges by picturing the truth behind the semblance.

Dickens, High Street and *Flicks Nightclub* depict the same side of the main street from different viewing positions. At first glance, both photographs portray an everyday street scene featuring commercial premises in a small town, although the upturned shopping trolleys and discarded tyres in *Dickens, High Street* and the charred door in *Flicks Nightclub* hint at something beyond the ordinary (see Plate 7). *Behind Flicks Nightclub* (see cover image), however, reveals the full extent of the facade. Whereas the former images still maintain the illusion of the main street, *Behind Flicks Nightclub* is the denouement of the series (see cover image). The rear of the street is devoid of buildings and comprises an open space with gravelled ground. The shallow brick frontage is held up by metal supports and girders; the illumination of the fake shop windows is explained by the electric cables that run from the encased windows. This third photograph places the viewer backstage, behind the painted facade. *Behind Flicks Nightclub* unmasks the mechanism of *trompe l'oeil*: it pulls back the curtain of the illusion and reveals the surface nature of the simulacrum.

Guards/Violent Man and *Behind Flicks Nightclub* demonstrate a different relation to similitude from those photographs that appear to maintain the illusion; they eschew external resemblance (to the simulacral model) and move further in the direction of difference. *Denton Underground Station, Lola Court, Job Centre, Transport Lane* and *Flicks Nightclub* are initially indiscernible from images of a real town. Others, such as *Victoria Road* (with the traces of rioting), suggest the truth behind the space's real purpose. *Guards/Violent Man, Semi-detached* and *Behind Flicks Nightclub*, however, clearly reveal the degree of semblance in the fictional Denton. The unmasking of the original Denton as a mere representation can be seen as a moment of disjuncture with the simulacrum as such. Deleuze describes simulation as operating through masking or a "process of disguising, where, behind each mask, there is yet another" (2004b: 300). The photographs in *Public Order* that most clearly reveal behind the simulacral facade (notably *Guards/Violent Man* and *Behind Flicks Nightclub*) are not a reversal of the simulacrum, however—they are not "good copies" of Denton. Moreover, what is revealed beneath the mask is neither "a face" nor "an originary model behind the copy" (Smith 2006: 104).

In *Public Order*, the revelation of the facile nature of the original simulacrum also negates the illusion of representational depth; it is as if the "phantasms of the surface have replaced the hallucination of depth" (Deleuze 2004b: 30). The photographs that reveal the phantasmatic semblance constitute a further liberation from *resemblance* (of Denton as model). Indeed, the permutations can be seen as part of the dynamic genesis of simulation where "simulacra ascend and become *phantasms*" (Deleuze 2004b: 354). The differential relation to similitude within the series (with some photographs appearing to maintain the illusion, and others clearly revealing the semblance) produces a divergence that comprises the rejection of the Idea of the illusion. *Public Order* comprises an internal disparity within its serial form that echoes Deleuze's account of modern art: "Difference must be shown *differing*. We know that modern art tends to realise these conditions … The work of art leaves the domain of representation" (2004a: 68). For Deleuze, "the domain of representation filled by copies-icons" was founded by Plato (2004b: 296). Deleuze's reversal of Platonism encompasses the affirmation of simulacra (via repetition with internal difference). The simulacrum's agility is contrasted with the stasis of representation, which: "mediates everything, but mobilises and moves nothing" and fails to capture difference (2004a: 67). Deleuze aligns the simulacrum with modernity, and particularly with pop art in its serial manifestation of a repetition with difference:

> pop art pushed the copy, the copy of the copy, etc., to that extreme point at which it reverses and becomes a simulacrum (such as Warhol's remarkable 'serial' series, in which all the repetitions of habit, memory and death are conjugated).
>
> *(2004a: 366)*

There is a conceptual relation between Pickering's *Behind Flicks Nightclub* (2004) and Jeff Wall's *Destroyed Room* (1978, which is itself a direct reference to Delacroix's *Death of Sardanapalus*, 1827). *Destroyed Room* appears to show us the aftermath of a crime or violent incident. Yet it also reveals its staging by depicting the wooden struts supporting the fake constructed walls of the set. Like *Destroyed Room*, much of Pickering's *Public Order* does not bracket off the edges of its constructed set; the staging of the *image* is visible within the photograph. One could situate *Destroyed Room* and *Public Order* within a specific subset of contemporary photography that not only presents simulated environments for the camera, but reveals the artifice behind its fabricated subject. However, there are distinct differences in the photographer's role with regard to the creation of these constructions. Whereas Wall's *Destroyed Room* is staged *for* the camera, Pickering's Denton has a real purpose that precedes its being photographed.

The inclusion of *Public Order* in the exhibition *Staging Disorder*[12] revealed its similarities to, and differences from, constructed and staged imagery. In this context, *Public Order* had most resonance with Claudio Hils's series *Red Land, Blue Land* and Broomberg and Chanarin's *Chicago*—which also comprise photographs of military training sites. David Campany's inclusion of *Public Order* in a number of "documentary projects" where "artifice is their subject matter" prompts reflection on their individual differences.[13] Campany highlights their aesthetic similarities—their "common visual style" that resonates with "the register of hyper-real simulation" with regard to virtual reality and the video game (2006: 10–11). However, the conceptual and political critique behind this work is elided when the emphasis is placed on the aesthetic. Moreover, Campany's assertion that the work is indistinguishable from "functional documents" produced by "military training facilities" overlooks the work's artistic and conceptual qualities (2006: 11). There is an *intentional* difference between these sites—or their functional documentation—and artistic reproductions. Although externally resembling the spaces that they reproduce, such work has an internal conceptual difference from the Idea of the original (and from its "functional documents").

Pickering's work is not concerned with artifice so much as unmasking what lies behind it. In an interview with Anthony Luvera, she states that her "ambition is for the work to hopefully go beyond questions of 'is it real or is it not?' I see it as being much more about the complicated social systems that are represented in the constructed scenarios" (Pickering and Luvera 2009: n.p.). Pickering's concern is with the politics of representation behind these sites, and with these spaces *as* representation (of the public, and perhaps most particularly of lower socio-economic groups).[14] *Public Order* produces an appearance that resembles the original (Denton), yet possesses an intentional difference. Moreover, its particular simulacral operation—much like that of Deleuze's simulacrum—enacts a positive difference that serves to question the hierarchy entailed in representation. Pickering's intention is not to revel in artifice but to reveal the insidious reality of the constructions and the socio-economic, political and moral judgements behind their design.

Public Order deconstructs socio-economic stereotypes in a similar way to Sherman's deconstruction of Hollywood's "stock personae" (Krauss 1984: 59). There are differences between Pickering and Sherman in their distinctive approaches to staging: whereas Sherman creates and performs the role of the stereotype—embodying the simulacrum—Pickering selects and documents a pre-existing simulacrum in a way that undermines its staging. Krauss highlights that, because Sherman is "both subject and object," then "the play of stereotype in her work is a revelation of the artist herself as stereotypical" (1984: 59). Pickering's deconstruction of the stereotype consists of a reproduction by different means—*Public Order* repeats the "original" simulacrum in order to reveal the stereotype. Yet both artists "reproduce what is already a reproduction" (1984: 59). Moreover, they both engage with the simulacrum in order to produce a deconstructive mechanism via a process of repeating *with* difference. Pickering produces a deconstruction of representation by highlighting the inherent stereotype and revealing the representation *as* representation (by going behind the representation to photograph its superficial reality). The correlation is further highlighted by Krauss's reading of Sherman: "the subject of her images is this flattened, cardboard imitation … her execution is no less preordained and controlled by the culturally already-given" (1984: 59). Like Sherman's, Pickering's use of photography constitutes a form of critique.

Pickering's work often engages reflexively with representation by depicting something that is already an image. In this regard, there is a confluence between her work and the genre of rephotography. The "Pictures" group—including Sherrie Levine and Richard Prince—were the most cited exponents of rephotography (a genre that was often aligned with the Baudrillardian simulacrum).[15] In his essay "Anti-Platonism and Art," Paul Patton reads the work of Levine (and others) as exemplars of postmodernist art, "concerned with the reproduction of appearances" (1994: 142). Patton asserts that these appearances are not simply "second-order" reproductions (of pre-existing images), but they entail a transformation through the artist's *conceptual* production (1994: 142). Whereas (modern) realist art aimed to eliminate the difference between the original and the copy, postmodernism inverts this goal by establishing difference through similarity (Patton 1994: 142–3). Pickering's work consists of a Deleuzian simulacral repetition (a semblance rather than a likeness) that possesses internal difference from the original. This is particularly evident in her *Art and Antiquities* series, which includes complex photographic "documentations" of the fakes produced by the notorious art forger Shaun Greenhalgh. Also comprising recreated scenes with genuine forgeries (as well as fake artefacts constructed for a television programme about Greenhalgh), this series manifests the irony behind Plato's *Sophist*—of searching for the true pretender. Greenhalgh's fake artworks also achieve 'authenticity' when they are photographed by an artist using a historic photographic technique such as the salt print. Pickering observes that, whereas appropriation art of the 1980s such as that by Levine drew on the work of (real) photographers such as Evans, her *Art and Antiquities* replicate something that is fake (2015).

In *Art and Antiquities* and in *Public Order*, photography is no longer aligned with representation but with repetition. Pickering's work demonstrates difference *from*, rather than identity *with*, that which it purports to copy. Writing on Prince, Michael Newman insists that rephotography does not produce a perfect copy: it is a resemblance that *bears difference* (2006: 54–5). For Newman, repetition is the means through which the simulacrum is manifested; he insists that this is a repetition *with* difference:

> It is not possible to 'penetrate' the simulacrum, as if to pierce through a veil, because there is nothing behind or beyond. The only way of getting some purchase on it as

> simulacrum, the only way to make the 'as' manifest, is to repeat it. Thus repetition can be understood as a way of creating a horizontal difference across the depthless surface of simulation.
>
> *(2006: 54–5)*

In *Public Order*, Pickering repeats Denton *as* simulacrum and pictures the veil itself in all its depthless surface. *Public Order* consists of photographs that repeat a model without origin, but they do not faithfully copy the *Idea* of Denton: the aesthetic resemblance belies the intentional artistic differences. Denton is already a simulacrum, but *Public Order* produces a simulacral copy—a simulacrum of a simulacrum—that challenges the original (mis) representation.

Representation and repetition are intrinsic to photography. Photography as a medium consists in copying; it repeats and often duplicates its referent as model. Photography's mediation—as re-production and re-presentation—can be seen to embody the Platonic "good copy" that repeats the identity of its model. Deleuze describes photography as an *analogical* medium that "proceeds by resemblance" (Deleuze 2003 [1981]: 80). For Krauss, though, photography's resemblance is such that it "raises the specter of nondifferentiation" and thus undermines the distinction that Plato seeks to make between the original and the copy (1984: 59). Krauss, then, reads a certain Deleuzianism into photography. In Krauss's analysis, photography's mimetic capacity enables its deconstructive mechanism. *Public Order* functions in such a manner—deconstructing the stereotypes behind the fake town, but also deconstructing the medium itself. The self-referential elements such as the photograph within the photograph (in *Victoria Road*) or the picturing of the props area in *Guards/Violent Man* or the back-stage area in *Behind Flicks Nightclub* are additional reflexive tools for this deconstruction. Reflexivity rejects conventional mimesis and disrupts our reading of photographs as transparent windows on the world. What is brought to the fore in *Public Order* is the conceptual difference between photography and its model.

Public Order functions like the Deleuzian simulacrum in its production of difference through repetition. *Public Order* may produce external resemblance, but there is an essential difference from the "original." Denton is a *model* town (though it has no original); *Public Order* produces an appearance of something that is already an image, but it is a repetition *with* difference. *Public Order*'s divergence from the "internal essence" of Denton—the refusal to be a "good" copy of the deceitful original—echoes Deleuze's simulacrum and its undoing of the Platonic hierarchy of representation. In refusing conventional photographic *representation*, these works provoke reflection on photography's potential as a simulacral repetition—one that possesses a *positive difference* from that which it appears to copy. Deleuze's simulacrum feigns resemblance through (external) "appearance-making" that disguises its internal dissimilitude (to the Platonic Idea). Pickering's work engages the Deleuzian simulacrum via its phantasmatic *appearance-making* in conjunction with intentional (internal) dissimilitude.

In its move from representation to repetition, *Public Order* embodies Deleuze's opposition to Platonic *iconology*. The affirmation of the simulacrum occurs through similitude and dissimilitude. In *Public Order*, we see photography as a "false copy" encompassing internal non-resemblance. That the simulacrum uses resemblance in order to produce *difference* undermines representation as such. *Public Order*, then, also produces a deconstruction of the documentary mechanism of photography as a medium of re-production. Rather than *proceeding by resemblance*, *Public Order* proceeds (by divergence) through semblance and dissemblance. The complex interplay of semblance and dissemblance in *Public Order* challenges photography's historic alignment with truth, although, in its divergence from the original, *Public Order* is a simulacral repetition that paradoxically engenders truth. Simulation reveals photography's truth.

Acknowledgements

My thanks go to Sarah Pickering for providing her artwork and copyright, and for all of her valuable input.

Notes

1 See *Between Deleuze and Derrida*, eds. P. Patton and J. Protevi (2003), for an interesting comparative study of those thinkers.

2 Roland Barthes characterises the photograph as not merely "a 'copy' of reality" but "an emanation of *past reality*" (Barthes 2000 [1980]: 88–9). We cannot deny that "*the thing has been there*"—*that-has-been* (Barthes 2000 [1980]: 76; original emphasis).

3 Camille references Benjamin's (1999 [1936]) "Work of Art in the Age of Mechanical Reproduction," which highlights the decline of aura in the era of technological reproducibility. Benjamin's "Small History of Photography" essay (1997 [1931]) is also pertinent.

4 See Lomas on this point of how Klossowski helped to translate Benjamin's "Work of Art" essay (2011: 44).

5 References to *Sophist* will follow customary Platonic methods of citation and be preceded by the abbreviation *S*.

6 Deleuze originally published this essay with a title that specifically referred to the reversal of Platonism in the journal *Revue de Metaphysics* in 1967—see the preface to *The Logic of Sense* where Deleuze notes that the appendices were revised from previous publications (2004b: x).

7 Baudrillard insists that, in the era of the hyperreal, we encounter a generation of signs that are no longer referential—"models of a real without origin or reality" (Baudrillard 1994 [1981]: 1–2).

8 This is something that analytical philosophy fails to grasp: in its alignment of photography with *automatism*, the agency and creativity of the photographer are denied.

9 See Pickering's book *Explosions, Fires and Public Order* (2010a). Images are also available on the artist's website: www.sarahpickering.co.uk/

10 Pickering has stated that training officers acting as rioters—and armed with baseball bats—would hit the trainees' shields and that one recruit retaliated by kicking (email from Pickering, 3 March 2016).

11 Pickering has spoken about the latent threat of violence in these images in an interview with Susan Bright (Pickering 2010b). She initially photographed the violent training exercises but did not want to produce reportage (Pickering 2015). Her subsequent decision to photograph deserted spaces surprised the participants, who assumed that the riot exercises would have made for more interesting action shots.

12 Curated by Christopher Stewart and Esther Teichmann—at London College of Communication in 2015. The exhibition catalogue *Staging Disorder* (2015), edited by Stewart and Teichmann, includes artworks and commissioned essays.

13 In Campany's (2006) essay "Straight Pictures of a Crooked World," he includes Pickering's *Public Order* series in a discussion of "documentary" work alongside: Broomberg and Chanarin's *Chicago*, An-My Lê's *Small Wars*, Larry Sultan's *The Valley*, and Steffi Klenz's *Nonsuch*.

14 Pickering states that, "All of the burning environments in *Fire Scene* are particular types of places, representative of a particular group of people—usually low income. There's always a suggestion of neglect or deviation" (2009).

15 Douglas Crimp's curation of the *Pictures* exhibition (1977) and his subsequent essay heralded a generation of artists concerned with the nature of the photographic image. Levine's *After Walker Evans* (exhibited at New York's Metro Pictures Gallery in 1981) is a paradigmatic example of rephotography.

References

Barthes, R. (2000 [1980]) *Camera Lucida: Reflections on Photography*, trans. R. Howard, London: Vintage.

Baudrillard, J. (1994 [1981]) *Simulacra and Simulation*, trans. S.F. Glaser, Ann Arbor: University of Michigan Press.

Benjamin, W. (1997 [1931]) "A Small History of Photography," in *One-Way Street and Other Writings*, trans. Edmund F.N. Jephcott and Kingsley Shorter, London: Verso, pp. 240–57.
Benjamin, W. (1999 [1936]) "The Work of Art in the Age of Mechanical Reproduction," in H. Arendt (ed.) *Illuminations*, trans. H. Zorn, London: Pimlico, pp. 211–44.
Camille, M. (1996) "Simulacrum," in R. S. Nelson and R. Shiff (eds.) *Critical Terms for Art History*, Chicago: University of Chicago Press, pp. 31–44.
Campany, D. (2006) "Straight Pictures of a Crooked World," in P. Seawright and C. Coppock (eds.) *So Now Then*, Cardiff: Fotogallery, pp. 8–11.
Cornford, F. M. (1935) *Plato's Theory of Knowledge: The Theaetetus and the Sophist of Plato, Translated with a Running Commentary*, London: Routledge & Kegan Paul.
Deleuze, G. (2003 [1981]) *Francis Bacon: The Logic of Sensation*, trans. D. W. Smith, London: Continuum.
Deleuze, G. (2004a) *Difference and Repetition*, trans. P. Patton, London: Continuum. [Originally published in French in 1968].
Deleuze, G. (2004b) *The Logic of Sense*, trans. M. Lester, London: Continuum [first published in French in 1969].
Deleuze, G. (2005 [1983]) *Cinema 1: The Movement Image*, trans. H. Tomlinson and B. Habberjam, London: Continuum.
Deleuze, G. (2005 [1985]) *Cinema 2: The Time Image*, trans. H. Tomlinson and R. Galeta, London: Continuum.
Derrida, J. (1981) *Dissemination*, trans. B. Johnson, Chicago: University of Chicago Press [originally published in French in 1972].
Klossowski, P. (1997) *Nietzsche and the Vicious Circle*, trans. D. W. Smith, London: Athlone.
Krauss, R. E. (1984) "A Note on Photography and the Simulacral," October, 31, pp. 49–68.
Krauss, R. E. (1986) *The Originality of the Avant-garde and Other Modernist Myths*, Mass: MIT Press.
Krauss, R. E. (1999) "Reinventing the Medium," *Critical Inquiry*, 25:2, pp. 289–305.
Krauss, R. E. and Deleuze, G. (1983) "Plato and the Simulacrum," trans. Krauss, *October*, 27, pp. 45–56.
Lomas, D. (2011) "Simulacra and the Order of Mimesis in Dalí and Glenn Brown," *Konsthistorisk tidskrift/Journal of Art History*, 80:1, pp. 23–45.
Newman, M. (2006) *Richard Prince: Untitled Couple*, London: Afterall.
Patton, P. (1994) "Anti-Platonism and Art," in C. V. Boundas and D. Olkowski (eds.) *Gilles Deleuze and the Theater of Philosophy*, London: Routledge, 141–156.
Patton, P and J. Protevi (eds.) (2003) *Between Deleuze and Derrida*, London: Continuum.
Pickering, S. (2010a) *Explosions, Fires and Public Order*, New York: MoCP/Aperture.
Pickering, S. (2010b) "Sarah Pickering and Susan Bright: Introduction and Public Order series 1/5," interview with Susan Bright on 31 March 2010, Aperture Foundation, on the occasion of the publication of Pickering's first monograph: *Explosions, Fires and Public Order*. https://vimeo.com/11904198 [Accessed June 2016].
Pickering, S. (2015) Interview with the author on 15 July 2015.
Pickering, S. (2016) Email from Pickering to the author on 3 March 2016.
Pickering, S. and A. Luvera (2009) "Fire Scene: Sarah Pickering in Conversation with Anthony Luvera," *Hotshoe* (April–May) and www.luvera.com/sarah-pickering-in-conversation-with-anthony-luvera/ [Accessed June 2016].
Plato. (1935) "Sophist," in *Plato's Theory of Knowledge: The Theaetetus and the Sophist of Plato, Translated with a Running Commentary*, trans. F. M. Cornford, London: Routledge & Kegan Paul, 165–332.
Smith, D. W. (1997) "Translator's Preface," in Pierre Klossowski *Nietzsche and the Vicious Circle*, trans. D. W. Smith, London: Athlone, vii–xiii.
Smith, D. W. (2006) "The Concept of the Simulacrum: Deleuze and the Overturning of Platonism," *Continental Philosophy Review*, 38:1–2, pp. 89–123.
Stewart, C. and E. Teichmann (eds.) (2015) *Staging Disorder* (from an exhibition at London College of Communication), London: Black Dog Books.
Talbot, W. H. F. (1844) *The Pencil of Nature* as cited by the Special Collections Department, University of Glasgow Library, file: //localhost/<http://special.lib.gla.ac.uk:exhibns:month:feb2007.html> [Accessed January 2009].

7

Five versions of the photographic act

Archival logic in the work of Andrea Robbins and Max Becher

Shep Steiner

Andrea Robbins and Max Becher's *Black Cowboys* (2008–2016) is a politically loaded, research-based project that this New York-based collaborative team has been working on for ten years (see, for example, Figure 7.1). The series goes to the heart of what we could describe as a system of picture *making* that not only confronts the ethical problems of picture *taking*, but broaches overlapping issues of aesthetics and politics in the process. As I go on to argue, the act of beholding—whether in the gallery context or in the form of the photobook—reproduces and refocuses these matters, and the problem of visibility thematizes them. In fact, we glimpse the photographic act less through the logic of mimesis or the all too familiar mechanical model of reproduction and more as a structural flaw that can only be read as the symptomatic stutter of a vastly extended biomechanical apparatus (*dispositif*), which compensates for failure by working overtime. The photographs of Fred Whitfield calf roping, of the four inmates at "Angola" State Prison, or of Myrtis Dightman by a statue of Myrtis Dightman exemplify the processes involved. Taken together, these pictures mark the variable threshold of visibility that surrounds the African American cowboy. The myth of the American West and the figure of the cowboy are such overdetermined constructs today that the black cowboy hovers unacknowledged on the ragged edge of the visible. Look at the figures in *Three Bull Riders, One Bronc Rider, Richmond Texas* (2016; see Plate 8). The three on the left, Dightman, Willie Thomas, and Freddie "Skeet" Gordon, are among the most famous of bull riders, yet ranch-hand attire and ball caps disappoint in a culture where a cowboy hat and get-up are mandatory. Dightman's split-second cameo riding a bull in Sam Peckinpah's *Junior Bonner* (1972) provides the thinnest of testimonials. Cultural mash-ups with soul, hip hop, and Islam, seen in the group photos of the "Brotherhood of Riders" and the "Four Cowgirls in Black" (two in hijabs) only obscure the issue as urban and religious phantasms hijack the image. The links between black rodeo and the Louisiana penitentiary system do not help, nor Whitfield's status as the winningest black cowboy on the circuit.

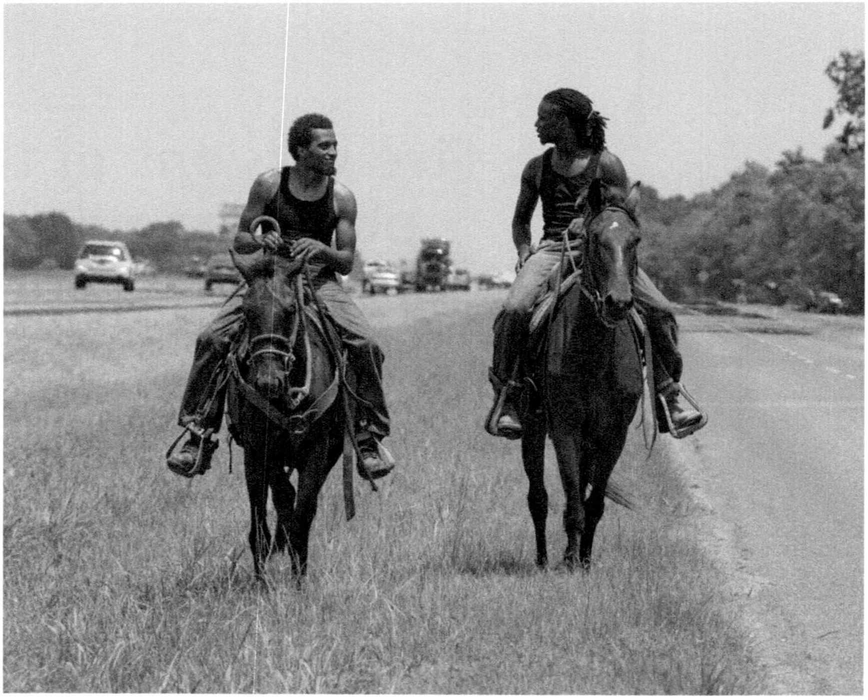

Figure 7.1 Andrea Robbins and Max Becher, *Two Riders Along Highway, Bounce Back Trail Ride, Welsh, LA* (2015). Courtesy the artists

Since 1991, Robbins and Becher have pursued no fewer than 27 loosely connected projects across the globe, each focusing on the legacies of colonial power. In all of these projects, photography brings into visibility a range of cultural and social hybridities, intentional communities, ideological and religious transplants, architectural morphisms, discursive airdrops, and chiasmic crossings between nation states. As with the example of the *Black Cowboys* (Robbins and Becher 2014b), their preferred subject matter tends at first to strike one as curiously humorous, decidedly minor or dealing with marginal issues, but the stakes are always high. This response is an occupational hazard for the photographers, who work within and against deeply ingrained hegemonic constructs such as the white cowboy of film history, the resolution of discrimination and segregation in America, and even the much larger problem of Southernization, all processes through which the artists would ultimately have us frame the *Black Cowboys*. As a consequence, both the enlightened student of history and the most politically correct among us will be put off their game. Face to face with Robbins and Becher's *Black Cowboys*, *German Indians*, or other ticklish subjects, we are placed in an awkward position and forced to perform in unusual ways. More specifically, as viewers of *Myrtis Dightman, the Jackie Robinson of Bull Riding* (2016), or *Living Legend, Bull Rider Willie Thomas* (2016), we are cornered into admitting something like: "Black Cowboys! There is no such thing." As I go on to argue, Robbins and Becher's practice demands we shift our basic understanding of documentary photography from its comfortable status as a container for describing or reporting on events to understanding photography (as well as its reception) as an act in its own right—a move that echoes J. L. Austin's distinction between the "constative" and "performative" utterance (Austin 1964). In their work, photography both performs acts of reporting or describing and incites acts of reporting or describing on the model of the speech act. This act, which is infinitely repeatable or quotable in different contexts, is at the crux of their work, and inasmuch provides the crucial *topos* around which this essay unfolds. In this regard, the essay attempts to rethink basic problems associated with the photographic enterprise that we usually take for granted. I expand the basic photographic act—defined by the click of the shutter—to include a set of pre-photographic and post-photographic acts, which, respectively, precede and follow that paradigmatic gesture. This expanded framework for thinking about photography is the result of confronting a range of contemporary photographic practices over the last ten years (Steiner 2005, 2011, 2013, 2015). Specifically, I extend the photographic act to include emergent processes constitutive of consciousness and find Austin's notion of the speech act also lurking in the viewers' response to the post-photographic situation of the gallery and the photo-book. These ideas raise three fundamental points about the photographic act as I trace it in the work of Becher and Robbins: (1) real-world examples of this repeatable linguistic act furnish the artists with their wide-ranging subject matter; (2) the general logic of the act finds at least five extensions in their practice; and (3) the repeatability of the act is a 'conduit' for power, the stakes of which are raised to an acute level in the case of *Black Cowboys*.

Ethically speaking, we cannot divorce our encounters with these photographs from the wider questions of race and identity that animate the current hegemonic moment. I suggest that the interference offered by a hegemonic regime of ethics is a constant factor in our encounters with these works; further, ideological violence, easily mistaken for irony, is constantly overcome through the performance of an ethical response to singular photographs; and, lastly, the tension between these two ethical measures marks an important threshold of Becher and Robbins' photography. This limit marks both a linguistic frame, or 'discursive mode', instituted in and as the act of viewing (what has been called "ethicity"), and an intrinsic organization of the subject (what the artists call "typology"), which gestures in turn to the outsides of photography (De Man 1979: 16). If we leave open for now the question of the self-organized system of rules that structure black cowboy culture, we can begin to understand the larger system of logic, aesthetic criteria, and organization implicit in Robbins and Becher's photographic corpus by isolating the very Western and arch-photographic problem of the trigger. This trigger is basic to the logic of modernist photography and is put under extraordinary pressure in Robbins and Becher's corpus.

Trigger

If one were to imagine the history of photography from Robbins and Becher's perspective, what would undoubtedly come under the most acute pressure is the category of hair-trigger photography. John Szarkowski's notion of "the photographer's eye," where "the central act of photography, the act of choosing and eliminating" divides what is inside from what is outside the frame, summarizes this aesthetic well (Szarkowski 1966: 9). For Szarkowski, the royal road to the art of photography is underwritten by the act of pressing the trigger at the right moment. However, if choosing the right moment to press the trigger is something reserved for the art of photography, then, for Szarkowski, the act of actually pressing the trigger itself is incidental. Shadowing the rigid protocols of J. L. Austin's research into speech-acts, the true and good photograph for Szarkowski privileges the model of the constative utterance that frames facts or a state of affairs. Given the lasting influence of modernist tropes in photography, it seems that very few practitioners or critics would contest this basic genealogy. Henri Cartier-Bresson's notion of the "decisive moment" is perhaps its sharpest articulation, but war photography as practiced by Robert Capa, Eddie Adams, Joe Rosenthal, or Luc Delahaye is no less representative. Framing on the fly or shooting from the hip in order to get the Pulitzer is the name of the game. The genre of street photography is no less a fit. Even if exemplars of the style from the 1970s such as Garry Winogrand, Lee Friedlander, or Diane Arbus privilege an internal rather than external trigger, the cause and effect relationship of the essential mechanism is marked. In all of the latter cases, the shutter is tethered to a subjective 'I' behind the lens on the lookout for motifs: in Arbus's case the odd-ball or outsider; in Friedlander's, the frame showcased as porous, transparent, and punctured; or, in Winogrand's, the utter contingency of elements barely captured in a tilted world. Equally relevant are the *Polaroid Photographs* (1975–1976) of James Welling. The incredibly banal and dozy scenes that crop up before his Polaroid are no less the document of a trigger event, the crux being that the banal and dozy are themselves transfigured or made unique by the photographic act. Our fascination with the category of photojournalism also captures much of its flavor, as does Michael Fried's privileging of the anti-theatrical tradition (Fried 2005). Even Roland Barthes' emphasis on singularity and contingency and his analytics of photographic surprise, shock, rarity, prowess, deskilling, and the *trouvaille* or lucky find share in the mystique of the trigger event (Barthes 1981: 32–33). What differentiates Robbins and Becher's perspective is the pressure they place on this symbolic moment of the high tradition.

The master fictions of the art of photography—all ruled over by the controlling metaphor of the symbolic trigger—hold value for Robbins and Becher only in so far as "the central act of photography" is made into a kind of echo chamber that gestures to other versions of the act. Their reasons revolve around a healthy skepticism about the modernist paradigm of "the photographer's eye" and the aesthetic experience it ostensibly offers up. Thus, in the case of portraiture, a genre that crops up quite often in their corpus, the problem of expression is placed under considerable strain (Berger 2008). Perhaps the symbolic genre *par excellence*—especially in the hands of a master of the quick encounter on the street such as Arbus, where the truth of the subject's interior life is apparently made immediately accessible on the face—portraiture is rubbed the wrong way in Robbins and Becher's work. One feels this pressure especially in the four photos of black cowboys from "Angola" State Prison. If the deep lines etched into the face of the oldest of these cowboys read as a transparent mirror of a long, hard life on the chain gang, the black and white stripes of his prison uniform place him in a unique relationship with the three younger men, as well as a more complicated relationship with black cowboy culture as a whole. In these extended syntactical contexts, the portrait as face is stripped of uniqueness and metaphysical truth and instead served up as a series of surfaces that exist within a number of differential systems of signs at the mercy of larger questions of ideology, including the institution of slavery and its contemporary manifestation as the chain gang and penitentiary system. As Robbins put it, "We look for subjects where surface defies subject and contradicts assumption" (Robbins 2010), a strategy that makes all of the portraits of black cowboys not only open to projection, but simultaneously quarantined against its effects, for the portraits do not militate against deep truth so much as bend or twist deep truth towards hegemonic values.

Equally pertinent to note with regard to the high tradition is that not even fresh experiences of the open road or new locations for shooting hold much water for these artists. We know, in fact, that, in order to get their shots, intensive research and extensive travelling are required (Lippard 2006). Thus, in the face of their project *Cracker Barrel* (2014)—which required extensive driving time to as many of the locations of the Cracker Barrel Old

Country Store as possible—all of the contemporary epigones of Robert Frank and William Eggleston, even Frank and Eggleston themselves, come across as spellbound by the myth of the open road. Indeed, for Robbins and Becher, the freedom of the open road is seen as inseparably correlative to the penal labor provided by the US prison industry, with its well-known high incarceration rates of African Americans. New experiences—whether of the exotic kind that we associate with travel photography or with the particularly American freedom experienced on the road trip—are just not what is up for grabs in this series, which centers on the 'eerily' similar accent wall and accoutrements above the standardized fireplace in the 630 franchised restaurants in 42 states of the Cracker Barrel Old Country Store system. The same applies to *Following the Ten Commandments* (2012–2014), another photographic series that hinges on a grueling travel regimen, this time to document the proliferation of Ten Commandments monuments across the continental US. The planning and travel time necessary to hit the trail rides and rodeos that make up the *Black Cowboys*—in Florida, Georgia, Louisiana, Texas, California, and Oklahoma—are similar. But again, none of these projects are a celebration of the dizzying experience of the open road, or the documents of an arduous performance. Rather, as I go on to suggest, these projects are all bracketed by a broader interest in Southernization, which the artists would describe as the slow but inevitable ideological processes by which Southern politics, values, and beliefs (including the taste for Southern cooking, religious conservatism, and racism) have spread and continue to spread across the United States.

System

These deviations from straight photography raise the question of Robbins and Becher's relationship to the variable mediations of photography performed in and as conceptualism. If we grant the systems-based photography of Bernd and Hilla Becher as the stiffest sounding board against which the practice might be profitably viewed, then we should also recognize the leverage gained through recourse to American versions of systems photography, especially Ed Ruscha's. In the first place, we might briefly gesture to the little-acknowledged, mirroric logic at the heart of Bernd and Hilla Becher's practice (Steiner 2015). Given the 19th-century plate camera the couple used, there is always an equivalence struck between the apparatus for picturing and the technical apparatus pictured. Furthermore, the identity established between the grammatical subject of the Bechers' photographs and the broad cross-section of technical buildings they photographed across northern Europe (winding towers, blast furnaces, water towers, etc.) is ultimately rooted in the finely balanced system of technological, economic, and environmental relationships implicit in the Siegen industrial region—Bernd Becher's home and a social formation that should be thought of as being as close to the model of an egalitarian society as the Bechers believed possible. In short, folded within the objectivity of the Bechers' special version of the documentary photograph is a system of prosthetic extensions that indelibly links the always-centered, well-lit and wholly visible object before the camera to the camera, the photographer(s) behind the camera, the particular system of relations implicit in the production of high-quality steel in Siegen, and, finally, the expanded field of this technical system outside Siegen. The Bechers' project of putting this system of relations into action in each and every photograph and, second, showcasing this system through the presentational form of typology provide the European heritage for Robbins and Becher's project. As should already be clear, not only do Robbins and Becher have more distance on their subject matter than the Bechers, but their key emphasis is to shed light on the negative effects of any one system of reproduction, what they call the "colonial conduit" (Robbins and Becher 2014a).

The importance of Ed Ruscha's systems aesthetic is different again. Take the artist's humorously classic photo-book, *26 Gasoline Stations* (1963). Given the repetitious subject matter, we imagine the instructions for the piece to be built right into the title. A similar kind of work is suggested by *Following the Ten Commandments*, with important qualifications. For instance, if, for Ruscha, the title as script to be performed is followed 'to a T' by the bumbling persona we assume to be behind the camera, then, in Robbins and Becher's work, the demands made upon the photographers are at least as contradictory and complex as the ways in which they themselves bend the system put into motion. For *Following the Ten Commandments* is precisely not about the apparently meaningless performance of a task by the artist, but the loaded question of the performative, which not only completes an act in and as the process of picturing, but so does in the shadow of the Ten Commandments monuments themselves. The ideological backstory and the local byways of religious fundamentalism and conservative politics spelled out in the didactics accompanying each photograph are the first clue. The steady proliferation of these monuments across the United States is the second clue. This process, which the artists identify as one aspect of Southernization, narrates the slow erosion of the Establishment Clause of the First Amendment by slowly chipping away at the separation between church and state, an issue sharply punctuated by the Supreme Court's *Van Orden vs. Perry* ruling (2005), which argued that the installation of a Ten Commandments monument in Austin, Texas, was constitutional. Third, in contrast to Ruscha, fidelity to a system is continually tested in *Following the Ten Commandments*. If, in *Bradford County Courthouse, Starke, FL*, the dreamy architectural photography of the likes of Julius Shulman frames the lightning-strike sharpness of the monument that looks as if just cut from stone, then, in other photographs from the same series, the monument is lost (see Plate 9). In *Bloomfield City Hall, Bloomfield, NM*, it blends in with a forest of other monuments and competing signs, the result of endless quibbling, court dates, and conciliation between city and city council on the unconstitutionality of the monument. In *Oklahoma State Capital, Oklahoma City, OK*, the monument is dwarfed by the architecture. Donated by a local Republican with an eye to further dissolving the separation between church and state in his own backyard, the monument was awaiting the results of lawsuits filed for its removal by the American Civil Liberties Union and American Atheists Inc., until it was driven over by a religious fanatic who claimed Satan made him do it. In *Connellsville Middle School, Connellsville, PA*, the Ten Commandments monument is boarded up awaiting a court decision. In 2012, the Freedom from Religion Foundation filed a court order for the removal of the monument, originally gifted by Cecil B. DeMille and the Fraternal Order of Eagles, but a local Baptist group calling themselves Thou Shall Not Move blocked the decision.

In short, if *Following the Ten Commandments* might well come off as a potentially pious act, a humorously random decision on the part of the artists, or even a conceptual script to be carried out, first and foremost the series should be read as investigative journalism of the kind made famous by *All The President's Men* (1976), where the phrase "Follow the money" opened up the floodgates to the Watergate Scandal. Reproducing a moment of reproduction in the world for the purposes of art *à la* Ruscha is very different from recognizing the reproduction or proliferation of Ten Commandments monuments as symptomatic of larger ideological processes, in the grip of which one may potentially find oneself (see also Plate 10). In this regard, Robbins and Becher balance the question of system with lessons learned from Hans Haacke, a point made nowhere more sharply than in the didactic panel accompanying *Bradford County Courthouse*. The text identifies a certain Joe Anderson Jr., "owner and president of a number of Florida road building companies," who commissioned and paid for the monument and who has stalled the monument's removal by claiming his organization's First Amendment Right to practice religion. In contrast to Ruscha's irony, irony for Robbins and Becher is not a stumbling block that militates against ideology critique. The quirky air of idiocy that is often implicit in Ruscha's projects is actually put to work in Becher and Robbins' photographs. Granted that the associations with Ruscha's "everyman" are a crucial fiction, the acts performed by this photographic team are not determined solely by the limited aim of finding new ways to make art on the model of photography. On the contrary, because the photographic act for Robbins and Becher is linked to a much broader, contested field of social and linguistic convention—what Benjamin Buchloh relates to the "open semiological system" of the *Neue Sachlichkeit*—their projects are as much about affirmative critique as about correcting our folkish ways (Buchloh 1994: 18). As such, the monuments pictured in *Following the Ten Commandments* are both exemplary examples of Ten Commandments monuments *and* exemplary proxies for yet to be documented monuments that find a place in the grammar of something like a stuttering world-sentence that is actively being written. Textuality as historical trace gains an edge in this photography.

The field of acts

With this conceptual backstory now sketched in and the trigger event situated within a system of like events, we can specifically turn to Robbins and Becher's various extensions to the basic logic of the photographic act. Balancing and negotiating the tensions implicit in each of the sites (or *topoi*) where photography happens constitute a pragmatic rule in their practice. All of these sites are linguistic knots of one kind or another with a purchase on what is taken as the paradigmatic act of photography: the vastly overvalued moment when the photographer looks through the viewfinder and takes a picture. The reproducibility of this basic logic—always turning on the photographic act, always framed as a linguistic encounter, always bracketing a fairly stable event structure hinging on relations between subject and object—constitutes the systematic core of their expansive practice. As a consequence, the fundamentally modernist understanding of photography as "trigger event" keyed to the discerning eye of the photographer is far too narrow a definition of the medium for this collaborative team who refer to themselves as artists who use photography, who identify as systems photographers, and whose content-rich practice belies any theoretical detour that would reposition the much venerated act within an expanded field of like acts. Shaped by the theoretical pressures that brought photography to the forefront of contemporary art in New York in the 1980s–1990s—especially allegory and the meta-theoretical leaps that characterized the expanding frame of reference implicit in the succession of forms of neo-avant-garde practice that took hold of the art field in the wake of modernism (e.g. minimalism, performance, conceptualism, institutional critique, etc.)—for Robbins and Becher, the problem of photography extends far before itself and far after itself. In their hands, the medium of photography is a far larger entity than we are used to handling. To the trigger event of modernist photography, they add what amounts to a set of pre-photographic supplements and post-photographic acts.

If we are to understand the complex processes that Robbins and Becher bring into visibility, the first step is to map out the broader field of photographic acts, which these artists claim as a working context. In the first place, and preceding the nominal definition of photography as trigger event, we need to acknowledge an operational version of the act that occurs (impossibly) before the digital recording of time and place or the chemical system of writing with light, and I have described this above as the conceptual framework of systems photography. Further, this prehistory or antecedent of the act proper presupposes an even more primordial act of archivization that Derrida describes as a "taking place" (Derrida 1995: 1). The double utterance that begins Walter Benjamin's "Talk About Collecting" captures some of the mystery surrounding this originary act (Benjamin 1968). With the opening lines "I am unpacking my library. Yes I am," the critic points to something taking place as he speaks, an allegorical act of unpacking that underwrites the literal saying by the literal doing. These retrospective moves by both critics are deeply counterintuitive, but the basic stakes of the game are the same for Robbins and Becher, whose photography makes a place for this "taking place." The aim of their performative notion of photography is to picture a notion of the support that the "decisive moment" only presupposes; that the street photographers of the 1950s–1960s hunted back to a subjective surface; and that conceptual-based systems photographers of the 1970s tethered in turn to a notion of the support that was keyed to the equivalence struck between subject and object.

In the second place, and succeeding the nominal definition of the trigger event, we need to acknowledge a set of photographic acts that post-date the paradigmatic act of photography. Thus, it is a small thing to note—and it can be easily blown out of proportion vis-à-vis the other versions of the act put into circulation—that each of the photographic series that make up Robbins and Becher's corpus are organized according to a system of color frames. The frame—whether as viewfinder, pictorial bracket, or system of classification—is never a neutral category for these photographers. For instance, the *Black Cowboys* have wooden frames; their earliest series, *Colonial Remains* (1991), bright yellow frames; the *German Indians* (1997–1998), beige frames; and, for what is perhaps their best-known series, *770* (2005–2014), blue frames. This assortment of frame colors, which are rightly associated with the color-coded folders of a filing system, should not immediately be conflated with what has been called an "archival impulse" (Foster 2004), "archive fever" (Enwezor 2008), or the logic of state control and the policing of bodies that is one of the key functions of the photographic archive (Sekula 1986). All of these global accounts of photography's relationship to the archive are not sensitive enough to singular acts. Thus, for Michel Foucault, a key theorist of the archive, singular acts—or "fragments" as he called them—found the archival enterprise (Foucault 1972: 147). So too for Robbins and Becher, who key their pragmatic notion of the archive to the photographic act and the variability of its reproduction. In order to reverse the defacement of the act in the name of the archive, we must resist filing Robbins and Becher's work under the heading of archival photography and instead see their photography as something actively written. One way to advance this protocol is to bracket the essentially meta-theoretical issue of the frame by way of a set of discourses that are familiar to the main lines of contemporary photographic practice. I refer to the example of the photo-book that preceded the presentational space of the gallery as a key site for the dissemination of photography. To be more precise, the *topoi* of the photo-book and the gallery wall are places where photography happens in excess of the moribund notion of the archive.

Robbins and Becher's practice leans on the models of both the photo-book and the presentational space of the gallery wall. They variously push, trouble, as well as mix and match the conventions of each. The colored frames of their various series garner another kind of significance in this context. Here, the frame functions across any one series to tie the discrete images together, much in the manner that the cover of a book works to para-textually bind the many pages of a narrative (Genette 1997). As such, the frames mark the presentational form of Robbins and Becher's photography as a kind of halfway house between the photographic image intended for the book and the photographic image intended for the wall.

Indeed, for Robbins and Becher, photography for the wall will never entirely detach itself from the form of the photo-book. In all but one of the photographic series they have produced since 1991, the scale of the images is small in comparison with contemporary trends, and, when confronted by any of these series, the viewer will inevitably read the individual photographs off one another. My point in mentioning all this is not merely to flag the fact that the act of looking and the act of reading are particularly porous things that bleed into the act of photography; I want to emphasize that Robbins and Becher's particular negotiation of the tension between the photo-book and the wall-mounted image is locked in a well-known set of generational debates that not only affected their own contemporaries, but centrally informed the work of Bernd and Hilla Becher. In its broadest sense, this tension is part and parcel of photography's slow emergence from out of the shadows of painting, via the book or photo-essay (Wall 2013: 14), to the limelight of *Photokunst* (Chevrier 1989) and, more recently, *Why Photography Matters as Art as Never Before* (Fried 2008). Granted, for a generation of younger photographers today, the particular coupling between photography and book is slightly anachronistic, given the new ties engineered between photography and computer screen. Nevertheless, I would emphasize that our encounters with all of these photographic *topoi* (and this includes the dusty archives that were Sekula's concern) should be thought of as extensions to the basic logic of the photographic act. Photography, whether keyed to the book, the wall, the screen, or the filing system, is always modeled on the reproduction of the original trigger event: the viewer steps into the shoes of the photographer and is placed beside the original event. As Barthes knew well enough from his own use of the performative, we are not returned to the past by the photograph, but only given proof that the event we see once happened ("Life/Death"; Barthes 1981: 92).[1]

Pre-photographic acts

To briefly summarize the foregoing, we can say that the photographic act, or trigger event, unfolds in two directions. In the first place, it folds out or flows downstream—as when one turns the pages of a book—to take shape as a unique set of methods of organization, codification, framing, or more simply archivization, that happen after the fact of photography; and, in the second place, it moves in a completely counterintuitive direction, opening upstream to a barely codifiable range of extant (always-already present) processes or systems of reproduction that involve filtering, indexing, focalizing, mediation, or lens work of one kind or another. Further, we should add that, if post-photographic acts blur the boundaries of reception with the making of photography, that far stranger species of pre-photographic acts turns the act of taking a photograph into a very odd act of viewing or reception. In this sense, if Robbins and Becher's paragon of the post-photographic act is grounded in the gallery context, based on a scaled-up model of the photo-book, and involves the lexicalization of singular photographs by their being strung into a photographic series (a sentence of sorts to be read), then the pre-photographic act gestures towards more obscure processes: history finding linguistic expression as the operations of mind, or vice versa—the action of mind seeing historical process as a semiotic operation. In a sense, the organization or policing of facts, which always happens in the discursive context of the book or the institutional context of the gallery, here bleeds off to the organization and policing of acts! In this highly fugitive zone patrolled by "unknown *actants*," the very possibility of taking a picture is inseparable from the problem of visibility itself (Latour 2014: 12). These operations are the processes of the archive proper: they are the ongoing, functional operations that are gestured to by the literal form the archive takes as series, book or image file. Though the processes of reproduction that follow from photography are more easily discernable, the reproductive processes that precede photography—and that provide a footing for the very system of classification that will become the visible manifestation of the archive—are given at least equal emphasis in this practice. These provide a systematic rule for the photographers to take a photograph in the first place. More crucially, these reproductive processes give their practice a purchase on the 'real'; thus, one of the recurrent tropes of Robbins and Becher's work is what they call "the transportation of place," a situation in which a geographical *topos* or place is subject to the laws of reproduction that we associate with photography (Robbins and Becher 1998). Regarding this action by which the ideological tensions of one place and time are reproduced in another place and time, they write:

> Everywhere, not only in the new world, such situations are accumulating and accepted as genuine locales. Traditional notions of place, in which culture and geographic location neatly coincide, are being challenged by legacies of slavery, colonialism, holocaust, immigration, tourism, and mass-communication. Whether the subject is Germany in Africa, Germans dressing as Native Americans, American towns dressed as Germany, New York in Las Vegas, New York in Cuba, or Cuba in exile, our interest tends to be a place out of place with its various causes and consequences.
>
> *(Robbins and Becher 2005: 81)*

What we should mark here, as the content-rich area of this collaborative team's research, are the processes through which iteration (or the action by which language is disseminated) gains a hold in the world. That is, "the transportation of place" is governed by what Derrida calls a general notion of iterability. Derrida tells us, "For something to be a sign, it must be able to be cited and repeated in all sorts of circumstances" (Culler 1997: 98). Or, more complexly:

> The status of "occurrence" or the eventhood of an event that entails in its allegedly present and singular emergence the intervention of an utterance ... can only be repetitive or citational in its structure, or rather, since those two words may lead to confusion: iterable.
>
> *(Derrida 1988: 17–18)*

In effect, then, Robbins and Becher's numerous projects provide analytics of the ways and means by which a local grammar—always an expression of power, economic interests, colonial expansion, globalization, and so on—extends or increases its sphere of influence through iteration. These are subtle processes, complexly disguised and variously smoothed out by a dominant ideology's fine-toothed comb. They operate at the micro-textual level, on a global scale, incrementally over time and they tether the political to the aesthetic in so far as these processes are part of the same weave that knots "the visible" to "the sayable and the thinkable" (Rancière 2006).

The principle semiotic chains, language systems, or linguistic knots that constitute Robbins and Becher's unique focus all have as their essential backstory some relationship of contiguity with the jackboot universalism of Germany or the gunboat capitalism of the United States of America. Most recently, their projects have zeroed in on what the artists call the Southernization of the United States, or the ways in which the South (or the old Confederacy) has managed to maintain and even extend its powers (both domestically and internationally), in spite of the historical defeats represented by the Civil War and civil rights. For Robbins and Becher, the process of Southernization is a large and broadly scattered set of practices occurring across a great many linguistic fields. They trace the process back to the reinvention of the Old South after desegregation in the 1950s and see it as part of a culture-wide process inclusive of everything from the recent run of presidents hailing from the South to the popularity of the genre of the Western film. Working within and against the variable forms of ideological closure that provide the terms of the very possibility of the visible is not the real difficulty here; rather, the crux is perceiving what is excluded from "the visible, the sayable and the thinkable" by the process of Southernization. Undoubtedly their most powerful project in this regard is *Black Cowboys*, where the busting of our collective myth of the cowboy is preceded by a general tittering set off by seeing black ones. The series sheds light on a "thriving and widespread" contemporary black cowboy culture; it plumbs one of the more startling byways of segregation in and as the history of the competitive rodeo circuit; and finally it traces our disbelief in the figure of the African American cowboy to "Hollywood's commercially-driven exclusion of black cowboys from western genre films and television" (Robbins 2010).

Crossing the lines of political correctness and brushing up against the prickliest questions of identity, stereotype, race, and creed are central to this practice, for it is a particularly tough and intractable set of issues they tackle. Maneuvering their corpus into a position in which they could poke at these ever so raw nerves has taken some time and obviously has an important relation to their own biographies. And, while Southernization itself gains momentum from the recurrent motifs of the corpus as a whole, it would seem to build upon a number of specific projects they have completed since 1991. Foremost among these is perhaps *The Americans of Samaná* (1998/2001), which focuses on the descendants of African American slaves who needed to flee to Haiti for their freedom in 1832. *Old Tucson* (1993), the film set for countless Hollywood Westerns, and *Global Village* (2003/2005), built by the global housing charity Habitat for Humanity as a "poverty theme park" in Georgia, also fall into place here. Recently, more purposeful research into Southernization also includes a number of projects pursued over the last seven years that never made the cut. These include photographs of protests in Sanford, Florida, around the Trayvon Martin shooting, rodeo photographs of black inmates at the infamous Angola State Penitentiary in Louisiana, research into the Jacksonville, Florida faction of the New Black Panthers, into Muslims in New York, and ongoing research into the descendants of a group of Confederates who left the American South for Brazil in 1865 because slavery had not been abolished there.

These forms of ideological extension through other means that Judith Butler would call "ethical violence" (Butler 2005: 5), and which Theodor Adorno would characterize as the problem of extending "moral norms of behavior" past their due date—the question of slavery in 1865, the persistence of segregation in the southern states in the 1950s, and the current incarceration rates of African American males are all historical anachronisms of this type—are part of the blind struggle for representation that is the unfolding of history (Adorno 2001: 16). Robbins and Becher's investment in Southernization hinges on an attempt to picture this otherwise invisible process of ideological creep. I should not worry about disparaging the world-historical shifts represented by abolition and desegregation by offering up in the same sentence my own preferences for Bobby Flay's barbeque sauce over say, Diana® Sauce, because Robbins and Becher's point about Southernization is precisely that the thing worms its way into the minutiae of everyday life. The humor we find in a portrait of a black cowboy is no different. Our apparently harmless surprise and chuckle at seeing these figures is a version of "ethical violence." "Collective ideas" that make claims about universality can only be "repressive and violent" (Butler 2005: 4)! These ideas are constitutive of subjectivity, which is not to say there is no room for movement. Rather, by using photography to tickle the collective ideas each one of us clings to, the idiosyncrasies of the symptom are isolated and given on the spot treatment. For the "collective ethos" always exists in tension with the concrete form in which individual morality is acted out. Hence, Adorno's emphasis elsewhere on a "Minima Moralia," which names precisely the distance from the hegemonic dominant (Adorno 1978). For Adorno as much as Butler, everything comes together around "the scene of address," which brackets the singular encounter with the other (Butler 2005: 54). The same holds for Robbins and Becher: processes such as Bavarianization, Americanization and Southernization can only be brought into visibility in the face-to-face encounter with a singular photograph from a photographic series. The differential between a collective and individual ethics is where the (future) politics of Robbins and Becher's work come into focus and, ultimately, where ethics is made habitable, or "appropriable by 'individuals in a living way'" as Butler, leaning on Adorno, puts it (Butler 2005: 5).

How exactly the artists identify what it is they will photograph—or, more succinctly, what it is that will constitute the focus of their intensive research projects and grueling travel regimes to visit entirely unremarkable sites—is one of a number of crucial questions. For example, how does one identify the processes of Southernization as manifest in and as the relatively new or emergent languages represented by the Ten Commandments monuments or Cracker Barrel Restaurants, currently popping up all across the United States? More specifically, how many monuments, restaurants, or for that matter black cowboys must one see (and, more precisely, not see or simply pass by) before one recognizes that they represent a language of one kind or another meeting the needs of a general notion of iterability, and, hence, also recognize the requirements of the three series known as *Following the Ten Commandments*, *Cracker Barrel*, and *Black Cowboys*? My line of questioning here is concerned with determining when and where the act of recall kicks in and we remember that the object seen is like another we have seen before. This inaugural moment of memory that is allegorical in nature, constitutive of each and every archive, and that establishes memory's relationship to language through iteration places serious pressure on the cause and effect relations implicit to the normative conception of the photographic act. Yet it is no less a version of the photographic act. For the salient condition at the heart of memory—or at least at the heart of each one of our own *mnemotechnic* systems (literally, memory tool or aid, but, more broadly speaking, data recovery system, index, archive, linguistic system)—depends upon the pre-emergent effects of stimuli reaching a saturation point. At some point, the pressure of the system will finally allow the registration of the self-same signs in the world; before this ceiling is reached, the landscape remains patternless and the structure of iterability invisible, but it is no less a triggering mechanism foundational to the paradigmatic photographic act.

A second aspect of this prehistory comes into focus by virtue of the special relationship between "ethical violence" and the problem of irony. Not taking black cowboys seriously is the crux of the matter: a hegemonic regime of ethics is troubled and tickled by the very existence of these individuals. Take the specific case of situational irony, which is a constant side effect of the disjunctions resulting from the "transportation of place" such as seen in *German Indians* (1997/1998), *Venice, Las Vegas* (2010–2011), *French Strip Malls (America in France)* (2003), or *Wall Street in Cuba* (1993), or the dislocation and unmooring of identity exampled in works such as *Kareem, Harlem, NY* (2010) or *Couple, Swainsboro, GA* (2010) from the *Black Cowboys* series (Figure 7.2). Irony in each of these cases raises what the artists call "the beholder's share," something the artists identify with a moment internal to reception that they believe can be harnessed (Robbins and Becher 2014a). *Doxa*, common assumptions, class constructions, or hegemonic stereotypes that we all carry in our heads enable these photographs to spur an ethical labor that Becher suggests "retraces the colonial gaze or process" (Robbins and Becher 2014a). As Robbins puts it:

> What if one could anticipate perceived 'personal' meanings that a work generates in the mind of the viewer ('feelings', cultural assumptions or stereotypes) and then transform them into a predictable outcome that 'feels' unpredictable for the viewer and 'in the doing' sheds a light on the process of reception … This flip is the grist of comedy and conceptual art: to purport to offer one thing and reveal it to be something else in the process of viewing, while making the viewer ultimately feel complicit and not ridiculed or diminished in the process.
>
> *(Robbins and Becher 2014a)*

Harnessing the viewing process in a way that both establishes comfortable access and mirrors the dominant order, yet ultimately subverts hegemony in the process of recognition, is what allows these photographers to enter into dialogue with such difficult, politically sensitive, and controversial subjects. It is what divides their work in two: they count on the fact that their symptomatic responses to a general subject such as black cowboys will be repeated in the mind of the viewer, and, second, that the viewer's encounter with, say, the specific man and woman in *Couple, Swainsboro, GA* (2010) will turn this regime on its head. For if it takes

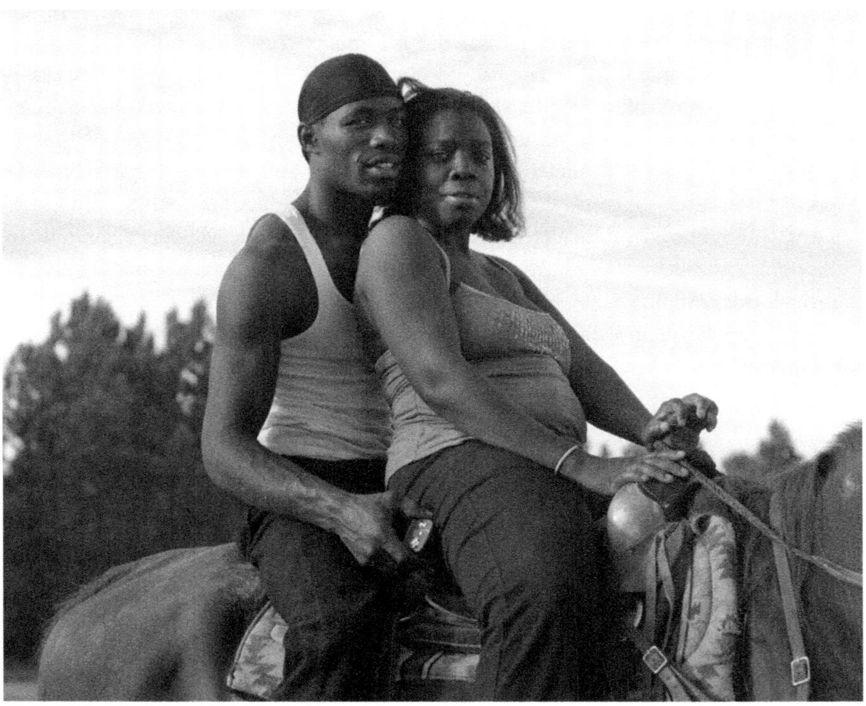

Figure 7.2 Andrea Robbins and Max Becher, *Black Cowboys: Couple, Swainsboro, GA* (2010). Courtesy the artists

but a moment to compute the do-rag, cell phone, wife beater, and bulging traps of the man, then who can resist the grace of the woman's smile and the way she leans into her man. The flip from othering to identification happens in the flash of an instant and, in this case, with the help of gender. This range of issues, which treats photography as a broadly inclusive set of event-like structures, is what compelled this collaborative team to divide their notion of the medium of photography into five versions of the photographic act. To reiterate: (1) There is "the central act of photography, the act of choosing and eliminating" what is inside from what is outside the frame, which is the darling of modernists (Szarkowski 1966: 9). (2) There is the artist's interest in the "transportation of place" that is governed by a general notion of iterability and designates a situation in which a geographical *topos* or place is subject to the laws of reproduction that we associate with photography (Robbins and Becher 1998). In the case of their wide-ranging project on Southernization, this tracking of iterative acts amounts to an attempt to keep pace with a history that is actively being written: *The Black Cowboys*, *Following the Ten Commandments*, and the *Cracker Barrel* series each take up a place in this ideological struggle for representation, which actively shapes consciousness. (3) There is what I have described as the murky prehistory of the act when memory's relationship to language has not yet reached its iterative saturation point. Here, I am thinking of the processes by which Robbins and Becher identify new subjects for series yet to come on the basis of previous research work. This is perhaps most productively thought of as the increasing pressure of the trigger finger as it closes in on a subject to shoot, such as the month-long Ramadan celebration of Washington's birthday in Laredo, Texas, or the Fourth of July celebrations of the Improved Order of Red Men in Tuckerton, New Jersey, who consider themselves the real descendants of the "Sons of Liberty"—two subjects for possible series that have emerged in the last year. (4) There is the set of acts keyed to photography's distribution and display in the photo-book and on the gallery wall. These acts of judgment turn on a process of editing down and distilling out successful photographs and syntactically arranging these in a larger series. In the broader context of contemporary photography today, these "act(s) of choosing and eliminating" easily rival Szarkowski's "central act of photography," and especially so in the case of Robbins and Becher, where each series is modeled on an act of writing and, hence, a sentence to be read. (5) Finally, as the latter suggests, there is the complex reproduction of these processes in the interpretative encounter, a multifaceted event that can only divide viewers against themselves. For, in Robbins and Becher's work, the viewer becomes one of the basic arenas where the ideological struggle for visibility takes place, and as such we catch a glimpse of the way in which ethics as a "discursive mode," rather than a "relationship between subjects" or even a "transcendental imperative," has made a home for itself in the language of photography (De Man 1979: 206).

Note

1 Barthes' performative is made clear later in Part II of *Camera Lucida*, where he "consent(s) to combine two voices, the voice of banality (to say what everyone sees and knows) and the voice of singularity (to replenish such banality with all the élan of an emotion which belonged only to myself). It was as if I were seeking the nature of a verb which had no infinitive, only tense and mode" (Barthes 1981 76).

References

Adorno, T. (1978) *Minima Moralia: Reflections on a Damaged Life*, trans. E. F. N. Jephcott, London: Verso.
Adorno, T. (2001) *Problems in Moral Philosophy*, trans. Rodney Livingstone, Stanford: Stanford University Press.

Austin, J. L. (1964) *How To Do Things With Words*, Cambridge: Harvard University Press.
Barthes, R. (1981) *Camera Lucida: Reflections on Photography*, New York: Hill & Wang.
Benjamin, W. (1968) "Unpacking My Library" in *Illuminations: Essays and Reflections*, (ed.) Hannah Arendt. New York: Schocken Books, pp. 59–67.
Berger, M. (2008) *Andrea Robbins and Max Becher: Portraits*, Center for Art, Design and Visual Culture, University of Maryland Baltimore County.
Buchloh, B. (1994) "The Architectural Uncanny in the Photographs of Andrea Robbins and Max Becher" in *Andrea Robbins and Max Becher*, (ed.) M. Catherine de Zegher. Middleburg and Kortrijk: The Kanaal Art Foundation, pp. 17–22.
Butler, J. (2005) *Giving an Account of Oneself*, New York: Fordham University Press.
Chevrier, J.-F. (1989) *Les Aventures de la forme tableau dans l'histoire de la photographie*, Photokunst exhibition catalogue, Stuttgart: Staatsgalerie Stuttgart.
Culler, J. (1997) *Literary Theory: A Very Short Introduction*, Oxford: Oxford University Press.
De Man, P. (1979) *Allegories of Reading: Figural Language in Rousseau, Nietzsche, Rilke, and Proust*, New Haven and London: Yale University Press.
Derrida, J. (1988) *Limited Inc.*, trans. Samuel Weber and Jeffrey Mehlman, Evanston: Northwestern University Press, pp. 17–18.
Derrida, J. (1995) *Archive Fever: A Freudian Impression*, trans. Eric Prenowitz, Chicago: University of Chicago Press.
Enwezor, O. (2008) *Archive Fever: Uses of the Document in Contemporary Art*, New York and Götingen: International Center of Photography and Steidl.
Foster, H. (2004) "An Archival Impulse," *October 110* (Fall), 3–22.
Foucault, M. (1972) *The Archaeology of Knowledge and the Discourse on Language*, New York: Pantheon Books.
Fried, M. (2005) "Barthes's Punctum," *Critical Inquiry*, 31:(3) (Spring), 539–574.
Fried, M. (2008) *Why Photography Matters as Art as Never Before*, New Haven: Yale University Press.
Genette, G. (1997) *Paratexts: Thresholds of Interpretation*, Cambridge: Cambridge University Press.
Latour, B. (2014) "Agency at the Time of the Anthropocene," *New Literary History*, 45, 1–18.
Lippard, L. (2006) "Out of Place" in *The Transportation of Place: Andrea Robbins and Max Becher*, (ed.) Maurice Berger. New York: Aperture Foundation.
Rancière, J. (2006) "Aesthetics and Politics: Rethinking the Link," Lecture given at the University of California, Berkeley, 2006; transcript posted on 16 Beaver Group website, www.16beavergroup.org/
Robbins, A. (2010) Correspondence with the author, March 1, 2010
Robbins, A. and Becher, M. (1998) Quoted in Hesse, Gary, "Introduction" in *Contact Sheet 98, Andrea Robbins and Max Becher: Bavarian by Law/German Indians*, Syracuse: Light Work.
Robbins, A. and Becher, M. (2005) "Andrea Robbins and Max Becher: German Indians at Bernard Toales Gallery," *Tema Celeste* (January–February), 81.
Robbins, A. and Becher, M. (2014a) Correspondence with the author, October 28, 2014
Robbins, A. and Becher, M. (2014b) *Black Cowboys*.. Available at www.robbinsbecher.com [Accessed October 23, 2014]
Sekula, A. (1986) "The Body and the Archive," *October 39* (Winter), 3–64.
Steiner, S. (2005) "Where World View and World Lines Converge: William Eggleston's Los Alamos," *Fillip*, 1 (Summer), 1–6.
Steiner, S. (2011) "Dialectical Inroads to a Post-Political Photography: Democratic Violence in the Work of Lidwien van de Ven," *Journal of the Philosophy of Photography*, 2:(1), 57–81.
Steiner, S. (2013) "Photography at a Crossroads: Studio as Genealogy, *Dispositif*, Spur," *Journal of the Philosophy of Photography*, 4:(2), Dec., 243–260.
Steiner, S. (2015) "Bernd and Hilla Becher: Spring Points, Technical Extensions, Degree Zero," *Enclave Review*, 13 (Autumn), 5–9.
Szarkowski, J. (1966) *The Photographer's Eye*, New York: The Museum of Modern Art.
Wall, J. (2013) "Introduction" in *Patrick Faigenbaum*, exhibition catalogue, co-curated by Katherine S. Bartel and Jeff Wall. Vancouver: Vancouver Art Gallery.

8

Jean Baudrillard's photography—a vision of his own strange world

Gerry Coulter

Introduction

Asked to comment about his photographs on display at the "The Ecstasy of Photography" exhibition (Institute of Modern Art, Brisbane, July–August 1994), Jean Baudrillard replied:

> I was conscious that there was something there—it was something new for me. On the one hand, I was disappointed because they seemed more aesthetic and more beautiful than I had believed them to be—and I didn't really want this aesthetic quality. On the other hand, I became more conscious of building a new vision of my own strange world.
>
> *(Baudrillard 1997a: 32 ff.)*

Photography was a strange attractor for Baudrillard (the most reluctant of artists) during the final two decades of his life: "I was always interested in the balance between the extreme banality of objects and their enigmacity" (1997a: 4). This is an extension of Baudrillard's view of philosophy and of writing, which was to discover the underlying unintelligibility of things. For him, the task of thought (including its expression in photography) was to take a world that is given to us as enigmatic and unintelligible and make it more so (Baudrillard [1999] 2001a: 151). This insight was not a recipe for nonsense for Baudrillard but an important way of resisting being drawn into rational supports for the system that exists—as most thought, including so-called 'critical theory', does. The first step toward a radical theory for Baudrillard involved a rejection of the effort to make the world either real or intelligible. As he put it to the "Baudrillard in the Mountains" Conference in Missoula, Montana, in May of 1989: "Just as the world drives to a delirious state of things, we must drive (slowly) to a delirious point of view" (quoted in Stearns and Chaloupka 1992: 26). Any rigorous or strictly coherent and organized understanding of Baudrillard's photography is a lie. I am not out to tell a lie here. Any attempt to make his images part of the system, or art, or any system, would constitute the betrayal of a friend.

The objects Baudrillard photographed—a car submerged in water (*Saint Clément*, 1987), the red salt beds (*Salins*, 1998), his own shadow projected against a wall by the setting sun

(*Punto Final*, 1997), trompe l'oeil advertising hoardings (*Rio*, 1998), graffiti during his travels (*New York*, 1997), a bicycle leaning up against a pole as though gazing into the water (Amsterdam, 1989), a broken statue of an ancient god-like figure (*Frontiera*, 1993), the impression left by the warmth of his own body on a blanket spread over a chair (*Sainte Beuve*, 1987), veil-like materials enshrouding tall building construction sites (*Rio*, 1997), a tall building with its windows bricked over (*Soho*, 1987), or the image of Place Bastille reflected upside down in a wine glass inside a restaurant (*Bastille*, 1998)—are images of the things that fascinated him.[1] In his photography, he defied the object, not unlike how he defied the concept in his writing (Baudrillard 1997a: 33). Photography for Baudrillard is an act of isolation—of excluding everything else in the world—often in a Baroque light that passes quickly in the late afternoon. If you want a coherent voice in Baudrillard's photographs, you will not find it—what you will find is the record of the fanciful moments when an object seized his attention enough for him to photograph it. While he did not wish to promote an object-based aesthetics, he did recognize that the subject does not possess all the power in any subject–object relationship. He was willing to bequeath to the object some responsibility for the fact that it was interesting enough to capture his attention and photographic effort (1997a: 38).

Photography was more than a pleasant diversion for Baudrillard and surprised even him when he came to assess how he was much more passionate for images than for texts (1997a: 37). Photography was a source of joy for Baudrillard; his photographs are records of what, ever so briefly, in a given light, gave him joy. Few things in this world were so important to him. In the end we must acknowledge that this great maker of theory was also a fine maker of images, and that each of his images was a kind of visual theorization of the world. For Baudrillard, photography was a kind of theory, different from writing, but theory all the same. The concept may ultimately be unrepresentable but so too is the image ultimately inexplicable. Between them is an insuperable distance. As a result, the image is always nostalgic for the text, and the text nostalgic for the image (Baudrillard [2000] 2003a: 2).

Contemporary thought is rich in understandings of concepts and of images but not in the poetic relationship between the two. From Baudrillard's writing on photography, we may better understand the poetic, mutual longing that concept and the image hold for each other. In so doing, we may better experience the seductive unintelligibility and enigmaticalness of both concepts and images. Even Baudrillard was deeply challenged by his own traversal of this very difficult and little-explored terrain. For many years, he maintained that his own writings and photographs shared no direct connection, but in the last decade of his life he came to see things differently:

> I know a little about photography ... but not very much. I came to it as a diversion or a hobby [...] and yet at the same time, it was also something serious, in the sense that it offered an alternative to writing—it was a completely different activity which came from elsewhere and had no connection with writing [...] finally I realized that there was a relation between the activity of theoretical writing and the activity of photography, which at the beginning seemed utterly indifferent to me, but it's the same process of isolating something in a kind of empty space, and analyzing it within that space, rather than interpreting it.
>
> *(Baudrillard 1997a: 34)*

Baudrillard began to take photographs in the mid-1980s and at first made no effort to theorize them. Although his writings and photographs originate from different desires—one to write a text, the other to write with light (Butler 2005)—there exists a point of connection between them. I think it was largely an accidental yet unavoidable connection, and Baudrillard only became aware of it very late in his life. It has everything to do with the poetic relationship existing between concepts and images. Baudrillard's thought on photography serves to illuminate his work as a whole because a point of richness exists between his written texts and his photography—both work to make the world more unintelligible and enigmatic. As such, Baudrillard's images possess a vital point of intersection at the core of his own thought on philosophy and theory.

Baudrillard's photographs may be viewed as another way for thinking the world against truth, meaning, the paradigm, or the real in favor of the unintelligible and enigmatic. A Baudrillardian photograph, whatever else it is, rebukes aesthetics and theories of scientific objectivity for assessing the photograph: "What I bemoan is the aestheticization of photography, its having become one of the fine arts, the photographic image, by its technical essence, came from somewhere beyond, or before, aesthetics" (Baudrillard 1999: 139–140). This is something a Baudrillardian image and Barthes' writing in *Camera Lucida* share. Indeed, I argue that one of the markers of the end of aesthetics and scientific objectivity in our time is the Baudrillardian photograph. The photograph is not merely theory but holds dramatic implications for how we think about theory and images.

Photographing an enigmatic world

> Consider the way the camera is used now. Its possibilities are no longer those of the subject who 'reflects' the world according to his personal vision; rather, they are the possibilities of the lens, as exploited by the object. The camera is thus a machine that vitiates all will, erases all intentionality and leaves nothing but the pure reflex needed to take pictures. Looking itself disappears without a trace, replaced by a lens now in collusion with the object—and hence with an inversion of vision.
>
> *(Baudrillard [1990] 1993: 56)*

To accept the world as unintelligible and enigmatic and to experience the joy and poetry of writing it (and photographing it) are defining characteristics of Baudrillard's later life. Photographs for Baudrillard are, like writing, a response to the world—a way of theorizing it. Baudrillard's photographs (like his writings) are traces of his thinking—light writings left behind by the moment of an object demanding the attention of a specific subject at a particular angle. Many, if not all, of his photographs, the ones he allowed us to see, as well as his writing, could be placed around a single question:

> 'Why is there nothing rather than something?' There is, ultimately, no answer to this, since the nothing originates in myth, in the original crime, whereas the something originates in what, by convention, we call reality. Now, the real is never sure. The question then becomes, not 'Where does illusion come from?', but 'Where does the real come from?' How is it that there is even a reality effect? That is the true enigma. If the world was real, how is it that it did not become rational long ago? If it is merely illusion, how can a discourse of reality and the rational even arise? But that is the question. Is there anything but a discourse of the real and the rational?
>
> *(Baudrillard [1995] 1996: 13)*

Baudrillard's photographs participate in a superior form of irony that he discussed in his writings even before he took up photography:

> Everything can be summed up in this: let's believe for a single instant the hypothesis that there is a fatal and enigmatic bias in the order of things. In any case, there is something stupid about our current situation. There's something stupid in the raw event, to which destiny, if it exists, could not be insensible. There's something stupid in the current forms of truth and objectivity that a superior irony could spare us.
>
> *([1983] 1990: 191)*

The desire to photograph and to write both appealed to similar aspects of how Baudrillard's mind worked. And Baudrillard's mind operated in a singular way, as his writing on seduction illustrates:

> The act of thinking is an act of seduction which aims to deflect the world from its being and its meaning—at the risk of being itself seduced and led astray. This is how theory proceeds [...] The object of theory is to arrive at an account of the system which follows out its internal logic to its end, without adding anything, yet which, at the same time, totally inverts that system, revealing its hidden non-meaning, the Nothing which haunts it, that absence at the heart of the system, that shadow running alongside it. [...] To duplicate the world is to respond to a world which signifies nothing with a theory which, for its part, looks like nothing on earth.
>
> *([1999] 2001a: 150)*

Baudrillard's photographs do not originate from the same source as his writing, but they are a way of theorizing an unintelligible and enigmatic world as even more unintelligible and enigmatic. And, when one of them does not increase the world's unintelligibility and enigmaticalness, we think it certainly does nothing to remove these qualities from the world. A Baudrillardian photograph offers us no more ultimate truth or meaning than does his writing. If anything, there is an effect of unraveling and often something mystifying about them.

There is often a quality of slowness at work in Baudrillard's photography and a sense of light and time being observed. Perhaps Baudrillard's photography, like his writing, resolves the world in ways which make it only vaguely recognizable—a world that looks like nothing in this world or that of mainstream professional photography. Further, his photographs often undermine the day-to-day visual truth we think we find in the world, and quite often nothing could be further from the 'truth' than a Baudrillardian photograph, despite the fact he used film (not a digital camera) and did not retouch his images.

Baudrillard resisted being led astray by language and the false security much of the philosophical tradition places in it. For him, as in Lacan, "language is not the reflection of meaning, it is there in place of meaning" ([1992] 1994: 92). From a thinker who took very seriously the idea "we no longer have any standards of truth or objectivity, but a scale of probability" ([2000] 2002: 85–6), we should not be surprised to find photographs that view the space between the true and false as one of random distribution. The world Baudrillard finds, the world that theory must precede, is a world where the real hides behind appearances, leaving us with the "gossamer thin difference between illusion and the real" (Baudrillard [1995] 1997b: 63).

Baudrillard's photographs are not the work of a pessimist but of a thinker for whom reality, like God, may well exist; he simply did not believe in either. Baudrillard's satisfaction rests in his understanding that it is precisely the unintelligibility of the world and its enigmaticalness that saves us from ourselves—as meaning givers:

> Do we absolutely have to choose between meaning and non-meaning? But the point is precisely that we do not want to. The absence of meaning is no doubt intolerable, but it would be just as intolerable to see the world assume a definitive meaning.
>
> *(Baudrillard [1999] 2001a: 128)*

Thought, for Baudrillard, assumed a catastrophic role:

> For me, thinking is radical in so far as it does not claim to prove itself, to verify itself in some reality or other. This does not mean that it denies the existence of that reality, that it is indifferent to its impact, but that it regards it as essential to keep itself as an element in a game whose rules it knows. The only fixed point is the undecidable and the fact that it will remain so, and the aim of the entire work of thought is to preserve that. ... Thought must play a catastrophic role ... concerned for the human, and, to that end, recapture the reversibility of good and evil, of the human and the inhuman.
>
> *(Baudrillard 2003b: 91–2)*

As writing was no more or less than a challenge to the real (Baudrillard [1977] 1987: 124), photography, as Baudrillard's photographs illustrate, could participate in the same game. Baudrillard's photographs, like his theoretical writings, precede the world—accelerating terminal processes. In them, as in his writings, a catastrophe of meaning is anticipated. The real cannot be written nor can it be photographed. What are written and photographed are the appearances behind which the real hides (the original illusion; Baudrillard 2000: 59 ff.).

Baudrillard's enigmatic car in the water (*Saint Clément*, 1987) can make us think about the catastrophe not of the car, but of all technological civilization. The drowned car is in ecstasy, its entire presence denoting an absence, a catastrophe in slow motion as it dissolves into the water. This photograph of a car evokes slowness, inertia, the absurdity and ultimate unintelligibility of progress, and of the nothing that underlies everything—the nothing that haunts modernity represented here by one of its greatest objects of fascination and desire, the motorcar. Like the world as a whole, this car in water will never be 'understood'; it is an image that raises doubt, at most a fragment that stands in for an ambiguous reality. Similarly, Baudrillard's enigmatic photograph of an empty red chair (*Sainte Beuve*, 1987) is a portrait of absence, of the impression left by a warm body on a cold blanket pressed into the chair by the weight of the body over time. It is an image of absence in ecstasy—a compelling emptiness, a fragment of the nothingness each of our lives traverses.

Baudrillard's *Salins* (1998) is like a photograph from another planet—one where the color of everything is not what we expect. The traditional directness and sentimentality of the landscape photograph is traded for a glimpse of the appearance of a world strange to formal landscape photography. *Salins* possesses the unintelligible quality of looking like nothing on earth, but it is precisely a fragment of the earth—not the earth that landscape photography has taught us to look for.

Perhaps it was Baudrillard's lack of formal photographic training that made his point of view possible. His photographs record moments of recognition that the real was near but the real never passes through the appearances behind which it hides. His photographs also partake of an indispensable quality of the enigmatic, its worrying and gloomy aspect—the dismal part of the enigma, the part that makes us feel as though something is very wrong. Yet, upon closer inspection, all is right in the world he photographed; what is wrong, what has been violated, is our expectation that the landscape image be comforting and agreeable. It is precisely this disagreeable quality that tweaks the unintelligibility factor in each photograph, forcing us to look beyond traditional photographic explanations of landscape.

For example, the unreality of the world of appearances is present in Baudrillard's *Bastille* (1998)—a photograph of the outside world reflected upside down in a glass of wine on a restaurant table. It reminds me that photography subjects the world to an anamorphosis, the gaze of a particular subject's position from a particular angle. Baudrillard as photographer was something of a mannerist—and this too is an undiscussed aspect of much of his writing. Any conception of truth, meaning, or the real is stretched and elongated while interpretation is denied in favor of brief illuminations and fragments of a world we thought we knew. For Baudrillard, the object 'takes' you, and one moves away quickly as from a scene where one has been apprehended for a moment by a question. *Bastille* is enigmatic in that it is almost baffling. It reminds us that everything we see is preceded by our training to understand it—that theory precedes the world. A quality that the images described here share is perhaps a desire on the part of the photographer to escape from meaning, to appreciate the fragments of the world, those perfect little singularities of light and color at the moment just before meaning is given, the moment of the closing of the shutter. In doing so, Baudrillard made us aware of our role as givers of meaning and the fact that it is the horizon of the object which we inhabit. The object gives no meaning of its own; as such, it can fascinate and seduce the subject:

> The object is what has disappeared on the horizon of the subject, and it is from the depths of this disappearance that it envelops the subject in its fatal strategy. It is the subject that then disappears from the horizon of the object.
>
> *(Baudrillard [1983] 1990: 113–14)*

We often like to think that objects only exist for us, but one thing we are constantly reminded of by Baudrillard is that neither subject nor object are possible without the other. It is the object that thinks us—it is the lens that focuses on us (Baudrillard [1999] 2001a: 89; see also Butler 2005). It is precisely the enigmatic quality of his photography that drove this awareness of seeing ourselves through the object, and it is this quality that perhaps best describes the yearning of Baudrillard's text and images for each other. Rather than the traditional photographic posture of supplying us with an image that fits into predefined categories, the photographs of Baudrillard baffle categorization and, in so doing, highlight the interpretive act of looking at a photograph. By forcing us to ask, "Is this what I think it is?" the moment of our awareness of the unintelligibility of the image is opened. It is this moment that frustrates notions of scientific objectivity and aesthetic theory—highlighting the personal nature of photography and its consumption that is at the core of Barthes' concept of *punctum*, as we will see in the next section.

Baudrillard's photograph *Toronto* (1994) is a perfect singularity, speaking to the presence and necessity of darkness to the writing of light. In it, the shadow of a man projected onto a white gas station wall follows him as he quietly retreats to the doorway. At the same time, our attention is pulled to the left of the photograph where a red truck races into the picture only a few feet from where the photographer is closing his lens. The image depends entirely upon darkness for its particular writing of light. The darkness of the deep-purple stormy sky over the gas station and the darkness of the shadows on the wall give Baudrillard's photograph a striking contrast with the harsh baroque light from the low-lying sun which writes the shadows on the wall. An impressive duality is created between points of light and points of darkness. The speeding truck in Baudrillard's photograph sends the light back in the opposite direction—into the lens. The duality of these images, which is an accidental quality, echoes in the multi-directionality of light. In *Toronto*, the light that writes the world is not merely the light writing of the photograph, but also its object. This is a quality that many of the photographs of Baudrillard share—a sense that photography is not merely the writing of light, but a meditation on this light writing, however brief and unsustainable during the moment just before the shutter closes. Other effects in these photographs are no doubt also the unintended and accidental outcomes of this meditation.

Baudrillard's photographs capture an essential irony of light writing, that darkness and gloom (the lack of light) are what highlights its presence. So, too, in (written) theory, where a passage through darkness, melancholy, and gloom bordering on nihilism is what often leads us to our own accord with the world and a kind of contentment with its indifference toward us. Imperfect light, often believed to be fatal to good photography, here make it possible. Similarly, in photography, the scarcity of light, or its obscurity, becomes essential to the enigmatic quality of the light writing. Light writing depends on the writing of darkness, of gloom, of the dismal and the obscure that rests at the heart of the enigma that is any photographic fragment of the world. Baudrillard photographed the world's indifference to us. It is this indifference, this sense that the world operates completely independent of us, that is more beautiful than the images themselves.

Baudrillard's *Punto Final* (1997) highlights the deeper nature of photography—that any photograph is never of any 'real' world, but, rather, is a record of the momentary appearances behind which the real hides. This is the enigmatic and unintelligible quality of the world and it is the product of every effort by every photographer to photograph the world. The difference with it and most other photographs of the world is that appearances are the intended target of the photographic lens. In *Punto Final*, Baudrillard photographs his own shadow projected onto a stucco wall by the bright sun setting behind him. The subject is the gossamer-thin difference between the world of shadows and the real. Our physical universe is thus photographed as light written on surfaces, without which we would be without appearances and our visual conception of the real. The story of visual existence (for sighted people), and its concept of the real, is very much the story of the writing of light. Shadows and ghostlike images represent the real, truth, and meaning in these photographs as their very concepts are liquidated. Light is the principle subject of the photograph as it is a central constituent of our ability to know, and be deceived by, the universe. *Punto Final* is an image concerning the act of seeing that rests at the core of photography.

Baudrillard's photographs serve to remind us that the "real is merely a simulation, a model for regulating and ordering the radical becoming, the radical illusion, of the world and its appearances; for reducing any internal singularity—of events, beings or things—to the common denominator of reality" (Baudrillard [1997] 1998: 69). This is as good a reason for taking photographs as any other—maybe the best one we have.

Many of Baudrillard's photographs record an absence. Most photographers aim to capture something rather than nothing. In his effort to write nothingness with light, his images, like his texts, ask us to look for less, less meaning and less to believe in, and to find contentment there in a world that always seems to be asking us to find more. If it is important for us to have things in which not to believe, then Baudrillard's photographs may be portraits of a world that defies belief.

I have no desire to define fully what it is that constitutes a Baudrillardian image, but, in the making of this article, certain questions inevitably arise that allow both author and reader to gather thoughts under the term 'Baudrillardian photograph'. It is doubtful that any kind of precise definition of 'Baudrillardian' is achievable, and, if one were possible, it would only constitute a danger. We can, at best, point to some problems and difficulties while allowing similarities in Baudrillard's writing and Baudrillardian images to speak for themselves—to cast a light on one another. It is the fact that they refuse to do more than this that serves to increase their value against truth and meaning. We find that both speak to the world's ultimate unintelligibility and enigmaticalness, accelerate terminal processes, and, as such, represent the catastrophe of meaning. Writing with light, like writing with a pen, constitutes a separate but related effort to speak to a world that is unintelligible and enigmatic, by making it even more unintelligible, even more enigmatic. Baudrillard makes no effort to duplicate the world in his images, and, as in his theoretical writings, the result is usually something that looks unlike anything on earth. The world is what it is to us because we have theorized it as such; theory, whose task it is to challenge the world's appearances, always precedes 'the world':

> The radical illusion is that of the original crime, by which the world is altered from the beginning, and is never identical to itself, never real. The world exists only through this definitive illusion which is that of the play of appearances—the very site of the unceasing disappearance of all meaning and all finality. And this is not merely metaphysical: in the physical order, too, from its origin—whatever that may be—the world has been forever appearing and disappearing.
>
> *(Baudrillard [1995] 1996: 85)*

And so, "at the heart of the photographic image there's a figure of nothingness, of absence, of unreality" (Baudrillard [1997] 1998: 93). Baudrillard says that the magic of photography comes from allowing the object to do all the work. For him, the object seduces us, calling upon us to photograph it as opposed to everything else around it (Baudrillard [1995] 1996: 86–7). Ultimately, photography involves the writing of light for Baudrillard: "no matter which photographic technique is used, there is always one thing, and one thing only, that remains: the light. Photo-graphy: The writing of light [...] this light is the very imagination of the image" (Baudrillard 2001b: n.p.). As such, the mutual yearning of text and image becomes a very complex business for Baudrillard and one that calls upon Barthes' understanding of *punctum*.

Barthes, the *punctum*, and Baudrillard's photography

The singular illusion in which the photographs of Baudrillard, like his texts, participate is an effort to live in a world that is indifferent to us. Here, the role of theory is neither to explain nor clarify, but to highlight, and if possible deepen, an unintelligibility and enigmaticalness already present in a world that hides behind appearances. The task of this photography, like writing, is to function as theory. At their respective best, both theory and photography lose their meaning at their limits, and this does not happen often enough; when it does, the photograph and the theoretical text do not participate in some truth-building exercise (Baudrillard [1977] 1987: 38). A provocative logic comes into play, one that recognizes that we can no longer occupy the space of truth ([1977] 1987: 129–30). Here, photography, like theory, can serve as a challenge to the real—a challenge to the real to expose itself as illusion. The photographs of Baudrillard highlight uncertainty—the only certainty we know. Photography, then, the 'Baudrillardian variety', is like theory, a kind of simulation—both simulation and challenge ([1977] 1987: 133). A striking thing that many of Baudrillard's photographs share is that the *punctum* of each of the photographs selected here can participate in a kind of simulation akin to Baudrillard's theory where the unintelligibility and enigmaticalness of the world are the subject.

Roland Barthes, like Baudrillard, understood photography to be an uncertain art (Barthes [1979] 1980: 18). In *Camera Lucida*, Barthes gives us the concepts of *punctum* and *studium*. The *studium*, or "the average effect," is a general enthusiasm that one has about photographs and photography—the *studium* is what allows us to share an interest in many different photographs and photographers, although it is highly unlikely that we will like all of the work of any one photographer ([1979] 1980: 26). *Punctum* is an accident in any particular photo; it is the point where it interests me more than any of the others. Barthes describes it as "a cut, a little hole, the accident which pricks me, but also bruises me, is poignant to me, a wound" ([1979] 1980: 26). For Barthes, the photograph is pure contingency, existing outside meaning.

Barthes says: "I imagine that the essential gesture of the operator is to surprise something or someone and that this gesture is therefore perfect when performed unbeknownst to the subject being photographed" ([1979] 1980: 32). Later, Barthes writes that he is "too much of a phenomenologist to like anything but appearances," and this is a liking he shares with Baudrillard. In Barthes' words: "the object speaks; it induces us, vaguely, to think. ... photography is subversive not when it frightens, repels, or even stigmatizes, but when it is pensive, when it thinks" ([1979] 1980: 38). Baudrillard's photographs not only record the capturing of light, but at the same time have been seized by that light (Baudrillard 1999: 146). On the *punctum* Barthes also says that:

> occasionally a detail attracts me, this detail is the punctum. I feel that its mere presence changes my reading, that I am looking at a new photograph, marked in my eyes with a higher value ... very often the punctum is a detail, a partial object ... the punctum shows no preference for morality or good taste, the punctum can be ill-bred ... paradoxically, the punctum, while remaining a detail, fills the whole picture ... the detail which interests me is not intentional and probably cannot be so.
>
> *(Barthes [1979] 1980: 42–7)*

How might we apply Barthes' concept of the *punctum* to Baudrillard's photographs? First, we should look for the unintentional details of these photographs—the details that fill the whole picture. This is, as Barthes stresses, a deeply personal undertaking. In *Saint Clèment*, the *punctum*, for me, is in the bubbles emerging from under the hood at lower right as representing some kind of last gasp of the car, or perhaps even the civilization that brought such a beautiful catastrophe into existence. In *Sainte Beuve*, I see the *punctum* in the long serpentine crease pressed into the blanket on the chair, which denotes absence. That point where the person is no longer present remains present to us. In *Bastille*, the *punctum* occurs at the moment when I realize that I know the location appearing upside down in the glass (Place Bastille in Paris). In *Toronto*, the *punctum* is the shadow of the man following him faithfully along the wall. This is also supplanted very quickly by a second *punctum*, the truck roaring silently into the frame—a rare experience of double *punctum* in one image. In *Punto Final*, the *punctum* is to be found, for me, in the texture and depth of the shadow of Baudrillard projected onto the wall. It appears thick, as if painted in asphalt.

Baudrillard refused formal photographic training, preferring to operate as a 'primitive' in his own culture. This is a characteristic Barthes recognizes himself as he analyzes photographs: "I am a primitive ... I dismiss all knowledge, all culture; I refuse to inherit anything from another eye than my own" (Barthes [1979] 1980: 51). For Barthes, the *punctum*:

> can be revealed after the fact, when the photograph is no longer in front of me ... the punctum is what I add to the photograph and what is nonetheless already there ... the punctum then, is a kind of subtle beyond—as if the image launched desire beyond what it permits us to see.
>
> *(Ibid.: 52–9)*

This describes precisely my own experience of the *punctum* in these Baudrillardian photographs. Perhaps for you, no wound?

Conclusion

> [I]t is the scene that demands to be photographed, and you are merely part of the décor in the pictorial order it dictates, the subject is no more than the funnel through which things in their irony make their appearance.
>
> *(Baudrillard [1990] 1993: 153)*

Barthes reminds us, against aesthetics and science, that we know only deep within ourselves the reasons why we like one photograph more than others (even of the same photographer). Writing of a photograph of his mother as a child in a winter garden, Barthes tells us that, "it would tell me what constituted that thread which drew me toward photography" (Barthes [1979] 1980: 73). This solitary photograph is, for Barthes, deeply personal. He tells us he cannot reproduce it in his book because:

> It exists only for me. For you it would be nothing but an indifferent picture, one of thousands of manifestations of the 'ordinary'; it cannot in any way constitute the visible object of a science; it cannot establish an objectivity, in the positive sense of the term; at most it would interest your studium: period, clothes, photogeny; but in it, for you, no wound.
>
> *([1979] 1980: 73)*

Like all writings on photography that share a Barthesian spirit, this essay offers a personal exploration of my own reaction to Baudrillard's photographic theory. Photography suffers when reduced to aesthetics and dies when reduced to science. The *punctum* is personal. This is why only part of its argument will find appeal with some readers, many of whom will find no *punctum* in any of the photographs discussed in this article. It is quite possible that I am the only person who will find the *punctum* I do in these photographs. If you do not find a *punctum* in them, they will remain at the level of *studium*, at the level of cultural interest at best. This article, then, like Barthes' *Camera Lucida*, is simply the record of our experience of "that unexpected flash which sometimes crosses this field of the studium" and it continues on to press owing to the patient tolerance of Baudrillard's images which consent, only somewhat reluctantly, to this treatment. The reader may decide for him/herself what is good, or what is beautiful, and I can only point to some interesting ways in which Baudrillard's writings and photographs cast a revealing light on one another. To appreciate a photograph as Barthes does is to stand in a world where aesthetics and science no longer exist. We are truly on our own, but is this not the case with any text? Perhaps this is the most important message we can take from assessing Baudrillard's images, that in photographs, as in writing, there is always a secret to be preserved (Baudrillard [1997] 1998: 89)—an unintelligibility and enigmaticalness that make both worthwhile.

I do not want to have to choose between meaning and non-meaning. Baudrillard's photography and both his and Barthes' writings remind me that, "the absence of meaning is no doubt intolerable, but it would be just as intolerable to see the world assume a definitive meaning" (Baudrillard [1999] 2001a: 128). When the Baudrillardian photograph and Barthes' notion of the *punctum* as personal occupy privileged places in theory, the terrorism of the disciplines, with their efforts to centralize and codify meaning, evaporates.

Photographs are vestiges of what remains after everything else is taken away: Baudrillard also wrote: "Every photographed object is merely the trace left by the disappearance of everything else. From the summit of this objective exceptionality absent from the rest of the world, you have an unbeatable view of the world" (Baudrillard [1995] 1996: 85). They float upon the nothing, after everything but our ability to read is taken away, and they are stronger than the will of aesthetics to control them or science to dissect them, and it is our interpretive abilities that lend to them a certain power. Objects, colors, light, and substance do not have a sentimental aura, and it is through photography that we can "add to the magical fact of their indifference, to the innocence of their staging, and thus bring out what is embodied in them: the objective illusion and subjective disillusion of the world" (Baudrillard [1995] 1997b: 96). Through images such as those shown here, the world "asserts its discontinuity, its fragmentation, its artificial instantaneousness ... photographs are a continuity of fragments ... merely the refraction of the world" (Baudrillard 1999: 130–31). Placed before photography as understood by Barthes and his concept of *punctum*, a concept that suited Baudrillard, science and aesthetics dissolve into the enigma and the void.

Each photograph by Baudrillard discussed in this chapter is intended to rouse a feeling of a kind of ecstasy—the ecstasy of the world of appearances disappearing into the lens of the camera. The photography of Baudrillard, like each of us as readers, and like Barthes with his *punctum*, stands alone and unarmed (Barthes [1979] 1980: 7). This is not a position occupied without moments of fear and frenzy, but it is, ultimately, as close to a feeling of freedom as we are allowed to feel, existing as we do along the horizon of the object. For Baudrillard, unknown even to himself for many years, photography can, like writing, work as theory in our efforts to poetically resolve the world. Photography in this view is not representation; like writing, like all theory, it is a fiction (Baudrillard [1999] 2001a: 142). Photography, or the writing of light, is thus simultaneously both a humbling and liberatory act. It becomes even more so when we acknowledge that, in photography, it is the object that does all the work. Everything else depends on our subjective vision—somewhere beyond, or before, aesthetics and science.

> There is perhaps but one fatal strategy and only one: theory. And doubtless the only difference between a banal theory and a fatal theory is that in one strategy the subject still believes himself to be more cunning than the object, whereas in the other the object is considered more cunning, cynical, talented than the subject, for which it lies in wait. The metamorphoses, the ruses, the strategies of the object surpass the subject's understanding.
>
> *([Baudrillard [1983] 1990: 181)*

After more than a decade of taking photographs, Baudrillard came to recognize one of photography's more radical implications—that, like writing, photography can isolate the object in a "kind of empty space" where it may be analyzed. As such, he slowly discovered, without intending to, that photography can be theory (Baudrillard [1997] 1998: 34).

Note

1 It is not possible to publish Baudrillard's images here, but many are available to view online. See, for example: www.ilsole24ore.com/art/SoleOnLine4/Tempo%20libero%20e%20Cultura/2009/04/fotografia-europea-baudrillard-gallery.shtml?uuid=afc3081c-2c25-11de-a184-094ac40c53f5&refresh_ce=1; *Saint Clément*, 1987, *Salins*, 1998, *Punto Final*, 1997—https://artphotobook.wordpress.com/2015/10/23/jean-baudrillard-photographies-1985-1998/; *Bastille*, 1998, and *Sainte Beuve*, 1987—http://chateaushatto.com/exhibition/ultimate-paradox-the-photography-of-jean-baudrillard/; *Toronto*, 1994—www2.ubishops.ca/baudrillardstudies/vol3_2/haladyn.htm

References

Barthes, R ([1979] 1980) *Camera Lucida*, New York: Hill & Wang.

Baudrillard, J. ([1977] 1987) *Forget Foucault—Forget Baudrillard*, New York: Semiotexte (ed.) Sylvere Lotringer.

Baudrillard, J. ([1983] 1990) *Fatal Strategies: Revenge of the Crystal*, trans. unknown, New York: Semiotexte/Pluto Press.

Baudrillard, J. ([1990] 1993) *The Transparency of Evil: Essays on Extreme Phenomena*, trans. James Benedict, New York: Verso.

Baudrillard, J. ([1992] 1994) *The Illusion of the End*, trans. Chris Turner, Stanford: Stanford University Press.

Baudrillard, J. ([1995] 1996) *The Perfect Crime*, trans. Chris Turner, New York: Verso.

Baudrillard, J. (1997a) *Art and Artefact*, (ed.) Nicholas Zurbrugg, trans. Nicholas Zurbrugg and Associates, New York: Sage.

Baudrillard, J. ([1995] 1997b) *Fragments: Cool Memories III—1990–1995*, trans. Emily Agar, New York: Verso.

Baudrillard J. ([1997] 1998) *Paroxysm: Interviews with Philippe Petite*, trans. Chris Turner, New York: Verso.

Baudrillard, J. (1999) *Photographies: 1985–1998*, Ostfildren-Ruit, Germany: Hatje-Cantz.

Baudrillard, J. (2000) *The Vital Illusion*, (ed.) Julia Witwer, New York: Columbia University Press.

Baudrillard, J. ([1999] 2001a) *Impossible Exchange*, trans. Chris Turner, New York: Verso.

Baudrillard, J. (2001b) "Photography, or the Writing of Light" in *Ctheory.net* (December). www.ctheory.net/articles.aspx?id=126 [Accessed June 9, 2016].

Baudrillard, J. ([2000] 2002) *Screened Out*, trans. Chris Turner, New York: Verso.

Baudrillard, J. ([2000] 2003a) *Cool Memories IV*, trans. Chris Turner, New York: Verso.

Baudrillard, J. (2003b) *Passwords*, trans. Chris Turner, New York: Verso.

Butler, R. (2005) "Baudrillard's Light Writing or Photographic Thought", *International Journal of Baudrillard Studies*, Volume 2: Number 1 (January): www.ubishops.ca/baudrillardstudies/vol2_1/butler.htm [Accessed June 9, 2016].

Stearns, W. and W. Chaloupka (1992) *The Disappearance of Art and Politics*, New York: Macmillan.

9

Visual episodic memory and the neurophenomenology of digital photography

Jill Bennett

A passage from Hilary Mantel's 1995 novel *An Experiment in Love* serves as an epigraph for this essay:

> Once you have begun remembering—isn't this so?—one image springs another; they run through your head in all directions, scampering animals flushed from coverts. Memory's not a reel, not a film you can run backwards and forwards at will: it's that flash of startled fur, the slither of silk between the fingers, the duplicated texture of hair or bone. It's an image blurring, caught on the move: as if in one of my family snapshots, taken before cameras got so foolproof that any fool could capture the moment.
>
> (Hilary Mantel 1995: 11)

Introduction

It is a paradox of human visual memory that it unfolds in time and yet seems to have more in common with still photographs than with the moving image. If ever this affinity were to be tested, it is now, in the age of smartphones and wearable action cameras, when video is as accessible as still photography. In fact, however, evidence emerging in experimental psychology, discussed below, indicates that certain forms of digital photograph are highly 'cognitively compatible' with human memory. They not only embody or represent memories but interact with memory processes in powerful ways, now verified by neuro-imaging.

This essay focuses on photographs produced by wearable automatic cameras and also phone cameras, attending to their subjective point of view and to how this links to memory. In contradistinction to analog photography, digital photography has been described as 'post-medium'. That is to say, it is reproducible and manipulable, and cannot be said to embody an indexical 'trace' of a real-world event in the way that was claimed for photochemically produced images. Digital photography has also engendered new ways of viewing and interacting with images, now rountinely encountered on screen. Both these factors must be taken into account in a phenomenology of digital photography.

A rich phenomenological tradition going back to Walter Benjamin has advanced analysis of the interactions between viewer and analog photograph. We are now at a juncture where diverse paradigms may start to converge in the study of memory and photography, not only owing to the shift from analog to digital, but with data emerging from neuropsychological studies of the use of photography. This essay examines the relationship between memory and photography, reflecting on my empirical work in collaboration with cognitive neuropsychologists. It anticipates the development of a new strand of thought that focuses on the felt experience of memory and cognitive process: a neurophenomenology that elucidates our interactions with digital photography.

Linking photography and memory

A means of recording events and of registering the photographer's presence at the scene, photography provides a functional analog for both episodic memory (memory associated with a particular time and place; Tulving 1983) and its subset of autobiographical memory (memory linking to the self; Conway 2005). It is, in turn, a means of activating memory: photographs can serve as external memory aids, or what cognitive psychologists call cues for memory retrieval.

Yet the metaphoric resonance between memory and photography rests as much on photography's limits and deficiencies as on its merits as a recording technology. A photograph captures a moment, a single time-slice rather than an event's unfolding in time; it can illuminate but also blur; it preserves but also wrenches the event from its temporal context. It is always a fragment.

The novelist Hilary Mantel's description of memory as a blurred snapshot evokes the qualities and experience of involuntary memory—the form of memory first described by Marcel Proust in *À la recherche du temps perdu* (*Remembrance of Things Past*; Proust 1961). Unlike memories mined at will, involuntary memory irrupts into consciousness—experienced as a flash, often triggered by a sensory cue. Photographs are themselves effective memory cues (as discussed below). For Proust, the mnemonic cue was the famous madeleine cake, a memory image suffused with sensation, establishing an embodied connection to place and to things past—things that might otherwise remain inaccessible to memory. Mantel focuses not on the trigger, but on the texture and feeling of the unfolding memory—its speed and dynamics. Images springing one from another, each imprinted with sensation: a set of rapidly self-compositing images rather than a seamless movie. Insisting that memory is closer to the still photograph than to film or video in this regard, Mantel locates the memory image in the pre-digital era of instamatic cameras, when 'Kodak moments' came back to us from developers in folders of prints—multiples of 12, of varying results. Memory, she suggests, feels like an image that now scarcely survives—the unintentionally blurred print that is today quickly and efficiently deleted at source.

If 'foolproof' digital cameras have not completely eradicated the blur, they have so dramatically expanded the reach and volume of personal photography that it matters less. An event is no longer condensed into a single print or limited to a film reel of 12, economically paced shots. At no extra expense, we produce near-identical multiples—a functional advantage that has effectively changed the way that we encounter personal photography. Unlike their predecessors, which nearly always took form as unique prints, digital photographs are stored electronically and viewed *en masse* as a data set. The discrete image that may in the past have been deliberately assembled into an album is now browsed via archiving software that enables relatively fast scanning or scrolling through sequences of images, and potentially many variations of the same image. This new condition of viewing may, by serendipity, bring the photograph even closer to the experience of human memory.

More is more

A form of everyday photography, emerging in the early 2000s, evinces the full effects of this shift from isolated images to the digital data set. Lifelogging refers to the continuous photo-documentation of everyday life and is associated primarily with small, wearable automatic cameras, such as the SenseCam invented in the Microsoft research labs in 1999 and the subsequent Autographer (Plate 11). Conceived as a "human black box recorder," SenseCam was designed to take photographs approximately every 30 seconds, or whenever a change in setting or conditions was detected by its sensors (Hodges et al. 2011; Wood et al. 2004). Hung around the neck on a lanyard or clipped to a lapel, the automatic camera functions unobtrusively without either the effort of deliberation or the disruption caused by using a point-and-shoot device. In order to compensate for the lack of a viewfinder, most models to date have been equipped with a wide-angle or fish-eye lens, designed to approximate human peripheral vision and maximize its field of view.

These features create a very distinctive experiential perspective. First, unfolding events are captured from a chest-level viewpoint, adhering to what psychologists and philosophers call a "field perspective"—a first-person, "own-eyes," embedded point of view, as opposed to a third-person, "observer" perspective (Sutton 2010, 2014). Second, nearly everything in view of the wearer is captured by the wide-angle lens. The 136-degree lens of the Autographer camera—used to capture the pictures in Plate 11—often picks up the wearer's hands, or parts of limbs, clothing, or hair, creating the sense of an embodied presence in the field. Thus, images include not only the extraneous details that are routinely excluded from deliberately framed shots, but the wearer's encounters with these minutiae.

If worn for an entire day, a SenseCam or similar camera might capture up to 5,000 images, presenting the challenge of how to store and access images. The dominant presentation paradigm for such data is known as 'rapid serial visual presentation', which allows for fast-forwarding of the images in sequence; software has also been developed to enable automated content analysis and event segmentation (Doherty et al. 2011).

The images in Plate 11 were taken by an Autographer worn by my friend and research collaborator Claire, as she sat drawing a map on the shore of Village Bay on St Kilda, a remote and depopulated island in the North Atlantic, 40 miles west of the Outer Hebrides. In terms of its field perspective, this camera captures something very different to the image of the same view that Claire might have taken from the same spot with her own hand-held camera. Looking back at these photographs, the wearer is confronted by images that manifest her own presence at the scene: images of the micro-encounters that unfolded across her whole field of view, knowable only from her position in the field. Imagine these reviewed via software that allows the viewer to scroll as fast or slow as she likes, so that images take on the quality of a time-lapse movie—or can be stilled and investigated. Viewing lifelog images in this way, many users report that they "remember more" than they otherwise would, and that the photos "foreground moments that would otherwise have passed unnoticed" (Fernyhough 2012: 177). (On another occasion, for example, Claire remembered a minor cut on her finger during an outing—the kind of episodic detail that is not commonly retained in event memories over time.) Most significantly, as I will discuss below, lifelogging images have had a dramatic effect on recall in cases of memory impairment, including amnesia (Loveday and Conway 2011) and Alzheimer's Disease (Woodberry et al. 2015), suggesting a "correspondence" with memory itself.

This auspicious empirical discovery is the somewhat accidental legacy of the lifelogging phenomenon. The latter was largely promoted in the spirit of memory expansion through total capture: "More pictures in order to remember more" was the selling point of one brand of lifelogging camera (Memoto). Gordon Bell and Jim Gemmell's book, originally marketed with the title *Total Recall*, exemplifies this focus (Bell and Gemmell 2009). Bell, a Microsoft researcher, documents the project *MyLifeBits* for which he wore his SenseCam each day from 2001 to 2007. His aim was to create a machine-enhanced photographic memory that captured and stored every bit of life data—though he abandoned the project when the volume of data amassed simply outgrew available storage capacity. More generally, by the mid 2010s—after the smartphone explosion—the market for lifelogging cameras had contracted in an environment of data fatigue where expansive capture and storage were no longer so appealing as ends in themselves.

In lifelogging discourse, the concept of enhanced personal memory, acheived through ever greater storage capacity, is inflected by a computational understanding of memory. Yet, in the realm of digital storage marketing, the photograph itself is casually elided with autobiographical memory; as I write, a banner ad describes the promise of cloud storage as "rescuing memories." This common conflation underlines the strength of the analogy between photography and memory, which, although axiomatic, rests largely and somewhat problematically on the process of capture.

Reconstruction

Photographic metaphors have permeated descriptions of memory from the nineteenth century (and, as Alison Winter's brilliant book *Memory* documents, the science of memory itself; Winter 2012)). In an 1875 essay on travel, the novelist Robert Louis Stevenson wrote, "We expose our mind to the landscape (as we would expose the prepared plate in the camera)"; as a result, "we have in our memories a long scroll of continuous wayside pictures" (Stevenson 1905: 107). Such allusions pertain directly to analog, photochemical photography, which, by virtue of being directly "imprinted" by light, is literally "an emanation of the referent," as Barthes put it (Barthes 1981: 80). The question of whether this analogy survives the shift to digital photography is moot. Clearly, it inflects commonsense perceptions that photographs *are* our memories—but, in theory, we have moved into a 'post-medium' age, when reproducible digital media no longer claim a singular relationship to a referent. Before we did so, critiques of the photograph as an indexical trace were well established. Notwithstanding the process of 'imprinting' or exposure of the photographic plate or film, it became clear that the photograph itself could never be reduced to an unmediated trace. In the post-medium condition, these critiques have been declared redundant (Doane 2007).

For memory psychologists, the photographic trace metaphor is as problematic as it has been for photography theory, to the degree that it equates the human mind/memory with the substrate of a photograph, passively imprinted from an external source. It has long been established within cognitive psychology that the relationship between visual memory and an original real-world event is not simply "reduplicative or reproductive" but "constructive" (Bartlett 1932: 204–205). More than 80 years ago, the pioneering British psychologist Frederic Bartlett proposed that memory is not a literal reproduction or replay of the past, but a continuously constructive process in which bits and pieces of information from various sources are pulled together. As such, memory is not free from distortion or further mediation (due to other perceptual input, emotion, beliefs, social influences, experience and so on). This same concept of memory, constructed or made anew each time remembering occurs, today underpins neuropsychological research investigating the neural basis of memory construction (Schacter and Addis 2007).

The trace in memory may be understood as always *re*mediated, in the sense coined by digital media theorists to evoke the impermanence of media recordings or creations, which may now be extracted from their original context and recombined into a new digital medium. Bolter and Grusin first described this mode of visible remediation as "a mosiac in which we are simultaneously aware of the individual pieces and their new, inappropriate setting" (Bolter and Grusin 1998), noting also that remediation may often remain invisible. For Bartlett, as Winter shows, the trace analogy was rejected completely:

> The analogy of a photograph belonged to a convention of memory that Bartlett had set himself against, the idea that what we observe makes its record in our minds as an impression stamped from without. Photography was not useful even as a foil because ... Bartlett did not want to measure memory against the idea of faithful record taking.
>
> *(Winter 2012: 213–214).*

In this respect, a much more promising analogy is presented by the process of digital production and remediation. The digital photograph no longer embodies the unique trace at the level of medium, but instead a referent whose relationship to the image is unstable, tenuous and dynamic—subject to continuous remaking. But my concern here is not specifically with the theoretical distinction between analog and digital photography. It is with the latter's phenomenological likeness to memory, for which the moving image becomes the foil as in Mantel's brief characterization above.

The moving image, which captures the scene in time-based form, such that it may replay itself from start to finish, manifests none of the obduracy of memory—the stops, starts, diversions and dead ends. Hence, it leaves no room for the interaction with memory, memory that actively recomposes itself from a vast "collection of moments," to use Esther Salaman's phrase (Salaman 1971). The compelling comparison of memory with photography is not with the singular image, characterized by stillness as opposed to motion; it is with the image in process, subject to imaginative reconstruction.

Even as it flows, memory is not a rerun but at best a stop-motion reconstruction, intersected at every step: "one image springs another; they run through your head in all directions" (Mantel 1995: 11). Memory is never like a single photograph; it is the thread of images, caught on the run—stilled and regenerated, but never existing in a fixed one-to-one relationship with an event or a scene.

Perspectives

"The Entire History of You" (a 2011 episode of the UK television series *Black Mirror*) envisages an implanted chip that allows mental replay of an event to facilitate enhanced perception of detail missed in an initial experience—in this particular case, affording the protagonist the opportunity to revisit conversations, searching for clues to his wife's infidelity. This sense that recording technology offsets the inability to be fully present is by no means a new theme: Benjamin writes of Proust that he is filled with the insight that none of us has time to live the life we are destined for—"we, the masters, were not at home"—for which reason our photographs have a capacity to surprise us, to reveal an optical unconscious (Benjamin 1968: 211).

The *Black Mirror* scenario might simply be read as underlining this experiential truth: that memory rarely yields in this way, for it holds no scene or event intact. The fantasy is not, in fact, to *relive* but to replay a scene, to perceive it not as it was perceived in life but with a disembodied forensic gaze, so that memory or the image in mind can be encountered as a piece of documentary evidence. This is a desire for something more than human memory: for the authenticating evidence, an image or sequence extracted from its perceptual context and removed to a space where it can be scrutinized for what was lived but not known. This is a fantasy surely based in part on our relationship to photography. It seems to imply the stasis of photography, the stilling of the moment so that it can be re-perceived under new conditions—conditions that enhance the visual, capturing the detail of the field or the close-up texture; indeed, the denouement of the *Black Mirror* episode turns on a revealing, portrait-like key frame, much like the key frame for a SenseCam or iPhoto event library, viewed in an on-screen video archive. It is this stilling that is the mark of photography—"in opposition to cinema," in Barthes' phrase (Barthes 1981: 3).

Such a return implies a shifting perspective. Motivated by anxiety, the remembering protagonist looks back at scenes with growing uncertainty and suspicion, doubting the perspicacity of his original viewpoint. In other words, the replay is not a repeat of his experience at the scene, but a more informed reinhabiting of this setting. In real terms, this remembering from an observer perspective may well occasion a departure from the visuospatial field perspective. The philosopher Peter Goldie draws attention to an important distinction between field and observer memories in this respect (Goldie 2012: 49–53): "in field memory one remembers 'from the inside', the events as they took place. In observer memory, one remembers 'from the outside', so that one is oneself part of the content of what one remembers," seeing oneself as others did (49). But, in contrast to the common presumption that "true" memory must reflect the subject's eye-view, he argues that, "there is no good reason to assume that observer memories are not genuine memories" (50).

Both of these perspectives are possible in autobiographical memory and empirically known (most people, it turns out, can switch between observer and field perspectives on the same scene in memory; McCarroll and Sutton 2017; Sutton 2010, 2014), but they are often driven by different emotions—and, crucially, by emotions from different times. Field memory implies remembering the emotion felt during the event remembered; observer memory may imply a subsequent reevaluation, as when one is retrospectively embarrassed by one's actions or simply when one is reflexively 'orienting' one's feelings.

If, hypothetically, Claire, the photographer, looks back at the above image, she may recall the wonderful view, sitting on the grass, the joy of drawing—or, conceivably, the difficulty of drawing, the dampness of grass, the irritation of the snapping of a pencil lead, and so forth. This sensory and embodied recall, corresponding to an embedded, first-person perception of the scene, is encouraged by the framing of this image which resituates her at the scene in an unusually vivid way, encompassing much of the detail of the immediate setting. On the other hand, she may (hypothetically, again) subsequently become self-conscious about what the others in the field were thinking of her and start to visualize herself as she appeared on the grass, absorbed in her drawing. At this point, she would be assuming an observer perspective on the scene and on herself, no longer remembering being in this spot, but retrospectively reconsidering her role at the scene (as in Goldie's example of when someone reflects on drunken behavior, experienced as fun at the time, but embarrassing afterwards).

SenseCam does not take us to the critical perspective as other forms of documentary photography might, nor to any kind of third-party observer position, but to the scene of experience. It is not the photography of rumination or a depressive position, which is always judgmental and self-reflecting, nor of aspiration and pretense or any kind of interpretative distance. It is not the photography of loss—which extends a gap between past and present: here-now, there-then—but of reinstatement. SenseCam takes us to the locus of firsthand experience. It is a photography of living presence and present emotion.

This is not the only form of autobiographical memory, but as a technique of remembering it is a particularly 'mindful' one in the sense that it engages sensory cues to recapture the feeling of being present—in other words, a primarily embodied experience.

Amnesia

> Every photograph is a certificate of presence.
>
> (Barthes 1981: 87)

In fact, Claire—whose photographs of St Kilda are seen in Plate 11—has dense amnesia, owing to a lesion on the right side of her brain. She relies on a camera to capture and retain information about her trip (the hypothetical scenario above does not play out for her in a simple way). Specifically, Claire has a profound retrograde amnesia for the period from her 20s to early 40s (she is, for example, unable to recall any episodic details about the birth or development of her children), as well as significantly impaired memory for specific autobiographical/episodic memories at all ages (Loveday and Conway 2011). In addition, she has what is termed 'anterograde' amnesia: an inability to form new long-term memories. Most of what happens to her on a given day is likely to be forgotten.

At the end of a day or at any time in the future, Claire might review her SenseCam images on a laptop, scrolling through hundreds of stills to reconstruct events in the hope of sparking recognition. Mostly, this does not happen. She has no sense of having been in the place in the photograph, but, even so, she can use the visual information it provides to infer what must have happened. Very occasionally, however, a memory is cued. This is a very big deal indeed.

Those of us with functioning memory may not immediately appreciate this distinction. We take for granted our ability to connect with the past through photographs—for memory to be casually jogged, either by the image of a time/place or by a sliver nested within. Viewing a snapshot of a childhood holiday, I might not recall the events of the day but might fasten on a recognized detail—the swimsuit I loved, the toy I played with all one summer—to establish 'memory'. We look at old school photographs and remember something of our schooldays, our schoolmates, the playground, the wearing of a uniform—if not the day of the photograph's taking.

Sometimes we know only ourselves. Barthes tells the story of a photographer presenting him with an image of himself that he cannot recall being taken. Confronted with the irrefutable truth that he is present in this otherwise strange image, he has no choice but to believe—"in the Photograph, the power of authentication exceeds the power of representation" (Barthes 1981: 89). Such "power of authentication" is no doubt part of the explanation for how photographs can promote so-called 'false memories'. A well-known example in cognitive psychology is Wade and colleagues' use of 'fake photographs' to convince experimental subjects that they had, as children, taken a trip in a hot air balloon that never in fact occurred. Over a series of interviews, 50 percent of the subjects created complete or partial false memories, evincing their readiness to believe the image—a result that throws into question the extent to which the shift from the indexical/analog (authentic trace) to the more unstable/manipulable digital makes any difference in the phenomenological condition of viewing. As Wade and colleagues suggest, "image-enhancing technology is readily available, people are frequently exposed to doctored images" (Wade et al. 2002: 597). Yet still authenticity is implicitly ascribed to the digital image.

For Barthes, the photograph is simply the "certificate of presence" and "never in essence a memory" (Barthes 1981: 91). There is "nothing Proustian in a photograph," he claims (Barthes 1981: 82). Conversely, the photograph for Claire is, at its most effective, an exemplary memory cue in precisely these terms. Psychologists Catherine Loveday and Martin Conway have monitored Claire's reviewing of SenseCam pictures, identifying instances of "Proustian moments" triggered by the images. A "Proustian moment" is their term for a moment of intense recollection, when images of the past flood into consciousness, leaving the subject with powerful experience of remembering (Loveday and Conway 2011: 697). For Claire, the 'flood' of episodic details into conscious awareness is dramatic—both personally exhilarating as she connects with a moment from her past and feels her memory to actually work, and neurologically significant. In an fMRI study of Claire recalling SenseCam pictures she viewed prior to going in the scanner, intense and widespread activation was observed in the occipital lobes and posterior parietal regions (Loveday and Conway 2011). The extent of this activation is noteworthy. The same activation occurs in non-brain-damaged individuals when they have "Proustian moments" in response to SenseCam cues, but it is more pronounced in Claire.

Embodied experience

When Loveday and Conway first published their experimental results, establishing the effectiveness of SenseCam images as memory cues, they presented the hypothesis that "SenseCam photographs are highly cognitively compatible with human memory" in a way that video, for example, is not. They reasoned that the success of SenseCam as a memory trigger could be due to the fact that, unlike the continuous flow of film or video, SenseCam photo sequences are perceived as sequences of discrete 'moments'. They are akin to episodic memory in that they are visual, they represent short time-slices of experience, are compressed and fragmentary, and are formed outside intentional awareness (unlike deliberately framed photographs); they are temporally ordered and preserve the perspective of the individual. These features, they suggest,

> overlap at least in part with features of episodic memory (Conway 2005), [and] make SC [SenseCam] images highly compatible with human episodic memory and because of this may increase the probability of containing an effective cue with which to stimulate memories.
>
> *(Loveday and Conway 2011).*

In other words, and importantly for a phenomenology of photography, SenseCam photographs both mimic the form of human memory and interact with and scaffold that memory in ways that are highly productive.

I came to know Claire when working as the visual theorist on a project led by artist Shona Illingworth with Loveday and Conway (Bennett in press; Bennett and Illingworth 2016). As part of this project, we travelled to St Kilda in 2014, both to make a film with Claire and to investigate further her use of SenseCam—a unique opportunity to spend time with her in the field, observing how she used SenseCam. Neuropsychologist Catherine

Loveday wanted to find out whether reviewing SenseCam photographs soon after shooting could enhance memory consolidation and retention. I was particularly interested in the specific qualities of images that were effective as memory cues, as previous studies had not sought to identify this or to compare the effectiveness of SenseCam with other kinds of personal photography.

Over the course of the trip and other meetings, several aspects of how Claire views SenseCam have struck me as significant. First, the particularly methodical way she reviews a batch of images. This is partly a function of the browser that encourages sequential viewing. But Claire has a tendency to proceed slowly, poring over each image. On one occasion, Shona and I sat with Claire looking back at St Kilda images, a large number of which were obscured by a hand in front of the lens. Our inclination was to pass quickly over these 'duds', but Claire will stay with the sequence. She does not immediately perceive the photos as mementos but engages with them as a means of orientation or scene-setting.

Second, I have been struck by the often physical or sensory-kinesthetic nature of recall with SenseCam. When talking about SenseCam images as she views them, Claire often alludes to walking or moving through a space—and she often responds to physical or gestural cues in the images. In other words, the experience of viewing is not simply optical or visual, but multimodal and embodied. This approach is enabled by the methodical review of a batch of images, which serves to set a scene or establish context. But, equally, it seems to arise from the consistent field perspective of SenseCam images, which are "experience-near" to use psychoanalyst Heinz Kohut's phrase (Froggett and Briggs 2012: n.p.). Such memories can often be of sensory-kinesthetic experience. For example, looking at SenseCam images of St Kilda in Claire's house one day, months after the trip, she works through sequences showing the remains of stone houses in the island's depopulated village. Claire says she remembers one thing: "I was talking aloud." She does not know why or to whom—maybe she was musing aloud about the inhabitants of the houses, perhaps she was talking to someone, although this is not apparent in the images. But she remembers the feeling of talking aloud. This 'memory' is distinctive for its lack of social narrative context; she has, at this point, a concrete sense of the village in place, of its significance and meaning as an abandoned settlement with no people, and she recalls her own act of speaking aloud—but without, as yet, any definite social context to make sense of this action.

My early interactions with Claire indicated that spatial orientation and/or an embodied relationship to location were beneficial to triggering memory. Rewalking the scene in mind, proceeding systematically across the space of the picture, seemed to increase the chances of remembering events. If SenseCam creates the conditions for this more effectively than other forms of photography, I wondered if 3D immersive imaging might enhance this experience further?

To test this, we developed Amnesia Atlas, a 3D browser, built in a Unity gaming engine, for viewing photographs taken by SenseCam (or the subsequent generation of wearable automatic camera, marketed as Autographer) in either a 3D immersive screen environment or a virtual-reality head-mounted display (Bennett and Kuchelmeister 2014; Bennett et al. 2014; Kuchelmeister and Bennett 2014). Using geo-tagging data, the browser relocates the photos into a 3D spatial setting, representing the sites at which they were taken. Users may then retrace their photographed journeys on terrain modeled in 3D, using a map on a tablet computer as a navigational interface. By developing an immersive experience, we enable a kinesthetic experience of this 3D space. So, for example, a viewer has the sensation of moving through the space—up and down hills and across modulated terrain—as they would have when they captured the photographs. Thus, in order to arrive at a given landmark, one may have to 'climb' a hill or navigate whatever terrain surrounds it.

One of the main advantages of the Amnesia Atlas immersive 3D browser (see Plate 12) is that it constitutes a powerful reinstatement of context—that is, not just of the physical setting itself, but of what is effectively the memory-encoding context. It has long been established in psychology that reinstating context, even in relatively weak forms, stimulates memory and increases recall (so-called 'context effects'). A compelling study by Godden and Baddeley showed, for example, that divers who learned material underwater had better memory when tested underwater (Godden and Baddeley 1980). Thus, we would expect that the doubly powerful reinstatement of context using lifelog photographs in an immersive 3D environment would lead to intense experiences of recollection and reliving. Building on Loveday and Conway's original protocol, we designed an experiment with the aim of comparing the effects of different photographic formats and viewing conditions, working with participants from the ageing population (65+). Specifically, we sought to test the nature of memory when cued with lifelog images as opposed to conventionally generated point-and-shoot photographs, and also the effects of viewing lifelog pictures in an immersive 3D environment, compared with viewing the images on a laptop, in order to evaluate the effects of greater physical presence and embodiment. The results of this study will be presented in full elsewhere; here, I offer some observations regarding how 3D imagery of spatial context impacts on the process of remembering.

Walking through a scene, methodically tracing the steps of a previous journey, establishes a setting. This might be understood as a kind of 'cognitive map' in the sense proposed by the urban planner Kevin Lynch in his work on wayfinding in the city, where key structural elements such as pathways render layout intelligible and navigable (Lynch 1960). In Claire's case, it lays down a context that cannot simply be brought to mind. More generally, it provides a background structure that supports the recollection of events/objects linked to its physical and architectural elements, somewhat in the spirit of the classical *method of loci*, where an architectural 'theatre' is designed to assist systematic recall of items (Yates 1966).

When participants review lifelog images in a 3D browser, we see very clearly the effect of reinstating a setting and of rewalking the route that was photographed. Participants are apt to describe both their walk and the process of orientation along the way, leading to significant recall of detail ("we turned and went up the hill, to the left there were some birds on a wall," and so forth). This sequential recollection of detail is more pronounced with the 3D immersive browser than with the regular 2D browser, but is the virtual reconstruction of place so powerful that the photographs themselves are no longer operative as memory cues? It is useful here to prise apart the notions of background and moment.

Salaman's prescient study of involuntary memory alludes to this distinction, arguing that, "In recreating the past we need [two] kinds of memory, the memory of the background and memories of moments" (Salaman 1971: 35). Backgrounding for her is a reconstructive process that draws on diverse available source material. She gives the example of fixing her various event memories of school in a classroom she remembers reasonably well:

> The school where I spent a year … I cannot reconstruct as a whole, but I can the classroom, and I use its space for the background of memories. I take four memories of events in that classroom, four islands fixed in space, and now I can see what filled the space between these islands. But I know for certain that they are separate in time; so it's as if I was learning to interpolate and, ignoring the time factor, to join up the four points and so get a geometrical picture of the room.
>
> *(Salaman 1971: 35)*

For Salaman, memories of events are easily distinguishable from memories of the background. She argues that *only memories of events come back involuntarily*, bringing with them strong emotions and giving a sensation of living in a past moment (Salaman 1971: 45). Background is a constitutive part of event memory—but one that is separable insofar as memory does not hold the scene intact but actively reconstructs it. If memory is indeed a composite image rather than an indexical trace of the visual form of what happened in the world, this sense of how background and event interrelate in the experience of remembering and of looking at photographs is instructive.

Viewing a day's SenseCam imagery, whether fast-scanning what is instantly recognizable, or methodically building up a map of the location, supports this process of scene-setting or backgrounding as the precursor or precondition for a more spontaneous or involuntary event memory.

Time and place

Barthes locates consciousness of a photograph across space and time dimensions:

> The type of consciousness the photograph involves is indeed truly unprecedented, since it establishes not a consciousness of the being there of the thing (which any copy could provoke) but an awareness of its having-been-there. What we have is a new space-time category: spatial immediacy and temporal anteriority, the photograph being an illogical conjunction between the here-now and the there-then.
>
> *(Barthes 1977 [1964]: 44)*

But is this an ontological condition of the analog photograph or simply an experiential one? For Barthes, it is experiential—a function of consciousness—but consciousness proceeding from the implicit claim to authenticity of the photograph (a claim that had an ontological base in the analog era, but no longer).

For Claire and others with impaired memory, temporal anteriority is not always self-evident, but must be actively established in the review of photographic data: the question is not only, "where were we then?" (then, in this picture of the past, this historical happening around which there are a general consensus and shared factual information), but, to borrow the title of a book by Lynch, "*What time is this place?*" Amnesia is often described as a condition of being trapped in a perpetual present; in Claire's words, "The past existing as a space you can't enter or feel—the future a space you can't imagine" (Bennett and Illingworth 2016: n.p.). It is hard to locate the past, but also the future, which can never be updated without recourse to memory. The 'then' is not instantly known to Claire, but the 'space' may be accessed through SenseCam. It is the feeling of space, and of moving within it, supported by these photographs that creates the conditions under which memory of the past can be momentarily accessed.

Feels like memory

In the Ullens Center for Contemporary Art in Beijing, in 2012, the artist Kan Xuan premiered the photographic installation *Millet Mounds* (shown subsequently in the Venice Biennale). This is a work that feels like memory—even if the pictured locations in rural China are places we have never visited. It looks somewhat similar to SenseCam or a lifelog installation, if one were to be constructed as an exhibit. *Millet Mounds* consists of 164 stop-motion videos, each documenting the artist's presence at an imperial tomb site (she visited nearly every known emperor's burial ground in China for this work). Each video is composed of between 400 and 500 photographs, taken on the artist's iPhone and looped into short narratives. The videos range in length from 30 seconds to two minutes. The photographs comprising the videos have all been sifted through a lo-fi filter using the camera app Hipstamatic. This is, in one sense, archetypical post-medium art: no longer a unique trace, but self-conscious in its production. Hipstamatic is generally used to create the illusion of lens and film choice, and to 'degrade' cell phone snapshots; it is a way of introducing variation and imperfection into digital images, as well as affecting a kind of photographic pictorialism. Yet, for Kan, "it is about trying to become closer to and trying to follow, in every moment, my wish to exist in that distance between 'thinking' and 'feeling'" (Lu and Watkins 2016: 18). Much like SenseCam, her hand-held cell phone camera tracks a pathway, close to the ground—a field position from which the texture of grass and footsteps in the grass are as pronounced as the monumental focal point.

Other passers-by transect these images so that there are multiple arcs of movement, often choppy and blurry as people come and go, falling by chance into the frame. The neuroscientist Michael Hasselmo evokes a new photographic metaphor for memory that resonates with visuospatial perspective:

> The traces left in my memory are not just discrete footprints but the continuous trace of my full body moving through three-dimensional space, as well as the continuous traces of other moving agents including our dog and cat. A more accurate analogy may be the streaks of movement in a long exposure photograph, where a movement appears as an unbroken fluid arc.
>
> *(Hasselmo 2012: 1–2)*

Digital photography, like Kan's stop-motion videos, in turn activates the experience of such traces, bringing into being a kind of photographic phenomenology of the journey in the landscape (the "long scroll of continuous wayside pictures" that comprises memory—if not in the manner of the exposed plate/film but through repeated recomposition). Kan's work is not "about memory" but it presents as memory: a neurophenomenology of memory—that is, the investigation of the *experience* aligned with cognitive and neurological processes of remembering. The work oscillates between the experiences of being in the field, of the way in which memories comes to mind, and of the body moving through space, which is never simply a visuospatial experience. In photography, this kind of internal memory experience requires a translation of the sensory, kinesthetic and proprioceptive dimensions—a trace of the full body in motion.

Future orientation

A neurophenomenological conception of photography is not focused on the interaction with an image of the past. That is to say, it does not operate on an axis from past to present in the way that other forms of phenomenological writing on photography might imagine the 'there-then' in a strange and confronting conjunction with the 'here-now'. Activating memory or an image of a past event—bringing it into mind—is a laborious, imaginative (even if fast and barely perceptible or acknowledged) process of construction. But, "remembering is not the re-excitation of innumerable fixed, lifeless and fragmentary traces," as Bartlett understood (Bartlett[1932]1997: 213). The metaphor of capture and storage alone is insufficient.

Technology positioned as an exemplary or complete method of capture (or, conversely, as the reverse—as digitally manipulable or 'false') is poorly positioned to explore memory process. The designation of 'post-medium photography' is more promising and not to be underestimated as a theoretical conceit. The post-medium condition (the possibility of manipulation, reproduction or remediation) does not in itself challenge the truth status of the image or imply falseness. The same argument is made on behalf of constructivism in memory studies; the fact that memory is not a perfect trace and is reconstructed does not make it false or 'bad memory'. The gold standard in memory never was or will be total or unmediated recall. Memory is inherently dynamic and flexible (Schacter and Addis 2007). It can be functional and true, while also being influenced, modified and imaginatively reconstructed. New forms of post-medium photography come as close as any art or documentary form to elucidating and accommodating this processual account of episodic memory.

This is not simply to say that a single digital image is more like memory than an analog photograph. The digital has shifted the study of photography beyond a focus on singular photographs, towards a concern with photography as a social, material and networked practice—because, it is argued, the manner of its production, consumption and distribution means that digital photography is inherently "processual, conversational and in constant flux" (Larsen and Sandbye 2014: xxx). A SenseCam or lifelog archive is *like* memory insofar as it is open to interactive engagement and remediation.

If memory contains a trace of the world, it is as much the trace of a sensing/perceiving body as of the object/event perceived; if the digital photograph—a lifelog image or something similar snapped by a cell phone camera—contains a trace, it is both the trace of a photographer and of the visual field. But, as Claire shows us, our memories are not our photos, secured in albums, digital archives or Cloud Storage; they are built out of a continuing process of engagement and remaking. Claire has become, of necessity, an astute user of SenseCam as a tool for memory reconstruction, an expert interpreter of the "image blurring, caught on the move". Such images are rarely of great memorial signfiance in and of themselves; in fact, they have life only insofar as they are connected and remediated. "One image springs another"—and is only as good as the next.

References

Barthes, R. (1977 [1964]) *Image, Music, Text*, Translated by Heath, S., New York: Hill & Wang.

Barthes, R. (1981) *Camera Lucida: Reflections on Photography*, New York: Hill & Wang.

Bartlett, F. C. ([1932] 1997) *Remembering: A Study in Experimental and Social Psychology*, Cambridge: Cambridge University Press.

Bell, C. G. and Gemmell, J. (2009) *Total Recall: How the E-memory Revolution Will Change Everything*, New York: Dutton.

Benjamin, W. (1968) *Illuminations: Essays and Reflections*, New York: Shocken Books.

Bennett, J. (2019) "New Subjects and Subjectivities," in Robinson, H. & Buszek, M. E. (eds.) *Companion to Feminist Art Practice and Theory*, Hoboken, NJ: Wiley-Blackwell., pp. 533–544

Bennett, J. and Illingworth, S. (2016) *Lesions in the Landscape*, Liverpool: FACT.

Bennett, J. and Kuchelmeister, V. (2014) *Amnesia Atlas*, Future Memory Wall, Liverpool: FACT.

Bennett, J., Kuchelmeister, V. and Del Favero, D. (2014) *Amnesia Atlas*, Science Park, Hong Kong: Exhibition associated with 20th International Conference on Virtual Systems & Multimedia.

Bolter, J. D. and Grusin, R. A. (1998) *Remediation: Uniderstanding New Media*, Boston: MIT Press.

Conway, M. (2005) "Memory and the Self," *Journal of Memory and Language*, 53:(4), pp. 594–628.

Doane, M. A. (2007) "The Indexical and the Concept of Medium Specificity," *Differences*, 18:(1), pp. 128–152.

Doherty, A. R., Moulin, C. J. and Smeaton, A. F. (2011) "Automatically Assisting Human Memory: A SenseCam Browser," *Memory*, 19:(7), pp. 785–795.

Fernyhough, C. (2012) *Pieces of Light: The New Science of Memory*, London: Profile.
Froggett, L. and Briggs, S. (2012) "Practice-Near and Practice-Distant Methods in Human Services Research," *Journal of Research Practice*, 8:(2). Article M9. Retrieved from http://jrp.icaap.org/index.php/jrp/article/view/318/276
Godden, D. R. and Baddeley, A. D. (1980) "When Does Context Influence Recognition Memory?" *British Journal of Psychology*, 71, pp. 99–104.
Goldie, P. (2012) *The Mess Inside: Narrative, Emotion, and the Mind*, Oxford: Oxford University Press.
Hasselmo, M. E. (2012) *How We Remember: Brain Mechanisms of Episodic Memory*, Cambridge, MA: MIT Press.
Hodges, S., Berry, E. and Wood, K. (2011) "SenseCam: A Wearable Camera that Stimulates and Rehabilitates Autobiographical Memory," *Memory*, 19:(7), pp. 685–696.
Kuchelmeister, V. and Bennett, J. (2014) "The Amnesia Atlas: An Immersive SenseCam Interface as Memory-Prosthesis," *Virtual Systems & Multimedia (VSMM)*, Hong Kong, 9–12 December, 217–222.
Larsen, J. and Sandbye, M. (2014) *Digital Snaps: The New Face of Photography*, London: I.B.Tauris.
Loveday, C. and Conway, M. A. (2011) "Using SenseCam with an Amnesic Patient: Accessing Inaccessible Everyday Memories," *Memory*, 19:(7), pp. 697–704.
Lu, L. and Watkins, J. (2016) *Kan Xuan*, Beijing: Exhibition, Ullens Center for Contemporary Art. http://ucca.org.cn/en/
Lynch, K. (1960) *The Image of the City. Publications of the Joint Center for Urban Studies*, Cambridge, MA: Technology Press.
Mantel, H. (1995) *An Experiment in Love*, Bath: Chivers.
McCarroll, C. J. and Sutton, J. (2017) "Memory and Perspective," in Bernecker, S. & Michaelian, K. (eds.) *The Routledge Handbook of Philosophy of Memory*. London: Routledge., pp. 113–126
Proust, M. (1961) *Remembrance of Things Past*. (12 vols), London: Chatto & Windus.
Salaman, E. P. (1971) *A Collection of Moments: A Study of Involuntary Memories*, New York: St. Martin's Press.
Schacter, D. L. and Addis, D. R. (2007) "The Cognitive Neuroscience of Constructive Memory: Remembering the Past and Imagining the Future," *Philosophical Transactions of the Royal Society B Biological Science*, 362:(1481), pp. 773–786.
Stevenson, R. L. (1905) *Essays of Travel*, London: Chatto & Windus.
Sutton, J. (2010) "Observer Perspective and Acentred Memory: Some Puzzles about Point of View in Personal Memory," *Philosophical Studies*, 148:(1), pp. 27–37.
Sutton, J. (2014) "Memory Perspectives," *Editorial, Memory Studies*, 7:(2), pp. 141–145.
Tulving, E. (1983) *Elements of Episodic Memory*, Oxford: Clarendon.
Wade, K. A., Garry, M., Read, J. D. and Lindsay, D. S. (2002) "A Picture Is Worth a Thousand Lies: Using False Photographs to Create False Childhood Memories," *Psychonomic Bulletin Review*, 9:(3), pp. 597–603.
Winter, A. (2012) *Memory: Fragments of a Modern History*, Chicago: University of Chicago Press.
Wood, K., Fleck, R. and Williams, L. (2004) "Playing with SenseCam" in *Proceedings of Playing with Sensors: Exploring the Boundaries of Sensing for Playful Ubiquitous Computing (W3)*, Nottingham: UbiComp.
Woodberry, E., Browne, G., Hodges, S., Watson, P., Kapur, N. and Woodberry, K. (2015) "The Use of a Wearable Camera Improves Autobiographical Memory in Patients with Alzheimer's Disease," *Memory*, 23:(3), pp. 340–349.
Yates, F. A. (1966) *The Art of Memory*, London: Routledge & Keegan Paul.

Part II
Politics

10

Seeing the public image anew

Photography exhibitions and civic spectatorship

Robert Hariman and John Louis Lucaites

Although photography may be many things to many people, its public character remains both omnipresent and difficult to recognize. Photography has been framed with respect to scientific research, the fine arts, police surveillance and forensic technologies, propaganda and other forms of ideological manipulation, advertising and commodity consumption, imperialism and other systems of domination, and other media such as writing and film, as well as vernacular practices of social bonding, memory work, and resistance. There has been good reason for doing so: it is deeply intertwined with all of those things. What can be lost in translation, however, is the idea that each of these frameworks can lead to misrecognition of how photography has become the primary way of seeing in a public world.

By focusing on the public image, we are part of a paradigm shift currently underway in photography theory and practice. That shift need not emphasize photography's involvement in public life, but public media, arts, and influence become more legible and perhaps more valuable than had been the case. Because of the changes, contradictions, and potential of the current habitus of photography, it also should be clear that any contemporary synopsis has to be provisional. Drawing on our recent work (Hariman and Lucaites 2016), we will outline the shift as we see it and then briefly summarize several thematic emphases we find useful for developing a critical sensibility for photography as a public art. Our work has its own limitations, however, and so we also suggest how a more engaged but also precarious commitment to civic spectatorship can be found in contemporary exhibition practices.

Rethinking photography

If you know anything about photography, you know what's wrong with it. That knowledge may range from simple awareness that digital photos can be altered to mislead the viewer, to powerful critiques of how images operate ideologically to maintain structures of inequity, exploitation, and violence. This constellation of critical skills developed over many decades in response to the rise of modern, industrialized, mass societies. Photography became a leading example of how a media technology could permeate all sectors of modern society, not least because of how it operated through commodity consumption. The critical sensibility that has developed is a superb example of how a focus on media specificity and media dependency can provide a powerful basis for social thought.

This critical apparatus has an impressive pedigree, developed by those in or aligned with the Frankfurt School, through a strong cadre of public intellectuals such as Susan Sontag and John Berger, to additional development by many fine scholars across many disciplines.[1] What may have been most important to subsequent developments—including this volume—is the transformation of photography from one technology among many to one that is central to understanding modernity and the risks of modernization (Hariman and Lucaites 2007: 243–86). And no one should be surprised that those dangers include technological envelopment of the lifeworld, transformations of value occurring through commodification and cultures of consumption in market societies, and the distractions, delusions, and emotional manipulation that are used to subvert liberal democracy and deny progressive government. What also developed, however, was an all-encompassing hermeneutics of suspicion: indeed, to follow the suggestion of W. J. T. Mitchell (Mitchell 2005: 26), thinking about images contained an iconoclasm that led to distortions and missed opportunities.

The strongest public statement was provided by Susan Sontag's *On Photography*, which began by declaring that "Humankind lingers unregenerately in Plato's cave, still reveling, its age-old habit, in mere images of the truth" (Sontag 1977: 3). Images are inherently suspect, as they are on the wrong side of a hard binary with truth. Aesthetic pleasure also is implicated by the allegory, as delusion and domination come from enjoying ("reveling in") the dumb show on the walls of the cave. Those caught in the image world forget that they ever were free to walk out into an unmediated world oriented toward reason and justice. No wonder that "the omnipresence of photographs has an incalculable effect on our ethical sensibility" (Sontag 1977: 24).

As Susie Linfield has pointed out, one of the oddities of this inheritance is that, contrary to thoughtful engagement in all other arts, critical judgment has been weighted heavily toward the negative (Linfield 2010: 3–31). Images are unreal, unrepresentative, and misleading, and photographic images are especially so because they conform so closely to reality. Scholars have developed an extensive catalog of how photographs fail as a mode of representation, disable viewers' capacity for critical response, and serve dominant interests. Linfield reviews many of the signature statements defining this critical optic, and the consensus is clear: photography serves those oppressive social structures already in place by creating a visual regime that saps the ability to see the world otherwise.

Much was forgotten along the way, however, or dismissed as sentimental and unreflective. By contrast, today we note that there always were dissenting voices: the early reviews of *On Photography*, for example, identify many problems that never were addressed subsequently. A related and much bigger discrepancy was that the slippage between theory and practice became a chasm: everyone, not least those writing against photography, participated in the image world in a myriad of ways and without becoming chronic 'voyeurs' or 'tourists' of reality, succumbing to compassion fatigue, or otherwise suffering the harms that had been predicted so emphatically. Additional incoherence in the critical discourse developed as many of its own assumptions were exposed as inadequate by the twinned processes of digitalization and globalization. What should be clear, moreover, is that those assumptions were not faulty owing to changes in technology and society, but rather that those changes highlighted what had always been problematic: for example, the denial of artistry in the image and pluralism in audience response, or the unexamined universalism and elitism underwriting critical judgment. Most notable, however, is the inability of the critical discourse to account for how photography succeeds as a form of life: for example, how it is used to recognize and relate to people, places, and things that would be ignored otherwise, and how it articulates civil society, the public sphere, democratic citizenship, human rights, and other institutions and ideas that define modernity.

Long story short, the theoretical discourse of the past 40 years regarding photography is both a remarkable intellectual achievement and one that has to be refigured in order to better understand actual practices of media use and better serve progressive ideals. Perhaps that is why thinking on photography now is undergoing a paradigm shift. Scholars, curators, editors, and photographers of many different backgrounds are working the edges, or aslant, or outside of the critical orthodoxy.[2] We use the term 'paradigm shift' because it seems to fit the current situation so well: as anomalies, inconsistencies, and other problems accumulate in the conventional understanding of a field of inquiry, basic assumptions begin to be questioned, and alternative approaches become more plausible. Eventually new works produce a shift in the attention space and conceptual vocabulary: old problems are not solved so much as subsumed under new problems, and advances come via work in new areas of interest or with new ideas or methods. These initiatives can be related to larger changes in technology, society, and culture, but they have to be worked out within the relevant communities of practice. Eventually, they solidify into another conventional wisdom that also will need to be refigured.

Such processes of change are not neatly organized. The habitus of photography today appears to be wide open and dynamic, with everyone caught up in what may be contradictory processes (e.g., that extend both personal agency and system control). Likewise, many are still caught in a language that no longer describes their media use, but a better language is not readily available. We need to recognize both that the conventional discourse—for example, as provided through the continued dominance of *On Photography* in classrooms and bookstores—does not provide the conceptual and attitudinal resources that are needed, and that the better alternatives still are a work in progress.

The need for change is captured by Trevor Paglen's observation that the traditional debates about photography

> have become largely exhausted. Simply put, there is probably not much more to say about such problems as 'indexicality', 'truth claims', 'the rhetoric of the image', and other touchstones of classical photography theory. And what remains to be said about these photographic 'problems' seems increasingly extraneous to the larger photographic landscape that we inhabit.
>
> *(Paglen 2014: n.p.)*

As one example of how a revisionary project might proceed, and to do so on behalf of a stronger conception of public art and spectatorship, we offer several theoretical reconsiderations and a critical practice.

Developing the public image

In *The Public Image: Photography and Civic Spectatorship*, we offer a provisional statement of how a more productive engagement with photography might develop. In order to get some room to move, there is need to reconsider media specificity in this sense: to recognize how photography has been saddled with the "burden of representation." The term comes from John Tagg (1988), but here has a different inflection: referring to the tendency, first, to blame media for social ills that have other or more widely shared causes and, second, to blame one medium for deficiencies that apply to all media. So it is that we are continually reminded that photographs are fragments of reality, although texts are as well; that photo manipulation is a grave concern, although deception is pervasive in public discourse; and that politics is being destroyed by digital media and not by a toxic combination of money, greed, and venality. This ascriptive habit, then, is coupled with a defective model of persuasion. The significant photograph is supposed to be uniquely compelling: applying a *direct encounter* that produces a *moral shock* that produces a *decisive effect*. Almost nothing works this way, however, and so images will never fail to disappoint. Yet they will continually be blamed while other media and not a few political actors escape accountability.

Once free of an arbitrary burden of accountability, photography can be taken more directly on its own terms. One next step can be to re-emphasize the importance of image interpretation. This commitment may seem odd given the constant flow and churn of imagery today; surely one should be tracking large patterns and dynamic processes, not individual images that are ever more likely to be displaced by others that in turn are lost in the ever-growing data streams. But in fact, the single image persists, and it is through that small portal that one can encounter larger patterns more reflectively. Indeed, a lot of work and a lot of free labor go into creating the images that constitute public culture, and an engaged spectatorship is needed if those creative energies are to be realized. The creative encounter with the image happens through interpretation. Much of the time that process is tacit, and often it is banal. Some of the time, however, the image becomes a place for challenging or enhancing one's experience of the world. Whether eliciting revulsion or awe, or revealing the familiar as strange, or fragmenting what had been whole, or joining what had been separate—whatever the encounter, the image is at that point prompting important reconsideration of how one lives with others.

To interpret the image, one can apply the conventional discourse on photography that one has at hand; interpretation always involves some prior conceptual scheme, and most will start with what is familiar to them. As long as the intention—or better, the need—is to resist media dependency and political manipulation, that should do. For a deeper and broader encounter with the image, however, one often has to break it out of the hermeneutics of suspicion and a corresponding contextual literalism. The most productive way to do that is to recognize the value of decontextualization. The conventional wisdom is that the meaning of the image has to be grounded in a verbal description of the specific event being recorded. Anything else is inauthentic or worse: a violation of the photographic subject and an invitation to delusion. But, if photographic meaning is radically plural, then it cannot be contained by any one interpretation, even one that provides literal fidelity to the immediate social and material context in which the photograph was taken. It can be difficult to accept the full force of this idea. Susan Buck-Morss provides the direct statement that is needed:

> The complaint that images are taken out of context (cultural context, artistic intention, previous contexts of any sort) is not valid. To struggle to bind them again to their source is not only impossible (as it actually produces a new meaning); it is to miss what is powerful about them, their capacity to generate meaning, and not merely to transmit it. ...
>
> Meaning will not stick to the image. It will depend on its deployment, not its source. Hermeneutics shifts its orientation away from historical or cultural or authorial/artistic intent, and toward the image event, the constantly moving perception.
>
> *(Buck-Morss 2011: 228–29)*

Rather than tether the image solely to literal reference, this reconceptualization emphasizes how image and interpretation alike involve decontextualization and recontextualization. This approach to image analysis features the deep pluralism of photographic meaning and audience response, features of public culture that are advanced comprehensively by digital technologies and global circulation.

The operations of de- and re-contextualizing operate within all media, but they become easily apparent with photography. As it has expanded across all societies and subjects, photography has indeed created an 'image world' in which all become accustomed to seeing images that are already somewhat dislocated, reproducible across multiple media, simultaneously situated in a specific place and an abstract space. The place is a conjuncture of (at least) a medium (a newspaper, billboard, or cell-phone screen), social practice (commuting, working, socializing), and topic (say, a presidential election). The space is the virtual archive created by the proliferation of images throughout the lifeworld for over a century. That continual concatenation of images makes any photograph fungible and interpretation inevitable; thus, no image is tied resolutely to a single event, while its meaning and significance emerge as one context or another is activated. Stated otherwise, photographic meaning is created as spectators move one way or another through the "museum without walls" that is photography's most comprehensive effect within modern societies.

By using the phrase "museum without walls," we are invoking the ghost of André Malraux: the English phrase is the publisher's translation of Malraux's *Le Musée imaginaire*. Malraux argued that photography and printing together had created a new capability for experiencing art: one that will "carry infinitely farther that limited revelation of the world of art which the real museums offer us within their walls" (Malraux 1967: 12). "Infinitely" is more a marker of enthusiasm than empirical assessment, but his vision has already been expanded beyond his own reach: instead of merely changing art, the concept now is used occasionally to valorize the photographic archive and the image world it has created.

Malraux's idea was that photography aided the emergence of modern aesthetics; the "museum without walls" signified that mentality, or habitus, of the modern art world in which 'art' could exist as such. Malraux saw this habitus as a civilizational achievement, albeit one not yet fully realized. To now say that photography itself is the museum without walls is to go further in that direction, and to value the image world accordingly. Photography's giant open-air museum includes not only the art and artifacts of the past but recordings of every visible feature of human existence. Instead of the museum being a refuge from the world, one where politics and other conflicts could be temporarily suspended in aesthetic contemplation, now the world has been brought into the museum. Everything can be subjected to aesthetic judgment, which becomes a more widely available resource for public thought.

Although speaking of specific exhibitions, Ariella Azoulay has put the point succinctly: "Visiting the museum, contemplating visual items, and passing an aesthetic judgment are all necessary actions performed by the modern citizen" (Azoulay 2008: 159). Contrary to fears of being trapped within an image world, the museum without walls cultivates opportunities and skills for civic reflection and engagement that can transcend other forms of enclosure. Although the spectator can never return to a condition of presumed innocence, the possibility of imaginative expansion and reconfiguration of the public sphere is always available; indeed, the means for doing so are in fact part of the exhibition.

Photography's comprehensive decontextualization has become the optical unconscious of modern public culture. That culture is defined by capabilities for expanded spectatorship, epistemic pluralism, and recombinant capability. What once could only be seen *in situ*—such as the great Buddha statues of Bamiyan—can be seen in Tel Aviv or Chicago or Lost Springs, Wyoming, even though they no longer exist. Likewise, photography does not provide the direct view of the object —and good thing, too, as it instead provides many different views. Front, back, below, above, microscopic, aerial, larger, smaller: the camera and related production processes see and share well beyond ordinary perception. Thus, the museum equalizes and combines without regard for material constraints or social conventions. Malraux featured the equalizing of major and minor artifacts—putting statuary and coinage on the same plane, for example, and the combination of images across nations, arts, genres, and styles. Following the globalism and neo-primitivism of early twentieth-century cultural modernism, such comparisons now are conventional, but we may not have recognized how they are examples of our inhabiting a public art world created by photography.

We also might note that these features are the specific targets of the iconoclastic critique of photography, as when Sontag excoriates the medium for its democratic leveling of the arts and their corresponding taste cultures, and for its mixing of its subject matter to make surrealism the default mentality of mass society (Sontag 1977: 51–82). Democratic accessibility and aesthetic impurity are easy precipitates of the new, relatively abstract space, one in which their status as images comes to the foreground, but not the only result. To push the point, the critique of the image world requires that one see images *as images*—that is, already decontextualized—and not as images in use within specific practices and specific environments, serving specific functions. The critique depends on the virtual reality it faults.

The point here is not merely to undercut doctrinaire thinking. Photographs both have specific uses and are the medium for a pervasive decontextualization of everything else. The museum without walls is the place where anything might be placed beside anything else: jewels and bedsores, birthday parties and atrocities, war and peace. The difference then is in valuation: whether to see loss of an original meaning or an emergent pluralism; a reproduction of prior social authority or a prompting of more comparative, creative, and interrogative capabilities; most important, a lost world where things knew their place or the surreal world of life as it is actually lived—a world, for example, where weddings and bombings can happen in the same time and place.

Decontextualization can lead to a loss of value, or to a revaluation of values. The choice is not between a surreal image world and the enlightenment provided by critical reason, but rather between an iconoclastic attitude toward the image world and another, more capacious understanding of the image world that provides the resources for insight, solidarity, and perhaps even reconciliation.

By placing an event within the museum without walls, that event is not stripped of meaning but rather presented for a wider range of judgment. The museum provides the social distance, provisional disinterest, embodied engagement, and slow temporality that makes reflection possible, a shift that is summarized by the term 'aesthetic judgment', but not limited to that. What is key, however, is the process of variable decontextualization and recontextualization that comes from the equality of artifacts, plurality of views, and comparison across boundaries. In respect to specific works of art, these can be the conditions for creativity; when distributed widely, they can enable less prominent but widely shared habits of civic spectatorship.

Interpretation on these terms also reconfigures the central predicament in understanding photography, which is that the recorded image is simultaneously trace and artifact. The problem is that twentieth-century critique advanced an unduly reductive and pessimistic conception of both realism and the imagination that has led to an implicit doctrine of literalism that inhibits civic spectatorship. What is needed instead is a reinvigorated realism that requires a stronger conception of the photographic imagination—one that encourages a way of seeing beyond ordinary observation or conventional belief. We begin with Siegfried Kracauer's observation on the media specificity of photography, which is that it includes a reality principle and an artistic principle; the former is primary, but we argue that the latter is necessary for the full potential of the medium to be realized (Kracauer 1960: 3).

So it is that photographic interpretation requires working through three levels of imaginative engagement: First, the literal extension of causal regularity that is known in the design world as closure; for example, we assume people in photographs have lower bodies even if not shown. Second, a similar extension regarding intentionality, whereby we infer, albeit with less confidence, that other people's behavior is legible, as when crying communicates sadness. The third extension of the photographic imagination occurs as it fills out what Hannah Arendt has called the "space of appearance" that is the habitus of public life (Arendt 1998: 198). That space consists of the places, media, and discourses in which people create a shared world that becomes the basis for collective organization and action. This is a world where 'innumerable perspectives' intersect, and a world that has to be re-created continuously out of that condition of radical plurality through interactions with others, as they are seen by others. As Roger Silverstone summarizes, that re-creation is defined by "the visibility of the other, of the stranger as well as the neighbor, the capacity for dialogue and the manifestation of discord, the presence of alternative views and the struggle for an audience" (Silverstone 2007: 32). It also is a continuing act of imagination, one in which we see images as reality and strangers as fellow citizens, while continually adjusting our conceptions of what other people are thinking, feeling, and doing. Through the complex intertwining of what was and what might be, the public image becomes capable of invoking photography's democratic vision.

Photography's public world

We offer a provisional definition of photography as a small language about vernacular life in a public world: small, because of its limited formal repertoire, familiar topics and settings, and low status relative to the other arts; vernacular because focused on or consumed by ordinary people in everyday settings; public because open, accessible, and shaping belief regarding the general welfare (Hariman and Lucaites 2016: 11–14). As it has been incorporated into news, entertainment, advertising, and other media, and become intimately woven into the practices of everyday life, photography has become the visual medium central to the constitution of public culture. That culture is the virtual reality created by media and other social practices regarding modern civil society, citizenship, governance, and other collective concerns.[3] 'The public'—for instance, as in 'the reading public' or 'the viewing public' and their attention to 'the public interest'—operates as a constitutive set of norms, attitudes, habits, and beliefs that are continually negotiated through media use defined by open access and voluntary response. You can look at the picture or you can turn the page (or change the channel, swipe the screen, etc.). As you do so, you participate in one of the modern spaces (along with the market and the state) for negotiating matters of collective concern. Public cultures make norms and actions more or less legitimate, questions of justice and sustainability more or less intelligible, and officials and institutions more or less accountable. Most notably for our purposes, they absolutely depend on spectatorship. So it is that public arts constitute public cultures, and one of the features of twentieth- and now twenty-first century spectatorship is that it is increasingly framed by photography.

The encounter with photography as a public art requires more than working aslant the conventional discourse on photography; nor should it be reduced to questions of method. It is not news that photography has been entangled with modernity, modernization, and the aesthetic and political ideals of cultural modernism. By seeing it merely as a medium rather than a public art, however, it is too easy to see it as an all-too-typical example of how modern technology colonizes the lifeworld. Instead, one might consider how the relationships are both deeper and more ambivalent than the conventional wisdom suggests. As an alternative, we maintain that the distinctive content of photography is modernity itself (Hariman and Lucaites 2016: 97–136). Put differently, whereas photography theory has traditionally focused on photography's relationship with the past, our concern is with how the medium reflects modernity's characteristic orientation toward the present as an implicit future. From this perspective, photographs can capture both utopian dreams and processes of dispersion, enact both allegorical and prophetic attitudes, and feature characteristic modern habits such as waiting for progress to prevent catastrophe. One result is that some images offer an archaeology of the present, which invites consideration of contemporary civilization as if it were in ruins.

Within the context of modern media and institutions, photography can also operate as a characteristic means for social thought (Hariman and Lucaites 2016: 137–70). Rather than begin with either conventional considerations of class stratification or conflict, the focus here is on how photography is aligned with society as such, that is, as a relatively autonomous dimension of modern life. From this perspective, photography is acutely attuned to social performance and social relationships—including those that it creates through spectatorship. Representative photographs articulate this performative optic and how it reframes ritual events, tracks social mobility, and provides an aesthetic awareness of social texture and social structure. This aesthetic can double as a basis for thinking about political and economic relationships during a time when it is becoming easier and more profitable to make labor invisible. When left with the asymmetry of the individual within a social structure, photography can thus feature both the unique moment and processes of repetition.

One sure process of repetition is the persistence of war, and so photography theory needs to rethink the medium's intimate relationship with warfare (Hariman and Lucaites 2016: 171–226). The conventional wisdom suggests that images of violence provoke either perverse pleasures or the moral anesthesia of compassion fatigue. Following writers such as Linfield and Azoulay, we focus on how photographers regularly provide an anthropology of violence. As images capture the changing nature of war, the spectator is confronted with untethered violence, regime-made disasters, and the refeudalization of the modern world, as well as processes for the normalization of war within otherwise civil societies. One conclusion is that photography documents more about violence than its most horrific traces—particularly how a war culture is becoming increasingly entrenched in everyday life across the globe. To face this danger, what is needed is not skepticism about the medium, but rather a more explicit ethic of spectatorship.

That ethic, we argue, requires an additional revaluation. In place of anxieties about the deluge of images, the overcrowding of the image world, and similar figures of excess, we offer an alternative optic that sees the image world as an expression of abundance (Hariman and Lucaites 2016: 227–60). This alternative is not without its problems, but they are not the problems of scarcity, which have dominated cultural criticism since the allegory of the cave. Instead of a few images capable of enchantment for want of better light, we follow Paul Feyerabend in extending the idea that abundance is an important feature of both the image world and any other world we might want to inhabit. Because doctrines of scarcity lend themselves to antidemocratic attitudes in aesthetics and politics, the vast, ever-growing photographic archive might provide a schooling in democratic habits of mind and feeling—if we give some attention to how to see on behalf of an abundant life for all.

The museum on the street

To make our argument as we did, not least by continuing a practice of image analysis that we had developed on our blog, www.nocaptionneeded.com, our attempt to rethink photography (and particularly photojournalism) required working with specific limitations. We allowed for use of work in respect to digitization and globalization, but not in respect to political and rhetorical problems from outside of photography that interfere with good civic use of the medium. Some would note our lack of attention to the problems of media industries and institutions today; others might want more attention to collective responses, whether through analysis of dramatic events (Black Lives Matter) or through empirical reception study. *The Public Image* focuses on freeing photography from the claims about its deficiencies as a medium, on demonstrating its potential as a public art, and on nurturing interpretive ideas and habits for civic spectatorship, but it remains open to claims that it is too abstract: looking only at the public image in the museum without walls, inattentive to the economic pressures and other factors changing (corrupting) journalism, and too focused on individual responsiveness (the engaged, reflective encounter with the single image) rather than on collective responsiveness and solidarity.

These concerns are exacerbated by another problem: a commitment to photography as a public art should confront the dysfunctional state of the public sphere today. It has become all too evident that public culture is wracked by extreme forces of political partisanship, financial corruption, and media irresponsibility. Discourse, institutions, governance, you name it: democratic institutions are undergoing a severe test. There should be small consolation in noting that, for once, it is difficult to pin the blame on visual media. We are witnessing a comprehensive degradation of language, and one brought about by those who benefit from destroying the critical reason and public accountability it can provide.

These various problems converge on the question of how practices of photography and civic spectatorship might provide both critical engagement in a culture of lies and solidarity without tribalism. How does expansion of the photographic imaginary work in conjunction with renewed commitments to public institutions and public goods, and to developing the alternative sources of social energy and political organization needed to overcome the challenges now defining the twenty-first century? Or if that seems too grand, perhaps it would be enough to simply maintain public spaces, norms, and ideals during a bad time. Whatever the aspiration, there is need to pay more attention to how the museum without walls is reconstituted frequently as a specific exhibition.

Photography exhibitions have become a regular feature within institutions such as art museums—where we now regularly can see strong commitments to a rich interplay of photographic genres. One affordance of a photographic exhibition is that it can bring the museum without walls inside the literal museum; no longer an enclave from a radically democratic image world, the arts institution can expand its role to draw on energies and challenges that world provides. As Malraux observed, "the museum was an affirmation, the museum without walls is an interrogation" (Malraux 1967: 162). The point is not to show a wider world, but to create conditions for critical reflection and to identify untapped resources for collective life. Thus, by channeling and condensing the larger archive, the photography exhibition might challenge fixed ideas of locality and history. For example, in a nation that defines itself according to assumptions of scarcity—some of them accurate—an exhibition might reveal untapped potential for change.

A converse process may occur within the many exhibitions that occur in vernacular spaces such as street markets and train stations, or online over time on specific topics. There the attention habits of public life—for example, habits of indifference to signage and strangers alike—are brought up short and refocused for aesthetic and moral encounters that converge in public judgment. Amid all of the anxieties about the deluge of images produced by digital technologies, it is notable that the image world also is continually being reconstituted in particular sites. Amid concerns about compassion fatigue, social isolation, and the acceleration of the news cycle, it is notable that effort is continually being made to slow people down, encourage them to look at images of a common world alongside other spectators, and do so on behalf of civic education and political advocacy.

Perhaps we should not be surprised that the most famous exhibition in the history of photography, *The Family of Man*, began in a high-status art museum, traveled extensively to many venues worldwide, and was distributed further as a book that is still in print. It also was the favorite whipping boy for those setting out the conventional discourse on photography (e.g., Barthes 1957; Sekula 1981), and its revisionary reconsideration recently is a good example of the paradigm shift now underway (e.g., Turner 2012; Azoulay 2013; Ferretti-Thelig and Krautz 2016). There were antecedents as well, not least in the political and artistic movements of Europe in the 1920s and 1930s, when surrealist montage and other curatorial techniques were developed. Many of today's exhibitions probably are driven primarily by recent technological and media affordances and the skills available to small organizations. With photo reproduction and display equipment ready to hand, mounting the exhibition may be the least of the difficulties involved.

The challenge for those thinking about photography today is to work out the terms for seeing both the limitations and the value of these venues. On one hand, they would seem to compensate for many of the stock criticisms of photography as a means of technological reproduction: they are situated, material, face-to-face encounters; they activate and interact with local contexts of interpretation; they disrupt the signage and other conventions of the image world as it already is structured by advertising and the state; and they hail spectators as citizens and as members of a public whose opinions matter. On the other hand, they remain subject to a host of problems: they are ephemeral, providing no ongoing place for collective reference or response; they are built for 'drive-by' consumption rather than capable of motivating collective action; they are likely to be absorbed into the surrounding décor, signage, and patterns of distraction and indifference; and, like the images they feature, they provide only a partial and exclusionary vision of public life.

Such concerns are always relevant to assessments of public art, but they also can distract from both more specific and more global issues. The specific issues involve those curatorial, presentational, and organizational decisions that define an exhibition. We emphasize as well how they are extensions, *mutatis mutandis*, of what are core capacities of interpretation. Active interpretation includes curatorial selection, both to establish a basic sense of genre or topic and much more creatively as well. To look at an image now includes the decisions to store, compare, or share it; sharing involves decisions about presentation (large file or small? Facebook or email?) and organization (Who is in the network? To what purpose?). Most of the time these decisions are tacit, instantaneous, and banal. But the exhibition raises the stakes while bringing the ends and means of interpretation to the foreground.

The exhibition—and the global distribution of exhibitions—also serves to both expand and shape the space of continuous interpretation on the spectator's terms that Malraux celebrates at the close of *Le Musée imaginaire*. Exhibitions make the audience part of the image. The spectator is always there, of course, as the photograph's reason for being, as one element in the event of photography, and as potential energy waiting to be released.[4] Stated otherwise, the exhibition is the visible form of what Azoulay has labeled the "civil contract of photography." The exhibition provides the "new form of encounter" that denominates spectators as citizens of photography, a public realm transcending other political boundaries, suggesting new forms of visibility for new forms of political action (Azoulay 2012: 24). The fact that it often is so demonstrably small, provisional, and contingent, or that "new" often means merely "hoped for," should take nothing away from the theoretical claim. The exhibition is a visible demonstration of how all photography coheres to create an abundant public space, a force field within which claims to justice, care, and solidarity can always be legible and occasionally capable of mobilization.

Staging a common world

Many exhibitions still take place in clearly demarcated institutional spaces, most prominently museums and professional galleries of one sort or another. These will continue to be important venues, but recent technological changes also have made it easier for photographic exhibitions to move into a wide array of increasingly vernacular public spaces. These spaces include train stations and airports, shopping malls, walls that otherwise divide and/or connect cities and communities, local/community-oriented galleries, or online locations such as Instagram and other social media outlets. The exhibitions invite passersby to become civic spectators.

The most prominent source of exhibitions of professional photography is organized by World Press Photo (WPP), which annually takes its award-winning photographs on a worldwide tour to 45 cities in more than 100 countries. The global audience for the WPP exhibitions exceeds 4 million people per year. It may be surprising that the tour is not seen as a contemporary Family of Man, but the differences probably do outweigh the similarities. In any case, the number of images submitted for the awards, the breadth and skill of the photographers and the photographs, the curatorial expertise, and the public exposure and commentary create a cultural statement—and professional controversy—each year. The exhibitions draw on these features of the WPP museum without walls, but provide more material and site-specific relationships as well. As many of the exhibitions are in cultural institutions, they then will be able to open those gallery walls via the public scenes and optics of press photography. When they are in public spaces such as the Berlin Hauptbahnhof, they convert a minimal sense of public interaction into a more deliberative encounter.

Many exhibitions are much smaller affairs: organized with fewer resources, more local subjects, and far less status. The exhibition on the street is particularly subject to these limitations, which, like the small language of photography itself, can become resources for artistic and political engagement in the face of controversy, trauma, and denial. Three smaller projects that illustrate the range of such exhibitions include the Activestills Collective, the Philly Block Project, and Everyday Africa.

Activestills

Activestills began in 2005 as a group of Israeli, Palestinian, and international photographers dedicated to "the power of images to shape public attitudes and to raise awareness on issues that are generally absent from public discourse." Working as documentary photographers, but on behalf of social justice rather than press neutrality, they view themselves as part of the struggle "against all forms of oppression, racism, and the violations of the basic right to freedom," including "the Palestinian popular struggle against the Israeli occupation, rights of women, LGTBQ, migrants and asylum-seekers, public housing rights, and the struggle against economic oppression" (Activestills, n.d.-a; Maimon and Grinbaum 2016: 31). Signing their work collectively, they also maintain long-term relationships with the communities where they bear witness, distributing their work through alternative and social media and as free exhibitions, both in the places where the photographs were taken and in cities throughout Europe, the Middle East, and the United States.

The collective also is attempting to open the visual field to create new public encounters. In place of simply showing victims, they feature and invite agency. Instead of trying to capture the decisive moment, they track the slower, more insidious forms of violence. Rather than rely on icons, they develop an archive and, foregoing much of the iconography of protest, they follow the odd, often chaotic angles of intimacy amid conflict and its devastating aftermath; this 'slow violence' too often appears invisible to the eye in any single iteration but builds across time and space to produce catastrophic results (Nixon 2013). And, rather than rely on the supposed power of the image to compel moral response, they assume that it has to work within complicated processes of interpretation, operating within the context of what Azoulay calls the civic contract of photography.

As an example, one might consider their #Obliterated Families Street Exhibitions (Activestills, n.d.-b), which puts on display family members who were killed and portraits of survivors of 50 of 142 families that lost three members or more during an Israeli military offensive on the Gaza Strip during the summer of 2014. The exhibitions, which have been on display in cities around the world, including Tel Aviv, Marseilles, Berlin, Warsaw, and Boston, are pasted on public walls, some of which disrupt the commercialization of the public space and others of which mark the very dissolution of the public and private. Figure 10.1 is symptomatic of the latter point.

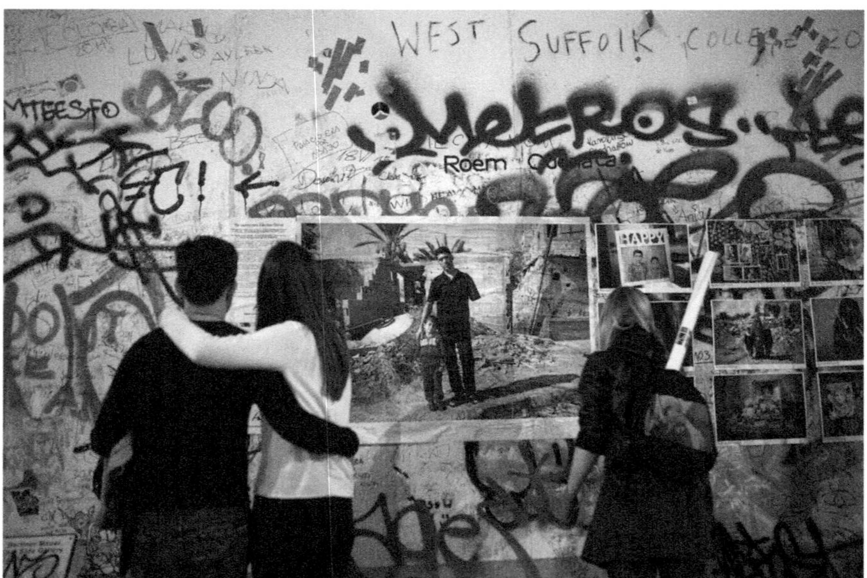

Figure 10.1 Anne Paq/Activestills.org, *Obliterated Families* in *Gaza* street exhibition, Berlin, Germany (November 7, 2015). Courtesy Activestills

The wall, a public space on a street somewhere in Berlin, has already been marked with graffiti that challenges the relationship between the public and private spheres of life. The Activestills exhibit, pasted to the wall, amplifies that dissolution as it layers photographs of family members apart from their families on a space that is now no longer clearly public or private, but somehow both at once. The photograph of the scene underscores the renewed sense of civic life animated by the exhibition, not least by the couple, arm in arm—spectators who also stand in for the families and potential families that are or could be exempt from the violence exposed by the exhibition. In short, the exhibition invites a unique and active spectatorship that in this case attends not just to the individuals who have been killed, but to the *civic* responsibility for the *private* lives that have been "obliterated" or mutilated in the process and otherwise *publicly* ignored. The exhibition confronts that process by restoring the lost families to public visibility and public accountability.

Just as the public art of graffiti transformed the wall from blank anonymity and enclosure to a display space for transgressive self-assertion, the photographic exhibition changes it again from a palimpsest of idiosyncratic signage to a call for engagement in a world of relationships and obligations. The multiple overlays created by the photograph of the scene and its online posting continue both lines of articulation: the exhibition becomes one part of a layered world in which each spectator can occupy multiple positions and reflect on specific encounters with the photographic subjects and other spectators. The continuous unfolding of the photographic encounter through repeated acts of spectatorship reflects back on the seeming endless continuation of the processes of destruction. Perhaps there is some counterpoint or consolation in the exhibition's other process: the way that it stops the passerby, slows down the act of seeing the destruction, and thus provides an example of how seeing can be the first of a series of disruptions. The vernacular exhibition collates subjects and spectators for moments of alignment and identification, but its chief benefit may be a template for small acts of resistance. If so, the inability to hold their attention for long need not be a concern.

Activestills also is available as a book (Maimon and Grinbaum 2016). By working through the volume, one's sense of inside and outside (and public and private, safe and not safe, etc.) begins to shift. Not to create the illusion that 'you are there', but to realize that violence extends beyond spasms of direct conflict to become a system of domination pressed into the fabric of life. Likewise, instead of looking for one image or signature event, one begins to appreciate the weight of the archive, the judgment of history, the profound need to work day after day, person by person, until justice and solidarity prevail. These ideas acquire personal texture in the interviews and statements within the book by photographers and other activists, whose understanding of their work, individually and collectively, reminds us of what may be the most important lesson of all: whatever the technology, artistry, or means of distribution, photography at its heart is an encounter with the world.

The Philly Block Project

Photo exhibitions often have a professional feel about them largely because amateur photographers lack curatorial skills or the opportunity to display their images in institutional spaces such as museums or art galleries. Their photos are consigned to family photo albums, old shoe boxes, and hard drives that never achieve a public audience and are rarely seen by anyone at all. The Philly Block Project addresses this problem—and much more—by bringing the members of Philadelphia's South Kensington neighborhood into collaboration with conceptual artist Hank Willis Thomas to "enable residents to image themselves" as a means of discussing "more challenging topics about the transition of their neighborhood" (Myers 2017).

South Kensington (aka North Philly) is a multi-ethnic neighborhood facing all manner of problems and transformations, not least the economic and social difficulties posed by gentrification. The primary task of the Philly Block Project was to construct a visual narrative that would preserve and celebrate the heritage of the community, past and present, by drawing upon the photographic memory of its residents (Crimmins 2016; Rupp 2016). The project operated in two registers: the first was to get members of the neighborhood to participate by contributing photographs from their family archives, in some cases going back five generations; the second was to persuade members of the neighborhood to be photographed by members of Thomas's team. Neither was a simple task. As one of the coordinators for the project put it, "There are a lot of reservations in the community about contributing images." In the words of one member of the neighborhood, "they don't want to expose their family. We're talking about family history" (Melamed 2016). In the end, the power of letting the people tell "their own story" prevailed, and the neighborhood archive grew to more than 15,000 photographs (Kinney 2016). A selection of more than 500 photographs were treated as bricks—or blown up to take the place of doors and windows (see Plate 13)—and used to recreate the neighborhood as a collage of the history of its diversity across time.

Added to these collages were life-sized photographs of the contemporary members of the neighborhood taken by Thomas and his team. The exhibit was then displayed at the Philadelphia Photo Arts Center, which became a site for the members of the neighborhood to gather and engage the multiple issues posed by its gentrification.

What makes the Philly Block Project especially unique is how it incorporated the members of a diverse and multi-ethnic neighborhood into the production of the exhibit itself. They were not just the subjects of the exhibit, but they had contributed a part of themselves as members of a community, either through photographs from their family archive or by being photographed themselves. This last point is illustrated clearly by Plate 13, for, although the "block" is made up of hundreds of individual photographs, it is defined by no single image but by the collection itself. The neighborhood, in short, was more than any one individual or family, or any one religion or ethnicity. That said, it was quite common for particular individuals to find the portions of the block in which their photographs were displayed and to have photographs taken of them observing the scene in which they were represented, using their spectatorship to activate a sense of the community by thus adding one more photograph to the neighborhood archive.

Just as it complicates the relationship between family and community, the Project complicates the relationship between interrogation and affirmation. By seeing one's family or clan or ethnic identity in the neighborhood, one also sees how it is but one piece of and one perspective on the neighborhood. (This panoramic view is not the typical perspective for most of us.) By bringing private photo archives into public display, they become open to questioning in terms of the norms of public life such as transparency, equality, and justice, yet, together, the archive produces a powerful elevation of the neighborhood into visibility, recognition, and legitimacy. The aggregation of individual images becomes transformed into an image of community. The Philly Block Project shows how photography's democratic distribution and accessibility, and its capacity for displaying pluralism within a commodity form, can be used to create models for collective association. And, once again, the exhibition can transform walls (material and virtual) of exclusion into the museum without walls, a space for imagining larger visions of collective life.

Everyday Africa

There is no news in recognizing that the public sphere has moved from a physical location to a virtual space. What makes the Everyday Africa project interesting is how it has used that space as a virtual museum to curate a local, vernacular retelling of the story of Africa. The project began in 2012 when Peter DiCampo and Austin Merrill, on assignment in the Ivory Coast with a grant from the Pulitzer Center, discovered that the mundane, everyday photographs they took with their cell phones told a more complex and nuanced story of Africa and Africans than was commonly represented in editorial assignments that featured refugees, famine and poverty, and the victims of war. As they tell the story, the western media showed no interest in the everyday Africa where scholars bent at their desks, shopkeepers tallied receipts, adults commuted to work, children played, families ate dinner at home—a world that included architecture, theater, high fashion, and other features of civilization (Estrin 2012; Merrill and DiCampo 2017: 15). To rectify this misrepresentation, they created Everyday Africa as an Instagram feed designed to tell stories that would challenge—or at least supplement—the stereotypes one finds regularly and commonly represented in the western press. They were soon accompanied by other photographers, many of them local to the African continent, and as of this writing the Instagram feed includes more than 3,700 photographs and 350,000 followers.

No single photograph from the project tells the whole story, and that is in some measure the point that is being made here. But perhaps the first photograph taken by DiCampo (Figure 10.2) is suggestive of the whole.

The caption reads "An elevator in a government building in Abidijan, Ivory Coast." The photograph is altogether ordinary; more so, it is altogether mundane. The man in the foreground is casually dressed, the elevator bears the markings of everyday usage, the angle of the photograph is somewhat askance, the colors are muted and subdued; there is certainly

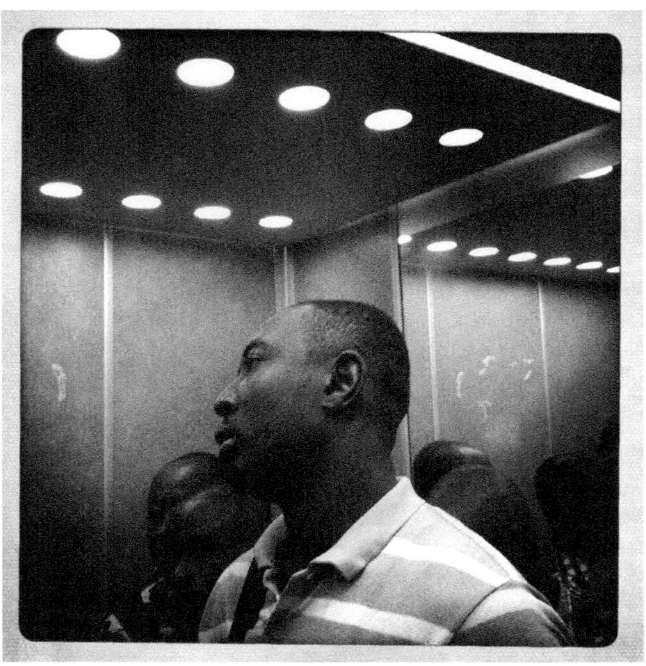

Figure 10.2 Peter DiCampo, *Man in Elevator*, in a government building in Abidjan, Ivory Coast, *Everyday Africa* series (March 1, 2012). Courtesy the artist

nothing exotic about the photograph or the world it represents. Indeed, how often do we think about government buildings in places like the Ivory Coast, let alone elevators, typical vehicles of modern urbanity? And yet the photograph offers a window into a regular and everyday aspect of such a life. The man's gaze and posture, like those behind him, suggests the casual indifference to strangers defining civic interaction in modern societies (Warner 2002: 65–124). Even the hushed green color scheme (not visible in the reproduction in this volume) marks something altogether commonplace if not actually monotonous when placed in contrast to the bright and vibrant colors typically used to make Africa exotic (Lutz and Collins 1993: esp. 87–118).

The banality of the image should not distract from its artistic qualities. The wash of color despite the bright white lighting suggests that one might look aslant at the scene, much as the man may be doing while waiting for his floor. The rows of lights repeated in the mirror image mime the operation of the camera, again suggesting a reflective moment. The turn from spectacular to vernacular optics does not produce a loss of meaning or responsiveness; instead, it recalibrates one's sense of scale and channels meaning and engagement into the small things and "ordinary affects" of everyday life (Stewart 2007). This process could be considered a way of re-enchanting the world, on secular terms. One important difference from the colonial optics that are being challenged by the exhibition is that this texturing and energizing of Africa occurs not in terms of its supposed primitivism or other civilizational differences, but in a manner that is directly continuous with the habitus of a spectator anywhere in the developed world. It is precisely the "casual inclusiveness" of such photographs that "[catalyzes] a new form of journalism that thrives not on the decisive moment but rather on a reality told in small pieces, from multiple perspectives" (Gottschalk 2017), and on behalf of multiple opportunities for identification.

Occupying a virtual space, Everyday Africa has opened itself up to a wide array of photographers who contribute at will. More than that, however, the project has expanded in a number of different directions. On one hand, it has developed a collaboration with the World Press Foundation to develop the African Photojournalism Database on Blink, connecting local photographers with the global media network and, thus, extending the reach of African photographers, as well as collaborating on exhibitions in Charlottesville, VA, and in the Netherlands (World Press Photo, n.d., Everyday). It has also begun to develop curricula as part of the Everyday Projects nonprofit organization that engages high school students by probing their stereotypical conceptions of Africa, exploring the roots of these conceptions, and then challenging them via the Everyday Africa project (Ruiz-Grossman 2017). Perhaps the greatest success here, however, is how the Everyday Africa project has been appropriated and adapted by other groups such as Everyday Middle East, Everyday Black America, Everyday American Muslim, Everyday Asia, Everyday Palestine, and so on, as well as some topically focused sites, such as Everyday Climate Change, all in the interest of using the virtual space of the internet to activate the civic spectatorship that is necessary for public recognition and institutional accountability.

Conclusion

There is no one theoretical discourse that can encompass all of photography, just as there is no one technology or practice that should represent the whole. A once radical discourse has become conventional, however, and photography's continued technological, demographic, and cultural expansions are prompting reconsideration of foundational assumptions and missed opportunities for artistic development, political advocacy, and scholarly understanding. Any alternative approach has to get beyond current habits of interpretation, and one such path is to consider how photography operates some of the time as a public art. *The Public Image* is our attempt to outline such an approach, and this chapter takes the additional step of looking to exhibitions and particularly vernacular exhibitions to move beyond the limitations of our own project.

An exhibition is located in a particular place or media site where one faces immediate constraints in terms of social, economic, political, and organizational circumstances. Even when limited to passersby choosing to stop unexpectedly, it displays the act of seeing in common and, by placing viewers in a direct encounter with public images, it materializes and performs the conditions of civic spectatorship and calls the viewers to a "civil contract" that can support solidarity and community. As Azoulay emphasized while defining that contract: "the citizen of photography enjoys the right to see because she has a responsibility toward what she sees" (Azoulay 2008: 144). The exhibition materializes these relationships and, thus, a shift from "the ethics of seeing or viewing to an ethics of the spectator" whose responsibility is toward the world and not merely the process of representation (Azoulay 2008: 130). These are the relationships that are most consequential and most at risk in any public culture, and the vernacular exhibition emphasizes how they always need to be recreated from the ground up.

For the same reason, the exhibition's ephemerality becomes another sign of photography's civic potential. It is episodic and, thus, might be capable of disrupting the 24/7 flow of information and misinformation that is the envelope of modern politics. It offers direct encounters and so cannot hide behind the combination of deceit, distance, audience segmentation, and repetition that is destroying the public sphere today. It something that can be done with relatively modest resources.

The question remains whether the many small exhibitions around the globe and throughout the global media environment can be more than flares of conscience. Indeed, it may be that more work needs to be done—that exhibitions and spectators alike need to be harnessed to political and social movements on behalf of photography's own democratic promise.

Notes

1 The conventional wisdom was promulgated by Roland Barthes, Guy Debord, Susan Sontag, Alan Sekula, John Berger, John Tagg, Victor Burgin, Rosalind Krauss, Abigail Solomon-Godeau, Martha Rosler, Carol Squires, and many subsequent scholars. It was preceded by and occasionally draws on Frankfurt School media theorists such as Siegfried Kracauer, Walter Benjamin, Berthold Brecht, Theodor Adorno, and Max Horkheimer. For the record, we find the latter group to be more sophisticated and less iconoclastic than many of those who came after them, not least in being willing to consider how media have both exploitative and emancipatory potential.

2 The community that is working out the paradigm shift includes writers such as Dora Apel, Ariella Azoulay, Geoffrey Batchen, Susan Buck-Morss, David Campbell, Lilie Chouliaraki, Geoff Dyer, Jae Emerling, Cara Finnegan, Paul Frosh, Liam Kennedy, Wendy Kozol, Susie Linfield, Nicholas Mirzoeff, W. J. T. Mitchell, Margaret Olin, Griselda Pollock, Jacques Rancière, Mark Reinhardt, Fred Ritchin, John Roberts, Vanessa Schwartz, Kaja Silverman, Sharon Sliwinski, Shawn Michelle Smith, David Levi Strauss, Barbie Zelizer, and ourselves, among many others.

3 An extended discussion of the concept of "public culture" is provided in Hariman and Lucaites (2007: 2–24) and Hariman (2017).

4 On the spectator's importance in the "event" of photography, see Azoulay (2008: 137–86; 2012: 26–27). On the spectator as potential energy in the camera, see Hariman and Lucaites (2016: 25–28).

References

Activestills (n.d.-a) *About Us*, from http://activestills.org/about.php [accessed June 27, 2017].
Activestills (n.d.-b) #Obliterated Families Street Exhibitions, from http://activestills.org/node.php?node=exhibition_307 [accessed June 27, 2017].
Arendt, H. (1998) *The Human Condition*, 2nd ed., Chicago::: University of Chicago Press.
Azoulay, A. (2008) *The Civil Contract of Photography*, Brooklyn, NY: Zone Books.
Azoulay, A. (2012) *Civil Imagination: A Political Ontology of Photography*, London: Verso.
Azoulay, A. (2013) "*The Family of Man:* A Visual Universal Declaration of Human Rights" in T. Keenan and T. Zolghadr (eds.) *The Human Snapshot*, Feldmeilen, Switzerland: LUMA Foundation, pp. 19–48.
Barthes, R. (1957) "The Great Family of Man" in trans. Annette Lavers, *Mythologies*. New York: Hill & Wang, pp. 100–2.
Buck-Morss, S. (2011) "Visual Studies in Global Imagination" in C. Bottici and B. Challand (eds.) *The Politics of Imagination*, Abingdon, UK: Birkbeck Law Press, pp. 214–33.
Crimmins, P. (2016) "Kensington Closeup Features Hundreds of Photos Assembled Block by Block," *Newsworks*, September 6, from https://whyy.org/articles/kensington-closeup-features-hundreds-of-photos-assembled-block-by-block [accessed June 27, 2017]
Estrin, J. (2012) "Picturing Everyday Life in Africa," *Lens, New York Times*, September 17, 2012, from https://nextcity.org/daily/entry/north-philadelphia-gentrification-art-history-display [accessed June 27, 2017].
Ferretti-Thelig, M. and Krautz, J. (2016) "Sprechende Bilder der Menschheit Relationalte Bildpraxis am Beispiel der Ausstellung 'The Family of Man'" in A. Glas et al. (eds.) *Sprechene Bilder, Besprochene Bilder, Bild, Bergriff und Sprachhandeln in der deiktisch-imaginativen Verständigungspraxis*, Munich: Bettinga (Hrsg), pp. 303–26.
Gottschalk, M. (2017). "How Everyday Africa Sparked a Movement that's Changing Western Stereotypes of Africa," *Artsy.Net*, May 31, 2017, from www.artsy.net/article/artsy-editorial-viral-instagram-account-changing-western-perceptions-africa [accessed June 27, 2017].
Hariman, R. (2017) "Public Culture" in J. Nussbaum (ed.) *Oxford Research Encyclopedia of Communication*, New York: Oxford University Press, from http://communication.oxfordre.com/view/10.1093/acrefore/9780190228613.001.0001/acrefore-9780190228613-e-32
Hariman, R. and Lucaites, J. L. (2007) *No Caption Needed: Iconic Photographs, Public Culture and Liberal-Democracy*, Chicago: University of Chicago Press.
Hariman, R. and Lucaites, J. L. (2016) *The Public Image: Photography and Civic Spectatorship*, Chicago: University of Chicago Press.
Kinney, J. (2016) "When Telling the Story of Changing Neighborhoods Becomes Part of the Story," *Next City*, October 31, 2016, from https://nextcity.org/daily/entry/north-philadelphia-gentrification-art-history-display [accessed June 27, 2017].
Kracauer, S. (1960) *Theory of Film: The Redemption of Physical Reality*, New York: Oxford University Press.
Linfield, S. (2010) *The Cruel Radiance: Photography and Political Violence*. Chicago: University of Chicago Press.
Lutz, C. and Collins, J. (1993) *Reading National Geographic*, Chicago: University of Chicago Press.
Maimon, V. and Grinbaum, S. (eds.) (2016) *Activestills: Photography as Protest in Palestine/Israel*, London: Pluto Press.
Malraux, A. (1967) *Museum Without Walls*, trans. Stuart Gilbert and Francis Price, London: Martin Secker & Warburg.
Melamed, S. (2016) "In South Kensington, Uniting a Neighborhood Through Photography," *The Philadelphia Inquirer*, March 22, from www.inquirer.com/philly/entertainment/arts/20160323_In_South_Kensington__uniting_a_neighborhood_through_photography.html [accessed June 27, 2017].
Merrill, A. and DiCampo, P. (2017) "All the Stories" in T. van der Heijden, P. DiCampo, A. Merrill, and N. Acquah (eds.) *Everyday Africa: 30 Photographers Re-Picturing a Continent*, Berlin and Heidelberg: Kehrer Verlag, 15–17.
Mitchell, W. J. T. (2005) *What Do Pictures Want?* Chicago: University of Chicago Press.
Myers, M. (2017) "A Yearlong Photo Project Captures the Spirit of a Philadelphia Neighborhood," *The Renewal Project*, April 10, 2017, from www.therenewalproject.com/a-yearlong-photo-project-captures-the-spirit-of-a-changing-philadelphia-community/ [accessed June 27, 2017].
Nixon, R. (2013) *Slow Violence and the Environmentalism of the Poor*, Cambridge, MA: Harvard University Press.

Paglen, T. (2014) "Is Photography Over?" *Still Searching*, March 3, 2014, from http://blog.fotomuseum.ch/2014/03/i-is-photography-over/ [accessed June 27, 2017].

Ruiz-Grossman, S. (2017) "Stunning Photos Bust Stereotypes of What 'Everyday Africa' Looks Like," *Huffpost*, June 14, 2017, from www.huffingtonpost.com/entry/everyday-africa-instagram-photos_us_5940406fe4b003d5948b9586 [accessed June 27, 2017].

Rupp, J. (2016) "The Philly Block Party Documents Life in South Kensington," *Philadelphia Weekly*, February 17, 2016, from www.philadelphiaweekly.com/news/the-philly-block-project-documents-life-in-south-kensington/article_4d600e22-c26c-5e17-9ac2-fa26bb54ab8e.html [accessed June 27, 2017].

Sekula, A. (1981) "The Traffic in Photographs," *Art Journal* 41 (1981), pp. 15–25.

Silverstone, R. (2007) *Media and Morality: On the Rise of the Mediapolis*, Cambridge: Polity.

Sontag, S. (1977) *On Photography*, New York: Picador.

Stewart, K. (2007) *Ordinary Affects*, Durham and London: Duke University Press.

Tagg, J. (1988) *The Burden of Representation: Essays on Photographies and Histories*, Amherst: University of Massachusetts Press.

Turner, F. (2012) "*The Family of Man* and the Politics of Attention in Cold War America," *Visual Culture* 24, pp. 55–84.

Warner, M. (2002) *Publics and Counterpublics*, New York: Zone Books.

World Press Photo (n.d.) "Everyday Africa and World Press Foundation Launch the First African Photojournalism Database on Blink," from www.worldpressphoto.org/news/2016-08-08/everyday-africa-and-world-press-photo-foundation-launch-first-african [accessed June 27, 2017].

11

Still images on the move

Theoretical challenges and future possibilities

Marta Zarzycka

In September 2015, a photograph of a drowned Syrian boy, Aylan Kurdi, lying face down in the sand on a Turkish island, was traveling across media contexts. As it did so, it underwent a number of material, aesthetic, affective, and spatial changes and evoked varying responses among audiences all around the world. On Facebook and Twitter, the photo was generally shown cropped, as a close-up, often oversaturated with color for more dramatic effect, and posted with the hashtag #Humanity Washed Ashore. It was further used in photoshopped memes that removed the small body from the original background. Thousands of shares online triggered reactions ranging from shock, horror, and doubts about its authenticity to anger at fellow users for converting the photograph into a piece of sentimental visual currency. In the mainstream press, the less-cropped (and therefore less-striking) version of the image was prevalent, sometimes in pixelated form. Many readers saw it as a powerful catalyst for the international community to support refugees' rights and likened it to the iconic 1984 image of the Afghan refugee girl by Steve McCurry. There have been claims that the image's reception shaped the refugee policy of certain host countries, generating further discussion of the impact of images on international policy-making. At the same time, the juxtaposition of the photograph with sensational captions in newspapers from European countries that refused to take in Syrian refugees sparked outrage at the hypocrisy of Western corporate media. Very quickly, the image was incorporated in art projects, often unsettlingly devoid of text, becoming a mournful allegory. In other projects, it transgressed the limits of a photographic medium, becoming a cartoon, a sand sculpture, or a mural. Eventually, the photograph made its way to banners used at political protests and inspired a reenactment by both European and Syrian activists staging the scene using their own bodies, lying motionless on a seashore. Most notably, Chinese artist Ai Weiwei was photographed lying face down on a pebbled beach on the Greek island of Lesbos, a key point of entry into the European Union, as part of a series of projects engaging with the refugee crisis. This action foregrounded the tangible presence of the boy's body, hardly acknowledged when scrolling the news on handheld devices.

Rather than speculating why this very image has been called 'iconic' (a word problematic in itself in the neoliberal economy of visual capitalism) and was claimed to move millions of global onlookers, I am interested here in a different set of questions: How can we, photography scholars and safely distant audiences alike, make sense of its migration in the era of digital connectivity, its relatively easy image manipulation, and the alarmingly short attention span of global publics? How can we map its changing meaning and impact as its travels impact dynamic processes of contemporary spectatorship and appropriation of, and engagement with, war images? Although "being a spectator of calamities taking place in another country [remains] a quintessential modern experience" (Sontag 2003: 18), the conditions of this spectatorship have changed drastically in the last decade. The increasing significance of citizen-produced photographs and art practices alongside established journalistic practices, as well as the entangled relationship between visual media and political uprising (e.g. in Egypt; Khatib 2013), makes it vital to consider image mobility and its stakes in the contemporary visual economy.

Building on a number of strategies to place photographic migration at the forefront of visual analyses, this chapter is an attempt to begin mapping this theoretical terrain and to make my own contribution to the development of a methodological agenda for this migration. Although there have been several attempts to develop a methodological framework and agenda for research on mobilities of mediated (visual) data (D'Andrea et al. 2011; Keightley and Reading 2014), visual and media studies have only recently sought to address the fact that this mobility is inescapable. The consequences of this mobility are remarkable: photographs migrate, passing through various distribution channels and before various audiences, assuming different forms, and undergoing mediation by different technologies and users as they do. Although the ethical case for considering war photographs is undisputable, we need sustained methodological reflection on how to make their contemporary travels our analytical lens. The ways in which photographs of war (understood broadly as images capturing armed confrontation as well as its aftermath: military and civilian casualties and survivors, destruction of households and urban spaces, poverty, forced displacement, the psychological consequences of trauma) are perpetually reshaped by, and implicated in, processes of image migration have yet to be engaged with fully and explicitly by photography scholars.

Different ways photographs migrate

The conditions for making, disseminating, watching, and using war photographs are radically different than they were just ten years ago. As a result, the contemporary spectator of war has splintered: her experience of distant conflicts is no longer limited to images encountered in one place, but rather consists of endless encounters as images travel across (sometimes overlapping) sites, spaces, and screens. Visual technologies themselves have become more portable, allowing the photographs of war and conflict to occur in new sites and to transform these sites. Next to professional journalism, for decades the chief context in which people encountered war photographs, other realms bring war to the attention of Western publics. Increasingly sophisticated mobile devices combining high-quality cameras and access to instantaneous online publishing have put powerful tools in the hands of social media users, both witnesses to and participants in violent conflicts (Andén-Papadopoulos and Pantti 2011). At the same time, appropriations of war photographs in artistic practices (frequently recasting photographic content in a new medium) propose increasingly critical readings of news images (Allan 2013; Pollock 2012), and their use in political interventions in urban space testifies to photography's power to form affective communities (Hesford 2011; Zarzycka 2016).

War photographs are exchanged on a scale unimaginable before; their compactness and instantaneousness—in contrast to video footage—enable them to move rapidly across mainstream magazines and newspapers, both print and online, social media such as Facebook,

Twitter, Instagram, soldiers' and civilians' photo blogs, museums, galleries (think of the work of Alfredo Jaar or Oscar Munoz), pop-up art spaces, biennales, and finally peaceful and armed demonstrations, and marking of urban spaces with posters, leaflets, and graffiti. A photo in a Gaza paramedic's Twitter post makes the front page of *The Guardian*, an embedded reporter's snapshot posted to Instagram becomes an exquisite (and expensive) prize-winning print in a professional photography contest, and a shot taken by a mobile phone camera is turned into an oil painting (think of Fernando Botero's paintings of the infamous Abu Ghraib photographs). This migration beyond the confines of a photographic medium can be found, for example, in Magnus Wennman's video documentary called *Fatima's Drawings*, where the drawings made by a five-year-old Syrian refugee in Sweden, recounting (in a voiceover) the trauma and loss she experienced in Syria and while fleeing to Europe, suddenly come to life through animation.

Finally, migration between various visual aesthetics (and consequently rhetorics) frequently takes place. At this time of upheaval of the boundaries of photojournalism (Cottle 2006), photographs produced by people living in the war zones and made available on social networks almost instantly are frequently blurry, shaky, and unedited, evoking debates on the *anti-aesthetics* of "raw" documentary footage (Foster 2002). Migrating to front pages of international newspapers, they undergo changes through photoshopping, cropping, digital enhancement, color adjustment, and other post-production tools. Western mainstream media continue to present images that are visually elaborate, 'cleaned', and perfected. The subtraction of color (images reproduced in black and white, either with artistic intent or simply to cut printing costs) or, conversely, the color saturation of originally black and white photographs (exemplified by the work of artist Sanna Dullaway, who 'adds' tint to historical photographs) can be seen as another technology of migration. Although they add another layer to our engagement with photography—the layer of gesture, of material involvement—such transformations, in the eyes of many, transgress standards of professional photojournalism, as witnessed in very recent controversies in prestigious photography contests. For example, the World Press Photo jury in 2015 disqualified more than 20 percent of proposed contest finalists owing to excessive (and often blatant) post-processing of a RWA file, often involving significant addition or subtraction to the image content, filters, dodging and burning, toning, color adjustment, conversion to grayscale, or cropping. The World Press Photo research project titled *The Integrity of the Image* was commissioned to assess what are the accepted standards relating to the manipulation of still images in photojournalism and documentary photography. However, in the times where all images are processed, depending on aesthetical judgment or political agenda, it becomes increasingly hard to argue for the 'integrity' of an image understood as pure, untouched, or fixed and immobile.

Image migration: reuse or rebirth?

Rather than 'dissemination' or 'circulation', terms commonly used in the cultural studies' 'mobility turn' (Bauman 2000), I propose to use the more embodied concept of 'migration' as an analytical lens that brings into view new constellations of socio-political relations. Instead of only portraying migration as a passive effect of new technologies (e.g. tracing the travels of the digital file in cyberspace, like numerous studies on digital photography to date), the ways in which images *change* in the process, as they are conscripted, appropriated (that is, adopted to signify new reality), and altered by their users, need to be thoroughly examined. The term 'migration' signifies here the broad, emergent cluster of ways in which war photographs travel. Photographic images are an irreducible constituent of the social experience of migration itself: while the global movement of individuals and communities has been a main feature of modernity, it has also played the key role in the expansion of visual culture in general, and photography in particular in, the imperialist and post-industrialist era. Millions worldwide are now forcibly displaced owing to war, persecution, the expulsion of minorities, land expropriation, natural disaster, or economic collapse. As this happens, national borders loosen and tighten, accommodating finance and trade while warding off mass movements of people. Photographic migration echoes the migration of human bodies, caused by war and imperialist politics; now, in the era of digital connectivity, photographs circulate across national borders (and technological devices) more freely than the subjects whose bodies they capture (Zarkov 2007).

These rapidly changing and destabilizing circumstances of photographic migration demand adequate and self-reflective ways of approaching the images of war. Whereas scholarship on war photography has usually been bound to one or another of these contexts of encounter, a new framework for understanding the dynamics and significance of the migration of war photographs across the multiple contexts of encounter, genres, aesthetics, and spaces is much needed. The ongoing wars have generated enormous quantities of grassroots and professional photojournalism, art-based activism, and public protest, while spawning massive citizen-made coverage and state-produced propaganda. The coverage of more recent conflicts has been informed by rich historic and iconographic traditions: of "war on terror" (Chouliaraki 2012), of mass displacement (Said 1986), and of extreme graphicness when representing civilian casualties (Baer 2002). Nonetheless, although war images have been the subject of substantial scholarship (e.g. Goodman et al. 2007; Mitchell 2005; Tumber and Palmer 2004), there has been little attention to the migration of photographs. The framework of existing photographic theory needs critical revision: claims regarding the veracity of the digital file (Becker 2013), its iconic status, its power to capture personal and collective trauma (Stallabrass 2012), or its belonging to a certain iconographic tradition (Boltanski 1999; Zelizer 2010) are underwritten by a set of assumptions that no longer hold true in the new media ecology of perpetual migration. The shifts in traditionally recognized characteristics of photography (documentary value, authenticity, correctness and truth) propel other shifts: in the power dealings, viewing practices, dialogic relations, image vulnerability, as well as the ways the audiences are constructed as they appear. The precise ways in which photographs are shaped by and implicated in processes of migration, and the ways in which the practices and experiences of migration are mediated have yet to be engaged with fully and explicitly by either photography scholars or media actors, or software engineers who design tools for scanning and classifying visual data online. The very recent example of the removal (and consequent reinstating) by Facebook of a photo of the 1972 image of a naked Vietnamese girl, Kim Phúc, running from a napalm attack, taken by Pulitzer Prize-winner Nick Ut of the Associated Press—,a fixture in our visual landscape—illustrates well contemporary dilemmas surrounding image mobility and the lack thereof. Facebook took action against the photograph as a result of the company's anti-pornography regulations, enforced both by human moderators and via a technology designed to scan for images related to child sexual exploitation. It consequently revoked its decision citing the photograph's 'iconicity' and 'global importance' as a reason to re-insert it into the visual sphere. In other words, it was the photo's institutional and historical gravity and its claims to inclusion in mass-mediated collective memory that have become its passport back to visibility. I cannot help thinking, however, that Ut's image's mobility, and its ability to *keep on* being mobile, happens at the cost of other images—the thousands of images of children afflicted by war in Syria, in Palestine, in Israel, in Ukraine, in Afghanistan, children who may or may not be partially or entirely unclothed, the corpses of children, children ailing among ruins, children far removed from the hopeful and cleaned-up images of NGO campaigns, taken off Facebook daily and unclaimed by outraged public. The abrogation and defense of the right to migrate across media platforms are important issues that contemporary conditions for disseminating documentary photographs demand that we face in the new media networks, where the issues of machine learning and scalability often overpower human judgment.

Moreover, in the times of endless circulation of photographs, photography research cannot afford to stand still, bound to one discipline only. Though various scholarly debates have addressed issues of context (Edwards and Lien 2014), framing (Minh-ha 1992), appropriation (Rigney 2012), intertextuality (Rancière 2007), re-mediation (Bolter and Grusin 1999), and transmediality (Kember and Zylinska 2012), to date, war photography has hardly been studied across the scholarly disciplines. Although a renewed interest in "media ecologies" or "transjournalism" is emerging in contemporary cultural studies (Appadurai 2013), a broader move to theorize how meanings and engagement are shaped by and implicated in the migration of images across contexts has not been undertaken. Some effort has been made to follow the travels of photographic icons, such as Nick Ut's shot of a napalmed Vietnamese girl or images of the Abu Ghraib atrocities (Hariman and Lucaites 2007; Perlmutter 1998), but this scholarship has remained limited to a handful of globally celebrated images rather than providing a systematic framework of analysis. Breaking through current discipline-bound debates to examine the media landscape in which art practices, social media, professional journalism, and political interventions in urban space are increasingly mutually referential and integrated into the fabric of everyday life is a much-needed practice. Whereas the debates around the "politics of the image" in the field of photography and visual culture tend to concentrate on the decoding of photojournalistic trophy shots, seen as static and immobile, current research ought to foreground the urgency of re-tracing and re-establishing as many links as possible between the photograph and the travels it undergoes, combining multiple disciplinary approaches and methodologies to bring into view a larger functional picture, one that allows comparison and contrast and encourages critical examination of multiple contexts for viewing war.

Although several scholars have called for such a breakthrough (e.g. Juhasz and Lerner 2006), the study of war imagery remains divided in academic research. Whereas scholarship on the global dissemination and connectivity of images has flourished with the rise of digital technologies (e.g. Lister 1995), scholars working on war imagery have usually been bound to their own specific, often clashing, interpretive contexts. Although we cannot account for *all* of the destinations of an image, photographic research should address multiple instances, rather than one instance, of its visibility: grassroots and professional photojournalism; art-based activism; public protest; state-produced propaganda; historical publications; international art fairs; gallery and museum exhibitions; pop-up art spaces; social media platforms such as Facebook, Twitter, and Instagram; blogs by participants in conflicts on both sides; subjects of forced migration and diasporic correspondents; online art initiatives; and newspapers and news sites.

Finally, as is the case with human migration, the questions of autonomy and agency are inevitable and demand constant consideration. Whereas some scholars argue that digitalization has helped the image become reproducible, curing it of its inherent passivity (Groys 2008), others claim that the perpetual removal of the image from itself—through the processes of reproduction and alteration—permeates it with non-identity and disassociation, creating a space where images become reproductions, copies, approximations, or quotations of themselves, governed as an amenable site of speechlessness (Steyerl 2012). Depending on their context, their aesthetic transformation, their use, and their audiences, war images may reinforce or dispute social and political hierarchies, perpetually reconfiguring and re-inscribing their stance.

Mobility and materiality

Researching photographs as transient and ephemeral sources of information has been dominant in photography studies (Sekula 2002). War images especially seem to rely on the cultural belief in (need for?) the transparency of the photographic medium, often suppressing the attention to the material properties of the images and their physicality in space for the sake of their representational value. War photographs, circulating in ever-increasing numbers and at multiplying speeds across our smartphones, laptops, and tablets, have come to be understood by Western audiences as ephemeral 'windows to the world', giving us visual access to distant conflicts. Cultural theory has largely neglected consideration of their materiality in favor of concerns with the aesthetics and frequently shocking content of these images (Sontag 2003). Those few scholars who have engaged with photography's materiality (understood here as a question not only of materials per se, but of activating material relations; Bruno 2007) have done so only in relation to the collector's fine print or cherished keepsake (Batchen 2006; Langford 2008), and increasingly as an archival object (Edwards and Hart 2004), often in an ethnographic rather than sensorial exploration. Moreover, although photographs' material properties have been examined by various strands of photography theory, either established or emergent (Barthes 1981; Fried 2008; Tagg 2009), none of the existing scholarship has paid attention to the *changing* character of these properties when photographs migrate, moving from analogue print to screen or from magazine to art installation.

And yet, to move is often to change material properties. Photographs have "volume, opacity, tactility and a physical presence in the world" (Batchen 1997: 2) that oscillate and waver as they travel. These transitions between digital volatility and the material, tangible 'objecthood' of war imagery (often becoming a painting, a sculpture, a part of animated footage, or an audiovisual installation) have large consequences for viewers' sense of spectatorship. As a result, rather than seeing screens, projections, posters, murals, or canvas as a neutral support for war images, the functional context of the changing materiality is integral to the construction of meaning.

This work has been predominantly done in artistic practice rather than academia. Going back decades, artists such as Hanna Hoch, Kurt Schwitters, John Heartfield, Andy Warhol, and Martha Rosler have used photographs in their montages, collages, and installations as powerful means to politicize artistic discourse. In their works, photographs become objects that are not only representational and visual, but also material and visceral. Still more recent transitions in the media landscape have enabled artists such as Thomas Hirschhorn, Alfredo Jaar, Jeff Wall, Sophie Ristelhueber, or Mark Wallinger to find an opportunity for tactile and spatial engagement with war and political violence that is often more corporeal and more reflective than is the case with either professional photojournalism or social media contexts, therefore upending the consumption regimes of contemporary visual culture. Among the strategies they use, for instance, are 'analoguing' or re-editing digital images for use in tangible installations; superimposing stills with other prints, objects, materials, or surfaces; making newspaper prints parts of audiovisual installations; or enclosing images in light boxes. All of these strategies foreground and exploit the material properties of photographs such as texture, scale, weight, tactility, surface, pixilation, stability/mobility, and screen multiplication, enhancing physical, kinesthetic, and multisensorial (involving senses other than vision, such as touch, sound, proprioception) engagements with the photograph. Interrogating and challenging the status of war photographs as transparent signifiers that travel seamlessly across cultural contexts, these recent art projects engender relationships between the images and their audiences that are different from the transactions that take place when we see photographs on computer screens and propose new affective, aesthetic, and ethical modes of engagement with the reality of war.

Thomas Hirschhorn's work might help illustrate this claim: his *Incommensurable Banner* (2010) provides a particularly compelling example of photographic migration that affects the materiality of images. The artwork consists of an 18-foot-long white fabric banner printed with photocopied, graphic photographs of mutilated bodies. In this work, Hirschhorn put photographs found on social media sites through a number of material changes. Part of an impromptu construction, they are printed on ostensibly cheap material, and their graininess and haphazard compilation—with some of the details lost in the folds of the fabric and others vividly standing out—disturb the seamlessness and ease with which we scroll the news on handheld devices. Bringing a sense of tangibility and palpability to the images, Hirschhorn's installation renders us aware of the physical presence of our own bodies, their spatial situation, and their separation from the bodies of the wounded and the dead.

Focusing on the material transformations of photographs in Hirschhorn's banner, we might consequently tackle several important questions that largely remain unasked in both cultural theory and photography studies: How does the placement of war photographs in art installations offer new modes of interactivity? How do their material transformations influence viewers' experience of space, temporality, proximity, and subjectivity? And, what are the particular qualities of the gallery and the museum as contexts that shape the active and embodied role of the visitor? Rather than seeing banners, screens, projections, posters, murals or canvas as a neutral support for war images, the scholarly attention to the material changes in migrating photographs might bring back the functional context of the materiality as integral to the construction of meaning, specific to changing sets of relationships and environments.

Photographic (im)mobility as social awareness

Both photographic and human migratory practices are driven or limited by national borders, political agendas, affective attachments, and spatial constraints. Although the relatively wide availability of communications technologies, transnational broadcasting, and international and diaspora journalism networks transcend former geographically based surveillance boundaries and local agendas, other factors foster the immobility of war images or their detour to other media. The motion or motionlessness of war photographs has for decades been determined by political propaganda and dissent, artistic agendas, grassroots activism, and editorial permissiveness or censorship (Papenburg and Zarzycka 2013). An increasing cultural interest in the power of photographs, propelled by the urgency of organizing and processing the ever-growing flow of images from conflict zones and the emergence of new communities around the sharing and repurposing of photographs and the participatory cultures that result, needs to include the examination of the forces that drive or limit the mobility of images in times of increasing neoliberalization of war and growing visual consumerism (Butler and Athanasiou 2013). What are the trajectories that photographs of war follow as they migrate across the contexts of professional journalism, social media, artistic practices, and political interventions in urban space, and what are the cultural/political forces that make them mobile *or* stagnant? These forces, simultaneously dictated and internalized by major photography stakeholders (publishers, news editors, curators, humanitarian aid workers, political activists), include the rigidity of national borders, contemporary copyright laws and conventions, licensing fees, threat of copyright violation, ownership laws, broadcast licensing and similar legal structures, commercially and market-based interests, editorial decisions made out of respect for the deceased and their families, social media platforms' policies regarding violent content, institutional infrastructures, cultural taboos and censorship, the presence of resonant cultural tropes and symbols, political agendas, historical momentousness, corporate or governmental propaganda, commodification of spectacle, processes of selection and homogenization, and artistic endeavors to raise awareness. The above example of Nick Ut's image illustrates how multiple forces determine an image's visibility and invisibility, its mobility and inertia.

Consequently, the flow and trajectory of an image of a drowned Syrian boy mentioned above have been determined by both state or counter-state. Some news outlets chose not to share it, but other outlets decided to do so, prompting the resurgence of a long-running debate about censorship, gatekeeping, voyeurism, and the ethics of spectatorship. The fact of the (non)reproduction of the photograph and the (lack of) permissibility of changes in its scale, resolution, motion, or color have been considered a litmus test for both highbrow journalism and participatory social media activism. Following these changing cartographies, the novel role of photography in cultural processes of 'occupying space' (or being denied that space) needs to be uncovered. The consideration of its access and limits, of its mobility and stasis, offers the possibilities for a new engagement with the photograph as it travelled and a deeper understanding of the affordances and limitations of photographic migration.

Gender and postcolonial issues in photography studies

Finally, interdisciplinary migration of current research on photographs needs to be addressed more rigorously. Images of war have been studied within the fields of art history, media and communication studies, journalism, literature, and peace, conflict, and refugee studies. My strong belief is that the conceptual framework of gender and postcolonial theory, with its ongoing commitment to recognizing empowerment and oppression under war, remains crucial in examining photographic representations of war. Research pertaining to cultural and ethical queries sparked by a new, decentralized, and interconnected circulation of images, concerned with the issues of gender, race, nationhood, and citizenship in the practices of Western spectatorship, is the only viable way to encounter these images in an ethical way. Although much scholarship has pertained to the "Western gaze" and the challenges of the cultural translation of text and imagery across geopolitical communities (Butler 2009), this gaze has been perceived as solid and fixed, rather than dynamic and diffracted. Scholarship concerned with gender, ethnicity, nationhood, and citizenship has provided important analyses of discourses and practices serving to represent subjects in the context of violence (Rentschler 2011). A new critical understanding of the ways in which collective and individual identities are shaped through the migration of photographs in times of war, decolonization, forced migration, globalization, and the process of European integration, and of the consequences of an often uncritical general use of images is urgently needed.

The fact of human migration has been used in gender studies to (re)shape notions of nationalism, citizenship, diaspora (Alexander and Hawkesworth 2008; Ponzanesi 2014; Sassen 2000), the enforcement of social and spatial boundaries and the designation of subordinated groups (Spivak 1993), the social control of belonging, exclusion, and identity (Benhabib 2002), and the ethical and political communities of spectatorship recognizing the "suffering of others" (Azoulay 2012). An important ethical stake of this scholarship has been to denaturalize the dissemination and reception of images by Western audiences (that is, media-savvy audiences worldwide, who read and comment upon journalism published in the centers of European and North-American powers), and to critically appraise the capitalist, neoliberal, postcolonial mechanisms that map the world into "spectator zones and sufferer zones" (Chouliaraki 2006: 19). Foundational gender and postcolonial theories expound on representations of non-Western subjects as a visually compelling spectacle (Nakamura and Chow-White 2012), engaging with enduring questions about the ethics of aestheticizing or even 'glamorizing' oppression.

Conversely, feminist theory has contributed to bringing several critical social theoretical themes to the forefront of studies on human migration, foregrounding the politics of scale, mobility as political force, and space as convergent to identity (Grosz 1995). Feminist geographers, for instance, have challenged colonial, imperial, and capitalist appropriations of space and national territorial enforcement practices (Massey 1994; Rogoff 2000), arguing that social relations are fundamentally spatial. The same assumption might be made when analyzing visual migration—images take on various meanings and acquire various affective power when circulating from the small individual screen of a phone to large protest banners held in urban space. Portraits of casualties of the state (such as Aylan Kurdi) or photographic testimonies of state-sponsored violence find their way from our smartphones to urban spaces we occupy with our fellow (non)citizens, to the off-line activism of mass demonstrations on the ground, to banners, posters, leaflets, graffiti, or murals. As they do so, they are changed by the power relations produced in these spaces and how, in turn, they invest these spaces with new power relations (Bhahba 1994; Rogoff 2000). An approach to photographic images that is driven by the question of how the idea of space, geography, and distance can be asserted photographically is necessary in developing a critical mode of analysis of visual imagery.

Moreover, feminist theory is particularly helpful to think about how the migration of images can produce novel modes of affective involvement, identification, or resistance. Affects, emotions, and feelings have become tangible commodities in neoliberalism and late capitalism (Zarzycka 2013, 2014). Critically expounding on scholarly claims that emotions are the main force that feeds the dynamics of revolutions such as the Arab Spring (Naghibi 2011), this strand of scholarship assumes that, profoundly shaping the experience of community and collectivity, emotions are frequently employed by political bodies to maintain global and local market consumerism, pro- or anti-war attitudes, social divisions, and notions of national belonging (Ahmed 2004; Anker 2014). There is no doubt that photographs of war undergo the changes of affective powers while migrating among contexts: for example, image dissemination on social media frequently challenges the more sanitized, reductive, or curtailed ways of mainstream journalism. Images that seem most mobile—shared, liked, cross-linked—become an integral part of a customized and participant-regulated affective system, a tool of exchange of emotions through a conversational and collaborative user experience. Although the concepts of mobility and its affective properties have taken prominent place in feminist and postcolonial theory concerned with violence and abuse of sovereign power (Cvetkovich 2007; Ngai 2005), they have never been applied to war photography.

Conclusion

Responding to still images on the move requires constructing their existence as something active, dynamic, either random or intentional, but never neutral or straightforward. The new conditions of fabrication, circulation, visibility, and, finally, possible intervention into photography have altered mainstream media, social platforms, streetscapes, and museum spaces. Mapping the trajectories of photographs' migration—several aspects of which have been outlined in this chapter—foregrounds particular claims regarding contemporary appropriation, engagement with, and impact of the visual representation of contemporary wars. The analytical trajectories in photography research proposed here need to be developed further and synthesized in order to form a model for the comprehensive analysis of the nature and consequences of the new mobility of photographs.

Consideration and examination of how photographic mobility can foster new relationships between photographic practices and their distributors and audiences are important research endeavors in today's profoundly changed media landscape. Aware of the ever-changing circumstances and cultural/political urgencies, we research and teach about the photographs of war, trauma, atrocity, and carnage. However, until we eschew traditional separations between audience, text, technology, and institution, our methods will keep pulling us back into their orbit, both in writing and in teaching praxis. The photographic migration marks the limit of what is possible with traditional visual analysis. The perpetual mobility of images cancels the promise of their transparency and uproots a visual logic patterned along terms such as 'indexicality', 'punctum', 'iconicity'. It must, therefore, be informed by both empirical analysis and methodological approach, as well as by the researchers' reflection upon the ethics and politics of the research itself.

References

Ahmed, S. (2004) *The Cultural Politics of Emotion*, Edinburgh: Edinburgh University Press.

Alexander, K. and Hawkesworth, M. E. (eds.) (2008) *War and Terror: Feminist Perspectives*, Chicago, IL: University of Chicago Press.

Allan, S. (2013) *Citizen Witnessing: Revisioning Journalism in Times of Crisis. Key Concepts in Journalism*, Cambridge: Polity Press.

Andén-Papadopoulos, K. and Pantti, M. (eds.) (2011) *Amateur Images and Global News*, Bristol: Intellect Books.

Anker, E. R. (2014) *Orgies of Feeling: Melodrama and the Politics of Freedom*, Chapel Hill, NC: Duke University Press.

Appadurai, A. (2013) *The Future as Cultural Fact: Essays on the Global Condition*, London: Verso.

Azoulay, A. (2012) *Civil Imagination*, London and New York: Verso.

Baer, U. (2002) *Spectral Evidence: The Photography of Trauma*, Cambridge, MA: MIT Press.

Barthes, R. (1981) *Camera Lucida: Reflections on Photography*, New York: Hill & Wang.

Batchen, G. (1997) *Burning with Desire: The Conception of Photography*, Cambridge, MA: MIT Press.

Batchen, G. (2006) *Forget Me Not: Photography and Remembrance*, Princeton, NJ: Princeton Architectural Press.

Bauman Z. (2000) *Liquid Modernity*, Cambridge: Polity Press.

Becker, K. (2013) "Performing the news," *Photographies*, vol. 6, no. 1, pp. 17–28.

Benhabib, S. (2002) *The Claims of Culture: Equality and Diversity in the Global Era*, Princeton, NJ: Princeton University Press.

Bhahba, H. K. (1994) *The Location of Culture*, New York: Routledge.

Boltanski, L. (1999) *Distant Suffering. Politics, Morality and the Media*, Cambridge: Cambridge University Press.

Bolter, J. and Grusin, R. (1999) *Remediation: Understanding New Media*, Cambridge, MA: MIT Press.

Bruno, G. (2007) *Atlas of Emotion: Journeys in Art, Architecture, and Film*, New York: Verso.

Butler, J. (2009) *Frames of War: When Is Life Grievable?* New York: Verso.

Butler, J. and Athanasiou, A. (2013) *Dispossession: The Performative in the Political*, London: Polity Press.

Chouliaraki, L. (2006) *The Spectatorship of Suffering*, London: Sage.

Chouliaraki, L. (2012) *The Ironic Spectator: Solidarity in the Age of Post-Humanitarianism*, Cambridge: Polity Press.

Cottle, S. (2006) *Mediatized Conflict: Developments in Media and Conflict Studies*, Maidenhead: Open University Press.

Cvetkovich, A. (2007) "Public feelings," *South Atlantic Quarterly*, vol. 106, no. 3, pp. 459–468.

D'Andrea, A., Ciolfi, L. and Gray, B. (2011) "Methodological challenges and innovations in mobilities research," *Mobilities*, vol. 6, no. 2, pp. 149–160.

Edwards, E. and Hart, J. (eds.) (2004) *Photographs, Objects, Histories. On the Materiality of Images*, London and New York: Routledge.

Edwards, E. and Lien, S. (eds.) (2014) *Uncertain Images: Museums and the Work of Photographs*, London: Ashgate.
Foster, H. (ed.) (2002) *The Anti-Aesthetic: Essays on Postmodern Culture*, New York: The New Press.
Fried, M. (2008) *Why Photography Matters as Art as Never Before*, New Haven, CT: Yale University Press.
Goodman, S. T., Grundberg, A. and Perez, N. (2007) *Dateline: Israel: New Photography and Video Art*, New Haven, CT: Yale University Press.
Grosz, E. (1995) *Space, Time, and Perversion. Essays on the Politics of Bodies*, New York and London: Routledge.
Groys, B. (2008) *Art Power*, Cambridge, MA: MIT Press.
Hariman, R. and Lucaites, J. N. (2007) *No Caption Needed: Iconic Photographs, Public Culture, and Liberal Democracy*, Chicago, IL: University of Chicago Press.
Hesford, W. (2011) *Spectacular Rhetorics: Human Rights Visions, Recognitions, Feminisms*, Durham, NC: Duke University Press.
Juhasz, A. and Lerner, J. (eds.) (2006) *F is for Phony: Fake Documentary and Truth's Undoing*, Minneapolis, MN: University of Minnesota Press.
Keightley, E. and Reading, A. (eds.) (2014) "Mediated mobilities: introduction," *Media, Culture & Society*, vol. 36, no. 3, pp. 285–301.
Kember, S. and Zylinska, J. (2012) *Life after New Media*, Cambridge, MA: MIT Press.
Khatib, L. (2013) *Image Politics in the Middle East*, London: I.B. Tauris.
Langford, M. (2008) *Suspended Conversations: The Afterlife of Memory in Photographic Albums*, Montreal: McGill-Queen's University Press.
Lister, M. (ed.) (1995) *The Photographic Image in Digital Culture*, London and New York: Routledge.
Massey, D. (1994) *Space, Place and Gender*, Minneapolis, MN: University of Minnesota Press.
Minh-ha, T. (1992) *Framer Framed*, New York and London: Routledge.
Mitchell, W. J. T. (2005) *What Do Pictures Want? The Lives and Loves of Images*, Chicago, IL: University of Chicago Press.
Naghibi, N. (2011) "Diasporic disclosures: social networking, neda, and the 2009 Iranian Presidential Elections," *Biography*, vol. 34, no. 1, pp. 56–69.
Nakamura, L. and Chow-White, P. (2012) *Race after the Internet*, London and New York: Routledge.
Ngai, S. (2005) *Ugly Feelings*, Cambridge, MA: Harvard University Press.
Papenburg, B. and Zarzycka, M. (eds.) (2013) *Carnal Aesthetics: Transgressive Imagery and Feminist Politics*, London: I.B. Tauris.
Perlmutter, D. D. (1998) *Photojournalism and Foreign Policy: Icons of Outrage in International Crises*, Westport, CT: Praeger.
Pollock, G. (2012) *Photographing Atrocity: Becoming Iconic*? in: G. Batchen, et al. (eds.) *Picturing Atrocity. Photography in Crisis*, London: Reaktion Books, pp. 65–78.
Ponzanesi, S. (2014) *The Postcolonial Cultural Industry: Icons, Markets, Mythologies*, Houndsmill: Palgrave Macmillan.
Rancière, J. (2007) *The Future of the Image*, London and New York: Verso.
Rentschler, C. (2011) *Second Wounds: Victim's Rights and the Media in the U.S.*, Durham, NC: Duke University Press.
Rigney, A. (2012) *The Afterlives of Walter Scott: Memory on the Move*, Oxford: Oxford University Press.
Rogoff, I. (2000) *Terra Infirma: Geography's Visual Culture*, London and New York: Routledge.
Said, E. (1986) *After the Last Sky*, London and Boston, MA: Faber & Faber.
Sassen S. (2000) "Women's burden: counter-geographies of globalization and the feminization of survival," *Journal of International Affairs*, vol. 53, no. 2, pp. 503–524.
Sekula, A. (2002) "Between the net and the deep blue sea: rethinking the traffic in photographs," *October*, vol. 102, no. Autumn, pp. 3–34.
Sontag, S. (2003) *Regarding the Pain of Others*, New York: Farrar, Straus & Giroux.
Spivak, G. C. (1993) *Can the Subaltern Speak*? in: P. Williams and L. Chrisman (eds.) *Colonial Discourse and Post-Colonial Theory*, Harlow: Longman, pp. 66–111.
Stallabrass, J. (2012) *Memory of Fire: Images of War and the War of Images*, Brighton: Photoworks.
Steyerl, H. (2012) *The Wretched of the Screen*, Berlin: Sternberg Press.
Tagg, J. (2009) *The Disciplinary Frame: Photographic Truths and the Capture of Meaning*, Minneapolis, MN and London: University of Minnesota Press.
Tumber, C. and Palmer, J. (2004) *Media at War: The Iraq Crisis*, London: Sage.

Zarkov, D. (2007) *The Body of War: Media, Ethnicity and Gender in the Break-up of Yugoslavia*, Durham, NC, and London: Duke University Press.
Zarzycka, M. (2013) "Feelings as facts: The World Press photo contest and visual tropes," *Photographies*, vol. 6, no. 1, pp. 177–184.
Zarzycka, M. (2014) "Save the child: photographed faces and affective transactions," *European Journal of Women's Studies*, vol. 23, no. 1, pp. 28–42.
Zarzycka, M. (2016) *Gendered Tropes in War Photography: Mothers, Mourners, Soldiers*, London and New York: Routledge.
Zelizer, B. (2010) *About to Die. How News Images Move the Public*, New York: Oxford University Press.

12

Interview with Ariella Azoulay

Ariella Azoulay and Justin Carville

Introduction, Justin Carville

In 2010, Tamara Lanier, a probation officer from Norwich, Connecticut, began to research her family's genealogy. Through historical records of US census information, Connecticut Historical Society genealogists and multi-generational familial oral histories, Lanier traced her ancestors to an African-American slave named Renty Thompson, who, she believes, was the son of a slave also known as Renty from a plantation in South Carolina (Barry 2011). This later Renty was notable as he was one of the subjects of fifteen daguerreotypes commissioned by the Swiss-born Harvard scientist Louis Agassiz. The daguerreotype of Renty, along with those of his daughter Delia and the other African-born slaves are a well-known chapter in the history of racial photography as one of the earliest examples of anthropological photography from Harvard University's Peabody Museum of Archaeology and Ethnology (Wallis 1995). Taken by the photographer Joseph Thompson Zealy in 1850, the daguerreotypes were commissioned by Agassiz to demonstrate the anatomical differences of the slaves and their descendants in support of his polygenesis beliefs that races had distinct origins, which validated nineteenth-century polygenic racial theories of white, western superiority over other racial groups.

Having traced her family's genealogy to someone whom she believed to be a direct descendant of the figure of Renty in Agassiz's collection of daguerreotypes of African-born slaves, in 2019 Lanier issued a lawsuit against Harvard University for ownership of the daguerreotypes (Hartocollis 2019: n.p.). The legal action against Harvard for its "wrongful seizure, possession and expropriation of photographic images of the patriarch of her family" claims that Renty and his daughter Delia were forced to "pose for the daguerreotypes without consent, dignity, or compensation," and that "their images like their bodies before, remain subject to control and appropriation by the powerful, and their familial identities are denied to them."[1] Although the law suit is bound to the legalities of the obstruction of property rights of slaves and their descendants, as a political act seeking the repatriation of ancestral identities through the photographic image, it is a reminder of Ariella Azoulay's call not to 'look' at photographs as evidence of something that was there, but to 'watch' them and the subjects they depict as an ongoing presence in the space of political relations constituted by photography (Azoulay 2008: 16). Indeed, Lanier's lawsuit to repatriate the image of Renty and his daughter from the power relations that subjugated their bodies as slaves is the type of political reimagining of the governing of photography and its uses that Azoulay's work has sought to claim for photography in its relations with a civil imagination that pursues social relations of solidarity between photographer, subject and viewer. Azoulay's tripartite model of the "participant citizens" incorporated into the act of photography—what she has termed the civil contract of photography—has marked a significant intervention into photographic theory of social power relations (Azoulay 2008: 17). Positioning the gaze of the viewer as restorative of the rights of photographed subjects to be citizens through their solidarity with those depicted in photographs in situations in which they have been subjugated, Azoulay's work has both sought to move beyond the limits of photographic theory that has focused on photography as constituting a new ethics of seeing, the empathetic gaze and compassion (and its fatigue) on the one hand, and the Foucauldian social power model of photographic historiography on the other. Indeed, as Azoulay prophetically notes in her own discussion of the Agassiz daguerreotypes of Renty and his daughter Delia, although subjected to the symbolic violence of the power relations that rigidly posed them before the camera, they were aware that they were "objects of a gaze that transcends the here and now," an addressee who is not present but whose gaze loosens the oppressive limits of the photograph and its taking (Azoulay 2008: 176–185).

With the exception of Steve Edwards' Baktinian-based dialogical model of social relations in photographic portraiture, John Roberts's rigorous dialectical interrogation of the political contradictions of photography, and Nicholas Mirzoeffs's tactics of countervisuality as reconfiguration of the politics of visuality, little photographic theory has challenged the limitations of the social power model of photography that has dominated photographic historiography since the first publication of John Tagg's ground-breaking work in the pages of *Screen Education* in the late 1970s (Edwards 1990; Mirzoeff 2011; Roberts 1998; Tagg 1988). The publication of Azoulay's *The Civil Contract of Photography* in 2008 both was a timely intervention into the rethinking of the social power relations of photography, and appeared at a salient moment in the visual culture of global geopolitics. Written during the Second Intifada in her native Israel—and published just as it was coming to an end—and throughout the period of 9/11 and the United States' invasion of Afghanistan and Iraq, *The Civil Contract* was published just before the emergence of anti-government protests and revolutions across the Middle East in 2010. Photographic theory had by degrees become enamoured of the spectacle of war envisaged by militarized technologies of visualization, and jaded by the saturation of images of conflict distributed with increasing velocity by the media industries and social media networks. Critics such as Susan Sontag sought to ameliorate the tiredness of photography theory and ethics by seeking comfort in the staged photography of Jeff Wall's *Dead Troops Talk (a vision after an ambush of a Red Army Patrol, near Moqor, Afghanistan, Winter 1986*; Sontag 2003: 110–113). As Azoulay bluntly put it: "they just stopped looking" (Azoulay 2008: 11). As *The Civil Contract of Photography* and her 2012 publication, *The Civil Imagination: A Political Ontology of Photography*, demonstrate that, although the politics of representation debates of the previous two decades remain important, they need to incorporate a more rigorous exploration of the politics of looking to understanding photography as a space of political relations that transgresses the normative artificial boundaries to social and political solidarity prevalent in the rise of populist nationalism in contemporary geopolitics.

Interview with Ariella Azoulay

JUSTIN CARVILLE (JC): I thought it might be useful to begin with what may appear to be a rather straightforward question, but one that is perhaps important in framing your particular approach to photography as a salient force in contemporary social relations within and between politically disenfranchised individuals and groups. In your writing photography as a cultural material process appears as central to your rethinking of social power relations, citizenship and the formation of the cultural politics of communities outside of the state. Why does photography as a material process and the still photographic image hold such a significant place in your articulation of the relations between photography and political theory?

ARIELLA AZOULAY (AA): It may be related to the fact that since I remember myself, I was surrounded by lies. Even when these lies could seem personal or intimate—such as those concerning my father's identity—they were vehicles of the reproduction of imperial structures. Photography played a role in their disclosure, or more accurately in their potential disentanglement. Contrary to the axiom that photographs lie—as if they could hold truth and betray their role, photographs were often a site of consolation as what they disclosed was closer to what I felt and confirmed that there is a certain tension of contradiction between what I have been told and what I could find out myself, reconstruct from the material environment in which imperial crimes were inscribed. The 'Frenchness' of my father is such an example. He was proud of being French, as if a European guy in the Levant, whose skin color is whitened as long as he adhere to the 'European' tag he was provided with. However, in one of the rare photographs he had of his mother, she is walking in the street. When I asked him once where the photograph was taken, he replied Oran. A broken narrative followed, insisting that Oran is part of France. He couldn't whiten his skin color, but he wanted us to pass as whites, to affirm our skin color—whiter than his—or in the Israeli context, as non-Sephardic Jews; but we were not. Even though it often worked out, the 'truth' was disclosed when our last name was said aloud, betrayed us in the plot he offered us, as for example when the teacher read students' names from her attendance list. Five years ago, when my father passed away, we stumbled upon the birth certificate of his mother, our grandmother, and to our surprise we learned that her name was Aysha. As a Jewish immigrant from an Arab country, he had to navigate between the racism that he experienced as indigenous in Algeria and the racist practices and premises he had to interiorize already in Algeria toward his fellow Arab neighbors and his Arab ancestors, and as a new immigrant to a state—Israel—that was founded on a racial technology against its Arab inhabitants. Photography became my companion in unlearning many lies, some of which I was even not aware that I was shaped by them. When I started to work on *The Civil Contract of Photography*, unlearning photography itself, and not only individual photographs, became necessary. It coincided with unlearning the knowledge provided to us by imperial institutions such as sovereignty and citizenship through which we learn to dissociate ourselves from others with whom we are governed in exchange for certain privileges offered for different patterns of loyalty and complicity.

JC: Your understanding of the political relations of photography from an autobiographical perspective here is interesting, and perhaps we can discuss that further in relation to activism a little later. However, for the moment I'm curious about the idea of both unlearning photography, and the role of photography in mediating unlearning in the cultural politics of the state. This seems counterintuitive to those cliché understandings of photographs as transparent windows onto the world; seeing is knowing; visual knowledge etc. What do you think is at stake in learning and unlearning photography in the context of the state and citizenship as you outline?

AA: With photography, we can see clearly how imperial technologies operate. Photography is an event of encounter among many, while we are incentivized to learn it either as the enterprise of individuals—photographers, or as a medium that enables to portray certain topics from the perspective of individuals. Think for example about the way plight is depicted—*by* individual photographers whose talent and approach to the topic matter in a kind of a parallel world of media, photojournalism, prizes and awards, and *of* individuals whose plight is at the centre of the frame as victims of perpetrators-less violence. This is how we socialized and trained to understand the plight of others with whom we are governed—as what we are 'concerned about'. I just visited the exhibition of Magnum Analog Recovery at Le Bal in Paris and was astounded to see how imperial plight at the end of WWII was shaped by Magnum/ICP photographers and yielded others' plight as a photographic style. This is predicated on the blurring of differences between different situations of plight in a way that perpetrators are depicted as victims or law enforcers and victims' plight is hollowed of its outrageous meaning. Thus, for example, three photos (1956) by Burt Glinn are shown only with the minimalist original caption "Palestinian Prisoners," as if there is no harm in reiterating an imperial narrative that when the photographs were taken enables the photographer to reiterate the voice of the plunderers and call these Palestinians "prisoners." These Palestinians are not imprisoned, but rather brutalized as they attempted to return to their home. They were expelled from Palestine six years earlier, and were forced to embody the imperial category of "refugee," and soon after "infiltrator" when they attempted to return to their homes. Unlearning photography is though inseparable from unlearning imperialism and the way we are expected to 'see' in photographs these political categories, that are given to us when we inhabit our assigned roles as citizens in a world in which others can be identified through them. Unlearning is a key term in my new manuscript—*Potential History*. Potential history is not an attempt to develop or invent a new theory, but rather to gain access to an old phenomenon—as old as imperialism. Saying it differently, my investment in unlearning is not an attempt to innovate but rather an attempt to join and reiterate previous attempts to unlearn, attempts that never cease to exist. The text that I recently wrote on the photographic work of Susan Meiselas, for example, is an attempt to identify, foreground and make available some such moments of unlearning photography of which her work on Kurdistan or the *Encounters with the Dani* consist.

JC: It is interesting that you appear to identify the unlearning of photography and unlearning of imperialism as requiring historical analysis rather than theoretical interrogation or philosophical reflection. As a cultural historian I was trained to prioritise the originary context of photographs; for example photographs from say the Afghan Wars of 1878–80 needed to be 'read' as emerging out of the historical context of those conflicts if their meaning was to be fully understood. However, it has always struck me that conceiving of the historical context of photography in this way can also be a burden to understanding, in that context imposes meaning and limitations on the types of questions we may want to ask of photography. Does the potential history you identify require critically rethinking historiography and specifically the historiography of the photographic image?

AA: Yes. Absolutely. Let me briefly go back to the example of Glinn's photographs. The original caption gains a kind of historical sacredness, an untouchable historical relic in the form of a document that we are required to worship and prioritize over the violence that these documents, which played a crucial role in the propagation of imperialism and the plight of colonized people, continue to exercise. So yes, photographs should be read in their context, but under imperialism and the way it impacted the photographic discourse, the 'context' is not neutral but shaped by a series of subsequent imperial events that form a chronological timeline of before and after. Thus, for example, the historical context of these photographs requires us to relate to the existence of the state of Israel and the destruction of Palestine as *faits accomplis*, and to Palestinians as they were seen and defined by the imperial sovereignty of the state—threats to its existence, and hence, from the moment they approach its borders they should be eliminated or arrested. We are in the realm of potential history and we are already in the process of unlearning imperialism from the moment we assume that what imperial violence defines as *faits accomplis* and historical milestones—for example, the establishment of states, the constitution of sovereignties or the end and beginning of wars—can be narrated differently, is not unavoidable, and is rather reversible, and still repairable.

JC: If we can, I'd like to turn to your earlier book, *Death's Showcase: The Power of Image in Contemporary Democracy* (2001), the first to have been translated into English. In your discussion of media images you focused on three contemporary sites for the display of imagery of death: the psychoanalyst's clinic, the museum and the television screen. For each of these sites you identify three respective types of imagery: the imaginary, the tangible and the virtual. You argue in the book that the display of death imagery within the three sites always refers to a lost or absent image, as you put it: "No matter how differently these three sites are organized, they share a similar motivation: to help the apparition of the lost image." Could you perhaps elaborate on how photography is implicated in these sites and forms of imagery in terms of the always recurring absence you identify in the display of death?

AA: I didn't go back to *Death's Showcase* since I wrote it, and I truly don't remember much from what I wrote there. I think it is quite far from the way I think today.

JC: It is obvious between *Death's Showcase, The Civil Contract of Photography* and *The Civil Imagination* that there is quite a radical shift in your theoretical framing of photography, what precipitated this rethinking of photography?

AA: Those are probably the kind of gaps that exist between what we are doing and what we have learned to think/say that we are doing. In a way, *The Civil Contract* was a refusal to occupy the position of an expert or a critic, a refusal to use critical theory and to excel in the use of its tools that interpellate us to provide sophisticated accounts that reveal the mechanics of power. When you ask me what precipitated this shift, I cannot but recall this intuition that I had that there is something wrong in the way that what can be understood from the position of a critic mirrors what power aims to achieve. This is linked to my objection to use the template of labor division between the photographer—being a subject, and the photographed person—being an object, in order to explain what was wrong about photography. I was maybe unable to fully articulate this at the time, but I resisted the role of the critic associated with an emphasis and affirmation of the structure of the asymmetric power relation between them, as if the one is active and the other is inactive. In this sense, the phenomenological account of the event of photography that I provide in *The Civil Contract* is a form of unlearning photography.

JC: Staying with *Death's Showcase* for a moment, I wonder if you could comment on how some of the theories and methods you explore in that book subsequently contributed to the ideas explored in *The Civil Contract of Photography* (2008) and *Civil Imagination: A Political Ontology of Photography* (2012) or do you see the later books as a complete reimagining of the relations of photography and political theory?

AA: Many of the theories and approaches that preoccupied me in *Death's Showcase* ceased to play a role in the later books. *The Civil Contract* emerged out of a rejection of critical theory, French post-structuralism and the male tradition of political theory. In this sense, *The Civil Contract* was my first serious attempt to unlearn 'theory' and let concrete modes of engagement with others and with objects generate my (non)theoretical accounts of explored phenomena. Rather than reading theories of photography and arguing with them, I was more interested in the way people who used photography under different capacities, including those who theorize photography, engaged with photography: with other participants, with the tools or with its product—the photographs.

JC: There are several issues raised here in your response about critical theory and your rejection of it, and about the field of photography theory that I would like to explore further. However, what has struck me about *Death's Showcase*, *The Civil Contract* and *Civil Imagination* is that Walter Benjamin's writings appear to be significant to your understanding of photography, politics and violence.

AA: Yes, in retrospect I think that Benjamin's single line on the incompleteness of history had an enormous influence on me in the sense that I could embrace it as a guideline even when I was still unable to understand it as it requires years of unlearning imperial temporality.

JC: Over the last decade with the proliferation of digital media platforms, mobile imaging devices, camera phones and social media, the still photographic image as a material object has been identified by some commentators as losing some of its relevance as a mobilizing force in the global cultural politics of resistance. The events around the Arab Spring of 2010–2011 for example have been referred to as camera phone or social media revolutions in terms of protests being as much visual as they were political. I wonder if you make any distinctions between the place of the still photographic image within social movements and, say, the more diffuse circulation of camera phone imagery in terms of their political affects?

AA: Your question is based on different assumptions that I reject, from the novelty of media, through the notion of revolution and up to the attempt to capture the essence of an era and to delineate it from what was before and what will follow. Photography was often mourned, declared dead, buried, and eulogized. These temporal markers of 'ends' are meant to renew our faith in progress, to make us believe that we are already in a new era, a 'next stage' of a sort. Mourning, in general, is one of imperialism's modes of promoting the new, and aiming to dispossess us from what we have and share with others. Unlearning imperialism is unlearning the conception of technology that reduces photography to a device that generates images, in a way that it can be distinguished from other devices that will be created later as more developed and up to date. Rather than the temporal distinction between 'old' media—still photography and 'new' media—camera phone, I insist on the existence of—and the duty to consolidate—different dividing lines, such as between imperial and the non-imperial uses of photography and photographic formations that undermine the temporal uses of photography.

JC: I understand your position on the division of imperial and non-imperial photographic practices. However, there are still those 'digital modernists' (that we might call them for want of a better term) who believe that digital imaging, its speed of distribution and instantaneous circulation bring with it new or novel potential uses in the cultural politics of resistances. I'm wondering if the imperial and non-imperial divide you identify is something that is not as easily identified or visible to those who are caught up in the digital media's perceived novelty. Does the perception of digital imaging's newness mask or obscure the divide you insist upon identifying?

AA: Yes, the newness creates a sui generis axis of progress that obscures opposition that cannot be interpreted in terms of improvement or regression, i.e., along a chronological timeline. Those 'digital modernists' conceive of what they are doing/thinking as temporally detached from what preceded them, while the divide that I propose between imperial/non-imperial resists this temporality and is predicated on a structural opposition between two incommensurable forms or formations. In this sense, the objection to slavery in the seventeenth or the nineteenth century cannot be approached in terms of progress or improvement but in terms of recurrence of the same—an anti-imperial position that sought to prevent imperial positions from propagating and defining the way things are.

JC: Is there perhaps another approach to thinking about the imperial/non-imperial divide as one that also involves appropriating or recontextualizing photography's serving of imperialism? I'm thinking of the political effects of imperial uses of photography in my own country, Ireland, and the appropriation of media images by organizations such as the Bloody Sunday Justice Campaign in annual commemorations and protests calling for justice or the victims of the Bloody Sunday atrocity in 1972 perpetrated by the British Army. This is just one example, but this contestation of imperial photography through appropriating its own imagery is also a historical phenomenon that has existed alongside and in opposition to imperialism since the nineteenth century.

AA: Sure. The fact that we have to insist on the divide in order not to lose sight of what is right and what is wrong doesn't mean that we live in a 'parallel world'. We share the world with those who are invested in the maintenance of the imperial condition, and we cannot but insist on our right to undo and unlearn the way images are shaped under regimes that generate imperial disaster. In the photographic archive that I created, *From Palestine to Israel*, the challenge was to unlearn photographs that originate in state archives and were used to adorn Zionists' narratives of war, victory and glory with the 'necessary price' victims had to pay.

JC: It might be useful to discuss a little about critical theory and power relations now that you have mentioned it. For historians and theorists of photography, social power has been one of the foremost historiographical approaches to photography since the 1980s. I'm referring specifically to what might be termed the Foucauldian social power model of photographic historiography developed by John Tagg, David Green (1984) and in a less overdetermined fashion by Allan Sekula (1986). You do not engage with these texts directly in your own writing, perhaps for the reasons you have just outlined, but this body of work nevertheless casts a shadow across any discussion relating to photography and politics for photography historians. How aware are you of this emphasis on social power within the historiography of photography and where does your own work sit in relation to it?

AA: As you could assume so far, I'm indeed trying to unlearn critical theory as well, or at least the particular tradition of critical theory by which I was shaped in the 80s and 90s. This is the critical theory that could completely ignore—and continue to ignore—the colonial and imperial condition under which it was shaped, its complicity with imperial interests that made it possible for its practitioners to have access to the treasures that were looted from others in order to study them, to be shaped by their appreciation, by the depiction of its victims as miserable by birth etc. etc., and by relating to the imperialism constitutive of political enterprises as side projects that could be left unstudied and assumed irrelevant to the genealogies of European formations. Think, for example, about Foucault's discussion of the penitentiary system in *Discipline and Punish* (1977) and his focus on the emergence of architectural reasoning in response to the plague. This long and influential discussion has no mention whatsoever of the imperial mega architectural reasoning that occurs at the same time by the same people, in the same port cities, in the form of the slave ship, the barracoon, plantations etc. It is not that Foucault was not aware of this history—he was. It just did not seem to him to be part of the histories that he was writing. Out of this denial, critical theory emerges and with it the position of the cultural critic that could be inhabited by descendants of perpetrators, who did not conceive it necessary for them to unlearn what they inherited from their ancestors, including of course the privileges, before or as part of acting as 'resisting subjects', completely in denial of those privileges, and also of the fact that others, oppressed by them, are denied access to these kind of positions, let alone the resources that are inseparable from them.

JC: In *Death's Showcase* you elaborate on how the sites for the display of visual images of death and violence contribute to how viewers ultimately experience death as an aesthetic encounter with different formations of imagery. Could you comment on how imagery circulating through social media or through web-based platforms is either an extension of the aestheticized experience of death or constitutes an alternative site of display with a corresponding alternative type of imagery?

AA: I wouldn't use the category of aestheticization today, certainly not in the form of a verb. In one of the chapters of *Civil Imagination* I propose to get rid of the opposition between the political and the aesthetic, and rather seek to engage with those who are regularly removed from such conversations defined as 'formative debates'. Today I would say it even more sharply—we have to disengage from many 'formative' debates and chronologies—such as first or second wave of … that shaped various disciplines with which we are associated. It is through these debates, among other mechanisms, that we are called to affirm and reaffirm the white histories of those disciplines with some "color correction" to use Brian Hochman's term.

JC: I originally read that argument in the essay "Getting Rid of the Distinction between the Aesthetic and the Political" (2011). At the time I thought back to all the exhibition reviews and essays I had written and remembered 'taking sides' as you term it, in falling along the lines of argument of work being too aesthetic. While not trained as an art historian, in my own way I was employing the professional gaze you identify as being oppositional to the practical and civil gaze explored further in *Civil Imagination*. Could you elaborate on what displacing the professional gaze might contribute to the re-thinking or re-imagining of the history and theory of photography and for the civil gaze you argue for? It's a big question but I'm interested in what questions could be asked of the history of photography if it was not burdened with the art-historical paradigm.

AA: Unlearning imperialism, including unlearning photography, is a slow process, with exciting moments of quasi revelation and painful moments of how much you could have been naïve to actually act as a spokesperson for systems that you were persuaded you are criticizing or opposing, followed by the tedious work of undoing the power of imperial idioms that are made to be reproduced through us while we act as knowledgeable experts. Unlearning is pursued through meticulous phenomenological accounts through which a non-imperial language is slowly regained. When I wrote this text to which you refer, unlearning photography qua art was the main focus. As I spent a few years as a curator, not surprisingly I was driven first in this direction but it was clear that this is only the tip of the iceberg, and that without unlearning art as an imperial form, some of the idioms

I'm using will continue to reinforce an imperial notion of art, and eliminate the foundational role of looting in the conception of art. It was only after this slow process of unlearning art that I was able to unlearn the photographic 'document' and study its emergence as part of the technology of the archive.

Note

1 A full PDF of the complaint can be found at: www.koskoff.com/content/images/Lanier-v-Harvard-Plaintiff-Complaint.pdf

References

Azoulay, A. (2001) *Death's Showcase: The Power of Image in Contemporary Democracy*, Cambridge, MA: MIT Press.

Azoulay, A. (2008) *The Civil Contract of Photography*, Cambridge, MA: MIT Press.

Azoulay, A. (2011) 'Getting Rid of the Distinction between the Aesthetic and the Political,' *Theory, Culture and Society* 27.7/8, pp. 239–263.

Azoulay, A. (2012) *Civil Imagination: A Political Ontology of Photography*, London: Verso.

Barry, A. J. (2011) 'Norwich Woman Thinks Famous Photo Shows her Slave Ancestor,' *The Day*, March 16, www.theday.com/article/20110221/NWS08/110229950

Edwards, S. (1990) 'The Machines Dialogue,' *Oxford Art Journal* 3.1, pp. 63–76.

Foucault, M. (1977) *Discipline and Punish: The Birth of the Prison*, New York: Pantheon.

Green, D. (1984) 'Veins of Resemblance: Photography and Eugenics,' *Oxford Art Journal* 7.2, pp. 3–16.

Hartocollis, A. (2019) 'Who Should Own Photos of Slaves? The Descendants, not Harvard, a Lawsuit Says,' *New York Times*, March 20, www.nytimes.com/2019/03/20/us/slave-photographs-harvard.html

Mirzoeff, N. (2011) *The Right to Look: A Counterhistory of Visuality*, Durham, NC and London: Duke University Press.

Roberts, J. (1998) *The Art of Interruption: Realism, Photography and the Everyday*, Manchester: Manchester University Press.

Sekula, A. (1986) 'The Body and the Archive,' *October* 39 (Winter), pp. 3–64.

Sontag, S. (2003) *Regarding the Pain of Others*, London: Penguin.

Tagg, J. (1988) *The Burden of Representation: Essays on Photographies and Histories*, London: Macmillan.

Wallis, B. (1995) 'Black Bodies, White Science: Louis Agassiz's Slave Daguerreotypes,' *American Art* 9.2, pp. 38–61.

13

Human rights practice and visual violations

Ruthie Ginsburg

Introduction

Light streams in through an oblong window at the center of a photograph documenting the activity of the non-governmental organization Physicians for Human Rights, Israel (PHRI) in the Palestinian village of Bidou. The light floods the interior and gently illuminates the five figures inside. One of them, in the corner of the photo, is bent over a table toward a little child lying in the arms of a woman covered by a bright headscarf. At the back, in the hallway, a bearded man holding another child looks on. The context makes it clear that the photo, taken by photographer Miki Kratsman, documents an Israeli physician examining a Palestinian child. Despite the blinding light that blurs some of the details, it is nonetheless discernible that this is neither a conventional medical clinic, nor a typical doctor in a white coat; rather, the professional appointment is held in an improvised space.

The light-framed human contact between physician and patients constitutes the object of the photograph. The eyes looking at the photo are led by the luminous innocence of the sight. It appears that the physician is guided mainly by knowledge and skill, while professional mannerisms are put aside. Moreover, the dichotomous matrix that distinguishes between the two sides of the Israeli–Palestinian conflict and operates as an organizing code for the relationship between the people involved is shed in favor of something more primary and fundamental, namely: care for a human being. We have here an utterly 'humanistic' photo in its reliance on an essential humanity beyond enmity and conflict, and a humanitarian gesture that crosses borders and sets up with visual means the inner space as diametrically opposed to the external, alienated, conflict-ridden environment of occupation.

The window marks the distinction or demarcation between the internal and external spaces of the image. But, although the photograph clearly maps out this distinction, its exposure of medical treatment is not experienced as a transgression into a forbidden area. The warm, bathing light and the absence of institutional insignia, such as a clinic or a professional appearance in a white coat, distract attention from what is taking place, from the otherwise obvious fact that the meeting is held for the purpose of medical treatment. In other words, the aesthetic and framing of the photograph induce a momentary amnesia around the notion that a medical appointment of the sort we are witnessing here is usually held under conditions of privacy.

The more the photo raises suspicion about the violation of accepted professional norms in the NGO's activity, the more it seems that the bathing light becomes invasive and violent, and the tenderness of the photo disappears. The exposure of the medical treatment to the photographer and to spectators alters the character of the light coming in. Baring the intimacy of this treatment to the camera is perceived from this perspective as a violation—both of the patients and of the picture in its initial tranquil, light-suffused aura.

In an interview I held with one of the NGO's employees, who was responsible at the time for the organization's public relations, she remarked:[1]

> In the mobile clinics there is a violation of medical confidentiality. Everybody hears the patients' medical problems. There was even a situation where a psychiatrist met with patients and [other] people were sitting there, including her son. And she would stop all the time to explain to him what the [medical] problem was and what could be done. In Israel it would never have happened.

Referring to the NGO's publications, she added:

> We [have] a double standard—it is permissible to show how miserable Palestinians are: children, women, sick and injured people, and dead bodies, but for Israelis we need to get a permit. In the [Occupied] Territories we publish the name of the Palestinian person appearing in the photograph (maybe because it gets to the High Court of Justice anyway, where the Palestinian's name gets published), but the names of Israelis are confidential. ... In the Territories, people have become an object, but when it comes to Israelis there is more sensitivity. There, in Palestine, they are a symbol, they do not have a face. I understand it intuitively. There is something base in appealing to the emotions—look how terrible it is for an old person in a senior home. [...] Over there [in Palestine] it is geographical photography. It's Africa.

The question I want to ask, then, informed by these statements from a PHRI employee as well as by the visual dynamic of the mobile clinic photograph, is not why norms of medical treatment are violated; nor is it why medical treatment is inadmissibly exposed in the photo; nor yet why a rights organization fails to protect the privacy of patients. Rather: What does this departure from the professional and formal norm teach us with respect to photography and human rights practice? As an answer to this question, I describe how photography can actualize the organization's practice as a political civil act through a set of socio-political spatial relations that transpire in the photograph(s). Whereas the common objections to photographs of human rights abuse are concerned with the exploitation of victimhood, I argue that we should not evaluate human rights photography just by the image product. Through a description of the organization's transgression of conventional socio-spatial delimitations, I show how it is performed as a political civil act. Political action is also exercised via disregarding medical confidentiality, where the photographs play a central role in revealing the treatment to the public eye.

The employee cited above points critically at the link between the violation of confidentiality in treatment and the portrayal of Palestinians during PHRI's activity.[2] She acknowledges the differential representation of injured parties in different spaces. Her remarks join a multitude of critiques directed against photography in general and photography in 'disaster zones' and wars in particular. Susan Sontag, Roland Barthes, and John Berger have argued that, even if a photograph conveys information about disaster and suffering, it is incapable of generating change in the spectators' consciousness (Barthes 1993; Berger 1991; Sontag 1977,

2003). The exposure of the injured in a photograph, therefore, may only cause additional suffering without the redemptive or compensatory benefits of epiphany, transformation, and response. Quite the opposite: Photographs of people hurt in war and/or disaster in fact reaffirm existing socio-political power relations (Rosler 2003; Sontag 2003). The division between those exposed to the camera lens and those whose privacy is protected embodies power relations both before and behind this selective viewing lens. Every photograph thus indexes a network of socio-political spatial relations and is itself woven into this network. Even if, as scholars have shown, a photograph contains an image of suffering, it at the same time (re)affirms the imbalanced power dynamic that dictates what is exposable and what is not. In addition, as Berger notes, photography of suffering may invoke horror in the spectators, but it may also reveal to them their own impotence in the face of this suffering. That is why, he argues, the exposure of spectators to violence through photography is twofold. On the one hand the viewers are exposed to an image of violence and, at the same time, to the violence endemic to their socio-political imprisonment, to their lack of influence and resources to right the wrongs they witness from afar (Berger 1991).

The photographs of PHRI's activities do not present an image of violence similar to war photography; the Palestinians treated by the Israeli physicians encounter no aggression. Rather, they expose the spectator to traces of violence. The provision of assistance by Israeli rather than Palestinian physicians may be interpreted as a shortage of medical services on the Palestinian side, just as the provision of assistance in a place that is not a clinic suggests a shortage of healthcare buildings and inaccessibility of health services. This shortage may be a product of the occupation, and as such a trace of violence. But, in the exposure of patients through the violation of medical confidentiality, the violence is of a different kind, embodied as it is in the image itself and in its production.

In *The Ground of the Image*, Jean-Luc Nancy usefully juxtaposes the violence of the image with the image of violence. In showing the complexity of the relationship between the two, Nancy defines violence itself, the violence of truth, and examines how violence and truth transpire in the image (2005: 20–26). He notes that violence depends on representation, on its image. To manifest its violent nature, violence will leave a mark. The truth is exposed precisely through such a violent image. In this way, Nancy demonstrates both the affinity and the difference between the image of violence and the violence of the image, and their collusion in the constitution of truth. By introducing the violation that can occur in production of the image—in this context, the extended event of photography—he offers a notion of truth that is exposed in the convergence of the act of violence and the violence of the image. In the PHRI photographs, both kinds of violence are given expression: the violence of the occupation and the piercing light of the image itself, of the space inside which the truth of a primal violence takes shape through photographic lighting and *mise en scène*. In the following, I will focus on the photographs of PHRI's mobile clinic, addressing the photographed image and its production. Describing the NGO's activity while referring to the photographs and to the photographic act itself will help us understand why the violation of confidentiality in the mobile clinic and the visual violation of the resulting images may be interpreted as a political civil act. Photographs of the mobil clinic that document the medical treatment represent the organization's actions at the Occupied Palestinian Territories (OPT) and in addition represent the political civil act of the exposure to the public eye. That is, the photographs not only show the medical care, but stand for the performance of revealing as well. The twofold aspects of representation show how, in the mobile clinic of PHRI, photography has a role in constructing the act as a political civil act.[3]

Physicians for Human Rights

PHRI was founded at the beginning of the first Intifada (1988) following the violation of the medical rights of Palestinian residents of Gaza and the West Bank. Its members have demanded, and continue to demand, the protection of their right to health in its broadest sense, encompassing such prerequisite conditions as freedom of movement, clean water, modern sanitary conditions, proper nutrition, adequate housing, education and employment opportunities, non-violence, and more. The NGO is active in four population groups: (1) Palestinian residents of the OPT, (2) prisoners and imprisoned detainees, (3) migrant workers and refugees, and (4) residents of Israel. The initiatives led by PHRI are shaped by the needs and distresses of the population. Regardless of the target population, the organization focuses on three channels of activity: individual assistance, medical assistance, and advocacy. The NGO has 23 employees on its payroll, and more than half of its 1,300 members belong to the medical profession, some of whom are regular volunteers in the clinics. In the mobile clinic, the NGO's volunteers provide diagnosis and initial treatment to Palestinians living in the OPT. In the 'open clinic', treatment is given to those lacking civil status, including migrant workers and refugees. The photographs I will discuss were taken in the mobile clinic.[4]

Almost every weekend, a group of roughly ten Israeli physicians goes out to a Palestinian village in the OPT. They visit a different village every Saturday. Palestinians from the village and from the surrounding area gather to receive diagnoses and medical treatment. Palestinian civil organizations, such as Palestinian Medical Relief, coordinate the medical day with the local population. The Israelis and the Palestinians meet in one of the public buildings, a school for example, and not in the existing clinics. For one day, the school is repurposed to receive medical patients.

On the NGO's website, as well as in its publications and reports, there are relatively few photographs. By contrast, the mobile clinic project, enjoying as it does the privileges of a flagship project, has been and continues to be the object of comprehensive visual documentation.[5] Thus the uniqueness of the project is double. First, it has a heroic aura: despite all barriers, Israeli physicians go to treat Palestinians in isolated villages in the OPT. Second, it is documented extensively and therefore receives a spotlight not given to PHRI's other projects. Well-known Israeli photojournalists, including Miki Kratsman, Nir Kafri, Limor Edri, Michal Heiman, Alex Levac, and others, have taken photographs during the 'medical days' in the OPT. And almost every single visit made by the physicians to a Palestinian village is covered by the press, especially by the Palestinian press.[6] In the published reports by the organization on its website and elsewhere, the volunteer physicians are seen in action. Medical treatments, diagnoses, and operations—activities usually undertaken behind closed doors—are exposed on the 'medical days' for all and for the camera to see. To be sure, the NGO does not publicly declare its violation of medical confidentiality during the 'medical days' in the OPT, but the conduct just described makes it clear that the large photographic archive is testimony to the organization's deviation from the accepted norm.

The violation of confidentiality

Ariella Azoulay notes that the act of photography is not identical to the photographed event. The spectators usually look for the 'thing itself' and are indifferent to the act of photography. That is to say, they observe the photographed event as framed by the photographer with the help of the camera, and they usually do not seek to learn through the photograph about the photographic act. Yet the act of photography does not exhaust itself in whatever is captured by the lens; rather, Azoulay argues, it begins with the appearance of the camera and perhaps even with the knowledge about its presence on the scene (2011: 137). If we return to the photo taken by Miki Kratsman in the mobile clinic, we see that the photographed physician and patients are indifferent to the photographic recording of their encounter. They do not look towards the camera, and it seems as if the photographic act is entirely alien to the photographed event. Ostensibly, the treatment is not contaminated by its documentation and remains uninfluenced by the spectators' gaze, disconnected from its witnessing by present and remote spectators. As the photograph is supposedly external to the event, it appears to be a voyeuristic transgression. The photo is thus akin to an alien force acting upon the encounter between the Israeli physician and the Palestinian patients, thereby also raising the possibility of its inherent violence in a gesture of aggression that mirrors the implied wounding that the medical act seeks to assuage. But can the act of photography in the framework of a rights organization be defined as a violent act *tout court*? How does a civil organization's protection of the rights of others become violent through the interposition of the camera lens? And is this violence compatible with the organization's protective activity, particularly the care administered in the clinic?

Protection within a community is purveyed not just actively, but also through the way physical and social spaces are organized. House walls, for example, carve out spaces that are demarcated off from the open, unmarked space and create a distinction between different social dimensions, between professional, commercial, and private realms. This distinction helps protect human and social life. The lines of demarcation also entail an ensemble of norms, regulations, and laws according to which individuals channel their behavior.[7] They define, for instance, when a person's entry into a certain area is considered as a form of trespassing and when, by contrast, the entry is deemed harmless and granted approval. One of the laws seeking to assemble within it a number of elements involved in the protection of rights is the Protection of Privacy Law. This juridical instrument often depends on the definition of the place in which an activity has been undertaken, or alternatively, on the question of where the norm has been violated. The various components of this law and the legal examples used to sustain it clearly articulate the link between physical space and social norm.

In professional relations, legal protection applies to the recipient of the service as a derivation of the right to privacy. Professionals such as lawyers, accountants, psychologists, and physicians need as much relevant information as possible for the provision of effective services (Birnhack 2007). In order to protect a citizen from the misuse of information transmitted without his or her consent, privacy is anchored in a legal norm providing the professional relationship with a safe framework, which is broken whenever information is transmitted outside formal procedures. The professional relationship is thus defined as an exchange between service provider and receiver, or, alternatively, it may be anchored in the location of the meeting: an office, an investigation room, a clinic, and so on.

It is on this emplacement of the professional contract that I wish to focus, and on its role in shoring up the right to privacy. Michael Birnhack has rightly noted how difficult it is to enforce the right to privacy owing to the fundamental ambiguity inherent in it, a lack of conceptual clarity, paucity of court rulings, but also owing to it being society- and technology-dependent. Technological developments and transformations may protect the right to privacy or they may challenge it. Cameras can take pictures of those entering a home, thereby offering protection from burglary. In the hands of strangers, on the other hand, they can expose and invade intimate spaces.[8] Birnhack notes that the legal protection of privacy rests on accepted categories, such as the dichotomy between private and public space. The work of the courts is facilitated by ruling on the basis of physical location, which absolves them of the need to examine the act in isolation from the place in which it occurred (Birnhack 2007: 52). But deploying the spatial dichotomy recognized in the Protection of Privacy Law can also serve to legitimize questionable human acts. That is to say, the very protection of privacy may sometimes render vulnerable those whose existence is conscripted to private spaces, such as women and children. In cases where an individual's home-based actions are exposed—the contents of phone conversations and sealed envelopes, their medical condition, sexual life, as well as, to a great extent, their economic condition—it is clear that their privacy is violated. In more nebulous cases, the question as to whether such violation occurs depends on a subjective judgment. Importantly, the source of the threat is usually the state and/or the market, rather than auxiliary entities such as NGOs.

In view of the definition of the right to privacy, I asked Dr. Ruchama Marton, founder and acting president of PHRI, if any complaint regarding the violation of privacy has been heard from Palestinians who had been treated in the mobile clinic. She replied that she had not been aware of such a claim and noted that, if anyone ever seeks privacy during the 'medical days'—for instance, by closing the door of the room in which the treatment is taking place—it is the Israeli physician rather than the Palestinian patient.[9] Whereas some of the Israeli physicians even refused to provide assistance under these circumstances, the exposure of medical treatment has not given rise to protest on the part of the Palestinian patients. The Palestinians are often accompanied by their partners, children, or neighbors. Hence, the sense of an unusual and disturbing non-observance of medical confidentiality usually occurs not so much among the Palestinians as among the Israelis. Postcolonial interpretive frameworks may help explain the cultural differences between the Israeli assistance providers and the Palestinian recipients of that assistance. Differences of this kind may also be unpacked through the postcolonial critique of humanitarianism and human rights as an imperialist project.[10] I would like to draw attention to a different aspect: that of understanding the violation of confidentiality and the production of the image as a form of civil protest. I will make this case by examining a photograph taken by photographer Miki Noam-Alon during a 'medical day' in the H-2 area of Hebron.[11]

In the photo, two PHRI volunteers are seen performing a surgical treatment in a grocery store (see Plate 14). The volunteers are bent over the patient, who lies face down on the counter. Light penetrates from the market alley into the dark store through the large metal door. The open door allows the physicians to do their work in the improvised operation room, while at the same time exposing their activity to the outside. The gaze of the surgeons and their patient is not turned toward the alley, and it appears that they do not see what is happening there. The photo thus stages an exposure to a concrete exterior, that of a commercial street, and to an imagined exterior encapsulated by the camera's presence. The exposure of the store's interior to the outside is doubled by the presence of two cameras, the one seen in the photo and the one with which the photo is taken.[12] The complex relationship between the social spaces made visible in this image dramatizes the dual character of the NGO's activity, which includes both treatment and photographic documentation (see Figure 13.1).

The first relationship is dependent, in our case, on the distinction between the store and the street—that is, a physical difference between internal and external space. The demarcation line between these spaces runs along the doorstep of the store, and the light outside underscores the opposition to the dark interior. The photograph frames the store as the interior, and the exterior expands into the alley and beyond. Rather than encompass the fullness of the exterior within its lens, the camera condenses the view by tracing the distinction between the two spaces. In other words, the exterior needs the interior in order to be defined as external, just as private space is needed for public space to be recognized as such. The division between store and alley is the difference between interior and exterior, and, apparently, inside the building the conditions for performing a surgical treatment are somewhat better than outside.

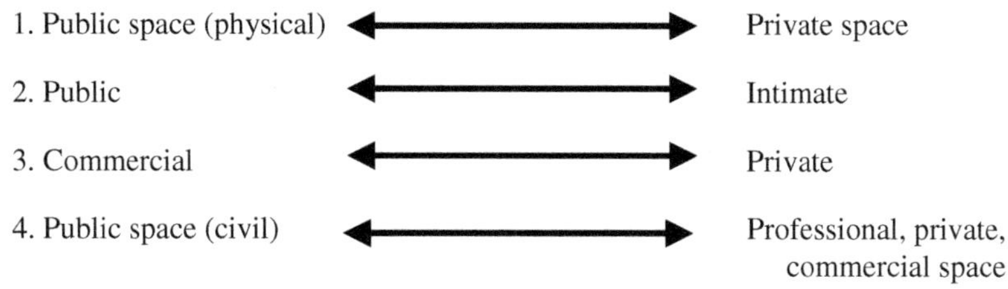

Figure 13.1 Ruthie Ginsburg, Diagram 1

The difference has to do with the media through which the events are unfolded and presented to the audience. In Alon's picture we see the camera that renders the events public. And yet, even without it, the surgery performed by the physicians is exposed to the public in the alley. The exposure of surgeries and clinical treatments to the public is usually rooted in the blurring of boundaries between care for the body and its investigation.[13] Other examples include the presence of an intern during practicum, which turns the intimate encounter between physician and patient into an encounter with more than two participants. Deviation from the norm is also brought about after injury resulting from human or natural disaster, with the site being declared a 'disaster zone.'

In a conversation I had with photographer Miki Kratsman on the photographs he had taken during the organization's 'medical days,' he recounted how physicians had referred patients to him at the beginning of his career, when he was making a living as a medical photographer:

> Some [of the patients] thought it was supposed to be an X-Ray screening, and when they realized they were being asked to be photographed with a regular camera, they would ask, 'What's going on?' Maybe they thought it was part of the treatment, but actually it was for the physicians, so they could publish articles with a visual documentation of the illnesses.[14]

In the context of PHRI's mobile clinic, Kratsman's reminiscence draws our attention to the dual motivation underlying the production of the photographs. In the story told by Kratsman, the physicians' interest in the public exposure of the treatment is primarily professional, whereas, in the case of PHRI, the treatment is made visible in a civil public space, exceeding professional interests. The difference, however, is not limited to the definition of the space's character, but also includes the relation of the photographed to the photographic act. Whereas the photographed mentioned by Kratsman have wondered about the photographic act, the Palestinians in the mobile clinics do not criticize the camera's presence, thereby collaborating with the documentation.

We mustn't forget that, compared with the private space of the home, the store would be defined as a public space revolving around economic exchange. Two main roles are recognized in the store: those of seller and buyer. As we can see in the photo, while the physicians are preoccupied with the surgery, the store's usual role players are absent, and the economic negotiation is suspended. The implicit dynamic is comprised in the third relationship suggested above—commercial space vis-à-vis that which is different from it.

The distinctions between private and public, community and intimacy, professional interests and commercial again converge to define the perimeter of this image as a civil public space. We see in this picture how the physicians, in their capacity as expert civilians assisting a Palestinian, redefine the space they inhabit as one that is neither commercial nor domestic or professional. Their definition is not a binary one, where one option cancels out another, but rather a *differentiating* one. In order to achieve visibility, a difference is needed in the social functions of space. Turning the store into a surgery room is what makes the physicians' activity visible—from both an ocular and a political perspective. The camera serves this production process in a twofold manner: It both creates a public image of the NGO's unusual activity and partakes in producing the very divergence that makes this activity susceptible to public interest and dissemination.

Drawing on this constitutive function of the camera in establishing and cementing social space, the key point I want to make is that the resulting framework may also be seen as a refusal to accept the separation between the Israeli public space and the Palestinians' private domain. Over and against the existing separation between the two societies, which makes it possible to disavow the Palestinians' rights, the 'mobile' social spaces redrawn in the mobile clinic indicate that the differences between these societies are not fixed. Instead of clear separation, an act of differentiation is what creates the condition of possibility for the recognition of rights. And it is the photograph itself that crosses boundaries between the social spaces and helps disrupt the division between them.

Humanitarian care of the providential kind is commonly associated with protection and even concealment aiming to secure the well-being of those whose rights are the objects of preservation. Yet the photo analysis just presented suggests that this kind of protection may not be compatible with protesting against the violation of rights of the same subjects and therefore sometimes demands the opposite. In order to point to injury and injustice, exposure and publicness are necessary, which in this case violate the demarcation lines between the social spaces—the very demarcation that may offer a shelter from abuse.

Ex-pose

In another photograph taken by Miki Kratsman in the mobile clinic, a picture titled *Identity Card* and included in one of PHRI's publications in 2009, we see the face of a woman touched by more than two hands (Figure 13.2). An analysis of this photograph helps us understand the connection as well as the difference between humanitarianism and PHRI's rights activity. I will examine this image by pointing to its instrumentalization of the photographed Palestinian woman in the NGO publication, to complete my argument that the photograph exposing medical treatment in the OPT is a form of civil protest.

Sontag comments that, "photographed images do not seem to be statements about the world so much as pieces of it" (Sontag 1977: 4), and Barthes regards the "photograph … [as] never distinguished from its referent" (Barthes 1993a: 5). Both stress the photograph's status as an image pointing at what *was* there. Nancy, on the other hand, conceives the photograph as a death mask ex(-)posing the image to the other (Kaplan 2005, 2010).[15] Once the image is posed out there, the image is what gets captured in the camera lens, but it also signifies that which is absent. In other words, the image discloses with its appearance a tension between the ex-posing and the absent. The woman's face in the photo taken by Kratsman is a public image, and at the same time an image of someone that no longer exists. Or, as may be deduced from Nancy's arguments, this image is one of an absence to the other.

In the interview I held with Kratsman, he recalled that the woman had arrived at one of PHRI's 'medical days' in poor physical condition, after having eaten hardly any food for three

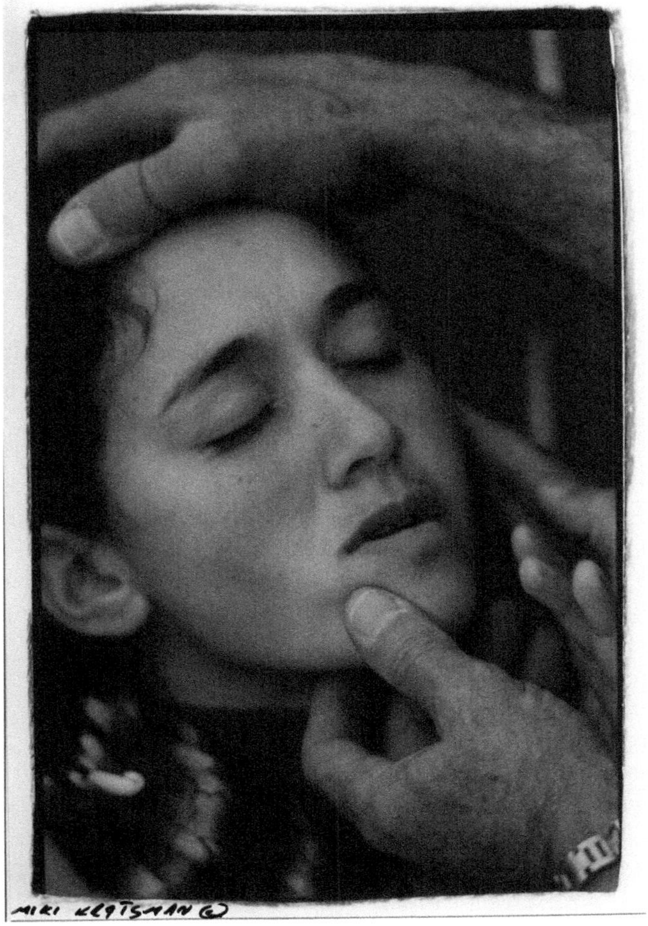

Figure 13.2 Identity Card, PHRI publication. Photo: Miki Kratsman (2000). Courtesy the artist

months. The clinic's activity coordinator representing PHRI added that she was around 20 years old, and he identified the hands in the photo as belonging to Professor Zvi Bentwich, a physician active in the organization. Following the physician's visit, the woman was transported to Israel for treatment at Tel Hashomer Hospital, where she was diagnosed with cancer. The belated treatment did not succeed in saving her from the illness that had already metastasized throughout her body, and she died shortly thereafter. A closure was imposed on the Jenin district in the OPT, and consequently the PHRI employees found it difficult to transfer her body for burial in her native village.[16] The image represents the gap between the bodily presence of the photographed and the photographic act itself, for, at the time of the photo being viewed, the photographed person is no longer alive. Recognizing this gap uncovers the three dimensions of violence: the violence of the occupation, the violence of the image truth, and the violence in the production of the image (Nancy 2005: 17–26). In other words: (1) the violence as it shows itself; (2) "truth is true because it is violent, and it is true in its violence," as Nancy puts it (p. 17); and (3) the process of producing the image can entail violence.

The angle chosen by Kratsman for documenting the encounter between the Israeli physician and the Palestinian patient focuses our gaze once again on the physical connection between helper and patient. The angle supposedly unites the perspectives of the photographer, the spectator, and the physician. The bodiless hands on the tortured face, as if providing the latter with a second frame, may for a moment appear to be the photographer's hands. Yet the reconstruction of the photographic act reveals that the photographer was holding the camera while documenting the moment. The photographer's presence thus attests to the existence of more than one gaze in the photo. The distinction, therefore, between documenter and caregiver splits the gaze resting on the Palestinian woman into (at least) two.[17] The split indicates the duality of PHRI's activity: documenting and care-giving. The former stems from and constitutes part of the NGO's work at the level of rights (advocacy), whereas the latter is the manifestation of its humanitarian activity. Both levels converge into one photograph, where they coexist and nourish each another, even as a permanent tension between them continues to sustain the image's visual appellation and vibrancy.[18] This duality reflects the statements of Dr. Dani Filc, former chairman of PHRI, in an interview I conducted with him:

> I think the tension characterizing the organization has to do not with whether it is a political or a human rights organization, but with whether it is a humanitarian or a human rights organization. A human rights organization is a political organization. As a humanitarian organization we engage in medical treatment. And as a human rights organization we deal with the more principled aspect. This tension does make the organization's work more difficult, but it also enriches it to a certain extent.[19]

Another physician active in the organization adds:

> The humanitarian aspect [of the mobile clinic] is a means [for attaining] an end, it is not an end in its own right. The organization's goal is to struggle for health rights. The mobile clinic sometimes serves this goal. It is a means to attain greater health, [and this goal exists] regardless of the clinic's activity or of whether that right exists or not. I think that the clinic is an excellent instrument because of the number of people exposed to it—there's nothing like it. That is its power. There are lots of people involved—service providers, patients. They are all exposed and are part of that exposure. The medical treatment is in fact the declared content. For us [the physicians] as service providers, the [treatment is rendered] in a very partial way. It is definitely insufficient, including usually in the eyes of medical functionaries on the Palestinian side.[20]

Indeed, the encounter between the physicians and those turning to them for help is usually a one-time encounter. The mobile clinic's activity takes place in different villages and does not return to the same place more than once a year. According to the coordinator of the clinic's activity, PHRI's strategic decision is to cover the entire area from the Hebron region up to Jenin. The standard medical treatment—comprising a patient's visit to the physician, an expert diagnosis (which sometimes requires further examination), provision of assistance, and follow-up until convalescence—is not possible. The clinic's political character is also evidenced by Dr. Marton's statement:

> In my view, it's a protest, and the second [goal] is to act in solidarity. We never go out without coordination and collaboration with Palestinian physicians, so in the past I haven't been willing to use the verb 'help.' It's not like the rich come to help the

> poor. We mustn't think or act that way. I'm always told how inefficient it is from a medical perspective. [But] we didn't come to open a medical center or to put a sentry whose job it would be to determine whether they are ill or not. Whoever wants to is invited to come. What is there, after all, in those villages? It should be a feast-like event. And why shouldn't the population get a serious examination on this occasion? ... If the goal is to express protest, [the protest] is about the health situation in the Territories, and now it's [also] about the military closures. And this protest does not change. ... [Therefore] part of our choice is to pick a village that has no clinic, and not to return to the same village, so as not to replace the conventional medical services. ... No routine is created, neither in principle nor in practice.[21]

It may be that the clinic is incapable of fully or even partially meeting medical needs, but its mobility exposes the organization's members to the medical problems that Palestinians are suffering from. The Israeli physicians learn from, and are enriched by, the encounter with Palestinians in the clinic. Another physician volunteering at the clinic recounted in an interview that, following the familiarization of the NGO's physicians with the problems on the ground, reporting on violations of Palestinians' medical rights has changed:

> It's not like what B'Tselem [an Israeli human rights organization—RG] does, sending out researchers, which [yields] more technical information. Here the documentation comes straight from the field, because our physicians witness it.[22]

So, on the one hand, the transition from one place to another and the one-time encounter prevent or limit the possibilities of purveying medical aid; yet on the other hand, they provide the NGO's members with an overall picture of the medical problems of the Palestinian population and the violation of its rights. And with the help of written and photographic evidence, this picture is conveyed to the society at large. For the organization's members, learning and understanding the state of Palestinians' rights in the OPT goes beyond merely providing care to 'others.' The physicians' activity and the exposure that comes with it also enrich their experience as citizens.

Photography, absence, rights

The idea of displacement at the core of the image, as formulated by Nancy, may also be appropriated, *mutatis mutandis*, for defining the discourse of rights. Nancy writes:

> The empty place of the absent as the place that is not empty: that is the image. A place that is not empty does not mean a place that has been filled: it means the place of the image, that is in the end, the image as place, and a singular place for what has no place here: the place of a displacement that the image is an empty space of absence.
>
> *(Nancy 2005: 68)*

As this statement suggests, the image appears in the place of absence, with its appearance leaving empty space intact. It helps to point to the problem of documenting human rights violation: that the image of violation is a shadow of the situation; it never renders the reality (if there is a reality). From Nancy's thoughts, we may deduce that the image renders the absence present, but nevertheless the image may mislead the spectator by creating a picture that might be perceived as full.

A similar claim may be made with respect to the discourse of rights. In 1948, the UN Declaration of Human Rights arose out of the distress generated by the absence of a definition of rights. In the aftermath of the Second World War, and especially after the violence of the Nazi regime, the need was acknowledged for a declaration of rights to which every human being is entitled simply by virtue of his or her humanity. But these rights have been, and continue to be, an empty space that is never entirely filled up. That is, the struggle for rights and the demand that they be enforced always emerge from the emptiness of absence. The construction of the discourse of rights around absence marks it as a continuous effort with no endpoint. As Susie Linfield notes, regarding the role of photography in the discourse of rights, photography stands as a medium reflecting that absence (and its apparent, albeit elusive, presence). Linfield asks how, for example, a 'right' may be photographed. What does a woman possessing rights look like? How is it possible visually to present a man who has a right? Her suggestion is, "like a person: that's all" (Linfield 2010: 37). Yet Linfield's assertion is problematic and itself gives rise to a question: How can a person be represented visually? Perhaps it is impossible for a photograph to represent an abstract concept such as 'human rights' and 'person' and it needs its context. In closing this chapter, I would like to tie these thoughts back to my reading of PHRI's photographs.

PHRI provides physical assistance to injured persons, but this assistance does not make it a humanitarian organization. To be sure, both forms of action rest on the Declaration of Human Rights and on international conventions, but, whereas humanitarian activity seeks to provide emergency assistance to the victims of disaster and war, advocacy demands that the sovereign powers prevent harm and take responsibility for the injured victims. Even if rights organizations help the injured, and even if many humanitarian organizations demand that the sovereign change their injurious ways and/or take responsibility for their subjects, the two modes of action adumbrate divergent sets of relationships between the organizations, the victims, and the sovereign. Whereas humanitarian organizations take on the role of the sovereign by providing assistance, the aid provided by rights organizations is focused on representation and mediation, as in advocacy, and their demand for ensuring and protecting the rights of the subjects is directed at the sovereign. As part of their activity, rights organizations seek to show the victims' suffering to the public. Consequently, many of them concentrate on reporting and producing documentation of the violation of rights.

My discussions with physicians and reflections on the images that document their involvement have led me to believe that PHRI's photography testifies to the organization's deliberate deviation from the accepted medical norm, in order to indicate that the physicians' activity consists of more than medical assistance. That is to say, the rights organization's activity in the OPT is not just humanitarian activity; hence, it is not conducted according to the ethically accepted procedure. By exposing the treatment to the public, they seek to unmask the problems that the Palestinians are suffering as a result of the violation of their rights. Through this reading, photographing the treatment given by physicians is understood as an instrument of protest, when the target of this protest is the absence of rights, an absence that photography, through its mediation of the past, is uniquely equipped to capture.

Notes

1 Interview with Maskit Bendel, July 23, 2007.
2 PHRI is not the only organization maintaining a differential protection of the confidentiality of Palestinians and Israeli Jews. In videos of B'Tselem, a human rights organization, faces belonging to the children of the Jewish settlers of Hebron are blurred out, whereas the faces of Palestinian

children are not. In this way, the confidentiality of Jewish settlers is preserved, whereas the Palestinians' is not. See www.btselem.org/ (accessed July 4, 2016). The same is true with respect to reports published by the NGO Breaking the Silence on the harassment of the Palestinian residents of Hebron by Jewish settlers: www.breakingthesilence.org.il/ (accessed July 4, 2016).

3 This understanding is based on the writing of Ariella Azoulay in her book *The Civil Contract of Photography*, where she opens up the possibilities of exploring how photography can be a form of political dialogue that transcends the limitation of representation by sovereignty. Her conception of photography aims to extend the social imagination in a way that sees it not only as an artifact, but also as an act of interpretation, a civil act of interpretation (Azoulay 2008: 16–17).

4 Gordon (2006), http://phr.org.il/ (accessed April 7, 2018).

5 Issues related to the OPT in which PHRI is involved are given greater media coverage than other issues. This gap may be observed in the conclusion written by Hadas Ziv, director general of PHRI at the time, in the organization's 2008 annual report. The mobile clinic receives more donations than other PHRI projects and is more documented by known photographers. The documentation is not an initiative of the organization, but rather the photographers. They ask to document the mobile clinic and no other projects.

6 Conversation with Salah Haj Yihyeh, mobile clinics coordinator, August 10, 2007.

7 See Foucault and Jay (1986).

8 The cameras' invasiveness is not restricted to the private sphere. Recently, we have been witnessing the production of images in the framework of Google Street View. This project, which seeks to photograph every street and every highway, exposes those not protected by house walls. Their privacy is violated in that they are documented without having asked for it, in the name of a corpocratic mapping project led by technological enchantment.

9 Interview with Dr. Ruchama Marton, March 2, 2009.

10 See, for example, the critique of human rights as a colonialist project by Talal (2000) and Spivak (2003). Reference to this critique may also be found in Ignatieff (2001) and in Hardt and Negri (2001). Talal starts his paper with the question about the gap between Third World countries and the Euro-Americas, and his answer is based on the idea that Third World societies are 'yet unredeemed' (2001: 14). Spivak focuses on the question of the human rights agency, while Ignatieff and Hard and Negri, by 'calling the global diffusion Western human rights' (Ignatieff, 2001: 4), cast human rights as a regime.

11 At the time, Miki Alon was a student. Now he is working as a photographer with another Israeli NGO.

12 The photos taken by photojournalist Limor Edri, who appears in this photo, have appeared in the newspaper *Ha'aretz* and in a photo exhibition following her documentary involvement in one of the 'medical days.' In a conversation I held with her (March 10, 2007), she said that she had joined the organization's activity on that day as part of preparing a newspaper article on PHRI. Unfortunately, the photos taken by Edri on the organization's medical day have not been found.

13 As Foucault writes: 'experience reads at a glance the visible lesions of the organism and the coherence of pathological forms; the illness is articulated exactly on the body, and its logical distribution is carried out at once in terms of anatomical masses. The "glance" has simply to exercise its right of origin over truth' (Foucault, 2003: 2).

14 Interview with Miki Kratsman, May 14, 2006.

15 'Nancy's turn to the death mask as the figure par excellence to speculate about photography as a discourse of exposure touches upon a number of aporias in light of its (impossible) contact with death. Nancy reminds us in *The Inoperative Community* that, "'to be exposed' means to be 'posed' in exteriority," to be in a relationship with the outside. … The expository approach to photography challenges the index by calling into question its logic of identity, identification, and representation and by foregrounding in its place the dynamics of exposure, expropriation, and alterity' (Kaplan, 2010: 49–50).

16 In the publication there is no trace of the identity of the girl in the photo. The story of her life and death as presented here has been pieced together from information gathered during conversations with those present on that medical day in the Jenin district. I have not found these details in any document relating to the photo.

17 I am putting aside here an additional gaze, that of the spectator, which is now embodied in the fact that I am looking at the photo.

18 On the distinction between humanitarian activity and the activity of rights organizations, see Feher (2007).
19 Interview with Dr. Dani Filc, December 2, 2007. It should be noted that some of the organization's employees and activists with whom I spoke defined the major distinction in the NGO's activity as that between activity assisting an individual person and 'principled' activity. The organization's employees routinely help in obtaining transit permits for the purpose of medical treatment. But, when similar cases accumulate, they appeal to the High Court of Justice in a 'principled' appeal, which does not focus on individual assistance, but on a given case as representative of a general problem they have identified. In contrast to humanitarian care, helping ill Palestinians to move through checkpoints constitutes advocacy action, wherein PHRI serves as a mouthpiece for those deprived of the possibility of negotiating with the appropriate authorities. The mediation between the parties does not replace missing services, as is the case with humanitarian organizations (for example, the international organization UNRWA's educational institutions and food distribution project).
20 The interview took place on July 7, 2007.
21 Interview with Dr. Ruchama Marton, July 6, 2007.
22 Interview with Dr. Ahmed Musawa, August 9, 2007.

References

Azoulay, A. (2008) *The Civil Contract of Photography*, New York, Zone Books.

Azoulay, A. (2011) "Photography," *Mafte'akh* 2: 65–80.

Barthes, R. (1993a) *Camera Lucida: Reflections on Photography*, London, Vintage.

Barthes, R. (1993b) *Mythologies*, London, Vintage.

Berger, J. (1991) *About Looking*, New York, Vintage.

Birnhack, M. (2007) "Control and Consent: The Theoretical Basis of the Right to Privacy," *Mishpat Umimshal [Law and Government]* 11: 9–73. (In Hebrew)

Feher, M. (2007) "The Governed in Politics" in M. Feher, G. Krikorian, and Y. McKee, eds. *Nongovernmental Politics*, New York, Zone Books: 12–27.

Foucault, M. (2003) *The Birth of the Clinic: An Archaeology of Medical Perception*, London, Routledge.

Foucault, M., and Jay, M. (1986) "Of Other Spaces," *Diacritics* 16 (1): 22–27.

Gordon, N. (2006) "Human Rights as Contingent Foundation: The Case of Physicians for Human Rights," *Journal of Human Rights* 5: 163–184.

Hardt, M. and Negri, A. (2001) *Empire*, London, Harvard University Press.

Ignatieff, M. (2001) *Human Rights as Politics and Idolatry*, Princeton, Princeton University Press.

Kaplan, L. (2005) *American Exposures: Photography and Community in the Twentieth Century*, London, University of Minnesota.

Kaplan, L. (2010) "Photograph/Death Mask: Jean-Luc Nancy's Recasting of Photographic Image," *Journal of Visual Culture* 9 (1): 45–62.

Kaplan, L. and John, P. R. (2010) "Introduction: 'Regarding Jean-Luc Nancy'," *Journal of Visual Culture* 9 (1): 3–10.

Linfield, S. (2010) *The Cruel Radiance: Photography and Political Violence*, London, University of Chicago Press.

Nancy, J.-L. (2005) *The Ground of the Image: Perspectives in Continental Philosophy*, New York, Fordham University Press.

Rosler, M. (2003) "In, Around, and Afterthoughts: On Documentry Photography" in L. Wells, ed. *The Photography Reader*, London, Routledge: 261–274.

Sontag, S. (1977) *On Photography*, New York, Dell.

Sontag, S. (2003) *Regarding the Pain of Others*, New York, Farrar, Straus & Giroux.

Spivak, G. C. (2003) "Righting Wrongs" in N. Owen, ed. *Human Rights, Human Wrongs*. New York, Oxford University Press: 164–227.

Talal, A. (2000) "What Do Human Rights Do? An Anthropological Enquiry," *Theory and Event* 4 (4). https://muse.jhu.edu/article/32601 [accessed April 8, 2018].

14

Love the bomb

Picturing nuclear explosion

Paula Rabinowitz

The photobomb

Stanley Kubrick's subtitle for his 1964 dark satire *Dr. Strangelove or: How I Learned to Stop Worrying and Love the Bomb* offered a weird and ironic comfort in the midst of Cold War anxiety. My title is meant quite literally: an expression of this love. How did the bomb, or, more pertinently, its photographic image—the photobomb, almost immediately named the "mushroom cloud" (O'Brian 2015a: 15)[1]—saturate the semiosphere to become an icon of desire? Not only in the psychoanalytic sense—that view is actually easier to discern as the image, and its imprint, oscillates between Eros and Thanatos, erotics and power, something clearly signaled in both the advertisement for the National Atomic Testing Museum, which features Miss Atomic Bomb of 1957, where the mushroom cloud conveniently covers the woman's breasts and pubis, and Bruce Conner's 1989 collage *Bombhead*, where the mushroom cloud replaces the head of a man in a business suit (see Figure 14.1). In J. Robert Oppenheimer's famous words upon the successful Trinity test detonation, he was reminded of the *Bhagavad-Gita*, declaring: "Now I am become Death, the destroyer of worlds" (quoted in Rhodes 1986: 676).[2] Instead, this image appears closer to home, in fact located within it, around the kitchen table. How did this pervasive image, the photobomb, crystallize the open secret of nuclear (family) annihilation?

The bomb was brought home through its photograph. Moreover, its metaphoric assimilation through the photograph meant it was a token of remembrance connected to others memorializing key events, whether official or private, and as such became intimately understood through discourses of marriage located within domestic space. It became impossible to separate the photobomb from the family. The nucleus of the atom and the home were fused in the national imaginary, and this process of literal and figurative domestication was central to acculturating citizens to mass destruction in the postwar years. At the end of World War II, the horrors of extermination camps and the atomic bombs' decimation of Hiroshima and Nagasaki became part of the media landscape; war's deaths were seared into mass consciousness through magazines, newspapers, movies, television, even postcards. Images of death—the corpses piled in troughs after the Allies entered Auschwitz, the utter leveling of Hiroshima after the bomb—are of necessity static. What distinguishes the photobomb, the still image of the explosion and its split second aftermath, is the way in which extraordinary

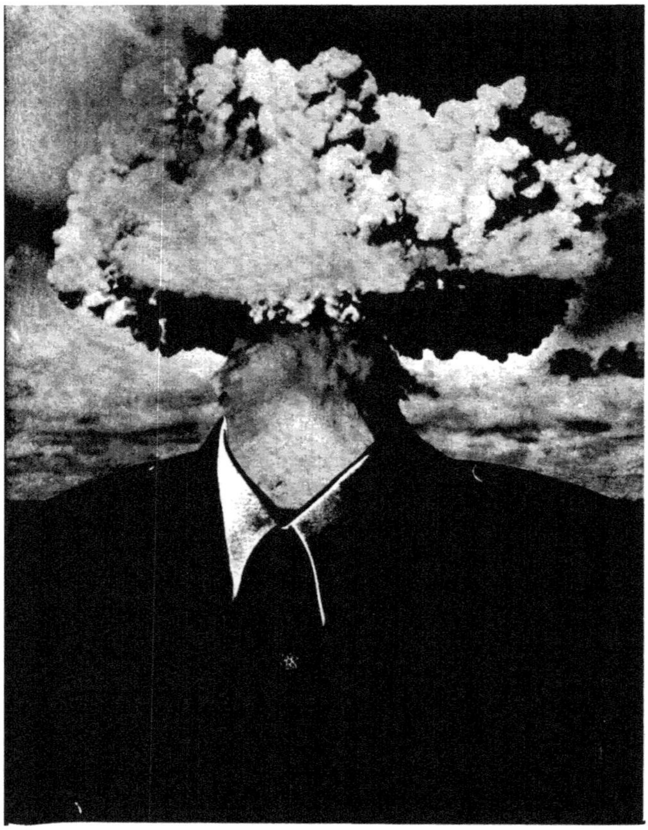

Figure 14.1 Bruce Conner, *Bombhead* (1989), $9\frac{3}{4} \times 7\frac{11}{16}$ in. offset lithograph and photocopy collage on paper mounted on paper board. © 2016 Conner Family Trust, San Francisco/Artists Rights Society (ARS), New York

velocity and force stabilized and ultimately was rendered iconic. Or, to put it another way, *medias* became *res* as the explosion was distilled, made still, through the photograph. How did the process of movement (atomic energy unleashed) become "caught" (in James Agee's terms [Agee and Evans 1941/2001: 30]) mid-explosion and objectified? This was both a technical process and an ideological one.

The bombs' enormous power shocked the world as the images of their explosive force, but not of their destruction of Hiroshima and Nagasaki, circulated globally in 1945 and registered that a new era—the Atomic Age—was beginning. This was its purpose according to Oppenheimer, who often declared "the atomic bomb is shit," because it was not a practical weapon; instead, "the visual effect of an atomic bombing would be tremendous," he argued, and Soviet scientists would understand its message (Rhodes 1986: 642, 648). The atomic bomb could be seen in both black and white and color within days of the detonation. What was kept under wraps, an open secret known among scientists in Japan and the US but kept from the American people, was its aftermath—the devastation caused by the fires and radioactive fallout that followed the two bombings. John Hersey's reporting in the *New Yorker*, which became the 1946 bestseller *Hiroshima*, was the first to breach this 'security' (Figure 14.2):

> General MacArthur's headquarters systematically censored all mention of the bomb in Japanese scientific publications, but soon the fruit of the scientists' calculations became common knowledge among Japanese physicists, doctors, chemists, journalists, professors … Long before the American public had been told, most of the scientists and lots of non-scientists in Japan knew … that a uranium bomb had exploded at Hiroshima and a more powerful one, of plutonium, at Nagasaki … They estimated that, even with the primitive bomb used at Hiroshima, it would require a shelter of concrete fifty inches thick to protect a human being entirely from radiation sickness. The scientists had these and other details which remained subject to security in the United States printed and mimeographed and bound in little books … Altogether, the Japanese scientists were somewhat amused at the efforts of their conquerors to keep security on atomic fission.
>
> *(Hersey 1948: 105–6)*

While the bombs' effects were hiding in plain sight, the photobomb could be found in the most unlikely places. Its power to disturb was diluted almost immediately as it took on its iconic proportions and entered the realm of kitsch. Milan Kundera defines the Cold War years as permeated on both sides of the so-called Iron Curtain by forms of "totalitarian kitsch," each "realm" encrusting it with its own trademark; but, for each, "the dictatorship of the heart reigns supreme … Kitsch causes two tears to flow in quick succession … moved, together with all mankind" (Kundera 1984: 250–51). Thus, an image, such as that of the "bomb cake" being sliced—"Vice Admiral W.H.P. 'Spike' Blandy and his Wife Cutting an Atomic Cake"—on the occasion of the first anniversary of the atomic test at Trinity 1946, signaled its complete assimilation into the domestic sphere and with it into US propaganda about the efficacy but also comfort of its national scientific and technical know-how, even as it spurred worldwide derision. In fact, the so-called "Atomic Age" began a few years before the A-bomb's first explosion with Enrico Fermi's experiments at the University of Chicago cyclotron on December 2, 1942. But the immediate and total surrender by Japan following Nagasaki's bombing meant the world now understood the implications of this newly harnessed device of mass destruction. The image of the bomb's first birthday cake, published in *Time* magazine and many other news outlets, including the society pages of the *Washington Post*, spurred an international outcry against the American trivialization of the A-bombings of Hiroshima and Nagasaki and of the destructive power of this new mode of weaponry that brought highly technological warfare directly into contact with mothers and children at family meals or on the way to school or work, the ones decimated when the bombs detonated.

> In Washington last week, at the Army War College's sumptuous officers' club, two admirals and their wives gave a little party to commemorate the dissolution of Joint Army-Navy Task Force No. 1, which staged Operation Crossroads at Bikini. An East St. Louis group of bakers sent a cake, made out of tiny angel-food puffs, in the shape of an atomic explosion. Vice Admiral W.H.P. ("Spike") Blandy, Crossroads commander, and Mrs. Blandy were photographed gaily cutting the cake, while Rear Admiral F. J. Lowry stood happily b y.
>
> *(*Time*, 18 November 1946: 32)*

*Time*speak was designed to absorb any occurrence anywhere on Earth into the sanitized domestic space of the American middle-class home. And surely cutting a birthday cake—but cutting it together, like a classic wedding cake cutting picture—lodges the bomb securely within the nuclear family. This assimilation was enabled by the already familiar image of the photobomb.

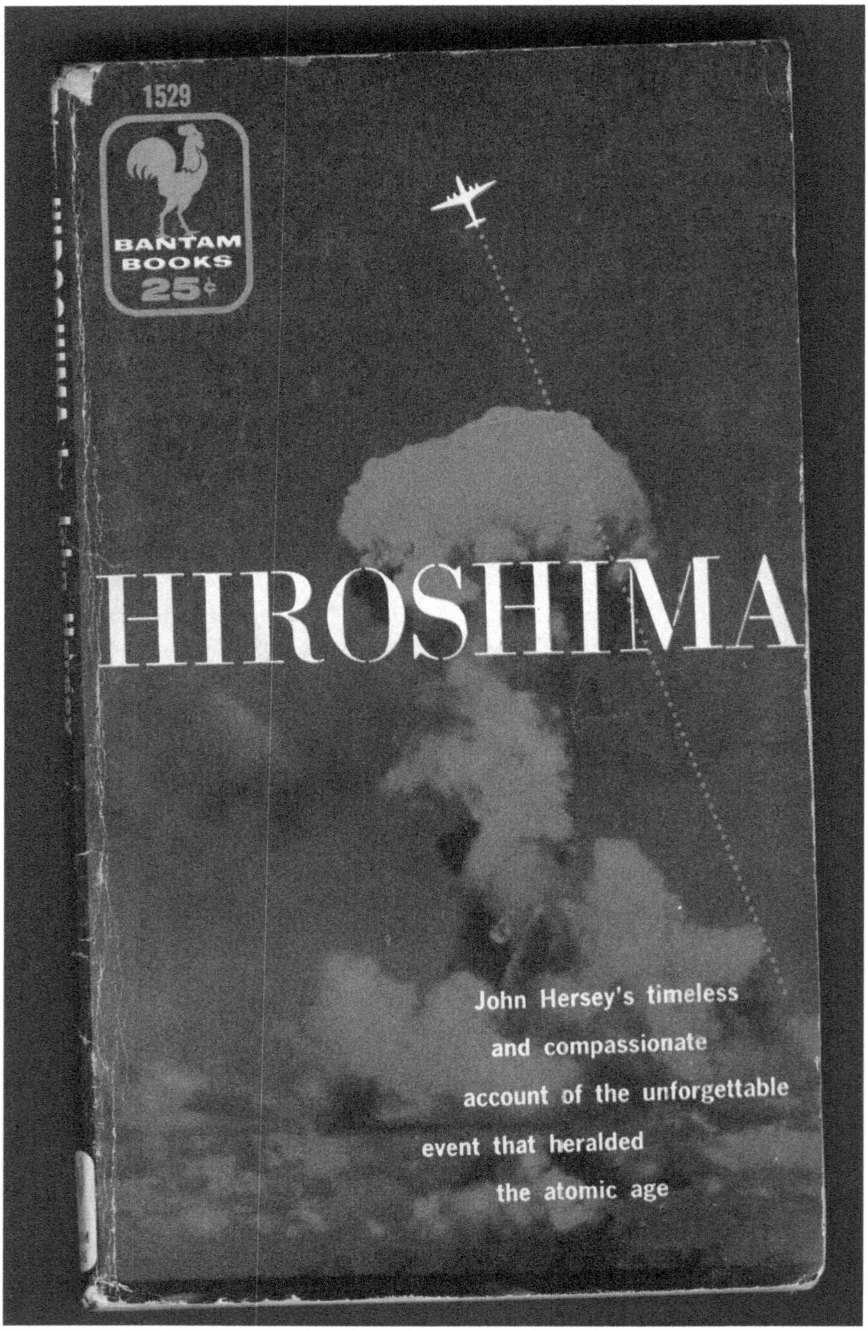

Figure 14.2 Cover: John Hersey, *Hiroshima* (1948), by Geoffrey Biggs

A still image/still an image

The photobomb is an example *par excellence* not only of the narrative device of *in medias res*, as it captures an instant already in process, but also of "In Media Res," Giulia Colaizzi's conceptual pun for the way in which media become matter, become thing, and, in an extension of her linguistic play, the thing also becomes nothing (*res* means nothing in Catalan).[3] It is at once utterly static and endlessly mobile. This mobility results from the instantaneous quality of the photobomb and the split-second timing of its image-making, but it is, in addition, a mobile image that travels across media as it was reproduced, parodied and reclaimed by artists, journalists, politicians and advertisers. The photobomb acts as the "crystal-image," according to Gilles Deleuze, because:

> time has to split itself in two at each moment as present and past, which differ from each other in nature, or what amounts to the same thing, it has to split the present in two heterogeneous directions, one of which is launched towards the future, while the other falls into the past.

In each case—present/past/future—its split and multiplying image sends us to death: "the gushing of time as dividing in two, as splitting" (Deleuze 1989: 81). Although not concerned with atom bomb photography, the connections Deleuze draws between the "time-image" and its emergence after World War II and the importance of the crystalline image as one forestalling but instantiating death point to the subterranean impact of the bomb (as well as, of course, that of the Holocaust) on European film directors.

The links between the still image and moving image—and thus the connection to memory and death—are contemplated by Laura Mulvey, but again, the photobomb is not the overt context of her meditation on the impact of the DVD and our ability to stop a film *in medias res*; however, her discussion of the scene in Pompeii of the recovery of the corpses in Roberto Rosselini's film *Viaggio in Italia* (1953), which are usually thought to convey the images of a destroyed Europe (as in *Germania, anno zero*), more closely refracts the afterimages of Hiroshima and Nagasaki in the ways in which instantaneous death appears as form (Mulvey 2006). In the case of the bomb, those forms were recorded as photograms in the shadows made by bodies and their clothing when the explosion happened. The photobomb reverses the trajectory of the photograph as *memento mori*, set in motion, according to Roland Barthes' readings, by our awareness of the implicit death of those photographed. Human form is evacuated from the photobomb as its appearance masks the bodies littering the ground below. Like any attempt to fix an event, it takes on the folly of seriousness.

> All those young photographers who are at work in the world, determined upon the capture of actuality, do not know they are agents of Death. This is the way our time assumes Death: with the denying alibi of the distractedly 'alive'.
>
> *(Barthes 1980: 2).*

In the postwar films that constitute Deleuze's "time-image," form presents stillness within the moving picture, and thus, Mulvey declares, instantiates "Death 24× a Second." The photobomb reverses this, inverting the process. In an instant, it arrests the motion of destruction—and this requires a highly technical procedure, which links the making of the image of the photobomb to the making of the atom bomb itself—and poses it as a form of pin-up, evacuating the actuality of the shit it congeals. Robert Frank found postcard racks displaying the photobomb of nuclear weapons tests in gas stations and drug stores in Nevada alongside scenic images of the desert when he traveled across the country documenting "The Americans" in 1958. The time of the bomb is at once elongated—it was years in the making, and its effects still play out over decades (as Barack Obama showed when he became the first sitting US president to visit Hiroshima in 2016; Broad 2016)—and compressed—its immediate destruction occurs within minutes of detonation. This ricocheting among past, present, future is akin to the "figures of oblivion" Marc Augé discerns in the process of memorializing: "where oblivion is concerned, all tenses are present tenses, because the past gets lost in it or finds itself again, and the future is only sketched out in it" (Augé 2004: 58). This is the "singular intermediary" linking photography to theater and the rituals of forgetting to remember Augé describes; it occurs "by way of Death" (Barthes 1980: 31).

Augé's meditation on oblivion comes from his ethnologist's observations of ritual, initiation and possession, but his insistence on the term oblivion to understand the processes of memory links the psychic and social practices of forgetting and remembering to the cultural work of the photobomb, which is at once a trace of an ineffable moment, a reminder that a new age has begun, and with it, the possibility of annihilation, and a repudiation (even as it is an extension) of all that has come before. We need to obliterate the past in order to live in it and to continue through the present into the future. The photobomb might be seen as a means to train populations to forget, but its presence is also a stubborn marker of the oblivion the bombs trace. The three figures Augé marshals for this complex imbrication of person into social are:

> *return* ... to find a lost past again by forgetting the present ... *suspense* ... to find the present by provisionally cutting it off from the past and the future ... *rebeginning* ... to create the conditions for a new birth that, by definition, opens up into every possible future without favoring a single one .
>
> *(Augé 2004: 56–57; original emphasis).*

Through these figurations, time is managed, socially and personally, as forgetting and remembering make the one at least two (Augé 2004: 59).

This management of time, and thus death, occurs through manipulations of scale; moving in and out of past, present and future reconfigures temporal relationships, because the duration of pastness and futurity, each of which is infinitely long, gets exchanged for the immediacy of the present instant. Time stretches and shrinks as forgetting enables memorialization. Photographer Daniel Blaufuks considers this as "one of the paradoxes of photography" as the process of retrieval of the past occurs at once in the present and the eventual future. "Memories are images from images from images. Do we need memoires? Do we need photography to remind us of memory?" he wonders (Blaufuks 2012: 26). This symbiotic process between memory and image within differential temporalities is fundamentally an ethical problematic ensuring that memory remains in constant flux, a permanency based on continual revision as personal experience is set in and against social practices. Thus spatial relations are also rescaled as the intimate becomes monumental or vice versa. The photobomb, seen in miniature—for instance, in the contact sheets Berlyn Brixner designed to record the unfolding of the bomb during the Trinity test—shrink the bomb's magnitude to the size of one's palm. These still images, 10,000 of them taken at intervals of less than a second, could be collated into moving pictures reanimating the bomb's force as energy is released. The monumental is miniaturized; violent movement is stilled. This alteration of scale and speed, like the counterintuitive work of oblivion for memory's sake, is a process of narration. It tells a story, but not the one of the bomb's destructiveness. Instead, it records the "brilliant flash" that blinded its observers, who later recall the sequence of unseen events as a series of sensations of light and heat (Rhodes 1986: 671–75).

In Walter Benjamin's words—*avant la lettre*—the photobomb:

> comes together in a flash with the now to form a constellation. In other words, image is dialectics at a standstill ... Only dialectical images are genuine images (that is, not archaic): and the place where one encounters them is language.
>
> *(Benjamin 1999: 462)*

The photobomb, which comes together in a flash, however, is not a "genuine image," is not "dialectics at a standstill." Instead, it functions as an antithesis of this "constellation" because it precludes, or at least seems to close off, language. Yet the photobomb has not only generated moving and other still images: it has been part of literary history since the Cold War; its situation is essentially that of fiction, of narrative. It is also a language bomb.

The art bomb

Not only does the photobomb freeze the incredibly destructive and speedy movement of the bomb almost before it happens (like lightning and thunder, its visual impact precedes its sonic effect, which can be seen in various declassified films on YouTube) and thus work to manage time, its stillness and size also manage space. Because these relationships are unstable, poised between memory and oblivion, they generate new forms. In the words of David Levi Strauss, they transform.

> To represent is to aestheticize; that is, to transform. It presents a vast field of choices but it does not include the choice *not* to transform, not to change or alter whatever is being presented. It cannot be a pure process, in practice.

This is true for photography and for "any of other means of representation ... To become legible to others, these imaginings must be socially and culturally encoded" (Levi Strauss 2005: 9). The photobomb as an icon strays into the middle of any number of other media—poetry, film, song lyrics, book covers, paintings, sculpture, and comics. In this migration across the peripheries of media, it continually returns to the center of things, the nuclear family and its home, or, more properly, the varied domestic remnants left in the bomb's aftermath.

In part, Kubrick's satiric movie and other films—short experimental ones (Bruce Conner's 1976 compilation film *Crossroads*), animations (John and Faith Hubley, *The Hole*, 1962), as well as numerous Hollywood B-movies (*Attack of the 50 Foot Woman* [1958])—helped inoculate American citizens against the horrific image of nuclear annihilation perpetrated by their government. The photobomb encoded oblivion by appearing seemingly everywhere. It could be found, as well, in the many photomontages (Bruce Conner, *Bombhead* [1989]; Figure 14.1]), sculptures (David Smith's 1950 *Star Cage*; Figure 14.3); poems (Gregory Corso's "Bomb" in his 1960 volume *The Happy Birthday of Death*, Figure 14.4, or Allen Ginsberg's "America" from *Howl*) and novels (Nevil Shute's 1957 *On the Beach* [made into a Hollywood film with Gregory Peck and Ava Gardner] and Judith Merril's *Shadow on the Hearth,* 1950 [made into the 1953 Motorola television drama *Atomic Attack*], and, later, E. L. Doctorow's

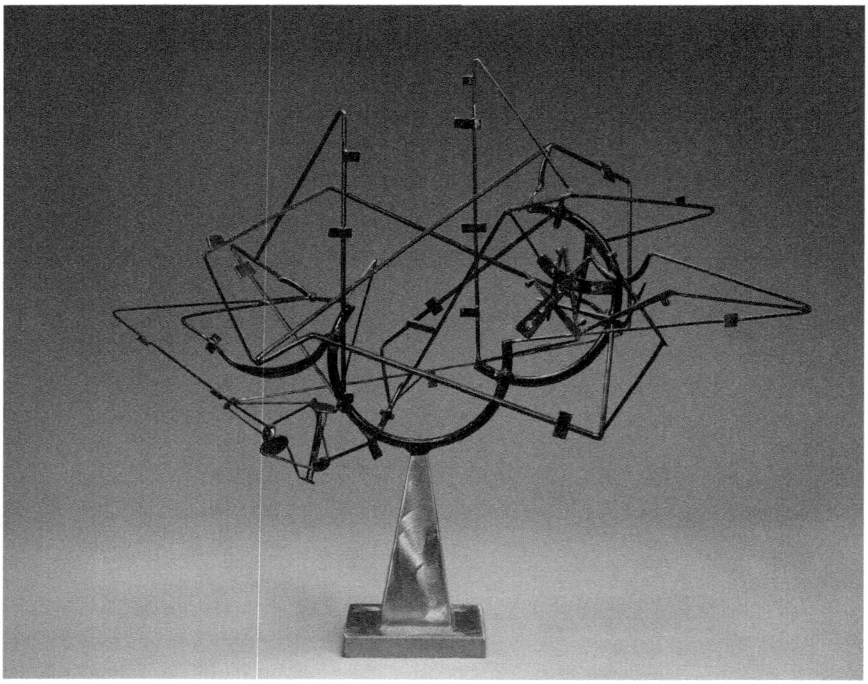

Figure 14.3 David Smith, *Star Cage*, 1950, painted and brushed steel, 44⅞ in. × 51¼ in. × 25¾ in., the Collection of the Frederick R. Weisman Art Museum at the University of Minnesota, Minneapolis. The John Rood Sculpture Collection. 1953.189

1971 novel, *The Book of Daniel* and Robert Coover's 1977 satirical condemnation of Cold War A-bomb and H-bomb hysteria, *The Public Burning*) circulating within popular and avant-garde cultures, often with a critical edge. It eventually refashioned women's clothing. Less than a year after the destruction of Hiroshima and Nagasaki, on July 5, 1946, Louis Réard's bikini went on sale. Réard said that, "like the [atom] bomb, the bikini is small and devastating." Fashion writer Diana Vreeland described the bikini as the "atom bomb of fashion" (quoted in Rosebush n.d.: n.p.). "What was once a symbol of dread [… has] become one more image in a lexicon of images. The mushroom cloud that is 'boiling' has a kitchen-stove familiarity that signals a certain domestication of turbulence," according to critic Edward Brunner, writing of its circulation within poetry (Brunner 2001: 195).

Brunner's critique of the banality of the mushroom cloud as icon is aimed at the poem bomb—best captured by Gregory Corso's 1958 concrete poem "Bomb," which appeared as a foldout, like in *Playboy*, in his 1960 volume *The Happy Birthday of Death*. But its effect depends on the visual image of the bomb. After all, Corso could not have fashioned his poem into a visual silhouette of the A-bomb without its photograph becoming a pin-up within the postwar imaginary. The process of domestication, Brunner so beautifully dissects, was central to another aspect of the aesthetic, political and ethical implications of the photo-bomb: paradoxically, its inherent violence and instability—once the chain reaction was unleashed, it could not be stopped—crucially served to prop up and stabilize the middle-class family in the US. In advertisements, Réard declared the swimsuit could not be called

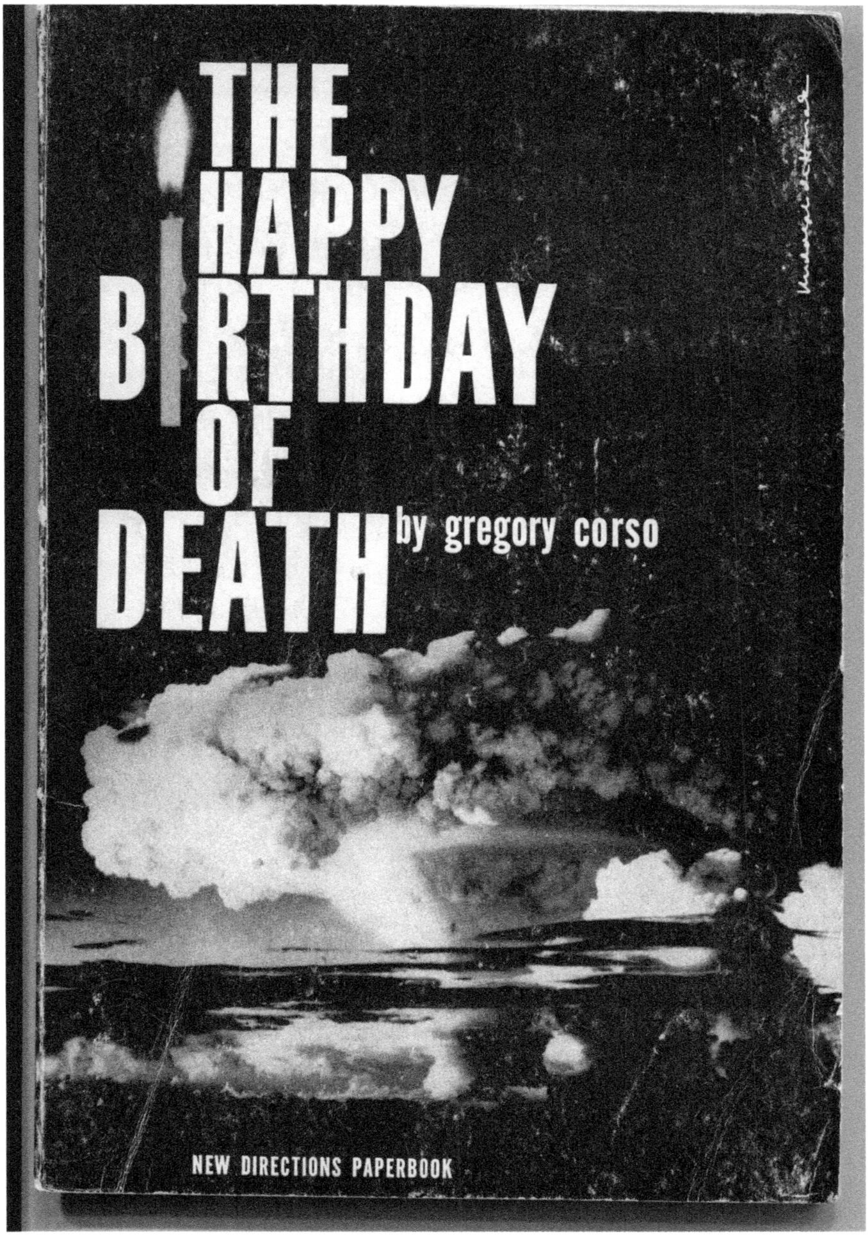

Figure 14.4 Cover: Gregory Corso, *The Happy Birthday of Death* (1960)

a genuine bikini "unless it could be pulled through a wedding ring" (Rosebush n.d.: n.p.). The miniaturization of the swimsuit, like the shrunken image of the bomb, was figured through a wedding ring; marriage was an essential aspect of this semiotic slippage.

The culture of bomb photography—usually performed under the auspices of the military—entered homes, and thus "aestheticization" (Levi Strauss 2005: 9), in very different ways:

incinerating them in Hiroshima and Nagasaki; decorating them in the United States. It is precisely this disjuncture—between security (in the US; refrigerators and bomb shelters) and destruction (in Japan; Hiroshima and Nagasaki)—that drives the discourse of domestication. Counterintuitively, as the threat of nuclear war receded, the photobomb's link to the home and family became much more prevalent, especially since the end of the twentieth century with Condoleezza Rice's invocation of the mushroom cloud as a *casus belli*, on the one hand, and the declassification of so many images of nuclear tests, on the other.

Two books on the photobomb, Peter Kuran's *How to Photograph a Nuclear Bomb* (2006) and Rachel Fermi's *Picturing the Bomb* (1995), are laid out to look like 1950s photo albums, with a horizontal format and black pages as background for the black-and-white snapshots on display. The 2015 exhibit at Toronto's Art Gallery of Ontario, *Camera Atomica*, cemented the technical and aesthetic connections between the photograph as event and as means to dislodge it, in general, as well as the specific ways in which the bomb was itself figured as a mechanism of photography as it froze the shadows of people and objects caught in its blast. As Julia Bryan-Wilson notes of the images of on-site observers of nuclear tests:

> The flash of the bomb often acts in place of the flash of the camera in these images, and this substitution demonstrates how there is a peculiar affinity between photography and atomic weapons, as the technology of sight and the technology of death are conjoined in an intimate marriage .
>
> *(Bryan-Wilson 2015: 118)*

Her metaphor of "an intimate marriage" of vision and death through technology makes clear how technologies of Cold War domesticity included refrigerators, toasters—and nuclear weaponry (as well as nuclear medicine).[4]

Within hours of the atomic bombings of Hiroshima and Nagasaki, images of the pluming mushroom cloud were circulated globally (O'Brian 2015b: 84). As John O'Brian succinctly notes: "Nuclear photography, like the nuclear era itself, is haunted by questions of excess" (2015b: 77). Even under the intense secrecy of national security, thousands of images of bomb tests circulated endlessly. Under the direction of Berlyn Brixner, at the inaugural Trinity test alone, even before the widespread coining of the phrase 'mushroom cloud' to describe the effect of atomic bombs attached a vegetal sensibility (rhizomatic, ubiquitous and potentially deadly, but strangely associated with a life force as they multiplied)[5] to it, more than 100,000 photographs were taken in fractions of the split seconds of detonation (O'Brian 2015b: 80). Most of these images were black and white, some still, others motion pictures, made from reconnaissance photographs and films shot from planes accompanying the Enola Gay to Hiroshima as well as the images of the Trinity and later Bikini tests, but three photobombs were taken in color by Jack Aeby of the Trinity test site bomb detonated July 16, 1945, weeks before Hiroshima was bombed. These were the ones used to dramatize the news articles appearing in October 1945 that publicly confirmed the A-bombings. These front-page images, bathed in yellows and oranges, became another stock-in-trade of nuclear iconography, as did the shadow images of those present in Hiroshima and Nagasaki when the bombs exploded. But it was the black-and-white mushroom cloud that ultimately signaled the Atomic Age, the nuclear age, even though the image of "Little Boy" captured from the Enola Gay by Bob Caron actually appears as a plume of smoke from the firestorm caused by the explosion (Broad 2016: D2). Elaine Scarry points out, however, that the *hibakusha*, survivors of the atomic bombings, saw no mushroom cloud, which is an image viewed from afar: "such pictures keep us safely outside the ground where terrifying injuries took place" (Scarry 2016: D).

The photobomb superseded the images of the devastated cityscapes and then of the few remnants—objects retrieved by survivors—which presented a stark contrast to the domesticated visions of nuclear survival gracing magazine covers and newspaper front pages. These were less widely viewed, especially in the US, than the mushroom cloud, though they did seep into the culture. Jackson Pollock's action paintings, such as *Convergence* (1952), recall the scenes of destruction, buildings flattened, corpses piled everywhere, found in the reconnaissance photographs and in those taken by the bomb survivors of the immediate aftermath of the "Flash-Bang" (Sasaki n.d.: 16). Many of these are currently exhibited in and around the Peace Museum (dedicated in1952, opened in 1955) in Hiroshima. Yuichiro Sasaki "roamed about the fire-ravaged city limits known as 'Hiroshima Desert' with no immediate signs of creatures around, carrying a camera as my solo [*sic*] companion," mapping the deaths across the "A-bombed city" (Sasaki n.d.: 2). When he spread his canvas on the floor and dropped paint on its field, Pollock mirrored the relationship of aerial bombardiers to their target. Mark Rothko's color fields partitioning the canvas into cloud-like sections, too, can be seen as gesturing obsessively toward nuclear weapons' aftermath, as can David Smith's 1950 sculpture *Star Cage*, which appears as a more direct rendition of the mushroom cloud. Despite Pollock's insistence that his postwar work resisted including recognizable figures and expressed his inner feeling as he dripped, flung and poured paint, he did acknowledge that "the modern painter cannot express this age, the airplane, the atom bomb, the radio, in the old forms of the Renaissance or of any other past culture" (Pollock 1999: 20).[6]

By the end of the 1940s, especially after the USSR detonated its first nuclear test in 1949, the bomb's presence as an icon and as shorthand for anxious modern living became a global household reality. This occurred in the US, in part, because its use became associated less with its powerful and brutal ending of World War II with Japan's total surrender following the bombing of Nagasaki, than with the hundreds of tests undertaken as the US sought to maintain nuclear superiority during the Cold War, as well as the new discourse of civil defense that was aimed at preserving the American nuclear family and its middle-class way of life through the many calls for constructing home bomb shelters.[7] Even the painter Georgia O'Keeffe had one built on the property of her Abiquiu, New Mexico, studio, not too far from the site of the bombs' development. Thus, the dimensions of the nuclear cloud, shrunken already from its extreme heat and fire and the black rain of radiation to the mushroom cloud, entered the realm of modern art, kitsch and popular culture, sutured at once to horror and security through the possibility of survival in a bomb shelter.

The home bomb

For instance, the 1953 B-movie *Split Second*, an amazing mash-up comprised of film noir, gangster and westerns with an atomic bomb plot twist, begins in the office of a US Army general modeled on Leslie Groves, who oversaw the Manhattan Project at Los Alamos, New Mexico. On each of the walls of his office in the Nevada desert, visible out the windows, where he is briefing newspaper reporters on the planned atomic bomb test scheduled for early the next morning, is a photograph of the mushroom cloud. It appears to be a photograph of the bomb used on Hiroshima or Nagasaki, but more likely is one of the many bombs exploded at the Nevada test site after January 1951. The photographs serve as decor connecting the desert view beyond the walls to the military preparations going on within the room. With each shot, from every angle, the image of the bomb is visible in the background in a photograph hanging on the walls. Never the direct focus of the scene or the camera, which sets up the dual plot of atomic test and prison escape, after the lead reporter is reassigned from covering the explosion to tracking down the escapees, the photograph is part of the scenery, a core reminder of the military's know-how both technically and aesthetically.

Directed by Dick Powell (who starred in films noirs), this B-movie is only one of many Cold War-era movies to address the threat of nuclear attack. Here, however, it is not the enemy destroying Los Angeles with a nuclear bomb (as in the later 1962 film *Panic in Year Zero* [d. Ray Milland]), but the US government itself that plans to destroy a ghost town in the Nevada desert. *Split Second* weaves together a series of characters all of whom end up in Lost Hope City, Nevada, after a prison break by a psychotic murderer—a World War II veteran—who takes a woman and her lover hostage, then stops the reporter and the B-girl he's picked up hitchhiking when the first car runs out of gas. As the clock ticks, the camera returns to the military base occasionally, but primarily remains trapped within the abandoned general store where various characters plot their survival. The movie concludes with the obliteration of the town shown in documentary style using the stock footage made at the Nevada test site of trees pushed parallel to the ground and houses imploding with the blast, as had occurred with Operation Upshot-Knothole Annie in March 1953, which was known publicly as "Operation Doorstep" and "Doomtown" (Kuran 2006: 103).

Listen to these three names: Operation Upshot-Knothole Annie (with its female-named and sexualized bomb [like Grable or Priscilla, and other tests named Nancy, Ruth, Dixie, Harry, even Climax]), Operation Doorstep (with its evocation of the front porch) and Doomtown (with its echo of Western oil or gold or railroad boomtowns). Each ties the bomb test to sex, the body, domicile or mythic spaces of a wholesome Americana—that is, it marks the semiosphere through biopolitics. The photobomb within the moving image interrupts the temporality of this short (85-minute) Hollywood black-and-white movie as it brings the bomb home—on the walls of the office and by creating a community of those stranded and doomed to annihilation. In this film noir, through the still framing of the photobomb, a nuclear explosion becomes an attribute of interior decoration (or rather office decor).

Walker Evans had photographed the calendars, magazine covers and advertisements pasted around tenant farmers' fireplaces for *Let Us Now Praise Famous Men* that he and James Agee found in Alabama in 1936, bringing the glossy world of unattainable things into the unpainted wood shacks of those who lived without them. Agee works through his prose to convey their process as "That of recall; of reception, contemplation, *in medias res*" (Agee and Evans 1941: 215). Nuclear iconography functions paradoxically in a similar fashion—as Lindsey A. Freeman notes of her memories of nuclear trinkets, such as irradiated dimes, and the pictures displayed at the "Atomic City" museum in Oak Ridge: "the souvenirs worked to domesticate the dangers of radiation" (Freeman 2015: 124). They were private mementos to bring home from a trip to grandma's house.[8] As with Julia Bryan-Wilson's conjuring of "marriage" as the metaphoric way to conceptualize the relationship of atomic weaponry and photography, Freeman's tokens connect nuclear annihilation to the home and extended family.

Rhetorically, it is almost impossible to detach the nuclear bomb and nuclear family, either in popular culture or in the metaphors writers and artists use to convey the horrors of nuclear weapons: the mushroom cloud, the emptied cities, the burned and vaporized bodies, and, more recently, nuclear power and its accidents, and so on, all eventually come home. The Nevada test site included clapboard homes, reminiscent of newly developed postwar suburban housing stock, complete with furniture and mannequins of mothers and children watching television, and set in various locations and directions to determine how to site a house for maximum survival in the event of nuclear war. Yuichiro Sasaki returned from Tokyo to his home to discover thirteen members of his family had perished:

> [I] began to take pictures of the sites where my relatives died … this 'Hiroshima Diary' is a photographic version of my energetic exploration of the sites where my kins [*sic*] met their fate. While clicking the camera, I realized that I had taken about 100,000 pictures … this hoard of negatives is everything to me.

Documenting what was no longer became a way—achieved through negatives—"of recording the miseries of war for future reference." Sasaki's search for the destroyed homes and lives of his family as he snapped hundreds of photographs, "recording the heat flash, heat blow, bomb-shell blast, blast pressure, etc. unique to the atomic weapon," was a means of instantiating memories, in Blaufuks sense, as images—even negatives—became the means for resuscitating the past in the future (Sasaki n.d.: 24–25).

Lorraine Hansberry's 1959 drama *A Raisin in the Sun*, which challenges red-lining—racial profiling in housing—that maintained segregated neighborhoods in postwar America, expressly links domestic spaces with atomic bomb tests. Set in Chicago's Southside "sometime between World War II and the present," the play makes clear that African-American dreams are stymied by money woes, and that decent housing, offering "peace and comfort," is under the constant threat of violence, including nuclear war (Hansberry 1988: 93): complaining about the unusual heat, Ruth notes: "Everybody say it's got to do with them bombs and things they keep setting off" (Hansberry 1988: 8). The bombs Ruth refers to—nuclear weapons—come closer to home when the vivid imagination of the Younger's neighbor repeats an imagined newspaper headline: "NEGROES INVADE CLYBOURNE PARK—BOMBED," recounting how, in the all-white neighborhood where Mama has purchased a small quasi-suburban home, "colored people … was bombed out of their place" (Hansberry 1988: 102, 100). Racialized violence in the US melds into the domesticated terror of nuclear weaponry, so that home is no longer shelter; hence the need for another subterranean bomb shelter.[9] In Nâzim Hikmet's poem, "STRONTIUM 90," written behind the so-called Iron Curtain a year before, domestic space, even the air—where milk and grass and freedom have been undone by "very strange weather"—the invisible fallout, rather than the photobomb of nuclear bomb tests, invades and deranges longing and love (Hikmet 2002: 202).[10]

By the end of the 1950s, "picturing the bomb"—and picturing it in connection to private life and the home—was inescapable. Rachel Fermi's volume *Picturing the Bomb* begins with a "Page from a photo album. Los Alamos, February 1944," with a house and a child and its mother on the lawn outside. "Learning to walk" says the white-inked inscription on the black paper (Fermi and Samra 1995: n.p. [6–7]). This page is followed by another "Page from photo album." This one is captioned "Hiroshima and Nagasaki, September–October, 1945. The first courtesy of Jean Critchfield, the second from Robert Serber." Together these constitute the visual remnants of domestication and destruction that Fermi (granddaughter of the so-called father of atomic energy) has juxtaposed. In 1961, her grandmother Laura Fermi's children's book *The Story of Atomic Energy* (a book I owned and loved, as did my children) described the building of the "secret cities" of the Manhattan District's Site X—Oak Ridge, Tennessee, growing "as fast as a mushroom." She explains: "Homes went up by the hundreds … with the facilities that hundreds of families need: schools, churches, stores, theaters, and eating places" (Fermi 1961: 102).[11] The atom cities were recalled in bomb shelter design and reconstituted through posters demarking fallout shelters, as well as in Gordon Parks's *Life* magazine layout in 1949 of the "Atom City" of Los Alamos. US citizens were asked to enter the nuclear realm through their homes (in the form of bomb shelters and refrigerators that resembled them) and vicariously through the images of the domesticated spaces generated by the making of the devices used to form the mushroom cloud.

When Lotte Jacobi photographed her friend and co-exile Albert Einstein in his Princeton University office in 1938, she could not have known what this playful image of the brainy scientist in a black leather jacket, surrounded by a messy desk and bookshelves overflowing, portended. But, the next year, Einstein would write the infamous letter (with the aid of Leo Szilárd, Eugene Wigner and Edward Teller) to Franklin Delano Roosevelt urging him to pursue further research into nuclear chain reactions, codified through the work of Enrico Fermi and Szilárd, because the Germans were already at work on "extremely powerful bombs … A single bomb of this type, carried by boat and exploded in a port, might very well destroy the whole port together with some surrounding territory" (quoted in Freeman 2015: 130). Jacobi made pictures of Einstein among his personal belongings—including the twin cups with baby pictures of him and his sister he carried with him from Germany when he fled the Nazis—domesticating this unruly scientist. He was only one of many wild-haired "egghead" geniuses that formed an essential part of the production of the uncanny nuclear *Heimlich* created through photographs and their unique ability to relocate history into the household.[12]

Maxine Hong Kingston remembers that, immediately after World War II ended, she

> went to a movie where the attendants gave each kid a free picture of an atomic bomb explosion. Smoke boiled in a yellow and orange cloud like a brain on a column. It was a souvenir to celebrate the bombing of Japan. … At the base of the explosion, where the people would have been, the specks didn't resolve into bodies.
>
> *(Kingston 1980b: 273).*[13]

Kingston's memory of "smoke boiled in a yellow and orange cloud" suggests that she received a copy of Jack Aeby's color photograph—the only extant one of the Trinity test of "Gadget," which, by mid-August 1945, when details about the bombings of Hiroshima and Nagasaki were still heavily censored in the United States, was published in newspapers and magazines around the globe.[14] Certainly, no bodies were anywhere near ground zero—and, had they been, they would not even be "specks." This fiery image inspired numerous popular cultural renderings of nuclear annihilation found on movie posters and paperback book covers, such as the first paperback edition of John Hersey's *Hiroshima* (Figure 14.2), often featuring a distraught white couple frantically fleeing the garish yellow and orange visuals filling the background. Kingston's memory of hiding the picture from her younger brothers and sisters to protect them, but later taking it out to study it when she was alone, reveals how memories of the mushroom cloud are inseparable from both the sublime fear and erotic pull the image of the bomb created within the private space of the home.

As the walls of offices or the secret recesses of bedrooms in 1940s and 1950s America became showcases for the photobomb, the photographed bomb image was firmly emplaced in the home and thrust into the public sphere through "civil defense." But, more than that, its incorporation into home decor was both facilitated by and inaugurated a rhetoric of domesticity to describe the bomb—the bomb necessitated home-y language. In its "redundancy," it was already wed (and I choose this word deliberately) to the social imaginary of domesticity (Flusser 2000: 65). Once cities became targets, domestic life, primarily made up of mothers, children and the elderly, became a battlefront. And, once the effects of radiation became widely recognized, the air itself could not be trusted; homes needed to secure themselves, and the photobomb became an emblem—along with the fallout shelter symbol—of this new kind of nuclear family/war. But this is not kitsch, it is deadly serious, deathly serious, as the photographs of Ishiuchi Miyako reveal (2016). Once the shadow images of kimono patterns left on the skin of *hibakusha* and their skin itself became disfigured by keloids, skin became a medium. When the transient remnants of those annihilated entered common vision, clothing became an element of war materiél.

The image of the mushroom cloud, invoked by Condoleezza Rice in the hyped-up bellicosity of the Bush administration's war in Iraq, has served as an aestheticized emblem of power, scientific know-how and death. Its ubiquity is a reminder of the role nuclear weapons were claimed to play as a deterrence of war through threats of assured mutual destruction, but its presence as a figure and icon also became part of a process of domestication that raises ethical and political questions about how terror is managed within and through the image. If the photobomb works as an image capturing reality *in medias res*, and thus fixes the ephemeral, it also cancels memory and memorialization as "one redundant photograph displaces another redundant photograph" (Flusser 2000: 65). It is also *media res*, image as thing, as non-thing. Despite the death behind and underneath the photobomb, it counters the melancholy associations of photography with mourning. It erases memory via the imprint of pure image—an image that represents the total erasure of life. It assumes totemic status—like the picture cards Kingston kept hidden from her siblings, or the bunny rabbits clutched by the children Gordon Parks found playing in Los Alamos, or the trinkets Leslie Freeman brought home from Oak Ridge—through its penetration of the walls of American homes. As such, its place is within the realm of family life, as war is transformative, akin to the ways in which, as Benjamin had it, fascism aestheticized politics, and even war (Benjamin 2008: 44). Picturing nuclear explosion, we learn to love the bomb. Following Benjamin's call, can we also learn to politicize its form—and in so doing annihilate it before it does us in? The photobomb has pervaded post-World War II consciousness; the ethical implications of seeing the mushroom cloud, now in its multi-sited appearances as an aesthetic yet kitschy vision of power and, paradoxically, naiveté, are part of the work of oblivion, of obliteration, of forgetting and annihilating—part of the work of photography. How can we theorize these images in ways that do not neutralize, do not disappear, what they represent?

Notes

1 Rhodes (1986) quotes from D. R. Inglis, a ballistics engineer, who described for the Manhattan Engineer District Records the explosion's climax: "the top of the slenderer column seemed to mushroom out into a thick parasol of a rather bright but spectral blue" (673). This may be the first use of the mushroom image (but as a verb); interestingly, it appears along with the image of a parasol—a Chinese invention later brought to Japan for sheltering one from the sun's rays. See O'Brian (2015a: 40–41) for the photograph "Mushroom Cloud, Test Baker, Operation Crossroads," taken by the US Army Photographic Signal Corps during the first atomic test on Bikini Atoll in the Pacific, on July 26, 1946.

2 See the footage of his remembrance at www.atomicarchive.com/Movies/Movie8.shtml

3 Giulia Colaizzi, organizer of the panels *In Media Res*, at the XVI International Conference of the Spanish Semiotics Association, November 2015, Bilbao, Spain. A shorter version of this essay was delivered as part of these linked sessions. This essay was completed while I was 2016 Visiting Fellow at the United State Studies Centre at the University of Sydney, Australia.

4 On the connection between refrigerators and bomb shelters in the 1950s imaginary, see Nekola (2008).

5 Weart notes the complex and ambivalent associations of the mushroom—with death, with transmutation, with visions (psilocybin), with children's literature (Alice, Babar), with a protective umbrella, etc. (Weart, 1988: 402–3).

6 For more on the "curious art-history of the mushroom cloud," see Jones (2002).

7 The Toronto AGO exhibit, "Camera Atomica," offers examples of bomb photography as it circulated in Canada and demonstrates, therefore, how, outside the USA, the image was penetrating globally.

8 I too had a nuclear memento: a gigantic radioactive clamshell brought home from Kwajalein where my father witnessed the final above-ground thermonuclear test.

9 For a detailed discussion of Hansberry's play in the context of other African-American protests against the bomb, see Foertsch (2009).

10 https://eddieplayfair.com/2015/04/12/nazim-hikmet-hiroshima-and-strontium-90/ [accessed June 5, 2019].

11 Fermi commented, "After I married, the only true vacation from physics that I ever had was the wartime period of secrecy. At the end of the war, the vacation was over" (Fermi, 1961: Flyleaf).

12 That picture is at the Tokyo Fuji Art Museum; many thanks to Ms. Hiritani, its photography curator, for showing these to me and Tajiri Ayumu for translation. Lecklider's 2013 work on eggheads of the postwar era shows how the image was at once a homey one—the egg—and an uncanny one as the egghead took on qualities of queerness.

13 David Bernstein, Kingston's contemporary in New York, also remembers trading color A-bomb prints, like large baseball cards, almost immediately after the war ended (personal communication).

14 Jack Aeby worked as a photographer at Los Alamos. He received permission to photograph the Trinity test on July 16, 1945, and was able to acquire a small roll of color film, extremely difficult to come by during the war. He snapped once; then made three pictures in rapid succession from a makeshift tripod. The second of the three was in focus; it was immediately seen by Leslie Groves and J. Robert Oppenheimer and the team at Los Alamos. The next three to view it were Winston Churchill, Josef Stalin and Harry Truman. There were 50 motion picture cameras trained on the atomic test netting about 100,000 frames of it, according to Berlyn Brixner, who headed up the photographic project at Los Alamos.

References

Abey, J. (2005) Interview with Robert Siegel, *All Things Considered*, National Public Radio (July 15).

Agee, J. and Evans, W. (2001 [1941]) *Let Us Now Praise Famous Men*, Boston, MA: Houghton Mifflin.

Augé, M. (2004) *Oblivion*, trans. M. de Jager, Minneapolis, MN: University of Minnesota Press.

Barthes, R. (1980) *Camera Lucida: Reflections on Photography*, trans. R. Howard, New York: Hill & Wang.

Benjamin, W. (1999) *The Arcades Project*, trans. H. Eiland and K. McLaughlin, Cambridge, MA and London: Belknap Press.

Benjamin, W. (2008) *The Work of Art in the Age of its Technological Reproducibility, and Other Writings on Media*, Jennings, M., Dogherty, B. and Levin, T. (eds.), Cambridge, MA: Harvard University Press.

Blaufuks, D. (2012) *Works on Memory: Selected Writings and Images*, Cardiff: Ffotogallery Wales.

Broad, W. (2016) "The Hiroshima Mushroom Cloud that Wasn't," *New York Times*, May 24: D2. www.nytimes.com/2016/05/24/science/hiroshima-atomic-bomb-mushroom-cloud.html [accessed January 18, 2017].

Brunner, E. (2001) *Cold War Poetry*, Urbana and Chicago, IL: University of Illinois Press.

Bryan-Wilson, J. (2015) "Posing by the Cloud: US Nuclear Test Site Photography in Process," in J. O'Brian (ed.), *Camera Atomica*, London: Black Dog, pp. 107–23.

Corso, G. (1960) *The Happy Birthday of Death*, New York: New Directions.

Deleuze, G. (1989) *Cinema Two: The Time-Image*, trans. H. Tomlinson and R. Galeta, Minneapolis, MN: University of Minnesota Press.

Fermi, L. (1961) *The Story of Atomic Energy*, New York: Random House.

Fermi, R. and Samra, E. (1995) *Picturing the Bomb: Photographs from the Secret World of the Manhattan Project*, New York: Harry N. Abrams.

Flusser, V. (2000) *Towards a Philosophy of Photography*, trans. A. Mathews, London: Reaktion Books.

Foertsch, J. (2009) "Against 'Starless Midnight of Racism and War': African American Intellectual Antinuclear Agenda," *Philological Quarterly* 88 (Fall): 409–30.

Freeman, L. (2015) *Longing for the Bomb: Oak Ridge and Atomic Nostalgia*, Chapel Hill, NC: University of North Carolina Press.

Hansberry, L. (1988) *A Raisin in the Sun*, New York: Vintage.

Hersey, J. (1948) *Hiroshima*, New York: Bantam Books.

Hikmet, N. (2002) *Beyond the Walls: Selected Poems*, trans. R. McKane, R. Christie and T. Halman, London: Anvil Press Poetry.

Ishiuchi, M. (2016) "Postwar Shadows," Getty Center, exhibition October 6, 2015–February 2, 2016.

Jones, J. (2002) "Magic Mushrooms," *The Guardian* (August 6) www.theguardian.com/artanddesign/2002/aug/06/art.artsfeatures [accessed March 21, 2016].

Kingston, M. (1980b) *China Men*, New York: Alfred Knopf.

Kundera, M. (1984) *The Unbearable Lightness of Being*, trans. M. H. Heim, New York: Harper Collins.

Kuran, P. (2006) *How to Photograph an Atomic Bomb*, Santa Clarita, CA: VCE.

Lecklider, A. (2013) *Inventing the Egghead: The Battle over Brain Power in American Culture*, Philadelphia, PA: University of Pennsylvania Press.

Levi Strauss, D. (2005) *Between the Eyes: Essays on Photography and Politics*, New York: Aperture.

Mulvey, L. (2006) *Death 24× a Second: Stillness and the Moving Image*, London: Reaktion Books.

Nekola, C. (2008) *Deep Freeze: The Cold War Makes Its Own Metaphors*. Liège, Belgium: Centre Interdisciplinaire de Poétique Appliquée (*CIPA*) Lectures in Humanities, University of Liège.

O'Brian, J. (ed.) (2015a) *Camera Atomica*, London: Black Dog.

O'Brian, J. (ed.) (2015b) "Nuclear Flowers of Hell," in *Camera Atomica*, London: Black Dog, pp. 75–105.

Pollock, J. (1999) "Interview with William Wright (1950)," in P. Karmel (ed.), *Jackson Pollock: Interviews, Articles, Reviews*, New York: MoMA, pp. 20–23.

Rhodes, R. (1986) *The Making of the Atomic Bomb*, New York: Simon & Schuster.

Rosebush, J. (n.d.) "1945–1950: The Very First Bikini,,," *Bikini Science*. www.bikiniscience.com//chronology/1945-1950_SS/1945-1950.html [accessed March 21, 2016].

Sasaki, Y. (n.d.) *Scens [sic] of an A-bomb City: Diary of Hiroshima*. Self-published pamplet obtained from Hiroshima Peace Memorial Museum.

Scarry, E. (2016) "Letter to the Editor," *New York Times*, May 31: D2. www.nytimes.com/2016/05/31/science/letters-to-the-editor.html

Time. (1946, November 18) "Atomic Age: Angel Food," p. 32.

US Army Photographic Signal Corps. (26 July 1946) "Mushroom Cloud, Test Baker, Operation Crossroads," photograph made during the first atomic test on Bikini Atoll in the Pacific.

Weart, S. (1988) *Nuclear Fear: A History of Images*, Cambridge, MA: Harvard University Press.

15

Twice captured

The work of atrocity photography

Molly Rogers

Photographs showing the victims of horrific events, particularly those perpetrated by one group of people against another, that are circulated with the purpose of inciting moral outrage have been around practically since the advent of photography itself. There are, for example, those images used by American abolitionists to raise awareness of the horrors of slavery. *The Scourged Back*, sometimes reproduced as *Gordon*, is probably the best known among these, both at the time of its making and now. The image shows a black man with his back turned to display a dense pattern of scar tissue, evidently the result of maltreatment under slavery (Figure 15.1). Made at a Union camp on the banks of the Mississippi in the spring of 1863, the image was reproduced as an etching in numerous publications with abolitionist sympathies and also widely disseminated by photography studios throughout the North (Rosenheim 2013: 156–7). The image also reached a large audience when it was published in the July 4, 1863, issue of *Harper's Weekly* flanked by two other images, apparently of the same man, called "Gordon" in the article, one showing him in tattered clothes and the other in a Union soldier's uniform. The accompanying article employed the literary tactics of the slave narrative to excoriate Southern slaveholders for their cruelty and thereby generate support for the war.

Although photographs of atrocity are thus nearly as old as the medium itself, the genre "atrocity photography" is a more recent phenomenon. The conventional definition of an atrocity photograph requires that the image shows a body that has been subjected to grievous harm, was reproduced along with a text explaining the image as a sign of moral degradation, and was intended to shock the viewer into recognizing that the form of harm depicted is not only terribly wrong but likely could have been averted—it seeks, in other words, to elicit action (Azoulay 2012: 249–50). *The Scourged Back*, by this definition, could be called an atrocity photograph. Broader definitions of the label allow for greater subtlety in the representation of violence, and even the complete absence of its effects visually, such that traces of the atrocity-event are not necessarily evident in the image but nonetheless played a part in its production (Hirsch and Spitzer 2012; Lowe 2012). In this vein, we could place alongside *The Scourged Back* any number of photographs from antebellum America showing enslaved men and women, including those made to satisfy scientific interest and slaveholder sentimentality.

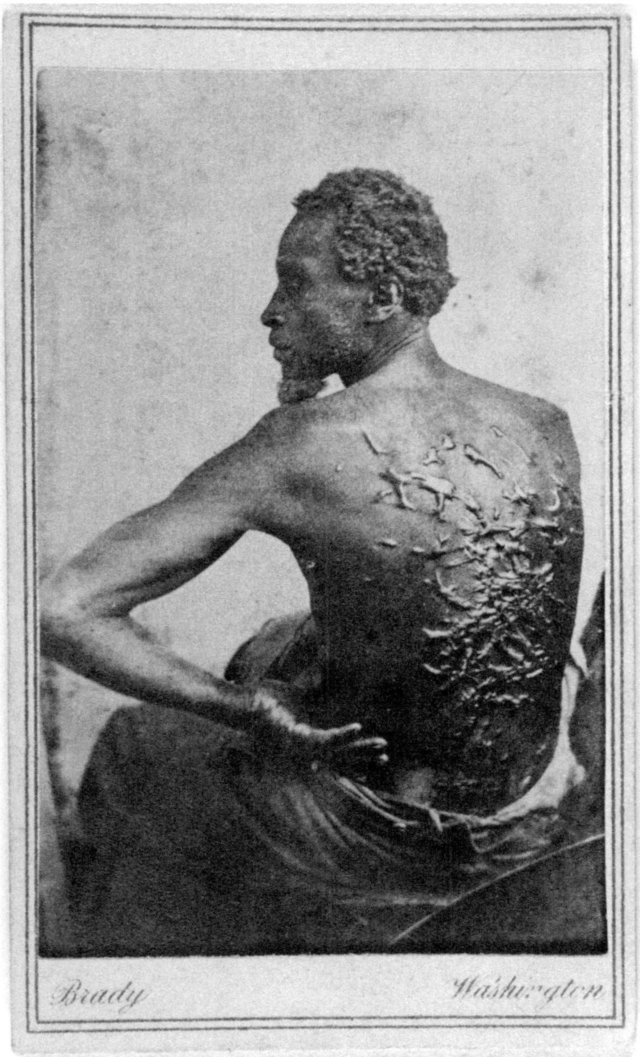

Figure 15.1 Mathew Brady Studio, *Gordon*, copy after William D. McPherson and Mr. Oliver, 1863. Albumen silver print, National Portrait Gallery, Smithsonian Institution

The idea of atrocity photography arose in the post-World-War-II era, when a vast number of images pertaining to Nazi atrocities bore witness to terrible crimes—the volume of images and heinousness of the crimes were, by most accounts, overwhelming. These images raised vital questions about the utility and limits of representation: here was a different sort of image, one demanding a new analytical approach (Friedlander 1992; Didi-Huberman 2012). Writing on atrocity photography specifically, however, was slow to develop and, initially, did not focus upon the Holocaust, although it remained a powerful touchstone.

Among the first to address general human suffering in photographs of particular victims was John Berger in his 1967 essay "Image of Imperialism." Berger took as his subject a then just-published post-mortem photograph of the Cuban revolutionary Che Guevara, which he examined in light of historical revolutions and contemporary wars. Concluding that the horror of Guevara's death is the horror of a world gripped by imperialism, Berger wrote: "It is an image which, as much as any mute image ever can, calls for decision" (Berger 2013: 9). Five years later, in "Photographs of Agony," Berger expanded his analysis to consider the effects of war photography, but his principal interest was why the "decision" called for by a photograph is rarely acted upon. He concluded that such images actually depoliticize the event they show by virtue of a "double violence." On the one hand, the war photograph virtually assaults the viewer with its graphic depiction of violence; on the other hand, it underscores the viewer's "moral inadequacy," her inability to do anything about the causes of violence—not just the people who wield weapons but the institutional apparatus of power that sanctions use of those weapons. In the end, the war photograph depoliticizes the atrocity-event because it "accuses nobody and everybody," leaving the viewer shaken but helpless (Berger 2013: 30–3).

Susan Sontag took this concern for the effects of photographs of atrocity still further in *On Photography*, worrying that "a saturation point may have been reached" (Sontag 1977: 21). There were simply too many images of atrocity in circulation for us to be able to digest their meaning and significance, she suggested, and this made atrocity less real and the horrible more ordinary. The outcome of this overexposure was a desensitized, apathetic viewer. Further, Sontag believed that the aesthetic tendency of a photograph contributed to this problem: "Even those photographs which speak so laceratingly of a specific historical moment also give us vicarious possession of their subjects under the aspect of a kind of eternity: the beautiful" (Sontag 1977: 109). The most horrific image might one day be called beautiful because, "The ethical content of photography is fragile." Images of atrocity thus "tend to be swallowed up in the generalized pathos of time past" (Sontag 1977: 21).

Nevertheless, there are exceptions. Sontag allowed that certain iconic images of atrocity do not lose their power to shock because they are now regarded as "ethical reference points" (Sontag 1977: 21). She repeated this idea in *Regarding the Pain of Others*, a book that struggles with the effects of painful images, and in which the term "atrocity photograph" first appears (Sontag 2003: 23). Sontag noted, "there are pictures whose power does not abate, in part because one cannot look at them often" (Sontag 2003: 83). Presumably, she has in mind here the images from Bergen-Belsen and Dachau that, as she wrote in *On Photography*, affected her profoundly when she first saw them as a young girl in 1945: "When I looked at those photographs, something broke" (Sontag 1977: 20). And so, it would seem, not all photographs anaesthetize: some move us profoundly and with lasting power. The most disturbing photographs may not lead to overt political activity, but they are nevertheless "an invitation to pay attention, to reflect, to learn, to examine the rationalization for mass suffering offered by established powers" (Sontag 2003: 117). Looking, in other words, is the very least we can do.

Building on the ground laid by Berger and Sontag, recent writing on atrocity photographs has been thoughtful, nuanced, and provocative, exploring the meanings of particular images with respect to the conditions under which they were made and are circulated and viewed. Much of this writing has also retained a note of alarm: photography, we are told, is "in crisis" (Prosser 2012: 12–13). The proliferation of images and the excess of meaning potentially found within an image, the reason an image is made, and how it may be used, the commodification of atrocity through images, censorship, aesthetics—the list goes on. Yet these concerns are applicable to photography generally and they are not new; if photography is in crisis, then it has been so since the medium's inception. The claim of "crisis" for atrocity photographs suggests a different problem, one to do with scholarship and writing about such images more than their production and circulation. More specifically, it is a symptom of what Sontag called "the frustration of not being able to do anything about what the images show" (Sontag 2003: 117).

What do photographs documenting human suffering do to us as viewers? What is the purpose of looking at atrocity photographs? Why don't photographs of atrocity prevent further atrocities? These are the questions typically posed in writing about atrocity photography. Here I want to ask a different set of questions: Why do we insist on there being a category "atrocity photography," and what constraints on our thinking does that category impose? Photographs of atrocity-events may serve as evidence, memorial, and object lesson, but what function does the generic branding of such photographs serve? What does it mean to correlate images made under vastly different conditions and for equally varied purposes, images such as those taken by the prison officials at Tuol Sleng in Cambodia, Nick Ut's picture of Kim Phuc suffering the effects of napalm, Richard Drew's "falling man," and the *carte-de-visite* of Gordon's scarred back? With the label "atrocity photograph" comes conventions, a canon, standard texts, and other hallmarks of generic description, including expectations—expectations of what we will see, what the image will signify, and how we are meant to feel and perhaps behave upon seeing the image. But why do we do this? Why is it not enough to call them war photographs, or photojournalism, or abolitionist propaganda, or even just photographs? Simply put, why turn photographs of atrocity into atrocity photographs?

To better understand the work of atrocity photography, I propose to consider what happens when we assign the label "atrocity photograph" to an image about which little has been written and which has no obvious (which is to say visual) connection with an atrocity-event and was not made or circulated under conditions that would suggest it was intended to function as an atrocity photograph. I am, in other words, reframing a historical photograph in order to see what this treatment reveals about our interest in the genre. The photograph I have chosen is A. F. Corning's image of Cynthia Ann Parker made in Fort Worth, Texas, in 1861 (Figure 15.2). Using a little-known photograph leaves me free to draw conclusions about its meaning, conclusions neither confirmed nor denied by others, a condition not permitted by well-known images or recent examples of photojournalism.

The effect of applying the label "atrocity photograph" in this way is threefold: the image, the person depicted in the image, and viewers of the image are all transformed by the designation. The label "atrocity photograph" makes the image iconic—perhaps not iconic in the sense that it is easily recognizable by a multitude, or that it becomes one of Sontag's "ethical reference points," but it does become representative of the atrocity-event. As a consequence of this transformation, the image loses something of its specificity. Moreover, the person depicted becomes locked in the iconic gesture of the image, which is to say he or she becomes an object of historical value such that the details of his or her own experience are overwhelmed by the atrocity-event. And, finally, by participating in this reframing of the image, we succeed in mitigating—if only to a small degree—the pain and frustration of viewing photographs of atrocity. That these transformations of image, subject, and viewer may be detrimental raises the question of whether the label "atrocity photograph" is at all beneficial.

***

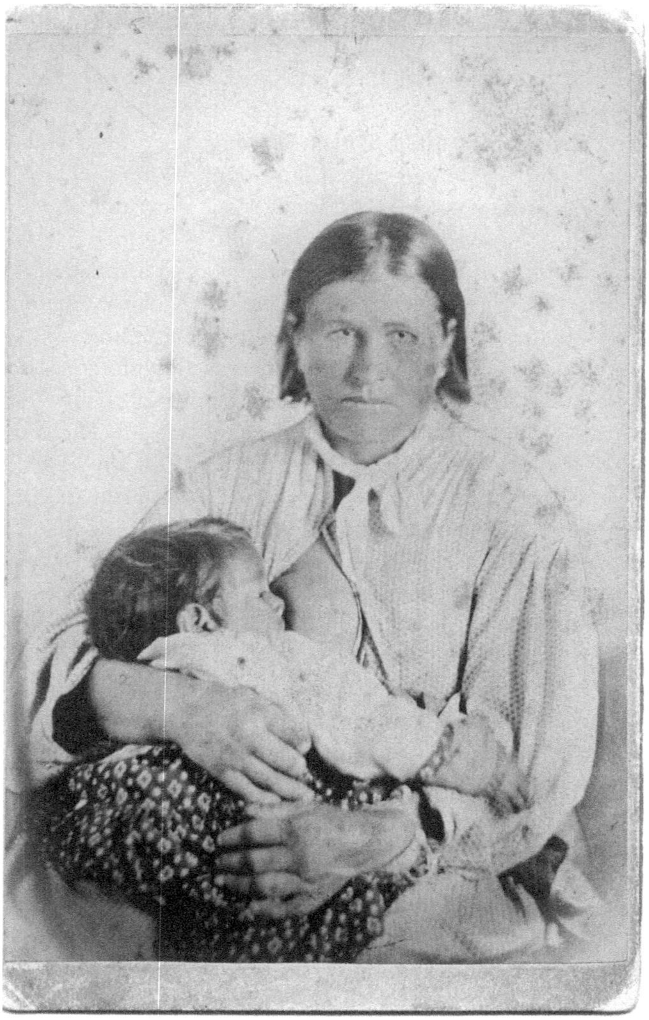

Figure 15.2 A. F. Corning, *Cynthia Ann Parker with Prairie Flower (*1861), albumen silver print. The Texas Collection, Baylor University, Waco, Texas

The Parker brothers—James, Silas, and Benjamin—together with their father, Elder John, and their extended families, settled in north-central Texas at the headwaters of the Navasota River. The land was fertile, permitting subsistence farming, but the location was isolated from other white settlements, and relations between settlers and Native Americans were uneasy at best. Wichitas and Kichais had long made their home along those same waterways, where they farmed and hunted. More troublesome for settlers were the Comanches, Apaches, and Kiowas who roamed the plains further afield. These more aggressive tribes sometimes launched raids against white settlers for the purpose of stealing horses or cattle. The whites, however, were known to launch raids of their own and sought security in their fortified settlements and firearms, despite the fact that they were greatly outnumbered.[1]

On the morning of May 19, 1836, a group of mounted Comanche and Kiowa—some reports claimed there were as many as 800—approached the Parker's fortified settlement bearing a dirty white flag. Upon first sighting, when the group was about a quarter-mile off, someone shouted, "Indians! Indians!" Panic ensued. More than half of the men were already away working in the fields, leaving behind six men, eight women, and a number of children. As the raiding party drew closer, one of the women slipped away to raise the alarm, while others simply grabbed their children and fled as quickly as they were able.

The mounted party paused some 200 yards from the entrance to the fort. Benjamin Parker, one of the men remaining behind that morning, approached them, unarmed. He was their first victim, clubbed senseless and then pierced with lances. Silas Parker, his brother, was also beaten to death, and his scalp taken with the aid of a butcher knife. The other victims were Samuel Frost and his son Robert, and Elder John Parker, whose skull was shattered and scalp and genitals cut from his body as his wife, Sally, was made to watch; she was later pinned to the ground by a lance through her chest, and the clothes were stripped from her body. In what came to be known as the Fort Parker Massacre, the Comanche–Kiowa raiding party killed five settlers and captured five others. The captives included two women, Elizabeth Kellogg and Rachel Plummer, and three children: Rachel's toddler son James, nine-year-old Cynthia Ann Parker, and her younger brother John.

After riding well into the night, the warriors stopped to celebrate their victory, for not one among them had been harmed during the raid. As they danced and replayed scenes from the day, they abused their captives, kicking and punching them if they dared speak or cry out. The adult women, Elizabeth and Rachel, were likely raped. The next morning, the group continued north, seeking to put as much distance as possible between themselves and white people. After riding for five days, they reached the High Plains. It was there that they divided up the captives. Elizabeth Kellogg was purchased by a group of Kichais and later passed on to Delaware Indians, and the others were claimed by different groups of Comanche. Kellogg was ransomed within a year, and Rachel Plummer the following year; the two boys ended their captivity after six years. Cynthia Ann Parker remained with the Comanche for twenty-four years.

Little is known about Parker's captivity. According to Comanche oral tradition, a childless couple adopted her, raising her as their own. From them she learned the Comanche language and skills required of Comanche women, such as cleaning and tanning buffalo hides. Her Comanche name was Naudah, meaning Keeps Warm with Us. She is thought to have married a chief, Peta Nocona, who as a young warrior had participated in the raiding party at Parker's Fort, and she had two sons, Quanah and Pecos, and a daughter, Topsannah. In these important respects, and undoubtedly many others, during her captivity Parker became one of the Comanche people, a view borne out by the testimony of whites who, from time to time, caught sight of her: "She refused to listen to the proposition [of returning to her white family], saying that her husband, children, and all that she held most dear, were with the Indians and there she should remain."

The years of Parker's captivity were marked by ever-worsening relations between white Texans and the Comanche people. Settlers had made survival in an already harsh environment difficult for the Comanche by depleting their food supply and bringing with them disease. Moreover, as settlers continued to establish homesteads along the frontier, the cavalry's ability to protect a growing and dispersed white population was tested. The legislature, responsible for the safety of its citizens, responded by establishing forts across the region and reinvigorating the Texas Rangers, along with assorted volunteer companies—essentially vigilantes. These measures led to more rather than less violence. Both Texans and native tribes initiated bloody raids that were warfare in all but name. The Battle of Pease River—also called the Pease River Massacre—on December 19, 1860, was one white-led raid among many, the details of which might not have been recorded, let alone burnished in the many retellings, had it not been the occasion on which the Texas Rangers captured Cynthia Ann Parker.

Accounts vary. Some claimed there were as many as 600 Comanche warriors camped alongside Mule Creek, near the Pease River. More reliable sources describe the encampment as a temporary home to a modest number of workers supporting a hunting party then some distance away. There were, maybe, fifteen women, children, and older men packing to leave when the Rangers and volunteer troops descended upon the camp at full charge. Panic ensued. Mounted troops chased down the fleeing Comanche who were already on horseback, sometimes riding for miles to shoot them and collect their scalps as trophies. Those fleeing on foot were summarily shot in the back. In the end, the "battle" lasted no more than thirty minutes during which time rangers killed seven Comanche, four of whom were women. "I was in the Pease River fight," one Ranger later said, "but I am not very proud of it. That was not a battle at all, but just a killing of squaws."

Among the Comanche fleeing on horseback was a woman wearing a heavy buffalo robe. When a ranger caught up with her and pointed a gun at her face she hastily cried out, "Americano!" The soldier, taken aback, held his fire and then was ordered by an officer—in some accounts, the future Texas statesman Lawrence Sullivan "Sul" Ross—to lower his weapon. The woman was white, the officer remarked: though dark-skinned from dirt and exposure, she had blue eyes. She also had a small child concealed in her buffalo robe. Cynthia Ann Parker had been captured a second time.

Her identity was not immediately apparent. She spoke no English and, fearing her husband and sons had been killed, and that her own life and that of her daughter were in danger, tried repeatedly to escape. An interpreter calmed her somewhat by explaining that no harm would come to her. She was subsequently taken to Camp Cooper, "where she could be properly clothed and cared for." Her own clothes were burned. Further interviews were conducted with an interpreter, and, although she offered no conclusive evidence as to her identity, other than that of a Comanche woman, officials believed her to be Cynthia Ann Parker and so sent for a relation to confirm their views. In early January of 1861, her uncle, Isaac Parker, arrived at the camp and questioned her, first through an interpreter and then directly, in English, but with little result. Isaac Parker turned to an officer and said, "If this is my niece, her name is Cynthia Ann," expecting him to translate, but then the woman spoke: "Me, Cynthia Ann."

With the promise that she would eventually be reunited with her sons, Parker was convinced to travel with her uncle to his home in Birdville, Tarrant County. On the way, they stopped at Fort Worth, where the "white captive" caused a stir. Children were let out of school in order to join the crowd at a local retail store that had gathered to see Parker. "She stood on a large wooden box," one spectator recalled:

> she was bound with rope, she was not dressed in Indian costume but wore a torn calico dress … she made a pathetic figure as she stood there, viewing the crowds that swarmed about her. The tears were streaming down her face, and she was muttering in the Indian language.

Matters were only slightly better at the photography studio of A. F. Corning, where Parker was taken to have her picture made. With spectators crowding the studio, Corning had a difficult time doing his job, and the disposition of his unhappy subject did not help matters. Witnesses claimed that the camera frightened Parker, that, when Corning pointed the device at her, "she threw up her hands before her face and said, 'oo-oo-oo-oo!'" Nevertheless, she consented after seeing others photographed to no ill effect. She would not, however, have her picture made alone: a woman offered to hold Parker's daughter, Topsannah, while she was photographed, but the child "drew back in fright and clung to her mother." When shown the photograph Corning had made, however, Parker appeared pleased by the representation of her daughter (Figure 15.2).[2]

The public's interest in Cynthia Ann Parker increased as the story of her return from captivity spread and likely reached a pinnacle in the spring of 1861 when, dressed in "neat garments, which she thought very uncomfortable," she was taken to Austin to observe the secession convention there. During a break in proceedings, the lawmakers also discussed their unusual visitor, voting to award Parker a league of land and an annual stipend for Topsannah's education. The deliberations, however, terrified the guest of honour, for she apparently thought the meeting's purpose was to decide her fate and that of her daughter. Once again, Parker took hold of her child and fled, only to be brought back by her uncle Isaac, who reassured her as best he could. During this visit to Austin, Parker sat for a second photograph, a tintype, posing alone and wearing the clothes given to her by the women of Birdville (Figure 15.3).

Cynthia Ann Parker never assimilated. Her return to the white world was fraught with misunderstanding and sorrow. She often feared for her life, and many times tried to run away, with only the repeated promise of seeing her sons, whom she thought lost on the prairie, convincing her to remain with her white family. At one time she stopped eating. Her Comanche ways—such as cutting her breast with a knife and applying the blood to tobacco, which she smoked as she lamented the loss of her sons—were met with perplexity by well-meaning but largely unsympathetic relations and neighbours. Nevertheless, she proved useful by spinning, weaving and sewing, and tanning hides, drawing on the skills she had learned as a Comanche squaw. One neighbour remembered her as "an open-hearted, good woman, and always ready to help somebody." And yet, to the end, Parker never stopped grieving for her lost Comanche family and the life she had shared with them. Her uncle Isaac claimed she was "the most unhappy person I ever saw. She pined for her children and her husband continuously. ... She was as much an Indian as if she had been born one."

When Topsannah took sick and died in 1863 (the date is disputed), Parker lost the only tangible connection she had with the Comanche people and their way of life. When she herself died in 1870 or 1871—no longer newsworthy, the particular circumstances of her death were not recorded—her uncle eulogized, "She was virtually a prisoner among her own loving kindred, but they did not realize it until too late."

★★★

It was Secretary of State Thomas Jefferson who coined the word "atrocity" as we now understand the term, which is to say, an act of extreme cruelty. On June 30, 1793, in a letter to the US Commissioners to Spain, Jefferson defended the fact that the United States had furnished the Chickasaw tribe with arms. Given the geopolitics of the North American frontier, Spain did not appreciate the gift. Jefferson explained: "We have given a few arms to a very friendly tribe, not to make war on Spain, but to defend themselves from the atrocities of a vastly more numerous and powerful people" (Jefferson 1793). The more numerous and powerful people to which Jefferson refers were not white Europeans or their

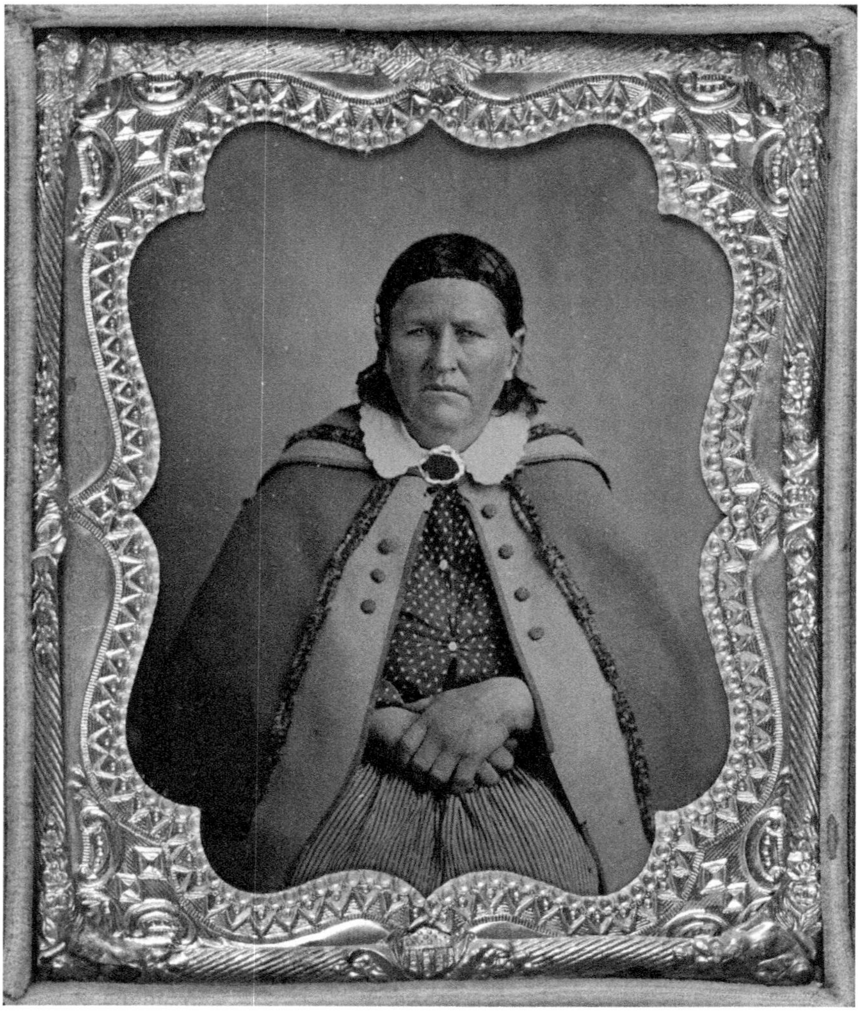

Figure 15.3 William W. Bridgers, *Cynthia Ann Parker* (1861). Sixth plate tintype, hand-colored; 7 × 8.3 cm. DeGolyer Library, Southern Methodist University, Lawrence T. Jones III Texas Photographs

descendants, but the Creeks, who "have now, for more than a twelvemonth, been committing murders and desolations on our frontiers." Atrocity, as it was first conceived, was a consequence of warfare between Native American tribes. It did not remain exclusively so for long.

Cynthia Ann Parker was a victim of this frontier bloodlust twice over, but before considering whether A. F. Corning's photograph of Parker may be called an atrocity photograph, we need to consider the image itself, to take account of what it actually shows and likely meant at the time it was made. Made just weeks after Parker's recapture, the image shows her cradling her daughter in her arms, her blouse parted for nursing. Her hair is cut short—a

Comanche sign of mourning—and her clothes and those of her child are unremarkable and unadorned. Her hands appear large and coarse from work, but she supports her child tenderly. Overall, the composition of the photograph is neat and balanced, but nothing here is beautiful or even arresting—there is no *punctum*, to apply Roland Barthes's term, except perhaps Parker's eyes (Barthes 1981: 27). Looking directly into the camera, she betrays no particular emotion or mental disposition, yet her blue eyes capture the light just so, giving them a penetrating aspect.

In some respects, the photograph resembles other "mother and child" portraits of the late nineteenth century in which white women are shown nursing infants. Yet these other images are idealized, whereas Corning's is completely lacking in sentimentality. We also know that the intent here was for Parker to be photographed alone, but that she and her daughter could not be separated. Topsannah's presence in the image is therefore circumstantial, rather than intended as a signifier of "motherhood." There is no allegorical intent here, no purpose other than to capture the likeness of a woman who happens to be holding her child. For this reason, the photograph seems to be straightforwardly a portrait, not unlike the second image made of Parker, the tintype in which she wears a heavy robe.

A portrait is the record of a person's appearance, yet it is rarely this alone, for how we feel or what we know about the person colours what we see in the image. To better understand the original meaning of a portrait, we must therefore ask for whom it was made and why—in other words, consider what the intended viewer may have seen in the image. The idea for the photograph of Cynthia Ann Parker appears to have originated with the photographer, Corning. He claimed to have "prevailed" upon her to accompany him to his studio, and more than twenty years later he was still in possession of the original image or its negative. Parker's fame as a "white captive" meant that securing her likeness held commercial possibilities, and, although it is not clear whether Corning sold copies of the image, if nothing else her presence in his studio raised a crowd and thus served to promote his services. The photograph is thus a portrait made to promote a photographer's trade. It is also, however, the portrait of a woman holding her "wild" child, as one contemporary labelled Topsannah, and consequently may have held meaning with respect to attitudes concerning the capture of white females by Native Americans.

Race mixture was a national preoccupation during the nineteenth century and captivity narratives, as well as frontier literature more generally, often fixated on the rape of white women by the native "savage," whether real or imaged. Frequently, the point was made by omission, as in the narrative written by Parker's cousin, Rachel Plummer, also captured at Fort Parker. Using strong if veiled language, Plummer managed to describe the very thing she could not bring herself to describe:

> To undertake to narrate their barbarous treatment [of me] would only add to my present distress, for it is with feelings of the deepest mortification that I think of it, much less to speak or write of it … my very soul becomes sick at the dreadful thought.

The disgust expressed in narratives such as Plummer's was informed by the belief that Native Americans were inferior to white people, which in turn served to justify the eradication of their cultures. That Parker had genuine affection for her husband and children, and thus did not share her cousin's status as sexual victim, was lost on contemporaries wholly convinced that Indian–white unions meant the end of civilization.

For white society, Topsannah was a symbol of Parker's supposed defilement by her captors, as the language used by one woman present in Corning's studio makes clear. In addition to noting that Topsannah was "wild," Mollie King said of Parker's daughter:

> The little girl was very pretty with a soft smooth reddish-brown complexion, about halfway between the natural complexion of an Indian and that of the white race. Her hair and eyes were very black (features more inclined to that of an Indian than white.)

The idea that the physiological traits of a mixed-race child fall "halfway" between those of the two parents was current scientific racial theory in 1861, and the woman further made a point of noting that Parker was "very fair," thus emphasizing her position among the "white race." Bearing in mind these indications of concern for race purity and mixture, particularly as they related to white captivity, Parker's portrait could have been viewed as an ethnographic document. It also might have been seen as a parody of (white) motherhood.

Let us not forget, however, that, despite what people may have thought about Parker or her child, and consequently what they may have seen in the photograph, the image was nevertheless *hers*. When Corning showed it to Parker and she saw Topsannah, she "seemed pleased with its [*sic*] picture." Although we do not know whether Parker ever owned a copy, the photograph was her portrait and that of her daughter, and so held meaning for her personally. It also held meaning for her son. In 1884, Quanah Parker placed a notice in the Texas newspapers, "stating that he wished to secure, if such a thing were in existence, a picture of his mother, Cynthia Ann Parker." Corning saw the notice and supplied the Comanche chief with a copy, which Quanah had enlarged as a painted portrait (Figure 15.4). Here the photograph takes on still different meaning by providing the son with a celebratory memento of his deceased mother and sister.

We can, therefore, identify multiple meanings in the Fort Worth photograph of Cynthia Ann Parker. It was a way for a photographer to drum up business by tapping into the spectacle of Parker's recapture. It was, simply, a portrait of a woman holding her child, but it was also a family photograph. At the same time, it may have brought to mind for some viewers the literature of captivity and the scientific racial theories of the day, in which case Walter Benjamin's oft-cited remark seems particularly apt here: "There is no document of civilization which is not at the same time a document of barbarism" (Benjamin 2007: 256). The Fort Worth image found further life in the early twentieth century when it was made into a real photo postcard, Parker's story by then having become the stuff of frontier legend, and later refashioned as a Hollywood movie (*The Searchers*, 1956, dir. John Ford).

And so, returning to our principal subject, may it also be said that Parker's portrait is an atrocity photograph? Does it show a body that has been subjected to grievous harm, or did violence play a part in its production? Has it been reproduced along with a text explaining the image as a sign of moral degradation? And has it been used to shock the viewer into recognizing that the form of harm depicted in the image is not only terribly wrong but likely could have been averted?

The atrocity-event that the Fort Worth photograph can be said to represent is neither the Fort Parker Massacre nor the Pease River Massacre, but rather the clash of cultures that made both of these events possible, and many others besides, resulting in the near extermination of the native peoples of North America. Similarly, the bodily harm represented in the Fort Worth photograph has as its source not the beatings Parker received from the Comanche nor the rope burns sustained when her family bound her so much as the sum of her

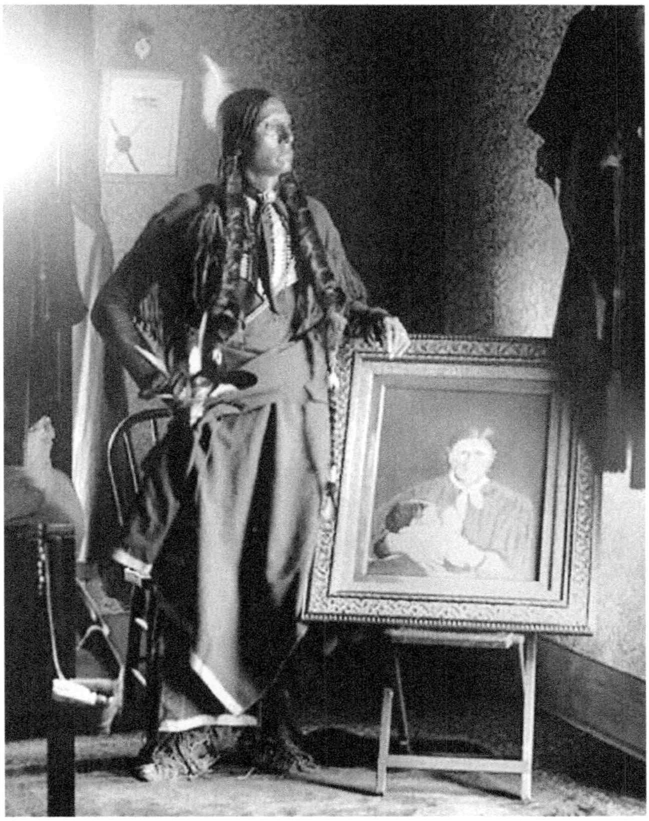

Figure 15.4 Photographer unknown, *Portrait of Quanah Parker,* c.1884. Collection of the author

experience. The physical abuse Parker endured during both her captivities pales in comparison with the violence done to her through cultural displacement and by being made to bear witness to the race war between both her peoples. Parker may not be visibly suffering the effects of violence in the Fort Worth image—although her eyes perhaps suggest otherwise—but her known story is shot through with violence and its after-effects.

It is impossible to know Parker's story, or understand her portrait as a sign of moral degradation, without benefit of a text, the second requirement of atrocity photography. No photograph's meaning is self-evident. Captions to describe what lies beyond the frame, as well as what happened before and after the image was made, are necessary to direct our understanding. This is especially the case with atrocity photographs, for there is always the chance that we will miss the atrocity in the image. The caption or narrative is how we know that the image is a representation of harm, and that this harm was both wrong and avoidable. Was the photograph of Parker copied and distributed, exhibited, or published in her lifetime with an explanatory caption? We do not know. Nevertheless, had it been so, the moral wrong conceived by the photograph's exhibitors would likely have been the depredations of Native Americans, not the effects of Manifest Destiny and race war. Parker's suffering and what her compatriots perceived as her suffering were not the same. Today, however, we see things differently. The historical narrative of Parker's life now provides the photograph's caption.

Atrocity photographs have a peculiar relationship to history. Looking at an atrocity photograph is not like looking at other kinds of photograph, because the enormity of the event lifts the image to the status of history, even if what is depicted occurred yesterday. If the image is truly representative of the atrocity-event, then it must not be forgotten: it is, rather, promoted to take hold of the viewer's imagination, becoming iconic like Nick Ut's picture of Kim Phuc and Richard Drew's "falling man." Parker's portrait was not viewed in this way during the nineteenth century, but it can be now. Indeed, in this essay, with the aid of contextual material about her two captivities and the wider circumstances that made them possible, the photograph is made to be representative of the Native American genocide through murder, displacement, and forced assimilation. It is, in other words, an atrocity photograph.

What then happens when we do this, when we make a photograph iconic of an atrocity-event? First, the meaning of the image shifts its focus from the specific to the general, from the particular time and place in which the image was made to the manifold time and place of the atrocity-event. In the case of the Fort Worth photograph, the subject of the image is no longer Cynthia Ann Parker, but the near extermination of Native Americans of which her experience is deemed illustrative. This has the effect of blotting out to a greater or lesser degree the person in the photograph: Parker is still the nominal subject of the photograph, but anything to do with her that does not confirm the atrocity-event may be discarded. Her pleasure at seeing Topsannah in the image, for example, does not speak to the greater issue of genocide and so may be dropped from the narrative or caption. With this, the circumstantial, subjective details that make the image hers are lost. Georges Didi-Huberman calls this effect the "hypertrophy of the image," which is to say we want to see everything in the image—the atrocity-event in its entirety—but at the same time we are inattentive to much that the image holds (Didi-Huberman 2012: 34). As a consequence of this, Parker becomes locked in the iconic gesture of the image and so rendered an object of historical value. This occurred with *The Scourged Back*, in so far as abolitionists and publishers largely fabricated the formerly enslaved man's story, and possibly also his name, to suit their political purpose, with the unintended effect that, by highlighting slavery's brutality, they cast the man himself into obscurity.

The remaining question, then, is this: Why describe an image as an atrocity photograph if it results in the loss of historical detail and objectifies the individual depicted in the photograph? Berger's observation that such photographs inflict a double violence on viewers—assaulting us with a depiction of violence and also underscoring our inability to prevent violence—points to an answer. The atrocity photograph acts upon us, Berger further notes, and so prevents emotional complacency by demanding that we act, that we "either dismiss it or complete its meaning for ourselves" (Berger 2013: 9). Many writers have acknowledged this affect by recounting their emotional responses to photographs of atrocity. Images from Bergen-Belsen and Dachau, for example, cut Sontag "sharply, deeply, instantaneously" (Sontag 1977: 20). Upon looking at similar images, Susie Linfield felt "sadness, indignation, disgust, and puzzlement," and, more pointedly, shame (Linfield 2010: xiii). Jenny Edkins describes the affect of such images perfectly when she writes, "There is something in the image itself that in any case exceeds the caption, some way in which the image speaks to us not through text but directly, through the surplus or excess that it reveals" (Edkins 2013: 141). This surplus is what causes us to feel and, as a consequence of this feeling, moves us to act, if only to make sense of the thing that hurts us, as these writers have done.

I became interested in Parker's portrait because it resonated with photographs of enslaved men and women I had studied: it was similarly painful to look at, despite the visual content being very different. By affixing the label "atrocity photograph" to Parker's image, I can at once contain this emotional content and complete its meaning. Elevating the image to the status of icon by emphasizing its historical and moral significance both exposes the injustice of the atrocity-event and honours the many victims of that event. The Fort Worth photograph of Parker is, on the one hand, merely a portrait, one made for commercial purposes; however, when aspects of its historical contingency are highlighted, it can instruct and inform and, in the process, mitigate to some degree the pain inflicted by the image upon the viewer and the resulting frustration of being powerless to prevent atrocity. By calling it an atrocity photograph I can, in other words, push back against the double violence described by Berger to give meaning both to the image and to the atrocity itself, and thus also to my own being. The unending recurrence of atrocity-events demands that we take notice in this way, that we examine the documents and judge the perpetrators, even generations after the event occurred, even if it hurts to do so.

There is no reason, however, why this act of pushing back should not also take account of the surplus found in emotional affect and historical detail. Calling an image an atrocity photograph should not necessarily push to one side or obscure these elements of the image. Although it is difficult to see everything in a photograph of atrocity—the many details, both horrific and banal, that make up the atrocity-event—one can nevertheless be attentive to what actually took place, including that which has little or no connection to the event. Photographs are not one thing or the other, but many, often in turn or even at once, and so, although we may be moved to apply labels that help us to understand an image, at the same time we must take note of all the image holds and promises—including the many details of its making—so that we may serve as witnesses to its testimony. Only by admitting this surplus, this multiple being of the image, will we know that Cynthia Ann Parker, despite her suffering on the day she visited Corning's Fort Worth studio, was delighted to see her daughter represented in a photograph.

Notes

1 My account of the Fort Parker Massacre, Parker's captivities, and the Pease River Massacre are derived from Carlson and Crum (2010); Exley (2001: Chapters 4, 5, 11, 13); Frankel (2013: Chapters 1–5); Hacker (1990); Manning (1919: 85); Parker (1844); DeShields (1886); and Araminta Taulman, "Interview of Mrs. Nunnally," 1926, Joseph Taulman Collection, box 2F263, Dolph Briscoe Center for American History, University of Texas, Austin.

2 My account of Cynthia Ann Parker's visit to Corning's studio, discussed here and subsequently, and of the image's afterlife, derive from Araminta Taulman, "Personal interview with Mrs. Mollie (Allen) (Mrs. R.H. King) King [*sic*], 901 Bennett St., Fort Worth, Texas, Monday, July 5, 1926"; "Personal interview with Mrs. King (82 years old), September 13, 1926," Joseph Taulman Collection, box 2F263, Dolph Briscoe Center for American History, University of Texas, Austin; *Fort Worth Daily Gazette*(1884: 7); and Clarke (n.d.: 70).

References

Azoulay, A. (2012) "The Execution Portrait" in: G. Batchen, M. Gidley, N. K. Miller, and J. Prosser (eds.) *Picturing Atrocity: Photography in Crisis*, London: Reaktion, 249–259.

Barthes, R. (1981) *Camera Lucida: Reflections on Photography*, trans. Richard Howard, New York: Hill & Wang.

Benjamin, W. (2007) "Theses on the Philosophy of History" in: trans. Harry Zohn, *Illuminations*, New York: Schocken, 253–64.
Berger, J. (2013) *Understanding a Photograph*, G. Dyer (ed.), New York: Aperture.
Carlson, P. H., and Crum, T. (2010) *Myth, Memory and Massacre: The Pease River Capture of Cynthia Ann Parker*, Lubbock: Texas Tech University Press.
Clarke, E. R. (n.d.) "YA-A-H-HOO, Warwhoop of the Comanches, the Cry that Struck Terror into the Hearts of the Pioneers in the Early Days of Texas," Elizabeth R. Clarke Papers, Eugene C(eds) Barker Texas History Center, University of Texas, Austin.
DeShields, J. T. (1886) *Cynthia Ann Parker: The Story of Her Capture*, St. Louis.
Didi-Huberman, G. (2012) *Images in Spite of All: Four Photographs from Auschwitz*, trans. Shane B. Lillis, Chicago: University of Chicago Press.
Edkins, J. (2013) "Politics and Personhood: Reflections on the Portrait Photograph," *Alternatives: Global, Local, Political* 38:2, 139–54.
Exley, J. E. P. (2001) *Frontier Blood: The Saga of the Parker Family*, College Station: Texas A&M University Press.
Fort Worth Daily Gazette (1884) "A Relic of Cynthia Ann Parker," May 26, 7.
Frankel, G. (2013) *The Searchers: The Making of an American Legend*, New York: Bloomsbury.
Friedlander, S. (ed.) (1992) *Probing the Limits of Representation: Nazism and the "Final Solution"*, Cambridge: Harvard University Press.
Hacker, M. S. (1990) *Cynthia Ann Parker: The Life and the Legend*, El Paso: Texas Western Press.
Hirsch, M., and Spitzer, L. (2012) "Street Photographs in Crisis: Cernauti, Romania, c.1943" in: G. Batchen, M. Gidley, N. K. Miller, and J. Prosser (eds.) *Picturing Atrocity: Photography in Crisis*, London: Reaktion, 179–87.
Jefferson, T. (1793) Letter from Thomas Jefferson to William Carmichael and William Short, June 30, Thomas Jefferson Papers, Library of Congress. www.loc.gov/resource/mtj1.018_1016_1034 [accessed December 20, 2015].
Linfield, S. (2010) *The Cruel Radiance: Photography and Political Violence*, Chicago: University of Chicago Press.
Lowe, P. (2012) "Picturing the Perpetrator" in: G. Batchen, M. Gidley, N. K. Miller, and J. Prosser (eds.) *Picturing Atrocity: Photography in Crisis*, London: Reaktion, 189–99.
Manning, W. (1919) *Some History of Van Zandt County, Volume I*, Des Moines.
Parker, J. W. (1844) *Narrative of the Perilous Adventures, Miraculous Escapes and Sufferings of Rev. James W. Parker: During a Frontier Residence in Texas*, Louisville.
Prosser, J. (2012) "Introduction" in: G. Batchen, M. Gidley, N. K. Miller, and J. Prosser (eds.) *Picturing Atrocity: Photography in Crisis*, London: Reaktion, 7–13.
Rosenheim, J.L. (2013) *Photography and the American Civil War*, New York: Metropolitan Museum of Art.
Sontag, S. (1977) *On Photography*, New York and London: Penguin.
Sontag, S. (2003) *Regarding the Pain of Others*, New York: Farrar, Straus & Giroux.

16

Presenting the unrepresentable

Confrontation and circumvention

Jane Tormey

In recent years, photographers have made use of documentary methods that stretch the capacity of the image to visually describe the subject matter addressed. Moving away from a preoccupation with 'self-sufficient' imagery, and having assimilated many of the conceptual attributes of art practice, artists/photographers can be seen to aim for something more expansive, particularly with regard to political content. As I viewed photographic projects at two different festivals in the summer of 2016—*Les Rencontres d'Arles 2016*, a festival of art photography promoted as "the cutting edge of developments in the photographic image", and *Visa pour l'image 2016*, the International Festival of Photojournalism at Perpignan—I observed differences in the methods of engagement and presentation. Although the functions of art and photojournalism have different agendas, both present images of trauma and conflict. My experience of viewing such images prompted questions concerning the nature of subject matter, the manner of presentation and its consequent affect, which coincidentally resonated with issues provoked by my reading of Jacques Rancière's essay "Are Some Things Unrepresentable?" (2009a [2003]).

In exploring some of Rancière's hypotheses about representation, this essay uses his discussion as a prompt to ask how photographic documents confront or circumvent subjects that might be described as 'unrepresentable'. In his writings on the relations between aesthetics and politics, Rancière usefully refers to specific methods of practice. With reference to these and with an emphasis on methods of presentation and my own experience of viewing—in most cases at Arles or Perpignan—I discuss examples of practice in relation to Rancière's questioning of subject matters, photographic strategies and the arguments presented in Georges Didi-Huberman's *Images in Spite of All* (2008). Applying Rancière's theoretical speculations about 'art' in general terms to practices that use photography specifically, I consider the limits of representation in two respects: those that aim to exceed visible subject matter to encompass complex political situations and those that challenge the ethical efficacy of representation by aiming to represent what might be considered too horrifying or tragic and is thereby 'unrepresentable'. As Rancière questions the efficacy of political art and the rationale for representing atrocity, I ask in what ways can photographies represent challenging subject matter and be effective for political purpose or for meaningful response.

Rancière's position in relation to aesthetics emerges from his concept of 'politics', which he conceives as a form of action that deviates "from the 'normal' order of things" (2010: 35) and causes a rupture with that order to effect a redistribution of power in some way: what he calls "reconfiguring the distribution of the sensible" (2009b [2004]: 25). It is a redistribution in which those individuals who are excluded from power acquire new forms of visibility, when people presuppose equality and take action. As both art and politics emerge from the primary motivation to assert identity and construct cultural visibility, acts of 'doing and making' are comparable to a 'primary aesthetics'. Rancière's "politics of aesthetics" (2006) is thus embedded in the theoretical frameworks for sensory experience that order and structure all forms of art and culture. His argument for the 'politics' of art starts from the aesthetic paradigms that dominate the direction of art practice and the nature of this 'redistribution' of the sensible. His conception of art as a form of dissensus establishes a relationship between aesthetics and politics that relates to their common social function of intervention. In these terms, art has the potential to intervene in social norms, adjust the distribution of power and reframe "material and symbolic space" (2009b [2004]: 24) by "tearing experience from ordinariness" (19). As a form of dissensus, the 'politics of art' lies in the process of reframing common experience at a more fundamental level than specific art forms might suggest. As he gives examples of very different art practices, which he categorises in various ways, Rancière is speaking of the conceptual principles—aesthetics—underlying the specific forms of art practice. In considering the distinctions that he draws between different practices, it becomes clear that he conceives the relation between forms of art (and photography) and politics as a fundamental social function.

In the "Paradoxes of Political Art" (2010), Rancière addresses art's political efficacy and the strategies that artists adopt to maintain political impact. Arguing that art presents a series of paradoxes that reflects its incapacity to reduce the distance between the original political context, the photographer's social intention and the affective impact, he describes the way in which representations of atrocity or social injustice are separated from emotional affect or political impact. Whereas, for example, collages by John Heartfield or Martha Rosler are forms that combine aesthetic experience and the realities of life, he suggests 'critical art' such as Rosler's *Bringing the War Home* (1967–72 and 2004), which aims to create political awareness, relies on a consensual understanding of critique and a common denunciation of commodity. Artistic endeavour to produce the correction of behaviour by aesthetic means of presentation relies on our familiarity with the subject, applies methods from a limited repertoire of strategies, such as parody, and therefore only confirms what we already know. In consequence, the inefficacy of critical art practices move between an emphasis on "testimony, archive and documentation" of common experience, and a social art practice that intervenes in "the 'real' world" (Rancière 2010: 145). However, despite the oppositional ideologies for art's function—its distance from life or its self-elimination—Rancière asserts this tension provides a political function (2009b [2004]: 46). And it is this tension between distance and immersion, both in content and in affective impact, that proves to be the running theme of my discussion.

Although it is assumed that art can subvert and incite, Rancière contends that, in order to sustain political efficacy, strategies have to be constantly rethought from ever-different perspectives. He considers that some of the most interesting works contributing to reframing the sensible are forms that, accepting their political inadequacy as "mere images" (2010: 149), interrogate representation without overtly providing a critique. One such example he gives is Sophie Ristelhueber's *W B* (2004), which documents Israeli blockades on Palestinian roads, many of which are photographed from the air. As a result, details of conflict disappear into the landscape, with the effect of displacing a reactive response that might be provoked by more spectacular imagery with the more discreet effect of curiosity (2010: 149–50). This circumvention of overt political comment is a common strategy that exploits repetition and forces the viewer to be actively reflective. Either way, as 'mere images' they are highly mediated and work critically, in a dilatory way. The strategy, which plays between explicit and implicit reference, and between empirical fact and restrained comment, achieves conceptual affect by circuitous means. We can understand this restraint from explicit meaning as a convention demonstrated in its most simplistic form by projects such as Yan Morvan's *Champs de Bataille* (2015),[1] which, in its documentation of 400 sites of battle, relies on each image's metonymic reference to historical conflict. This convention of visual understatement inherits an understanding of the power of photography from Barthes' critique of horrific images that are so over-constructed by the artist that we are immobilised "between the literal fact and the overestimated fact" and "can no longer *invent* our own reception." In consequence, the images fail to affect us because there is no room left for our own judgment: "someone has shuddered for us, reflected for us, judged for us ... for us they have no history" (Barthes 1997 [1979]: 71–3). Barthes articulates the paradoxical fact that documenting horror for the purpose of drawing attention to political injustice can be ineffectual if too pointedly directing our response. It is this awareness of the ambiguous photographic apparatus that encourages strategies that use insinuation or persistent repetition, as with Ristelhueber and Morvan, rather than use illustrative political mediation or photography's capacity for pictorial spectacle.

The circumvention of spectacular imagery is amplified in *The Future of the Image* by Rancière's observations concerning the representation of challenging or tragic subject matter. Sceptical about the notion of the 'unrepresentable' in relation to traditions in art, he asks under what conditions can something not be represented. To say that a subject is unrepresentable either means that the manner of representation is not adequate to the specific experience, or that some subjects *must not* be represented for aesthetic purpose. Discussing the material manifestation of difficult ideas, he distinguishes between representations that simply avoid some subject matters as being ethically inappropriate and those that confront the problem by inventing a strategy, a "new fictional logic," to render that subject matter "tolerable." In the example of staging Greek tragedy, he suggests the difficulty of representation results from the interaction between emotions and ethical concerns, between "what can be seen and what can be said" and "wanting to know, not wanting to say, saying without saying and refusing to hear." Ultimately, he concludes, there is disjunction between the experience that motivates the work, what it means, and what subsequently happens in its viewing: between the relationship to its origin and its destination; between what is conceptually absent and what is materially present (Rancière 2009a [2003]: 111–8).

Rancière's speculations suggest parallels with current documentary practices that either accept the inappropriateness of representation, as seen in Gideon Mendel's use of discarded objects as trope for the human tragedy in Calais (2016),[2] or attempt to counter the disjunction between experience and viewing by: choosing to make understated rather than explicit statements (Ristelhueber); placing the event 'off stage' and making reference without visible representation (Morvan); or constructing a fictional logic of 'characters' that deflect direct visibility (Walid Raad). Each of these strategies relies on some sort of conceptual absence by reference to implications outside the frame or by prompting identification with the subject, while simultaneously creating distance from it. With the many practices that have testimony, archive and documentation in mind or that attempt to engage in the 'real world', it follows that the insufficiencies inherent in representing tragic subject matters will dictate the direction of methods that perpetually swing between ethical representation, political mediation and the propensity to aestheticise. This can be seen in a notable tendency in photographic projects that adopt ever more elaborate strategies for photographic documentation. The complexity of emotions and ethical concerns involved characterise the dilemma for artists who are concerned to represent horrific events. Aware of the conditions of power involved, the possibility of objectification, the nearness of subjective fiction and the demise of the authentic image, artists/photographers display a super-self-consciousness of their position and political agency.

Unrepresentably complex

Methods used to represent political histories and/or trauma must first be able to encompass a range of concerns. Certainly there is a tendency towards the use of "testimony, archive and documentation" when engaging with subjects that can be described as being unrepresentably complex and cannot be defined in a single image, and which in turn are often political or concerned with traumatic events. Projects such as the *Atlas Group Project* (Walid Raad, 1989–2004) and *Forest Law* (Ursula Biemann and Paolo Tavares, 2014), or *Method of Loci* (Stéphanie Solinas, 2015) and *The Jungle Show* (Yan Gross, 2016), both presented at Arles,

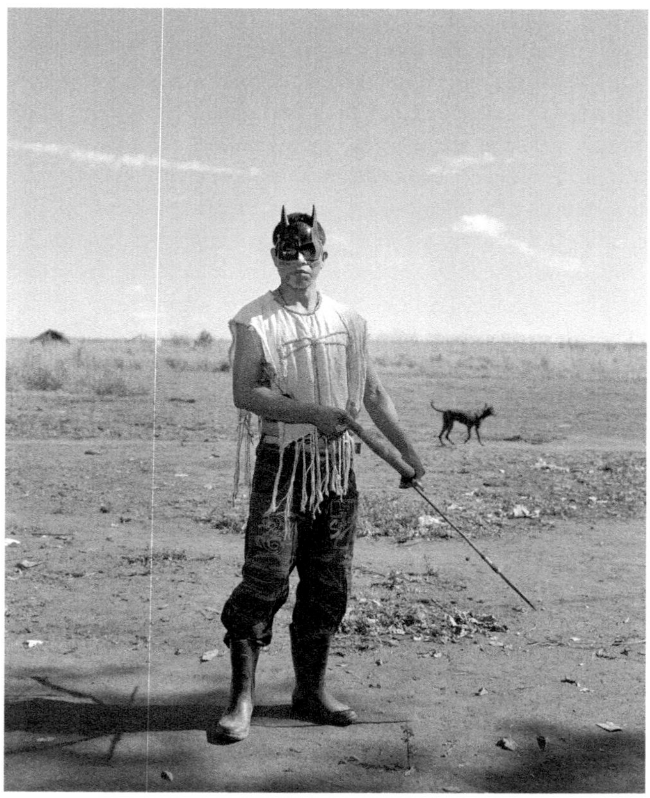

Figure 16.1 Yann Gross, *Dulcídio Gomes, Guaiviry, Brazil,* from *Jungle Book* series (2016). © Yann Gross

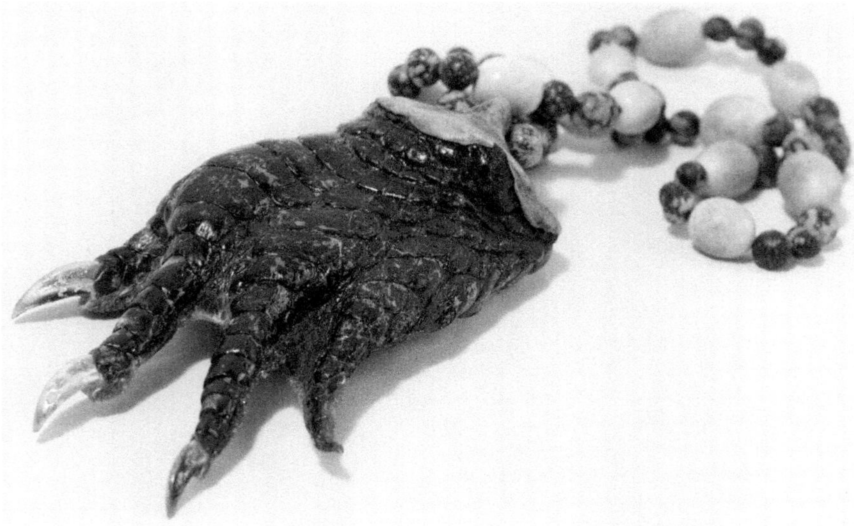

Figure 16.2 Yann Gross, *Pendant with Caiman Foot,* from *Jungle Book* series (2016). © Yann Gross

are each quietly political, but do not overtly protest, as with more traditional documentary formats. Each of these projects adopts the appearance of documentary in the use of procedures that avoid directorial authoring and assert localised difference over general statement. Each incorporates many elements that present the possibility of different configurations. As an example, Gross's *Jungle Show*, picturing the detail and behaviours of a community, only implies the impact of global forces on its complex social relationships, culture and functions. The traumatic effects of change are referenced indirectly, in the nuanced and disputed consequences of exchange between subjects and objects: endangered species and curious objects; traditional myth and American pageantry; the proximity of river and the impact of highways; the harvesting of latex and the cultivation of coca; the primacy of jungle and the potential of pharmaceutical product; the incongruity of symbolic relics and the possession of rifles (Plate 15 and Figures 16.1–16.3).[3]

Stéphanie Solinas's project *The Method of Loci* is typical of contemporary practices tempered by cultural awareness that follow the premise that detailed study of a locale in all its many dimensions will tell us something of the wider political situation (see Figure 16.4].[4] Incorporating photographs, film, drawings and objects, it presents a socio-political study of the Halle Lustucru in Arles and the people dependent on it (1906–2003). The project exhibits a multi-perspectival view of a place that is no longer visually accessible, except in archival record. Central to her work, she says, are questions relating to "how reality is organised," particularly if the reality is socially and historically complex. She asks: "How can one go back in time through photography, what elements will allow you to gain access to a reality that today is invisible?" (De La Fresnaye 2016). *The Method of Loci*, with its various photographic incarnations and archival illustrations, tests the limits of photography to document the network of consequences of a place and its many uses. Presenting a Foucauldian critique of colonialism, global

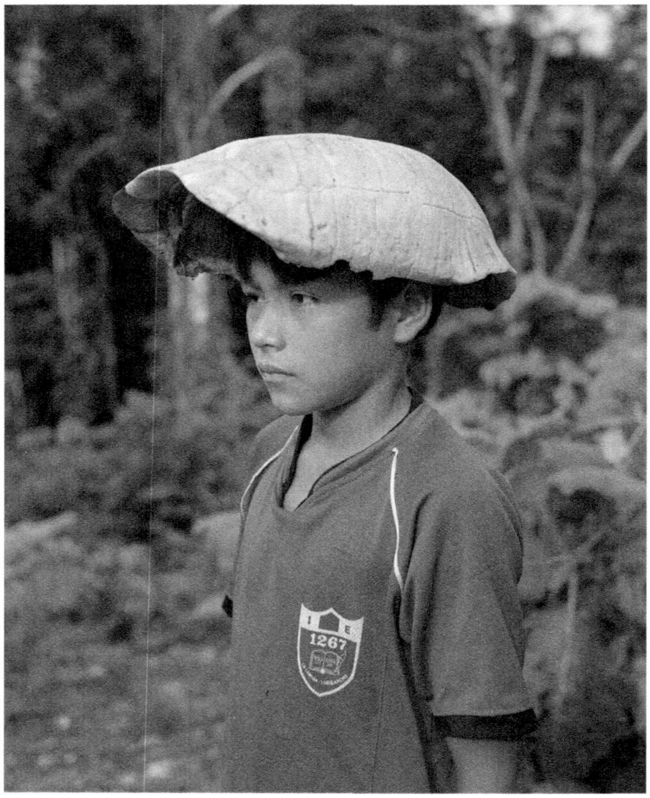

Figure 16.3 Yann Gross, *Turtle Shell Cap, Bolivar Community, Peru*, from *Jungle Book* series (2016). © Yann Gross

capitalism and social expansion, it signals the far-reaching implications of industry and immigration told from different disciplinary perspectives and from singular familial accounts. So surprising and remarkably complex was the content and history of this place that I did wonder if Solinas had resigned herself to the impossibility of its documentation and resorted to fiction, in the manner of Walid Raad's process in the *Atlas Group Project*.[5]

Raad's *Atlas Group Project* attempts to visualise the conflict in Lebanon geographically, psychologically and as it has developed historically, so that the difficulty is not only that the subject matter is hugely complex, but also that it is tragic. As comprehensive representation is not possible, what is significant is the project's focus on matters/conditions/events that commence before, and extend and develop beyond, the instant of a photograph. The subject matter is therefore the *experience* of a situation, rather than the factual evidence normally associated with a photograph and visually available within its frame. Objects and 'facts' presented in photographs are assumed to provide 'objective' information, whereas the representation of experience needs to be diverse and far-reaching and to include uncertain or disputable positions. Bruno Latour and Peter Wiebel's exhibition *Making Things Public* (2005), exploring the ways political or public concerns can be represented, demonstrated an

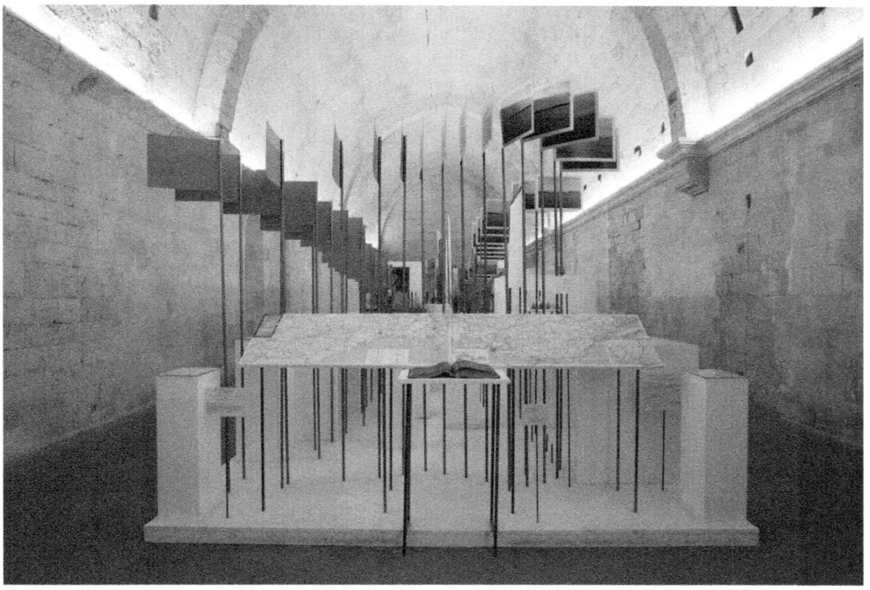

Figure 16.4 Stéphanie Solinas, *The Method of Loci (Mind Palace)* (2016). © Stéphanie Solinas

approach that focuses on "matters-of-concern" rather than "matters-of-fact" (Latour and Weibel 2005: 16). The conception of gathering together numerous factors, across disciplines and through history, emphasises representation as a coalescence of things that *re*presents the subject of concern. Weibel conceived the exhibition as an "assembly" describing the *relationship* between technologies, networks, media and 'things' that give rise to the public sphere and that integrate the usually separated fields of science, art and politics (2005: 1015).

Representation as a network of relationships assumes the need for interdisciplinary forms of knowledge, besides scientific certainty, and therefore includes facts, interpretations and fictions. Photographic projects that incorporate such networks (Solinas) underline the significance of context, exemplified by Allan Sekula's contra-definitive documents, collectively describing the effects of capitalism, and his insistence on reading across different perspectives in series. Raad's strategies develop this methodology with the introduction of contradictory and fictional accounts or fanciful extension. Fictions expose the fragility of photography as testimony or authentic document, and reflect the tensions of authority, power and the veracity of political agency. And artistic play, such as developed in *Atlas Group Project* or *Cotton Under my Feet* (2007, exhibited at Arles 2016),[6] introduces emotional experience by confusing and thus circumventing the physical signs of conflict or horror with subjective trivial observation.

Each of these projects has a political agenda driving the manipulations of document and, in their self-consciousness, can be accused of hiding in sanitised fictional realms of art practice, entirely separated from the experience of life (Raad), or of being so inclusive of localised and tangential content as to remove any chance of affect (Sekula, Solinas). But they each demand that audiences become active agents in the construction of meaning, in the effort of making connections between different elements. Rancière identifies the significant factor of recent practices as their "polemical function," shifting from "provocative dissensus" to something more circuitous, which he insists on categorising with another set of strategies: "the play, the inventory, the encounter and the mystery" (2009b [2004]: 52–8). Many such projects use the strategy of 'mystery' by linking different elements in an extensive 'play of analogies'. Certainly, Raad uses the "ludic register"; Hans Peter Feldman's *100 Years* (2001)[7] presents an inventory "testifying to a history and a world in common"; Solinas and Gross are "archivists of collective life" using the potential of images to display a common history; and Tobias Zielony's project *The Citizen* (2015), documenting African refugees in Germany, ruptures the usual relation between 'encounter' and response by publishing the refugees' stories in the newspapers of their respective countries of origin.[8]

Unrepresentable atrocity

Artists/photographers who endeavour to represent situations of atrocity confront the problematic of ethical representation: what it is possible to represent, and what intrudes on private despair.[9] Alfredo Jaar (whose practice Rancière refers to as an ethical example) clearly acknowledges the disjunction that exists between a tragedy—that is unrepresentable—and what it is possible to record photographically (Jaar in Levi Strauss 2003: 91). His *Rwanda Project* (1994–2000) exemplifies a strategic use of photographic documentation that aims for a responsible telling of history or trauma that counters the fleeting viewing of photographs. Having taken more than 3,000 photographs and recorded numerous accounts of witness to the genocide in Rwanda, Jaar did not show these photographs for nearly two years while he considered how to present them. Facing the disjunction between the experience and its representation, he was concerned to not merely add to ubiquitous news imagery that has no impact. He subsequently devised methods of display that avoided direct depictions of scenes of violence and destruction, and his first installation, *Real Pictures* (1995), shows no photographs at all. In 2016, at Art Basel, Jaar's *The Gift* confronts another image of unrepresentable tragedy—Alan Kurdi's dead body lying face down on a beach at Bodrum—by not showing it. Instead, an image of that beach is wrapped around a gift box along with a call for donations for the NGO Migrant Offshore Aid Station.[10] A slight gesture as a critical work, as Rancière argues, the level of political impact relies entirely on the extent and reach of the image's previous exposure and on a consensual understanding of political injustice.

Rancière is concerned to understand the purpose in presenting images of atrocity and what is supposed to be provoked—sympathy, anger, rebellion, indignation—what is art supposed to be doing? He asks, "which models of the efficacy of art govern our strategies, hopes and judgements regarding the political import of artistic practice" and how is this reflected in prevailing strategies? (2010: 135). What strategies are used to combat the distance from the original situation and context? I found myself confronted by such questions while viewing examples of photojournalism at *Visa pour l'image*. Although clearly not serving the same function as exhibition in venues associated with aesthetic focus, as in Arles. the same questions of purpose are raised. The Perpignan festival is a showcase for a profession serving the very necessary function of informing the world of the consequences of war and atrocity. But, as I cruised through numerous displays following the same unvaried format, I began to wonder why I was looking at all these images of pain, and what the purpose of displaying them in this sanctified space of festival was. The purpose of presentation appeared confused by multiple agendas. I was interested by the tone of the editorial for *Visa pour l'image*, which appears to defend photojournalists for 'doing an honest job' as simple "witnesses" and to justify the use of methods "without indulging in artifice or concept" (Leroy 2016). It pointed also to the precarity of their profession, dependent as it is on grants and awards, which needs the support of the festival to generate funding for further projects. The editorial reference to "major and recurring stories," which "featured the same pictures, the same scenes of horror," signals the principal aim of bringing newsworthy 'stories' to the world's attention. Nonetheless, the editorial and the many commentaries accompanying the images signaled a tension between introducing knowledge of a situation by communicating visual evidence and the mediation of photographic affect caused by seeing "scenes of horror." The editorial identifies a conflict in purpose and an assumption that a choice has to be made between either the use of artifice and concept or the job of simple witness. It brought to mind Barthes' argument that it is the news agency photograph, the "literal photograph," that, lacking artifice, "compels the spectator to a violent interrogation" (1997 [1979]: 71–3). The tension between distance and immersion is further complicated by the im/possibility of separating witness from artifice.

The problems associated with viewing images of pain are well rehearsed. In speaking of photographs of genocide, Rancière echoes Sontag and Barthes in saying images of horrific events can generate anger, but can also "turn the victim's pain into an aesthetic matter" (Rancière 2010: 136) Sontag points out that the photograph gives us mixed signals: "Stop this, it urges. But it also exclaims what a spectacle!" Photographs can divert attention from the suffering, from any obligation to act, and can create the illusion of consensus or lull us into a state of acceptance. She suggests that to be effective as political instruments or alter opinion or behaviour, photographs need to shock (2003: 68–72). Far from shocking me, my inhibited and passive experience in Perpignan is testament perhaps to the influence of a systematic presentation without clear purpose. It contrasted with my viewing in 2009 of Jaar's *The Sound of Silence*, which demonstratively confronts photojournalism, responsibility and ethics in the photographing of trauma. It is one of the few times that I have encountered an image that has profoundly shocked me out of my measured appraisal—entirely owing to the artifice of a presentation designed for maximum emotional affect. It only features the one Pulitzer Prize-winning photograph by Kevin Carter, and yet it exposes a series of tangential facts with the one simple purpose of shocking my complacency by simultaneously confronting the many implications of that image.[11]

The Sound of Silence demonstrates the photographic event and its consequences as extensive. What once seemed common sense in regard to images of pain and suffering has been problematised by more recent discussions by, for example, Judith Butler (2009) and Ariella Azoulay (2008, 2012). Azoulay implies that Sontag does not sufficiently consider the circumstances of those who are photographed. Following an established understanding of photography as an apparatus that includes all processes associated with its making, distribution and consumption, Azoulay has developed the analysis as a "civic practice" that is "within the framework of citizenship as a status, an institution, and a set of practices" (2008: 24). She has argued that the ethical implications of image production extend beyond the object to include individual responsibility. In her terms, the photograph is a political space and an act of interpretation shared by all the partner participants involved, including the audience. Azoulay advocates the event of the photograph as a continuing process in which the subjects of the photographs are not over and done with in the past, but are testament to that civic contract each time they are viewed.

It follows that subsequent publications of a 'newsworthy' photograph continue to construct its meaning, "its legibility, its illegibility, and its very status as reality" (Butler 2007: 958). Whether published in newspapers or shown in galleries, how photographs are shown and described can remove the specific brutality from the original scene.

Responding to Sontag's discussion (2004) of the Abu Ghraib images, Butler emphasises the significance of conditions that 'frame' the relation between the photographer, the camera, the subject of suffering and its presentation. Integral to this frame is the photographic apparatus that supports the event of photography and that is seldom an explicit part of the story, and yet how that frame circumscribes what can be called reality affects ethical responsiveness. For example, if the destination for the photograph is the international scene, it will endorse the commodification of newsworthiness and the specific methods adopted by the photographer. Echoing Rancière's comment that interpretation can only be critical when there is consensual understanding, Butler states that a photograph only becomes effective politically if it is viewed within the context of a relevant political consciousness. Making the frame visible facilitates "critical scrutiny" (2007: 952). It is possible that presentation can extend the photographic event by providing a history and a means for visual reflection so that "visual evidence and discursive interpretation can play off each other" (Butler 2007: 957). And, in expansive photographic studies, such as described here, content is extended to include the wider frame and its implications. Methods of presentation that are more discursive than definitive require the viewer to find relationships and interpretations that more readily suit that situation and context.

Representing the unrepresentable

Butler points to the assumption by some that to show photographs of torture or of the Holocaust not only minimises the horror by defining a situation that exceeds description, but also defines us as perpetrators in viewing that horror. Significant for this exploration of the distanciated or affective impact of content is the profound argument provoked by Georges Didi-Huberman's book *Images in Spite of All.* Founded on the existence of four photographs taken by a Jewish prisoner bearing witness to the mass killing at Auschwitz, Didi-Huberman responds to a series of arguments prompted by his catalogue essay and their exhibition in *Memoirs des Camps*, 2001: the representation of a horror that is 'unrepresentable'; the bearing witness to imminent death; the proximity of testimony to forgetting that horror ever took place. "Snatched from hell," two of the photographs were taken furtively from within the dark space of a gas chamber. Framed by black, these are but momentary glimpses of a clandestine process that expose what humans are capable of doing. The fourth photograph, taken we imagine in haste and fear, shows us no evidence of death or killing, but is testament to the risk taken by the photographer as a consequence of hiding, running, escaping from those who are perpetrating the horror, but who are unnamed. Seen in sequence, and not cropped or altered, the photographs are themselves evidence of resistance to that horror: the "image is metaphorically out of breath: it is pure 'utterance', pure gesture, pure photographic act without aim" (Didi-Huberman 2008: 36–8).

Didi-Huberman pursues the arguments made against showing these photographs throughout the book. He argues for the ethical need for these images to be seen, in contrast to the critical positions taken by Elizabeth Pagnoux and Gérard Wajcman and exemplified in Claude Lanzmann's refusal to include any archive image or film footage in his 1985 film *Shoah*. Lanzmann privileges the oral testimony of memory rather than archival images, which he says "petrify thought and kill any power of evocation" (Lanzmann, quoted in Didi-Huberman 2008: 93). Didi-Huberman is accused by Pagnoux and Wajcman of over-interpreting images and of exploiting what is unrepresentable. Wajcman points out "the social, ethical and *political* dangers" of elevating "the image to the status of relic" typical of the Christian religion and idolatry: "it is as though he were under a sort of hypnotic captivation of images" and in "fetishistic denial" of the event itself (Wajcman, quoted in Didi-Huberman 2008: 52–3). As relic, more damning than fetish, they become a leftover of what is past and a useless thing; they are "attractive substitutes" that cover up the absence of the event, reducing it to a "televisual ideal." They do not show the extermination of the Jews, but hide that horror, which is unrepresentable. Countering this argument, Didi-Huberman states that these images do not only represent what has gone but, as relics, they remind us of what is present, of what humanity is capable. They demand that we confront our absence from what is shown, which is not the same as "usurping the place of the witness" as Wajcman suggests. In addition, the act of producing these four images was one of affirmative power, and, for us today, to reject all such images rejects also the debt owed to the photographer's political act of resistance and "amounts to the impotence of pure avoidance, a symptom of *psychic resistance* in the face of the horror that gazes at us from these photographs" (2008: 64).

Pagnoux's view emphasises the difference between mere knowledge of an event and experience of it, and that to look again disrespects the reality of the original horror, the experience of which cannot be wholly imagined. She argues that analysis of the images is a form of voyeurism, a "reconstitution, fiction, creation" that amounts to a nullification of memory. Besides the fact of invention, to make us witness of the scene is to distort the reality of Auschwitz, because once we 'know' of this horror, we cannot revisit it (Pagnoux, in Didi-Huberman 2008: 54–5). Pagnoux argues that we should maintain distance from the horror, and that to look at the photograph and to believe oneself to be there denies us that distance and is a form of betrayal. Didi-Huberman acknowledges that Pagnoux's attitude is a form of respectful silence, like a prayer, but argues that it is in itself useless. It turns the refusal to look into some sort of abstract metaphor for a principled statement that acknowledges the existence of horror. "If the horror of the camps defies imagination, then *each image* snatched from such an experience becomes all the more necessary" (2008: 26).

At the core of this relentless polemic is the significant difference between knowing and experiencing: between the intention of imparting knowledge and that of trying to duplicate experience. Wajcman argues that either we know "or we do not know, meaning we do not want to know or that in one way or another, radically, secretly, insensitively … we deny it took place." Didi-Huberman counters that *knowing* does not end with "its capture in a revealed certainty," that *knowing* is "without end," and certainly does not end with one image. He asserts that Wajcman's arguments emerge from confusion "between a *certain* knowledge of what is represented and an *uncertain* recognition of what is seen; between the uncertainty of having *seen* and the certainty of having *experienced*," and that Wajcman is "confusing the unimaginable with the unrepresentable." In order to know we must also imagine, and to imagine does not mean that we believe ourselves to have been there: "imagination is not identification" (2008: 81–8). Didi-Huberman pinpoints that what is significant for the validity of the image's affect is the difference between seeing and knowing. Images will not tell all of anything, but, in seeking the impossibility of "a unique and integral image of the Shoah"—the 'all-image'—Wajcman dismisses all images (124). And, by insisting on not looking, Wajcman has not understood that some images may have the capacity to displace, rupture and push knowledge to the limit.

Rancière comments on this debate in his essay "The Intolerable Image," observing that not only do these images make no claim to represent the total reality of the horror, but, because of the manner in which they were taken, their presentation declares that the horror *is* unrepresentable. He identifies Wajcman's argument as based on an assumption that privileges the validity of spoken testimony over the evidence of imagery, whereas *both* are only ever partial representations, and neither duplicates the entire horror. Wajcman understands images as being presented as proof of an act, when there is no need of proof; they lie because they do not represent the experiential reality of the Holocaust; there is something unrepresentable that cannot be made visible in an image; the horror should not be shown, or even witnessed. Rancière challenges this argument that identifies the image with "idolatry, ignorance or passivity" and that centres around the assumption that, if the real can never be entirely visible or known, the opposite view must be that it can, whereas this oppositional logic, which denies us looking or representing at all, does not get anywhere near the complexity of the relationship of an image to the real or to its validity as witness. Photographic representation is not a duplicate, but "a complex set of relations between the visible and the invisible" (Rancière 2009c [2008]: 89–95). It is complex because it results from a series of contradictions inherent in our expectation of images: we expect evidence but distrust it; we recognise that they can only be partial, and, ultimately, they diminish experience. Images are not complete; they work together with memory and the imaginary; they are both fact and fetish and are neither wholly illusion nor wholly fact. The 'facts' displayed in images can never be free of values and will always be in dispute but, as Didi-Huberman observes, if we label them 'document', they become more manageable for us, more justifiably accessible. And in that process, we remove them from their history and from their specificity (2008: 33).

Two points of particular significance for this discussion emerge from this debate. First, Didi-Huberman argues that there is a distinction between terrifying images that remain in the "sphere of consensual experience," which is on the level of a general and depersonalised acknowledgement, and those that provoke a "*tearing experience* that causes the upheaval of territories and thus of limits" (2008: 81) or, in Rancière's terms, a dissensus that reconfigures common sense. In the course of his argument, Didi-Huberman cites Barthes' discussion of the over-mediation of horrific images and suggests that what is needed in the face of this difficulty, and to avoid the mere 'coverage' of atrocity, is a doubting gaze, a "critical gaze" (2008:70). My experience confirms that the frames of reference and the manner of presentation are significant in effecting an active critical gaze, or whether the viewer experience is measuredly consensual or "tearing." Second, despite his alignment that privileges the spoken word (testimony) over photography (evidence), Wajcman's differentiation between the validity of testimony and the partiality of evidence is significant for the effective use of photographs (Rancière 2009c [2008]: 89–95). The implication of 'testimony' here is that it is involuntary, authentic and speaks of more than can be told in an image. There is a subtle difference between 'testament' that suggests written document as proof and 'testimony' that serves as a sign of an event or quality. It follows that there is a significant difference between images intended as matters of fact and images presented as testimony to matters of concern, and to something more than can be seen.

Presenting the unrepresentable

The argument that imagery cannot represent what is considered 'unrepresentable' demonstrates the power and fear of images, and Wajcman's and Pagnoux's view presents a challenge to photographers who try. Their invective confronts how we interpret and understand images by implying that there is some boundary or limit to what a photograph can refer. If there are such limits, they will depend on who is drawing those limitations that determine what is too horrific to be shown: the state, the institution or the consensual values and expectations of the audience. Applying Wajcman's argument to the conditions of horror displayed at Perpignan would render many of them unrepresentable. But the stated aim of photography in this context seems simple—to bear witness to events so that they are available and can be seen. For example, the photojournalist Yannis Behrakis states his intention to "establish a feeling of shared responsibility for the misfortune of others" and to "be the voice of the persecuted and the eyes of the global audience."[12]

Dominic Nahr's project *Fractured State* (© Dominic Nahr for *Medecins Sans Frontieres*), which documents the civilian victims of South Sudan's civil war, was exhibited in both Arles and Perpignan, using different methods.[13] In Perpignan, the presentation followed the uniform format at the festival of regularly spaced images accompanied by brief descriptions of the circumstances and context below. In Arles, a smaller selection of images, of various image sizes and formats, was presented; the venue was a shabby but atmospheric space; the hanging was more ambivalent, less formal and less informative than in Perpignan. The photographs were shown alongside a video installation by Marc Hofer, specifically produced for the venue,[14] that recounted stories of five individuals and their experience of displacement and later return to South Sudan. Perpignan encouraged the reading of captions over the looking at photographs, so that written information was privileged over visual testimony. I noticed how we all moved in convoy from one to the next—fleetingly. I tended to look at *what* was photographed rather than *how*, but in an appreciative way—it was perhaps a "consensual experience." In Arles, I looked longer and more closely at the images, and with more engagement—it was a focused and disturbing experience. Labelled as 'art' in this context (supported by the Swiss Foundation for Photography and the Manuel Rivera-Ortiz Foundation for Documentary and Film), the exhibition blurb confirms a different purpose from Perpignan, although no less complex. The project is described as multifaceted and displaying the hard facts of conflict together with a subjective view and states Nahr's purpose as aiming to document "crucial stages" in a history. It implies his intention to focus on the people and their struggle rather than the visible evidence of conflict and to emphasise the "dissonance" between the hope that followed the founding of an independent state and the difficulties people have endured since. The statement suggests that it is possible to document and to display this network of complexity: to separate or integrate subjective view and facts; to differentiate stages of a conflict; to contrast individual lives beside international conflict; to contrast hope and despair. Despite the unremitting anguish evident in the images, I doubt the possibility of achieving these various aims without strategic focus in presentation.

Butler sums up the complex contextual and psychological influences that frame response to photographs and explains in part the perturbation I felt in viewing the images in Perpignan. Before we can say how the photograph affects us, "we have to make sure that the photograph still has the power to affect us at all. Sometimes it seems to bespeak our numbness, and other times it seems to establish our prurience and tendency to respond to sensationalism" (Butler 2007: 955). Perhaps the manner of display contributed to the photographs somehow losing their "power to affect us all," or perhaps I respond more readily to strategies designed to shock, rather than these measured narratives. Perhaps, when the purpose of communication is confused with the aim of affect, images have less impact. Certainly, the nature of presentation in Perpignan encouraged a hurried viewing and diminished reflection to the extent that my experience was one of a distanciated interest over critical engagement, whereas some presentations have compelled me to look and go on looking, so that I am taken elsewhere, out of the present, and made to think, to wonder and sometimes to feel. Nahr's most affective image—a body floating face down in water—records the aftermath of horror, but not the act (see Plate 16). Exploiting the metonymic capacity of photography to make spectacle and to evoke the imagination from its fragmentary reference, this image is somehow more potent when isolated as it was in the exhibition at Arles. But then I am mindful that my viewing, although thoughtful, is one of curiosity and intrudes on that private horror.

The tension between artifice and witness in photographing scenes of horror is complicated in both contexts by unclear statements of purpose: in Arles, the expectation of the exhibition was one of evoking the imagination and memory in various ways; in Perpignan, the stated functions were defensive. Despite aiming to satisfy a different expectation and assume a different significance, distinctions have become blurred between the appearance of photojournalism and many projects presented in an art context: it is commonplace for artists to have assimilated journalistic strategies of documentation in their work. And it is noticeable that, despite the denial of concept and artifice and a plea for simple witness, photojournalists increasingly insert individual perspectives or 'artifice and concept' into the reporting. The tradition of photojournalism expects to draw the world's attention to situations of concern. The tradition of documentary has expected to provoke a desire to change situations, but, as is understood, there is no "straight line between perception, affection, comprehension and action" (Rancière 2009c [2008]: 103). And an increased awareness of the political agency of images and the fear of artifice or intrusion have resulted in a growing critical sensitivity in devising strategies, of which Ristelhueber's displacement and Mendel's "fetishistic denial" are examples.

In *The Emancipated Spectator*, Rancière discusses the possibility that artistic strategies can construct ethical testimony and tolerable images. His argument with Wajcman's view asserts photographic representation as a means of contributing to knowledge and understanding that can be as valid as the spoken word. He reiterates that photographs do not equate with proof, and that their association with facts is an assumption: he disputes the division between facts and their interpretation, and the hierarchical status of philosophical or scientific discourse that is assumed to explain hidden truth; he argues that there are different ways of telling a story, different 'levels of discourse', and that what is necessary is the invention of methods appropriate to the content. To provoke meaningful reflective response to atrocity, strategies must navigate a whole system of relations between the emotions present at the scene, and the methods used to transpose those emotions in an image (Rancière 2009a [2003]: 12). As an example, Rancière describes Lanzmann's strategy that uses displacement as a means to create distance between the traumatic experience and how that trauma is perceived in the present (2009a [2003]: 127–9). He describes the scene in *Shoah* in which the space of extermination at Chelmno is magnified by its present silence, in contrast to what is absent—what that space was witness to. To provoke meaningful reflective response, he suggests that confronting the reality of what materially remains of an event is more effective than "the representation of causes which resist any explanation."

He also proposes solutions regarding the distance between subject and affect by amplifying the possibility of active viewing. His "emancipation" advocates the blurring of "boundaries between those who act and those who look" (2009c [2008]: 19). In the context of photography, there is an expectation that passive viewing and distanciation inevitably follow 'spectatorship'. Rancière problematises the expectation that looking is passive, which assumes a uniform transmission of knowledge and energy from the artist to the spectator, by suggesting a redistribution of the oppositional positions that are assigned to the spectator who views and the artist who acts. He emphasises two factors: besides the distance between artist and spectator is the work itself, which *actively* exists between the artist's idea and the viewer's sensation; the spectator is active as "she observes, selects, compares, interprets" its meaning, which "is owned by no one" (2009c [2008]: 13–15).

A redistribution of the boundaries between those who act and those who look can be seen in expansive documentary productions that place spectators in the middle of performative presentations of imagery, as with Solinas's, Gross's or Biemann's installations. Projects such as these are immersive: they redistribute the distance from the original subject by making the spectator engage with different levels of material reference—photographs, films, documents, commentaries. Exhibition forces a discursive encounter that prolongs consideration of the matter of concern by requiring us to physically move around a situation, from one tangential issue to another, some of which may be contradictory or disputable. As with Sekula's presentations of *Fish Story*, the process repositions expectations of the engagement with photographs to one that is analogous with reading a novel (Sekula 2003: 107). When reading a book, we expect to encounter contradictory stories, different points of view from each of the protagonists; we expect to respond to elements of the book in both conceptual and emotional ways, and according to our experience.

I emphasise Rancière's mention of "polemical function" as being a dimension that makes the difference between mere acknowledgement and affective impact. Heartfield's montages prefigured the possibility of a polemical function, by placing one reality alongside another to make visual argument. Discursive presentations of political content extend the practice of visual juxtaposition and of purposeful 'documentary' by disrupting the possibility of simplistic cause and effect. The premise of producing a visual system of relationships that navigates between fact and fiction, ideology and expression, is one that necessitates a durational response and a less oppositional relationship between linguistic and visual representations. It is a procedure that demands thought and participation in a space of enquiry and testimony that is not one of finality. As eventful rather than definitive, it exploits the photograph's dynamic as active rather than relying on static, nominative qualities; meaning does not stand still: it is mobile and malleable and can accelerate and delay—dilatory in Barthes's terms (1977 [1970]: 95).

If it is assumed that representations of atrocity claim to duplicate the experience of suffering, it is clear that "some things are unrepresentable." In considering the ethics and efficacy of valid presentation and of confronting the distance between original event, representation and affect, it is necessary to draw the distinction between the representation of experience, which is absent, not accessible or duplicable, and the present experience of meaningful response to its performative representation. The tension between distance and immersion works by contradiction: images may depict experience in all its manifestations, but cannot duplicate it; we cannot approach the total event, yet can be immersed in its representation; images may keep material reality distant from us, but keep what is conceptually absent reverberating for us, caught in a web of implications with no resolution. Perhaps the degree to which the viewer is immersed determines the level of active engagement and the nature of response, and it may be that the use of photography can be effective for information and for the provocation of feeling—but not perhaps at the same time. A discursive aesthetic can be effective in contemplative ways that create a quiet dissensus, which is circuitous, even devious in its confrontation of political matters of concern (Raad); it may be emotionally affective by exploiting the ambiguous nature of photography and its reference to absent content. Presentations that utilise evocation of the imaginary and memory, which are banished in Wajcman's view, exploit the fact of our absence, expose the frame in a violent way and construct emotional response (as in Jaar's work).

In reviewing presentations that might counter the refusal to look at the unrepresentable, the 'production' of presentation is key in differentiating response as being one of "consensual" understanding or the "tearing" experience of immediate affect—as demonstrated by the different displays of Nahr's *Fractured State*. Although I have highlighted examples of discursive presentation that challenge the apparatus of looking and experiencing images, the purpose and fabrication of their performative role are not always articulated—to communicate information, to produce knowledge or to transpose emotion—at least not to the same extent as has been examined in documentary film. As Rancière suggests, the relationship between artist/photographer, viewer and subject matter can be redistributed with the strategic construction of a durational viewing and by 'emancipating' audience engagement. The proposition offers an interesting challenge for the polemical use of photography.

Notes

1 Exhibited at *Les Rencontres d'Arles*, 2016, www.rencontres-arles.com/CS.aspx?VP3=CMS3&VF=ARLAR1_460_VForm&FRM=Frame%3AARLAR1_364
(NB: all websites in these notes accessed September 6, 2017).
2 As a photojournalist, Mendel has exhibited at Perpignan and won the Pollock Krasna Foundation Prize 2016 awarded to "an outstanding artist whose work embodies high creative standards and exemplifies the impact of art on individuals and society," www.instagram.com/gideonmendel/?hl=en
3 Yann Gross, *The Jungle Book*, http://yanngross.com/?page_id=188, and *The Jungle Show*, Arles 2016.
4 Stephanie Solinas, *Methods of Loci*, Les Rencontres de la Photographie, Arles, http://stephaniesolinas.com/stephaniesolinas/la_methode_des_lieux___le_palais_de_lesprit.html
5 Walid Raad, see for example, "Files Type A—Authored files" and "Files Type AGP—Thin Neck File" *in The Atlas Group Project*, www.theatlasgroup.org
6 www.rencontres-arles.com/C.aspx?VP3=CMS3&VF=ARLAR1_460_VForm&FRM=Frame%3AARLAR1_372&LANGSWI=1&LANG=English</URI>. The exhibition *Nothing but Blue Skies* (Arles 2016) curated projects in response to September 11, 2001. It included Raad's *Cotton Under My Feet* (2007) that presents images of the New York skyline on that day, each of which have had the objects obscuring the sky, such as the World Trade Centre, cut away leaving only blue. He states: "I still cannot remember the exact color of the sky on that fateful September day, but the trials in Seattle, Portland, Detroit, and Alexandria have helped me narrow it down to ninety-six shades of blue," Freize Art Fair 2011, http://katemariecarter2ndyear.blogspot.co.uk/2011/10/frieze-art-fair.html
7 http://momaps1.org/exhibitions/view/83
8 Tobias Zielony, http://myartguides.com/exhibitions/tobias-zielony-the-citizen/
9 See examples in Batchen et al. (2012)
10 See also Jaar (2010).
11 Kevin Carter, www.theguardian.com/media/2014/jul/30/kevin-carter-photojournalist-obituary-archive-1994
12 Yannis Behrakis, *Paths of Hope and Despair*, 2016, presents images of the migration from the Middle East to Greece, www.pulitzer.org/winners/photography-staff-reuters
13 Dominic Nahr, first image in the series *Fractured State; South and North Sudan*, http://dominicnahr.com/sudan-border-war/
14 Marc Hofer's *South Sudan: 5 Years On* is a "talking heads" presentation of interviews with people who returned to South Sudan following its becoming an independent state in 2011. They talk of their experience of diaspora, their identity and speculations about the future, https://vimeo.com/173884695

References

Azoulay, A. (2008) *The Civil Contract of Photography*, New York: Zone Books.
Azoulay, A. (2012) *Civil Imagination: A Political Ontology of Photography*, New York and London: Verso.
Barthes, R. (1977 [1970]) *Image Music Text*, trans. Stephen Heath, London: Fontana Press.

Barthes, R. (1997 [1979]) *The Eiffel Tower and Other Mythologies*, trans. Richard Howard, Oakland: University of California Press.

Batchen, G., Gidley, M., Miller, N.K. and Prosser, J. (2012) *Picturing Atrocity: Photography in Crisis*, London: Reaktion Books.

Butler, J. (2007) "Torture and the Ethics of Photography", *Environment and Planning D: Society and Space*, Vol. 25, No. 6, pp. 951–966, April 19.

Butler, J. (2009) *Frames of War: When Is Life Grievable?* London: Verso.

De La Fresnaye, M. (2016), "Arles 2106: Interview with Stéphanie Solinas La méthode des lieux", July 7, *The Eye of Photography*. www.loeildelaphotographie.com/en/2016/07/07/article/159913632/arles-2016-interview-with-stephanie-solinas/ [accessed November 14, 2016].

Didi-Huberman, G. (2008) *Images in Spite of All: Four Photographs from Auschwitz*, Chicago: University of Chicago Press.

Jaar, A. (2010) "Global Africa: Alfredo Jaar", lecture and interview, Smithsonian Latino Center. www.youtube.com/watch?v=G89kO0DQpt0 [accessed November 8, 2016].

Latour, B. and Weibel, P. (eds.) (2005) *Making Things Public: Atmospheres of Democracy*, Cambridge, MA: MIT Press.

Leroy, J. (2016) Editorial, *Visa Pour L'Image: 28th International Festival of Photojournalism*.

Levi Strauss, D. (2003) *Between the Eyes: Essays on Photography and Politics*, New York and London: Aperture.

Rancière, J. (2006 [2000]) *The Politics of Aesthetics*, trans. Gabriel Rockhill, London; New York: Continuum.

Rancière, J. (2009a [2003]) *The Future of the Image*, trans. Gregory Elliott, London and New York: Verso.

Rancière, J. (2009b [2004]) *Aesthetics and Its Discontents*, trans. Steven Corcoran, Cambridge and Malden, MA: Polity Press.

Rancière, J. (2009c [2008]) *The Emancipated Spectator*, trans. Gregory Elliott, London and New York: Verso.

Rancière, J. (2010) *Dissensus: On Politics and Aesthetics [various essays from 2000]*, trans. Steven Corcoran, London and New York: Continuum.

Sekula, A. (2003) *Titanic's Wake*, Liege: SNEL.

Sontag, S. (2003) *Regarding the Pain of Others*, London: Hamish Hamilton.

Sontag, S. (2004) "Regarding the Torture of Others", *New York Times*, May 23. www.nytimes.com/2004/05/23/magazine/regarding-the-torture-of-others.html [accessed November 14, 2016].

17

The eco-anarchist potential of environmental photography

Richard Misrach and Kate Orff's *Petrochemical America*

Conohar Scott

Introducing *Petrochemical America*

This essay examines a publication entitled *Petrochemical America*,[1] which is a collaboration between the photographer Richard Misrach and the graphic illustrator Kate Orff. The publication highlights both the difficulties and possibilities associated with photography when it is used to bring about awareness of environmental problems associated with industrial pollution. Misrach's photographs of petrochemical pollution in the Mississippi Delta region are discussed in relation to a subgenre of photographic image-making that I term 'environmental photography'. The term refers to examples of photographic practice that seek to promulgate the ethical values of environmentalism as a social movement, which has a history in the USA dating back to Rachel Carson's seminal publication *Silent Spring* (Carson 1963). Although photography is the dominant aesthetic medium in this practice, it is further defined by the inclusion of additional modal forms—cartography, infographs, textual passages, and so on—which are combined with the photograph in order to provide an appreciation of the environmental problems associated with the site of photographic documentation.

The subject of *Petrochemical America* is an industrial corridor some 150 miles along the Mississippi river in Louisiana, located between the cities of Geismar and Baton Rouge. This area produces "a quarter of the nation's petrochemicals" (Misrach and Orff 2014: 17), and the extensive nature of the pollution in this region has resulted in increased cancer rates in the local populace, which "have earned the area the dubious nickname of 'Cancer Alley'" (Sun 2012). In the first of three sections in the publication, Misrach takes the term *Cancer Alley* as the basis for his own photographic series. Misrach's photographs are illustrated in the traditional format of a monograph with imagery placed on the right side of a double page spread, accompanied by a title and caption on the facing page, which serve to anchor meaning in the image by summarizing an environmental problem closely associated with the viewpoint. Kate Orff's contribution forms the basis of the entire second section of the photobook, and this is subtitled an *Ecological Atlas*. Here, Orff's extensive research into the environmental implications of pollution in Cancer Alley is conveyed through a mixture of textual passages and visually compelling infographs. On some occasions, Orff takes Misrach's photographs as the basis for computer-rendered diagrammatic overlays that illustrate the degradation of the environment and resulting environmental health impacts. The final section of the publication is once more authored by Orff and is entitled: *Glossary of Terms & Solutions for a Post-Petrochemical Culture*. As the name suggests, this closing segment attempts to inform the reader of the need for alternate environmental protocols, while also profiling activist groups who are engaged in resisting the substantive environmental health threats emanating from corporate industrial producers operating within the region.

My reading of *Petrochemical America* is informed by three theoretical schools of thought. The first is Jane Bennett's concept of vital materialism (Bennett 2010), which argues that non-human and abiotic objects have powers of agency that have the potential to effect change in culture. This observation leads Bennett to conclude that political agency also belongs to non-human and abiotic entities. In the context of this essay, I use Bennett's argument to suggest that pollutants dumped into the Mississippi bayou can have a profound effect upon culture by causing illness or even death, and as such they should provoke in us a reconsideration of what constitutes our notion of 'the public'. Taking non-human agency into account, Bennett argues it is possible to develop a more empathic sense of environmental awareness. Importantly, her approach also creates a justification for the notion that aesthetic objects such as the photobook can be judged to have their own political agency in culture—an observation that justifies the political use value of art. For this reason, I pursue a twofold strategy in this essay. First, I consider the political efficacy of both Misrach's and Orff's artistic contributions with regards to the ongoing political situation in Cancer Alley. Second, I consider the potential of the photobook as a mass-produced artefact to bring about new forms of environmental awareness through the use of aesthetics.

If Bennett's vital materialism provides an emotive and philosophical basis for understanding that culture is intrinsically part of a vibrant material world that surrounds and interacts with us, then Murray Bookchin's concept of social ecology provides the basis for defining environmentalism as an eco-anarchist political theory, which advocates an abandonment of capitalism in favour of small autonomous eco-communities that persist sustainably. Bookchin's reasoning for this is that he believes there is a direct correlation between social inequality and the perturbation of the natural world through pollution, resource depletion, and habitat loss. The ideal society is by definition an ecologically harmonious one. One key aspect that Jane Bennett's notion of vital materialism and Murray Bookchin's concept of social ecology share is a belief in the horizontal distribution of power and resources, which both theorists argue is in keeping with the interdependency of ecosystems. In the context of *Petrochemical America*, I argue that activist groups working to resist pollution in the region are engaging in autonomous forms of resistance, which have much in common with both Bennett's and Bookchin's conceptual schemas. The challenge of this essay then is to draw a parallel between a theoretical reading of the politics of environmental activism and the potential of the photobook to articulate this political intentionality through the medium of aesthetics.

The third and final theoretical perspective I employ comes from the artists Trevor Paglen and Aaron Gach (2003), who make a distinction between artworks that maintain an 'attitude' towards political subject matter by simply referencing it, and projects that take up an engaged 'position' to political struggles by actively trying to promote change within a given locality. In essence, what Paglen and Gach argue is that art, which is tactically 'positioned' in dialogue with local activist struggles, succeeds as a form of politics mediated through aesthetics. This is because the artwork exists within a sociopolitical context in which it has a use value for citizens who are actively engaged in resisting the various privations that have been imposed upon them. In the context of the ongoing political situation in Cancer Alley, I also borrow Henry Giroux's (2017) and Linda Ottinger's (2013) criticisms of neo-liberalism in the present era, in order to argue that the environmental threat facing the disenfranchised communities of the Mississippi Delta is ideologically motivated. As a form of resistance to neo-liberalism's disregard for environmental standards, I also profile the efforts of citizen scientists in Louisiana (the Louisiana Bucket Brigade) who challenge dominant sources that claim a substantive environmental threat does not exist in this region. Finally, this essay questions how the genre of environmental photography, and the photobook in particular, can aid and contribute to the struggles of autonomous groups active within the region.

Richard Misrach's environmental photography

Misrach's photographs contained within *Petrochemical America* are representative of environmental photography, which can be understood in the first instance as the photographic documentation of industrial or man-made forms of pollution, whether they be in the land, sea, or air. Second, this genre can be characterized by a willingness to move beyond the indexical representation of pollution *alone*, in order to include additional modal forms, which provide a further evidential basis for the artist's environmental claims. Examples of additional modes might include: textual captions, graphic design icons, environmental science data, political manifestos, cartography, legal statutes, infographs and diagrammatic overlays. The resulting multimodal assemblage is then employed in order to make the case for environmental remediation, or to attribute blame to a third party—for example, an industrial polluter. This extraneous modal information provides the function of anchoring meaning to the image, but it also makes an appeal to the social imaginary by calling for environmental remediation and redress for those communities, individuals, and non-human entities affected by pollution. In essence, multimodality is the design process through which the photograph acquires a cogent sense of political intentionality, which cannot be obtained by looking at the image singularly. This is not to say that photography is a mere appendage. Rather, in its indexical capacity to represent disenfranchised individuals or polluted ecosystems, photography is the medium through which the hard, quantitative data of environmental science, or the struggles of environmental activists, can be reified and amplified within the cultural sphere. In this sense, the power of environmental photography lies in the image's capacity to engage the audience emotively as a means of promulgating praxis, while the non-visual 'evidence' of a substantive environmental threat is provided by other modal forms.

Not all contemporary photographers who tackle the subject matter of pollution are concerned to inform the audience as to the nature and identity of the pollutants addressed by the image. One such photographer is Edward Burtynsky who, over the course of his career, has remained true to the notion that his images form "an open-ended narrative" that amplifies environmental concerns associated with mining while simultaneously lauding the technological achievements we have gained as a species (Burtynsky, cited in Campbell 2008: 43). This ambivalent political approach clearly benefits the artist when it comes to gaining admission to sensitive industrial locations. Burtynsky admits that mining companies "usually give me access because I'm not going in there as an environmental activist," and, significantly, the artist also maintains an ambiguous political stance towards his audience, believing that, "forcing an issue down someone's throat is not an effective strategy for communication"

(Campbell 2008: 46). In contrast to Misrach's commitment to multimodality as a means of providing a politicized reading of the image, Burtynsky uses only brief captions to describe his subject matter. The absence of extraneous modal information results in a privileging of the aesthetic over an awareness of the political or socio-economic context in which the image is framed. In this sense, Burtynsky creates a spectacle of environmental despoliation, and he does so without the counter-position of contextual information, which could serve to anchor the aesthetic in a political paradigm that openly questions the status quo. Arguably, the difference in approach between artists who exhibit only a political intentionality that is ambiguous and others who choose a method of working in which an environmentalist agenda is overt and to the fore represents a schism in the contemporary practice of documenting environmental issues photographically.

Within the context of the photobook as a printed artefact, an archetypal example of environmental photography would be Eugene Smith's *Minamata* (Smith and Smith 1975), which examines the plight of the Japanese villagers from the southern island of Kyushu, many of whom contracted severe mercury poisoning from eating fish and shellfish after the Chisso Corporation's chemical factory had flushed methyl mercury into Minamata Bay over an extended period of time. Aside from Smith's harrowing images of the stricken population and the surrounding environment, the publication is defined by a polemic essay from the photographer's partner, Aileen Smith, that examines victims' testimonies, detailed autopsy reports concerning the prevalence of mercury inside the human body, and data detailing the distribution of the pollutants across Minamata Bay. In previous publications, Misrach has employed a similar approach. In *Bravo 20: The Bombing of the American West* (1990), he collaborated with his wife Myriam Weisang Misrach, who wrote a similarly polemic essay to Aileen Smith's, in order to convey the extent of the environmental health problems associated with Misrach's photographs. Misrach's partnership with Kate Orff further suggests the act of collaboration with additional authors and/or activists is in itself a predominant characteristic of what constitutes environmental photography as an ontological category.

Another more recent example of environmental photography is David T. Hanson's *Waste Land: Meditations on a Ravaged Landscape* (1997) series, which documents sixty-seven destinations across the USA which have been judged by the US Environmental Protection Agency (EPA) to be 'Superfund' sites—i.e. locations requiring a long term remedial planning in order to clean up hazardous contaminants. Throughout the series Hanson's strategy is to present in a triptych format—take for example his *California Gulch, Leadville, Colorado* (2005; Figure 17.1). Typically, an aerial photograph of a toxic location is accompanied by an enlarged segment of a US Geological Survey map showing both the scale and geographical positioning of the site—in this instance, the town of Leadville sits adjacent to the mining complex. The third element of Hanson's triptych comes in the form of a written statement from the EPA that details the history of the location, the scale and variety of pollutants present, the potential of the site to impact upon surrounding ecosystems and communities, and the remedial action required in order to make the location benign. By such means, Hanson's artworks are encoded with a cogent environmentalist message. The publication *Petrochemical America* uses a similar tripartite structure: Misrach's *Cancer Alley* provides the photographic element, Orff's *Ecological Atlas* cartographically maps the polluted ecosystems of the Mississippi Delta, and the concluding glossary section provides the textual solutions necessary for the remediation of the polluted topography. The resulting assemblage combines to articulate: cause, impact, and redress.

In the *Cancer Alley* portion of the publication, the subjects of Misrach's photographs are varied but include numerous views of the Mississippi River, homesteads and habitations

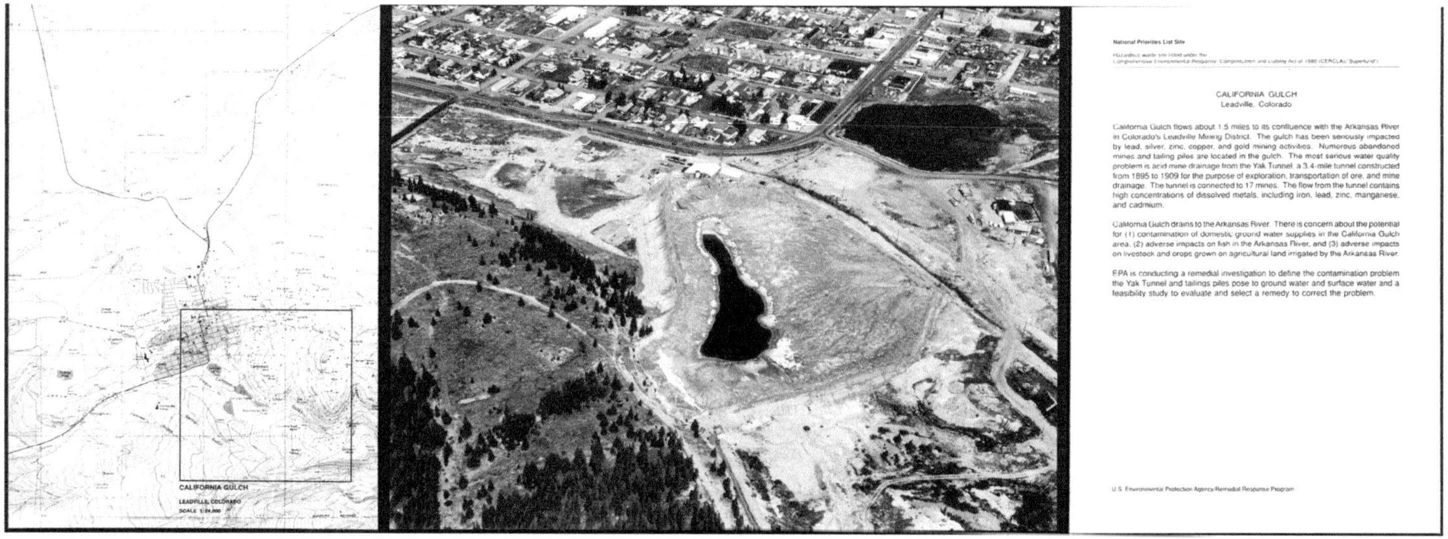

Figure 17.1 David T. Hanson, *California Gulch, Leadville, Colorado*, from the series *Waste Land* (1986). Ektacolor print, modified topographic map and gelatin silver print, 44 × 119 cm. © 2017 David T. Hanson

adjacent to petrochemical works, arable land, and the bayou for which the Louisiana region is noteworthy. Given the extensive nature of petrochemical production in this region, which hosts "over one hundred behemoth industrial plants" (Misrach and Orff 2014: 17), it is difficult to summarize the sum total of petroleum products produced. To take one company in the vicinity at random, BASF, located in Geismar, Louisiana (see Plate 17), represents a typical multinational petrochemical operator. BASF started production in 1958, and today the company hosts more than 1,000 employees who manufacture a range of petrochemical products including hydrochloric acid, solvents, plastics, pesticides, herbicides, detergents, foams, polyester fibres, and swimwear (BASF 2018).

Historically, Misrach's choice of the Geismar region as subject matter has significance to the environmental movement in the USA because it was in petrochemical plants such as those located in Cancer Alley that DDT, and other environmentally damaging pesticides and herbicides, were first manufactured for domestic consumption. In *Silent Spring*, Rachel Carson notes the effects of DDT upon the bird population in the same year that the BASF plant first opened when she observes "blank spots weirdly empty of *all* bird life" (Carson 1963: 85). As Carson demonstrated to the American public throughout the 1960s, the battle to undermine ecosystems for increased profit had taken a sinister turn in the post-World War II years, as the development of new forms of petrochemical pesticides resulted in the death of apex predators such as birds of prey on an endemic scale. As a form of political activism and as a social movement, environmentalism emerged from the counter-cultural 'hippy' scene prevalent in the United States during the 1970s. Such politically radical voices were given further credence by a host of influential scientists who began to talk openly about global environmental concerns such as peak oil and resource scarcity. In the early 1970s, a succession of high-profile publications emerged, such as Paul Ehrlich's *The Population Bomb* (1968), Barry Commoner's *The Closing Circle, Confronting the Environmental Crisis* (1973), and the Club of Rome's *The Limits to Growth* (Meadows et al. 1972), which did much to raise the profile of environmentalism in US culture. Such scientific publications were given further credence by widespread media coverage of environmental disasters, such as the 1969 Santa Barbara oil spill (Swift et al. 1969). One unexpected positive outcome from exposure of this disaster by the media came in the form of the US Senator for Wisconsin, Gaylord Nelson, who was so moved by the incident that he founded Earth Day (Earth Day Network 2017) as a means of raising the profile of environmentalism nationally. Given the sudden explosion of environmental rhetoric in North America during this period, it is not surprising that Friends of the Earth was formed in 1969 and Greenpeace in 1972.

In the 1970s, the US government's EPA sponsored a nationwide photographic survey of the USA, which was known as the *Documerica* project (US National Archives 2017). The EPA hired approximately seventy freelance photographers to document a varied range of subject matter including the urban environment, air and water pollution, industrial waste, and mining scenes. Approximately 113 images from the survey were displayed at the Smithsonian Museum in 1974 under the title *Our Only World*, and the show subsequently toured the USA until 1978. In an article assessing the significance of the exhibition, Gisela Parak argues that the initiative was the first example of a photography exhibition in which a national government employed "photographic eco-images to emphasize the complexity of environmentalism and to sanction specific behavioral patterns" (Parak 2013: 53). *Documerica* demonstrates the extent to which environmental issues had come to be at the forefront of US government policy by the mid 1970s, and it underscores the gains made by the environmental movement since the advent of Carson's *Silent Spring* (1963) more than a decade before. As Parak observes, photography in this era was employed as a form of 'visual mediation' and as a 'vanguard' for how the US administration sought to inform the American public. Not only does Parak's observation highlight the historical importance of the role that

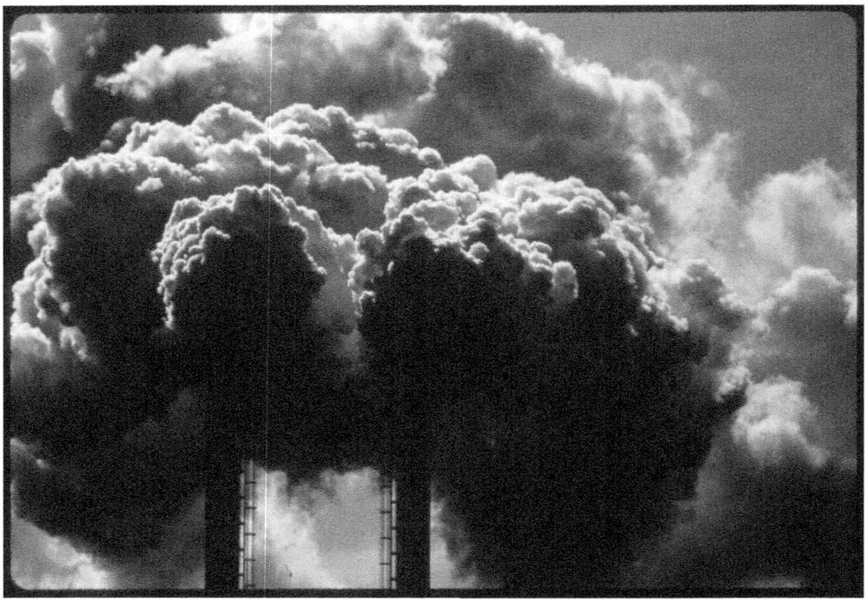

Figure 17.2 Marc St. Gil, *Burning Discarded Automobile Batteries* (07/1972), from *The Documerica* project. US National Archives' Local Identifier: 412-DA-11382

photography has played in bringing about greater awareness of environmental issues, it also suggests that contemporary projects such as *Petrochemical America* can only be considered as activist in so far as they are oppositional to the current state administration's stance towards environmental welfare.

Hard-hitting images from the *Documerica* project, such as Marc St. Gil's *Discarded Automobile Batteries* (1972; Figure 17.2), should be regarded as being in opposition to the modernist credo of conservationism espoused by Ansel Adams. Adams' pictorial images from the same era undeniably sought to venerate the sublimity of the natural world by documenting the unspoilt vistas of national parks such as Yosemite. However, as Rod Giblett observes, Adams's preoccupation with conservationism was largely centred upon the documentation of "sanctuaries, those special places for plants and animals and those aesthetic landscapes" (Giblett 2012: 141), which are distinct from the vast majority of the American continent. In this sense, Adams's photographic pictorialism functions as a form of protest against the various ecological and societal privations that arise as a result of the rapid transformation of the USA, but they do so without ever *directly* addressing the very subject matter of environmental despoliation that Adams was reacting against. In contrast, images such as *Automobile Batteries* can be understood as an aesthetic counterpart to Adams's vision of an untrammelled nature because they confront environmental degradation head-on.

In its depiction of the bayou at the outset of the twenty-first century, *Petrochemical America* situates itself firmly in the tradition of environmentalist discourse in the USA, which can be traced back to the likes of *Documerica*. Perhaps the most evocative feature of Misrach's *Swamp and Pipeline, Geismar Louisiana, 1998* (Plate 17) is the rusty pipeline, which spans the width of the frame and signifies an imprisoning lattice, suggesting that the marsh has become gridironed by a network of pipes. Indeed, part of the caption accompanying the image states: "Since 1903, oil companies have routed an estimated twenty-six thousand miles of pipeline throughout the oil-laden Southern parishes and across the Southern coastal wetlands" (Misrach and Orff 2014: 153). In counter-position to the pipe spanning the breadth of the frame, dead Cypress trees stand mournfully in the background, signifying a defeated ecosystem in terminal decline. In Misrach's photograph, the wetland is depicted as a space of capitalist production, a thoroughfare through which oil is transported to the petrochemical factories. Accordingly, the swamp becomes nothing more than a source of water for the manufacturing process and a dumping ground for unwanted effluents. Lurking ominously out of the frame, the bayou of Geismar is implicitly conjoined with the apparatuses of petrochemical production—distillation tanks, unit and fluid systems, power plants, and so on—which constitute the totality of the industrial infrastructure in the region. Capitalism's transformation of the bayou as a space of economic productivity has therefore produced a situation whereby companies such as BASF produce synthetic swimwear while also contributing to the transformation of the marsh into an ecological dead zone wherein nothing swims, and in which the conditions for endocrine disruption and carcinogenic poisoning in humans have become an elevated statistical possibility (Misrach and Orff 2014: 145).

Eco-anarchism as community resistance

Henry Giroux is known in the USA for his outspoken views, which often challenge racial and social inequalities, and for championing universal democratic participation. In his publication *America at War with Itself* (2017), Giroux observes that it is significant the local population of the Mississippi Delta are predominantly non-Caucasian and economically disenfranchised. Giroux draws a comparison between the people of the Mississippi Delta, who, in the aftermath of Hurricane Katrina in 2005, were left to fend for themselves in the face of widespread destruction and pollution, and a more recent scandal that emerged in 2016 in Flint, Michigan, when it was discovered that the town's drinking water contained alarming levels of lead. Giroux argues that it is the fate of certain communities in the USA to live in what he describes as "zones of abandonment" (Giroux 2017: 104). For Giroux, these are sites of habitation in which the local population has no say over the institutional practices of "domestic terrorism [and] state violence" that are foisted upon them (Giroux 2017: 104). Here, Giroux's use of the term "domestic terrorism" is intentionally provocative, but it is a phrase he returns to on many occasions throughout his publication. Citing scientific reports in the aftermath of the 9/11 disaster, in which the public were warned of the dangers of a possible terrorist attack on the public water system (Jones et al., cited in Giroux 2017: 127), Giroux argues that the state's failure to provide a safe environment for these communities amounts to a comparable act of domestic terrorism committed by the state on its own people.

For Giroux, the explanation for the domestic violence enacted upon the citizenry emerges from his realization that "savage neoliberal polices" have created a situation whereby disenfranchised communities find "the state at war with them" (Giroux 2017: 104). Neo-liberalism's emphasis on decentralizing government departments, the privatization of public services, and its emphasis on trusting business to self-regulate directly undermines the mandate for state authorities such as the EPA to monitor environmental standards in the USA. Significantly, Giroux's description of the contemporary neo-liberal era of governmental policy stands in stark contrast to that of the 1970s in which the state promoted initiatives for improving environmental welfare standards and attempted to foster public awareness through the EPA by instituting projects such as *Documerica*. Reagan slashed environmental expenditure significantly upon coming into office, and, although funding has varied somewhat with successive neo-liberal administrations, it has remained significantly depressed when compared with the budgets of the 1970s' era (Barnett 1994: 51). Giroux makes an important observation when he identifies that the cuts, which have affected the state's capacity for environmental stewardship, are the result of ideological policies that have been intentionally put into practice. This can be seen in the ongoing situation in Cancer Alley, which often requires citizens to stay indoors when the air becomes noxious with chemicals, and it has created a situation whereby autonomous community activist groups have emerged as a means of resisting this tyranny.

One such group is the Louisiana Bucket Brigade (LABB), which encourages citizens to report incidents of water pollution so they can be mapped and viewed on its website. LABB also maintain a high level of visibility as a pressure group in the local media, and the group's campaigners act as advocates for remediation, both regionally and nationally. Moreover, LABB also conducts 'citizen science' by educating community members on the construction and use of homemade air quality testing devices, or 'buckets', in order to monitor air quality. Constructed from plastic containers, the buckets are sealed at the top with a rubber tube. Inside, a simple computer circuit helps to create a vacuum that draws air into the bucket, where it can be held in a plastic bag and laboratory tested. Examples of LABB conducting citizen science by providing bucket training are readily available on the group's Flickr photostream (LABB 2017a, 2017b).

In her publication *Refining Expertise: How Responsible Engineers Subvert Environmental Justice Challenges* (Ottinger 2012), the environmental commentator Gwen Ottinger relates at length a campaign led by LABB against a refinery owned by a company named Orion that was complicit in releasing toxic gases adjacent to the fence-line community of New Sarpy in Cancer Alley. As Ottinger explains, the combination of bucket readings and residents' testimonies created a powerful dossier of evidence that served to challenge the scientific studies conducted by the industrial producers, which failed to explain the cause of residents' respiratory illnesses. Ottinger observes that this type of DIY action can be considered as "a key theoretical justification for democratization—that science is never politically neutral and thus should not be given a privileged position in democratic decision making" (Ottinger 2013: 18). Although results from a bucket device do not provide measurements of the standard necessary for legal enforcement proceedings to be taken against a polluter, this collating of evidence is one method of challenging the narratives promulgated by the state industrial apparatus. Ottinger states that, "the policies of neoliberalism create a kind of market rule that undermines participatory democracy [...] and further disadvantages economically and socially marginal groups" (Ottinger 2013: 25). Yet, as Ottinger also acknowledges, the policies of neo-liberalism open up new opportunities for participatory democracy by shaping "the possibilities for collective action and social change" (Ottinger 2013: 25). In the context of Ottinger's remarks, it can be argued that the work of activist groups such as LABB shares much in common with a model of autonomous direct action referred to by Murray Bookchin in his eco-anarchist writings.

Bookchin's theories are referred to using the term social ecology, which is summarized in his assertion that, "The imbalances man has produced in the natural world are caused by the imbalances he has produced in the social world" (Bookchin 1986: 85). The core principle of social ecology is that ecological problems arise as a direct result of hierarchical structures of power and oppression that form the basis of the neo-liberal capitalist state. For this reason, social ecology asserts that the concept of the nation-state and its regimes of representative power should be abandoned (Biehl and Bookchin 1998: 4). In their place, Bookchin advocates a return to smaller eco-technological communities that are governed by municipal assemblies. At the core of Bookchin's concept of public assembly is a commitment to participatory democratic decision-making wherein power and governance are accessible to *all* political subjects (Bookchin 1997: 1). Importantly, Bookchin's commitment to community structures of self-governance arises out of an awareness that ecosystems cannot be understood "from a hierarchical viewpoint" (Bookchin 1991: 271) owing to the interdependency and interrelatedness of ecosystems. At the core of social ecology as a political project is a belief that social structures should effectively mirror the organizational principles of ecosystems. If Bennett argues vital materiality "is the rubric that tends to horizontalise the relations between humans, biota, and abiota" (Bennett 2010: 112), then Bookchin's concept of social ecology represents a political theory that proposes a restructuring of society on principles that also emphasize horizontal distributions of power in keeping with ecosystem sustainability.

As means of resisting, and ultimately overcoming, the hegemony of the capitalist state, Bookchin is typical of left-libertarians more generally in advocating the use of direct action as a revolutionary strategy that can be deployed in order to "assert the identity of the particular within the framework of the general" (Bookchin 1986: 23). In the face of propaganda from the media and state institutions, Bookchin argues that individual personalities have been largely "effaced" (Biehl and Bookchin 1998: 139) because personal identity is tethered to the demands of the capitalist economy. The implication is that individuals cannot imagine themselves as political actors in control of their own destiny but only as passive consumers of the status quo. Such an observation leads Bookchin to claim that, in a capitalist society, "there can be no fulfilled self" (Bookchin 1986: 67). In the face of such privations, Bookchin advocates a rediscovery of the self through the use of direct-action tactics. In the context of the ongoing struggle for remediation in Cancer Alley, LABB's use of the bucket for DIY testing is one method by which individuals can regain a sense of pride and belonging. Direct action therefore has the potential to alter subjectivity by transforming passive citizen-consumers into active democratic participants, and in turn this has the potential to bring about the conditions necessary for the revitalization of communities.

Kate Orff's *Ecological Atlas*

In the second section of *Petrochemical America*, the *Ecological Atlas*, Kate Orff's infographs display the mechanisms through which petrochemical production can lead to chronic illness in humans. Like activists working in the region such as LABB, Orff's infographs represent a challenge to the politicization of science by the industrial state apparatus. Take, for example, her *Requiem for a Bayou*. Here Orff's illustration reproduces Misrach's photograph of the same name, which appears in the opening section of the publication. The primary importance of Orff's contribution is that, on many occasions, she extends and augments Misrach's photographs by plotting what is referred to as 'throughlines' over the image (see Plate 18). This additional information details the ecosystem's organic interdependency as a metabolic food web within which humans are implicated. In her infograph, Orff extends Misrach's original photographic to a panoramic format with the addition of a computer-rendered forest to the left. As the image moves to the right, Misrach's view of the stricken swamp is overlaid with a list of inorganic pollutants entering the ecosystem from the oil industry. To the side of the infograph, a caption written by Orff provides further anchorage by describing how the dead Cypress trees and the lattice of canals and pipes are only the most visible signs of ecosystem distress—the real, insidious dangers come from pollutants such as PAH (polycyclic aromatic hydrocarbons) compounds which cannot be observed by the human eye but are known carcinogens. It is precisely because photography often cannot visualize pollutants within an ecosystem—but instead must be content to document the decline of an ecosystem as a whole—that it becomes necessary to supplement an indexical representation of the polluted topography with additional modal forms such as Orff's infographs.

The act of visualizing and articulating the complex environmental problems that are endemic to Cancer Alley is especially important when it comes to describing the privations suffered by the disenfranchised communities of the region. As Orff notes in the caption accompanying her infograph, humans, as apex predators in the ecosystem, ingest a variety of chemicals and metals that emanate from the petrochemical industry (Misrach and Orff 2014: 171). This accumulation of pollutants, which builds up over the course of a lifetime, is further exacerbated by the danger of inhaling a host of carcinogenic gases emanating from the petrochemical works, not to mention the threat posed by the inhalation of agricultural pesticides in the region. Given the endemic presence of various types of pollutant in Cancer Alley, it is significant when Orff comments that, if citizens fall ill from exposure to pollutants, "the burden of [legal] proof lies with those whom the chemicals affect" (Misrach and Orff 2014: 145). Very often, the attribution of blame to a particular party is something that may be suspected but cannot be easily proven in a court of law. As a result, many Louisianans suffer debilitating illnesses or even premature death, leaving their families with no means of redress. This is precisely why Giroux's justification for his claim that the US government is enacting a form of "domestic terrorism" (Giroux 2017: 104) upon its citizens is so apt in this scenario.

Taking a closer look at Orff's throughlines, it is possible to interpret the combination of abiotic and biotic elements, which are integrated in the ecosystem's feedback loops through a series of dotted lines, as a horizontally distributed interpretation of scientific research. Viewed from this perspective, Orff's mark-making is reminiscent of Murray Bookchin's observation that social ecology as a political philosophy advocates a horizontalized and non-hierarchical distribution of power within social structures, which is in keeping with how ecosystems function and operate (Bookchin 1991: 271). Arguably, Orff's ecological illustrations can be considered as an aesthetic representation of social ecology's predominant ethical values, which are imbued in the materiality of the art object itself. If Orff's inclusion of the infographs in *Petrochemical America* provides the publication with political intentionality, then it is also important to consider to what extent the publication as a printed artefact can be considered as an active political agent within culture. One method of assessing the publication's potential for enacting praxis is to borrow Bennett's notion of the 'vital materiality' of non-human actants, which is outlined in her publication *Vibrant Matter* (2010). Orff's illustrations provide a means of understanding Bennett's argument for the potential of any object, whether it be animate or inanimate, to influence politics and therefore the formation of culture. Bennett asserts that an actant, as "neither an object or a subject but an 'intervener'" (Bennett 2010: 9) in the social sphere, can potentially take the form of an animal, an artefact, a commodity (e.g. a photobook), or even a substance, such as the PAH compounds listed in Orff's illustration.

At the heart of Bennett's insight is the realization that, although an actant such as a book or a chemical may not possess intelligence, or even life, this does not mean to say that it cannot exert a profound influence upon culture. In Orff's illustration, carcinogenic actants are seen to enter the food chain through the pursuit of traditional activities such as fishing and hunting. Applying Bennett's notion of the 'vital materiality', it becomes possible to understand that such abiotic actants can exert agency upon the community (or culture) in any number of ways. Most obviously, this may be by impacting upon the well-being of individual human lives as pollutants enter into the food web and then into the body. In turn, the proliferation of abiotic actants on the local population may increase the burden facing health services. Understood from a broader socio-economic perspective, it is also possible to see that these actants have the potential to influence markets by affecting real estate prices in the region (if the area acquires a reputation for ill-health), which in turn could also contribute to a decline in educational standards in local schools—and so it goes on. In this respect, it is reasonable to consider that abiotic actants have the potential to exert a profound influence upon communities by contributing to a decline in the quality of life for those citizens who are conjoined in ecosystems with them.

Bennett also outlines how individual actants can work in conjunction with each other by forming what she terms an assemblage, which is capable of acting in a collective unconscious manner, often with chaotic and unpredictable results (Bennett 2010: 24). Bennett's concept of the assemblage is especially useful for an understanding of the unpredictable nature of inorganic pollutants, which upon release into an ecosystem can combine with other (in) organic compounds to create a toxic soup that has no natural precedent and is impossible to simulate in the laboratory. Returning to Orff's observation that residents of Cancer Alley often cannot make a binding legal case capable of implicating an industrial polluter (Misrach and Orff 2014: 145), it is possible to use Bennett's notion of the assemblage to understand that, from a legal perspective, the attribution of blame is difficult to ascribe. Pollution is insidious: ingested pollutants that have combined with other compounds in the ecosystem, before being transferred into the food web, may emerge as a form of cancer in individuals decades later, with no indications as to who was responsible for the release of the pollutants in the first instance. For this reason, the dumping of harmful pollutants into the environment is a crime that goes largely unpunished.

Bennett's philosophy of vital materialism is the belief that politics and our normative concept of what constitutes 'the public' are largely insensitive to the affects and effects that non-human actants can exert upon culture. By taking a broader perspective and thinking about the potential agency of non-human entities, it becomes possible "to *experience* the relationship between persons and other materialities more horizontally, [which] is to take a step toward a more ecological sensibility" (Bennett 2010: 10). Here Bennett argues that a consideration of the emergent properties of how actants and assemblages can affect culture has the potential to bring about a greater empathic awareness concerning the integral role that humans play as actors within ecosystems. As an alternative to the status quo, Bennett argues that thinking from a vital materialist perspective encourages the need for alternative environmental protocols when it comes to identifying habits of consumption and waste management. In the case of Cancer Alley, the present epoch's cultural dependence upon petrochemical products must therefore be called into question, and with it the need for such a concentration of refineries within the Mississippi Delta region.

Taking into consideration *Petrochemical America* as a singular object, Misrach and Orff's contributions can be considered as a multimodal assembly of aesthetic modes that are all the more powerful because they have been brought together within the confines of the publication. In the variety of Orff's infographs alone, which cover diverse subjects such as consumerism, slavery and historic disenfranchisement of people in the region, the economy of food production, the threat to traditional industries such as fishing, and the role that petrochemicals play in the contemporary home, *Petrochemical America* does not attempt to privilege one narrative strand over another. Instead, the reader is presented with a broad swathe of environmental and socio-economic issues affecting Cancer Alley, without being offered an easy solution for these entrenched problems. Rather like the efforts of citizen science activists who want to demystify science as a discipline of enquiry exclusively carried out by state agencies, *Petrochemical America* is a publication that aspires to the democratization of knowledge through the communication of complex ecological and socio-economic problems that are simplified by the process of visualization. The publication does so from a non-hierarchical standpoint, but this is not to say that *Petrochemical America* is not without problems that have great significance for those interested in the potential of environmental photography to contribute to environmentalist struggles in the world at large.

The eco-anarchist potential of *Petrochemical America*

In the final section of the publication entitled *Glossary of Terms and Solutions for a Post-Petrochemical Culture*, Orff presents the case for radical change to the status quo in Louisiana. This is conveyed through a range of alphabetized glossary terms. In some instances, glossary entries are listed in order to help the reader with subject specific terminology, whereas, on other occasions, it guides the reader towards an understanding of environmental legislation. The glossary itself varies greatly in content: some entries list relatively modest initiatives such as buying vegetables from farm shops, not supermarkets, or advocating the purchase of eco-friendly household cleaning products. It is significant, however, that such relatively uncontroversial inclusions sit equally alongside politically cogent examples of direct action and community resistance. In her reading concerning the limitations of *Petrochemical America*, Gwen Ottinger (2012) singles out the glossary as a particular weakness of the publication when she comments that it does not distinguish between relatively minor and significant environmental solutions. Here, Ottinger makes an insightful point, because the format of the glossary necessarily aggregates information. Discussing the shortcomings of the glossary, Ottinger concludes that the failure of *Petrochemical America* to envision a post-petrochemical society is due to "an important omission from the main substance of the book: people" (Ottinger 2012). Ottinger's criticism therefore shifts from the shortcomings of the glossary as a mode of presentation to a lack of attention given to the privations suffered by the population as a whole: "Populations are represented by stick diagrams, not residents using their inhalers." As an alternative, Ottinger calls for documentary photographs that show "community members at refinery gates, or taking air samples under a raging flare [and] images of a joyful family reunion going on against the backdrop of an industrial facility"—all of which would engender a greater sense of empathy in the audience. It is striking to note that the very sorts of image Ottinger calls for are discernable in activist photostreams such as the example of LABB's Flickr account (LABB 2017b) but are absent from *Petrochemical America*.

In a recent retrospective entitled *Being(s) 1975–2015*, exhibited at the Fraenkel Gallery, San Francisco (2015a), the human presence is explored as a recurring theme throughout Misrach's artistic career. In a publicity video created for this exhibition, Misrach states that his long-standing approach to photographing people is not concerned with an exploration of individual human identity. Instead, the human figure appears as a diminutive presence in the landscape—'the stand-in'—for all of humanity (Misrach 2015b). Returning to Ottinger's criticism of *Petrochemical America* concerning the failure of the glossary, the inclusion of images that document individuals' dignity and lived experience in Cancer Alley would not be typical of the approach Misrach has taken to the documentation of people throughout the course of his career. Ottinger's criticisms are misplaced, however, in suggesting that the burden of community documentation should have fallen upon Misrach and Orff. Instead, the potential for *Petrochemical America* to articulate or embody the autonomous values of social ecology could have been substantially improved by giving the glossary over to the activists themselves. Such a tactical approach would have allowed members of the community an opportunity to autobiographically document their dignity and suffering in the face of what Giroux describes as "domestic terrorism" (Giroux 2017: 104).

In their argument for a tactical reappraisal of what constitutes politicized artistic practice, the multimedia artist Aaron Gach and the political geographer/photographer Trevor Paglen make a distinction between two different approaches when they employ a categorical distinction between "artworks which have an 'attitude' towards a given reality and works that inhabit a 'position'" (Gach and Paglen 2003: n.p.). The first distinction pertains to art that addresses political subject matter but does not engage directly with the politics of activism. According to Gach and Paglen's argument, works of this type evince an 'attitude' to political struggles but remain "situated outside the discourse or material conditions that [they are] intended to reflect comment upon" (Gach and Paglen 2003: n.p.). The example provided is art that is displayed in a location "secondary to its content" (Gach and Paglen 2003: n.p.)—

this might be in a metropolitan art gallery, in which both the audience and the geographical display of the work address a particular grievance remotely, but without direct recourse to those affected. Conversely, what Gach and Paglen identify as an engaged form of practice is one that takes up a 'position' with reference to a political struggle. This means that the artwork contributes directly to a groundswell of resistance, which is existent or emergent within that locality. To this end, Gach and Paglen assert that cultural producers have an obligation to situate their practice, and its subsequent dissemination, within "the context of political activist infrastructures" (Gach and Paglen 2003: n.p.). They comment that this can be done by "using various resources for building coalition and alliances, assisting activist groups with media production, or any number of approaches to creative problem solving" (Gach and Paglen 2003: n.p.) that would require the skills of an artist or a visual communications expert. Taking Gach and Paglen's argument into consideration, it is pertinent to consider what the use value of environmental photography is within the context of community resistance to the hegemony of industrial pollution.

Arguably, the failure of the glossary in *Petrochemical America* to overtly profile the ongoing activist struggles within the Mississippi Delta region represents a missed opportunity to extend Misrach and Orff's collaborative ethos further, thereby limiting the eco-anarchist potential of *Petrochemical America* significantly. This is not to say that *Petrochemical America* merely takes up an 'attitude' towards the environmental problems facing Cancer Alley, but it is to suggest that the potential of the photobook to amplify the struggles of eco-anarchist activist groups such as LABB is diminished by a refusal to enter into an extended form of collaboration with such groups. *Petrochemical America* does exert influence as an environmentalist actant within the broader social sphere; however, Gach and Paglen's tactical approach suggests that the publication's potential to alter the social imaginary in the Cancer Alley region could have been improved by full integration of the artwork into the struggles of autonomous community resistance groups active within the region. Doing so would have placed *Petrochemical America* in the heart of community relations in a way that is simply not possible otherwise. The inclusion of activist groups as co-authors could have created the conditions for a new-found sense of resistance in fenceline communities such as New Sarpy, which are among the most affected by petrochemical pollution. Indeed, there is no reason why Misrach and Orff's photographs and infographs should not occupy a prominent position within the community as educational tools in schools or community associations, as billboards or posters in shop windows, and as advocacy materials that can aid activists in their deliberations with representatives of the petrochemical industry or the state. As a result, although *Petrochemical America* remains a cogent example of the capacity for environmental photography to illustrate the problems of industrial pollution, the publication falls short in its capacity to inhabit a 'position' within a political reality in the manner that Gach and Paglen describe.

If environmental photography is to enjoy future prominence as a form of political art practice that can aid activists in their struggle against the threat of industrial pollution and resource depletion, then it is essential that artists move away from a model of dissemination based upon the notion of intellectual ownership. Certainly, *Petrochemical America* is a publication that redefines the possibilities of environmental photography as a tool for advocacy; this is in no small part owing to the quality of Orff's infographs, which advance the possibilities of environmental illustration significantly. However, because an art monograph is an expensive publication to own—it is undeniably a luxury product—and acquiring a copy is beyond the means of many citizens who live in the Cancer Alley region, it is important that political art is accessible to those in most need. Working in conjunction with activists, as Gach and Paglen propose, could not only have resulted in the creation of advocacy documents that had a direct use value for autonomous groups, it may also have bolstered support for activism within the communities of the region as well. Cultural producers who are committed to political praxis therefore have an obligation to share their intellectual property by making art accessible to all. In the case of *Petrochemical America*, this might have occurred by distributing digital files of infographs or photographs to activists for copyleft reproduction, while the artistic copyright remained with the authors in the form of the hardback monograph or exhibition-quality prints. By such means of collaboration with local activist networks, the eco-anarchist potential of *Petrochemical America* could have been realized to a much greater extent.

In conclusion, environmental photographers should remain mindful of the need to situate their artistic practice firmly on the side of activists and their struggles, as Eugene Smith did with *Minamata* (1975). As the twenty-first century progresses, it is inevitable that environmental politics will emerge as one of the key areas of contestation throughout the world. In the struggles that will ensue, environmental photography must not remain aloof. Instead, it must perform the role of *directly* confronting the environmental calamities that urgently require redress. It can do so by aiding emancipatory struggles that point the way towards new forms of social organization that are in keeping with the core libertarian values of environmentalism.

Note

1 *Petrochemical America* was originally published as a hardback first edition monograph in 2012 but was later reissued as a cheaper and more accessible paperback in 2014. It is this second edition that is referred to throughout.

References

Barnett, H. (1994) *Toxic Debts and the Superfund Dilemma*, Chapel Hill, NC: University of North Carolina Press.

BASF. (2018) *About BASF In Louisiana*, www.basf.com/us/en/company/about-us/Locations/featured-sites/Louisiana/about-louisiana.html [accessed June 17, 2018].

Bennett, J. (2010) *Vibrant Matter: A Political Ecology of Things*, Durham, NC: Duke University Press.

Biehl, J. and Bookchin, M. (1998) *The Politics of Social Ecology: Libertarian Municipalism*, Montreal, London: Black Rose Books.

Bookchin, M. (1986) *Post-Scarcity Anarchism*, 2nd edition, Quebec, Canada: Black Roses Books.

Bookchin, M. (1991) *The Ecology of Freedom: The Emergence and Dissolution of Hierarchy*, revised edition, Montreal: Black Rose Books.

Bookchin, M. (1997; 1993) "Deep Ecology, Anarchosyndicalism, and the Future of Anarchist Thought," in Bookchin, M. (ed.), *Deep Ecology and Anarchism: A Polemic*. London: Freedom Press, pp. 31–40.

Campbell, C. (2008) "Residual Landscapes and the Everyday: An Interview with Edward Burtynsky," *Space and Culture: International Journal of Social Space*, vol. 11 (1), pp. 39–50.

Carson, R. (1963) *Silent Spring*, London: Hamish Hamilton.

Commoner, B. (1973) *The Closing Circle: Confronting the Environmental Crisis*, 2nd edition, London: Jonathan Cape.

Earth Day Network. (2017) "The History of Earth Day" [Homepage of Earth Day Network], www.Earthday.Org/About/The-History-Of-Earth-Day/ [accessed June 5, 2017].

Ehrlich, P.R. (1968) *The Population Bomb*, New York: Ballantine Books.

Gach, A. and Paglen, T. (2003) "Tactics without Tears," *Centre for Tactical Magic* [Online],, www.tacticalmagic.org/CTM/thoughts/TacticsWithoutTears1.htm

Giblett, R.J. (2012) *Photography and Landscape*, Bristol, UK: Intellect Books.

Giroux, H.A. (2017) *America at War with Itself*, San Francisco: City Lights Books.

Hanson, D.T. (1997) *Waste Land: Meditations on a Ravaged Landscape*, New York: Aperture.
LABB. (2017a) "Louisiana Bucket Bridge: Flickr Photostream," www.Flickr.Com/Photos/Labucketbrigade/Albums [accessed April 28, 2017].
LABB. (2017b) "The Bucket," www.Labucketbrigade.Org/Content/Bucket [accessed April 28, 2017].
Meadows, D.H., Meadows, D.L., Randers, J., and Behrens III, W.W. (1972) *The Limits to Growth: A Report for the Club of Rome's Project on the Predicament of Mankind*, New York: Universe Books.
Misrach, R. (2015a) "Richard Misrach: Being(S) 1975–2015," *Fraenkel Gallery*, https://Fraenkelgallery.Com/Videos/Richard-Misrach-Beings-1975-2015 [accessed April 28, 2017].
Misrach, R. (2015b) "Richard Misrach: Being(s) 1975–2015," https://vimeo.com/127248223 [accessed July 7, 2017].
Misrach, R. and Misrach, M.W. (1990) *Bravo 20: The Bombing of the American West*, Baltimore: Johns Hopkins University Press.
Misrach, R. and Orff, K. (2014) *Petrochemical America*, 2nd edition, New York: Aperture.
Ottinger, G. (2012) "Petrochemical America, Petrochemical Addiction," *Southern Spaces*, https://Southernspaces.Org/2013/Petrochemical-America-Petrochemical-Addiction [accessed April 28, 2017].
Ottinger, G. (2013) *Refining Expertise: How Responsible Engineers Subvert Environmental Justice Challenges*, New York: New York University Press.
Parak, G. (ed.) (2013) "Eco-Images: Historical Views and Political Strategies," *RCC Perspectives*, (1), pp. 53–59 [Online]. www.environmentandsociety.org/perspectives/2013/1/eco-images-historical-views-and-political-strategies [accessed June 6, 2017].
Smith, W.E. and Smith, A.M. (1975) *Minamata*, New York: Holt, Rinehart, & Winston.
Sun, F. (2012) "Revisiting the South: Richard Misrach's Cancer Alley" [Homepage of *Time Magazine*, Online], June1, http://Lightbox.Time.Com/2012/06/01/Richard-Misrach/?Iid=Lb-Gal-Viewagn#3 [accessed June 10, 2012].
Swift, W.H., Touhill, C.J., Haney, W.A., Nakatani, R.E., Peterson, P.L., and Des Voigne, D.S. (1969) *Water Pollution Control Research Series: Review of Santa Barbara Channel Oil Pollution Incident*, 20. Richland, WA: U.S. Department of the Interior.
U.S. National Archives. (2017) "Documerica: The Environmental Protection Agency's Program to Photographically Document Subjects of Environmental Concern, 1972–1977" [Homepage of U.S. National Archives, Online], https://Catalog.Archives.Gov/Id/542493 [accessed June 6, 2017].

18

Counter-forensics and photography[1]

Thomas Keenan

From the instrumental to the operational image

Silently, and for just a few seconds, a pair of pale green images appear on a screen as a man in uniform inspects them. About half an hour into *The Forgotten Space* (2010), the epic film Allan Sekula made with Noël Burch about ocean-going commerce and container capitalism, the film turns abruptly from a panoramic aerial view of the Port of Los Angeles/Long Beach to the interior of an office and its screens at the port complex.[2] The sequence is designed to introduce the motif of the container as Pandora's Box and the scene from Robert Aldrich's *Kiss Me Deadly* (1955) to which Sekula and Burch return at the conclusion of the film. To get there, *The Forgotten Space* shows us some unusual images: not simply images of the port and its activities, but images produced by it as part of its everyday operations (see, for example, Figure 18.1).

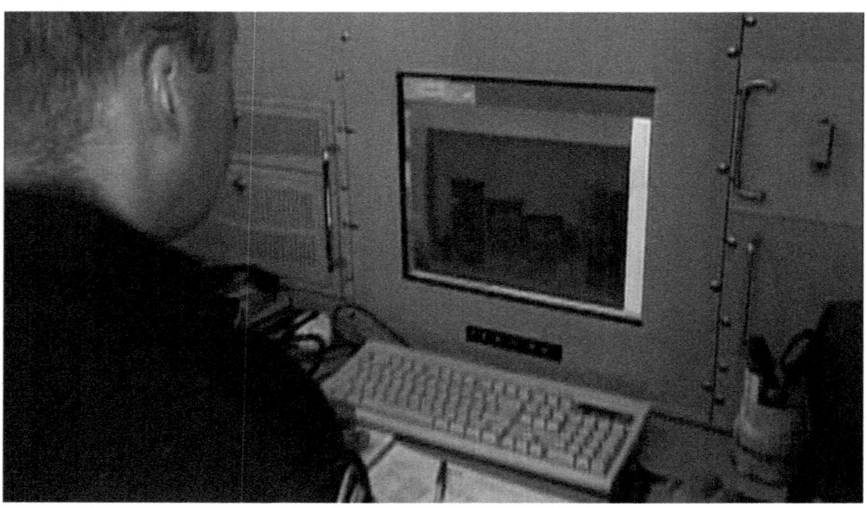

Figure 18.1 Allan Sekula and Noël Burch, directors, *The Forgotten Space* (2010). Video still

Within the scene are two short sequences that, from their texture, appear to come from stock footage. They show a US Customs and Border Protection (CBP) officer operating a cargo scanning system, part of what is called a "nonintrusive inspection" regime to examine the contents of containers passing through the port.[3] The scanner produces images that are analyzed by software algorithms designed to identify shapes and materials, detect suspect or anomalous objects, and then highlight these on a screen for a human operator.[4] The scene, thematized in the voiceover as a matter of "the American obsession with counter-terrorist security," shows a customs officer looking at such images, as well as the scanning device doing its work outside, and then two other officers opening up and entering a container.

With these sequences, Sekula and Burch show us, twice, the reading of an image or, more precisely, the mechanical reading of a technical image. They do not say that this is what the CBP officer is doing. In fact, they do not even mention in the voice-over that images are being produced or examined. Like the men in the scene, they are more interested, here, in getting into the container, opening the box.[5] But "scanning the can," as this procedure is apparently known, is for many reasons worth attending to. By starting with these images we can begin to appreciate Sekula's patient exploration of the relationship between photography, evidence, and humanism—and, with it, the politics of human rights.

What happens in these scenes of reading? In the first sequence, where the screen appears to show a wheeled vehicle inside a container, the operator examines the image and, in effect, queries it with the mouse, generating a second image of the same contents from the reverse side. Icons are lit up on the left side of the image. The wipe across the computer screen shows us that new information is being presented, and then the cursor hovers over one of the objects, lingering for a second until it begins to blink. The film leaves the monitor for a moment to show the actual scanner, which appears to be a gamma-ray imaging device called a mobile Vehicle and Cargo Inspection System, at work outside.[6] It then returns inside to the officer, now viewing on his screen the contents of another container, presumably, and another wipe, although not much can be said about it. The film shows, but does not pay a lot of attention to, these screen images.[7]

They are almost forgotten, these technical pictures. Together, the man and his machines read these images, which are nothing if not instrumental. *Instrumental image* and *mechanical reading* are terms drawn from Sekula's 1975 essay on Edward Steichen's work in the First World War as the commander of American aerial reconnaissance operations in France (Sekula 1984a). By exploring Sekula's reading of those photographs in "Steichen at War," we can begin to understand something about the pictures from the border.

The gamma-ray images are less images to be looked at than images to be used. Referring to a number of aerial images produced by the Photographic Section of the Air Service in the American Expeditionary Forces (he notes that 1.3 million images were made), Sekula insists that we attend to the ways in which "their meaning relates to the ways they have been used" (Sekula 1984a: 33).

These are images, he says, designed to make things happen, to record and display a situation so as to intervene in it (see Figure 18.2). "Simply put," he writes, "the problem was to decide what was there [on the battlefield] and to act on that decision before 'whatever it was' moved." The images are understood as evidence, then, but a special kind of evidence that aspires to be almost immediately operational: "The value of aerial photographs, as cues for military uses, depended on their ability to testify to a *present* state of affairs." The photographs bear witness to a particular, limited situation, recording it so as to enable operations in it. They are made to be actionable evidence, cues to be used, and they are linked in a network or a chain with a set of actors and agents that respond to them (Sekula 1984a: 34).[8]

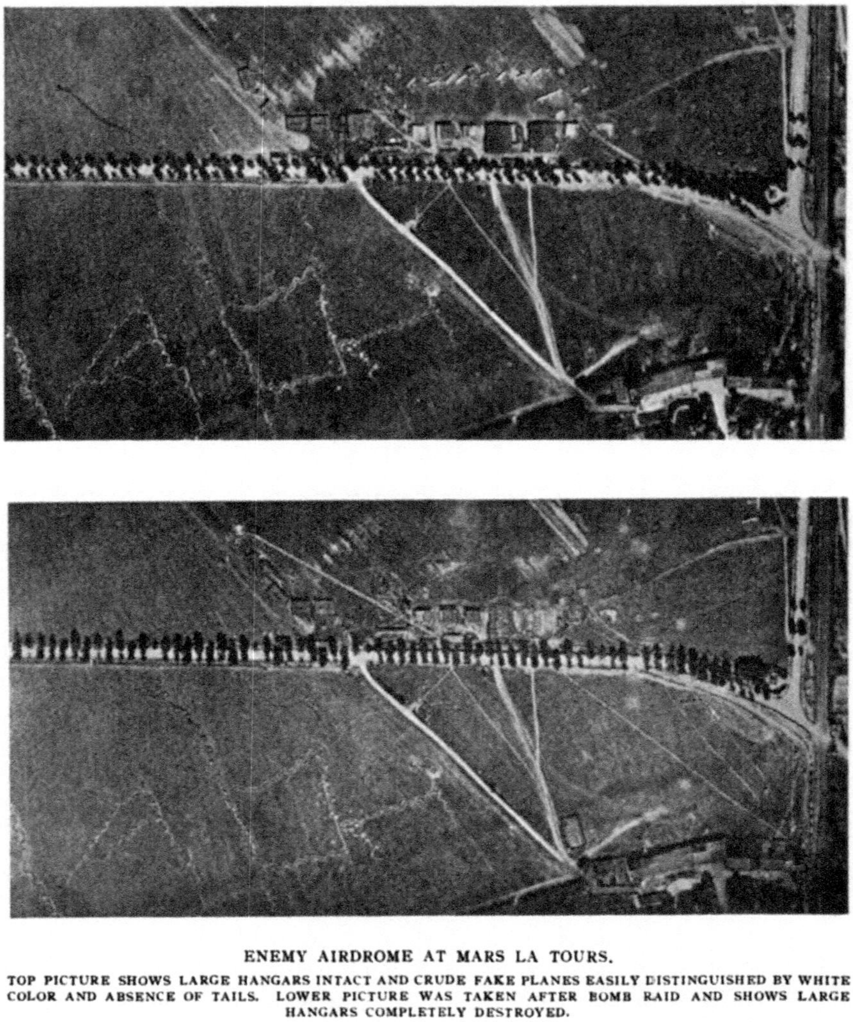

Figure 18.2 *Enemy Airdrome at Mars La Tours*. Illustration from Major Edward J. Steichen, A.S.A., "American Aerial Photography at the Front," *US Air Service* 1, no. 5 (June 1919)

In this sense, Sekula says, the images are produced and interpreted out of "fundamental tactical concerns," and as tactical media they function in conditions where the goal is to minimize the mediations of time and signification as radically as possible (Sekula 1984a: 35). They aim, that is, for a certain self-effacement, not so much to represent as to instruct, to effect, to enable a transformation in the reality they depict. Sekula writes,

> Few photographs, except perhaps medical ones, were as apparently free from "higher" meaning in the common usage. They seem to have been devoid of any rhetorical structure. But this poverty of meaning was conditional rather than immanent. Within the

> context of intelligence operations the only "rational" questions were those that addressed the photograph at the indexical level, such as: "Is that a machine gun or a stump?" In other words, the act of interpretation demanded that the photograph be treated as an ensemble of "univalent," or "indexical" signs, signs that could only carry one meaning, that could point to only one object. Efficiency demanded this illusory certainty.
>
> ... The systematic investigation of a landscape for traces of an enemy, coupled with the destruction of that enemy, was surely a mechanical process. ... "Reading," as it was ideally defined, consisted of a mechanical coding of the image.
>
> *(Sekula 1984a: 35–36)*

Sekula is interested, then, in how the utility, the instrumentality, the performativity of the image—under certain conditions and in certain contexts—can restructure it so radically as to void it, effectively, of rhetorical structure, not simply reduce it to its indexical origins but render it unequivocal and uniquely referential.

A process existed for doing that. Sekula describes the interpretive grid that was overlaid on the aerial images, translating them into operationally effective documents, guides for the destruction of the enemy. The grid includes both the codes of representation generated by a camera flying over a three-dimensional object (what does a farmhouse look like from overhead, or a person, or a machine gun, or a tree?) and a secondary set of codes that conventionalized the process of identification and allowed similar objects to be compared to one another ("a triangle stood for a dump, a circle with a central dot stood for a trench mortar"; Sekula 1984a: 35).

Sekula calls this decoding and recoding of the images, which had to be done as quickly as possible on a fluid and reactive battlefield, "mechanical." Efficiency not only demands certainty, however illusory it might be, but makes the illusions real by automating or mechanizing their processing. Reading, practiced as "a mechanical coding of the image," assumes and ratifies, realizes, this empiricist epistemology. For Sekula, photography consists of more than this, but the radical and originary instrumentalization of these images commands his attention.

Reading becomes mechanical coding. The ideal goal of such an interpretive machine would be to incorporate the "reading" of the image into the very technology that generates it in the first place, to produce images that arrive before the eye bearing their own translation into the terms required *for* intervention and then to link that directly to the means *of* intervention.

The Forgotten Space shows us something like this process in action. The images from the scanner in the film, like the aerial reconnaissance images from Steichen's unit, in effect seek to suspend the question of interpretation, to build it into the production of the image itself. The ideal mode of reading them would be not to have to read them at all.

All sorts of pragmatic obstacles stand in the way of achieving this goal—camouflage and deception; camera angles; shadows, blurs, and reflections; unexpected materials; and so on—but they are precisely practical ones, for which better technical solutions might be found.

The very structure of communication or signification itself must also be considered, though. No message can avoid being read, however apparently automatic the reading may be. In "On the Invention of Photographic Meaning," Sekula outlines this epistemological position; its escalating series of steps can be summarized by arranging quotations from the first five pages of the essay:

1. "All communication is, to a greater or lesser extent, tendentious; all messages are manifestations of interest."
2. "With this notion of tendentiousness in mind, we can speak of a message as an embodiment of an argument. In other words, we can speak of a rhetorical function."
3. "This ... implies, of course, that a photograph is an utterance of some sort, that it carries, or is, a message. However, the definition also implies that the photograph is an 'incomplete' *utterance*, a message that depends on some external matrix of conditions and presuppositions for its readability. That is, the meaning of any photographic message is necessarily context determined."
4. "Every photographic message is characterized by a tendentious rhetoric."
5. "[But] the photograph is seen as a re-presentation of nature itself, as an unmediated copy of the real world. The medium itself is considered transparent. The power of this folklore of pure denotation is considerable. It elevates the photograph to the legal status of document and testimonial" (Sekula 1984b: 1, 3, 5–6).

In his reading of the aerial images, Sekula marks the fact that the rhetorical structure is irreducible—and that the photograph is not really an unmediated copy of the world—with qualifying phrases such as "*apparently* free from 'higher' meaning" and "*seem* to have been devoid of any rhetorical structure." But he is not interested in simply proving that the instrumental/mechanical approach is "illusory," that the force of the indexical is not immanent, that everything is rhetorical or needs to be interpreted. On the contrary, here the tendentiousness, the argumentative force, of the image is not a secret, and so he is interested in the "conditions" that make it work, in how well it can be made to work, and in the consequences of that "conditional" workaround.

The conditions generate a particular rhetorical structure that, in fact, verges on transparency. The "folkloric" demediation is more or less accomplished in the battlefield situation, where the image re-presents elements of the real world successfully enough to allow their targeting and destruction. And, in its machinery, its mechanical reading, it tends toward a system in which the loop between production, interpretation, and reaction can be further and further reduced and closed, to a point where the image would no longer require reading in anything like the sense we currently mean.

Today, all sorts of images are at work that do not require human eyes to see them or to function. The examining officers in *The Forgotten Space* are mere accessories now. The images can operate on their own. For instance, here are some examples from spaces of interest to Sekula:

- Robots assemble cars in automated factories using combinations of live camera feeds and object recognition software to ensure that the robot and the car move at the same speed and that each added part fits into the right space.[9]
- Cruise missiles fly to their targets using Global Positioning System data, as well as by comparing stored three-dimensional terrain maps of their flight path with real-time imagery as they fly over the territory depicted in the maps (the software is called Digital Scene-Mapping Area Correlation). Course corrections happen automatically, generated by the image correlation.[10]
- The International Space Station (ISS) and other orbital platforms are now regularly serviced by automated cargo vehicles. Although the docking could be remotely controlled from the ground, the berthing of the cargo craft is in fact done automatically, with the cargo ship being guided to the correct spot on the space station by cameras that capture

reflected laser light and respond to it by manipulating the thrusters on the arriving vehicle. Video documentation viewed and recorded by scientists on the ground shows what it looked like in June 2013 when the French Automated Transfer Vehicle 4, the "Albert Einstein," arrived at the ISS on its own (see Figure 18.3). The images are not simply from or of something flying; they are doing the flying.[11]

None of these images needs to be seen by human beings, however interesting they are to look at. They need no interpretation in order to work; or, rather, they include something like interpretation as part of the image-making process. They are about as purely instrumental as images can get, and to that they add a feedback loop—what happens in the image guides, produces, and creates effects in the world that is imaged. They are, as Harun Farocki would say, operative or "operational images," "images that do not try to represent reality but are part of a technical operation."[12]

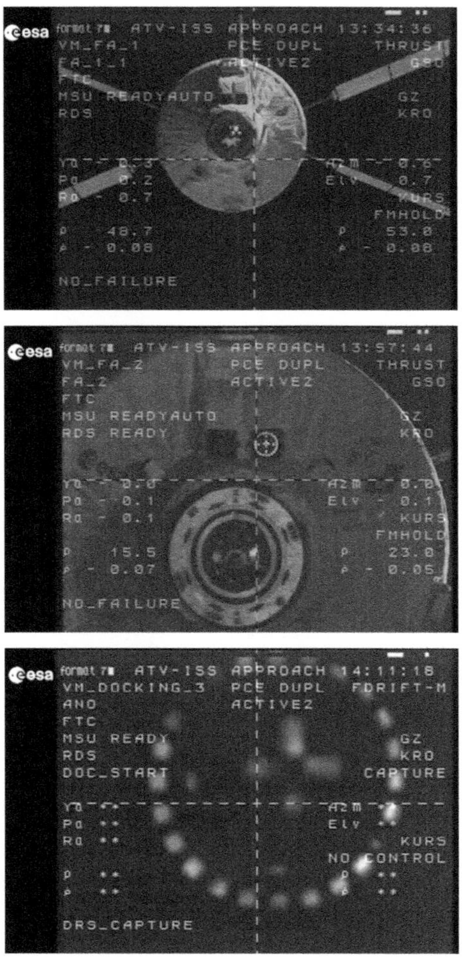

Figure 18.3 European Space Agency. *ATV-4 Docking to the International Space Station–Transmission Replay* (June 15, 2013). Video stills

A direct line extends from Steichen's unit's aerial imagery and its "mechanical" reading—Sekula had needed to put the word *mechanical* in quotation marks—to the algorithmic analysis of the gamma-ray images in *The Forgotten Space* and on to the image-based guidance systems that make spacecraft dock and missiles impact.[13] The questions remain the same: who or what is there, is it a target, and where is it? The tools for answering them have simply become more powerful and faster.

Contemporary intelligence analysts practicing what is known as "activity-based intelligence" work with vast geo-referenced databases of information collected, interpreted, and stored virtually automatically. Leticia Long, then director of US National Geospatial-Intelligence Agency, described the practice in a 2014 article:

> ABI systems must have the sensors and algorithms—preferably on the sensor suite itself—that processes the data, detects anomalies, and alerts the analysts. The automated tools must identify and integrate patterns of activity from multiple sources so we can establish "watch boxes" with persistent, broad area collectors ... that can stare at an area as often as needed or track objects continuously.
>
> *(Long 2013: 11)*

"Algorithms ... on the sensor suite itself" means that the gap between the production of the image and its interpretation has been reduced effectively to nothing. The camera/sensor that acquires the image also processes it, which can involve not only identifying and locating objects in it but linking those objects to all sorts of other data, and even prompting the action that intervenes in the space pictured.

As Trevor Paglen has pointed out, it is only by an accident or a sort of courtesy that humans can see the vast majority of images produced today: "What's truly revolutionary about the advent of digital images is the fact that they are fundamentally machine-readable: they can only be seen by humans in special circumstances and for short periods of time." From automated license-plate readers to face recognition, machines now produce images to be read by machines—to be taken, read, and acted upon. "Images," Paglen writes, "have begun to intervene in everyday life, their functions changing from representation and mediation, to activations, operations, and enforcement" (2016).[14]

Steichen knew this. Sekula quotes him mournfully realizing that, "the photographs we made provided information that, when conveyed to our artillery, enabled them to destroy their targets and kill. A state of depression remained with me for days." Sekula calls this "negatively-instrumental communication" and tracks Steichen's photographic conversion, as it were, to the "positively-instrumental"—namely, to "a humanist, life-affirming art" (Sekula 1984a: 48–49).

Sekula finds the inversion, which culminates in Steichen's exhibition *The Family of Man*, dubious in the extreme. If the technical or mechanical image can enable killing, the artistic and humanist image is not much of an escape; he writes, "'a global vision of life,' even in its 'humanist' and liberal manifestation, may serve to mask another vision, a vision of global domination" (Sekula 1984a: 51).

Readers of Sekula know that he uses few words with more implacable contempt, more corrosive criticality, than *liberal* and *humanist*.[15] Nevertheless, this masking operation seems to be not the only thing that a turn toward the human can do; it can also generate what Sekula, equally corrosively, calls "pity." From "liberal esthetics," he writes in "Dismantling Modernism, Reinventing Documentary," comes "compassion rather than collective struggle. Pity, mediated by an appreciation of 'great art,' supplants political understanding" (Sekula 1978: 875).

What would a properly political understanding, even a global one, look like in relation to photography? What else is possible? Are there other tactical operations with images, ones that can do something besides destruction while resisting the masking of domination, on the one hand, and the compensations of compassion on the other?

From evidentiary promise to counter-forensics

I think the answer from Sekula is a qualified yes. His argument turns on a notion of witness or testimony that recurs, without being underlined, in a number of his writings on photography. We have already seen it in statements such as, "The value of aerial photographs as cues for military uses, depended on their ability to testify to a *present* state of affairs," and later in the claim that, "the power of this folklore of pure denotation is considerable. It elevates the photograph to the legal status of document and testimonial."

Although Sekula is wary of the realist restriction of photography to testimonial status, he is, as we have seen, also interested in how and when this cueing happens. In "The Body and the Archive," he notes that, from the beginning of Henry Fox Talbot's explorations with the calotype, the "evidentiary promise" of the image was prominent (Sekula 1986: 6). And in "Dismantling Modernism, Reinventing Documentary," he begins his consideration of new documentary modes by reminding us of the necessity of "expos[ing] the myth" of documentary and underlining what he again calls "the *folklore* of photographic truth." But he does this in order to return to a reinvented form of documentary.

What is the myth? "The rhetorical strength of documentary is imagined to reside in the unequivocal character of the camera's evidence, in an essential realism" (Sekula 1978: 862). And why is this not correct but rather mythic, folkloric, imaginary? The point is not that the camera does not record what it sees, that the camera lies. As Sekula told Debra Risberg, "the old myth that photographs tell the truth has been replaced by the new myth that they lie" (Sekula, in Risberg 1999: 23).

Neither is correct. Sekula's argument is more complicated than the mere exposure of the myth that so often simply inverts an allegiance to the indexical truth into its opposite. He argues that we need to understand the evidence provided by the photograph not in terms of its relation to the reality it presents, as if the photograph offered a proof that was not only indexical but decisive or definitive. Rather, photographic evidence must be considered in terms of the forum or the debate into which its testimony is entered, what he calls in his Steichen essay its "conditions" and what he calls in "Dismantling Modernism" its "presentational circumstances."

Without saying so explicitly, Sekula turns to the surveillance camera images of Patricia Hearst, caught by the automated gaze in the midst of a bank robbery with her Symbionese Liberation Army captors-turned-colleagues, and to the fate of those images in a courtroom (see Figure 18.4). He is again talking about mechanical, technical images, and how they are to be read:

> I shouldn't have to argue that photographic meaning is relatively indeterminate; the same picture can convey a variety of messages under differing presentational circumstances. Consider the evidence offered by bank holdup cameras. Taken automatically, these pictures could be said to be unpolluted by sensibility, an extreme form of documentary. If the surveillance engineers who developed these cameras have an esthetic, it's one of raw, technological instrumentality. "Just the facts, ma'am." But a courtroom is a battleground of fictions. What is it that a photograph points to? A young white

> woman holds a submachine gun. The gun is handled confidently, aggressively. The gun is almost dropped out of fear. A fugitive heiress. A kidnap victim. An urban guerrilla. A willing participant. A case of brainwashing. A case of rebellion. A case of schizophrenia. The outcome, based on the "true" reading of the evidence, is a function less of "objectivity" than of political maneuvering.
>
> The only "objective" truth that photographs offer is the assertion that somebody or some thing—in this case, an automated camera—was somewhere and took a picture. Everything else, everything beyond the imprinting of a trace, is up for grabs.
>
> *(Sekula 1978: 863)*

Sekula's argument is nominalist in the extreme—evidence is that which is presented to the eye, that which is made evident in the image or in the trace. The "imprinting" of the trace decides nothing, settles nothing, determines nothing, forces no conclusions. Conclusions, decisions, happen in an altogether different realm and depend on "differing presentational circumstances" and conditions of use. This "indeterminacy" of meaning does not hold in spite of the indexicality of the image but because of it: Because there is a trace, an imprint, there is the possibility of interpretation, the opportunity for meaning, fiction, and hence the "battleground of fictions." Because there is a trace, there is a battle. Sekula demonstrates this with his rapid-fire rehearsal of some of the positions in the argument, competing ways of reading even the documentary image. Around the image, a debate can begin—we decide what it says; it does not, it cannot. This is what the word *evidence* means:

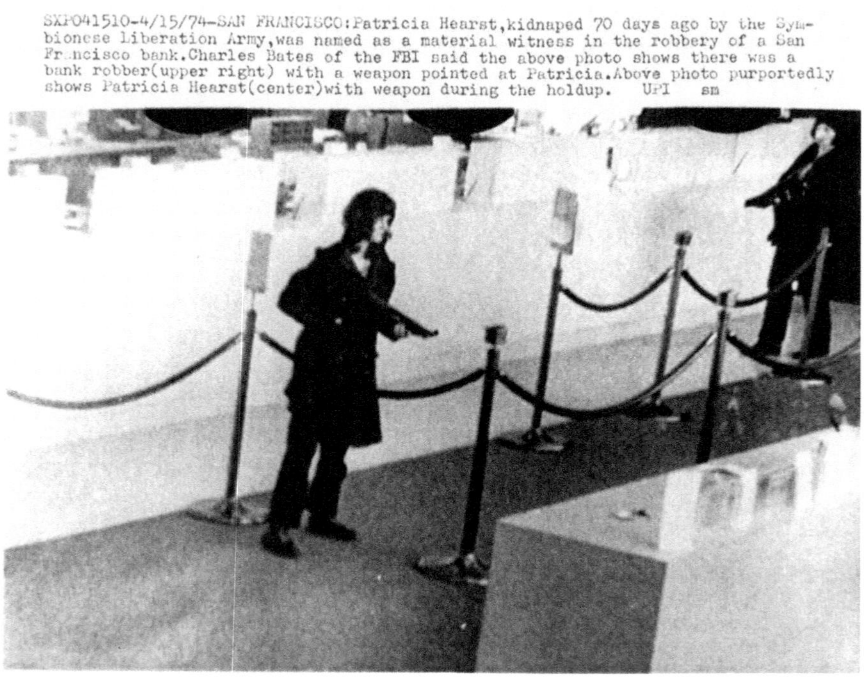

Figure 18.4 Security camera image showing Patricia Hearst during the robbery of Hibernia Bank, San Francisco (April 15, 1974). Federal Bureau of Investigation press release image

"everything beyond the imprinting of a trace, is up for grabs." The reading of the evidence, which is the only thing one can do with evidence as it does not speak for itself (this holds even with nonmute evidence, such as testimony in a courtroom), will always be a matter of "political maneuvering." That is what "up for grabs" means. The interpretive grid created by Steichen's unit, or a contemporary analytic algorithm, would represent an extreme form of such maneuvering.

Sekula presents this claim about indexicality, realism, indeterminacy, and the "up for grabs" as a challenge, a provocation, a charge, a demand for responsibility. This at least is how I understand his interpretation of the anti-apartheid photographs of Ernest Cole as a testimony of their own:

> The example of Cole's work suggests that we would be wise to avoid an overly monolithic conception of realism. Not all realisms necessarily play into the hands of the police, despite Theodor Adorno's remark, designed to lampoon a Leninist epistemology once and for all, that "knowledge has not, like the state police, a rogues' gallery of its objects." If we are to listen to, and act in solidarity with, the polyphonic testimony of the oppressed and exploited, we should recognize that some of this testimony, like Cole's, will take the ambiguous form of visual documents, documents of the "microphysics" of barbarism. These documents can easily fall into the hands of the police or their intellectual apologists. Our problem, as artists and intellectuals living near but not at the center of a global system of power, will be to help prevent the cancellation of that testimony by more authoritative and official texts.
>
> *(Sekula 1986: 64)*

We could call this persistent commitment to evidence, testimony, and the document—and to the necessity of making arguments, in courts and elsewhere—a "forensic" sensibility. Forensic in the sense of a commitment to ambiguity, polyphony, and, hence, to the forum and to the interpretive dispute—and its resolution, however provisional—that must follow from the trace and its "relative indeterminacy." Forensics is not simply about science in the service of law or the police but is, much more broadly, about objects as they become evidence, things submitted for interpretation in an effort to persuade. The word is derived from the Latin *forensis*, which refers to the "forum" and the practice and skill of making an argument before a professional, political, or legal gathering (Keenan and Weizman 2012: 28). Perhaps, in honor of the oppositional and critical politics of someone like Cole, we ought to call this sort of practice "counter-forensics."

I owe this unusual formulation, *counter-forensics*, to Sekula, a master of the neologistic inversion. A few years ago, Carles Guerra and I latched onto his beautiful word *anti-photojournalism*, from *Waiting for Tear Gas* (1999–2000), but it is only one in a long list of such contrarian maneuvers, perhaps oppositional or dialectical or perhaps something else (Sekula 2003: 87). Others include the "counter-image" and the "counter-display" and the "counter-sites" he examines in *Fish Story*; the practices of "counter-testimony and counter-surveillance" he explores toward the end of "The Body and the Archive"; and, most richly, the "counter-reenactment" represented by the "anti-*Titanic*" voyage of *The Global Mariner* he so admires in "Between the Net and the Deep Blue Sea."[16]

Counter-forensics is almost surely a notion of Sekula's invention, although, since he first published it in 1993, it has become a term of art for something else.

Today, if *forensics*—in common parlance—refers both to the scientific investigation of physical and digital objects (including documents and photographs, as well bodies, bones, bombs, bullets, and buildings) and to the presentation of those objects as evidence in legal proceedings, then *counter-forensics* refers to all sorts of efforts designed to frustrate or prevent in advance the analysis of those objects. When one suspects one might be, in the course of doing something, leaving behind traces that would allow a forensic anthropologist or archivist or accountant to reconstruct, at a later time, what one had been doing, one might want to take precautions, or even active countermeasures, to preemptively impede that future production of evidence. Those efforts belong to what is today professionally called counter-forensics.[17]

Although Sekula might have been sympathetic to some of these efforts—he did often take the side of the oppressed, the protester, the dissident, the rebel, against the forces of the police, the military, or the corporation—the professional meaning of counter-forensics is not at all what he meant by the term. Sekula meant something almost exactly the opposite. With the term, he refers to nothing less than the adoption of forensic techniques as a practice of "political maneuvering," as a tactical operation in a collective struggle, a rogues' gallery to document the microphysics of barbarism. He uses the term in a short essay on the photographer Susan Meiselas and her work in and on Kurdistan in the aftermath of the first Gulf War in the early 1990s. The essay, called "Photography and the Limits of National Identity," was published in 1993 and updated in 2006.[18]

Sekula makes a compressed, complex argument. Photography has often served as an instrument of "surveillance and cataloguing." This is particularly so in the case of the Kurds, whom Sekula calls "a people defined from without by multiple oppressors and scientists and adventurers: Ottoman Turks and Persians and Europeans in the nineteenth century, Turks, Iraqis and Iranians in the present period, with periodic bursts of 'Western' journalistic intervention" (Sekula 1993: 54–55). In Kurdistan, the administrative uses to which photography could be turned went hand in hand with "torture and extermination." Both surveillance and cataloguing, as Sekula argues about the "new juridical photographic realism" of the Paris police official Alphonse Bertillon in "The Body and the Archive," depend on a process of individuation and identification. Bertillon, he argues, "invented the first effective modern system of criminal identification," a process that aimed to link the "metrical accuracy of the camera … a medium from which exact mathematical data could be extracted" with "a bureaucratic-clerical-statistical system … [whose] central artifact [is] … the filing cabinet," in order to produce nothing less than "proof of identity" (Sekula 1986: 5, 16–18, 25).

In that sense, Sekula writes about Kurdistan, "forensic methods (detective methods focusing on evidence and the body) offer a tool for oppressive states." But, he somewhat unexpectedly continues, "forensic methods have also become tools of opposition." To demonstrate this, he produces a simple and apparently symmetrical diagram, which he refers to as a "sequence of actions: Identification–Annihilation–Identification" (Sekula 1993: 55).

The association of the first two terms is already hinted at in "The Body and the Archive," where Sekula proposes a sort of correction to what he sees as Michel Foucault's overly strong distinction between disciplinary and repressive power, writing that:

> we need to understand those modes of instrumental realism that do in fact operate according to a very explicit deterrent or repressive logic. These modes constitute the lower limit or "zero degree" of socially instrumental realism. Criminal identification photographs are a case in point, since they are designed quite literally to facilitate the arrest of their referent.
>
> *(Sekula 1986: 7)*

Then, returning us silently to Steichen and the "negatively-instrumental" aerial imagery, he adds in a footnote, "Any photographs that seek to identify a target, such as military reconnaissance photographs, operate according to the same general logic" (Sekula 1986: 7 n.7).

Sekula sees this process of identification, and especially the kind of identification in which photography is a basic element, as the essential accomplice to or even the instrument of ultimately genocidal operations:

> The oppressor state catalogues its victims as precisely as possible, typing them as a group, but seeking to register and track individual members. The key to ideological power over the "other" lies in typing; the key to functional power lies in individuation. In other words, stereotypes are ideologically useful and necessary, but in the end it is individuals who must be reduced to ashes.
>
> *(Sekula 1993: 55)*

However, documentary and identificatory practices have another side or another potential. We would be wise to avoid an overly monolithic conception of indivuation as well, it seems. Sekula hints at this, somewhat dismissively, toward the end of his discussion of Bertillon, when he refers to a "curious aspect of Bertillon's reputation"—namely that his method "could be regarded as a triumph of humanism." Bertillon, he says, "contributed to this 'humane' reading of his project: 'Is it not at bottom a problem of this sort that forms the basis of the everlasting popular melodrama about lost, exchanged, and recovered children?'" (Sekula 1986: 34)

Although Sekula then drops this line of reasoning in the "Body and the Archive," the problem of the missing—whether children or political prisoners or simply enemies—returns in his reading of Meiselas's photographs from Kurdistan. They, and the forensic effort they chronicle and assist in, differ both from the state's surveillance archive and from the melodramatic canon (see Plate 19). What is missing in Kurdistan is not this or that child who can become the object of pity or compassion, but something more radical: the missing are the objects of a systematic political campaign of extermination. A people has been targeted for disappearance, he says, but the project has left its traces and can be challenged:

> Counter forensics, the exhumation and identification of the anonymised ("disappeared") bodies of the oppressor state's victims becomes the key to a process of political resistance and mourning. The work of the American forensic anthropologist Clyde Snow, first in Argentina, with the victims and survivors of the "dirty war," then in El Salvador, at the massacre site of El Mozote, and then again with the remains of the Iraqi campaign of extermination of the Kurds, has provided the technical basis for this project. In Argentina, this work combines with that of psychoanalysts in the study and therapy of the interrupted work of mourning in the psyches of those who suffer from the indeterminacy of the "disappearance" of their loved ones. These are dismal sciences, but fundamental in their basic humanism, a humanism of mournful re-individuation, laying the groundwork for a collective memory of suffering.
>
> *(Sekula 1993: 55)*

And so the sequence "identification–annihilation–identification" turns out to be not exactly symmetrical. Just as the forensics is different when linked to a process of political resistance to oppression, so is the identification. Assigning names and histories after the event of annihilation is something very different from fixing identities before it. Knowledge needs this rogues' gallery of bones and images, memories and traces, when the aim of the genocidal assault is to erase not just people, but also their history and their rightful claim to share the Earth with others.

Likewise, who is doing the killing and who the identifying makes a difference. Typically, the state has a monopoly both on killing and on identifying, but in some cases the practice of identification is done by others, in order to learn about those killed by the state. Snow once remarked,

> of all the forms of murder, none is more monstrous than that committed by a state against its own citizens. And of all murder victims, those of the state are the most helpless and vulnerable since the very entity to which they have entrusted their lives and safety becomes their killer.
>
> *(Snow, cited in Joyce and Stover 1991: 217)*[19]

The history of human rights forensics is marked by this asymmetrical reversal of state policing techniques into tactics for resisting and challenging injustice.

And that implies that the humanism at work here is different as well. The "humanism of mournful re-individuation" that restores names and identities to the disappeared is nothing like "the celebration of abstract humanity" Sekula had denounced earlier, the one that, "in any given political situation," simply amounts to "the celebration of the dignity of the passive victim" (Sekula 1984b: 21),[20] for Sekula, Snow, and Meiselas in Kurdistan practice a different humanism:

> It is here, at the "individual" and forensic level, that the project of building a usable archive of the Kurdish "nation" begins. Without recognition of this level, all assertions of national identity are just that, mere assertions, liable to become dangerous fictions. The individual and mass graves and intimate grief must never become sepulchral excuses for abstract monuments. And it is precisely in this sense that photography's incapacity for abstraction is valuable.
>
> *(Sekula 1993: 55)*

Photography, then (and this is what Meiselas's Kurdistan projects attempted to do), can join the dismal science of mass-grave exhumation in the project of recording and recovering the traces of the disappeared, of re-individuation. Their humanism is neither the merely sentimental and compassionate kind nor a mask of domination, but a *basic* one, basic precisely to the extent that it refers not to abstract metaphysical foundations but rather to the traces of specific individuals and events, the testimony of the bones and the images.

Counter-forensics, whether Snow's or Meiselas's, produces evidence, documents individual and specific things, names names, and attaches names to bodies. Both practices do this as part of a political struggle—not because the images and the bones are self-evident but because they are not. They operate like the police, but differently. Identification can assist annihilation, and it can resist it. "Not all realisms necessarily play into the hands of the police," Sekula said about Cole. As in Cole's South Africa, "some of this testimony … will take the ambiguous form of visual documents, documents of the 'microphysics' of barbarism." As traces, precisely, the images and the bones are up for grabs, and I think Sekula sees in this counter-forensic presentation one more effort to confront and block the monopolization of testimony and narrative by the authorities, and with it the second silencing of the dead. Meiselas herself remarked on the convergence between Snow's forensic work and her own photographic practice in Kurdish Northern Iraq:

> Forensics is very meticulous work. It paralleled where I was at the time. I was ready for that type of careful examination and I became absorbed in the minutiae of the process —how to track the bones, what the bones tell us.[21]

So, photography, thanks to its trace-structure, its "incapacity for abstraction," takes a paradoxical but necessary turn in the direction of another abstraction, that of humanism, but this time rethought and repracticed as political struggle, as human rights advocacy. Sekula underlines the fact that this turn does not happen automatically, either for the forensic anthropologist or the counter-forensic photographer:

> [Meiselas begins] with the sense that where bodies are buried in secret there must also be a buried archive, limited in scope but immense nonetheless, waiting for resurrection. An archive, but not an atlas: the point here is not to take the world upon one's shoulders, but to crouch down to the earth, and dig.
>
> *(Sekula, in Lubben 2008: 344)*

To dig is to climb into the grave with the dead, to share a space with them, and to confront the fact of their death, not in order to undo what has happened (which cannot be done) but to transform their silence and disappearance into names, stories, and claims. Listening to, and allowing others to hear, "what the bones tell us" is a practice with no guarantees. Forensics and photography both traffic in "the ambiguous form of visual documents," documents that are up for grabs in law and politics. But they have important things to say, and Sekula's work itself bears witness to the ongoing struggle "to help prevent the cancellation of that testimony by more authoritative and official texts." In the age of the algorithmic image, that counter-forensic struggle—which encompasses both images themselves and the circumstances of their presentation—is more urgent than ever.

Notes

1 An earlier version of this article was published as "Counter-forensics and Photography," *Grey Room* 55 (Spring 2014), 58–77. © 2014 by Grey Room, Inc. and the Massachusetts Institute of Technology, reprinted by permission of the MIT Press.
2 Allan Sekula and Noël Burch, dir., *The Forgotten Space* (2010; Brooklyn: Icarus Films, 2012), DVD.
3 See Cross (2006) and Rundle (2009).
4 On the automated image analysis of cargo containers, see, for example, Chalmers (2007) and Orphan et al. (n.d.).
5 In a helpful reading of this paper, Ben Young (co-editor, with Marie Muracciole, of the special issue of *Grey Room* 55 (Spring 2014): "Allan Sekula and the Traffic in Photographs") suggested that Sekula and Burch are less interested in the scanning technologies and the contents of the containers (the operational or technical dimensions of the process) than in the "political theater" of the scanners, "the image or idea or wish for functional security." This is certainly the case for the film.
6 The VACIS system installed at the Port of Los Angeles is explained in Orphan et al. (2005).
7 Writing in *Wired* in 2002, Steven Johnson described his surprise at the automated detection algorithms in a similar device as he watched the image of a car being scanned for radiation: "I'm so transfixed by the shot of the Mercedes, I don't notice the rainbow stripe that appears beneath the outline of the trunk, shifting from green to bright red as the scan continues. 'It's already detected the radiation,' Callerame says. 'Green indicates something's there, red is more serious. Even this very small source reveals a potential danger. And you can see that the source is localized to the back of the vehicle'" (Johnson (2002): n.p.). For a good description of the algorithmic identification process, see: Westminster International (2011). This product brochure describes "a real time

threat identification operator alert software package that automatically screens for potential explosives and other threats by utilising advanced material classification and atomic density analysis by drawing a coloured ellipse around the area of suspicion."

8 A vast literature explores the role of images, especially photographic ones, as evidence in legal and political cases. An exemplary visual introduction is Phillips et al. (1997). Piyel Haldar argues that, in evidential practice, "in order to acquire meaning, ... images have to be torn apart and rendered unstable. Or, put differently, a form of iconoclasm is enacted under evidential examination according to which images are defaced and destroyed in a manner that seems to contradict the judicial faith in images" (2008: 140). Jennifer L. Mnookin shows that, as photography entered the domain of the law and established itself there in the nineteenth century, "the meaning and epistemological status of the photograph were intensely contested, both inside and outside the courtroom" and, even more important, that "the judicial response to photographic evidence helped to bring about broader changes in both courtroom practice and the conceptualization of evidence" (1998: 6). Thomas Thurston (n.d.) has authored a valuable online resource about the early history of this question. More broadly, John Tagg's *The Burden of Representation: Essays on Photographies and Histories* remains an essential resource on "the coupling of evidence and photography in the second half of the nineteenth century" (1993: 5). Lorraine Daston and Peter Galison's work—in "The Image of Objectivity" (1992) and *Objectivity* (2007)—explores the history of photographs and other "mechanically objective" images as evidence in scientific practice. Georges Didi-Huberman makes a powerful claim for the importance of "look[ing] at images to see that of which they are the survivors" in *Images in Spite of All* (2008: 182). And Ariella Azoulay's pages on how "everything could be seen" in *The Civil Contract of Photography* (2008: 190–203) are for me the richest analyses of the paradoxes of the linkage between evidence and photography.

9 "Spacecraft Dockings Improve Car Assembly," European Space Agency, January 20, 2010, www.esa.int/Our_Activities/Technology/TTP2/Spacecraft_dockings_improve_car_assembly.

10 Carlo Kopp (2009: 55–57). For an illustration of this process, see "Tomahawk Cruise Missile (BGM-109)," YouTube video, 7:04, n.d., posted by "TheMilitaryConceptChannel," May 11, 2012, www.youtube.com/watch?v=a6yio1ZGFw0

11 "ATV-4 Docking to the International Space Station—Transmission Replay," European Space Agency: Space in Videos, June 15, 2013, http://spaceinvideos.esa.int/Videos/2013/06/ATV-4_docking_to_the_International_Space_Station_-_transmission_replay

12 The "operational image" is the essential category of Farocki's three-part installation series called *Eye/Machine* (2000–2003) and the corresponding film *War at a Distance* (2003). In the notes for his online catalogue, Farocki writes, "The third part of the *Eye/Machine* cycle structures the material around the concept of the operational image. These are images which do not portray a process, but are themselves part of a process. As early as the Eighties, cruise missiles used a stored image of a real landscape, then took an actual image during flight; the software compared the two images, resulting in a comparison between idea and reality, a confrontation between pure war and the impurity of the actual. This confrontation is also a montage, and montage is always about similarity and difference. Many operational images show colored guidance lines, intended to portray the process of recognition. The lines tell us emphatically what is all-important in these images, and just as emphatically what is of no importance at all. Superfluous reality is denied—a constant denial provoking opposition" ("Eye/Machine III," Harun Farocki [website], n.d., www.harunfarocki.de/installations/2000s/2003/eye-machine-iii.html). The second quotation comes from Harun Farocki, "Le point de vue de la guerre," *Trafic* 50 (Summer 2004): 449; quoted Didi-Huberman (2009: 48). Farocki's essay "War Always Finds a Way" (2009: 102–112) also has a lot to say on the operational image. The essential theoretical resource on this is the work of Paul Virilio, especially *War and Cinema* (1989) and *The Vision Machine* (1994), especially the last chapter on "sightless vision."

13 Some news reports have suggested that overhead image analysts in the US military, distant successors to the men of the aerial reconnaissance unit Steichen commanded, can be overwhelmed by the imagery acquired by airborne drones. Christopher Drew of the *New York Times* reported in 2010 that, "the Air Force and other military units are trying to prevent an overload of video collected by the drones" and that, "while the biggest timesaver would be to automatically scan the video for trucks and armed men, that software is not yet reliable" (2010: A1).

14 In a lecture at Davos, Paglen summarized the argument this way: "Right now *the cameras themselves* are doing the operations. In other words, you have a traffic camera; *that camera* can detect if somebody is doing something wrong and automatically issue a ticket" (2018: n.p.). And, in an essay

devoted to Farocki that finds that his "dramatic exploration of the emerging world of operational images is now anachrononistic," Paglen argues that, "nowadays operational images are overwhelmingly invisible, even as they're ubiquitous and sculpting physical reality in ever more dramatic ways. We've long known that images can kill. What's new is that nowadays, they have their fingers on the trigger" (2014: n.p.).

15 The best example would be the withering critique of the liberal humanism of Steichen's *Family of Man* exhibition in Sekula (1981).

16 Sekula (2002b: 51, 103, 113, 120; 1986: 62; 2002a: 26, 32–33).

17 The first Lexis/Nexis citation for the term *counter-forensics* is from March 2005. For a fascinating description of the sophisticated counter-forensic (in the current sense) tactics of the Irish Republican Army, see the chapter on "The Forensic Battlefield" in Geraghty (2000).

18 Sekula (1993); revised with an afterword as "A Portable National Archive for a Stateless People: Susan Meiselas and the Kurds," *Camera Austria* 95 (2006): 9–11. The revised version, once again titled "Photography and the Limits of National Identity," is included in Lubben (2008: 342–344). The final version is reprinted in the issue of *Grey Room* (no. 55, Spring 2014) where the present essay first appeared. I am very grateful to Ben Young for first calling this text to my attention.

19 See Joyce and Stover (1991: 217). Joyce and Stover quote from an address Snow gave to the American Association for the Advancement of Science in May 1984.

20 Sekula ends with a compelling critique and reversal: "This is the final outcome of the appropriation of the photographic image for liberal political ends; the oppressed are granted a bogus Subjecthood when such status can be secured only from within, on their own terms" (21).

21 Kristen Lubben, "An Interview with Susan Meiselas," in *Susan Meiselas: In History*, 242. Meiselas's photographs are included in the report that Human Rights Watch produced on Koreme: *Iraqi Kurdistan: The Destruction of Koreme During the Anfal Campaign* (New York: Human Rights Watch and Physicians for Human Rights, 1993). Diane Dufour included valuable documentation of this decisive moment in her exhibition chronicling the uses of photography for forensic purposes (2015: 169–185).

References

Azoulay, A. (2008) *The Civil Contract of Photography*, New York: Zone Books.

Chalmers, A. (2007) "Cargo Identification Algorithms Facilitating Unmanned/Unattended Inspection at High Throughput Portals," in *Proceedings of SPIE*, vol. 6736, Unmanned/Unattended Sensors and Sensor Networks IV, ed. Edward M. Carapezza, Bellingham, WA:SPIE.

Cross, E. (2006) "A Visit to CBP's Port of Los Angeles/Long Beach," *CBP Today* 4, no. 6/7 (June–July): web.archive.org/web/20111023193144/www.cbp.gov/xp/CustomsToday/2006/jun_jul/1a_visit_la_port.xml

Daston, L. and Galison, P. (1992) "The Image of Objectivity," *Representations* 40 (Autumn): 81–128.

Daston, L. and Galison, P. (2007) *Objectivity*, New York: Zone Books.

Didi-Huberman, G. (2008) *Images in Spite of All*, trans. Shane B. Lillis, Chicago: University of Chicago Press.

Didi-Huberman, G. (2009) "How to Open Your Eyes," in *Harun Farocki: Against What? Against Whom?* ed. Antje Ehmann and Kodwo Eshun, London: Raven Row/Koenig Books.

Drew, C. "Drone Flights Leave Military Awash in Data," *New York Times* (11 January 2010): A1; https://www.nytimes.com/2010/01/11/business/11drone.html

Dufour, D. (2015) *Images of Conviction: The Construction of Visual Evidence*, Paris: Le Bal, Editions Xavier Barral.

Farocki, H. (2009) "War Always Finds a Way," in *HF/RG*, ed. Chantal Pontbriand, Paris: Jeu de Paume/Blackjack Editions.

Haldar, P. (2008) "Law and the Evidential Image," *Law, Culture and the Humanities* 4: 139–155.

Johnson., S. (2002) "Stopping Loose Nukes," *Wired* 10, no. 11 (November), www.wired.com/2002/11/nukes–2/

Joyce, C. and Stover, E. (19991) *Witnesses from the Grave: The Stories Bones Tell*, Boston: Little, Brown.

Keenan "Counter-forensics and Photography," *Grey Room* 55 (Spring 2014), 58–77.

Keenan, T. and Weizman, E. (2012) *Mengele's Skull: The Advent of a Forensic Aesthetics*, Berlin: Sternberg Press.

Kopp, C. (2009) "Cruise Missile Guidance Techniques," *Defence Today* 7, no. 5: 55–57, www.ausairpower.net/SP/DT-CM-Guidance-June-2009.pdf

Long, L.A. (2013) "Activity-Based Intelligence: Understanding the Unknowns," *The Intelligencer: Journal of U.S. Intelligence Studies* 20, no. 2 (Fall/Winter), pp. 7–15.

Lubben, K. (ed.) (2008) *Susan Meiselas: In History, New York: International Center of Photography*, Göttingen, Germany: Steidl.

Mnookin, J.L. (1998) "The Image of Truth: Photographic Evidence and the Power of Analogy," *Yale Journal of Law and the Humanities* 10, no. 1 (Winter): 1–72.

Orphan, V., Muenchau, E., Gormley, J., and Richardson, R. (n.d.) *Advanced Cargo Container Scanning Technology Development*. San Diego: Science Applications International Corporation, www.trb.org/Conferences/MTS/3A%20Orphan%20Paper.pdf

Orphan, V., Muenchau, E., Gormley, J., and Richardson, R. (2005) "Advanced Gamma Ray Technology for Scanning Cargo Containers," *Applied Radiation and Isotopes* 63: 723–732.

Paglen, T. (2014) "Operational Images," *e-flux Journal* 59 (November 2014), https://www.e-flux.com/journal/59/61130/operational-images/

Paglen, T. (2016) "Invisible Images (Your Pictures Are Looking At You," *The New Inquiry* (8 December 2016), https://thenewinquiry.com/invisible-images-your-pictures-are-looking-at-you/

Paglen, T. (2018) "Invisible Images of Surveillance," World Economic Forum, Davos, 24 January 2018, http://opentranscripts.org/transcript/invisible-images-of-surveillance/

Phillips, S.S. Haworth-Booth, M. and Squiers, C. (1997) *Police Pictures: The Photograph as Evidence*, San Francisco: Chronicle Books, San Francisco Museum of Modern Art.

Risberg, D. (1999) "Imaginary Economies: An Interview with Allan Sekula," In D. Risberg, *Dismal Science: Photo Works 1972–1996*, Normal: University Galleries of Illinois State University, p.247.

Rundle, E. (2009) "Port Security Improves with Nonintrusive Cargo Inspection and Secure Port Access," *Government Technology* (July 28), www.govtech.com/featured/Port-Security-Improves-With-Nonintrusive-Cargo.html

Sekula, A. (1978) "Dismantling Modernism, Reinventing Documentary (Notes on the Politics of Representation)," *Massachusetts Review* 19, no. 4, (Winter 1978): : 859–883

Sekula, A. (1984a) "The Instrumental Image: Steichen at War," In A. Sekula, *Photography against the Grain: Essays and Photoworks, 1973-1983*, Halifax: Press of the Nova Scotia College of Art and Design, pp. 32–51. The article was first published in *Artforum* 14:4, December 1975, 26-35.

Sekula, A. (1984b) "On the Invention of Photographic Meaning," In A. Sekula, *Photography against the Grain: Essays and Photoworks, 1973-1983*, Halifax: Press of the Nova Scotia College of Art and Design, pp. 3–21.

Sekula, A. (1986) "The Body and the Archive," *October* 39 (Winter 1986), pp/ 3–64.

Sekula, A. (1993) "Photography and the Limits of National Identity," *Culturefront* 2, no. 3 (Fall 1993), pp. 54–55.

Sekula, A. (2002a) "Between the Net and the Deep Blue Sea (Rethinking the Traffic in Photographs)," *October* 102 (Autumn 2002).

Sekula, A. (2002b) *Fish Story*, 2nd ed. Düsseldorf: Richter Verlag.

Sekula, A. (2003) "Preface to *Waiting for Tear Gas [White Globe to Black]* (1999–2000)," In *TITANIC's Wake*, Cherbourg-Octeville, France: Le Point du Jour Éditeur, p. 87.

Tagg, J. (1993) *The Burden of Representation: Essays on Photographies and Histories*, Minneapolis: University of Minnesota Press.

Thurston, T. (1991–2001) "Hearsay of the Sun: Photography, Identity, and the Law of Evidence in Nineteenth-Century American Courts," http://chnm.gmu.edu/aq/photos/index.html

Virilio, P. (1989) *War and Cinema*, trans. Patrick Camiller, New York, Verso Books.

Virilio, P. (1994) *The Vision Machine*, trans. Julie Rose, London: British Film Institute; Bloomington: Indiana University Press.

Westminster International. (2001) *WG IS1517DV X-Ray Cargo Scanner (180kV)*, Banbury, UK: Westminster International, www.wi-ltd.com/security/Scanning_and_Screening/X_Ray_and_Screening_Systems/Pallet_and_Cargo_Scanners/WG_IS1517DV_X_Ray_Cargo_Scanner

Part III
Theories

19

Derrida and photography theory

Malcolm Barnard

Introduction

There is a sense in which all Derrida's work has been about photography, and that it has all been the theory of photography, even if that sense is "unfamiliar in the milieus in which a competent discourse on photography is practiced" (Derrida 2010b: 14). This is the sense in which Derrida's various accounts of the constitutive role of difference, delay and the absent in what is perceived and experienced as the identity and immediacy of the present are also an account of photography. What works for Derrida in the history of philosophy, in the analysis and deconstruction of the conceptual oppositions and binary logics of western thought, also works in the theory of photography. As he says:

> Ghosts: the concept of the other in the same, the *punctum* in the *studium*, the completely other, dead, living in me. This concept of the photograph *photographs* every conceptual opposition; it captures a relationship of haunting that is perhaps constitutive of every 'logic'.
>
> *(Derrida 2007: 272)*

That which is supposed to be dead and departed returns and lives on as a ghost or *revenant* to haunt and make possible the living present. And that which is supposed to be other and is consequently excluded from the same is present in that identity and makes it possible. We have seen Derrida make these moves and these claims with regard to such founding philosophical conceptual oppositions as writing/speech, expressive/indicative and nature/culture, and we have become increasingly familiar with them. The history of philosophy supposed the dead letter of writing to be exterior to speech, 'a dangerous supplement', but Derrida demonstrated that its representational detour was interior to and a condition for living speech. What is less familiar are the ideas, first, that this haunting and this supplementarity is a conception of photography at all and, second, that this conception of photography photographs every conceptual opposition, capturing the haunting that makes every logic possible.

Although it will not have time or space to show how this conception of photography captures the haunting that is constitutive of *every* logic, or even how this conception of photography photographs *every* conceptual opposition, this essay will identify and explain the sense in which prosthetic supplementarity, 'the concept of the other in the same', is a conception of photography. It will show how some of the founding conceptual oppositions and some of the central debates of photographic theory can be explained in terms of this conception of photography. For example, it will outline Derrida's account of the two ways that the *punctum*, which is supposedly an instant and different from the *studium*, is actually a duration and thus thoroughly cultural: first as an explanation of the structure of the photograph and second as an explanation of the experience, or phenomenology, of the photograph. It will also show how, if the *punctum* is duration, it is also *technê* or 'art/craft', and that, if all photography entails *technê*, then there is a point at which all photography is art. The question as to whether or to what extent photography is art has occupied photography theory since the beginning, and not only through Benjamin's notion of aura. The conception of photography as document or documentary and the relation of that conception to the rhetorical and ideological functions of photography are also raised by Derrida's critique of the supposed binarity of *punctum/studium*. I will try to show here that, if the *punctum* is duration, then there is time and space for cultural difference, ideology and rhetoric, and the integrity of any innocent documentary function is automatically compromised. And I will show how Derrida argues that the notion of aura, supposedly destroyed by technical reproduction, may be reinstated by exactly the *technê* that Benjamin alleges destroys it. In doing these things, it will explain how Derrida's work is a form of photography theory.

The claim that all of Derrida's work has been about photography may appear contentious (although I hope to demonstrate the sense in which it is true), but the claim that all Derrida's work follows from his conception of time and temporality is surely not at all contentious. This much has been clear since the publication of *Speech and Phenomena* (*La Voix and le Phénomène*) in 1967, where he shows that Husserl is forced to suppress or ignore his initial and profound insight into the constitutive role of the temporally non-present in the temporal present in order to make his phenomenological arguments work. This essay will explain Derrida's account of time and temporality before going on to show how that account is central to his photography theory and how it makes his critique of the *punctum* in "The Deaths of Roland Barthes" and in *Copy, Archive, Signature* possible. It will then show the consequences of those arguments around the *punctum* for the theoretical debates concerning photography as art, the documentary or rhetorical functions of photography and finally how they paradoxically transform the notions of *technê* and aura as they are found in Benjamin's theory of photography.

Because it is so central, it is worth explaining briefly that Derrida's argument concerning photography as art uses the term 'art' in the sense of the transformation of material and as being the product of *technê*. These ideas will be further explained in the section entitled "Photography and *technê*" below, but it might help to understand that the very technology of photography guarantees some transformation of material, and that, as the transformation of material through technology, all photography is a form of cultural production, and therefore art. Derrida's argument makes explicit the link between the sense of *technê* that gives us our understanding and experience of technology and the sense of *technê* that gives us our understanding and experience of 'art', and it does this by showing how the latter is made possible by the former.

Derrida on time

In the chapter of *Speech and Phenomena* entitled "Signs and the Blink of an Eye," Derrida introduces and takes apart the 'myth' of the punctual instant. This is a myth that we will meet again in his *Copy, Archive, Signature* (2010b). Derrida argues that, as the blink of an eye has duration, closes the eye and introduces non-perception and absence as a condition of present perception (Derrida 1973: 65), so both the opening and closing of the camera's shutter and the *punctum* have duration, and that duration introduces variation and difference as a condition of the identity of the instant (Derrida 2010b: 8–9). Derrida's account of time effectively consists in taking Husserl's radical rethinking of time more seriously and applying it more rigorously and more consistently than Husserl does himself.

In *The Phenomenology of Internal Time Consciousness* and *Ideas*, Husserl presents a conception of the present moment or instant in which that present moment is complicated by references to the past and to the future; the present is made possible by the relation to that which is not present. Husserl argues that the present contains protention and retention: he says that what makes the present moment possible is a relation to remembrance, which he calls retention, and to expectation, which he calls protention (Husserl 1975: 197–8, 1964: 62). Every present perception that we have is colored by or happens in the context of a relation to what we remember of past perceptions and to what we imagine or expect from future perceptions, and Husserl argues that the present moment and the perception that takes place within it would not be possible without those relations. The presence of the present is thus conditioned or made possible by a relation to the other and the different (to what is by definition not present; the past and the future).

While I do not want to prejudice the discussions in the following sections, it might be worth providing some brief comments explaining how this conception of time affects the notion of the photographic instant. There are two main consequences, as we shall soon see. The first is that, if the structure of time is not simple, if what is experienced and conceptualized as a simple self-same present moment is actually duration and refers to the past and the future, then there can be no simple present to be experienced in the *punctum*. Second, if there is no simple moment in which the photograph can simply and passively record the instant, then there can be no documentary photography, at least as it is routinely or naively conceptualized.

Derrida shows in this chapter that Husserl is forced to suppress or ignore the very insights that he has presented in his rethinking of time in order to make other parts of his phenomenology work. For example, Husserl is committed to the idea of "primordial dator intuitions" (Husserl 1975: 83). These primordial dator intuitions are foundational and authoritative perceptions and experiences: they provide incontrovertible evidence for his phenomenological investigations and, according to Husserl, they happen in "the blink of an eye," in a punctual present instant. This, of course, is where Derrida locates the moment or the place at which Husserl's argument begins to self-deconstruct. Husserl is "trying to retain two apparently irreconcilable possibilities": he wants to insist on both the punctual present that is needed for his dator intuitions to work *and* the construction of the present from the relation to what is necessarily absent (Derrida 1973: 67). It is clear that he cannot argue that there is a punctual 'now' in which fundamental intuitions may be had and that the 'now' is made possible by its relation to the not-now of protention and retention. However, this is what he is forced to do, and Derrida has great fun identifying the points at which Husserl's text begins inevitably to creak under the strain.

Derrida's conception of time is thus based on his critique of Husserl's account of time in his (1973) *Speech and Phenomena.* He insists on the constitutive role of the absent and the other in the supposed identity of the self-same present instant. A self-same present instant would be a moment of time that contained no reference to anything that was not itself: Derrida's argument is that there can be no such self-same present instant as every supposedly present instant is made possible by the existence within it of something that is not it, something that is different from the present—the past and the future. This, as I suggest, indicates that Derrida takes the Husserlian insight concerning the construction of the present from the elements of protention and retention more seriously and applies it more rigorously and more consistently than Husserl does. The way that the alleged presence of the present is actually made possible by the relation to what is other than and different from the present (the past, memory or archive of retention, and the imagination, future or 'to come' of protention) permeates and structures all of Derrida's thought. It should come as no surprise, then, that this conception of time is found almost unchanged in his accounts of photographic time to be found in his essay on the death of his friend Roland Barthes (2007), and his *Copy, Archive, Signature* (2010b). As suggested in the quote in the Introduction above, this conception of time may even be understood as a conception of photography, and, as Husserl's rethinking of time began the break with the Aristotelian conception of time (Derrida [1967] 1973: 61), so Derrida's conception of photography, based on that rethinking of time, may signal the beginning of the end of "a certain conception of photography" (Derrida 2010b: 5). In order to explain and support these claims, it is now appropriate and the time to consider the *punctum* and the *studium*.

Time, Barthes, *punctum, studium*

Derrida's complicated notion of time, in which what is other than and different from the present moment constitutes or makes possible that present moment, is the basis of his account of photography; as noted, it may even be photography. It is also the basis of Derrida's critique of Barthes' account of the *punctum* in "The Deaths of Roland Barthes" and *Copy, Archive, Signature*.

In *Camera Lucida*, Barthes explains the *punctum* as the detail or element of a photograph that pierces him or wounds him, like the point of an arrow pricking his skin (Barthes 1984: 26–7, 40–3). Throughout the text, Barthes identifies the *puncta*: in one photograph he sees only a boy's bad teeth, in another he concentrates on another boy's crossed arms and in a third he is pierced by the boy's huge collar and the girl's finger bandage. He distinguishes *punctum* from the *studium*, which is a kind of "unconcerned," general or "vague" interest in a photograph. *Studium* is the sort of interest in things that one finds "all right," that is generated by one's membership of a culture and one that is therefore almost involuntary (Barthes 1984: 27–8). The *punctum* is an instant, a point, and it is presented by Barthes as existing outside of or apart from the culture that produces the *studium*. This is to do with time because Barthes says it is a point, an instant, and because Barthes opposes it to culture, which inevitably involves or demands a reference to history, or time. The *studium*, then, is coded, it is thoroughly cultural and it is even described as a form of connotation, or cultural meaning, by Barthes (1984: 26, 51). The *punctum* is not coded, it is not a cultural product but an uncoded and even unnameable instant (Barthes 1984: 51).

Although he sometimes hints that Barthes actually experiences the same desire to hold two irreconcilable positions on the *studium/punctum* dichotomy as Husserl does in his account of time (Derrida 2007: 272–3), and, as we shall see in a moment, Barthes himself gives the game away at one point, it is nevertheless quite clear that the conception of photographic time supposed by the *punctum* is going to attract Derrida's attention. Derrida begins by observing that Barthes' interpretation of photography is governed by the "logic of the punctual *stigma*" and, with a reference back to Husserl's blink of an eye, he explains the instant or the *prise de vue* of the photographic 'shot' as duration (Derrida 2010b: 8). As duration, the 'instant' is a "heterogenous time," it supposes "a differing/deferring and differentiated duration." In this duration, then, difference has space and time to happen: "the light can change ... subevents can occur ... micrological modifications [and] effects" can take place (Derrida 2010b: 8). If there is no present moment or 'atomic instant', then there can be no instant that is 'captured', and there can be no *punctum*, even if it feels like there is: each supposedly atomic instant will have duration, and one way in which this duration may be understood is as the temporal difference that Derrida insists on in Husserl's radical rethinking of the structure of time. The differentiated duration is the complicated notion of time that we saw above, in which the 'to come' of a future and the archive or trace of a past are the conditions for the presence of the present.

Derrida's conception of time as found in this critique of Husserlian phenomenology has two main consequences for Barthes' account of photography, which, as Derrida reminds us, is also presented as a phenomenology (Derrida 2007: 270, and especially 288). The first is that the *punctum* is not an instant, either in the 'impact' it has on Barthes himself, in his experience and perception of the *punctum*, or in the conception and explanation of the conceptual element of the photograph. The first consequence may be seen in Barthes' account of the photograph of Lewis Payne in *Camera Lucida*. Barthes is explaining what he presents as "another *punctum*" or a "new *punctum*," one that he says has to do with "intensity" rather than form. He describes and explains his experience of the *punctum* in this photograph by saying that "*he is going to die*. I read at the same time: *this will be* and *this has been*" (1984: 96). The *punctum*, or this aspect of the *punctum*, is not a simple and present instant: it is as complicated as Derrida's account of the allegedly or supposedly simple and present instant in Husserl. Barthes' account refers to the past in "this has been," it refers to the present in "he is going to die" and it refers to the future in "this will be." As Husserl's present contained protention (references to the future) and retention (references to the past), so Barthes' *punctum* refers to past and future as well as the present. What has been presented as the experience of a simple present point is also a structure of past, present and future and it thus refers to a duration. The second consequence may be seen in Derrida's assertion that, "the punctum is not what it is" (2007: 288). The *punctum* cannot be a simple instantaneous moment in Derrida's account of photography because, as we have seen in his critique of Husserl's account of time, there can be no simple self-presence that does not contain reference to what it is not. According to Derrida's argument, the present must contain references to what it is not, the past and the future, and thus the *punctum* cannot but contain references to what it is not, the past and the future. Thus Barthes' *punctum* is not what it is: as a present moment, it is made possible by reference to what it is not, the past and the future.

There are other consequences of this argument, and they are all relevant to photography theory. For example, this notion of the photographic instant or present as differentiated duration, as being constituted by the relation to the past and the future, to what is absent and not-present, explains the possibility of photography as art, as archive or documentary and paradoxically reinstates the possibility of a Benjaminian concept of a photographic aura. Benjamin's account of aura is relevant to the arguments here because where Benjamin explains art as the presence of aura and argues that *technê* in the sense of technology destroys aura and thus art, Derrida explains that *technê*, in the sense of art, is part of all photography.

Photography and *technê*

Derrida remarks that, having thought the entire photographic enterprise as undeniably marked by *technê*, we are now enjoined to "rethink the essence of *technê*" (Derrida 2010b: 10). The following paragraphs will explain why Derrida argues this and outline the consequences for photography.

Technê is an Ancient Greek word meaning art, or craft/craftsmanship, and it refers to a human capacity to transform material. This material that is worked on and transformed by our human ability to make and to do is often, and most originally, conceived as nature and it is often presented as *physis* in Derrida's writing. *Technê* is the origin of our understanding and practice of technology, and the technological is classically conceived of as being external to the body and as something artificial, something added to an existing body or perception. The most obvious examples of such a conception of technological addition or supplement would be spectacles or replacement limbs. The spectacles are added to our body to enable us to see more clearly, and the replacement limb is added to the body to enable us to walk, for example. Derrida's argument is that *technê*, the technological, is the condition for there being any body and any perception 'in the first place'. Although there can, of course, be no simple origin or originary source in Derrida's photography theory, technology is not a substitutive prosthesis, but rather a constitutive or "originary" prosthesis (Derrida 2010b: 13). It is (paradoxically) an addition that makes the thing to which it is added possible 'in the first place'.

One of the earliest and best-known examples of *technê*, of prosthetic technology, in Derrida's work, is writing. Supposedly a mere tool, an external and 'mechanical' form of representation that is added to speech as a supplement and that threatens the presence of living speech, writing is actually the condition for the presence of 'living' speech. The 'detour' into some form of external, written representation is the condition for speech, and speech could not exist or work without that originary tool or prosthesis. Another, equally early, but less well-known and potentially more controversial example of *technê* is perception. Derrida argues in *Speech and Phenomena* that, "perception does not exist" and that, "there never was any 'perception'" (Derrida [1967] 1973: 45, 103) because perception must always be represented in some external system: "the perceived present can appear as such only inasmuch as it is continuously compounded with a nonpresence and nonperception, with primary memory and expectation (retention and protention)" (Derrida [1967] 1973: 64). Representation in the form of memory and anticipation is the external and prosthetic condition for the possibility of what is called perception.

This is the basis of the sense in which Derrida is using the word *technê*. Consequently, when he argues that, in the *punctum*, there is duration and that that duration is "constituted by a *technê*," and when he concludes that the entire photographic enterprise is "undeniably marked" by that *technê* (Derrida 2010b: 10), this is what he is trying to explain. And this is why Derrida says in *Copy, Archive, Signature* that perception is marked by *technê*: perception is dependent on "re-tention and re-presentation" by the technical, and there can be no "pre-technical perception" (Derrida 2010b: 9). If this is the case, if there can be no perception that is not made possible by *technê*, then perception is itself a form of photography. Derrida provides another gloss on this when he argues that the technical is not a threat to photographic authenticity, that the technical, *technê*, or what has hitherto been theorized as 'artistic' input, is not a threat to the document but rather the condition for all documentation and all archivization (Derrida 2001: 72).

Perception is dependent on *technê* because it is dependent on some external system, which, since *Of Grammatology*, written in 1967, Derrida has characterized as 'writing' (Derrida [1967] 1976: 15, for example). Derrida's argument is that, for perception to be possible, it is necessary for it to be represented to us—we have to be able to say what it is that we are perceiving, for example, for the perception of that thing to be possible. Being able to identify and say what it is that we are perceiving requires the use of language, the words and concepts of a language, in order for that perception to be a perception of anything at all. The language, the words and concepts, along with the grammar of that language, are not us, they are different from us and external to us: they are an external system in which the perception has to be represented in order for it to be a perception. Given that our language is not us, it is a tool or a prosthesis, it is *technê*, and that is why perception is a form of *technê*. It is worth reminding ourselves of Derrida's point (above) that it is an originary conception of prosthesis, not a substitutive conception of prosthesis: paradoxically, in Derrida's account, the prosthesis is an addition or substitute that makes possible the thing that it supplements. These are not easy arguments, but they are Derrida's arguments.

It is interesting to tie Derrida's account of the prosthesis back to Barthes' account of photography. Barthes acknowledges an element of this understanding of the originary or constitutive prosthesis and, as noted above, almost gives the game away regarding his uncertainty about the *punctum*. When he says that the *punctum* "is an addition: it is what I add to the photograph and what is nonetheless already there" (Barthes 1984: 55), he is acknowledging that the *punctum* is a supplement. Saying that the *punctum* is what he adds to the photograph admits the cultural, his general interest, the interest he has as a member of a culture, to the *punctum*. The idea that the *punctum* is added conflicts with, or, as Derrida has it, "composes with," the idea that the *punctum* is already there in the photograph, ready to rise out of the photograph and pierce him (Derrida 2007: 271). In Derrida's account, this is no longer a simple binary. The *punctum* is something added to a photograph but that is already there: the *punctum* is now more akin to Derrida's idea of supplementarity, of the originary or constitutive prosthesis that is an addition to something but that makes the thing possible by being added.

Technê and aura

One of the things we are also surely obliged or enjoined to rethink is the role of *technê* in the mechanical or technical reproduction of the photograph. We are obliged to rethink this because the notion of time that Derrida uses in his critique of Barthes and the photograph involves the concept of *technê*, and the technological has consequences for the notion of aura, which Benjamin uses in his arguments around whether the photograph is a work of art or not. This phrase is intended to recall Benjamin's essay on the work of art, the German title of which is *Das Kunstwerk im Zeitalter seiner technischen Reproduzierbarkeit*. It will be noted that the word in the title that traditionally or usually gets translated into English as 'mechanical' is *technischen* in the original German text. *Technischen* means 'technical', rather than 'mechanical', and this slightly different translation restores and authenticates the link made in the present essay to Derrida's use of the word *technê* and, therefore, to art.

Benjamin's argument in this essay is that aura in the work of art is destroyed by technical reproduction. The argument to be pursued in this section is that, if, as Derrida says, the *punctum* is duration, and if the duration of the *punctum* allows or permits *technê*, then there is a sense in which the uniqueness of the photograph is not destroyed by reproduction. Paradoxically, there is also a sense in which all works of art are technically reproduced, and that, therefore, no works of art possess aura.

The argument in Benjamin's essay is that some works of art possess aura and others do not; more precisely, technically reproduced works of art do not possess aura. Aura is explained as the sense of uniqueness and authenticity that one feels before a work of art (Benjamin 1992: 217). Uniqueness has its source in the work of art's place in "the fabric of tradition"; the sense that there is a single unique work of art derives from the specificity of that work of art's location at a point in a tradition. Authenticity is a product of the work's place in ritual or cultic practices (Benjamin 1992: 214, 217). However, in the age of technical reproduction and for the first time, technical reproduction "emancipates the work of art from its parasitical dependence on ritual" and "to an ever greater degree, the work of art ... becomes the work of art designed for reproducibility" (Benjamin 1992: 218).

Technical reproducibility takes two forms in Benjamin's essay: woodcuts and lithography. Some eighty years after Benjamin wrote the essay, we may add electronic and digital forms of reproduction, but the effect is the same: the aura of the work of art 'withers' in the face of all such forms of reproduction. Reproduction destroys aura in two ways: by making possible many copies of the work of art and by making it possible for the work of art to "meet the beholder" wherever they are (Benjamin 1992: 215). The existence of many copies of the work destroys the sense of the uniqueness of the work, and the image meeting the beholder in their own 'particular situation' destroys the authentic cultic or ritual location of the work.

Benjamin has analogue photography and film in mind in this essay but it is clear that his arguments apply to electronic and digital forms of image and text production. Indeed, Derrida suggests that the new digital technology only makes clearer the role of activity and art in the old analogue technologies (Derrida 2010b: 6). The existence of the technically reproduced analogue or digital photograph in many copies (or even in only potentially many copies) destroys the sense of the uniqueness of the work of art. The idea that any one of those many copies could come to meet us in our particular situation, wherever we happen to be, at any time of day or night, likewise destroys any possible sense of ritual or cultic value. Consequently, Benjamin argues that technical reproduction destroys aura in the work of art.

However, if the *punctum* is duration, and if duration is the condition for the possibility of *technê* in the photograph, and if *technê* is understood as the artistic alteration or formation of material, then there is a sense in which the work of art remains a work of art even after technical reproduction. It is this for two reasons or on two levels. First, there is the presence of artistic choice and decision-making, the human elements, the selections and choices made by or on the part of the human hand and eye and the compositional choices of the artist in the production of the photograph. If the *punctum* as duration is the condition for the possibility of those elements of *technê* in the photograph, then it is hard to deny the artistic (or crafty) components of photography and difficult to see how they could be destroyed by reproduction. Second, there is the sense of *technê* in technical reproduction. It is tempting to argue that the very means of reproduction guarantees some level of 'artistic' or creative content simply because *technê* is the transformation or working of material, and each individual reproduction will by definition be different from the last and from the one to come. As the transformation or working of material, it is cultural and thus a form of cultural production, or 'art'. On this account, all technical reproduction is art.

The 'reverse' or negative of this argument would be to say that, if there is no non-technical, non-prosthetic perception, then all image construction, including all perception, is technical reproduction, and no works of art retain aura. This argument uses Derrida's idea that there is no "pretechnical perception" to make the point that all perception and all image-making are forms of technical reproduction. No perception and no image-making have aura, because they are all the product of representation: some form of external representational system must have been used to (re)produce them 'in the first place'. They are all, to that extent and as Derrida says, "iterable," and none is the result of an "un-iterable" experience; consequently, none is unique, and none has aura (Derrida 2010b: 9).

The duration of the *punctum* may also be seen as the condition for the possibility of the ritual and cult that Benjamin refers to in his account of the aura of the photograph. The creative decisions, along with the selections and discriminations of hand and eye, are what make the work of art a work of art, and Derrida argues that the time of the *punctum* is a duration, and that change can occur within it. Thus, the things that make the work of art a work of art, which are inevitably connected with the rituals and cultic practices of the artist's studio—precisely the commonly fetishized discriminations and 'special' decisions that the artist makes—are present in the time of the *punctum*. If they cannot not be present, then there may be another reason for suggesting that the aura of the work of art is not destroyed by technical reproduction.

And if this time or differentiated duration of the *punctum* is when and where technics enter the photograph, when decisions and transformations may be made, when difference happens, then it provides the sense of Derrida's saying that, "The process here would begin before what is referred to as processing" (Derrida 2010b: 11). In the dialogue that makes up *Copy, Archive, Signature*, Michael Wetzel talks about how "art … enters into the development process" of photography when the photographer can change the decisions s/he has made about the length of time they allow for the image to develop, for example (Derrida 2010b: 11). In his reply, Derrida immediately suggests that this process of processing has always already begun: "technics intervenes from the moment a view or shot is taken," and technics can involve the choice of viewpoint, the aperture and so on (Derrida 2010b: 12). It is not that the photograph is 'taken' and then the photographer begins the process of processing the image: the duration of the *punctum* ensures that the process has begun; it means that the process has always already begun. Although Derrida does not explicitly refer to Barthes or the account of the *punctum* in this passage, it is clear that there is some implied critique of the notion of the self-same instant of the *punctum*. Derrida's argument is, of course, that there can be no simple present, that the present is always infinitely divisible and divided; this is what allows for or makes possible change and, therefore, history and culture. Consequently, there is always some processing; there is never a simple 'natural' moment that is captured, as a straightforward result of the nature of the technology, the technics, that is involved.

In *Copy, Archive, Signature*, Derrida makes one or two final points concerning aura. At one point, the discussion turns to the nineteenth- and early twentieth-century practice of presenting signed portrait photographs of oneself to people as gifts. Derrida speculates on the way in which the signature on the photograph (re)introduces something like authenticity to the image and on the way in which the signature and the portrait form and the fact that it is a gift (re)introduces something like uniqueness to the gift (Derrida 2010b: 22–3). There is no claim that Benjamin's destruction of the aura has been simply reversed, or that aura is fully and unproblematically present in these photographs, but the situation is said to bear witness to the "irreplaceable fetish" of the "absolute rarity," of the "unique event," and thus the authenticity of the artwork (Derrida 2010b: 23). Later, Derrida refers to the attempt to reconstitute, rescue or recapture some element or vestige of aura from the people involved in the production of photographs or from the processes of photography. Where some will argue that a photograph that was personally processed, that was hand-developed or hand-printed by the 'artist', still retains aura, Derrida refers to the photograph of Nietzsche's typewriter and the way in which it is used in biographies of Nietzsche. He says that, "an attempt is being made to reconstitute the aura around something that has or is bound to have the effect of dispelling the aura" (Derrida 2010b: 29). Like the photographic negative, the typewriter is held to have some special connection to the person using it. The attempt is being made in these arguments to reconstitute something like the cult or ritual value around the photograph (from which uniqueness and aura were held to derive in Benjamin's account), and, if the typewriter was subsequently discovered not to have been Nietzsche's, then "it would no longer hold any interest" (Derrida 2010b: 29).

Photographic archive and memory

Notions of the archive and memory are clearly of central importance to much photography theory. The photographic representation stands for, or substitutes for, the person, and representation is therefore conceived here in terms of one thing replacing something that is absent, or as one thing substituting for another thing. The thing that is absent, be it a person or a place, is conceived metaphorically as death or the dead, and the photograph is consequently conceived as a form of memory, or a form of mourning for that which is absent or dead. This traditional conception of the relation between the photograph and the thing it is the photograph of is the origin of memory and an account or explanation of the archive. The photograph is an example of the substitutive 'prosthesis', where the photographic representation comes after, and substitutes or stands in for, the thing, the person, event, landscape or whatever is now missing or lost.

However, in Derrida's account of the prosthesis, the prosthesis is not substitutive and it does not come after: rather, it is originary and constitutive. The constitutive prosthesis is the supplement that is added; as noted above, it is (paradoxically) the addition that makes the thing to which it is added possible "in the first place" (Derrida 2010b: 13). So, the photographic representation does not 'stand in' for the person; the photographic representation constitutes any and all representations we have of that person 'in the first place'. And this prosthetic structure works at the level of perception, as well as at the level of the photograph: Derrida comes close to arguing that perception is a version of photography. And this is because there is and can be no "pretechnical perception" (Derrida 2010b: 9).

Any pretechnical perception would depend on there being a *punctum* that was not duration, in which we were the entirely passive receivers of the material that comes through our senses. Derrida's argument, against Barthes, is that there is not a duration-free *punctum*, and thus that we are not simply passive receivers of whatever flows through the *punctum*. Because there is duration, we are 'active': because there is the inevitability of difference in duration, there is, therefore, active discrimination and decision on our part. This radically complicates the notion of active and passive as they apply to perception (and photography), and this is why Derrida casts around for neologisms with which to describe the new situation. He tries "actipassivity" in *Copy, Archive, Signature* (Derrida 2010b: 12) and he tries "passactivity" in *Athens: Still Remains* (Derrida 2010a: 67).

This has consequences for the photographic theory of memory and the archive. If this entirely passive exposure that is supposed in Barthes' account of the *punctum* were possible, it would mean that an "immediate and natural" perception, and an immediate archive, would be possible (Derrida 2010b: 10). However, because this entirely passive exposure is not possible, because there is duration and there is, therefore, both difference and decision, there can be no immediate, natural or (precisely) pre-technical (pre-mechanical) perception. As Derrida argues in his *Archive Fever* (1996), as well as here, this means that there can there be no immediate or unmediated archive or memory; each archive or memory has to be mediated, and this can also happen only through representation and the trace, traces and representations of what has happened. This is why the prosthesis of memory has to be the originary or constitutive prosthesis described in Derrida (2010b). It is also worth noting, very briefly, that, because memory and archive can happen only through representation, they can happen only institutionally. One of the consequences of the debate between Derrida and John Searle in and following Derrida's *Limited Inc* (1997) is that it is now possible to understand representation as an institution. Searle agrees that the decision that x stands for or represents y is the first institution (Searle 1995: 43–46), and, following Derrida's arguments in *Copy, Archive, Signature* (2010b), we can see that representation (as originary prosthesis) is necessary for any archive or memory to be made possible or, precisely, instituted—set up and established.

The photographic image and mourning

The image, and the photographic image, are no different from any other form of the trace in Derrida's work, and this is another reason for arguing that all that work is photography theory. As Michael Naas says, "every trace implies the death of its author not in some future present but already and structurally from the beginning … death comes from the very beginning to work over all writing, all photographs, all traces" (Naas 2003: 1845). Every representation, every written, spoken or otherwise inscribed mark, every gesture, speech act, painting, drawing and photograph exists on the basis of or in relation to death, to that which is absent and not present. The most powerful of these absences or deaths, which make the iteration of inscription possible, is the death of the author. And it is the trace, the relation to the absent and non-present that precedes and makes any and all representation possible on Derrida's account. Derrida says that "death, or rather mourning" opens up the possibility of the image and, without an understanding of the role of death and mourning in the possibility of the image, "one understands nothing of the power of the image" (Derrida 2001: 146).

What we have seen above as the living present in Husserl's work is fractured and put out of joint by the relation to the absent past and the future; any presence is therefore non-simple and complicated by the relation to the absent, or death. As Dick and Wolfreys point out, "The ostensibly living present of phenomenology is no longer re-presented as such by the image, but called forth as the non-simple presence that, divided from originary presence and the living present, allows the thinking of its other" (Dick and Wolfreys 2013: 272). For Derrida and Marin, this relation to the always already absent, to death, is the condition for the possibility of the image: it is death and mourning—the relation to the always already absent—that makes the image possible, that "propels it to 'vision'" (Marin, quoted in Derrida 2013: 146), or calls it forth. As Derrida says, "only death, which is not, or rather mourning … can open up this space of *dynamis* … the possible as such" and make the image possible (Derrida 2001: 146). The being, the condition, of the image is force, and force is not a being, not part of ontology, and it is explained in terms of *dynamis* in Derrida's text.

On this account of the photographic image, death is not the simple absence of presence, the absence of something or someone that or who was here but is no longer here: death as absence is now understood as constitutive of presence, of the living present—presence and the living present are only understood in relation to the constitutive role of absence or death within it. The image and the photograph have to be able to 'work' or be meaningful in the absence of the subject, the person who made the image or who took the photograph, the people in the image or photograph, as well as in the absence of any spectators of the image or the photograph. This is why Derrida tends to speak of reference, or even "the referencial," rather than the referent (Derrida 2007: 288). As Derrida argues in "The Deaths of Roland Barthes," reference is strictly impossible because it can and will never be finally or fully achieved, but the desire or impulse towards it is also never ending; as Derrida says, the *punctum* "suspends the referent and leaves it to be desired, while still maintaining the reference" (Derrida 2007: 284, 292). The absence of the referent, death, is structurally presupposed as a condition of any form of representation, it is not an accident that happens to the subject. Any system of representation has to be able to operate in the absence of any subjects: differences between elements and the relations between those different elements have to be in place, but their being in place means that there do not have to be any subjects at all. The absence of the subject is one aspect of what is referred to as death here.

Consequently, if the image and the photographic image are understood as representation, and if representation is understood as reproduction, as simple mimesis (the resemblance of one thing to another thing), for example, then they are barely understood at all, according to Derrida and Marin. Or, rather, they are understood in the reductive terms of ontology and philosophy. This is because to understand the image and the photograph in this way is to miss the constitutive role of absence or death in the image and the photograph. On this account, the image relates to death insofar as it can represent, or reproduce, an image of someone or something who is no longer here (who is dead, maybe), but they cannot account for how death makes the image or the photograph possible in the first place. It is not that the photographic image simply represents someone who is or may not be here, poignant as this may be, and even with the famous Winter Garden photograph of his mother, as Barthes describes it in *Camera Lucida* (Barthes 1984: 63ff.). It is that the relation to death and mourning makes the photographic representation possible 'in the first place'. Death in the form of the absent subject is the condition of the image and of the photographic image: the contingent representation of subjects who will inevitably die or who are already dead is itself made possible by this more originary and structural form of death.

Recognizing the role of death and mourning in the image and in the photographic image involves understanding how death and mourning take place 'in advance' and make the image as reproduction and mimesis possible. Much conventional photography theory would have it that death and mourning follow the manifestation or coming to vision of the image, rather than making the manifestation or appearance of the image possible. For example, the first chapter of David Bate's *Photography* (2009) is entitled "History," and the relation between photography and memory is present from the first page. And Graham Clarke's *The Photograph* (1997) begins from the notion of the "historical significance" of the photograph, in terms of its functions of recording and fixing (Clarke 1997: 7, 11). It is also interesting that Bate refers to the 'prosthetic' nature of the photographic representations that are held to constitute memory, to help us keep something and not lose it. He says, for example, that the portrait of a person "stands in" for that person (Bate 2009: 9). In these accounts, the photographic representation comes after, stands for, or substitutes for, the person, and representation is therefore conceived here as the substitutive prosthesis, in terms of one thing replacing something that is absent, metaphorically dead, or as one thing substituting for another thing. In Derrida's account of the prosthesis, the prosthesis is originary, it is the (cultural) addition that makes the (apparently natural) photograph possible.

Derrida and Marin argue that absence, or the dead, along with the memory of what is dead and gone in the photograph, rather make the photograph possible, and that the constitutive role of what is absent and dead actually accounts for the power or *dynamis* of the image: rather than being a "weakened reproduction of what it would imitate," the image can now be thought and understood in terms of its power and its authority, in terms of what makes it possible (Derrida 2001: 147). Derrida's arguments here concerning the constitutive role of death and mourning in the photograph follow directly from his arguments around time that were explained in the second section of this essay, above, and they lead directly to the idea that Derrida's work is all about photography, which will be explained in the following section. The references in the present to the absences of the past and the future, which we saw were part of Derrida's critique of Husserl's conception of the present as a self-same instant, are the condition for representation as they are the condition for our experience of whatever presence there is. The constitutive role of the absent, or metaphorically 'dead', past in the experience of the present is what Derrida and Marin are referring to when they talk of death and the place of mourning in representation. Work on these concepts and processes is what Derrida refers to throughout his writing as mourning, or the work of mourning; his consistent and repeated references to mourning (in the 2005 essay on friendship, for example, and in *Specters of Marx*, 1994) are the consequence of thinking the role of what is lost, and how we are to relate to what is lost. The absent, what is dead and to be related to in or as mourning, are the conditions of friendship and hospitality, as much as they are the conditions of representation. The dead, what is absent and to be mourned, but returns and has an effect, as the or a ghost, is thus the condition for the possibility of photography as a form—perhaps, as Derrida says (2007: 272), the most "representative" form, or the best example, of representation.

Derrida's work is all photography theory

The first sentence of this essay claimed that there is a sense in which all of Derrida's work has been about photography and that it is all photography theory. This is because there is something about photographic representation that is true of all representation, that is also true of conceptual, perceptual and linguistic representation. It was suggested that the notion of time provided the link here. The role of the past, the absent or the dead was to make the present, the presence of the present and the living possible. The following quote was used in the opening paragraph to introduce these issues:

> Ghosts: the concept of the other in the same, the *punctum* in the *studium*, the completely other, dead, living in me. This concept of the photograph *photographs* every conceptual opposition; it captures a relationship of haunting that is perhaps constitutive of every 'logic'.
>
> *(Derrida 2007: 272)*

A ghost is supposed to be dead and gone, but in Derrida's case that which is supposed to be dead and gone, which is supposed to have left or been excluded once and for all, is seen to have a constitutive or originary role in the present. Various aspects of the photograph and of photography were shown to share this structure or this economy: as well as the *punctum/studium*, there was aura, memory and archive. Derrida's critique of Barthes' concept of the *punctum* was shown to provide the key to these "logics." In Derrida's critique, there is duration in the *punctum*—duration and difference are the basis of the explanation for how *technê* and art and culture (the *studium*) are actually active and present in the supposedly natural and passive instant from which they are believed to have been excluded in Barthes' account.

Consequently, the moment is fractured, and time is "out of joint," as Derrida says elsewhere (1994: 3), because there is a necessary and inescapable reference to past and future in the photographic 'instant' and the *punctum*. The time of the present is out of joint because it necessarily contains and is complicated by the presence of that which is absent from it: as we saw with Husserl's account of time, each supposedly simple present instant is knocked out of joint by the parts played by the future and the past in making it possible. There is a paradox here in that (because of this disjointedness) the present instant is, or is able to present itself as, its own memory or archive, and it has to do this in an image or representation (one thing standing for another thing). It has to do this in an image, or representation, because there is nothing else. And because there is already a history, an available and re-iterable history of prior representations, we have to argue that the present is only what it is because of the archive, because of the trace, of what has passed (on) in it. Thus, as noted above, the supplement or originary prosthesis of the archive makes the present possible 'in the first place'.

This structure (or economy, as it is always changing) is the structure (economy) of the photograph as well as of representation, logic and thought, and this is why I have argued that all of Derrida's work is an account of photography. Because the structure of photography is and can be no different from the structure of any other form of representation, photography captures, or photographs, every other logic, because every other logic will have to follow the logic of representation. These logics include the logics of friendship, hospitality, the gift and cosmopolitanism, as well as those of writing and the trace in Derrida's work. This is why Derrida says that the haunting/mourning that is photography is found "everywhere" (Derrida 2007: 279). And this is why he says that, "the photograph photographs every conceptual opposition," and that it captures the relationship of haunting (of one thing that is supposedly dead and gone actually being the condition for the living present) that constitutes every logic (Derrida 2007: 272).

References

Barthes, R. (1977) *Image–Music–Text*, Glasgow: Fontana/Collins.
Barthes, R. (1984) *Camera Lucida*, London: Fontana.
Bate, D. (2009) *Photography: The Key Concepts*, London: Bloomsbury.
Benjamin, W. (1992) "The Work of Art in the Age of Mechanical Reproduction," in *Illuminations*, (ed.) and introduction Hannah Arendt, London: Fontana Press, pp. 211–244.
Clarke, G. (1997) *The Photograph*, Oxford: Oxford University Press.
Derrida, J. ([1967] 1973) *Speech and Phenomena and Other Essays on Husserl's Theory of Signs*, trans. and introduction by David Allison, Evanston: Northwestern University Press.
Derrida, J. ([1967] 1976) *Of Grammatology*, Baltimore: Johns Hopkins University Press.
Derrida, J. (1994) *Specters of Marx: The State of the Debt, the Work of Mourning and the New International*, trans. Peggy Kamuf, with introduction Bernt Magnus and Stephen Cullenburg, London and New York: Routledge.
Derrida, J. (1996) *Archive Fever: A Freudian Impression*, Chicago: University of Chicago Press.
Derrida, J. (1997) *Limited Inc*, including 1988 "Afterword," Evanston: Northwestern University Press.
Derrida, J. (2001) "By Force of Mourning," in *The Work of Mourning*, (eds.) Pascale-Anne Brault and Michaeil Naas. Chicago: University of Chicago Press, pp. 139–164.
Derrida, J. (2005) *The Politics of Friendship*, London: Verso.
Derrida, J. (2007) "The Deaths of Roland Barthes," in *Psyche: Inventions of the Other Volume 1*, (eds.) Peggy Kanauf and Elizabeth Rottenberg, Stanford: Stanford University Press, pp. 264–298.
Derrida, J. (2010a) *Athens: Still Remains*, New York: Fordham University Press.
Derrida, J. (2010b) *Copy, Archive, Signature: A Conversation on Photography* (ed.) and introduction by Gerhard Richter, Stanford: Stanford University Press.
Dick, M.-D. and Wolfreys, J. (2013) *The Derrida Wordbook*, Edinburgh: Edinburgh University Press.
Husserl, E. (1964) *The Phenomenology of Internal Time Consciousness*, Bloomington: Indiana University Press.
Husserl, E. (1975) *Ideas: General Introduction to Pure Phenomenology*, London: Collier Macmillan.
Naas, M. (2003) *Taking on the Tradition: Jacques Derrida and the Legacies of Deconstruction*, Stanford: Stanford University Press.
Searle, John R. (1995) *The Construction of Social Reality*, New York: Free Press.

20

Image, affect, and autobiography

Roland Barthes' photographic theory in light of his posthumous publications

Kathrin Yacavone

As central to the theory of photography as Roland Barthes has become since his death in 1980, he was always reluctant to be considered an expert on the subject. In a late interview, he described *Camera Lucida*, his most important contribution to the field, as a "modest book" that would disappoint photographers, not least owing to his lack of in-depth knowledge of the medium (Barthes 1985: 357). In the same interview, Barthes professed unfamiliarity with canonical photographic works reproduced in important monographs and catalogs, stating that he selected the images for *Camera Lucida* from contemporary journalism. He adds that his choice of material was largely a matter of his own taste and the "pleasure" certain images held in store for him (Barthes 1985: 357–359). Similarly, shortly after the publication of the book, Barthes wrote on one of his filing cards (his equivalent of a writer's notebook), "[I am not an expert of Photography], I am only an expert of myself" (quoted in Nachtergael 2012: 121 [my translation]). These comments and notes, albeit partial and anecdotal, speak to several characteristics of Barthes' approach to photography, as well as his reception in the field of photography theory. First, his theoretical reflections on the medium are always specifically linked to personal life experiences and his tastes and, rather than pursued in isolation, are a significant part of his larger intellectual projects and methodologies, be they structuralist-semiotic or, later, an affective and phenomenological approach to reading, writing, and visual culture, conjoined with a pronounced self-reflexive interest in autobiography. Second, his approach to writing on the medium, from his early semiotic works to his later more personal and impressionistic engagements with photography, takes its cues from specific photographic images. An exception is one short but influential text, "The Photographic Message." In this essay, Barthes, at the time part of the Centre for the Study of Mass Communication at the École Pratique des Hautes Études, members of which sought to establish a systematic (i.e. semiotic) framework for the study of mass culture, analyzed photography in general as a system of communication, without reference to individual images, photographers, and specific styles or genres. The result was his famous definition of the photograph as a "message without a code" (Barthes 1977: 17). This notable exception aside, Barthes' writings on photography are centered on his perceptual and affective as well as intellectual engagement with particular and personally meaningful images.

This broadly speaking phenomenological orientation, inflected by a specifically Barthesian idea of pleasure, is equally prominent in several posthumous publications that deal with photography. These include the *Mourning Diary* (first published in French in 2009), his 1978–1980 lecture series at the Collège de France titled *The Preparation of the Novel* and his seminar "Proust and Photography" (published in the lecture series in 2003), and his final, never completed or published project, "Autobiography in Images." Barthes worked on these projects during the relatively short span of 1977–1980, a period framed by his mother's death on October 25, 1977 and his own on March 26, 1980. Recent developments have contributed to a reassessment of Barthes' oeuvre; these include the transferal of the Barthes estate from the IMEC (Institut Mémoires de l'Édition Contemporaine) archives to the Bibliothèque Nationale de France in 2011 and a relatively more open accessibility to unpublished material resulting from it; and a plethora of publications during the centenary year of Barthes' birth in 2015, seeking to make public hitherto unpublished material from his entire career, including correspondences, drafts, and notes from his famous (yet still largely unpublished) filing system. This reassessment should extend to his thoughts on photography, going as far back as to his second book, the 1954 biography of Jules Michelet, seldom mentioned in the context of his writing on photography, although clearly relevant.

Against this background, the present reconsideration of Barthes' contribution to the theory of photography has three main aims: (a) to introduce Barthes' posthumously published texts into the (English-language) discourse of photography theory; (b) to situate these texts within Barthes' overall engagement with the medium; and (c) to evaluate the extent to which they shed a new or different light on some of his well-known arguments and ideas. From a critical-conceptual perspective, I shall map these questions against the wider binary discourse in Barthes' oeuvre on photography and (or versus) language. In other words, Barthes' rejection of an authoritative position on photography is, on some level, entirely justified, of course, and not (only) a sign of (false) modesty. Primarily a literary critic and throughout his career first and foremost interested in language, Barthes' approach to photography remained indebted to this primary field of study, coupled with the question of the ideology and violence that language also always conveys, in his view. At first (in the 1950s) subsuming all images—photographic or other—under the paradigm of the linguistic sign, Barthes moved on (in the 1960s) to define the photograph as distinct from language, while still adhering to a linguistic and semiotic vocabulary. From the early 1970s onwards, he began to dissociate the photograph from language, clearly wishing to distinguish, for example, between the photographic album that opens his autobiographical *Roland Barthes by Roland Barthes* and the main text. His late and posthumous publications, finally, indicate that Barthes not only attempts to wholly separate photography from language, but that he increasingly uses photographs *in the place* of it, given his increasing experiences and conceptualizations of language as violent, even "fascist," as he provocatively suggests in his inaugural lecture at the Collège de France in 1977 (Barthes 2000: 461). This neat trajectory notwithstanding, throughout his career, Barthes always draws attention to the paradox that a photograph 'speaks' most powerfully precisely when it points beyond language or when it arrests language (as he argued, for example, in "The Photographic Message," with respect to the potentially traumatic impact of certain photographs); this stoppage of language, in turn, places (some) photographic images outside not only discourse, but the dominant ideology that is inescapably bound to it. And it is no coincidence that this insight is gained through viewing, responding to, and being powerfully affected by specific images, the leitmotif of Barthes' approach to photography, as I shall argue.

Michelet's gaze: the photographic portrait and biography

Barthes' first analysis of photography came in his well-known semiotic works on popular culture, including *Mythologies* (published in book form in 1957), where the medium is considered under the umbrella of an all-encompassing language paradigm. In other words, photography is seen to work in much the same way as language, at least with respect to cultural and ideological connotations, and he reads and analyzes photographs as texts whose ideological message must be demystified and critiqued. Transposing the semiological and, more specifically, Saussurean model of the linguistic sign (consisting of the arbitrarily linked signifier and signified) to the photographic image, Barthes' subsequent writings evidence a shift in his initial conception, culminating in his controversial proposal that the photographic image is "a message without a code" in 1961. This understanding of photography's specificity ran against the grain of prominent semiotic perspectives on visual culture, such as Umberto Eco's, which insisted on the coded nature of all cultural productions, including photography and film. The positing of photography as the 'other' of language is, however, one of the major themes of Barthes' writing on photography from this point on and represents one of the theoretical challenges he grappled with throughout his career and that resurfaces in a pronounced way in his late work.

This language-related strand in Barthes on photography runs in parallel with another, complementary one: the emphasis on the specific viewing experience and the impact and effect of a photograph on its viewer. This is a well-known and -discussed aspect of his relevant late works, and *Camera Lucida* specifically. However, recently published sections of his correspondence reveal that even the young Barthes was fascinated by the affective power of photography, one that he not only succumbed to, but actively orchestrated in his biographical work on the nineteenth-century French historian Jules Michelet. Published in 1954 as Barthes' second book, *Michelet* appeared in Seuil's *Écrivains de toujours* series (the same one in which *Roland Barthes by Roland Barthes* appeared about two decades later), consisting of monographs dedicated to canonical French writers, philosophers, and intellectuals, in a format that typically juxtaposes biographical narrative with historical documents, such as facsimiles and autographs. Painted and photographic portraits of the authors in question provide further stock material characteristic of the series. Barthes intensely studied Michelet (for a planned, but never realized, PhD thesis), while confined to a hospital bed in the hope to cure his tuberculosis (first in the Saint-Hilaire-du-Touvent sanatorium and then in Leysin, Switzerland) from the mid-1940s onwards. In 1945 Barthes wrote to his close friend Robert David demanding, in no uncertain terms, to be sent a specific photographic portrait of Michelet, telling his friend in which little Parisian shops he might find the image (Samoyault 2017: 526). The photograph he had in mind, which he most likely saw in publications consulted for his biography of the historian, cannot be identified with certainty. It is likely, however, that it was either the photograph (by an unknown photographer) that Barthes chose for the cover of the original edition or Nadar's portrait of Michelet, from 1854/1855, taken against a plain background, letting the personality of the sitter fully emerge without the distracting decorum of the then typically stuffy bourgeois settings. The photograph by Nadar appeared in Barthes' biography as the only image reproduced over two pages in the middle of the book, making it the most prominent image in the monograph. (The English translation features the photograph of Michelet as a smaller, oval frontispiece illustration and thus also emphasizes its importance.)

Although it may seem that Barthes simply followed a convention of biographical discourse with the inclusion of photographic portraits of his subject, his foreword clearly speaks to a more reflexive and conscious principle at work. Referring to the illustrations in the book, Barthes foregrounds the visual aspects of his biography as part of his "impassionate gaze" (Barthes 1987: 3), akin to Michelet's guiding use of visual material, including portraits, in his historical investigations. Barthes' selection of images goes hand in hand with his critical approach: in her majestic biography of Barthes, Tiphaine Samoyault has recently drawn attention to the sensory categories, invoking touch, smell, vision, and so on, borrowed from Michelet's own work and used by Barthes as chapter headers in his Michelet biography, labelling Barthes' approach an "affective" form of criticism (Samoyault 2015: 277–278 [my translation]). Although by no means as explicit as in his much later *Camera Lucida*, the use of photographs as first and foremost affective and emotional vehicles, for both Barthes and his readers, is thus already evident on the pages of *Michelet*. The prominent place of the Nadar portrait in his early work further resonates with his last book on photography, where Barthes states that Nadar is the "world's greatest photographer" (Barthes 1993: 68) and where he includes three images (of an original selection of ten) by this nineteenth-century photographer.

Moreover, after he was given the photograph of Michelet by Robert David, Barthes placed it on his desk while studying the historian's work (Samoyault 2017: 197); much in the same way, at the end of his life, he placed the much-discussed photograph of his mother as a child on his desk while writing *Camera Lucida*. In a further striking parallel between the two portraits, upon receipt of the portrait from Paris, Barthes again writes to his friend and describes its powerful, unsettling effect, indicating that he struggles to describe what he calls the "Kindness of a face" (Samoyault 2017: 526), a description that fits better with the photograph by an unkown photographer rather than the Nadar image, where Michelet's gaze is skeptical. Kindness is the very same characterization Barthes uses later to describe the photograph of his mother, in *Camera Lucida*: the word *bonté* occurs three times in the same paragraph that grapples with the description of the impact of this image on the author (Barthes 1993: 69). Although language apparently fails to accurately reflect Barthes' visceral experience of both portraits, there is one striking difference in his treatment of the portrait of Michelet and that of his mother as a child: he reproduces the former and withholds the latter. The different strategies employed by Barthes at the beginning and end of his career are most likely owing to his increasingly self-aware and reflexive use of photographic images in his work, as well as his evolving thought on photography more generally. In other words, even if the primary experiences of the two photographic portraits are similar in certain ways, the theoretical contexts of *Michelet* and *Camera Lucida* within which these viewing experiences are conveyed are not only separated by a proverbial and actual lifetime, but also marked by the death of the mother in 1977. This difference may be belied, however. Chantal Thomas has suggested that the affinity between the two books (or between Michelet, the historian, and *Camera Lucida*) lies precisely in the meditation on death, characteristic of Michelet's oeuvre (Thomas 2015: 92). Taken together with the new insights gained from the publication of hitherto unknown material, in both *Michelet* and *Camera Lucida* the contemplation of the photographic image and its emotional impact on the viewer are far from representing mere biographical anecdotes. Rather, as I have suggested above, the roots in biographical circumstances of Barthes' engagement with photography speak to what is one of his distinctive contributions to photography theory: namely the emphasis on the viewing experience and, concomitantly, the affective and potentially transformative power of the photographic image on the viewer.

Although Barthes wrote on landscape photography throughout his career (including, for example, on the rural scenes photographed by Daniel Boudinet in a 1977 article for the French fine art photography magazine *Créatis*), his overall preference apparently was for photographic portraiture, an aspect that is confirmed and further emphasized by his posthumously published works, as well as being the grounds on which his theory of photography has often been critiqued, most comprehensively by James Elkins (2011). For Barthes, the human face in photography is the locus for the most effective conveyance of the affective power of photography, and his major interest in what may be classified as family snapshots rather than artistic portraiture, for example, further speaks to his intensified search (starting in the mid-1970s) for a 'neutral' form, one that escapes the binary structures of meaning and classification (a topic he explores explicitly in the 1977–1979 lecture series on *The Neutral*). In other words, a form not a priori shaped by ideological forces—for example, in the form of connotations or second-order meanings—and therefore possessing a certain "*innocence*," as he found, at least once, in his mother's childhood image (Barthes 1993: 69).

Camera Lucida through the lens of mourning

Considering the similar uses of photographic portraits in Barthes' early and late books, as well as the publication of his *Mourning Diary*, new insights can be gained from rereading *Camera Lucida* in this light, especially in relation to its writing process, the origin of a number of key ideas, and the deeper meaning of individual photographic images for Barthes. In addition to the extensive scholarly commentary *Camera Lucida* has received in the context of photography theory, scholarship focused on the evolution and production of Barthes' last book has mainly been concerned with the development of the text itself, with surprisingly little attention paid to the reproduced photographs, their provenance, and meaning for Barthes. For example, Jean-Louis Lebrave's 2002 essay has analyzed the intricate layering of notes and quotations fueling the writing of *Camera Lucida*, emphasizing the Proustian resonances in handwritten drafts and related filing cards that were even more pronounced than in the published version. The 330 dated notes (on the typical card format Barthes worked with of one-quarter of standard-sized paper) making up the *Mourning Diary*, written between October 26, 1977 (the day after the death of Barthes' mother) and September 15, 1979, further confirm the close connection to Proust, but also draw attention to new textual and visual connections and influences with respect to *Camera Lucida*.

Neil Badmington has recently argued that the notion of *punctum* developed in the first part of *Camera Lucida*, as pertaining to a particularly poignant detail of a photographic image that speaks more or less powerfully to the individual viewer, has a cinematic origin rather than the usually assumed photographic one (Badmington 2016: 44–54). In a similar fashion of displaced origins or recontextualization that have become apparent only by virtue of posthumous publications, Barthes' differently oriented definition of the *punctum* in the second half of *Camera Lucida* as photography's noema or essence, that is, the "that-has-been" (Barthes 1993: 96), is equally prefigured in his diary. Barthes repeatedly refers to Donald Woods Winnicott's text "Fear of Breakdown" (Barthes 2010: 122), in which the psychoanalyst considers the long-term impact of early trauma. This text provides Barthes with a formulation that both captures his own psychological state as well as applying to the paradoxical temporal structure of the photographic image (as showing something in the present that has already happened in the past). In his *Mourning Diary*, three references to Winnicott are directly linked to Barthes' experience of his mother's death: first, he writes about the "*fear of what has happened*," which he then reformulates as a "*catastrophe that has already occurred*" (Barthes 2010: 122, 158, 203; original emphasis). This latter phrasing anticipates the verbatim reference in *Camera Lucida*, where Barthes adds that "every photograph is this catastrophe" (Barthes 1993: 96). Both examples show the extent to which Barthes' primarily psychological and individual reactions to cinematic images and to the event of the loss of his mother are later transcribed to fit the conceptual context of his discussion of photography in *Camera Lucida*.

With respect to photographic images, more specifically, I have already discussed the significance of a perceived kindness in Barthes' viewing of selected portrait photographs and the concomitant difficulty of description and, hence, a silencing of language in both his early *Michelet* and *Camera Lucida*. His *Mourning Diary* confirms this correlation between affective visual impact and silencing of language in Barthes' preoccupation with photography. On January 20, 1979, a few months before the writing of *Camera Lucida*, Barthes notes in his diary:

> *Maman*'s photo as a little girl, in the distance—in front of me on my desk. It was enough for me to look at it, to apprehend the *suchness* of her being (which I struggle to describe) in order to be reinvested by, immersed in, invaded, inundated by her kindness.
>
> *(Barthes 2010: 226 [translation modified])*

Barthes here perceives the kindness of the face of the mother as a child as the essence or "suchness" of her being and, just as in his letter to Robert David from 1945 in relation to Michelet, laments the difficulty in describing this kindness. The four synonyms with which Barthes seeks to capture the effect of the image on him point towards the inner struggle to speak (about) the photograph's impact. This short diary entry prefigures a further key aspect of Barthes' engagement with photographic images, one that he embeds into the theoretical framework of *Camera Lucida* (which is necessarily lacking in his diary), that is, the self-consciously and, hence, meta-theoretically naïve reading of the photographic image as, at least hypothetically, devoid of connotations. Hence, his wish "to be a primitive, without culture" (Barthes 1993: 7). The evidential power of the photographic image and its affective force lead to an inevitable silence of language, or, inversely, language is reduced to a deictic function only: "Here it is" (Barthes 1993: 5), in Barthes' view. On his final account, language would either "tame" the image or subject it to ideology inherent in any meta-language (Barthes 1993: 117). In a meta-reflexive mode, not long after the above-quoted entry, the diary itself enters a period of silence (with only one brief entry between the end of March and mid-June 1979), a silencing that Éric Marty describes as a "process of extinction" (Marty 2010: 24 [my translation]), during which Barthes turns to writing his book on photography.

There are two further observations to be made on the entry from January 20, 1979. First, Barthes casually mentions that the photograph of his mother as a child lies in front of him on his desk, confirming his working methodology that he already explored in writing *Michelet*: the text emerges out of a close and presumably constant dialog with the central portrait; Barthes literally works under the leading (photographic) gaze of his mother/child that he describes, later, in an entry from December 29, 1978 as a "measure" and a "judge" that "guides" him (Barthes 2010: 220) and then, in *Camera Lucida*, as his "Ariadne" in the photographic labyrinth (Barthes 1993: 73). Curiously, he also draws attention to his simultaneous distance from and proximity to the photograph. This dynamic recalls Walter Benjamin's famous evocation of "aura" as a "unique appearance of distance, no matter how close it may be" (Benjamin 1999: 518 [translation modified]) with respect to nineteenth-century photographic portraits in his "Little History of Photography," which Barthes, as preparation for *Camera Lucida*, read in the French translation of the *Nouvel Observateur* special photography issue (Yacavone 2012: 19–26). Second, the above entry (and others) from Barthes' *Mourning*

Diary confirms what has previously been a matter of debate and contention (at least in an English-speaking context), namely the actual existence of the notoriously absent photograph of the mother in *Camera Lucida*.

As I have argued elsewhere with reference to photographic evidence showing Barthes at his desk with the portrait of his mother as a child in front of him (Yacavone 2012: 164–166), the posthumous *Mourning Diary* leaves no doubt about the fact that the so-called Winter Garden Photograph, the existence of which has been disputed, does exist. (It is in fact preserved in the Barthes archive, in a separate box from the other photographs and not open to public viewing.) Barthes' diary entry from June 13,1978 captures the discovery of the photograph: "This morning, painfully returning to the photographs, overwhelmed by one in which *maman*, a gentle, discreet little girl beside Philippe Binger (the Winter Garden of Chennevières, 1898)" (Barthes 2010: 143). In one of his last interviews for French television, a melancholic Barthes recalls the same episode in a disarmingly open account of the encounter with the image of his mother (Thomas and Thomas 2015), highlighting that the speculation on the missing photograph in *Camera Lucida* was perhaps due to a lack of accessibility of (at the time) widely circulating visual material and information, rather than a deliberate strategy, beyond the logic of the arguments in *Camera Lucida*, that is, on Barthes' part. In addition to the television clip, in 1979, Barthes was willing to be photographed at his desk together with the childhood portrait in front of him, as I noted. This color portrait of Barthes circulated on the cover of the first edition of the 1981 collection of interviews *Le Grain de la voix* (Yacavone 2012: 165).

The real existence of the Winter Garden Photograph has implications for Barthes' wider theses on the theory of photography to the extent to which his ontological quest in *Camera Lucida* is not imaginary, but rooted in an actual photographic image. The missing image is thus neither fiction nor literature nor writing, but a photograph—not more, but also, crucially, not less than this (Yacavone 2012: 170–171). By the same token, posthumous publications have brought to light the slowly evolving process whereby Barthes' book on photography represents a unification of two, initially separate preoccupations in his life: the death of the mother in 1977 and his subsequent desire to acknowledge her existence through a "monument" (Barthes 2010: 133), on the one hand, and the commissioning of a book, in the same year, by the Cahiers du cinéma label (under which Barthes had previously published during the 1960s), on the other. The synthesis of the two events is evident in the *Mourning Diary* where reference to *Camera Lucida* is first made as the "book about Photography," followed by the expression "book around *maman*," which finally becomes "*Photo-Maman* book" (Barthes 2010: 105, 133, 136). It is also interesting to note that the last entry *pre*dates the discovery of the Winter Garden Photograph, which suggests that the idea to combine autobiographical discourse and photography theory in his last book *ante*dates the finding of the object that became the (visually absent) nodal point of the book. Once the two strands were consciously combined, Barthes was impatient to get to work on the book, as is clear from his diary as well as from a recently published letter to his life-long friend Philippe Rebeyrol, dated March 25, 1979. Barthes describes his book as "profondément lié aux images de maman"—that is, "profoundly related to the images of his mother"—and tells his friend that its writing is "affectively essential" for him, which is why he no longer wishes to postpone his work on it (Barthes 2015: 253 [my translation]).

Although the dates Barthes provides at the end of *Camera Lucida* suggest a swift writing period of only about six weeks, between April 15 and June 3, 1979, Badmington has rightly pointed out that the *Mourning Diary*, by contrast, reveals that the preparation of the book took much longer, and that Barthes struggled to begin writing for more than a year (Badmington 2016: 44). In part also owing to his lecturing commitments at the Collège de France, most notably his *Preparation of the Novel* series, as Barthes laments in the same letter to Rebeyrol, the groundwork for *Camera Lucida* also included intense exploration of photographic material. Apart from the search for his mother's essence in old family photographs—only one of which is actually reproduced in his book, that is, the "La Souche" or "The Stock" picture, a portrait of the mother as a child, depicted together with her brother Philippe Binger and their grandfather (Barthes 1993: 104)—Jean Narboni's recent testimony of the publication process of *Camera Lucida* sheds novel light on Barthes' selection of images.

Then the production editor of the Cahiers du cinéma imprint, Narboni received the original manuscript of *Camera Lucida* and collaborated with Barthes on its final layout during the summer and autumn of 1979. Together with the manuscript, Barthes submitted a list of illustrations containing 56 images, but quickly afterwards recalled his original propositions, indicating in a letter to the editor dated June 18, 1979 that he wishes to "greatly reduce" the number of illustrations (quoted in Narboni 2015: 44–46 [my translation]). Just as in the case of his first illustrated book, *Michelet*, Narboni's account confirms that Barthes paid close attention to the text-and-image dynamic in *Camera Lucida*, not only by selecting the images himself, but also by closely considering the place of images in his text and their captions. But, if the published text contains only 25 images, less than half of the initially proposed amount, omitting images that Barthes was initially keen on including, such as photographs by Robert Mapplethorpe, portraits of Rossini and Offenbach by Nadar, and a Duane Michals portrait of Andy Warhol (Narboni 2015: 79), it is reasonable to assume that aspects of the final selection were also due to circumstances beyond Barthes' control. Indeed, Narboni writes about the circuitous process whereby planned illustrations were discarded, replaced, and substituted by others, and that Barthes once, albeit halfheartedly, expressed the wish to renounce any kind of illustration with the aim of "facilitating" the publication process (quoted in Narboni 2015: 78 [my translation]). And yet, his suggestion that this process lacked a "plan" (Narboni 2015: 78) on Barthes' part is not fully convincing, not least given that the illustrations together represent both "another little history of photography," with images representing almost every decade of photographic history from 1820 to 1970, as Geoffrey Batchen has argued (Batchen 2009: 262), and a "history of the faceless," that is, the forgotten faces of history, as Magali Nachtergael has recently proposed (Nachtergael 2015: 66 [my translation]). Barthes insisted on including other images from the original list. As Narboni testifies, Barthes asserted his plan to reprint Daniel Boudinet's blue-green Polaroid photograph of a curtain in color and on special paper (Narboni 2015: 58), which affirms Diana Knight's argument that the frontispiece image is linked to Barthes' description of his mother's eyes as "blue-green" (Barthes 1993: 66), hence establishing an intermedial link between the only color image in *Camera Lucida* and the missing photograph of the mother (Knight 1997: 266).

As these new findings and details on the production process of *Camera Lucida* indicate, although idiosyncratic in many ways, Barthes' approach to photography theory may be described as generally inductive—that is, moving from contemplation of specific images to a formulation of the wider theoretical implications and conceptual insights gained from this close viewing. His original text, intended as a blurb and published for the first time in full as a facsimile in Narboni's book, is telling in this respect: much less enigmatic than the published (French) version of the Tibetan contemplation on death as a "super-illusion" (Barthes 1980; omitted in the English translation), Barthes' original draft is a glossing of his loosely phenomenological approach and an explanation of the intended word-and-image interplay. He writes for example:

> This search takes the form of a wandering: its author looks at some photographs that have a personal interest for him and seeks to define step by step where that which holds him, fascinates and moves him resides in these photographs.
>
> *(quoted in Narboni 2015: 72 [my translation])*

There is no straightforward and linear connection between images and text or ekphrasis here, but a back-and-forth meandering that is guided by emotion and affect as much as intellectual inquiry. Barthes thus goes on to define his discourse as both "intellectual and affective" (quoted in Narboni 2015: 72 [my translation]), of which the Nadar portrait of his wife Ernestine, reproduced as the first image of the second part of *Camera Lucida*, is a telling example.

Narboni quotes from the first manuscript version of Barthes' book, where he explicitly drew attention to the substitution of his own mother with the old woman depicted in Nadar's portrait: "It was as if [...] I had substituted my own mother with the mother of Nadar" (quoted in Narboni 2015: 94 [my translation]). Even before the publication of this explicit comment by Barthes, I have shown the level of confusion and/or substitution at work here: Nadar's portrait shows his wife Ernestine rather than his mother (already long dead when the photograph was taken in 1890), a mix-up aided by Beaumont Newhall's misleading dating of the image in his classic *History of Photography*, which Barthes consulted in preparation of *Camera Lucida* (Yacavone 2012: 170). Barthes' subsequent deletion of his commentary on the image emphasizes the extent to which he sought to protect his mother and her image from the theoretical discourse at the center of which he nonetheless places her—absent—photograph. "In the Mother," Barthes writes, "there was a radiant, irreducible core: my mother" (Barthes 1993: 75). However, as Narboni's account makes clear, Barthes at the time was informed that the Nadar photograph depicts the photographer's wife rather than his mother, which led Barthes to add to the image caption "mother" an ambiguous "or of his wife, one does not know" (quoted in Narboni 2015: 98 [my translation]). This suggestive practice of text-and-image relation that deliberately favors personal reading over historical accuracy is deployed throughout *Camera Lucida*. However, it is used to the most powerful effect in relation to the Winter Garden Photograph of the mother as a child, where the image disappears entirely 'behind' language. In other words, the ekphrastic account of the image evokes it in much detail, but replaces it and denies the reader the opportunity to scrutinize the image for him- or herself, owing to Barthes' fear, as he suggests, that the photograph may be seen as banal (Barthes 1993: 73). If language, in Barthes' last book, replaces the central and most important photograph, the posthumously published seminar on "Proust and Photography," as well as his highly fragmentary project "Autobiography in Images," move in the opposite direction: both texts evidence an attempt on Barthes' part to replace language by the photographic image.

A seminar on Proust and an "Autobiography in Images"

As I indicated in the introduction to this chapter, Barthes' posthumous publications that address photography date from the short period of 1977–1980. In parallel to working on *Camera Lucida*, he wrote the *Mourning Diary*, for example, but much of his time and energy in these years was taken up by the preparation of lectures and seminars at the Collège de France, as letters and diary entries from this period frequently emphasize. Mainly concerning the question of creative writing—more specifically, how one actually writes a novel—Barthes' *Preparation of the Novel* series, delivered in two installments in 1978–1979 and

1979–1980, also addresses photography. In one session, from February 17, 1979, Barthes discusses the reality aspect of the short poetic form of the haiku, harkening back to his 1968 discussion of the 'effect of the real' in Flaubert's fiction. If he analyzed detailed descriptions of a room's décor in Flaubert's short story "A Simple Heart" as an example of realist literature's production of a rhetorical effect of the real, here the emphasis is on the visual and its dominance over language in producing the reality effect. In the lecture, Barthes makes a strong analogy between a figurative disappearance of language in haiku ("language fading into the background, to be supplanted by a certainty of reality" [Barthes 2011: 70]) and photography's particularly powerful reality effect. With his future *Camera Lucida*, which he started writing a few months after the February session, likely in mind, he remarks that the specificity of the photographic image and this effect have not yet fully been explored and he continues by formulating the hypothesis that photography is defined by a "that has been" (Barthes 2011: 71), which represents the first occurrence of this expression in Barthes' work. Before the lecture moves on to discussion of individual haiku poems, Barthes proposes that a "*Theory* of photography"—here, as in *Camera Lucida*, contrasted with cinema, of which there is no theory but only a "culture"—"might be possible" (Barthes 2011: 71; original emphasis). If *Camera Lucida* can be seen to pursue such a theory or its possibility, his two unfinished projects, the seminar on "Proust and Photography" and his notes on an "Autobiography in Images," both explicitly turn away from any systematic theory of photography. Still closely related to the use of photographic images, they instead epitomize an even more creative and experimental probing of the affective, (auto)biographical, and imaginary effects and impacts of the photographic image that Barthes pursued during the final months of his life.

"Proust and Photography" was posthumously published in 2003 (and translated into English in 2011), as an appendix to *The Preparation of the Novel* lecture series. Planned as an "Examination of a Little-Known Photographic Archive," as the subtitle specifies, Barthes selects around 50 photographic portraits of Marcel Proust, his family, friends, and acquaintances, taken by Paul Nadar, son of Gaspard-Félix Tournachon Nadar, whose portraits were important to *Camera Lucida*. Yet Barthes never delivered the seminar. The evening before he had arranged to begin the projection of the images in a darkened seminar room at the Collège de France, he crossed the Rue des Écoles with the intention to check the image projector. He was hit by a van, later dying from the consequences of this accident in the context of long-term health problems (Samoyault 2017: 6). Even more elliptical than the rest of his lecture notes (where existing voice recordings complement the written notes, which has led to a re-edition of *The Preparation of the Novel* in French in 2015, taking account of the spoken comments), the posthumous publication of "Proust and Photography" consists only of some introductory notes, followed by the Paul Nadar photographs, which are arranged alphabetically as per the sitter's name and accompanied, in turn, by brief biographical comments on the sitter and his or her relation to Proust and his novel (information Barthes chiefly takes form George Painter's two-volume biography of Proust from 1959–1965).

"Proust and Photography" not only relates to Proust's importance for, and wide-ranging influence on, Barthes, but also shows the extent to which Barthes' use of Paul Nadar's photographs is based on the specific realist ontology of photography developed in *Camera Lucida* (Yacavone 2009: 105–109). However, recent research carried out in Barthes' archive (by myself and, most importantly for our context, by Magali Nachtergael) has brought to light the fragmentary notes for an autobiographical project "in Images," intended to consist exclusively of photographs, which leads to a different, forward-looking interpretation of the seminar. "Proust and Photography" and "Autobiography in Images" represent Barthes' turning away from the more theoretical considerations of *Camera Lucida*, and both exemplify an expression of the same autobiographically and affectively oriented intention vis-à-vis photography. But "Proust and Photography" takes a negative approach in the sense that it draws attention to everything that it does *not* attempt to do. Barthes begins his seminar by anticipating several likely "disappointments" on the part of his audience, with the first one consisting in "keeping [his] interventions to a minimum" (Barthes 2011: 308). Having become a cultural celebrity in the late 1970s (owing to the far-reaching success of his *A Lover's Discourse: Fragments*), Barthes' name alone drew large audiences to his lectures and seminars at the Collège de France, and his intention to disappear in the semi-dark projection room may well have disappointed potential members of his audience. Barthes imagines the audience as comprising what he calls "Marcelians," that is, only those interested in Marcel as a "social being" rather than in Proust, the established French literary author (Barthes 2011: 309). With this focus on Marcel's life, social habits, and peculiarities comes the next wave of disappointments, according to Barthes. Introducing the topic of his seminar, he again defines his aims negatively: neither an analysis of the links between Proust and photography nor even a seminar on 'Proust,' as he clarifies (Barthes 2011: 309). He will not analyze the photographs: "no ideas, no literary or photographic remarks, no attempt" to find correspondences between them and Proust's *In Search of Lost Time*, nor is the aim of the seminar "intellectual," and "there'll be no 'theory'" (at least, not beyond the few introductory remarks; Barthes 2011: 310). What then, one may wonder, is the purpose of Barthes' endeavor?

From our perspective, Barthes aims to fully exploit the affective power of the photographic image, against the background of reading Proust's novel. In his characteristically expressive language on the subject, he wishes to "produce an intoxication, a fascination," which he goes on to define as "particular to the Image" (Barthes 2011: 310). Put differently, Barthes' presentation places images before discourse to replicate the photographs' effect on the viewer that he himself experienced; intoxication is therefore not to be read in a pathological sense, but as a form of excitement and exhilaration. In a similar manner, he defines the identification of biographical "keys" or clues in relation to Proust's novel, that is, the supposed real model for the fictional character, as an "excitement" and a "cryptological energy" (Barthes 2011: 314). Further twisting the traditional understanding of the identification of keys (for which Proust's work has been a particularly rich field of exploration), Barthes states that the deciphering of clues does not refer to Proust's life, but to the reader and his or her imagination (Yacavone 2009: 104–105). Keys therefore "strengthen and develop the *imaginary* link with the Work" (Barthes 2011: 314; original emphasis). The specific role and function of photography in this context is to excite and ignite the 'cryptological energy,' on the one hand, and to affect a "confrontation," as Barthes notes, "between the Dream, the Imaginary of reading and *Reality*," on the other (Barthes 2011: 314; original emphasis). In other words, the photographic portraits by Paul Nadar as shown by Barthes are aimed at confronting the reader with his or her imaginary image of the characters in Proust's novel, a clash that can lead to (further) "disappointment" or, indeed, the intended "intoxication" (Barthes 2011: 315).

Barthes' selection of photographs for the purpose of intoxicating his audience and his sparse comments on them reflect his rejection of establishing the keys to Proust's novel in the traditional sense, while simultaneously playing on loose biographical links between the photographed person and Proust's life and literary work. But, he also goes further and connects the images to his own biography, for instance, when he comments on the portrait of

Professor Édouard Brissaud that he is the father of the "Dr. B. who treated [Barthes]" for his pulmonary ailment, the sons of whom he attended school with (Barthes 2011: 328). Or, pondering the death in 1952 of the Comtesse Greffulhe in light of her iconic portrait showcasing the back of her lily-covered dress and her facial reflection in a mirror, he exclaims "I was writing *Degree Zero*!" (Barthes 2011: 345). This kind of sudden short-circuiting of his own biography with that of Proust is reminiscent of Barthes' captioning of one of his childhood photographs included in *Roland Barthes by Roland Barthes*, which reads: "*Contemporaries? I was beginning to walk, Proust was still alive, and finishing* À la Recherche du temps perdu" (Barthes 1995: 23; original emphasis). Two other portraits included in his seminar are childhood portraits of girls: Jeanne Pouquet and Gabrielle Schwartz. Barthes remarks in the same personal tone: "I like the little girls from this period. [...] Perhaps because it's more or less that of my mothers' childhood" (Barthes 2011: 362). It is in the photographic section of "Proust and Photography" that his use of photographs is more positively affirmed: unlike the preliminary comments that indicate everything the seminar is *not*, Barthes' fusion of the Nadar portraits with his own biography experiments with a new form of biographical writing (Nachtergael 2012: 125), one that finds its positive expression in the notes for a planned autobiographical project "New Look" (Fonds Roland Barthes n.d., card no. 37 [Barthes uses the English expression]).

His intended, although of course not complete and literal, silence in front of the photographs by Paul Nadar in his seminar is congruent not only with Barthes' understanding of "fascination" as having "nothing to say" (Barthes 2011: 310), but also with the wider trajectory of his probing of photography's affective power as a silencing of language. This would have been fully achieved, however, in "Autobiography in Images," given Barthes' plan to tell the story of his life through an arrangement of photographic images without, or with only very minimal, accompanying text. Preserved in Barthes' archive in the Bibliothèque Nationale de France, an envelope belonging to his photography-related projects contains 54 handwritten index cards, as well as a number of images: postcards from Japan and the negative of the aforementioned "The Stock" family photograph (included in *Camera Lucida*), as well as a postcard showing an aerial view of Urt (Barthes' usual summer residence and where he wrote *Camera Lucida*).

These images are part of what Barthes, on the note cards from the same envelope, refers to as "My life in images/New attempt at autobiography/An autobiography New Look" (Fonds Roland Barthes n.d., card no. 37 [my translation]; underlining in the original). Penciled on the side of this card is a further comment that speaks to Barthes' intent to assemble 50 photographs of his life to extract and choreograph (in a Brechtian fashion, as he hints) a new form of visual autobiography (Nachtergael speaks of Barthes' "scénographie," 2012: 123). Although Barthes explicitly refers to the seminar on Proust and photography as a parallel project (Fonds Roland Barthes n.d., card no. 8), his emphasis on affect establishes a further connection between the two planned projects, based on the use of photographs as powerfully affective vehicles: "an autobiog [*sic*] with real images, centered on affect," Barthes notes (Fonds Roland Barthes n.d., card no. 39 [my translation]). Although Barthes wonders whether his 1975 autobiography represents a precursor to his current project, "Proust and Photography" and "Autobiography in Images" together represent a more radical approach to photography than the one explored in the photographic preface of his *Roland Barthes by Roland Barthes*. In the Proust seminar, Barthes planned to abandon general theoretical considerations and minimize discursive commentary in order to provide a platform for the full affective power of the photographic image to emerge; in the "New Look" project, he proposed to abandon language (almost) entirely. Any kind of meta-language in the form of ekphrasis or explanation, for example, is thus rejected and implicitly seen to hinder rather than help the viewing of photographs. Barthes here, in practice, reaches the logical conclusion of his own theoretical considerations, namely that the photograph is experienced as most affectively powerful in the absence of language.

In sum, Barthes' posthumously published correspondence, notes, lectures, and draft projects shed significant new light on his relationship with photography, from his use of photographic portraits in his early biography of Michelet, and his seeking to establish a theory of photography closely tied to the contemplation of individual images (both private and public) and their affective impact on viewers (*Camera Lucida*), to his subsequent turn away from theory and language more generally. This now expanded picture of Barthes' thinking on and through photography demonstrates, for instance, that his famous semiotic-structuralist analysis of the medium and its uses was a kind of intellectual detour —albeit a highly insightful and influential one—from the existential and affect-based account of photography initiated (in practice) in *Michelet* and later renewed and elaborated, but with clear continuity, not only in *Camera Lucida*, but also later, never fully realized work. Here, Barthes no longer attempts to describe his personal experience of photographs, but instead tries to provoke such experience for his readers and listeners. And it is clear that, even in such a paradigmatically personal work as "Autobiography in Images" would have been, this silencing of (meta-)language in the face of the image itself would have come to full fruition had Barthes lived long enough to realize it.[1]

Note

1 I wish to thank the British Academy and the Leverhulme Trust for the award of a Small Research Grant that has supported research in the Barthes archive. I am grateful to Éric Marty for granting permission to consult the archive, as well as Thomas Cazentre at the Bibliothèque Nationale de France for his help in accessing material.

References

Badmington, N. (2016) *The Afterlives of Roland Barthes*, London and New York: Bloomsbury.
Barthes, R. (1977) *Image Music Text*, trans. by S. Heath, London: Fontana Press.
Barthes, R. (1980) *La Chambre claire. Note sur la photographie*, Paris: Cahiers du cinéma/Gallimard/Seuil.
Barthes, R. (1985) *The Grain of the Voice: Interviews 1962-1980*, trans. by L. Coverdale, London: Cape.
Barthes, R. (1987) *Michelet*, trans. by R. Howard, Oxford: Blackwell.
Barthes, R. (1993) *Camera Lucida. Reflections on Photography*, trans. by R. Howard, London: Vintage.
Barthes, R. (1995) *Roland Barthes by Roland Barthes*, trans. by R. Howard, London: Papermac.
Barthes, R. (2000) "Inaugural Lecture," in S. Sontag (ed.) *A Roland Barthes Reader*, London: Vintage, pp. 457–478.
Barthes, R. (2010) *Mourning Diary*, trans. by R. Howard, New York: Hill & Wang.
Barthes, R. (2011) *The Preparation of the Novel. Lecture Courses and Seminars at the Collège de France (1978–1979 and 1979–1980)*, trans. by K. Briggs, New York: Columbia University Press.
Barthes, R. (2015) *Album. Inédits, correspondances et varia*, ed. É. Marty, Paris: Seuil.
Batchen, G. (2009) "*Camera Lucida*: Another Little History of Photography," in G. Batchen (ed.) *Photography Degree Zero. Reflections on Roland Barthes's Camera Lucida*, Cambridge, MA, and London: MIT Press, pp. 259–273.
Benjamin, W. (1999) "Little History of Photography," trans. by E. Jephcott and K. Shorter, in M. W. Jennings (ed.) *Selected Writings*, Cambridge, MA, and London: Belknap Press, vol. 2, pp. 507–530.
Elkins, J. (2011) *What Photography Is*, New York and London: Routledge.
Fonds Roland Barthes, "Autobiographie en Images," NAF 28630, Département des Manuscrits, Bibliothèque Nationale de France, Paris.
Knight, D. (1997) *Barthes and Utopia. Space, Travel, Writing*, Oxford: Clarendon Press.

Lebrave, J.-L. (2002) "La Genèse de *La Chambre Claire*," *Genesis*, 19, pp. 79–107.

Marty, É. (2010) *Roland Barthes, la littérature et le droit à la mort*, Paris: Seuil.

Nachtergael, M. (2012) "Vers l'autobiographie *New Look* de Roland Barthes," *Image and Narrative*, 13(4), pp. 112–128.

Nachtergael, M. (2015) *Roland Barthes contemporain*, Paris: Max Milo.

Narboni, J. (2015) *La Nuit sera noire et blanche: Roland Barthes, La Chambre claire, le cinéma*, Paris: Les Prairies ordinaires/Capricci.

Samoyault, T. (2015) *Roland Barthes. Biographie*, Paris: Seuil.

Samoyault, T. (2017) *Barthes. A Biography*, trans. by A. Brown, Cambridge: Polity.

Thomas, Ch. (2015) *Pour Roland Barthes*, Paris: Seuil.

Thomas, Ch. and Thomas, TTh. (dirs.) (2015) *Roland Barthes: Le théâtre du langage* [DVD], Paris: INA Editions.

Yacavone, K. (2009) "Reading Through Photography: Roland Barthes's Last Seminar 'Proust et la Photographie'," *French Forum*, 34(1), pp. 97–112.

Yacavone, K. (2012) *Benjamin, Barthes and the Singularity of Photography*, London and New York: Continuum.

21

Ideation and photography

A critique of François Laruelle's concept of abstraction[1]

John Roberts

Abstraction, mimesis, and photography

In *The Concept of Non-Photography* (2011), François Laruelle outlines an ambitious bid for a theory of photography that jettisons what he calls the "ontological distinctions and aesthetics notions" of the humanities (2011: viii); in other words, a theory of photography that demotes the interpretative and technical categories that hitherto have laid claim to photography's singular realism, or world-disclosing capacities. This expulsion of photography's normative "appeal to the World, to the perceived object" is to be pursued (2011: 3), not unsurprisingly, through an intellectual withdrawal from the organizational character of the social particulars, genres, styles and historicity of the photograph. This is why Laruelle is so insistent on the need for a theory of photography that rejects what he terms—familiar from his non-philosophy more generally—a decisionist interpretation of the photograph's manifest content, a form of interpretation that simply 'moves meaning around', as a "complement, a rectification, a deconstruction, [or] a supplement" (Laruelle 2010: xxii). This 'post-interpretative' approach he calls an *abstract* theory of photography. Standard photographic theory accumulates stories and multiple historical truths and as such registers the quality and range of photographic affects; an abstract theory of photography, on the other hand, dispenses with them. Abstraction, then, in classically scientific terms is a subtractive move—an axiomatic and reductive operation—rather than a hermeneutic exercise. Or, as Ray Brassier explains in an early, relatively sympathetic account of Laruelle's non-philosophy, decisionism constrains what philosophy might do: "the possibilities of philosophical invention, whether formal or substantive, are already delimited in advance by [a philosophical] decisional syntax" (Brassier 2003: 33).

But this move is not built out of a new language of photographic form. By abstraction Laruelle does not mean the creation of a photographic theory that interrogates the immanent spatial relations of the photograph, as opposed to the semiotic analysis of a scene or setting as a focus for the presence or absence of human activity, or that draws out the insignificant or overlooked detail (as in Salvador Dalí and Roland Barthes) as a means of defamiliarizing photography's manifest content. There is no recourse to the 'abstractedness' of the internal relations of photography, or nothing of this sort that would turn his concept of abstraction into a new version of formalism. Furthermore, his understanding of abstraction has nothing in common with the production and reception of photography under the law of real abstraction (photography's commodity form), and therefore with the notion of real abstraction as source of photographic truth (as in photography's reliance since the 1960s [Ed Ruscha] on repetition and the sequence as a metonym of 'reified vision').

Nor has his theory anything to do with photography's relationship to social abstraction as the correlative of real abstraction or the value form (the socially heteronomous impact of capitalist competition on the material world, or what Henri Lefebvre (1991) called "representations of space": the production and reproduction of the built environment) in photography's capacity for the panoramic bird's eye view. Rather, for Laruelle (2011), abstraction is what happens to photography when thinking about photography discards the mechanics of photographic interpretation as such—its "realist illusion" (8), its "already made 'interpretative frameworks'" (70)—to concentrate on photography as a specific order of the scientific, what he calls its infinite field of materialities: a "manifold of determinations without synthesis" (53). That is, photography is not a support for something else, something to be explained or narrativized on the basis of its manifest content, but an "unlimited theoretical space" (72).

In this respect, Laruelle follows, in a standard way, what other philosophers and theorists of photographic representation, from Charles Sanders Peirce onwards, have necessarily foregrounded: What is photography's relationship to the real? Why does photography continually recall us to the problem of the real? But for Laruelle, dramatically, this is pursued without any attachment to what has usually defined all schools—realist and anti-realist alike—within this tradition: namely photography's particular and vivid *worldliness* or social embeddedness. Thus, if realists and anti-realists differ on the conventionality or non-conventionality of the interrelationship between index and icon in photography, they at least both necessarily recognize that photographs establish a definite social-relational encounter with the world. Even Umberto Eco (1976), in his defence of the photograph as an autonomous symbol, recognizes this. Laruelle, however, pursues a conventionalist anti-realism and anti-Peircian position on the index–icon interface to the point where the photograph becomes absolute and pure idea. Indeed, abstraction is another word for the photograph's *ideational distance* from its depicted objects. "A photo manifests a distance of an infinite order or inequality to the World," rendering things as "inert and sterile" before they appear (Laruelle 2011: 100). "Photography allows one to see what a thing that is photographed resembles: the photo is only ever the photo *of* that which it *appears* to be the photo" (2011: 102; original emphasis). In other words, Laruelle, wants an abstract theory of photography that brackets the idea of photography as a possible mimetic doubling of the world. Photographs for Laruelle are definable not through what they represent—their perceivable objects—but what they represent as a photographic act or force itself—"a vision force"—and as such are absolutely distinguishable from their extra-representational objects. He talks of photographs as being apparitional in this sense.

Thus, for all photo-theory's commonplace talk of photo-*realism*, photographs in fact, do not share a common space of objectification with perception at all; represented objects in photographs are one thing, their objective referents another. This is why he insists it is more appropriate to talk of photographs resembling *other* photographs than it is of photographs resembling their depicted objects. Indeed, contrary to the research-scientific, legal and social uses of photography, photography has never been nor can ever be an objective aid. That is, every claim on photographic naturalism and realism suppresses the "infinite uni-verse that every time, every single photo deploys" (Laruelle 2011: 58).

Unsurprisingly, then, abstraction is a transcendentalizing process that runs in *parallel* with the world, as opposed to being in intimate association with it (in the Hegelian and dialectical sense), and, as such, is a mode of appearing that is wholly exterior to appearances as a source of knowledge. In the photograph: "There are only pure 'phenomena', with no in-itself hidden behind them"; the photograph is a "pure irreflective manifestation of the phenomenon-without-logos" (Laruelle 2011: 95, 96).

A strange disjunction emerges. On the one hand, photography invites an "unlimited theoretical" production, but, on the other hand, it resists as a condition of its essence—what Laruelle calls the photograph's 'literalness' or reproduction of the real-as-identity—any social and discursive encounter with its depicted objects. This is perhaps why abstraction takes on a heightened figural character for Laruelle, as opposed to its possessing any kind of socially productive and discursive identity: in creating this flattened and parallel universe, all photographs (not just staged or digitally composite ones) are an "absolute fiction" (2011: 20).

Indeed, *The Concept of Non-Photography* would appear to read, in part, like a hypertrophic extension of Martha Rosler's 1981 critique of the photo-document—a clean sweeping away of all documentary practice's social horizons and presumptions. But whereas Rosler presents an ideological critique of humanist approaches to documentary practice and talks disparagingly about the "liberal sensibility," "victim" ideology, "trophy hunting," "weep[ing]" vision, "sentimental mythification," and "aesthetic eternality" of traditional documentary practice (Rosler 2006: 176–186), Laruelle ignores the humanist atrophy of documentary practice and photo-writing and talks simply of the photo-document's ideological blankness. What concerns him is not that documentary photography and thinking are a haven for aestheticist and humanist idealizations of everyday life, but that photography is quite simply a blank art, an inert registration of things. Thus, whether photo-documents appear to aestheticize, idealize or humanize appearances (in the interests of bourgeois ideology) is neither here nor there, because photography is nothing other than a flat fictionalization of the world. Blankness is what Laruelle sees, therefore, as the distance between what always appears in the image and the world of things it references; there is no correlation. And because there is no correlation, worrying about 'aestheticization' and 'idealization' is irrelevant, given that there is no stable photographic truth that such 'aestheticization' and 'idealization' can be measured against. Talking about photographs as things that might be found wanting in matters of realism is, then, a category mistake. This allows Laruelle to treat the photograph's 'inertness' as the essential expression of the photograph's fictiveness—that is, blankness, as the space for absolute fiction, becomes the name precisely for the capacity of the photograph for both formal experiment and theoretical speculation—without fearing a loss of realism. So, if the loss of realism is an irrelevance, then the gap between what appears in the image and the world of things it references can form the basis for speculative modes of contextualization and reframing, of conceptual invention and chiasmus.

The basis for a socially discursive account of the production and reception of photography is obviously threatened here. Photographs lose their socially determined, causal-historic-genealogical identity—their identity as *concrete* abstractions derived from appearances—to become things operating transcendentally at the limits of thought, that is, irreducible to representation and causation. This dissociation of the photograph from its depicted objects and conditions of production, however, is hardly novel within conventionalist photo-theory, even within montage theory. Post-Kantian realists and idealists and avant-gardists and modernists have, of course, long attacked the false conflation between resemblance and truth. As such, there is nothing progressive in photo-theory about defending the powers of resemblance of the singular photo-documentary image and its pure or formal integrity, separate from multiple strategies of image-text production. Photography's claims on the truth of photography are irreducible to the naturalistic photo-document. But why, here, the *irreal inversion* of photography under the heading of abstraction? Why the absolute dismantling of indexicality and mimesis, and the reification of the photograph-as-symbol, in the name of a fictive abstraction? Why do photography and photo-theory need to become this parallel vision-force?

Photography, totality, and anti-decisionism

Laruelle's critique of decisionism more broadly is predicated upon on what we might call a fear of philosophical propinquity or subjective intimacy. If Peter Sloterdijk (2012) has denigrated Western philosophy as a tragic history of *epoché* and ascetic contemplation, of maddening distance, Laruelle (2010) sees it, from the opposite perspective, as a febrile and maddening entanglement of the philosophical subject with its objects. Western philosophy, or Greco-Occidental thought, is always damagingly caught up with the arbitrary judgements and circularity of 'doublet-thinking': the endless passage back and forth from one contrary to another. Even deconstructionism cannot escape this: as soon as the bifurcate logic is dismantled through the introduction of a suspensive third term, the circularity of meaning is restored at a higher level, a mere "softening" (Laruelle 2011: 133) of the would-be perils of decisionism; 'either/or' is changed for 'neither one nor the other', a mere supplementarity of alterity. Laruelle's post-metaphysical, post-dialectical, non-differencing-as-decisionism solution, then, is bracingly simple, if technically convoluted: a kind of non-subjectivist halting to philosophical scission and aporetic scrupulousness, in order to situate thinking at the border between the universalizing ambitions of philosophical conceptualization (the normative) and the axiomatic demands of science; a thinking that rejects 'more or less' an alterant turning; a thinking that incorporates difference without decisionism into a philosophy that knows itself like a science as a practice of the real. But this is not an invitation to let science take over the reins of philosophy. On the contrary, if philosophy for Laruelle needs to renew its vows with science—in order to clear out all the epistemological machinery of interpretation and Western philosophy's decisionist intimacy with its objects—these vows do not in turn produce a new unified scientized philosophy. If philosophy needs science to rid itself of decisionism, this new science (of philosophy-as-science) refuses to forfeit philosophy's special claims on the speculative. This is why Laruelle's abstract theory of photography does not actually set out to explain photography scientifically—give it an ontology, or provide a topology of its effects or a taxonomy of its attributes through a discussion of its uses—but, rather, to render it generically available for "unlimited theoretical" production. This is because photography's would-be non-resemblance to its objects provides not just a new formal set of possibilities for photographic production, but a new *philosophical-scientific* context for its non-decisionist reception. In the abandonment of external interpretative frameworks, photography is able to open itself up to a new photographic ideational immanence. That is, in detaching photography from the binarisms and 'stable' totalities of perception and representation, the "photographic state of things" can be rethought in a "more 'internal'" way (Laruelle 2011: 78). And, therefore, it is precisely here, around the trope of a new 'internality', that Laruelle's post-mimetic theory of photography meets up with his critique of decisionism and his non-philosophy.

Nature, contingency, and the object

In an article on Laruelle's speculative methodology, Andrew McGettigan has called Laruelle, pejoratively, a philosopher as strong poet (in Richard Rorty's sense), in which, frustratingly, the philosopher's critical 'intuition' does the philosophical work, separate from any adequate historical and theoretical account of his objects of critique (McGettigan 2012: 41). There is some truth in this, but Laruelle's commitment to theoretical speculation at the expense of the messy ideological, historical and social entanglements of objects and concepts is less a failure of methodological judiciousness and explanatory clarity than a familiar collapse of the critique of dialectics into an abstract rationalism, which it shares with some aspects of speculative realism. So, the idea that we can subjectivize Laruelle or Laruelle's anti-decisionist non-philosopher as a 'strong poet' figure conflicts with the scientific reassertion of the object here. There is, in fact, no subject at stake in Laruelle's non-philosophy (Laruelle 2015). Indeed, both Laruelle and speculative realism represent forms of rationalism that depose post-Kantian philosophy in the name of a *new thinking of the object* (a thinking of the object irreducible to the subject).[2] The unlimited production of theory, consequently, derives from the possible ways in which the object casts its materiality as a vector of forces *over* the subject.

In this light, mathematicized science and theoretical speculation, in their immanent analysis of the object 'in-itself', become the privileged means by which the thinker exposes the false or weak abstractions (ideological thinking), and their forms of intellectual support, in the consensual intersubjectivity of the philosophical cogito. In a crucial sense, then, the enemy is not exactly appearances here, but the metaphysical projection of thought into appearances, in an echo of the classic post-Kantian and post-Hegelian post-subject 'scientism' of Rudolf Carnap (1997). If Laruelle calls the outcome of the philosophical cogito decisionism, Quentin Meillassoux calls it correlationism and the "becoming-religious of thought," in these terms, or the "religionizing of reason" (Meillassoux 2008: 46–47). Indeed, this link between the idea of correlationism/decisionism and religious thought is fundamental to this return *to* the object. Thought *of* the object in-itself offers a resistance to the object as a metaphysical, or even dogmatic metaphysical, prop for spiritual values, 'language games' or various forms of historical probabilism.

For Meillassoux, this requires a fundamental temporalization of the object. As he argues in *After Finitude* (2008): philosophy's task against this current becoming-truth of belief (fideism, or faith independent of reason) is in the re-ontologization of the scope of mathematics as an absolutization of contingency; that is, the truth of mathematics lies in the fact that it subjects all things to the conditions of impermanence. And, therefore, the only convincing and non-circular way of exposing idealism and dogmatic metaphysics—and as such avoiding a clash of incommensurable secular and non-secular faiths—is *absolutizing* the contingency of all appearances, natural and social:

> critical potency is not necessarily on the side of those who would undermine the validity of absolute truths, but rather on the side of those who would succeed in criticizing *both* ideological dogmatism and sceptical fanaticism. Against dogmatism, it is important that we uphold the refusal of every metaphysical absolute, but against the reasoned violence of various fanaticisms, it is important that we re-discover in thought a modicum of absoluteness [in defending the contingency of all things].
>
> *(Meillassoux 2008: 49)*

In nature, therefore, things may have primary qualities and essences, but these primary qualities and essences can be at some future point *other than they are*. One day, our moon, millions and millions of years hence, may well not be the moon we know now; its movement and form may change, thereby changing scientific laws. Thus, by exposing nature as well as human production to the rigours of non-human timescales, the basic scientific principle that necessity cannot be derived from appearances (of science inductively arriving at lawfulness through appearances) provides an anti-metaphysical shock to 'interpretative', 'religionist' and 'creationist' thought. Nature is massively indifferent to our human-centred meanings and explanations, no matter how sophisticated. Thus, on this cosmological scale of things, the absolutization of contingency frees up human thought and human praxis from the anthropological limits of thought, thereby allowing us to accept the *non-necessity* of necessity as the ontological ground of all non-metaphysical, scientific and emancipatory theory.

For Laruelle, similarly, the "authentically scientific" critique of metaphysics is the problem of philosophy's reduction of thinking to anthropological meaning, hence his attack on post-Kantian philosophy (Laruelle 2010: xviii). Here, though, the focus is primarily on the hermeneutic privileging of difference in post-Kantian thought. In post-Kantian philosophy, ontologization of difference (contingency, heterogeneity), far from freeing philosophy from closed totalities, produces a new metaphysical move: the 'coupling' and mutual constitution of *differences*. That is, philosophies of difference are merely localized *redistributions* of essences, a rearrangement and displacement of them, creating new idealist unities and totalities. The fundamental problem of decisionist post-Kantian philosophy, therefore, lies in its inability or unwillingness, to "acquire a scientific, non-aporetic knowledge" of itself (Laruelle 2010: 11), beyond this distribution and rearrangement of differences (2010: xxii). Laruelle argues, then, that the failure to achieve these ends is due to the abandonment of the real as a *non-reflexive reality*, or what he calls the One. The One is a kind of cognate of an extra-discursive real (although this is not to be confused with matter as such, in a kind of positivistic or empirical sense), insofar as the One is immediately given *transcendentally*, that is, constitutes an "all-preceding" reality (2010: 153). The One or Indivision is:

> Absolutely immediate: … given (to) itself without passing through the mediation of a universal horizon, a nothingness, extasis or scission, a 'distance'. It is strictly non-reflexive, that is to say absolutely singular and autonomous as such before any universal (form, meaning, relation, syntax, difference, etc.).
>
> *(Laruelle 2010: 18–19)*

As such, the One is distinguished from the empirical and ideality:

> by a pure transcendental distinction that is immediately a 'real' distinction … the real no longer designating the ontic but rather [a] sphere of non-reflexive immanence. Transcendental distinction is here grounded 'in the nature of the thing'.
>
> *(2010: 185)*

The One is the object of an indivisible transcendental experience that is given to itself, "as what it is" (2010: 53). Hence, for Laruelle, the One is not that which is other to Difference, but is coextensive with the One. Difference is not what thought 'exits' from and 'returns to', but is the very ground of the "real absolute" (2010: 20). This means that "we do not exit from philosophy into the One; we describe the vision-in-One of philosophy" (155). The indivision of the One-as-Difference therefore guarantees the non-decisionist "immanent Unity" of philosophy and science (152).

In this respect, Meillassoux and Laruelle share a certain objectivist, de-subjectivizing spirit: the adaptation of science as a would-be enlargement of philosophical judgement outside the vicissitudes of a 'critical–critical' and aporetic thought of the object—a leap beyond finitude and hermeneutics we might say. But, if these moves, rightly, question the valorization of human-centred meaning, the cost of the rejection of the limits of being-thought is the demotion and disconnection of the links between praxis, meaning and abstraction. In freeing praxis from thought, as a consequence of freeing thought causally from its objects, praxis and thought are reunited under the auspices of a new speculative rationalism; thought leaps over mere appearances to announce a thought indifferent to the 'givens' and 'necessities' of the world. In this, the emphasis upon contingency *all the way down* returns philosophy to the spirit of a pre-Kantian Gnosticism. Because all things are contingent, then, thought should, at all points, be equal to this. This turns crucially on Laruelle's and speculative realism's understanding of the critique of sufficient reason.

Contingency and sufficient reason

To claim the necessity of non-necessity, and as such reject that things have good reason to be as they are rather than otherwise, is by definition to reject the claims of sufficient reason. There are no immutable reasons why things should *be* as they are, even movement of the planets. As Frank Ruda says (2012: 61): "the only sufficient reason for things to be how they are is that there is no sufficient reason for them to be how they are at all." But if this releases objects in the long run from the logic of necessity and dogmatic positivism, nevertheless, in the short run, it makes it impossible to infer that one set of objects, state of affairs or events is more probable or feasible than others, and therefore that a given set of objects, state of affairs or events is necessarily preferable; that is, that there is good reason for one thing to exist and take a particular form over another. The critique of sufficient reason, therefore, casts a chronic ontological instability or insecurity over such claims, insofar as such claims can always be held to be arbitrary. Now of course, this is precisely what drives this rationalist materialism's non-circular claims to post-metaphysical liberation: yes, the absolutization of contingency is destabilizing, but this is precisely its strength, because it allows extensive scope for "unlimited theoretical"—as we have noted in Laruelle—as a result of the unlocking of thought from the givenness of objects. Because things can always be other than they are means that philosophy loses its *fear* of the object, insofar as thinking is no longer forced to subject itself to the causal trajectories, pregiven histories and ontic intricacies and phenomenal stabilities of its objects—hence, Laruelle's rejection of photography's representational, social-relational intimacy with world, city and history.

Undoubtedly, the critique of sufficient reason is fundamental to the critique of any naïve realism or historicism; objects in and for themselves are not foundational for the natural sciences or social sciences, and, concomitantly, the present is not the pregiven outcome of the past. This is something that all post-Spinozan materialist philosophies (including Hegel's) share with speculative realism. But the absolutizing of contingency here as a de-subjectivizing of the philosophical cogito is unable to overcome a debilitating paradox: if *everything* is contingent, theories, social objects, natural kinds, then something might not be contingent; if everything is possible, then, something might not be possible —that is, the possibility of 'everything is possible' might include the possibility that 'everything is not possible'. There is always a possibility of non-possibility, always a possibility of non-contingency. Thus, in presupposing, therefore, that the non-necessity of necessity is the answer to dogmatic metaphysics on the grounds that it blocks off metaphysical language games and arbitrary interpretations, rationalist materialism of this stripe is guilty, as Ruda says, of a "non-dialectical generalization of un-totalizability" (2012: 68). That is, once contingency becomes the name for necessity and therefore precedes existence, the absolutization of contingency becomes a metaphysical and abstract notion itself, destructive of the continuity necessary for thought and practice and scientific enquiry in mortal, non-cosmological time (Macintyre 1990: 196–215). As Ruda explains:

> Contingency can only be logically anterior to any existence *if* there already is existence. Contingency is the retroactive anteriority to any existence *because* there is existence (thus it is not contingency that generates existence, but existence that generates insight into the very anteriority of contingency and hence already determines contingency).
>
> *(Ruda 2012: 68)*

The *necessity of contingency is itself contingent* (Hegel 1977). Or rather, the only necessity is not necessarily that of contingency.

Hence, the major outcome of the absolute release of contingency, of the liberation of the object from necessity, is that in the short term, paradoxically, it *leaves everything as it is*, because, if there is no reason why things *are* the way they are (within a given mortal time frame), then objects and their relations lose all traction as things that may change or *necessarily* resist change, or conversely may necessarily require change because they resist change. On this account, inferring change, on the basis of a probabilistic account of a given set of tendencies, is ruled out of court from the beginning. This is because such probabilistic tendencies are *themselves* held to be contingent or arbitrary under all conditions.

The political, and philosophical and scientific consequences that emerge from the absolute necessity of contingency, then, are deeply unappealing: as in Gnosticism, thought is uncoupled from the mediations between contingency, conceptualization and the real and, as such, unmoored from its embodiment in (self-constrained) practices and living subjects. This presents certain challenges, consequently, to this would-be new unity of science and philosophy. That is, it is unclear what the relationship between this new speculative unity of science and philosophy and practice actually is, and thus what it might enable faced with the intractabilities of the world.

Philosophy as science?

When science speaks about the mind-independent world, this does not mean that science believes that it is matter alone that guarantees materialism or the real for science, as if the truth *of* things is secured by the physicalist appropriation of a mind-independent nature. The real, rather, is produced at a conceptual level, out of this encounter with matter and the object, insofar as science works to produce the real through this process. The conceptualizations of science, therefore, do not mediate the real of a mind-independent world: they actively *produce* the real. However, they do not produce the real simply as idea, but as a space for further enquiry into, and transformation of, the real. This is why the discursive-real/real antipode of decisionism, correlationalism and speculative realism appears to misunderstand how science actually works in the world, given their reliance on a commonplace or naïve realist view of scientific practice perpetrated by many scientists themselves: that science posits the truth of an external nature separate from the subjective interests of scientists. In other words, the non-correlationist model of science is a phantasm, a science that denies the subjectivity of the scientists who produce it. Thus, contrary to the positing of truth as externality to the untruth of internality, science opens up a space in which scientific discourse has "real[existential] consequences," as Alexenka Zupancic puts it. As she argues:

> The fact that the discourse of science creates, opens up a space in which [scientific] discourse has (real) consequences also means that it can produce something that not only becomes a part of reality, but that can also change it.
>
> *(Zupancic 2014: 27)*

> Modern science literally creates a new real(ity); it is not that the object of science is mediated by its formulas, it is indistinguishable from them; it does not exist outside of them, yet it is real.
>
> *(Zupancic 2014: 25)*

Science *returns* to the real; therefore, effectively, the conventionalist argument about the real being an effect of discourse—which drives the critique of correlationism in the new rational materialism—is functionally misconceived. In other words, the conceptual production of scientific knowledge does not *subjectivize* the world—and as such produce it *as* discourse and philosophical speculation—it is the *answering call* to the real that the conceptualization of the real *necessarily* demands.

The temptations of scientism

One can see, then, why these forms of rational materialism have a certain scientistic and secular appeal at the moment, under the pressure of what we might call the Žižekian-type pincer movement of contemporary liberal fideism and fundamentalist dogmatisms. The neoliberal rationalization and tolerance of stupidity and ignorance as 'personal belief', and the justification of 'revealed truth' as 'spiritual flourishing' in various religious fundamentalisms spread the dogmatic subjectivization of thought into every nook and cranny of capitalist life, producing, as a counter to this, a tempting scientistic reaction or point of objectivist intolerance, *inside* contemporary philosophy, in its critique of both subjectivism and positivism—particularly in the light of the perceived radical impotence of post-Kantian philosophy. *After Finitude* and Laruelle's speculative scientism, thus, have a certain family resemblance to the post-ideological invective of Richard Dawkins (2006): *a plague on all your ideological plagues.*

Indeed, this is a new version of an old debate within the legacy of the Enlightenment. The new philosophical scientism eschews the historicity of reason (as in the immanent spirit of Hegel), in order to *re-scientize* reason in philosophy as the antithesis of ideology.[3] True emancipation, on its watch, lies in protecting science from the discursive cage of theory and embracing truth in philosophy as a knowledge of the 'great Outside', as a big, bold clear out of the "religionizing" of thought—or, in a slightly different register, philosophy doing to death the death of the death of God. But back on earth, in the day-to-day workings of ideology and practice, objects are not simply contingent essences that need liberating from the subjectivist grip of correlationism or decisionism (in order to resist the lures of fideism), but contradictory sites of subject-object mediation. This means that the 'object-liberation movement' of the new rationalist materialism fails (or more precisely rejects) a principle test of the dialectical tradition: the *unity* of appearance and reality. In this tradition, there are no mere appearances or mere illusions; appearances and illusions are a product of the movement of the real itself. And, therefore, all appearances and illusions contain some measure of truth; that is, appearances and illusions reveal as much as they conceal the reality that is manifest in them (Sayers 1985). If the conceptualization of science answers the real, then, it answers it on these terms: thought and praxis are immanent *to* illusion. This requires a subject who is transcendentally constituted not through a scientifically neutral access to the object-in-itself, or the indivisibility of the One, but through the vicissitudes of struggle and failure (Roberts 2011). This means, in turn, a fundamental *re-correlation* of subject and object. As Slavoj Žižek argues:

> we cannot gain full neutral access to reality because *we are part of it*. The epistemological distortion of our access to reality is the result of our *inclusion* in it, not of our distance from it ... the very epistemological failure (to reach reality) is an indication and effect of our being part of reality, of our inclusion within it.
>
> *(Žižek 2012: 646)*

The absolutization of contingency breaks this dialectical link, in its non-dialectical totalization of things, by treating *all* appearances as subjective illusions. As a result, what Marx calls the "relative necessity" of appearances (the explanatory link between appearances and objective/subjective 'real possibilities' in the world) is made incomprehensible.[4] Indeed, in Laruelle's concept of photography, it is made utterly trivial. This is why conceptualization as the theorization of appearances is an answer to the immanent transformation of the real, and not simply the means by which appearances' 'lack of reason' are exposed.

Flattening of the real

Laruelle's concept of non-photography (and non-philosophy) is particularly guilty here of this anti-dialectical flattening of appearance and the real—if one can actually assign culpability to a system that does not see the real as a philosophical problem at all in these terms and, therefore, has no sense of the relationship between appearances and knowledge, indeed, refuses it out of hand: the object of philosophy is not the conceptualization of the real as a delimited manifestation *of* the real, of an intervention into the real, but the "specularization of real objects" (Brassier 2003: 32). In other words, given that for Laruelle the photographic image is an *image-thing*, rather than an *image of the thing*, appearances have no constitutive relationship to truths that possibly stand 'behind them' inferentially. Photographs harbour "nothing invisible" (Laruelle 2011: 105). In other words, appearances have no immanent relationship to the real. This is why his abstract photo-theory wants nothing to do with photography's would-be relational, conceptual claims on its real objects (the world, history, the city): "Far from giving back perception, history or actuality, etc., in a weakened form" (2011: 53), photography reveals an "immanent chaos" that is derived directly from the gap between the image-thing and the image of the thing (2011: 95). Because, as Laruelle declares, a photograph is a semblance that resembles nothing—a flat identity in the last instance—there is no requirement on the part of an abstract theory of photography for thought in fact to be 'accountable' to appearances; indeed, for theory to be accountable to appearances is to undermine the very possibility of speculative thought itself. "A photo is more than a window or an opening, it is an infinite open, an unlimited universe from vision to the pure state" (2011: 108). Photographs are, on the contrary, *algorithms*—transitional states—not schemas, he says, and, as such, opposed to every philosophical synthesis that would hierarchize their contents based on a notion of inferential truth.

Consequently, photographic appearances do not *disclose* abstractions (social division, spatial relations, the unconscious); they are *themselves* abstractions, that is, manifestations of photography as a field of infinite materialities. And Laruelle calls this algorithmic potential photography's essential fractality (that is, its immanent resistance to philosophical synthesis as a condition of the gap between image-thing and image-as-thing, and not empirical evidence of the photograph's hidden geometric relations, in the manner of chaos theory). Fractality, then, is the intensive excess derived from photography's irreducibility to representation.

As such, in his later refinement of this theory in *Photo-Fiction, a Non-Standard Aesthetics* (2012), fractality as a critique of representation becomes more precisely the "onto-vectorial" and "quantic" aspect of the photograph (58), "liberating possibilities of new virtualities" (9). He calls this process, more broadly, photo-fiction or thought-art, in which the "photo is now the end of realism via an excess of the real and the absence of reality" (21). Indeed, the photographer 'loses' his or her causal and historico-conceptual relation to the world, in exchange for an art of "interweaving disciplines" (26). The quantic and the onto-vectorial, consequently, are forged by, and folded into, the "impossibilities of representation" (30). This in turn provides the jumping off point for a philosophy (non-philosophy) that builds off the absolute fiction of the photograph, without the conventional props of description or metaphor. Such descriptive and metaphoric moves are simply *photo-centric* (that is decisionist) and, accordingly, *tied* to appearances and the legacy of realism. As a result, the meaning of the photograph cannot be produced historically or dialectically, only quantically, through the immanent operations of the photo-fictive operations of the photograph itself. In such photo-fictions and their theoretical production, the conceptual image takes on an "objective appearance" (80) and, therefore, denies the world-determining mimesis and realist social-relation of standard photography and critical-theoretic or genealogical-historical criticism.

> In [photo] fiction the objective appearances are materially the same as in the photograph ... but they do not auto-conform themselves according to sufficiency, and it is in this that they form a probable chaos via the absence of the world and its sufficiency.
>
> *(Laruelle 2012: 81)*

In these terms, abstraction as a non-consistent multiplicity here is a version of the absolutization of contingency at the level of perception and returns us to all the problems of the post-dialectical tradition that beset this rationalist materialism and speculative realism.

The giving and asking for reasons

Photographs clearly are not simply windows on the world or fictive symbols; they are indeed abstractions, as Laruelle correctly insists, but they are abstractions not simply because they constitute in their theoretical reception a "transcendental creative force" (2012: 141) or refuse the "complacencies of recognition" (109) and "perceptual normality" (79), but because they are the outcome of, and instate, a specific set of social determinations. In this sense, photographs are properly concrete abstractions (socially embedded signs) that are also real abstractions (that is, subject to and the product of conflicting processes of social and technological reproduction and commodity exchange that operate trans-individually behind the backs of producers and spectators alike).[5] And this is why the appearances of photography, therefore, are not 'pure phenomena' or blank surfaces waiting for unlimited quantic speculation, but the objective concretization of these processes of abstraction and, as such, recoverable in theory and interpretation. Photography, then, is both a process *of* (real) abstraction and a system of appearance-generating mechanisms by which social abstractions are produced as signs as the outcome of this objective process. Consequently, the appearances of photography are caught up in the conflicts and contradictions of these processes as the source of photography's (abstract) truth-claims.

Thus, at one level, Laruelle, in the spirit of the critique of sufficient reason, is right: traditional photo criticism is happy to take most photography on trust (indeed, he calls his theoretical move a critique of the principle of sufficient photography). Accordingly, we need a theory of abstraction *in* photography and not as a formal afterthought or critical addendum; photographs are always more than their given or assumed appearances. This is in order to tell us that photographs are not mere things, not mere appearances, not mere illusory symbols, but conflictual ideological entities that, in their very fallen and fractured ideological condition, open out onto the world. Consequently, we also need a theory of abstraction that resists the received categories and generic assumptions of naïve realism; a theory of abstraction that is, as Laruelle puts it, resistant to false or pregiven syntheses and historicist closures of the dull machinery of generic interpretation. Laruelle is correct to insist, therefore, that, as abstractions, photographs demand an active theoretical engagement.

What we *do not* require, however, is a theory of abstraction in which a version of the absolutization of contingency dismantles the link between appearances and truth-telling as the necessary precondition of abstraction as speculation ("photography is a representation that neither reasons nor reflects"; Laruelle 2012: 37). This is a wholly *underdetermined* account of photography in which the inferential powers of photography—of photographic appearance as conceptually contentful in a determinate fashion—are weakened, diminishing the place of the photograph in a socially discursive account of representation as a "giving and asking for reasons."[6] In reifying singularity—in Laruelle's language, the quantic and fractal—therefore, the truth-producing aporias of the photograph's production disappear into the indeterminate and non-dialectical abstractedness of photography as a *non-consistent* multiplicity; a theory of abstraction *without* abstraction, so to speak, without social-relation and the real.

Abstraction and world-building

What kind of relationship between science and representation, then, best serves photography as a form of abstraction? How does photo-theory avoid the pitfalls of both naïve realism and the Gnostic theoreticism of photography as a parallel 'vision force'? This turns, I believe, on how we think about photographic practice and theory as *actively* possessing appearances. In this way, the active possession of appearances in photography is closer to *Darstellungsmethode* in Marx's sense (the capacity to produce truth from the active displacement or inversion of appearances; representation as the non-mimetic organization of particulars) than it is to simple *Vertretung* (replication, copying).[7] Hence, it is closer in theory and practice to representation as a form of staged production, as 'acting on', than it is to the conventional notion of representation as 'acting for', or the naturalistic reproduction of appearances. *Darstellungsmethode*'s active possession of appearances as a process of abstraction in the production and reception of the photograph, consequently, is not a matter of epistemology (of reflection), but, rather, an act of *world building*. That is, the work of possession (judgement) already begins from the process of abstraction (conceptualization) that is involved in taking the photograph and in its reception and judgement; abstraction works on abstraction.[8]

Nevertheless, it is *Vertretung* that is invariably identified with abstraction in photography, given the idea that copying presupposes an instrumental and self-distancing relation to the world. The idea of the possession of appearances as a reflexive and active process (as an answering response to the demands of the real as 'not-all'), so crucial to the practice of abstraction in *Darstellungsmethode*, is forgotten. Yet, it is precisely abstraction in these terms that is able to think the relationship between appearances and the demands of the real, discursiveness and the extra-discursive, as a condition of transformative practice. For it is precisely abstraction as *Darstellungsmethode* as the dialectical possession of appearances, as a claim on the inferential content of appearances—and, therefore, of the production of the real as the conceptualization of the 'not-all'—that creates a "new space of the real," in our theories and interpretations (Zupancic 2014: 28, 26). The real is not an essence or substance to be 'found' discursively or extra-discursively: it is a limit-condition to be defined by theory and interpretation. Laruelle and speculative realism, however, in their respective versions of 'world building' as abstraction offer a version of *Darstellungsmethode* without this necessary torsion. Indeed, they want abstraction without the real of the 'not-all' of appearances—without the inferential 'truth' of appearances—and, therefore, without a subject who, as an active part of this process, is part of this transformative and consequentialist struggle inside, and for, the real.

Finally, then, photographs maybe opaque, but their opacity is grounded in the irreducible sociality of appearances; things appear and have meanings because other things have happened before the photograph was taken, and, therefore, knowing why these other things happened will provide an entry point for the 'giving and asking of reasons' in front of the photograph. But this move is not an updated version of the social history of photography. Laruelle's resistance to this covert positivism of photographic theory is correct. Photographs cannot be made transparent by better theorizing, or better modes of interpretative (decisionist) understanding. But this does not mean that the causality of photographs cannot be reclaimed, for good reasons, and made to work in the interests of abstract truth. As an abstraction in these terms—as something that produces modes of abstraction from out of its sociality—the photograph is, therefore, above all else, a 'contentful' intentional act.

Notes

1 A shortened version of the essay was presented at the University of Westminster, June 2014, and published in *Photographies*, 2016.
2 There is much discussion about the heterogeneity of the term 'speculative realism'. Ray Brassier's short and barbed conspectus on its recent history, 'Postscript: Speculative Autopsy' in Peter Wolfendale's, *Object-Oriented Philosophy: The Noumenon's New Clothes* (2014) emphasizes this. However, despite the very different philosophical approaches to realism internal to its recent life on the 'philosophical market', as a broad church 'speculative realism', nevertheless, does share across its varied participants a certain kind of post-dialectical dissociation of truth from appearances (illusion); hence, the 'scientism' of its move against correlationism. Yet, as Brassier, point outs, Graham Harman's object-theoretics owes a greater debt to Heidegger's *anti*-scientism than it does to the anti-correlationism of a Rudolf Carnap. Indeed, the aesthetic content of this move has become increasingly apparent (see Harman 2018). So, if, for convenience sake, 'speculative realism' at the moment *stands for* a certain kind of post-metaphysical rationalist move within philosophy, its philosophical fortunes will, in the long run, certainly not be determined by the term 'speculative realism' itself; at some point, the crucial differences between participant positions will overspill the term, shattering whatever remains of the term's (fragile) self-identity. In other words, the inflationary or deflationary scientisms currently built into the term's 'popular' reception (certainly in the philosophically gullible and ahistorical constituencies of the artworld) will have to find their feet in the wider world as part of a dialectical account of realism and representation that has long preceded it.
3 For a Dawkinsesque defence of the legacy of the Enlightenment, see Jonathan I. Israel (2012).
4 This is principally an attack on Epicurus's speculative critique of necessity: 'It is a misfortune to live in necessity, but to live in necessity is not a necessity' (Epicurus, quoted by Marx, 1975: 43).
5 For a discussion of the transindividual function of real abstraction, see Alfred Sohn-Rethel (1978).
6 For a defence of the inferential role of representation, see Robert B. Brandom (2009: 184).
7 See Hans Friedrich Fulda (1978: 180–216).
8 For a discussion of abstraction and concrete abstraction, see Alberto Toscano (2008).

References

Brandom, R. B. (2009) *Reason in Philosophy*, Cambridge, MA, and London: Harvard University Press.

Brassier, R. (2003) "Axiomatic Heresy: The Non-Philosophy of François Laruelle," *Radical Philosophy*, No. 121, September/October, pp. 24–35.

Carnap, R. (1997) *The Unity of Science*, trans. with an introduction by Max Black, Bristol: Thoemmes Press.

Dawkins, R. (2006) *The God Delusion*, London: Bantam Press.

Eco, U. (1976) *A Theory of Semiotics*, Bloomington: Indiana University Press.

Fulda, H. F. (1978) "Dialektik als Darstellungsmethode von Marx," *Ajatus. Suomen Filosofisen Yhdistyksen vuosikirja*, 37, pp. 180–216.

Harman, G. (2018) *Speculative Realism: An Introduction*, Cambridge: Polity Press.

Hegel, G. W. F. (1977) *Phenomenology of Spirit*, trans. A. V. Miller, Oxford and New York: Oxford University Press.

Israel, J. I. (2012) *Democratic Enlightenment: Philosophy, Revolution, and Human Rights 1750–1790*, Oxford: Oxford University Press.

Laruelle, F. (2010) *Philosophies of Difference: A Critical Introduction to Non-Philosophy*, trans. Rocco Gangle, London and New York: Continuum.

Laruelle, F. (2011) *The Concept of Non-Photography*, trans. Robin Mackay, Falmouth: Urbanomic.

Laruelle, F. (2012) *Photo-Fiction, a Non-Standard Aesthetics*, trans. Drew S. Burk, Minneapolis: Univocal.

Laruelle, F. (2015) *Intellectuals and Power: The Insurrection of the Victim*, François Laruelle in conversation with Philippe Petit, trans. Anthony Paul Smith, Cambridge: Polity Press.

Lefebvre, H. (1991) *The Production of Space*, trans. Donald Nicholson-Smith, Oxford: Basil Blackwell.

Macintyre, A. (1990) *Three Versions of Moral Enquiry*, London: Duckworth.

McGettigan, A. (2012) "Fabrication Defect: François Laruelle's Philosophical Materials," *Radical Philosophy*, No. 175, September/October, pp. 33–42.

Marx, K. (1975) "Difference Between the Democritean and Epicurean Philosophy of Nature," in Karl Marx and Frederick Engels, *Collected Works*, Vol 1, London: Lawrence & Wishart.

Meillassoux, Q. (2008) *After Finitude: An Essay on the Necessity of Contingency*, preface by Alain Badiou, trans. Ray Brassier, London and New York: Continuum.

Roberts, J. (2011) *The Necessity of Errors*, London and New York: Verso.

Rosler, M. (2006) "In, Around, and Afterthoughts (on Documentary Photography)." Originally published in *Martha Rosler: 3 Works*, Nova Scotia College of Art and Design Press, Halifax, 1981. Reprinted in Martha Rosler, *Decoys and Disruptions: Selected Writings, 1975–2001*, Cambridge, MA, and London: MIT Press.

Ruda, F. (2012) "The Speculative Family, or: Critique of the Critical Critique of Critique," *Filozofski Vestnik*, Vol. 33, No. 2, pp. 53–76.

Sayers, S. (1985) *Reality and Reason: Dialectic and the Theory of Knowledge*, Oxford: Basil Blackwell.

Sloterdijk, P. (2012) *The Art of Philosophy*, New York: Columbia University Press.

Sohn-Rethel, A. (1978) *Intellectual and Manual Labour: A Critique of Epistemology*, London: Macmillan.

Toscano, A. (2008) "The Open Secret of Real Abstraction," *Rethinking Marxism*, Vol. 20, No. 2, pp. 273–287.

Wolfendale, P. (2014) *Object-Oriented Philosophy: The Noumenon's New Clothes*, Urbanomic, Falmouth.

Žižek, S. (2012) *Less than Nothing: Hegel and the Shadow of Dialectical Materialism*, London and New York: Verso.

Zupancic, A. (2014) "Realism in Psychoanalysis," in Lorenza Chiesa, ed., *Lacan and Philosophy: The New Generation*, Melbourne: re.press, pp. 21–34.

22

Fractal photography and the politics of invisibility

Daniel Rubinstein

This quote serves to introduce the key concepts of this chapter and draw attention to the importance of the non-rational—which is its main theme:

> We use systems to keep the wolf from the door, I thought. And systems are nothing but vast complexes of notions and concepts. Everything that helps us lose sight of the petty, pathetic and meaningless parts of our own selves. That is the wolf. The awkward, twisted or stupid part of the soul, the grudges and the envy, the hopelessness and the darkness, the childish joy and the unmanageable desire. The wolf is the part of human nature that the systems have no room for, the aspect of reality that our ideas, the firmament that the brain vaults above our lives, cannot fathom. The wolf is the truth.
>
> *(Knausgaard 2015)*

Preface

One approach to thinking about the way photography contributes to political theory and practice is to consider it as a tool for documentation, testimony, and reportage of the way political power operates on human subjects. Photography would then be defined as a critical medium posited against political power and offering a way of exposing the machinations of post-industrial society and the damage it inflicts on the environment, on animal and human life, and on the fates of individuals and of nations. One might have a political situation such as mass migration, low-wage labor, poverty, racism, exploitation, occupation, apartheid, or genocide and then ask what fitting photographic approach will adequately represent the political situation to be examined. One way of contemplating photography as political would be, therefore, as the creation of images about visible manifestations of hegemony, be it in the Houses of Parliament, on a council estate, in a fast-food joint, in a refugee camp, or in a gold mine. To do so would be to study photography as a "quantum of truth" and "moral leverage" (Berger 2013: 23–8) located outside the events and situations it attempts to represent, while simultaneously conceiving of them as spectacles that can be more or less adequately captured by optical means. The popularity of this approach to 'doing' photography is widespread and stretches across numerous projects, from Dorothea Lange's portrait of Florence Owens Thompson as "Migrant Mother" to the deliberately deadpan pictures by Martin Parr to the hyper-dramatic compositions of Sebastião Salgado. The common denominator of this way of working is that photography is conceived as a window that opens up onto a certain event. Vilém Flusser remarked somewhere that a window in the wall of a house is only capable of showing what is happening on the street beneath, but a photographic window is capable of showing things that are far away, either very small or very large, at the bottom of the ocean, on the face of a comet, and so on. In every case, photography is understood as capable of taking a slice of the real world and presenting it to the eye in the form of a two-dimensional picture. Photography, then, is regarded as a privileged technology that accurately represents the order of the world thanks to its grounding in industrial-scientific production, backed up by a transparently rational process of reliable recording. The danger in this way of thinking is that it determines photography as a discourse about exterior events, dominated entirely by the force of signification rather than by its own *materiality*. Questions are always asked about what the image is of, and what does it say about the state of the world, and this precludes submitting representation itself to radical critique.

Against the popular view outlined above, one that considers photography as a representation of objectively given reality, this chapter proposes the notion of 'fractal photography' as a way of thinking through the distinct political potential of the digital image. This move is indebted to post-structuralist philosophy's and queer theory's rejection of representational thinking, because of its reliance on universal totalities that are unable to account for the fragmented, discontinuous, non-binary, and multi-gendered realities of contemporary life. As Johnny Golding (2010) explains, the move towards fractal thinking in art and philosophy is motivated by the need to confront representation itself as a force that exerts considerable influence on human life. By interrogating representation and its effects, it is possible to restage photography, not as the more or less passive window onto the world, but as an active political agent that not only bears witness to the contemporary age, but is taking active part in seizing the 'out there' through algorithmic processing, discontinuous logics, and non-representational art.

Fractal photography is not a copy, a map, or a replica, but a force that acts in the world, and, through its action, it presents to the gaze the dynamic and fragmented forces that constitute the real political structures that shape the Earth. As will be discussed below, far from being a reliable depiction of an external reality, images harbor within themselves notions of incompleteness, randomness, mutation, and change—which also happen to be the key characteristics of contemporary life. For that reason, this chapter is not about photography as a window but about the inroads into the construction of experience afforded by it.

However, these departures from the logic of representation bring to light a problem encountered by anyone attempting to theorize photography as a fractal process constructed with algorithmic loops, glitches, viral assemblages, and data packets. This is because the theoretical instruments available for discussing photography dovetail with the paradigm of representation, and therefore the terminology of photography is rooted in the representational discourse, whether in its traditional iteration as objectively valid truth statement or in its more recent version as the expression of the subjectivity of the maker of the image.

The task of this essay, therefore, is two-pronged: its first aim is to explore the impact of representational thinking on photographic practices. Its other aim is to assemble a conceptual toolkit apt for grasping and inhabiting a form of photographic practice that is not dependent on paradigms of representation and its eternal bedfellows: image/model, subject/object, figure/ground.

From self to selfie

It is surely one of the most natural things to approach photographic images as legible visual surfaces that open a window onto the world outside the image. But what if the 'outside', not to mention the 'world', is not the stuff that is external to the image, but the very stuff the image itself is made of? If an image is not an expression of a point of view, but a process that organizes information, not a platform from which to observe the state of things, but itself a state of things, then perhaps before there can be an image of any kind, there has to be a relation of some sort that is required to produce the image. I would suggest that we ought to consider this relation as the first rule of politics for the twenty-first century. The continuous *transformation* of reality via infinitely proliferating code and the associated incessant creation of new landscapes by means of ballistic missiles, drone strikes, dark web, fracking, leaktivism, cyber warfare, sex trafficking, 'honor' killings, slave labor, or the melting of polar ice caps suggests that the image has to be rethought to accommodate within it relations of movement, flow, and transformation.

As an example of one such relation, consider the way Facebook 'friends' are not a window onto real (physical) friendships, but an autonomous and real (but not in a physical sense) entity that evolves according to an algorithmic logic (that is rapidly becoming integrated into living bodies). Although it is certainly possible to view Facebook as a (distorted) representation of one's social reality, there is also a possibility that Facebook is a symptom of life that is detached from its biological origins, and is re-oriented towards fuller integration into computational and algorithmic systems. Then Facebook might be explored as an image of a human condition that becomes truly immaterial, not interested in the production of spatial-temporal objects such as chairs, sausages, and tea for consumption in the 'real' world, but instead focused on manufacturing information rather than commodities. Social media industries such as Facebook, Twitter, and Snapchat can be understood not as leisure activities, but as sites of immaterial labor: an infinite process without an end product in which communication is work and work is communication.

Labor and play are, then, not two separate and dialectically opposed activities but one continuous process of transmission of signals that obliterates the distinction inherited from Marx (1859) between base (hardware) and superstructure (software). In this new economy of information capitalism (Pasquinelli 2011), surplus value is generated not from the traditional market activities of manufacturing, buying, and selling, but from updating one's status on Facebook, swiping right on Tindr, playing massive online multiplayer games, and navigating with Google Maps.

As Colebrook (2001: 697) observed: "There are not communities who *then* rely on channels and vehicles of communication. The immaterial communicational networks, the very machine of production, *is* the community." This conception of life as algorithmically, rather than biologically or socially, determined also suggests that the historical foundations of the rational self are being replaced by a new conception of subjectivity that is created, codified, and configured by always-on, instantaneous communication. Deleuze famously said: "We no longer find ourselves dealing with the mass/individual pair. Individuals have become '*dividuals*'" (1992: 5; emphasis in the original). When the focus of the scientific, cultural, and political discourse shifts from the individual towards networks, subjectivity itself becomes fragmented and dependent upon the apparatuses of knowledge production. As the visual incarnation of algorithmic processing, photography is not accidental to this practice of subjectivization, but it is the nexus of forces that establish information capitalism as irresistible visual spectacle by helping us to imagine virtual selves and seductive futures while simultaneously normalizing and naturalizing the transition from physical to online spaces.

For instance, the selfie phenomenon draws untold millions into a pleasurable game of self-representation, while Facebook constructs massive server farms in the Arctic Circle to host this treasure trove of facial data (Harding 2015). In what way it will be used is anyone's guess. But it is possible to consider the selfie not as a voluntary exercise in mass self-surveillance, but as a genuinely new art form that does not follow the ingrained perspectival ideal that places the spectator/artist at the apex of the cone of vision. The selfie might point towards an entirely different aesthetic criterion, based not on the subordination of the world to the eye, but on a radical decoupling of the eye from the body (exemplified by the selfie stick). The selfie then is not the vulgarized version of the self-portrait, but a provocation that questions the dominance of the eye and inquires after the politics that utilize the optical field in the construction of identities.

The sharing and dissemination of selfies through social networks point to a break between photography in its narrow sense as representation and the expanded field of photography that forgoes the domination of the absolute values of identity in favor of instant intimacy through online distribution. By going beyond the sovereignty of the eye over the organism, the selfie uncovers a state of pre-visual visuality, in which the image is not a signifier of an absent signified, nor is it a linguistic sign; rather, it is a demarcation of a constructed and unstable identity randomly fabricated from bits of landscape, body parts, accidental props, and spatial relations. Uncoupled from the discourse of 'truth' and from the metaphysical baggage of representation, the selfie resembles a "primitive territorial sign" that neither reflects pre-given reality nor reacts to universal concepts. It can be thought of as a self-validating reaction to a local and specific environment:

> The primitive territorial sign is self-validating; it is a position of desire in a state of multiple connections. It is not a sign of a sign nor a desire of desire. It knows nothing of linear subordination and its reciprocity: neither pictogram nor ideogram, it is rhythm and not form, zigzag and not line, artifact and not idea, production and not expression.
>
> *(Deleuze and Guattari 1996: 203)*

In its traditional form, photography expresses the potential for representation located within the capitalist organization of society. But when photography is detached from its ability to produce representations and considered as a flow of image-data, one arrives at another fully real force that springs from photography's ability to produce rhythms and not forms, reproduce and not represent, proliferate and not identify, self-replicate and not copy. As a process of instantaneous distribution, photography is being detached from objects in space as it poses a question about the condition of seeing as such. Instead of evaluating images on the basis of their similarity to actual events or situations, instead of re-examining their indexical or symbolic content, what is required is to inquire after the conditions that make something like an image possible.

By exploring the rules of engagement that govern the use of images, it might be possible to free thought from its dependence on the Platonic concepts of *original* and *copy*. For as long as the rule of this binary model persists, it is impossible to escape what Deleuze branded as "the four iron collars of representation: Identity in the concept, opposition in the predicate, analogy in judgment and resemblance in perception" (Deleuze 2004: 330). Thought that relies on representation cannot free itself from the transcendental; it is bound to remain metaphysical and theological. One of the installation pieces by the artist Jimmie Durham[1] (2015) bears the inscription:

> Humans and their gods seem to naturally create opposites-as-a-system. When one thinks 'white' one's next thought is usually 'black', for example, and then one declares a polarity that may not necessarily reflect a natural truth. (Do you really think the North Pole is really 'up' in the universe?—that the earth is bobbing along in space happily right-side-up?)

Colonizing representation

Foreshadowing aspects of post-modern philosophies of simulacra and virtual reality, Martin Heidegger has observed that the two most decisive events of modernity are that the world is transformed into an image and man into a *subject* (Heidegger 1977: 133). Heidegger's criticism of what we might call today 'representational turn' locates its origin in the philosophy of Descartes: it is with the inception of the *cogito* that representation has become the basis of truth and of being (Heidegger 1967: 99). The modern subject maintains his hold over the world by representing it to himself as a picture. "World picture, when understood essentially, does not mean a picture of the world, but the world conceived and grasped as picture" (Heidegger 1977: 129). What, then, is the power of *this* picture that can cause the world to take on the appearance of an image, or a ghost? For Heidegger, modernity is "the age of the world picture," because the modern subject is the product of a philosophical regime that declared representation to be the limit and the possibility of all knowledge. Representation configures the basic ideas about identity, subjectivity, and truth in two interrelated ways: on the one hand, it is the idea that the world can be known by being rendered as a picture; on the other hand, representation is the reduction of knowledge to a set of standardized and repeatable procedures (Judovitz 1988: 68).

Photography is still and, for the most part, studied as a mode of representation anchored in the metaphysics of light (Bolt 2000), on all the colonial connotations of bringing light to dark places. But there are indicators that the commanding position of the eye and the dominion of vision are being undermined by technologies that replace ocular logic with algorithmic architectures (Parisi 2014). Similarly, the transformation of the world into information, and of the human being into a nodal point in a social network, has decisive consequences for the role of photography within these new cultural formations. As Foucault argued in the *Order of Things*, ideas such as 'life', 'truth', 'man', and 'knowledge' are not eternal, transcendental values but the outcomes of specific configurations of knowledge, tied to mechanisms of collection, division, and distribution (Foucault 1989). More specifically, Foucault explained that practices and discourses of representation are decisive in determining what constitutes 'truth' for a society. For this reason, the idea of 'truth' sustained by the Age of Enlightenment up to and including the twentieth century is based on representation as a form of knowledge in which the image 'stands in' for the absent object. The image then becomes a diagram by means of which the absent object can be known. What is at stake here is not simply a model–copy relationship, but a political agenda of mapping, superiority, and conquest. As Bruno Latour (1986; quoted in Bolt 2004: 15) indicates, Western imperialism is a representational project because its intellectual justification always was to map the world—that is, to represent it in a way that allows first conquest then exploitation and finally tourism. The only way this can be accomplished is by establishing a subject–object relationship with the world. In this context, photography is the visual aspect of a vast colonizing project that subjects the world to the rule of technological rationality, which is a form of totalitarianism (Marcuse 2012: 73). As Barbara Bolt sums up: "representation [is] a mode of thinking and a relationship to the world that involves a will to fixity and mastery" (Bolt 2004: 17).

It is possible to argue that the traditions of liberal democracy take their bearings from a form of truth that sees the world as an extension of man's mind. This worldview finds reassuring confirmation in the photographic operation that asserts the correspondence between images and things. It is assumed that the image has a proper value that contains within it a valid statement about the world. The failure of post-colonial photography to offer an effective critique of colonialism can be attributed to the fact that, for the most part, photography relies on the same representational logic and on the same strategies of visual appropriation that give succor to colonialism. Salgado's *Workers* series surveys the world of labor from the vantage point of an all-seeing eye, unable to acknowledge the connection between photographer's urge to witness, to record, and to represent and the capitalist's urge to accrue, exploit, and dominate. Both the photographer and the capitalist are engaged in a game of conquest (the word *document* is from Latin *docere*: to teach, i.e. to assume a position of authority). Both strive to conceal their own process of production, preferring for us to focus on the end result and not on the road that led to it. To better adhere to the principles of the Albertian frame, and to preserve the illusion of optical innocence, the photographer excludes all traces of himself and his own *work* from the pictures. The photographer can honestly claim that he held nothing back, yet he has presupposed that photography has a natural capacity for truth, forgetting that it is the notion that reality exists independently of inscription that is ideological (Cohen et al., 2016: 59–60). The problem is that this notion of representation as objectively valid and true is grist to the capitalist mill, as it corresponds with the belief in the fairness of the free market exchange, in which wages are said to be a true and fair representation of labor. Like the photographer, the capitalist can claim innocence, for the wages he is paying are as objectively representative of labor as the pictures are representative of reality.

There are two points, then, that can be made about photography as a representational mechanism: the first is that it is conservative, the second that it is infantile.

Conservative

No matter what the subject of an image, no matter what the content of a photograph, it is always a representation of something or other. Therefore, although the content is different at every instance, representation remains the same. This persistence of representation creates an impression of stability and continuity, it suggests that, whereas people, events, and situations depicted in an image can change, the act of representation itself is internally constant. Under the rule of representation, it is impossible to conceive the prospect of genuine revisionism, of a situation where representation, as a mechanism that has subjectivity at its core, is replaced by another way of knowing and thinking. For that reason, representation offers itself as the economy of infinite exchange (Osborne 2010) that does not allow to imagine a way of being in the world outside subject–object relations. Photographic representation ensures that subjectivity, as the way by which humanity expresses its hold on the world, has the right to continue. In short, by accepting representation as the *sine qua non* of photography, we make it impossible to imagine the potential of a human being who is not experiencing the world as a subject, for whom the world in not an image or a picture.

Infantile

Representation is a law that is enshrined in the order of the world; its authority cannot be questioned, because nothing, not even questioning itself, is posited outside of this law. Whatever cannot be rationally represented remains outside of knowledge and immune to it.

Representation is true because it is rational and has its origin in the ability of the subject to present the world to himself as an image. Representation is transcendental because it is the visual manifestation of a logic that permeates all that can be known about the world. The authority of representation is unassailable because it underwrites the possibility of rational knowledge. The rationality of the human subject, his ability to make decisions for himself and have autonomy over his destiny, is assured by representation because it provides a true (i.e. rational) image of the world.

Iconic images and algorithms

Another politics of the image is possible, one that explores the photograph not in terms of the reality it represents, but as a dynamic system of forces that does not stand in for the 'real', and yet it has an authenticity all of its own. We can begin by thinking about photography not as a method for the production of symbolic surfaces, not as two-dimensional projection of a three-dimensional space, but as a device that disrupts signification and introduces elements of otherness or strangeness into it. It means, in other words, to abolish the distinction between images (copies) and things (originals), by accepting that the same transformations of energy, the same forces and processes operate in both. Neither reality, nor the image, can be labeled as the more original, or the more primal than the other, as both form the same, techno-bio-political surface. In the Information Age, to 'read' an image is no longer a question of interpreting its signifying content, but one of identifying the mechanisms, protocols, and devices that channel, store, guide, and block flows of energy and packets of data.

Photography's social and political agency is often more intimately connected to the fractal distribution of the image than to its content. For instance, consider the social media response to the death of Alan (Aylan) Kurdi, the three-year-old refugee who drowned during a sea crossing from Turkey to Greece, while his family was escaping the war in Syria. Was it the content of the image or perhaps the dissemination on social media that caused it to have an impact that surpassed anything achieved by many comparable images? It might be helpful to recall that, one year before the images of Alan Kurdi shocked the world, visually similar photographs of children who were killed by an Israeli missile attack while playing on the beach in Gaza (Barnard 2014) failed to provoke a comparable reaction.

The images of Alan Kurdi were viewed, searched for, and reposted online by 20 million individuals; as such, they testify to a new regime of visuality that is driven, not by subject–object relations, but by algorithms and the technical networks of social media (Vis and Goriunova 2015: 5). There is no shortage of photographs with similar content, and yet, for whatever reasons, images of Alan Kurdi's death stuck in the Wi-Fi networks and fiber optic cables and refused to disappear from the screen, from the feed, from the page. These images were 'liked', retweeted, searched for, hashtagged, and commented on by millions. Clicking the 'like' button or pressing the 'retweet' icon are affective as well as performative actions; there is pleasure and enjoyment in these gestures, insofar as they give rise to sensations. To 'like' an image is not to comment on its verisimilitude, but to register an intensity of emotion. This intensity is channeled through the feedback mechanisms of social media back onto the image itself, causing it to disseminate further and faster. Everything we experience online is always already technical, possible only because it is enabled by algorithmic processes that operate infinite feedback loops. The point is not only that, in order to arrive at the threshold of visibility, an image has to be approved by algorithms that censor the more 'graphic' scenes, the very ability of the internet to disseminate an image is enabled by a system that has pre-visual and pre-cognitive processes at its core.

When representation is augmented by algorithmic processing and repetition, the image becomes detached from its point of origin in a specific 'real' event and acquires 'nomadic' qualities. Central among them is the ability to be inserted into many discourses, narratives, and mashups (Vis and Goriunova 2015: 54). A whole new dimension of visual culture opens up when the logistics of dissemination, the discursive powers of reproduction, and the incalculable effects of algorithms bear on the production of meaning. It is possible that the images of Alan Kurdi became iconic not only because of what they represent, but because the fractal proliferation and dispersal of these images place something real, unimaginable, and for that reason horrific on our screens. In other words, the formal compositional elements of this photograph are not inevitable or necessary; rather, they become the subject not because of their connection with a specific time and place, but because they concentrate the libidinal energies of interface users in a way that is visible to the endless and anonymous algorithmic structures of the web.

Fractal theory of photography

Given the cultural, moral, and scientific investments in representation, this chapter's proposition that we think of images (photographic and otherwise) not in terms of what we see, but in terms of what it took to produce what we see might seem implausible if not outright perverse. Nevertheless, there are clear signs that excessive reliance on the visible as the essence of the image is a very bad strategy for attempting to grasp something authentic about the morphology of the world, because the world always escapes being fully grasped by rational and logical propositions (Stengers 2010), particularly, as Golding (2014: 218) puts it, "in light of the strange materialities, curved temporalities, and sliced dimensions expressed in, through and by the digital world." There are at least three reasons why this is so.

First, as Benoit Mandelbrot (1982) showed, many natural forms cannot be adequately described by any fixed measurement system that uses the yardstick of representation. From coast lines, fern leaves, pine cones, and cauliflower, to clouds, DNA molecules, mountain ranges, and snowflakes, self-similar or fractal patterns abound. All these shapes—which Mandelbrot named *fractals*—are made of structures and forms that self-replicate at different scales. The bud of romanesco broccoli is composed of a self-similar pattern of smaller buds, and each smaller bud is composed of a series of even smaller buds. As Mandelbrot amply demonstrated, fractal principles explain the construction of many natural phenomena. In an essay titled "How long is the coast of Britain? Statistical self-similarity and fractional dimension," he explains: "Geographical curves are so involved in their detail that their lengths are often infinite or more accurately, undefinable" (1967: 636). A geographical curve such as a coastline cannot be adequately represented by a broken straight line, because its length is entirely dependent on the unit of measurement. The smaller the unit of measurement, the longer the measured length, and any attempt at an objective, or measurement-independent, representation is going to come up short. Instead of imagining the coastline as constructed from linear segments, it is more productive to see it as a self-replicating fractal. Fractal-like behaviors are not limited to coastlines and mountain ranges: they are also found in society, where large groups are formed from small groups, which are in turn formed from even smaller groups. The topology of the web can be characterized as a scale-free, continuously self-replicating fractal (Berners-Lee 2009).

When self-replication is thought of not as an aesthetic dimension, but as core technical and scientific aspect of the image, it becomes possible to analyze photography as a fractal system (Laruelle 2011: 73). A fractal theory of photography would be one that responds to the problem of dissemination: not engaging with the aesthetics of the picture, but with those qualities of the photographic image that are imposed by its own modes of production and distribution. Fractal forms open up a way of describing the world not through an image that replicates the real, but through the specific ways repetition, symmetry, self-replication, and distribution enter the photograph. The inherent repeatability of the photograph opens up a way of thinking about reality not as a shadow on the wall of Plato's cave, not as a fixed entity represented as an image, but as a sequence of repetitions that establishes a 'synthetic unity' that is simultaneously technical-seductive-visual-immersive and infinitely expansive (Golding 2012). The difference between the representational worldview and the fractal can be summarized thus: whereas representation is a way of comprehending the world through images, fractal logic abstains from the visual aspect of the image, allowing one to focus on rhythms, self-referential segments, and scale-independent patterns, restaging the image as an infinite structure of self-replicating assemblages. Because fractals can be found in nature, in society, and in productive processes, they are exceptionally well suited to describe practices of growth, learning, and proliferation. As Golding (2012: 114) explains:

> [Fractal] sequencing creates pattern; the pattern re-loops to create 'synthetic unity'; the process is repeated. It is a process found throughout nature; it is in every pattern of growth; it is at the basis of artificial intelligence, and how robots 'learn'.

Fractal geometry has a particularly significant relationship to the analysis of networked images. Considered from the perspective of a single image, photography is static: it represents an object as fixed in space and attached to a frozen moment in time. But, considered from the perspective of the process, photography is a "dynamical system" (Baranger 2000), infinitely changeable and malleable as the algorithmic procedures continue to reshape and alter the image, while at the same time bifurcating and disseminating versions of it.

Mandelbrot's self-replicating forms cannot be adequately represented by a methodology that focuses solely on the pictorial. By drawing analogy with the coast of Britain, it is possible to suggest that migration of human beings seeking refuge from the sufferings of war cannot be adequately represented in an image. But the infinite, simultaneous, and instantaneous distribution of a single image of Alan Kurdi, which for a time becomes the most-viewed image online, provides a conduit to something that transcends visibility and can be described as an *experience* that is beyond experience. Conceptually, this image can be only grasped as content: it can be related to previously seen scenes, to other signs or to the semantic messages within, but as an encounter this image has affective power that transcends memory and language. What is given in the image is not so much a figure of a child lying face down in the sand but the very act of giving the given itself. As the outcome of millions of online operations, the image is something unquantifiable, gigantic, and incomprehensible. Its conformity to pictorial conventions is at odds with the manifold human and algorithmic operations required to produce this illusory presence. In its instantaneous dispersal, the image momentarily succeeds in grasping the enormity of the event of which it speaks. But this grasping occurs in the intuitive seizing of the non-visual and algorithmic structure of the image that makes the pictorial aspect perhaps not redundant, but certainly not exclusive. It is the immeasurable dimension of this image, its gigantic scale, its unlimited magnitude and incalculable range that make it stand in front of us as a virtual obelisk.

Second, as Nigel Thrift argues, the failure of representational approaches to capture movement, change, and affect requires a "non-representational theory." Thrift observes that contemporary capitalism is able to divert many of its tasks into non-representational jurisdictions that operate not with semantic or coded messages, but through flows, shapes, forms, tactile surfaces, and hypnotic rhythms (Thrift 2008: 17). The point is not only that some messages are better communicated through sensations than through semantic codes, or that forms of expression exist independently, or alongside, forms of content, but that, "human life is based on and in movement" (Thrift 2008: 5). For photography not to lose its social and cultural relevance, it must follow not only the visible manifestations of capital, but also the invisible forces of production and flows of speculation.

As the old-school distinctions between the conscious subject and the inanimate object are dissolved in favor of a continuous process of transmission and feedback, Thrift observes that, in the age of information and communication technologies, space ceases to operate as a three-dimensional, Euclidian topology and acquires streaming and performative qualities (Thrift 2008: 43–4). When cities, streets, and buildings come pre-loaded with information that is for the most part invisible, and yet absolutely essential for their functioning as public and political spaces, the ability of photography to adequately deal with space is severely compromised.

For as long as photography is obsessed with the representation of the visible it allows the non-visible to slip through the fingers, without being taken to task, examined, and criticized. But the non-representational is an active dimension of strife, manipulation, and life-altering hand-to-hand combat of energies (Massumi 1992). For instance, money no longer represents a quantity of gold. Instead, since the abolition of the gold standard and introduction of quantitative easing in the post-2008 financial crash, money has speculative, rather than representational, value. One consequence of this is the reshaping of urban spaces by international capital, as can be seen for instance in the conversion of flats and houses into "deposit boxes in the sky" (Booth 2014). As Andrea Phillips (2013) has shown, European cities are defined by the concept of a public space; however, as public spaces are converted into privatized areas with public right of passage (aka PAPO—public access, privately owned), they appear visually unchanged, but structurally, politically, socially, and culturally these are radically different entities from the democratic urban spaces beloved by the street photographers of the twentieth century.

For an example of the invisible forces that naturalize the politics of everyday life, consider Granary Square in London, one of the largest public spaces in Europe. It is framed on all sides by grand buildings: an art school, the headquarters of a national newspaper, multinational IT companies. At its heart is an 'urban beach' with fountains, street food stalls, canal bars, and restaurants. For the public, it is a popular escape from the hullabaloo of a major train station nearby. But, as the whole area is owned and developed by a private investment company, the public are only allowed in as consumers, visitors, and spectators. The idea of public space as an *agora*—a political entity related to citizenship, public debate, demonstration, protest, and specific performance of *truth* (Phillips 2013) is made absolutely impossible, not least because the area is monitored 24 hours a day by private security who would immediately act to prevent any civic activity, even the distribution of leaflets. China Miéville's novel *The City and the City* (2011) imagines life in a town where all residents are taught from birth to ignore aspects of urban life that do not fit with the current political arrangements, but the truth is that, for a number of years, the most significant, real changes in the structures of European cities have been taking place outside the optical field of view. What is most remarkable is that the gradual transformation of the city by the forces of international capital and the concomitant depoliticization of public space appear all the more natural for not leaving visible stress marks. In a very real sense, this is a different civic entity, in which the possibility of public engagement with politics is significantly altered. The irony—if irony it is—is that photography is still celebrated as the primary means of capturing and representing this new entity.

Third, since the triumph of digital and networked photography, computation and algorithmic processing have become the dominant cultural logic of the visual image. A number of recent studies have focused on the uncertainty, undecidability, and contingency embedded in the notion of the digital-born image (Marenko 2015; Parisi 2014; Rubinstein and Sluis 2013). As Parisi says:

> [Algorithms construct] digital spatiotemporalities that do not represent physical space, but are instead new spatiotemporal actualities. The contagious architecture of these actualities is constructing a new digital space, within which programmed architectural forms and urban infrastructures expose not only new modes of living but also new modes of thinking.
>
> *(2014: xiii)*

This means that computation is much more than a mechanism that produces, disseminates, and distributes images across the web. Algorithms not only perform instructions, they are also agents that create the material reality of the world by selecting, evaluating, compiling, and manufacturing data. Even more significantly, algorithmic processing of image data introduces glitches, noise, and mutations that contribute to the production of new forms of experience that encompass "embodiment, sensorial participation and the situated apprehension of materiality" (Marenko 2015: 111).

One of the consequences of photography being underpinned by an algorithmic, rather than representational, logic is that it introduces randomness, undecidability, and automation into the photographic process. Whereas twentieth-century photography could be more or less convincingly understood from within a totalizing system of dialectical opposites, such as the opposition between the original and the copy, such idealistic pretensions are unable to cope with the notion of the image as a product of algorithmic operations that not so much represent reality, but progressively create realities, cultures, and ways of thinking that are inherently computational. And, whereas the representational content of the photograph confirms the experience of perception by situating objects within a perspectival frame, the algorithmic processes that produce said photograph "represent abstract patterns [...] that extend beyond the limit of perception" (Kostas Terzidis, quoted in Parisi 2014: 66).

The picture of the world constructed by contemporary photography has undecidability—rather than representation—at its core, but, in a paradoxical way, this does not make it less true but, I would like to argue, opens up the photographic image to new forms of materiality and performativity. The reason for this is that, since the first half of the twentieth century, undecidability has emerged as one of the underpinning features of modern (fuzzy) logic and as one of the foundational principles of computation. In mathematics, the principle of undecidability was proven by Kurt Gödel (1992), but it was put to practical use a little later when Alan Turing employed it in the construction of the Turing Machine—the theoretical prototype of the digital computer and the device that he used to decipher the Enigma code during World War II that ultimately led to the surrender of Germany.

As a conceptual formulation that limits certainty and introduces an element of indeterminism into computation, undecidability is a non-dualistic entity that bypasses such oppositional pairs as original/copy, true/false, and form/matter, in favor of continuous deferral and a state of irresolvable complexity. The digital-born and algorithmically processed image is undecidable because the material processes involved in its production cannot be fully determined, and its structure continues to evolve and morph throughout its life cycle (see Figure 22.1).

As Marenko argues (2015: 112), the aesthetics of algorithmic processing are, to a large extent, connected with the concept of the glitch, as the unforeseen 'procedural stutter' that forms the immersive materiality of digital images. For that reason, in the transition to algorithmic imaging, photography did not simply replace one mode of image production with another, but passed from a closed system to an open, undecidable environment that makes room for expression that seeks not to 'make sense', but to inhabit states of indeterminacy that allow for chaotic and random movement that points to a world outside the domain of rational and logical representation.

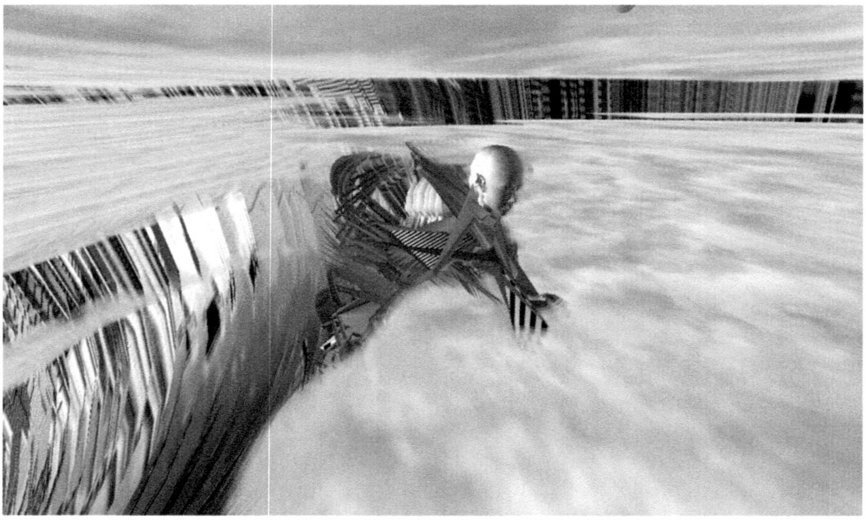

Figure 22.1 Rosa Menkman, *Acousmatic Videoscapes: Compress Process* (2012). Screenshot. Courtesy the artist

The compound proposition put forward by fractal geometry, non-representational theory, and algorithmic processing is that there is no reason to accept the postulate that underpins all theory of photography: that photography operates as an inscription of reality which is external to it. Reality is not first given to be later inscribed in an image, but rather reality inscribes itself as an image through a process of repetition and self-replication. It is not photography that represents reality, it is reality itself becoming photographic through a process of continuous self-replication.

Erasure and repetition

As should be clear at this stage of the story, the emphasis on visual representation as the *sine qua non* of photography is not without its conceptual pitfalls. Although there is no denying that representation offers access to reality, the access it offers is both limited and one-sided and tends to ignore those dimensions of existence that do not fit within a rational worldview. Stated succinctly, the prominence of representation smuggles into the photographic discourse all the staple doctrines of Western metaphysics: binary oppositions (image/object), signifiers, and subjectivism. Because of this allegiance to the sacred cows of rationality and visuality, photography is construed as a spectator's sport rather than an active participant in the fragmented and fractured logic of the 'age of technology' in all its internal paradoxes, fractal proliferation, and non-representational modalities of communication and art.

The conventional view of photography, because it assumes that a photograph is an imprint of the real, is based on philosophical and scientific ideas about vision, light, and optics, and, although these ideas are correct in their mathematical analysis of perspective, they are inadequate to describe what is actually happening when we look at an image. Challenging this logocentric standpoint requires us to attempt to recover something from a photograph besides its 'message', something that frustrates our habits of 'reading' pictures and falls outside communication protocols that privilege clarity and fetishize the index.

The truth is that, in addition to any content, the photograph always 'finds itself' in specific circumstances created by its modalities of production and distribution. The values involved in the production of the image determine to a large extent how we interpret it, which features we tune into, and which we suppress. Attention to the modes of production is not a rejection of representation, but a sensitivity to the deep integration of materials and practices in the creation of meaning. A photograph is not an image that also happens to be algorithmically or chemically produced; rather, production is the original state of the image that holistically combines sensual and logical elements. Should we be surprised if it is the production of the image that brings us face to face with the reality of the world and allows us to conceive of reality itself as a continuous process of self-replicating inscription? In the next section of this chapter, I will look at two time-honored strategies that step outside the representational framework: erasure and repetition.

Erasure

First among the practices that can open the doors of perception to aspects of reality that are not accessible to representation is the process of erasure. It just so happens that, in photography, the question of non-being and of nothingness is not only a speculative, metaphysical proposition, but something much more sensual and physical, embedded in the very core of image-*making*. Understood from the perspective of photographic production, it is erasure—rather than inscription—that is the essential component of imaging. Paradoxically, the imprinting of content that is taking place in the recording of a photo-mechanical image is the product of a process that has erasure at its core. This primacy of erasure over inscription is captured by the Latin expression *tabula rasa*, which translates crudely as 'blank slate', forgetting that *rasa* is of the same root as the English verb *erase* and means being removed, abolished, scraped away. In Greek and Roman times, the *tabula rasa* was a recording device: a wooden block covered with wax that could be written on with a stylus. But, before a new inscription could be made, the tablet had to be erased—or, as we might say nowadays, 'reformatted'—by the wax being heated and smoothed over, with a spatula scraping away all that was previously inscribed on it. It is not by accident that the writing instrument of antiquity required erasure prior to inscription, as the same principle underpins inscription in modernity as well: solid-state (flash memory) disks and memory cards have to be erased to make room for new recordings, a process that is known as Fowler–Nordheim tunneling (Tyson 2001). Nor is erasure limited to digital photography. The invisible *latent image*—produced by the exposure of photosensitive material to light—has to be subsequently obliterated by photographic development that converts the exposed silver halide crystals to silver grains (Tani 1995). Image creation involves not only the production of a visible surface, but also the obliteration of the invisible image. The paradoxical condition of photography is that it is both an inscription and a destruction at the same time.

It seems that photography erases, hides, and obliterates at least at the same rate as it imprints, writes, and records, so perhaps it is opportune to ask in what ways these operations of deleting and forgetting come to bear on the image. When Heidegger says that, "a thoughtful glance ahead into this realm of 'Being' can only write it as ~~Being~~" (Heidegger 1958: 81), he proposes that we think about erasure and forgetting as ontologically prior to remembering. The only way this primacy of nothing over Being can be captured in language is by crossing out the word Being and then leaving it, still crossed out, in the text. Armed with the understanding that every photographic inscription is done under erasure, and yet that erasure does not refer to any external reality but captures the internal condition of photographic production, we can begin to ponder the way erasure is pointing towards the non-representational origin of the image. Erasure seems to partake in two worlds at once: on the one hand, it is part of the representational mechanism, and, on the other, it smuggles into photography something sensual, non-identical, and irrational.

Where is the image that I have erased from my memory card? Doesn't it survive to some extent as the erased trace, in the absence of which nothing new would be recorded? And isn't it the case, then, that an image always bears witness to the removal that preceded it? Perhaps deletion is not merely a prerequisite for inscription, but one of the factors that determine the power of the image, either as its ground or as its destination. If that is so, then photography is not only a universally comprehensible language, but a portal into something prior to any language, namely the trace of erasure that is essential for any inscription to occur. However, because erasure is prior to inscription, it itself cannot be represented. Is it surprising that the history of erasure is absent from the theories and analyses of photography? As the non-representable trace, erasure contains no information, it does not communicate, and, yet, it proclaims that something had to be destroyed for *this* image to come into view. Photography in this case is a monument to forgetting, oblivion, and nothingness.

It goes without saying that *erasure* and *nothingness* are the staple preoccupations of twentieth-century artists, from Kazimir Malevich's *Black Square* and *4.33* by John Cage to *Erased De Kooning Drawing* by Robert Rauschenberg and Peter Eisenman's *Memorial to the Murdered Jews of Europe*. But let us consider, for example, the *Protographs* of Oscar Muñoz (exhibited in 2014). Here, the physical disintegration of the image just before or after it is being 'fixed' evokes the inherent instability and transience of memory, and the chaotic and uncontrollable forces that envelope any attempt at rational representation. As an artistic strategy, *erasure* introduces forgetting, disintegration, and disappearance into the heart of photography. It is a move that aims to re-move the content of the image, getting to a semi-emptiness that is filled with the memory of something that has been there previously but is now destroyed. By effacing the image, the gesture of removal also quietly suggests that there is a trace of non-signifying, pre-rational, and pre-subjective experience that nevertheless persists within the image. Miroslav Tichy's image production (1926–2011) involved leaving his homemade photographic prints to lie in the dirt, to be nibbled by rats, and used as coasters until such time when he considered them sufficiently 'developed' to be ready for display. An image that is defaced, obliterated, and damaged connects with the life-experience of the artist not by representing destruction—like so many immaculate photographs of catastrophes—but by intimating that the human subject and the image share the same experience: the individual disintegration of the former is mimicked in the physical obliteration of the latter.

Repetition

Although many other kinds of images can be copied, photographs are pictures that explicitly carry the directions for their own copying within themselves. Photography's ability to reproduce without any noticeable loss of information sets it aside from other visual forms, but the techniques that enable continuous reproduction not only safeguard logical and rational continuity between the original and the copy, but also give photography the affective powers of sharing, disseminating, reaching out, and touching. When an image is repeated, the second iteration overlaps with the first without becoming fully dissolved in it. This results in a series of ostensibly identical images that are nevertheless distinct from each other. Prints from the same photographic negative are said to be identical, but they bring into view a "reality segment" (Golding 2010) that can be named "multiplicity." The very ability of being repeated several times suggests that the logic that operates within a multiplicity is different from the logic of representation, because, no matter what is denoted in the visual content, repetition puts forward a non-dualistic and non-representational logic of production, distribution, and dissemination. Rosalind Krauss (1984) considered the destabilizing effect of photographic repetition by pointing to the way identical copies from the same original undermine the very notion of originality:

> By exposing that multiplicity, the facticity, the repetition and stereotype at the heart of *every* aesthetic gesture, photography deconstructs the possibility of differentiating between the original and the copy. [...] The practice of the multiple, whether one speaks of the *hundreds of prints pulled from the same negative or the hundreds of fundamentally indistinguishable photographs* [...] this practice has been understood by certain artists as not just a degraded or bad form of the aesthetic original. It has been taken to undermine the very distinction between original and copy.
>
> *(Krauss 1984: 59; my emphasis)*

It is, however, possible to think about photography not as the generation of *indistinguishable* copies (as Krauss would have it), but as the production of difference by means of reproductive technology. In *The Arcades Project*, Walter Benjamin proposes another way of thinking about repetition, not as sameness but as the eternal return:

> The idea of eternal recurrence transforms the historical event itself into a mass-produced article. [...] The idea of *eternal* recurrence derived its lustre from the fact that it was across any interval of time shorter than that provided by eternity.
>
> *(2002: 340; original emphasis)*

As Eduardo Cadava (1997: 31) observes, for Benjamin the main effect of technology is not the production of identical copies, but the creation of a world without identity, a world of perpetual becoming in which what is being produced through repetition is not sameness but radical, a-rooted difference formed through the interplay of singularity and repetition.

Repetition is never on the same plane as the content: content inscribes the image with meaning by treating it as a signifying surface. Content is semantic denotation that orders the world as a legible structure. But repetition does not deal with signification; rather, it mimics the labor vested in the production of commodities: things that are mass-produced usually do not carry with them the legend of their own production. For instance, my smartphone does nothing to remind me of the way it was manufactured; on the contrary, one could say that all traces of fabrication, assembly, and labor were surgically removed to impart on my senses that its origin is not production but immaculate conception. As an ethical strategy, repetition strips the veil of innocence from objects, revealing their secret logic of labor, made invisible and hidden from view by mass production. Bernd and Hilla Becher (2004) have explored the productive tension between representation and repetition in a series titled *Typologies of Industrial Buildings*. While adhering to the formal logic of classification based on visual resemblance between industrial constructions, the Bechers' work simultaneously exposes the ideological underpinnings of any such classification, for it requires the suppression of dissimilarities and the privileging of identity over difference. Representation operates on the level of content where each single image denotes an industrial object. But repetition operates between the images themselves, pointing out differences and suggesting that industrial production is not represented in photography, but that photography is essentially an industrial process. The Bechers' achievement lies in demonstrating that photography is not a form of visual communication: rather, it embodies the logic of technological production that commands all forms of aesthetic expression.

Repetition is not accidental to photography: it is the mechanical gesture that ties together discrete representations and, in so doing, creates its own accidental and profound meanings that use the contents of images as launching pads towards the forming of new sensations. What is being repeated is the content, but repetition is not on the same plane as the content. Most classic operas, pop songs, spaghetti westerns, and reality TV shows make skillful use of folding and refolding content to create repetition and, therefore, to communicate something entirely independently from the content in its unfolded state. 'Reality' shows such as *The Apprentice*, for instance, adhere to a fixed pattern of scenes, so that the story of each episode is told by identical means, with only the content changing, and the format remaining strictly the same. Here, repetition is much more than an organizing device: the viewer knows exactly what to expect at each moment and anticipates the next emotional peak, not owing to the actions of the contestants but because there is a rhythmic sequence that marks the boundaries between acts. The rhythm itself becomes expressive of the main messages of the show as it gets tied to motifs of sexual aggression, territoriality, and domination (Deleuze and Guattari 2003: 315).

The industrial process that makes photocopies is nothing if not a process of repetition, even if what is being repeated is symbolic representation of space. Representations follow one after another, representing this and that part of the world, but the repetition of the action of representation itself is a rhythmic beat that flows through all the photographed spaces, establishing another, deeper murmur of noises, glitches, and distortions. Because representation repeats itself it creates a rhythm, and because it is a rhythm it is temporal, which is to say, it involves a process that folds and unfolds over time. Thus, photography has an exterior body made of temporal processes of production, and an internal body made of framing devices and objects that are being framed, and an additional body made of ideological investments in questions of perception, truth, and resemblance. All three of its bodies are coded, which is to say, they are subject to the rules of repetition, because code is that which must be infinitely copied to ensure its operational validity.

Conclusion: the practice of fractal photography

The two strategies of non-representational photography, erasure and repetition, reveal something about the one-sidedness of the pictorial-representational approach, about its inability to deal with anything that is processual, temporal, and fluid. Practices that reproduce, disseminate, copy, and mutate constitute the primary photographic activity: they operate discretely, away from the signifying surface of the image. All the usual operations of indexical signifiers, decoding, and reading are secondary processes that emerge out of the photographic unconscious: the invisible process of repetition.

Photography, however, is not one image system among many, but the basic unit of visual communication of the technological age. Peter Osborne has already pointed out that: "[T]he photographic is not best understood as a particular art; it is currently the dominant form of the image in general" (Osborne 2010: 62). If photography is the basic semantic unit of the post-industrial society, it is possible that an inquiry into its conceptual makeup can reveal something about the way sense and meaning are being produced.

Photography can function successfully as representation precisely because the qualities that account for its own production are generally excluded from the content of the image. But the creative power of photography lies not so much in the visual surfaces it is capable of producing, but in allowing us to inhabit a state that is prior to the formation of the visual image. It is precisely because photography is an image produced through the means of modern technology that it is at one and the same time an event in the history of image-making systems and an event in the history of thought.

The fractal processes of production that operate beneath the optical surface of the photographic image are pre-subjective and pre-individual, but they create the connections between photographic production and production as such that constitutes the spatiotemporal reality that the photographic image represents. Photodigital culture can be studied as an archive, a memory, or visual communication, but this approach risks forgoing the possibility that the digital paradigms that produce visible surfaces are doing more than serving us data. Reality is not out there waiting to be photographed, but the photographic process that algorithmically shapes the image out of data is the same process that is shaping the environment, that has to be understood as located "within the algorithmic object" (Parisi 2014: 36).

The arrival of a photodigital environment suggests that, rather than understanding photographs as discrete units of information that capture specific time and space coordinates, photography should be understood as an infinite flow that cannot be equated with rational representation or reduced to individual images. To insist on the primacy of the visual image is to be deaf to the truly radical message of photography: that the 'visual image' is conjoined to processes of construction and distribution and through them to life itself. There is no possibility of distinguishing between form (content) and functions (code) because both are merged in the fractal image. The consequence of this fusion of technology with meaning is that any critical theory that takes the opposition between form and content as its starting point is bound to miss the role undecidability, incompleteness, and dissemination play in constructing the ground of the digital image. The decisive aspect of photography is the way it allows us to grasp the real not as 'part of the whole', but as a slice of self-replicating fractal multiplicity. This is not a representation of something, nor is it an expression of subjectivity; rather, photography gives visual expression to a part of life that escapes representation because it is not adequate to any concept: labor, desire, reproduction, self-replication, forgetting, and erasure—the essential and sensual organic singularities performed by humans in figuring through play and fight what humanity consists of.

Note

1 Jimmie Durham, "Various Items and Complaints," Serpentine Gallery, London October 1–November 8, 2015.

References

Baranger, M. (2000) "Chaos, complexity, and entropy: a physics talk for non-physicists," New England Complex Systems Institute, Cambridge. Available at: http://necsi.edu/projects/baranger/cce.pdf [accessed December 20, 2016].

Barnard, A. (2014) "Boys drawn to Gaza beach, and into center of Mideast strife," *The New York Times*, July 16.

Becher, B. and Becher, H. (2004) *Typologies of Industrial Buildings*, Cambridge, MA: MIT Press.

Benjamin, W. (2002) *The Arcades Project*, Translated by H. Eiland & K. McLaughlin. Cambridge, MA, and London: Harvard University Press.

Berger, J. (2013) *Understanding a Photograph*, London: Penguin.

Berners-Lee, T. (2009) "The scale-free nature of the Web," Available at: www.W3.org [accessed December 20, 2016].

Bolt, B. (2000) "Shedding light for the matter," *Hypatia*, 15 (2), pp. 202–16.

Bolt, B. (2004) *Art beyond Representation: The Performative Power of the Image*, London and New York: I.B. Tauris.

Booth, R. (2014) "Londoners miss out as homes built as 'safe deposit boxes' for foreign buyers," *The Guardian*, Dec. 3.

Cadava, E. (1997) *Words of Light: Theses on the Photography of History*, Princeton, NJ: Princeton University Press.

Cohen, T., Colebrook, C. and Miller, J.H. (2016) *Twilight of the Anthropocene Idols*, Open Humanities Press. www.openhumanitiespress.org

Colebrook, C. (2001) "Certeau and Foucault: tactics and strategic essentialism," *The South Atlantic Quarterly*, 100 (2), pp. 543–74.

Deleuze, G. (1992) "Postscript on the societies of control," *October*, 59, pp. 3–7.

Deleuze, G. (2004) *Difference and Repetition*, London: Continuum.

Deleuze, G. and Guattari, F. (1996) *Anti-Oedipus: Capitalism and Schizophrenia*, London: The Athlone Press.

Deleuze, G. and Guattari, F. (2003) *A Thousand Plateaus*, London: Continuum.

Foucault, M. (1989) *The Order of Things: An Archaeology of the Human Sciences*, London: Routledge.

Gödel, K. (1992) *On Formally Undecidable Propositions of Principia Mathematica and Related Systems*, New York: Dover.

Golding, J. (2010) "Fractal Philosophy, Trembling a Plane of Immanence and the Small Matter of Learning How to Listen: Attunement as the Task of Art" in Zepke, S. and O'Sullivan, S. (eds.), *Deleuze and Contemporary Art*, Edinburgh: Edinburgh University Press, pp. 133–54.

Golding, J. (2012) "Ana-materialism and the pineal eye: becoming mouth-breast (or visual arts after Descartes, Bataille, Butler, Deleuze and Synthia with an 's'," *Philosophy of Photography*, 3 (1), pp. 99–121.

Golding, J. (2014) "Ecce homo sexual: ontology and Eros in the age of incompleteness and entanglement," *Parallax*, 20 (3), pp. 217–30.

Harding, L. (2015) "The node pole: inside Facebook's Swedish hub near the Arctic Circle," *The Guardian*, September 25. www.theguardian.com/technology/2015/sep/25/facebook-datacentre-lulea-sweden-node-pole

Heidegger, M. (1958) *The Question of Being*, New York: Twayne.

Heidegger, M. (1967) *What is a Thing?* Translated by V. Deutsch and W.B. Barton. Washington DC: Gateway Editions.

Heidegger, M. (1977) "The Age of the World Picture" in Heidegger, M., *The Question Concerning Technology*, New York: Harper & Row, pp. 115–154.

Judovitz, D. (1988) "Representation and its Limits in Descartes" in Silverman, H.J. (ed.), *Postmodernism and Continental Philosophy*, Albany NY: State University of New York Press, pp. 68–84.

Knausgaard, K.O. (2015) "The terrible beauty of brain surgery," *The New York Times*, Dec. 30. Available at: www.nytimes.com/2016/01/03/magazine/karl-ove-knausgaard-on-the-terrible-beauty-of-brain-surgery.html [accessed December 31, 2015].

Krauss, R. (1984) "A note on photography and the simulacral," *October*, 31, pp. 49–68.

Laruelle, F. (2011) *Le Concept de non-photographie/The Concept of Non-photography*, Falmouth: Urbanomic.

Latour, B. (1986) "Visualization and cognition," *Knowledge and Society*, 6, pp. 1–40.

Mandelbrot, B.B. (1967) "How long is the coast of Britain? Statistical self-similarity and fractional dimension," *Science*, 156 (3775), pp. 636–38.

Mandelbrot, B.B. (1982) *The Fractal Geometry of Nature*, San Francisco: W.H. Freeman.

Marcuse, H. (2012) *One-Dimensional Man*, New York: Beacon Press.

Marenko, B. (2015) "When making becomes divination: uncertainty and contingency in computational glitch-events," *Design Studies*, 41, pp. 1–16.

Marx, K., (1859) "Economic manuscripts: a contribution to the critique of political economy," Available at: www.marxists.org/archive/marx/works/1859/critique-pol-economy/index.ht [accessed December 21, 2017].

Massumi, B. (1992) *A User's Guide to Capitalism and Schizophrenia: Deviations from Deleuze and Guattari*, Cambridge, MA: MIT Press.

Miéville, C. (2011) *The City and The City*, London: Pan.

Osborne, P. (2010) "Infinite exchange: the social ontology of the photographic image," *Philosophy of Photography*, 1 (1), pp. 59–68.

Parisi, L. (2014) *Contagious Architecture. For an Aesthetic Computation of Space*, Cambridge, MA: MIT Press.

Pasquinelli, M., (2011) *Machinic Capitalism and Network Surplus Value: Notes on the Political Economy of the Turing Machine*. Available at: https://immaterialiresistenti.noblogs.org/post/2011/10/13/machinin-capitalism-and-network-surplus-value/ [accessed December 12, 2016].

Phillips, A. (2013) "Public Space [Crossed Out]" in Dragset, I., Elmgreen, J., and Mellinger, N. (eds.), *A Space Called Public*, Munich/Köln: Walter Koenig, pp. 248–59.

Rubinstein, D. and Sluis, K. (2013) "The Digital Image in Photographic Culture; Algorithmic Photography and the Crisis of Representation" in Lister, M. (ed.), *The Photographic Image in Digital Culture*, London: Routledge, pp. 22–40.

Stengers, I. (2010) *Cosmopolitics I*, Minneapolis and London: University of Minnesota Press.

Tani, T. (1995) *Photographic Sensitivity*, Oxford: Oxford University Press.

Thrift, N. (2008) *Non-representational Theory: Space, Politics, Affect*, Abingdon, UK: Routledge.

Tyson J. (2001) "How removable storage works," May 28.. Available at: http://computer.howstuffworks.com/removable-storage.htm [accessed April 23, 2016].

Vis, F. and Goriunova, O. (eds.) (2015) "The iconic image on social media: a rapid research response to the death of Aylan Kurdi," *Visual Social Media Lab*.. Available at http://visualsocialmedialab.org/projects/the-iconic-image-on-social-media

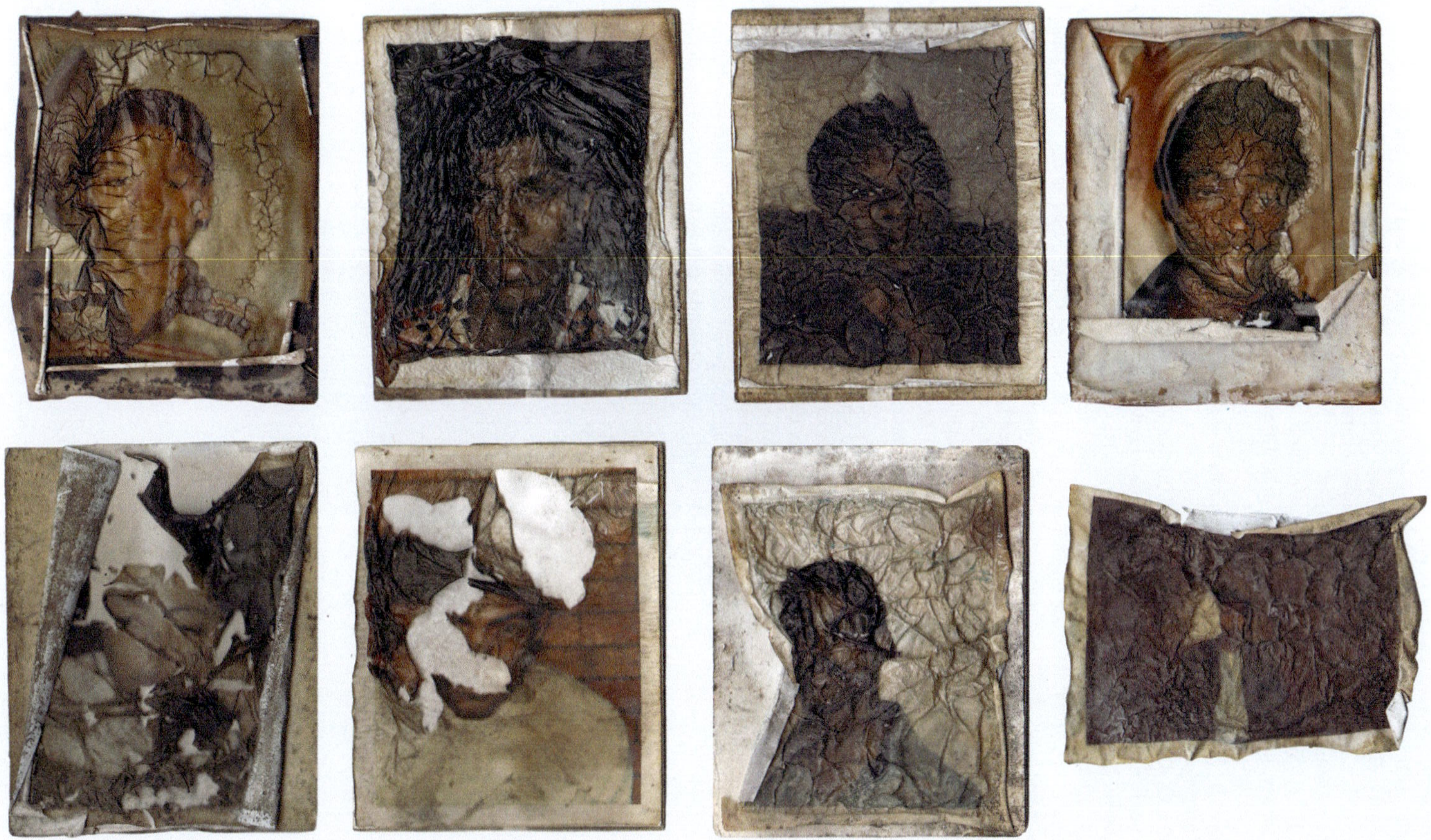

Plate 1 Arianna Arcara and Luca Santese, from *Found Photos in Detroit* (2012). Courtesy the artists

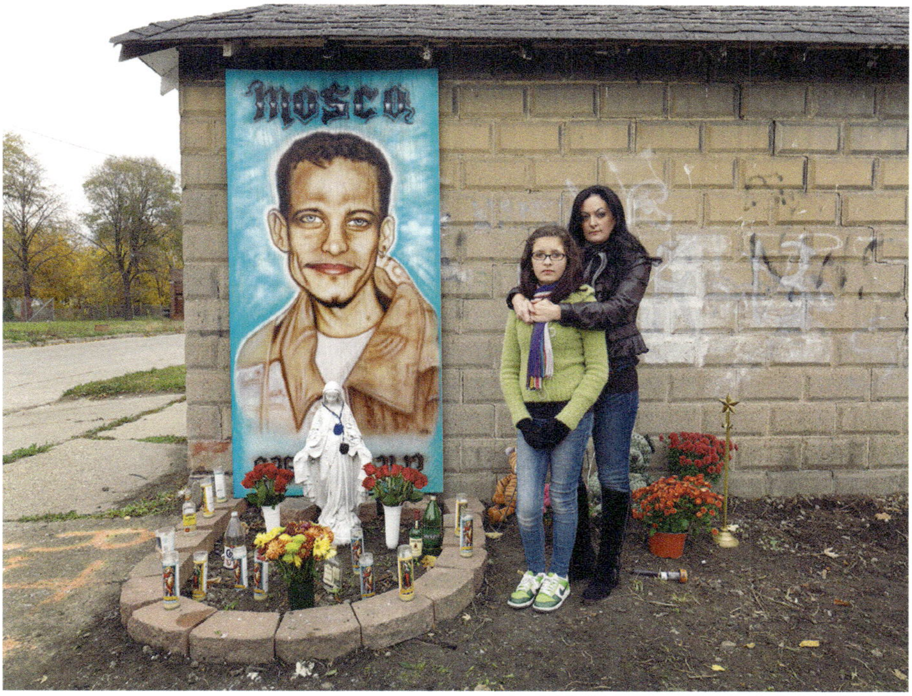

Plate 2 Dave Jordano, *Stacey and Carlitha, Jason's Memorial Site, Southwest Side, Detroit* (2012). Courtesy the artist

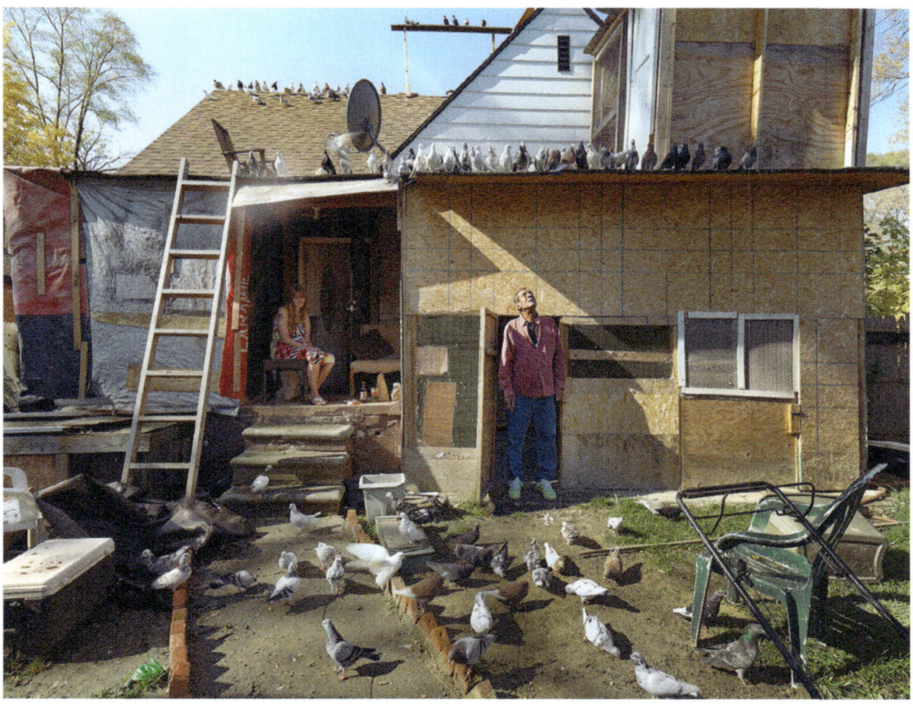

Plate 3 Dave Jordano, *Mo, Birdman of Detroit* (2012). Courtesy the artist

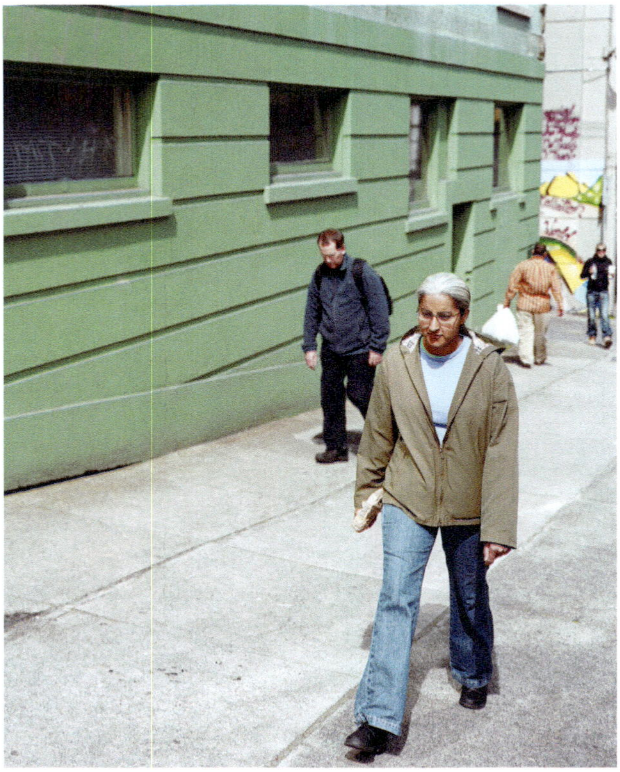

Plate 4 Jeff Wall, *Figures on a Sidewalk* (2008). Courtesy the artist

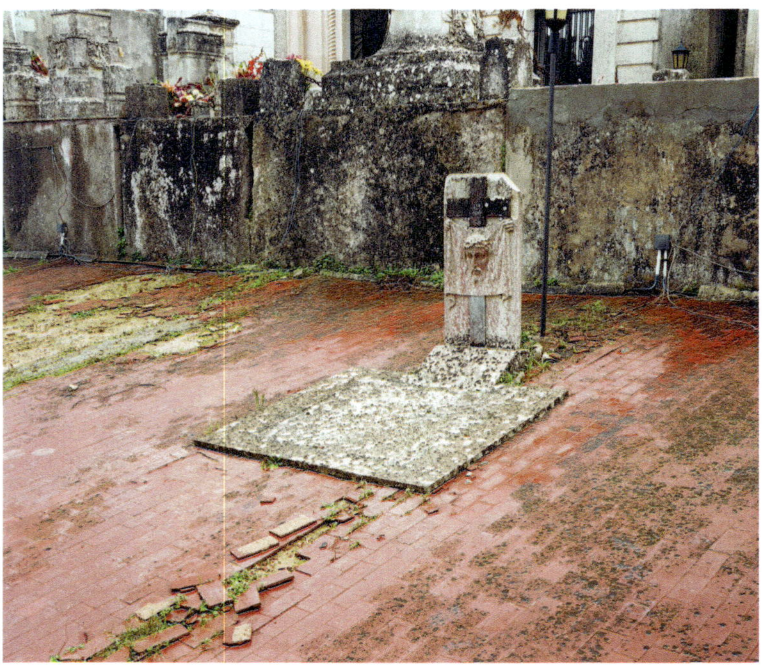

Plate 5 Jeff Wall, *Ossuary Headstone* (2007). Courtesy the artist

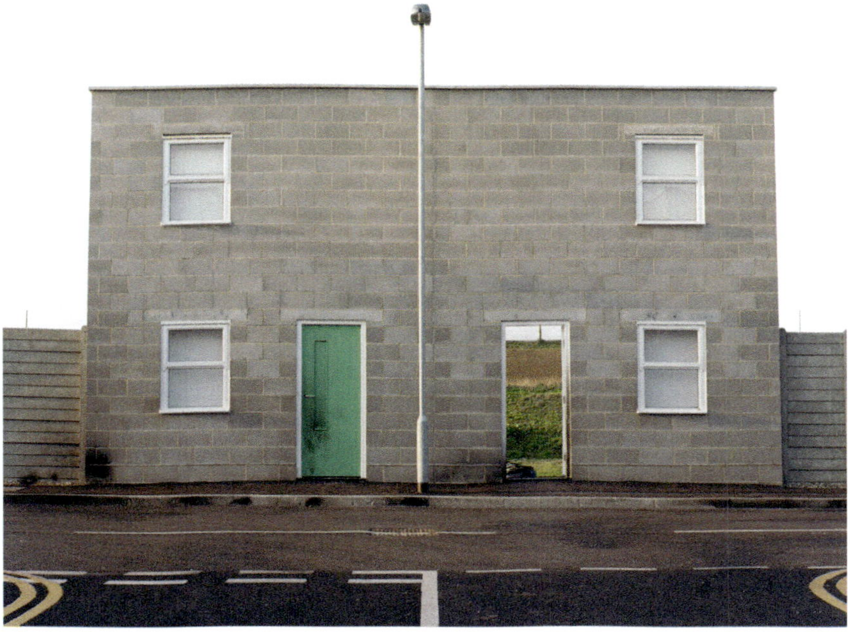

Plate 6 Sarah Pickering, *Semi-detached* (2004), from *Public Order* series. Courtesy the artist

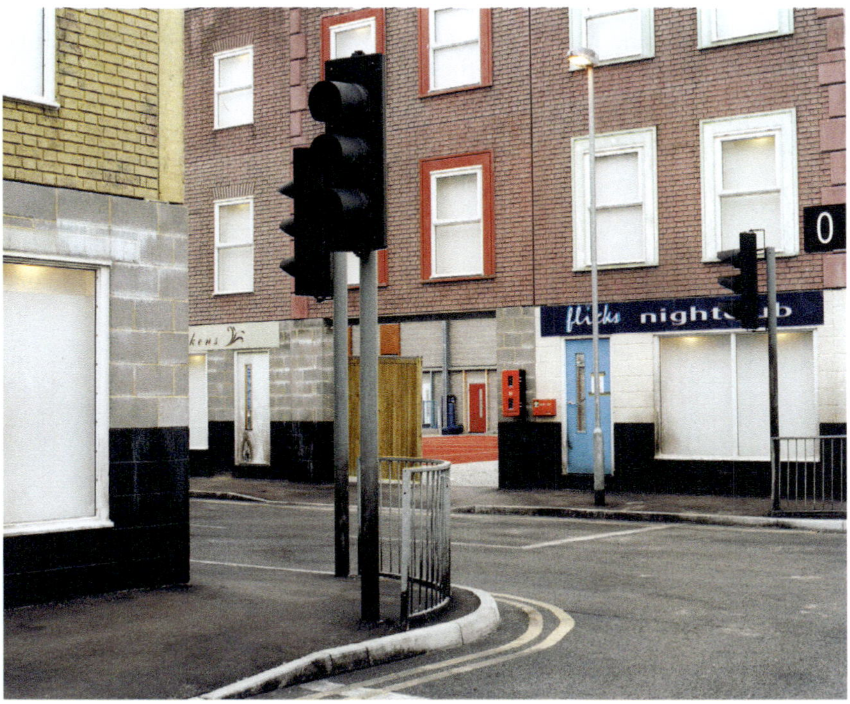

Plate 7 Sarah Pickering, *Flicks Nightclub* (2004), from *Public Order* series. Courtesy the artist

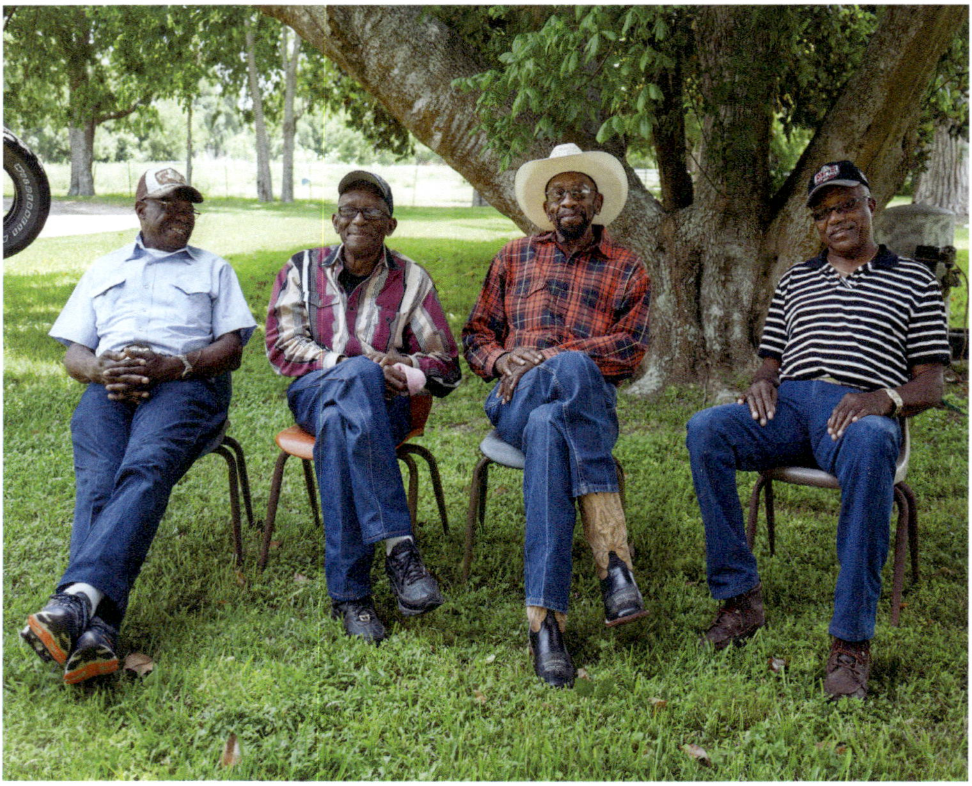

Plate 8 Andrea Robbins and Max Becher, *Black Cowboys: Three Bull Riders, One Bronc Rider, Richmond Texas* (2016). Courtesy the artists

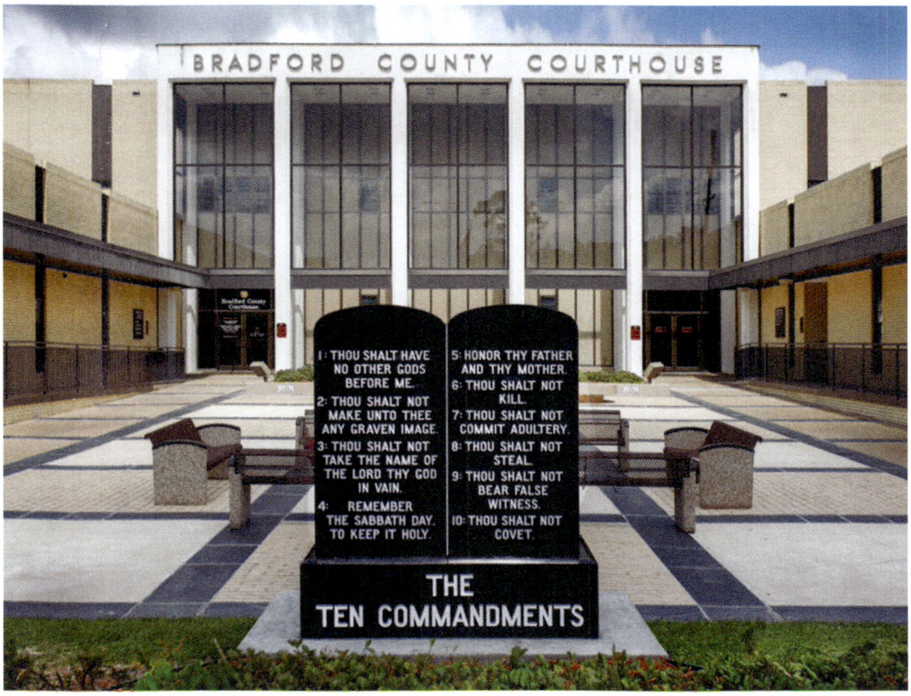

Plate 9 Andrea Robbins and Max Becher, *Bradford County Courthouse, Starke, FL* from *Following the Ten Commandments* series (2012–2014). Courtesy the artists

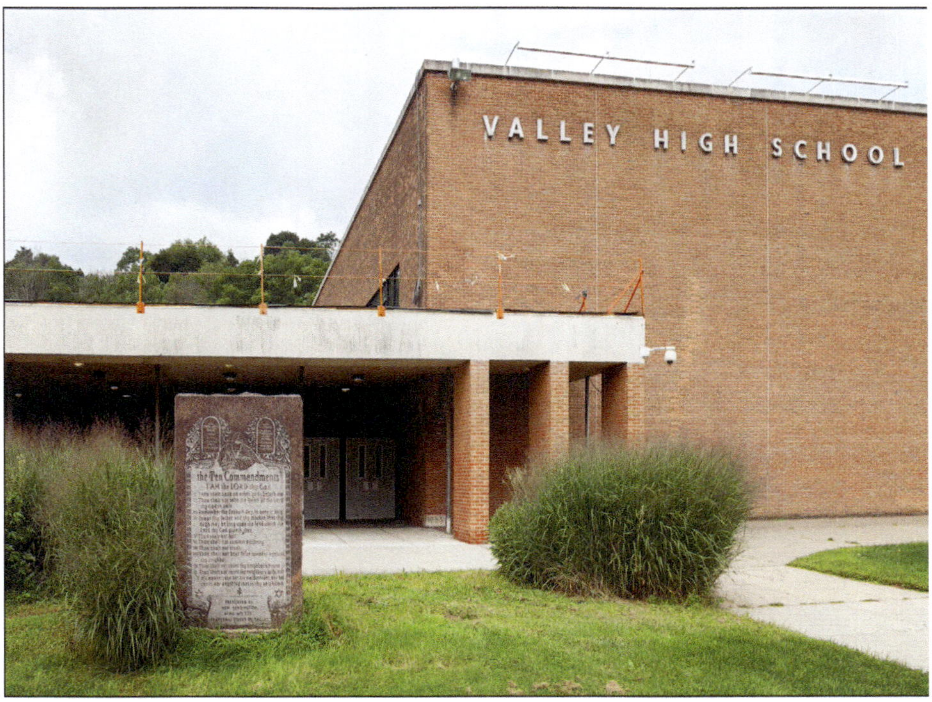

Plate 10 Andrea Robbins and Max Becher, *Valley High School, New Kensington, Pennsylvania*, from *Following the Ten Commandments* series (2012–2014). Courtesy the artists

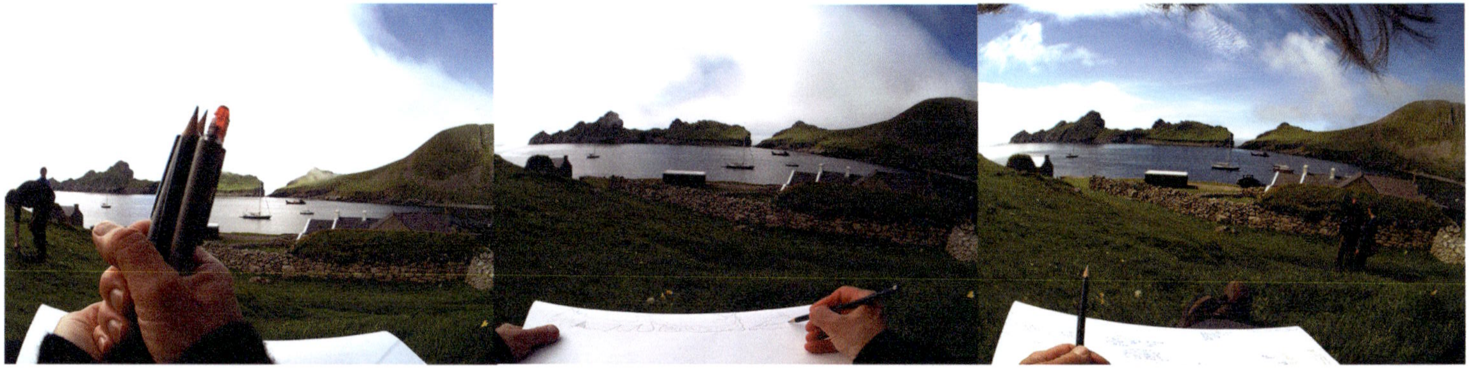

Plate 11 Sample images taken by an automatic camera, worn by Claire, St Kilda (2014). Courtesy the author

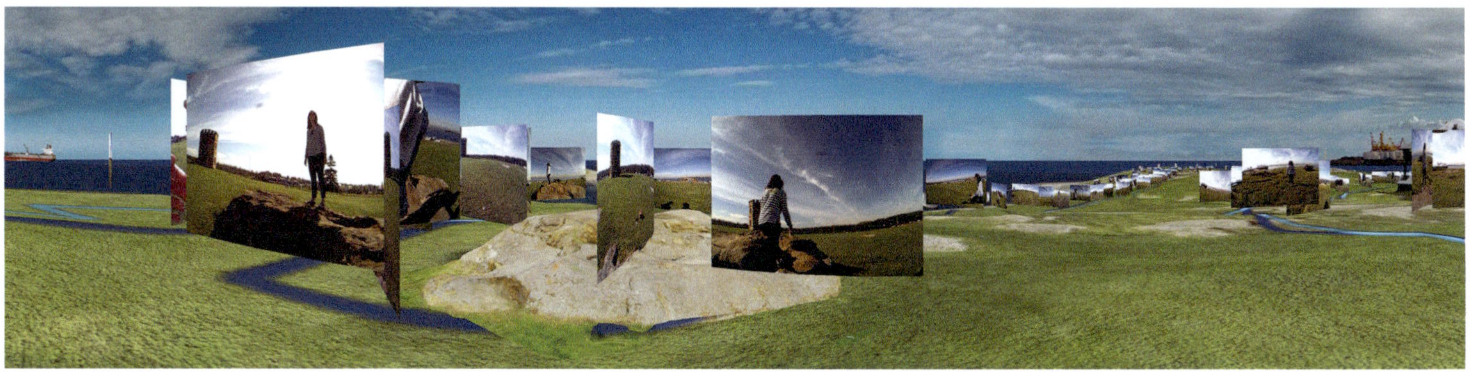

Plate 12 Amnesia Atlas, 3D immersive browser for viewing images taken by an automatic camera, Volker Kuchelmeister and Jill Bennett, detail (2014). Courtesy the author

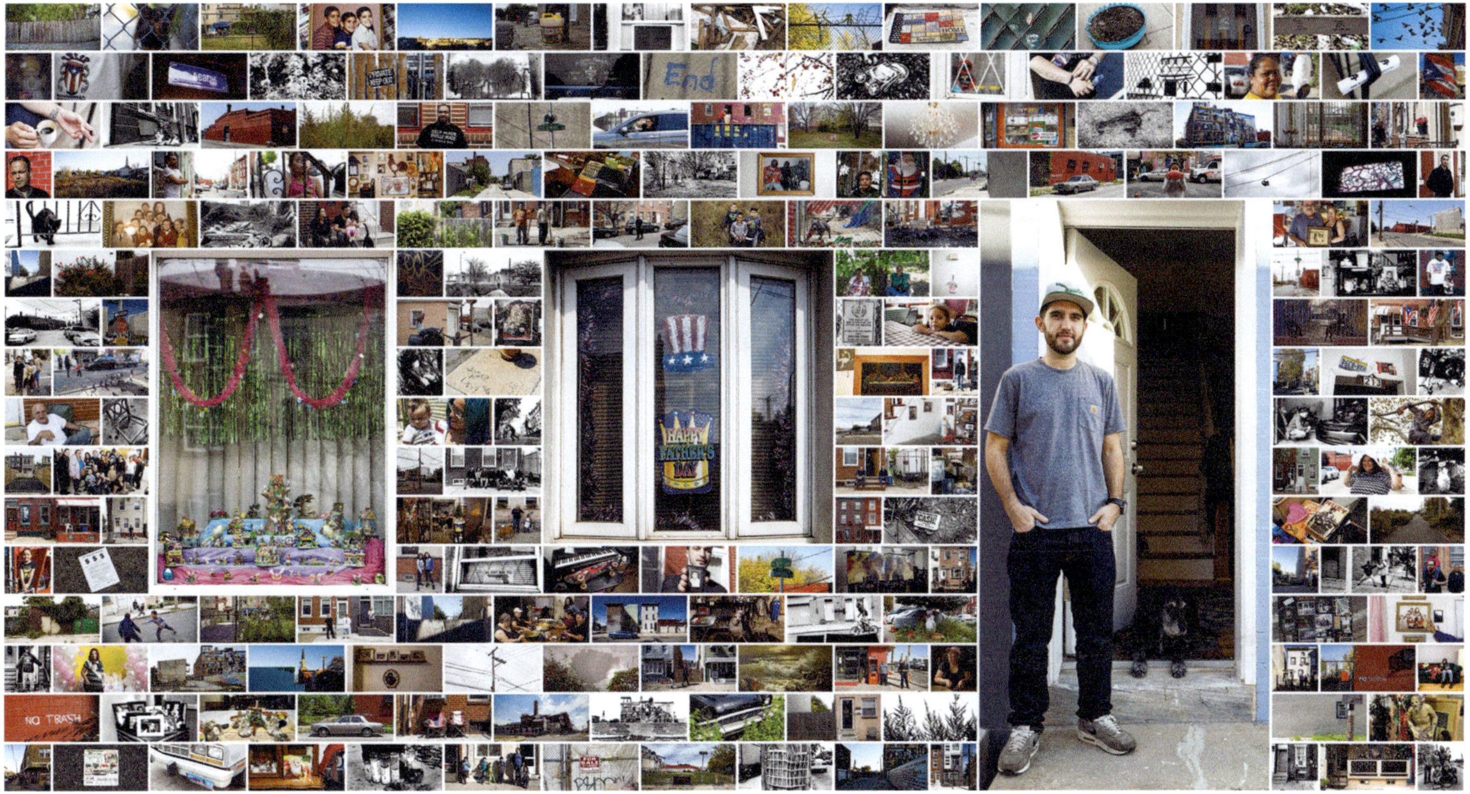

Plate 13 This image is one of four digital photo-brick composites installed as floor-to-ceiling prints in "The Block" exhibition in Philadelphia Photo Arts Center's gallery (September–November 2016). Wyatt Gallery, Marion Misilim, and Hank Willis Thomas created the composites and features photographs by Wyatt Gallery, Lisa Fairstein, Hiroyuki Ito, Will Steacy, and Hank Willis Thomas

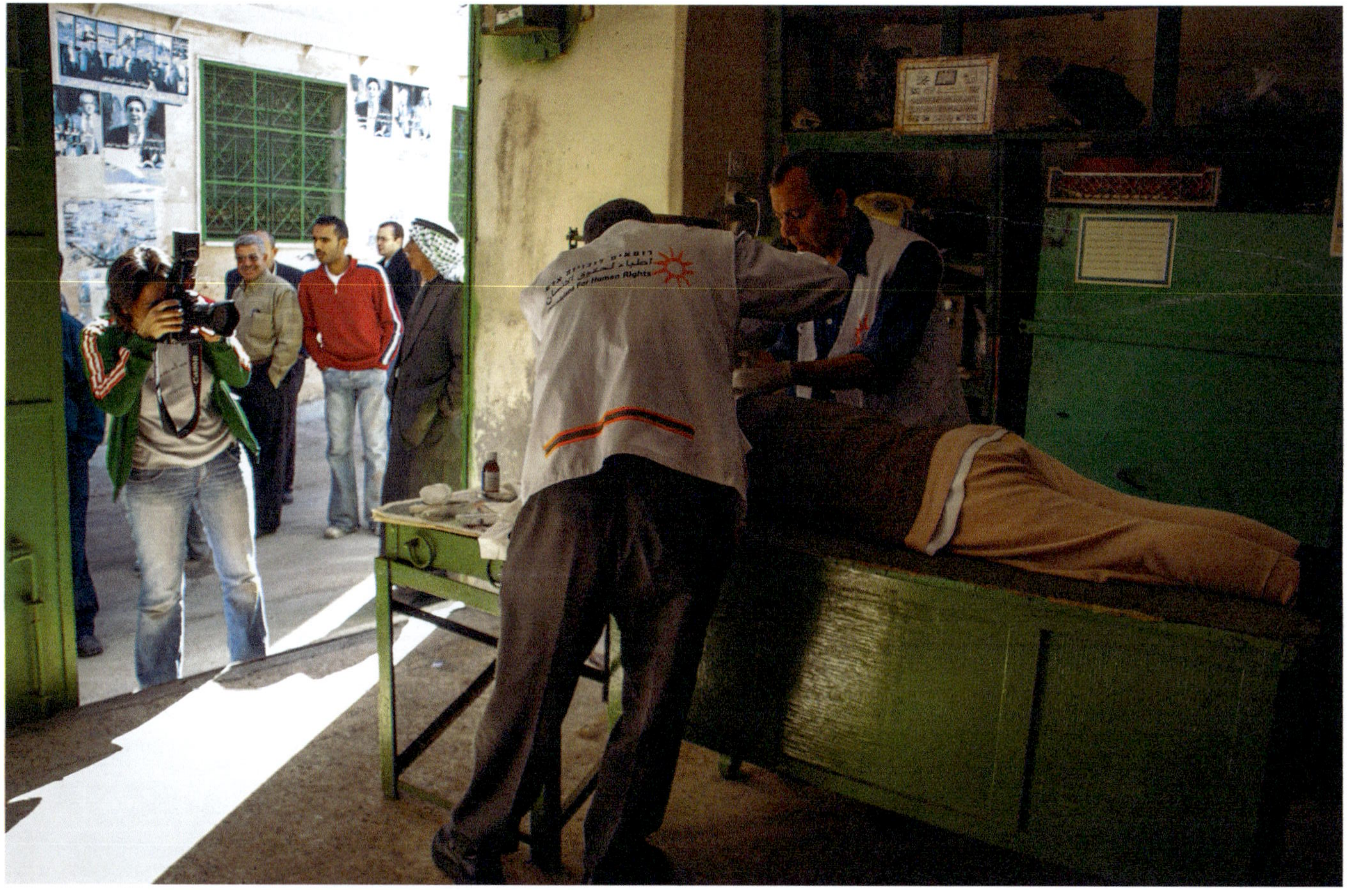

Plate 14 Mobile Clinic at Hebron. Photo: Miki Noam-Alon (2007). Courtesy the artist

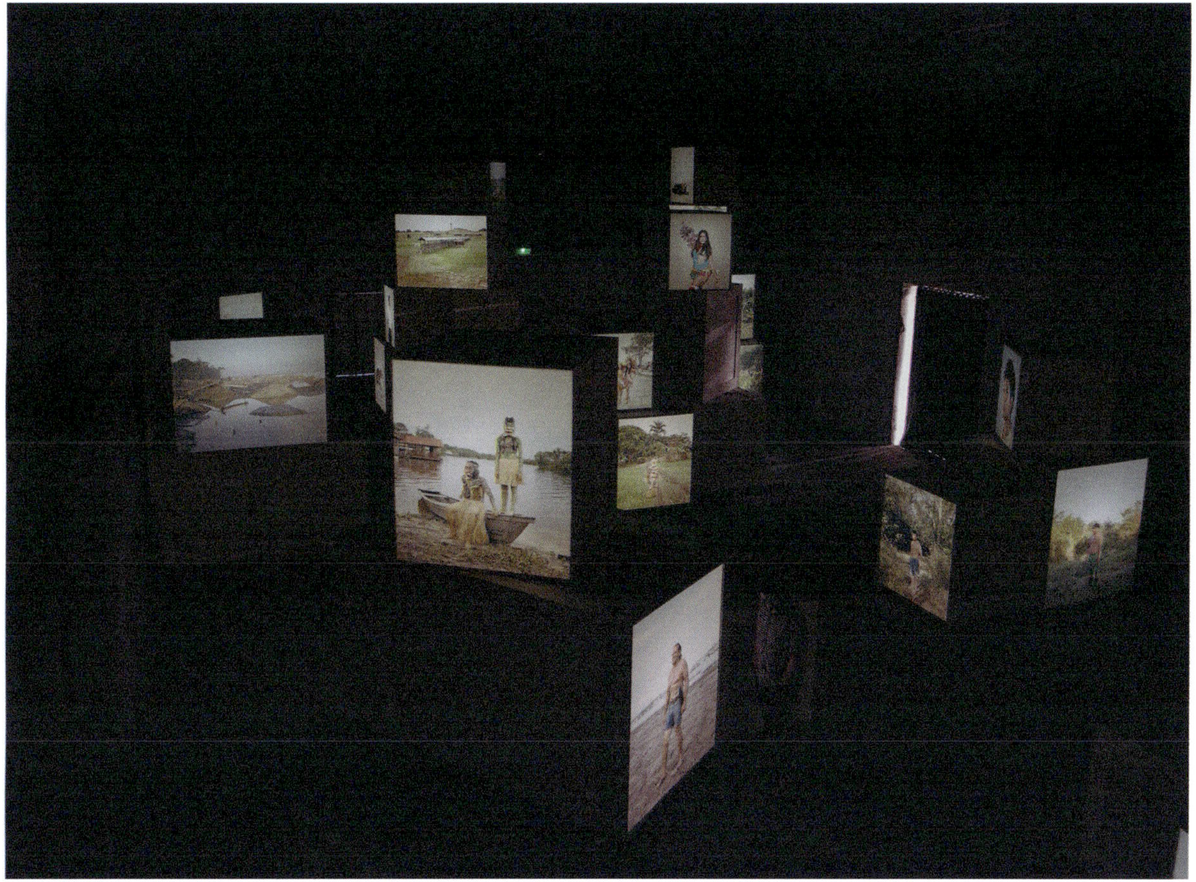

Plate 15 Yann Gross, *Jungle Book*, Installation view Arles (2016). © Yann Gross

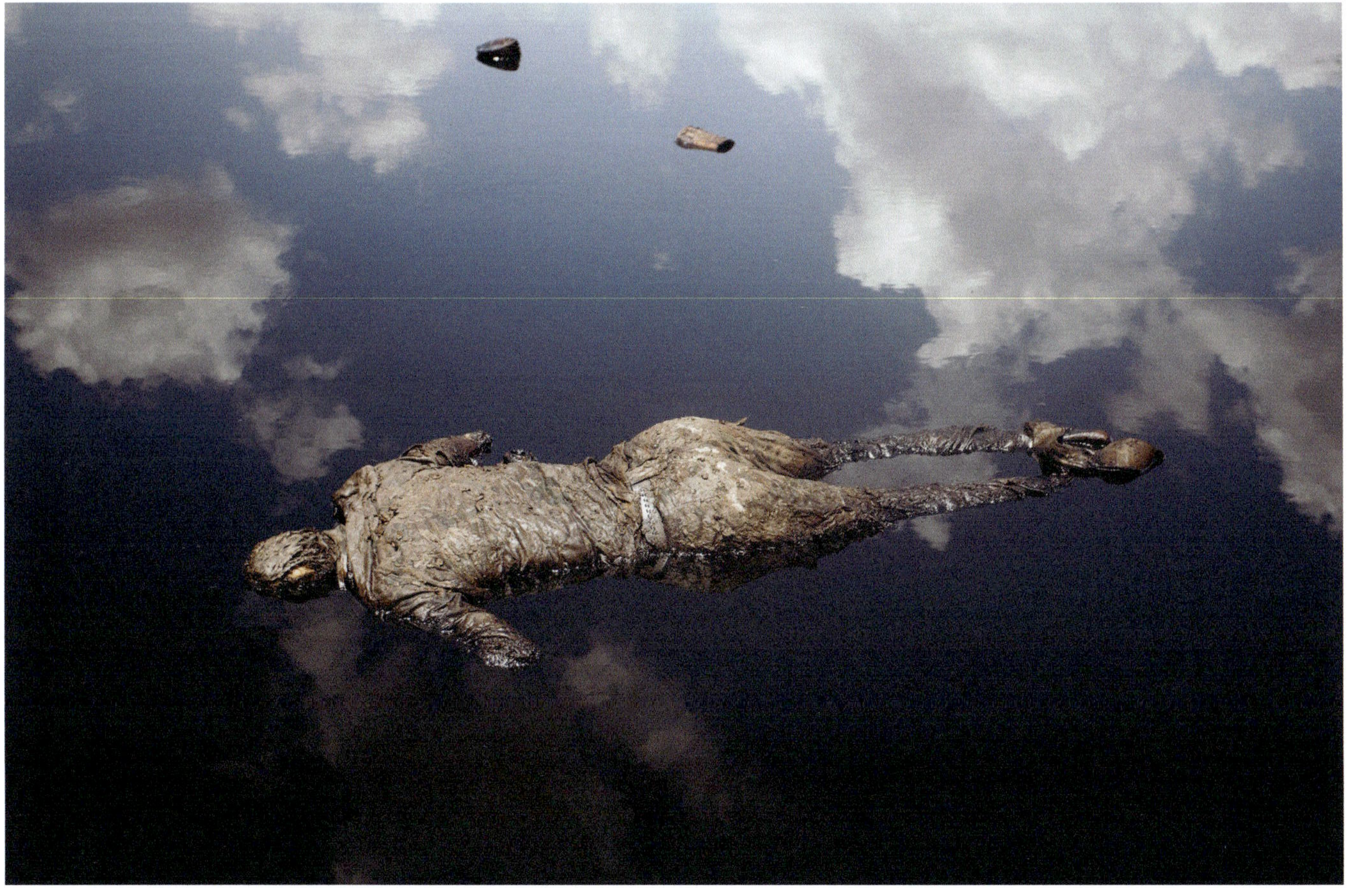

Plate 16 Dominc Nahr, *Fractured State, South and North Sudan* (2015). © Dominic Nahr/Agentur Focus

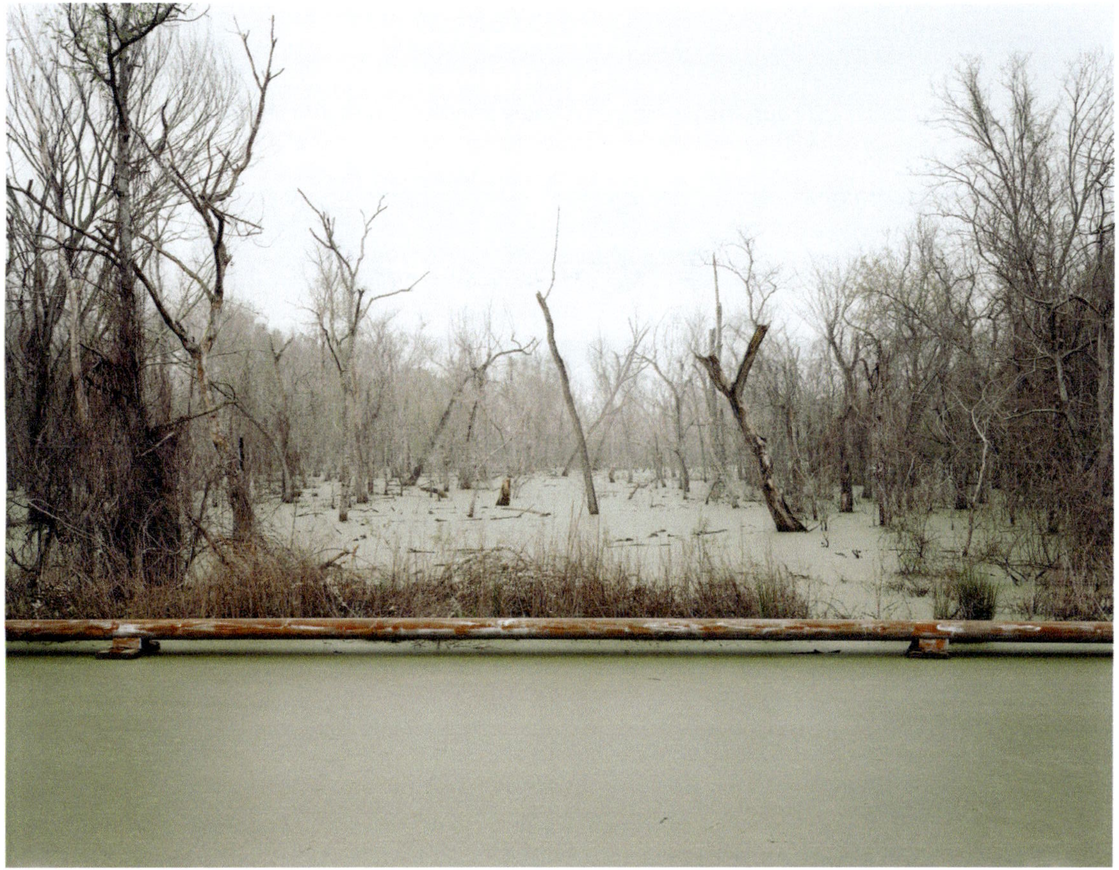

Plate 17 Richard Misrach, *Swamp and Pipeline, Geismar Louisiana* (1998). © Richard Misrach, courtesy Fraenkel Gallery, San Francisco, Pace/MacGill Gallery, New York, and Marc Selwyn Fine Art, Los Angeles

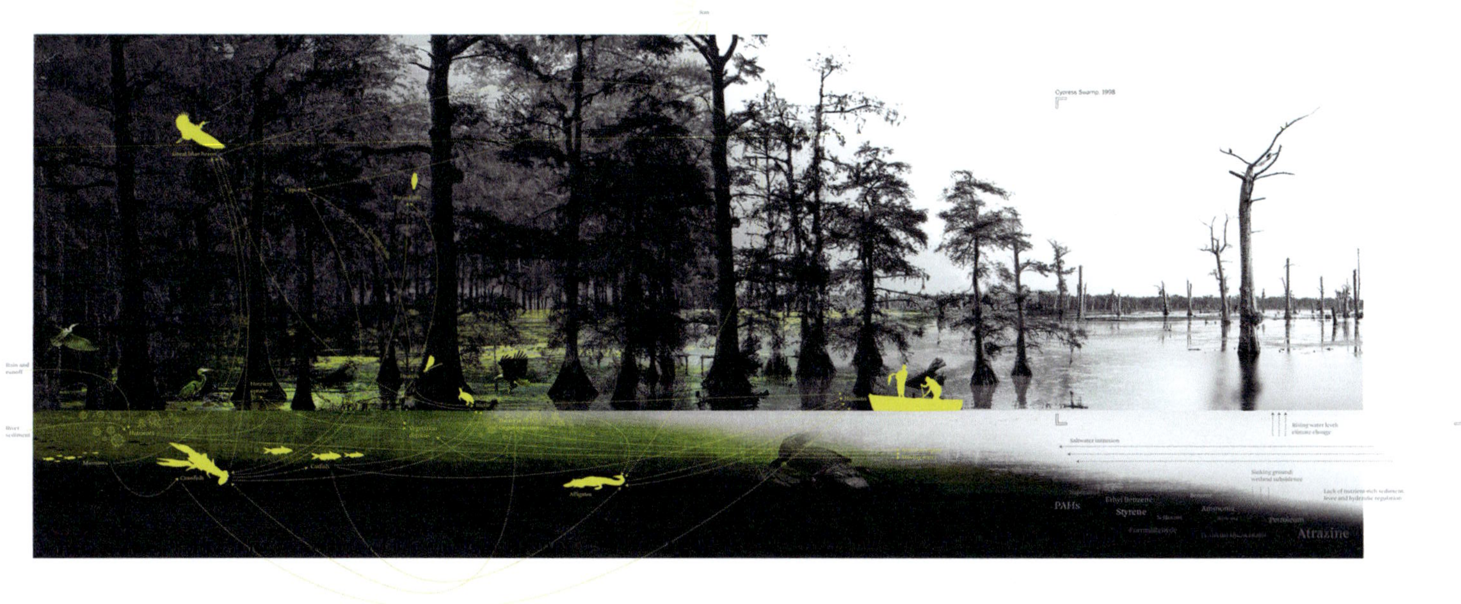

Plate 18 Kate Orff, *Requiem for a Bayou*, from the series *Petrochemical America* (2012). © Kate Orff

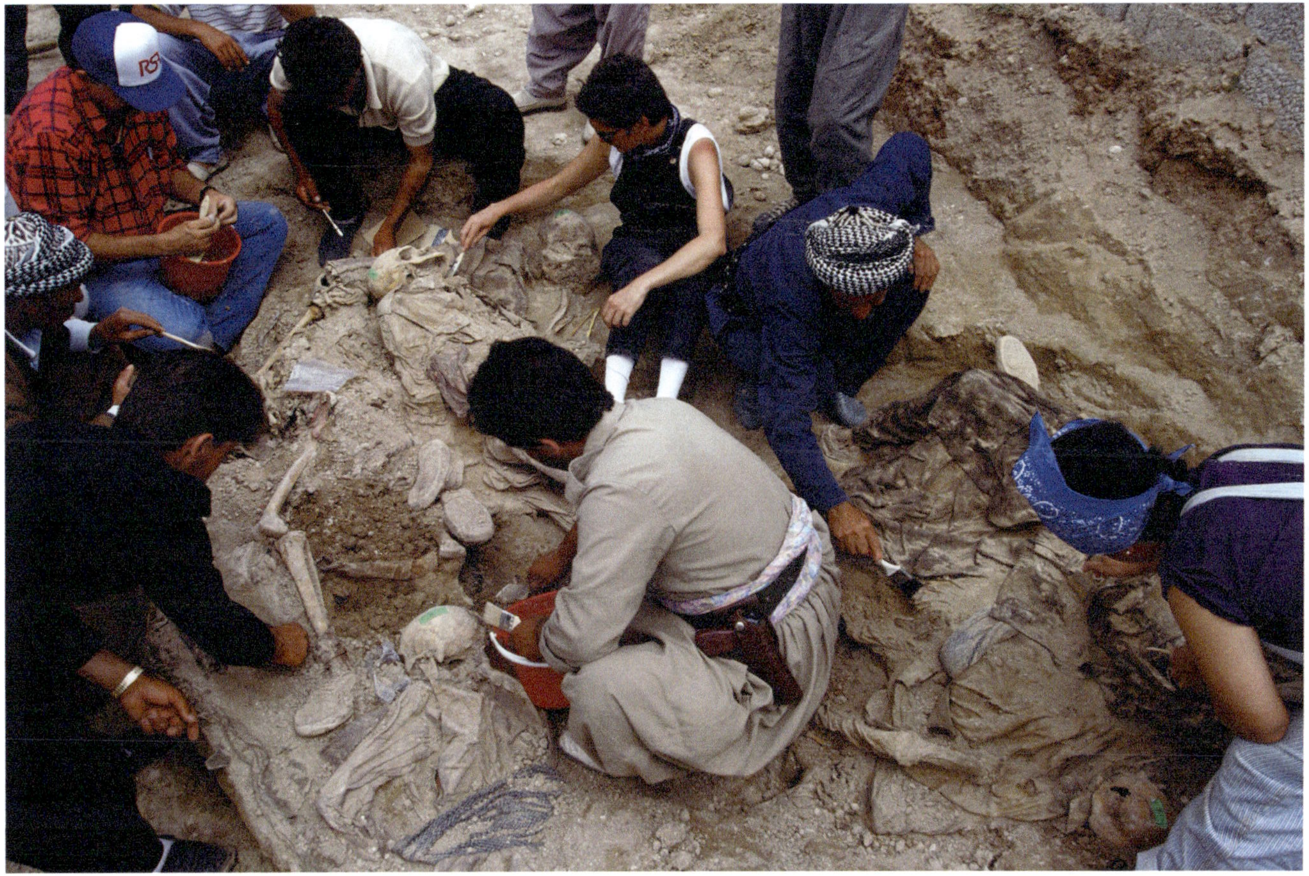

Plate 19 Susan Meiselas. *An international forensic team organized by Middle East Watch and Physicians for Human Rights work at a mass grave site in Koreme, Northern Iraq (Kurdistan)*, June 1992. © Susan Meiselas/Magnum Photos

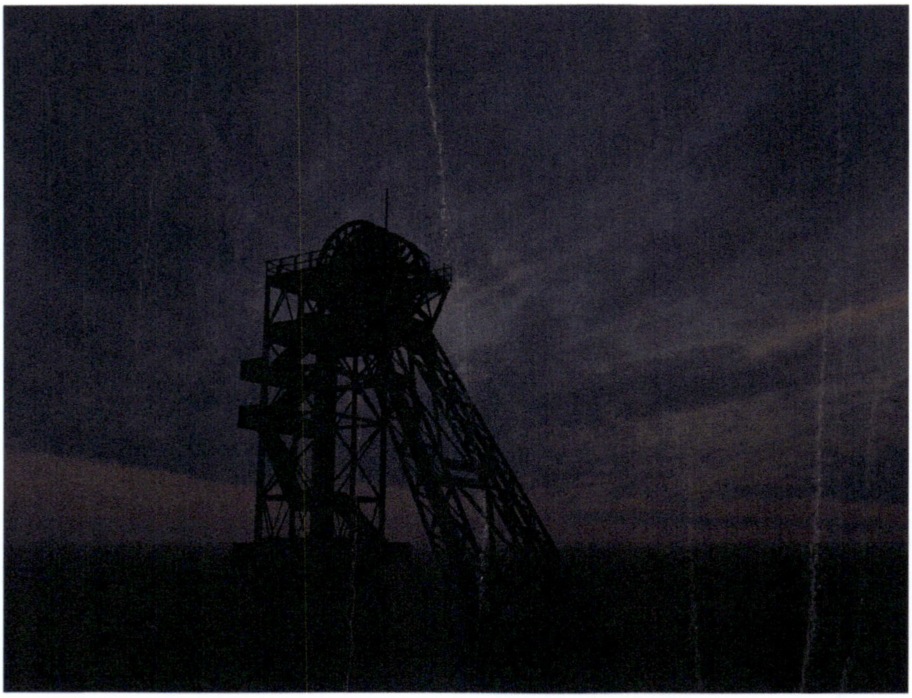

Plate 20 Victor Burgin, from *Occasio* (2014). Video still courtesy the artist

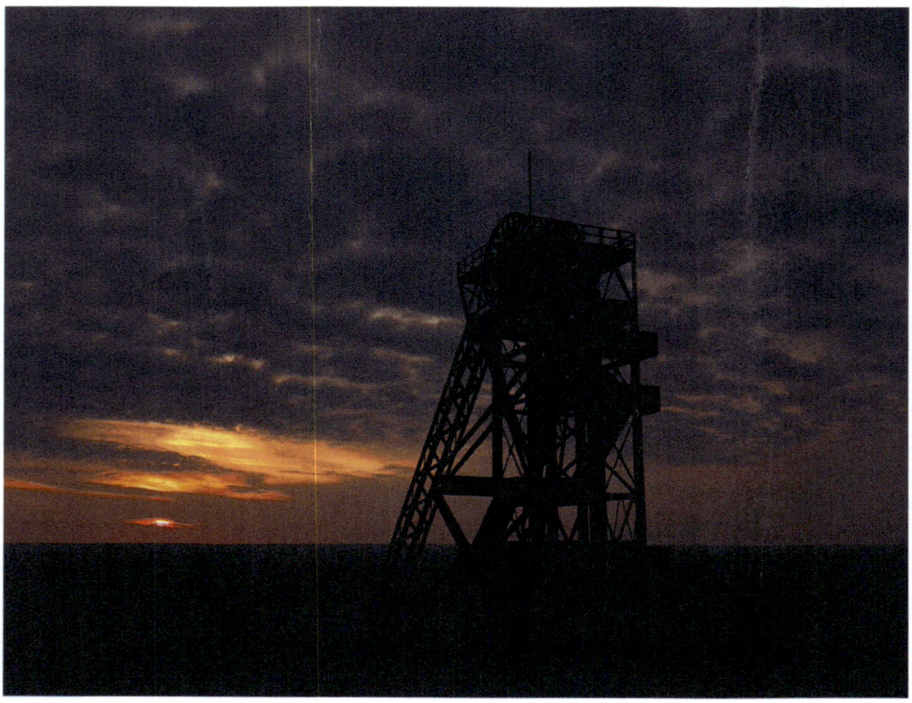

Plate 21 Victor Burgin, from *Occasio* (2014). Video still courtesy the artist

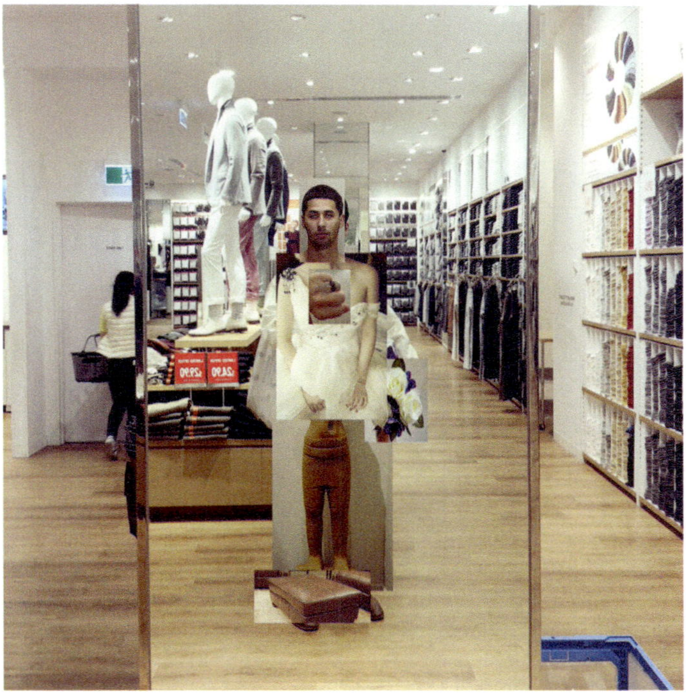

Plate 22 Jackson Eaton, *Melfies 2* (2014). Courtesy the artist

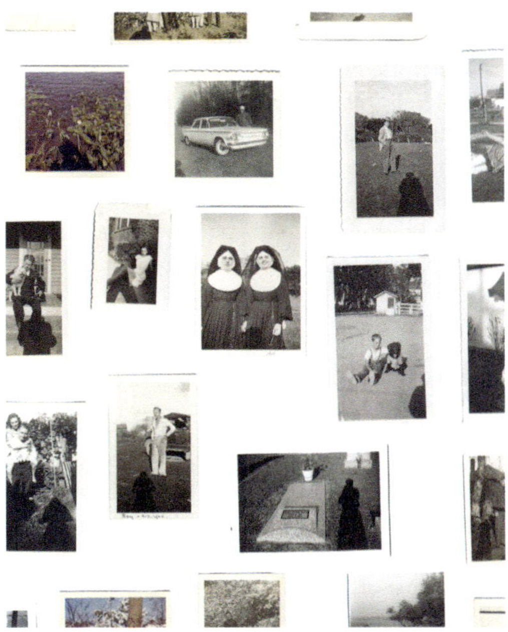

Plate 23 Patrick Pound, *The Photographer's Shadow* (2000). Detail from an ongoing collection of photographs. Courtesy of Station Gallery, Melbourne; Darren Knight Gallery, Sydney; Hamish McKay Gallery, Wellington; Melanie Roger Gallery, Auckland

23

Photographic apparatus in the era of tagshot culture

Mika Elo

In his essay "Little History of Photography," Walter Benjamin takes up Lazlo Moholy-Nagy's claim that the illiterate of the future will be those who cannot read photographs. For Benjamin, the key question is whether inscription, or more literally "scripting" (*Beschriftung*) "will become the most important part of the photograph" (Benjamin 2005: 527). Today, in the era of digital connectivity, we need to ask a similar question concerning the role of algorithmic processes in photography. How do photographs we take, share and look at relate to invisible metadata and computational processes? How is the 'script' of photographic phenomena now constituted? Benjamin helps us to explicate how metadata structures incorporated in the photographic apparatus introduce new discursive structures in society. This essay aims at outlining a structural shift in photography culture fostered by the variegated forms of tagging prevalent in digital networks: a shift from snapshot culture to tagshot culture. The photographic apparatus is hereby characterized as an assemblage facilitating intersemiotic entanglements in processes that convey sense. The essay relates these structures to Benjamin's philosophy of language, Giorgio Agamben's reflections on 'apparatus' and certain aspects of Gilles Deleuze and Félix Guattari's assemblage theory. Towards the end of the essay, Jean-Luc Nancy's ontological exposition of the 'struction' of sense is superimposed on Benjamin's notion of *Beschriftung* in order to highlight wider philosophical and media aesthetic implications of tagshot culture.

Dispersion of 'the photographic'

Questions concerning the relation between visibility and readability raised by Benjamin have become more compelling than ever, albeit within a new constellation of practices and technologies and their discursive framing. In Benjamin's time, bits of information helpful in reading the photographs (archival, technical and personal notes, as well as captions, etc.) were often inscribed on a paper next to the images, on the negative or on the back of the photographic print. Today, such markings—in contemporary vocabulary, 'metadata'—are not necessarily visible alongside the images or even legible to us. Contemporary image metadata standards, such as EXIF or XMP, supplement the image files themselves with informational elements that can serve many kinds of computational processes.[1] The term 'metadata', originally coined in the 1960s in the context of extensible programming languages' development, has, with the rise of the internet, shifted its predominant meaning from 'data about data' (also called 'structural metadata') to data about online resources (also called 'descriptive metadata'; Voß 2013: 20, 39). The shift from data to metadata marks a noteworthy step beyond the visible. It also challenges accustomed conceptions of writing and reading. In the 1930s, Benjamin theorized photography and other imaging technologies as forms of writing in terms of whether and how they could "keep pace with speech" (Benjamin 2002: 102). Today, the photographic script operates well beyond the human scale, both in terms of time and space.

In the new technological environment of photography, characterized by the heterogeneous mixture of old and new media technologies and practices, not only is photography culture undergoing a rapid transformation, but the mythical basis of 'the photographic' is eroding as well. It is becoming increasingly apparent that the reductive identification of photography as a cultural form with a limited set of technologies cannot offer more than a metonymic model of an imagined unity of photography (Osborne 2013: 123–125). The familiar questions concerning the identity, specificity and essence of photography have a new resonance. They are no longer questions about the unity of a medium. Photography is now distributed across various sites and circumstances in such a complex manner that conceptual delimitations of the photographic apparatus relying on the principle of containment appear increasingly obsolete and powerless.

Olia Lialina's GIF animation *Summer* (2013) offers a self-reflective response to this dispersion. Lialina has constructed an unusual experiential image sequence that relies on the computational management of metadata. The images show a woman (the artist herself) swinging on a swing that is seemingly fixed to the top of the browser window. The series is presented as a strange kind of animation: each frame is played back from a different website. There is a minimum of 18 individual hosting parties to support all frames of the animation, and it is the responsibility of the owner of the work to sustain the community of hosts at this minimum level. As the swing moves back and forth—in real time, if the internet connection is fast enough—one can see the rapidly changing URLs in the menu bar as the browser quickly redirects across a number of websites. The project makes up a distributive unity within a network of webpages using the most generic means of computational management of connections enabled by metadata.[2]

Summer hints at a plethora of issues related to metadata, mobile communication, social media, copyrights, online archives, surveillance technologies and robotics that force photography theory to face the dawning challenge of combining the conceptualizations of the photographic apparatus as a historically variable mesh of technologies, practices and discourses with the insight that photography was always already on its way to being beyond the visible and even beyond the human, that "all photography is to some extent nonhuman" (Zylinska 2015: 134). Dynamic data objects, such as Lialina's GIF animation, networked CCTV cameras and surveillance drones only make explicit that the photographic condition was never based on a seamless co-operation between a human photographer and the photographic apparatus. There is a gap between the two metonymical figures in this relation: the human eye and the camera eye.

This gap, constitutive of the photographic condition, is a historical variable. This can be explicated by comparing three different technological settings in the expanding field of photography. Eadweard Muybridge's famous serial photographs of a galloping horse from 1878 were taken with cameras set in a row along the horse's path and triggered in a sequence as the horse raced down the track in front of the cameras (Brown 1992: 42–47). When shown with a synthesizing instrument, such as a zoetrope, these images give an impression of a continuous movement shown from a seemingly real point of view. Time slice technology developed by Tim Macmillan in the 1980s uses a very similar principle, but here the cameras are set in a curved formation. When these cameras are triggered simultaneously, and the images are shown as an animation sequence, we get an impression of a virtual camera movement within one moment of time.[3] Retroactively, the time slice technique reveals that the camera is virtually moving in Muybridge's setting as well; the frontal arrangement only disguises this fact. In Lialina's *Summer*, the technological setting is radically different, even if the animation effect is seemingly rather conventional. The metonymic counterpart of the human eye is shown to be dispersed by means of networked relations. Here, unlike in the case of serial photographs and the time slice technique, the animation effect is not aiming at bridging the gap between human eye and camera eye in terms of visual illusion. This arrangement does not imitate human vision; it invites the viewer to read the operations behind the visual surface offered to the eye.

This schematic comparison indicates that photography theory is facing the task of mapping an "expanding field of photography" (Osborne 2003); the terrains of aesthetic, political, ethical and epistemic dimensions of photography are not only expanding but are also in the process of transformation and dispersion. We are now witnessing, after a long period of latency, how photography becomes readable as a hybrid hinge between the phenomenal horizon of experience and algorithmic processes (Fisher and Rubinstein 2013: 8).

The imagined unity of photography is being superseded by a new dominant cultural form: the computational management of metadata. A prominent example of the visual culture of industrialized societies, photography is now showing its latent potential for serving practices that find their motivation beyond the visible. It is more evident than ever that the photographic apparatus is entangled with invisible affordances. One of the central claims of this essay is that the current tendencies of this entanglement constitute a shift from snapshot culture to tagshot culture. As explicated in the course of the essay, this transformation finds its parallel in a shift from snapshot-like fixed digital documents to dynamic data objects. Whereas the snapshot, as a common visual record of lived experience, has for a long time epitomized the ubiquity of photography in visual culture, the current inclination of consumer photography towards hybrid forms of recording marks the rise of a new culture, where various methods of attaching metadata to images—that is, tagging—play an increasingly important role. Even if photographs are still taken on the spur of the moment, their 'tagability' has become the key to their networked afterlife. Whereas the visual record of a view used to be the most relevant frame of reference in snapshot culture, selective filtering of information now takes forms that are independent of the logic of our visual environment. Flickr, for example, allows searching for images with the help of various combinations of visual texture, colour, tag words, date, format, location data, as well as various user-related metadata. The invisible affordances of tagshot culture can be demonstrated through a simple search on different platforms: today, a Google image search for "land" gives a selection of landscapes and Land Rovers, whereas the same search in Flickr results in a juxtaposition of landing planes, birds and bees, as well as landscapes. A few days later, the result might be different; the whole setting is dynamic.

From semantic anchoring to intersemiotic encounter

The analogy between Benjamin's remarks on inscription and contemporary understanding of metadata can be made productive only by unpacking Benjamin's notion of *Beschriftung* and its hidden philosophical background motivations. The root of the term is *Schrift*—writing.

Schriftung refers to the operation of writing, and the prefix *Be-* adds to this a relational twist: *Be-schriftung* means literally "to provide (something) with writing"—in a word: scripting.

In "Little History" and in "News about Flowers," we find the famous passages where Benjamin discusses the "optical unconscious." He contends that, in a way similar to psychoanalysis, which opens access to the psychic unconscious, photography shows us a previously invisible area of experience: "A geyser of new image-worlds hisses up at points of our existence where we would at least have expected them possible" (Benjamin 2004b: 156). "For it is another nature which speaks to the camera rather than to the eye" (Benjamin 2005: 510). The technologically pre-scribed 'second nature' disconnects the visible from the human eye and its innate capacities; it *speaks* to the eye through the camera. Through photography, the eye gains access to areas of visibility where vision needs to be readjusted. Photography destabilizes the phenomenological ground of sense experience by showing even the most familiar things in a new light, as the catchy title of Benjamin's review of Karl Blossfeldt's plant photographs aptly expresses: "News about Flowers" (Benjamin 2004b: 155).

In the expanding field of photography, we continuously come across images that challenge our capacity to read them. In the processes of acquiring photographic literacy, we often rely on verbal language and linguistic models of signification, as the metaphor of reading suggests. It first seems that this is what Benjamin relies on, when he makes an appeal for inscription or 'scripting':

> The camera is getting smaller and smaller, ever readier to capture fleeting and secret images whose shock effect paralyzes the associative mechanisms in the beholder. This is where inscription (*Beschriftung*) must come into play, which includes the photography of the literarization of the conditions of life, and without which all photographic construction must remain arrested in the approximate.
>
> *(Benjamin 2005: 527)*

Benjamin links here the question of photographic literacy with a shift in societal relations that he, alluding to Brecht's estranging technique of combining images, gestures and texts in epic theatre, calls "literarization." A camera can capture the material circumstances of social life in the smallest detail, but the relational setting of these visible indices needs to be constructed cunningly. One easily thinks that conditions of life that are 'literary' are legible for those who know the code. Photographic literacy would then simply be a question of decoding skills. However, if we follow Benjamin's argumentation in "Little History" attentively enough, we will notice that he is not simply highlighting the importance of contextualization and the semiotic anchoring of images into the realm of verbally articulated representations.

Benjamin is known to make use of crafty textual strategies in his argumentation, such as the embedding of theoretical kernels in individual words (Petersson 2013: 74–79). In "Little History," we encounter this kind of gesture that links Benjamin's political-historical analyses with his philosophical-metaphysical reflections. These two registers relate to each other much like the two sides of the same coin, or like figure and background in an ornament. In "Little History" this kind of constellation is the connection between Benjamin's media aesthetic reflections and language philosophy. In Benjamin's view, technologies and techniques—literary, photographic, theatrical, etc., depending on context—partake of the relations of production and signification on the level of material arrangements and linguistic articulations. Technological operations are embedded in the horizon of their own application, which, for Benjamin, implies that they need to be thought in historical terms. For Benjamin, the question of photographic literacy is loaded with "historical tension" (Benjamin 2005: 527).

In "Little History," this elemental role of technics comes to the fore especially in a passage where Benjamin emphasizes that the "new image-worlds" opened up by photography "make the difference between technology and magic visible as a thoroughly historical variable" (Benjamin 2005: 512). The word "magic" paired with "technology" hints at the latent theoretical background of Benjamin's argument. According to Benjamin's philosophical account of linguistic communication, language is a historical process characterized by a tensional relation between mediation and immediacy (Elo 2007: 143–167; Elo 2018). On the one hand, language is liable to processes of instrumentalization. It tends to become a means of communication—that is, *Technik*, a 'technology'. On the other hand, it essentially is, by its own means, communication, or, more exactly: 'imparting', *Mitteilung* (Weber 2008: 38–44). Insofar as language communicates, it does so immediately—that is, it is 'magical' (Menninghaus 1995: 78). This polarity inherent to all languages (both verbal and non-verbal) becomes tangible whenever a language encounters another language. This implies that the task of translation emerges at the interface of two languages not only as the task of negotiating between their different ways of making sense, but also as the task of constructing a viable relation between linguistic technics and magic.

For Benjamin, the role of scripting (*Beschriftung*) in the "literarization of the conditions of life" marks an essential moment in the encounter between two different languages (in this case, photography and the written word). It gives rise to a resonance between their ways of making sense. The peculiar convergence of languages that, in Benjamin's view, constitutes the precondition of readability cannot be reduced to an exchange of pre-established meanings. Benjamin's call for scripting echoes his understanding of reading as something more than just the decoding of what there is. For him, reading involves tracing new trajectories that, because they are first discovered through reading, can only be "pre-scribed" (Weber 2001: 28). This implies that scripting is actually a gesture of translation, and it does not involve just semantic anchoring. At stake is something we might call, in Roman Jakobson's (1992) terms, an "intersemiotic" encounter that involves negotiating the relation between mediation and immediacy, across the divide of two different modes of articulation, in this case verbal language and photography. In following sections, the intersemiotic bundling of processes in photography addressed by Benjamin will be further explicated in terms of the photographic apparatus.

Language and apparatus

The theoretical perspective opened by the analogy between captions and metadata reaches a dead end unless its potential is explicated with regard to the new technological environment of photography. Two steps are needed. First, contemporary conditions of the photographic apparatus and its linguistic qualities need to be outlined. The media aesthetic approach suggested here involves consideration of the intersemiotic encounter between languages in terms of an "assemblage"—that is, as a moment of reconfiguration through relations of exteriority, both material and expressive in kind (Deleuze and Guattari 2014: 88, *passim*). Second, the notion of metadata needs to be differentiated. Here, the main challenge will be to describe the multiple implications of computational management of metadata in experiential terms.

When confronted with the eroding unity of 'the photographic', it is necessary to conceptualize photography, beyond any limited set of technologies, as a historically variegated apparatus consisting of technologies, practices and discourses. The conceptual move needed here finds its parallel in Giorgio Agamben's way of expanding the Foucauldian notion of *dispositif* that he makes with implicit reference to Benjamin's theories of language and translation. For Agamben, apparatus (*dispositivo*) is "literally anything that has in some way the capacity to capture, orient, determine, interpret, model, control, or secure the gestures, behaviors, opinions, or discourses of living beings" (Agamben 2009: 14). Agamben's list of examples is wide and heterogeneous: the pen, writing, literature, philosophy, agriculture, cigarettes, navigation, computers, cellular phones and language (14). For him, the key issues at stake in such apparatuses are "processes of subjectification," "humanization" and "the possibility of knowing the being as such," which, in the Heideggerian perspective that Agamben is building on here, implies the possibility of "constructing a world" (12–14). Apparatus, in other words, is an assemblage of technical arrangements and material circumstances that disposes or formats—as the etymology of 'apparatus' (*apparare*—'make ready for') hints at—the phenomenal horizon of human experience.

Against this background, *Beschriftung* marks the heterogeneous setup of the photographic apparatus in terms of an assemblage of different languages, verbal and non-verbal, an assemblage of gestural relations, signifying elements and recorded traits. In fact, the peculiar convergence of different languages that Benjamin writes of could be rephrased in terms of an inherent tendency of languages to assemble with each other into apparatuses. As Rosalind Krauss notes, Benjamin fosters a deconstructive attitude toward the idea of a self-contained medium and conceptualizes photography as a form that actually erodes its own specificity (Krauss 1999: 45).

Here, a note concerning the relation between the notions of language and apparatus is needed, as both Benjamin's "language" and Agamben's "apparatus," serving as the main points of reference here, are rather plastic notions (cf. Elo 2018: 288–289). For Benjamin, any kind of expression counts as language; in fact, "we cannot imagine a total absence of language in anything," not even in the world of things (Benjamin 2004a: 62–63). Agamben, in turn, expands the notion of apparatus beyond the historical specificity of Foucauldian knowledge/power settings to include virtually all kinds of "cultural techniques" (*Kulturtechniken*). In his exposition, language turns out to be, in terms of its ontological effects (subjectification, humanization and constructing a world), a metonymic model of apparatuses in general, and as such it comes very close to Benjamin's notion of language. Both Benjamin and Agamben, furthermore, insist on the multiplicity of languages/apparatuses. As medial settings of sense, they never appear alone, they are embedded in each other's co-appearance and they intersect and intermingle in multiple ways. Exposed to this multiplicity they are impure, insofar as purity implies self-containment.

Benjamin's idea of "pure language" helps us to find another footing for the linguistic purity of the photographic apparatus—or perhaps we could call it, in Deleuzian vein, 'consistency'? This would open up the possibility of considering the assemblage, through which the difference between technology and magic becomes visible as a historical variable in photography, in terms of a "plane of consistency." Benjamin emphasizes that all languages aim in their own singular ways at one and the same thing (Benjamin 2004c: 257). His term for this is "pure language"—a dimension of language that cannot be attained in any single, separate language, but only in the multiplicity of different languages mutually supplementing each other (ibid.). In short, "pure language" becomes a name for the origin of sense. 'Origin' here, however, is not a ground or a stable point of reference. Rather, it is an eddy (the word Benjamin uses here is *Strudel*) that brings heterogeneous elements together according to a logic that is historical (Benjamin 2009: 45). As sense-making apparatuses, languages are assemblages both in terms of their supplementary relations and in the sense that, instead of speaking of things from a meta-perspective, they speak "*on the same level as* states of things and states of content," to borrow Deleuze's and Guattari's concise formulation (Deleuze and Guattari 2014: 87; original emphasis). For Benjamin (as well as for Deleuze and Guattari), language is essentially *in medias res*; it participates in the world of things. His notion of language is both wide and abstract, but "in no way metaphorical" (Benjamin 2004a: 62).

To sum up, language-apparatuses are always exposed to reconfiguration through relations of exteriority; they are assemblages. This applies also to the language-apparatus of photography. The imagined unity of photographic apparatus is an effect of its consistency, its capacity to originate sense. It makes up a "distributive unity," to use Peter Osborne's apt term (Osborne 2013: 122–123). Osborne develops the notion in relation to the Kantian idea of aesthetic unity of experience—that is a unity without any rational ground other than the fact of its practical continuity and contiguity. For Osborne, "distributive unity" is the "logical form of the historical unity of empirical forms"; it is a pragmatic unity (ibid.). Lialina's *Summer* shows in clear terms that this pragmatic aspect of the photographic apparatus is especially tangible on the level of the interface. Interface is the pre-scribed place for linking the algorithmic processes to and with visual representations. It generates sense by establishing continuities and contiguities at the same time as it facilitates specific forms of reception, use and behaviour. In terms of its peculiar way of being distributed on the web, *Summer* indicates how the operative logic of an interface pre-scribes ways of making sense as well as shapes the ramifications of human experience.

Against this philosophical background, the contemporary photographic apparatus appears as a distributive unity of an assemblage of processes, technics, arrangements, material circumstances, regulations and articulations that format the experiential horizon of photographic imagery. With regard to this scenario, one of the key challenges of photography theory today is to grasp this distributive unity in terms of its ontological effects on the level of processes of subjectification, humanization and constructing a world. Attention has to be paid to the *ontological consistency* of distributed processes instead of the proprieties of a conceptually delimited photography. Here, a shift of focus from an instrumental view on technology (technology seen as an external factor affecting beings) to technics of being is needed. In the following, this refocusing is undertaken step by step.

Layers of metadata

The first step is a multilayered characterization of the new cultural form of computational management of metadata. As noted above, photographs have always been accompanied by more or less systematically recorded bits of information concerning their technical parameters, as well as by contextual notes, such as captions, in a word: 'metadata'. Today, the large variety of metadata does not only specify and contextualize individual photographs. Layers of metadata may also describe the moments of choice and adjustment incorporated in photographic processes. Cameras have not just gotten smaller and smaller, as Benjamin noted, they have also become more diverse, interconnected and intelligent. Processes of capturing, altering, sharing, copying, embedding and publishing can be interconnected in automatic fashion. Many of the technical adjustments are no longer mechanical and irreversible: they are computational and reversible. An illustrative case in point is the light field metering technology used by Lytro that makes explicit the vast optional space implicit in RAW files.

The computational affordances of contemporary cameras plug into networks where layers of metadata are created and managed, in variegated ways. These services and sites enable users to add metadata such as keywords and other kinds of markings—that is, tags—to various assets and internet resources without relying on a controlled vocabulary or categories.

This implies a shift from more or less hierarchical taxonomies and their optimized searchability to nonhierarchical and experiential taxonomies relying on user-generated metadata. This tagability is in fact one of the key features of the internet since Web 2.0 (Rubinstein 2010: 197). In Benjaminian terms, tagging is the eddy of sense-making in tagging systems, an originary feature that brings heterogeneous elements together according to a logic characteristic of the technological conditions fostering tagshot culture.

When the moments of capturing, processing, presentation and distribution of photographs are computationally interlinked in ways that go beyond the visual mastery of spatiotemporal relations, an individual photograph is no longer primarily a spatiotemporal fragment retrieved from the flow of visual experiences of the world. It appears, instead, as a placeholder in a multifunctional network of references, a nodal point in pre-formatted narratives and dynamic connections; it has become a tagshot. In more technical terms, this development reflects a shift from the predominance of snapshot-like fixed digital documents to dynamic data objects (Voß 2013: 38).

Broad lines of this ongoing shift can be pointed out by roughly distinguishing four generations of photo sharing platforms (Gerling 2015: 288–292). The first generation consists of explicit photo communities, such as Flickr (2002), where it is expressly photographs, both professional and non-professional, that are shared, traded and discussed—and tagged, for all these purposes. The second generation comprises social networks, such as Facebook (founded in 2004), where photographs are embedded in multifaceted social communications and their computational management. An illustrative example is the timeline profile introduced by Facebook in 2011 that uses an algorithm to organize photographs, videos and other assets into an editable narrative. Platforms of the third generation, such as Instagram (founded in 2010), foster especially mobile photography and instantaneous sharing. The fourth generation, exemplified by Snapchat (founded in 2011), one of the most popular photo sharing platforms to date with its 9,000 pictures shared each second,[4] shifts the emphasis to an ephemeral communication: snapchat pictures are not stored on a server or shown publicly on the web. This rough outline shows a development towards increased connectivity, instantaneity and ephemerality. The technological conditions of tagshot culture are shifting rapidly.

The computational management of metadata marks one of the key ontological effects of tagging systems, blurring the difference between online and offline experience. Evan Spiegel, the CEO of Snapchat, expresses this in apt terms in a keynote lecture from 2014 describing how our old conception of the world based on a clear difference between offline and online spaces is eroding: "We no longer have to capture the 'real world' and recreate it online—we simply live and communicate at the same time."

In terms of data patterns, tagability implies transformative potential: user-generated metadata structures can develop into ethnoclassification systems or 'folksonomies' (Mathes 2004) —that is, into new grassroots taxonomies with potentially wide impact. Tagging systems are not only flexible, they are also plastic in the sense that they not only adapt to changes, they also give rise to new forms and have the capacity to erase old ones as they can offer starting points for new mappings, vocabularies and connections.

From a technical point of view, tagging, in the wide sense used in this essay, involves organizing and managing the descriptive metadata that accompany the various online resources, such as photographs or videos, as well as linking these markings to structural metadata. Lialina's *Summer* offers a rich point of reference here, again, as it highlights and interconnects the technological operations fostering tagshot culture. In terms of its conceptual structure, technical realization and aesthetic presentation, it relies on a peculiar convergence of connectivity, instantaneity and ephemerality. The technological operations used and addressed in *Summer* can be schematized in terms of data modelling processes that involve three levels. Jacob Voß speaks of the "reality realm" of experienced phenomena, the "conceptual realm" of mental models and the symbolic abstraction and "data realm" of logical schemas and their implementation (Voß 2013: 33). Frieder Nake, in turn, describes the levels involved in data modelling in the more experiential terms of "surface," "interface" and "subface" (Nake 2008: 102–107). When generating metadata, users orient themselves in accordance with the phenomenal surface and rely on the functionalities of an interface. Substantial parts of data processing operations, however, take place automatically on the subface, on the level of algorithmic processes that operate beyond the user's notice. In Lialina's work, the rapidly changing URL line in the quickly redirecting browser window functions as an intriguing visual reminder of this. Intentionally produced markings are accompanied by non-intentional traces. Only a small part of user-generated metadata produced through operations such as labelling, marking, embedding and sharing—or simply by clicking—is visible on the surface, that is, on that side of the interface that faces the user. Data modelling processes entangle with experiential structures, as soon as the user gets cognitively and affectively engaged with what is afforded. In Nake's terms, the interface links causally determined processes of the subface with intentional processes of the surface and composes them into "algorithmic signs" (ibid.).

Struction

The second step in refocusing the question of photographic apparatus involves pondering the ontological implications of tagshot culture, specifically with regard to how the invisible operations taking place on the subface contribute to the multifaceted structuration of different dimensions of sense. In his essay "Of Struction," Jean-Luc Nancy gives an insightful analysis of the current erosion of the metaphysical paradigm of construction that has been the key principle of Western notions of the world. He describes the operative principle of construction reaching its limits and overshooting itself in the form of a whole industry of montages, arrangements and composition of forces (Nancy 2015: 47–48). Read with regard to the fact that photography has thoroughly been part of this paradigm, Nancy's diagnosis of the saturation and implosion of the paradigm of construction sheds light on the current dispersion of 'the photographic'. His discussion of struction offers a perspective for understanding how the plurality of technics destabilizes the paradigm of construction associated with analogue photography and hints at its ultimate collapse.

Nancy develops struction into an ontological concept that bundles a whole array of questions related to the emergence of sense through contiguity and connectivity. What is left over of construction, when its projects and counter-projects are losing their sense and direction, is 'struction'. The Latin root of the word is *struo*, which means 'to heap'. Without a prefix, struction does not imply any form of organization. First, con-, de- and in-, of 'con-struction', 'de-struction' and 'in-struction', introduce into the heap an ordering point of view. Struction, in other words, is about contiguity and co-presence, without any principle of coordination. It is a non-coordinated and contingent simultaneity of forces, forms, pulsions, projects and elans (Nancy 2015: 49).

Nancy follows Martin Heidegger in suggesting that the architectural paradigm of construction shows expansive metaphysical traits. In Heideggerian terms we could speak of technology as the rationale of a whole epoch (Heidegger 1977: 20–32). Nancy, however, adds to this scenario another turn by pondering technics with regard to singular–plural being. For him, the very existence is a question of plural technics (Hörl 2010: 137–138). With regard to the question of the phenomenon of world, this implies a challenge to conceiving the world as being in itself and of itself broken (Nancy and Tyradellis 2013: 43). This implies also that sense (in all senses of the word 'sense') is without an end, it does not have any finality (*finalité*); it is embedded in instable assemblages and associations. In Nancy's diagnosis, the plurality and existentiality of technics destabilizes the ground of the paradigm of construction and hints at its ultimate collapse.

Tagging systems constitute but one context for detecting symptoms of this implosion. It is worth noting that, in this ontological scenario, technics is not limited to what we are accustomed to call technologies; it involves, furthermore, structuration of ends (Nancy 2015: 44). Technics does not only provide a means to an end; furthermore, it multiplies, relativizes and transforms ends. When the ends intertwine in complex ways (as they do in tagging systems, for example), the various ends and means change their roles incessantly. In the last instance, at stake are the struction processes of sense.

Ontologically, struction names the state of 'with'—*avec*—without sharing; it only puts into play the simple contiguity and its contingence. In Heideggerian terms, it is the *mit* of *Mitsein* in a categorial sense. It is the pure and simple juxtaposition that does not make any sense as such (Nancy and Tyradellis 2013: 50–55). Against this background, the ontological consistency of the photographic apparatus that has incorporated into itself computational management of metadata subsists in the processes of struction of sense distributed across its three operative levels: surface, interface and subface. It operates through algorithmic signs. Here we can recall Agamben's characterization of apparatus as something that has "the capacity to capture, orient, determine, interpret, model, control, or secure the gestures, behaviours, opinions, or discourses of living beings" (Agamben 2009: 14).

The light that Nancy's ontological exposition of struction (of sense) sheds on the eroding unity of photography situates the shift from snapshot to tagshot within a wider frame of what Eric Hörl has termed "technological displacement of sense" (Hörl 2015: 1–3). He describes this currently ongoing displacement—with reference to both Nancy and Heidegger, among others—in terms of an emerging object culture that operates in micro-temporal regions and makes use of cybernetic processes. In his exposition, this new culture reverses the transcendental operating system shaped by media technologies and points to a transcendental technicity underlying all experience. This conception ends up shattering the entire sense culture based on processes of signification and hermeneutic types of subjectivity (Hörl 2015: 3). Computational management of metadata creates experiential shortcuts that tend to bypass human capacities rooted in embodied experience. The shift from snapshot culture to tagshot culture displaces the transcendental frame shaped by lens-based photographic processes—the visual horizon of time and space—and entangles it with a mesh of invisible computational processes. Unlike the mechanics of the locomotion of Muybridge's galloping horse, the logic of the galloping URLs in Lialina's *Summer* is a puzzle that cannot be pieced together within Euclidian space.

Experiential tagging

The third step in outlining the ontological consistency of distributed processes of tagshot culture involves highlighting the experiential aspects of tagging. As indicated above, the constellation of distributed processes and material circumstances operative in the photographic apparatus in the era of tagshot culture fundamentally displaces spatiotemporal structures of visual culture. The computational possibilities of manipulating the photographic flow of events go well beyond the mechanical click that marks the moment of capture in snapshot culture.

As a hybrid hinge between the phenomenal world and the data realm, tagshot has three faces. First, it has a distinct phenomenal face; it appears as an image, cut off from its visual environment. However, it needs to be pointed out that the distinctness of an image builds on dissimilarity; it involves discreteness and detachment, both spatiotemporally and in terms of identity. The way in which an image cuts itself off from everything else in order to appear as an image introduces a mute interval that fosters many kinds of speech: ekphrasis, commentary, captioning, tags. In the vocabulary of structural linguistics, this implies that an image is liable to intersemiotic encounters. Second, the tagshot has a conceptually formatted face that establishes mediations between the phenomena and algorithms. It is embedded in a functional setting. Third, tagshot has its hidden face that schematizes its visible aspects and functional connections with regard to the logic of technical implementation. A somewhat uncanny example of this three-faced configuration of the tagshot is the face recognition technology integrated in many consumer cameras today. It superimposes all three operative levels right on the human face.

Nodal points between phenomenal and algorithmic struction processes of sense, such as the tagshot, facilitate experiential structures. This co-operation of human tagging and non-human management of metadata might be called *experiential tagging*, as its aim, insofar as the co-operation is experientially motivated, is to attach pieces of information to perceivable assets in combinations that can be used to enhance meaningful relations. The wide popularity of transitory image sharing, such as snapchatting, suggests that these meaningful relations are often essentially integrated in digital networks. Experiential tagging of photographs involves multilayered bundling of markings (data and metadata) and computational operations, which aims at establishing connections across the three levels of data modelling processes that enable images to be attached to an experiential context. In many cases, the logic of experiential tagging greatly influences both the motivations for taking images and the ways in which images are captured. The AirDock auto-follow drone equipped with a GoPro camera, for example, automatizes the control of angle and distance of the camera during the physical activity that is to be filmed from an aerial point of view.[5] Alongside numerous other computational affordances of networked cameras, this kind of visual scoring of physical activity is a good example of a pre-scribed setting that contributes to fitting lived experience to its computationally managed image. With AirDock, a bike ride in a desert, for example, unfolds as a tracing of traces that are anticipated as seen from above.

Here, it is noteworthy to pay attention to the intimate link between conceptions of spatiotemporal coincidence and the idea of full presence. In order to function as a hybrid hinge between surface and subface, the tagshot needs to establish contact between them on the level of the interface. Even if this contact itself is mediated in many ways, its experiential effects, in terms of realistic feel, build on the idea of spatiotemporal coincidence, the epitome of which is the phenomenon we are accustomed to call 'real time'. The tagshot assembles phenomenal and computational elements and brings them into touch with each other—in the ideal case—in a seamless way.

The experiential rhetorics of seamlessness makes up the guideline for mainstream interface design, the logic of which is multiple targeting: it singles out functional gestures; builds up selected patterns of social and affective behaviour; and prioritizes certain ways of making contact and staying in contact (Elo 2012). All these targeting operations make use of the manageability of various layers of metadata. This means that the effects of computational management of the connections between the three realms of data modelling are not restricted to the level of practices and attitudes—that is, the mediations of epistemic, aesthetic, social and ethical relationships—but contribute significantly to the constitution of subjectivity (Boothroyd 2009: 330–345).

To sum up, the questions of contiguity and association of different elements in the dynamic data object 'tagshot' constitute the key issue with regard to the multifaceted experiential effects of tagging. As scalable, transferrable and parametric images, photographs are, in a sense, predetermined for experiential tagging: Photography as a bundle of technical operations has always been reaching out beyond visual representations, in ways that we now are witnessing in digital networks.

Struction and scription

The multilayered argument presented above constitutes a successive reconceptualization of the photographic apparatus with regard to the rise of tagshot culture. Nancy's ontological exposition of struction of sense was used to situate this theoretical endeavour in a wider philosophical and media aesthetic frame. One of the key points made is that tagging, from an ontological point of view, establishes new connections and relations of neighbourhood and bordering. Even if these connections are nonsensical as such, embedded in an apparatus they originate sense and contribute to the struction processes of sense. It can now be stated that it is not sufficient to theorize these settings from a phenomenological point of view only, as their configuration involves both phenomenal and non-phenomenal elements. Without the recognition of the hybrid character of the photographic apparatus as an assemblage, our understanding of it remains "arrested in the approximate," as Benjamin might put it.

As the concluding step, we need to return to the Benjamin quote discussed at the beginning of this essay:

> The camera is getting smaller and smaller, ever readier to capture fleeting and secret images whose shock effect paralyzes the associative mechanisms in the beholder. This is where inscription (*Beschriftung*) must come into play, which includes the photography of the literarization of the conditions of life, and without which all photographic construction must remain arrested in the approximate.
>
> *(Benjamin 2005: 527)*

In the last pages of the "Little History of Photography," from which this quote is taken, Benjamin presents the key problem related to *Beschriftung* in the form of a tensional combination of four points of reference: (1) 'photographic construction' related to Brechtian didactics and the Russian avantgarde, (2) surrealist 'destruction', (3) the uncritical welcoming of the artification of photography expressed by some painters and photographers alike, and (4) Baudelaire's famous denouncement of photography as an art form. From the contemporary perspective, the stakes are different. We need to go beyond the questions of construction, destruction and artification. When appropriately refocused, Benjamin's way of outlining the challenges and possibilities of inscription reverberate through the contemporary photographic apparatus. The key point that Benjamin helps us to highlight is that the event of inscription —'scripting'—urges us to consider the ways in which intersemiotic encounters within the photographic apparatus introduce new discursive structures in society. In Benjamin's exposition, scripting is an operation through which something invisible becomes readable—and the other way around: attached to a text, the image shows something that escapes words. In terms of the tagshot, the intersemiotic moment of scripting called 'tagging' pushes photography beyond the phenomenal horizon of experience and introduces computational processes and algorithmic signs in human interaction and sense-making.

Marking a hinge in the constellation of verbal and imaginal modes of *description*, *transcription* and *inscription*, Benjamin's *Beschriftung* shows affinity to Nancy's notion of struction and could, in accordance with this reference, be revamped into *scription*. Analogously to Nancy's notion of struction, which relativizes all programmatic aspects of sense, scription marks the limits of the semantic anchoring of photographs to a pre-established discursive setting. It thus reveals that 'photographic construction' cannot be made into a programmatic starting point for turning the "new image worlds" made accessible by photography into a basis for a new image of the world, as both the sense of 'image' and 'world' need to be rethought. In other words, scription turns our attention to the medial setting, in respect of which the different registers, parameters and elements of photography come together to constitute an apparatus that contributes to formatting the phenomenal horizon of experiencing images, the world and images in the world.

In light of their affinity, scription and struction appears as a productive double point of entry to the key challenges of photography theory in rethinking the transforming and dispersing field of photography. From this perspective, tagshots can be said to function as platforms for struction and nodal points of scription. Experiential tagging, in turn, appears as a plastic composition of hybrid sets of forces and operations. It tends towards seamlessness and composes image-events into entities that can be both looked at and clicked on. Making use of the rhetorical means of co-ordinating human tagging and computational management of metadata, experiential tagging introduces into these platforms or nodal points a pattern, an ordering point of view, thus, at least seemingly, reaffirming the schema of construction and reproducing the image of the world as a navigable whole.

According to Nancy's diagnosis, our history has reached the point where the paradigm of construction is not valid anymore. For him, there is more to this crisis than a simple wearing out of a paradigm. The very *principle* of construction has been unsettled (Nancy 2015: 50–51). The world is not anymore an image, and its measure is no longer human. This shift needs to be taken into account when theorizing digitally mediated photography today. As the tentative characterization of the emerging tagshot culture presented in this article suggests, we are facing the rupture and saturation of the paradigm of construction. This condition reveals that photographic construction already carried the seeds of its own deconstruction. The heterogeneous assemblage of photographic technologies, discourses and practices combined with the computational management of metadata has created a situation where photography theory is facing the abyss of the construction called 'the photographic'. What becomes readable in the ruins of the spatiotemporal framework constructed with the help of lenses, shutters and light-sensitive surfaces are the dispositional—that is, 'apparative'—processes of struction and scription informing the distributed unity of photography.

Notes

1 For a comprehensive visualization of the metadata universe, consult Jenn Riley's "Seeing Standards: A Visualization of the Metadata Universe", www.dlib.indiana.edu/~jenlrile/metadatamap/seeingstandards.pdf [accessed 13 July 2015].

2 Olia Lialina's *Summer* (2013) can be viewed starting, for example, here: http://1x-upon.com/~despens/olia/summer/[accessed 14 July 2015].

3 Cf. https://vimeo.com/6165108 and http://timeslicefilms.com/[accessed 30 May 2016].

4 Cf. statistics from January 2016: http://expandedramblings.com/index.php/snapchat-statistics/ [accessed 30 May 2016].

5 Cf. www.kickstarter.com/projects/airdog/airdog-worlds-first-auto-follow-action-sports-dron [accessed 26 February 2016].

References

Agamben, G. (2009): *What is an Apparatus? and Other Essays*, trans. David Kishik and Stefan Pedatella, California: Stanford University Press.

Benjamin, W. (2002): "The Work of Art in the Age of Its Technological Reproducibility" [1936], in *Selected Writings*, vol 3, eds. M. W. Jennings et al., trans. Edmund Jephcott and Harry Zohn, Cambridge, MA: Harvard University Press, pp. 101–133.

Benjamin, W. (2004a): "On Language as such and on the Language of Man" [1916], in *Selected Writings*, vol 1, eds. M. W. Jennings et al., trans. Edmund Jephcott, Cambridge, MA: Harvard University Press, 6th printing, pp. 62–74.

Benjamin, W. (2004b): "News about Flowers" [1928], in *Selected Writings*, vol 2. part 1. eds. M. W. Jennings et al., trans. Michael Jennings, Cambridge, MA: Harvard University Press. pp. 155–157.

Benjamin, W. (2004c): "The Task of the Translator" [1923], in *Selected Writings*, vol 1, eds. M. W. Jennings et al., trans. Harry Zohn, Cambridge, MA: Harvard University Press, pp. 253–263.

Benjamin, W. (2005): "Little History of Photography" [1931], in *Selected Writings*, vol 2. part 2. eds. M. W. Jennings et al., trans. E. Jephcott and Kingsley Shorter, Cambridge, MA: Harvard University Press, pp. 507–530.

Benjamin, W. (2009): *The Origin of German Tragic Drama*, trans. John Osborne, London and New York: Verso.

Boothroyd, D. (2009): "Touch, Time and Technics. Levinas and the Ethics of Haptic," *Theory, Culture & Society* vol 26 (2–3), pp. 330–345.

Brown, M. (1992): *Picturing Time—The Work of Etienne-Jules Marey (1830-1904)*, Chicago and London: University of Chicago Press.

Deleuze, G. and Guattari, F. (2014): *A Thousand Plateaus. Capitalism and Schizophrenia*, [1980], trans Brian Massumi, Minneapolis and London: Minnesota University Press, 15th printing.

Elo, M. (2007): "The Language of Photography as a Translation Task" in *Toisaalta tässä/Here Then. Photographs as Work of Art and as Research*, ed. M. Elo, Helsinki: University of Art and Design Helsinki and The Finnish Academy of Fine Arts, pp. 134–187.

Elo, M. (2012): "Digital Finger: Beyond Phenomenological Figures of Touch," *Journal of Aesthetics and Culture* vol 4. DOI: 10.3402/jac.v4i0.14982.

Elo, M. (2018): "Ineffable Dispositions," in *Transpositions—Aesthetico-Epistemic Operators in Artistic Research*, ed. M. Schwab, Leuven: Leuven University Press, pp. 281–295.

Fisher, A. and Rubinstein, D. (2013): "Introduction: On the Verge of Photography," in *On the Verge of Photography. Imagining Beyond Representation*, eds. D. Rubenstein, J. Golding and A. Fisher, Birmingham: ARTicle Press, pp. 7–14.

Gerling, W. (2015): "Moved Images—Velocity, Immediacy and Spatiality of Photographic Communication" in *Photographic Powers. Helsinki Photomedia 2014*, eds. M. Elo et al., Helsinki: Aalto ARTS, pp. 287–307.

Heidegger, M. (1977): *The Question Concenring Technology and Other Essays*, trans. Willliam Lovitt, New York: Harper & Row.

Hörl, E. (2010): "Die künstliche Intelligenz des Sinns," in *Zeitschrift für Medien- und Kulturforschung*, vol 2/ 2010, pp. 137–138.

Hörl, E. (2015): "The Technological Condition," *Parrhesia* vol (22), pp. 1–15.

Jakobson, R. (1992): "On Linguistic Aspects of Translation" [1959], In*Theories of Translation*, eds. R. Schulte and J. Biguenet, Chicago: Chicago University Press, pp. 144–151.

Krauss, R. (1999): *"Voyage on the North Sea"—Art in the Age of the Post-Medium Condition*, London: Thames & Hudson.

Mathes, A. (2004): "Folksonomies—Cooperative Classification and Communication through Shared Metadata," www.adammathes.com/academic/computer-mediated-communication/folksonomies.html [accessed July 8, 2015].

Menninghaus, W. (1995): *Walter Benjamins Theorie der Sprachmagie*, Frankfurt am Main: Suhrkamp.

Nake, F. (2008): "Surface, Interface, Subface: Three Cases of Interaction and One Concept" in *Paradoxes of Interactivity. Perspectives for Media Theory, Human–Computer Interaction, and Artistic Investigation*, eds. U. Seifert, J. H. Kim and A. Moore, Berlin: Transcript, 2008, pp. 92–109.

Nancy, J. (2015): "Of Struction" [2011], in *What's These Worlds Coming To?* eds. J.-L. Nancy and A. Barrau, trans. Travis Holloway and Flor Méchain, New York: Fordham Universty Press, pp. 42–58.

Nancy, J. and Tyradellis, D. (2013): *Was heißt uns Denken?* Zurich and Berlin: diaphanes.

Osborne, P. (2003): "Photography in an Expanding Field: Distributive Unity and Dominant Form" in *Where is the Photograph?* ed. D. Green, Kent and Brighton: Photoworks and Photoforum, pp. 63–70.

Osborne, P. (2013): *Anywhere or Not at All—Philosophy of Contemporary Art*, London: Verso.

Petersson, D. (2013): *The Art of Reconciliation—Photography and the Conception of Dialectics in Benjamin, Hegel, and Derrida*, New York: Palgrave Macmillan.

Rubinstein, D. (2010): "Tag, Tagging", *Philosophy of Photography* vol 1 (2), pp. 197–200.

Spiegel, E. (2014): AXS Partner Summit Keynote, January 25,www.snap.com/en-US/news/post/2014-axs-partner-summit-keynote

Voß, J. (2013): *Describing Data Patterns—A General Deconstruction of Metadata Standards*, Berlin: Humboldt-University Berlin. urn:nbn:de:kobv:11-100212118 [Accessed July 22, 2015].

Weber, S. (2001): "Globality, Organization, Class," *diacritics* vol 31 (3), pp. 15–29.

Weber, S. (2008): *Benjamin's Abilities*, Cambridge, MA, and London: Harvard University Press, pp. 38–44.

Zylinska, J. (2015): "Creative Power of Nonhuman Photography" in *Photographic Powers. Helsinki Photomedia 2014*, eds. M. Elo et al., Helsinki: Aalto ARTS, pp. 132–154.

24

Artistic representation and politics

An exchange between Victor Burgin and Hilde Van Gelder

Victor Burgin and Hilde Van Gelder

Introduction, Hilde Van Gelder

In his highly influential book *Thinking Photography*, Victor Burgin famously warns artists not to succumb to the romantic myth of inspiration and originality (1982: 81). He argues that, as all artistic 'creation' necessarily depends on pre-established codes and norms, naïve intuition is an insufficient basis for the creative process. Drawing on Walter Benjamin's essay "The Author as Producer," which he places at the beginning of the book, he insists that artistic representations should always include a reflective stance with regard to their own conditions of production. In retrospect this can be seen as one of the most consistent basic premises of his work. The original publication of our exchange (2011) elaborated on that premise toward a closing focus on a 'political' debate raging in visual art creation: artistic research.[1] Both Victor Burgin's oeuvre and his long academic career stand out as a pioneering, leading example within this domain. We concluded that visual art production is embedded in a historically grown, mature research praxis determined by specific paradigmatic conditions. This resulted in a joint plea for granting artistic research an independent place within the Art Academy. Seven years later, the greater urgency of the debate on 'artistic representation and politics' no longer is to be found in the internal politics of visual art. Sadly, the country where Victor Burgin presently lives, France, finds itself in a state of emergency that has been extended five times by the parliament since November 2015. Amnesty International reports that French emergency measures have 'disproportionately' restricted human rights in the country.[2] Even more unsettling is the 'wide range of new laws and policies' in my home country (Belgium) in the aftermath of the 'Brussels Attacks' (March 2016), as these have been implemented without the prior proclamation of a state of emergency.[3] On top of it all, the UK, Victor Burgin's native country, has unilaterally declared it will sail its own course. This rather unexpected sequence of events in the old heart of liberal democratic Europe has urged us to shift the focus of debate in the final part of our exchange towards an in-depth analysis of the politically allegorical projection work that is Victor Burgin's *Occasio* (2014).[4]

Exchange between Victor Burgin and Hilde Van Gelder (HVG)

HILDE VAN GELDER (HVG): You figure prominently among a pioneering group of artists that, as of the late 1960s, rejected American modernist aesthetic ideals. In your comments on the writings of Clement Greenberg and John Szarkowski, you dismantled their critical position as formalist and their theory as detached from reality. What you seem to have disliked most in Modernist discourse was the belief its adherents seemed to express in "the ineffable purity of the visual image"—a conviction that you trace back to a Platonic tradition of thought in which images have the capacity to reveal mystic truths enshrined in things "in a flash, without the need for words and arguments" (Burgin 1982: 214). I wonder if you can say today, some 30 years later, how exactly you feel that words in your work have come to counteract such illusions of pure visibility of the image?

VICTOR BURGIN (VB): I do not believe, or rather *no longer* believe, that my work can 'counteract' such illusions. Although I realise that your question refers to my photo-text work, I can perhaps more directly answer it by reference to my written work. At the time of *Thinking Photography*, I thought that a more broadly informed photographic criticism would eventually dispel the unexamined assumptions that then dominated writing and talking about photography. The notion of the 'purely visual' was prominent amongst these, as was the naïve realist idea that photography is a transparent 'window on the world'. The former belief dominated 'fine art' photography at that time, while the latter provided the ideological underpinning of 'social documentary'. When I first started to teach film and photography students, after having first taught in an art school, the 'art' and 'documentary' approaches were mutually antagonistic—ironical, given the fact that their founding assumptions are different formulations of the same Platonic idea. The Film and Photography department where I went to teach in 1973 was at the time one of only two schools in Britain openly dedicated to a documentary project and hostile to 'fine art' photography. The BA theory course I was asked to construct there, of which *Thinking Photography* is a trace, did for a while succeed in putting critical discussion—the "reflective stance" you refer to—in place of the acting out of inherited ideologies. But that period is now, as a friend of mine put it, a 'parenthesis in history'. There has since been a massive return of 'previous' frames of mind that had never in fact gone away, even among some of those who participated in the initial project—as if the mere fact of having acknowledged the validity of the arguments advanced in the 1970s and 80s now provides exemption from acting in response to them. In retrospect I can see—which should not surprise me, given my theoretical inclinations—that reason rarely prevails where there are professional and emotional benefits to be derived from irrationality. We are again confronted, as so often, with the psychological structure of disavowal: 'I know very well, but nevertheless …'.

HVG: You conclude your essay "Modernism in the Work of Art" by stating that the "division of labour" between 'theorists' and 'practitioners' is problematical ([1976] 2008: 120). In 1986, you add to this that the main problem of this divide is that it hinders peoples' attempts "for a truly critical cultural initiative" (1986: viii). The label 'critical', or stronger even, 'political' art, has often been attached to, particularly, your earlier practice. It seems, however, that, with regard to your work, this notion needs some clarification. It seems doubtful that you would agree with your art being identified as 'critical realist', a term Benjamin H.D. Buchloh coined in 1995 (196 n. 10) in order to describe Allan Sekula's photography.

VB: I have heard references to the time when my work "used to be political." My work has never ceased to be political, what has changed is my understanding of the form of politics specific to *art*, rather than, for example, investigative journalism or agit-prop. Benjamin

Buchloh's expression seems to me a symptom of the disavowal I just cited, not least because the issue of *representation* has simply dropped out of the picture. Beyond the attempt to rebrand what used to be called 'social documentary' it is difficult to see what work the expression 'critical realist' is intended to do. Either of the two terms Buchloh associates requires careful specification. To simply conjoin them as if their meanings were self-evident is inevitably to fall into complicity with the doxa—in terms of which to be critical is to *criticise*. Here the 'critic' assigns the 'artist' a position analogous to the one he himself assumes—that of a literally *exceptional* person who surveys, discriminates and judges. Where such a position is assigned, we do well to ask if there are not blind spots in the critical view. In the early to mid-1970s, when my work had an unambiguously obvious political content, there was very little such work in the art world. Forty years later, 'political art' is the new orthodoxy, but it is 'political' only in the way the media understand the term. For example, the enthusiasm for 'documentary' in the art world of the past quarter-century has provided a spectrum of gallery-sited narratives—from intimately anecdotal 'human interest' stories to exposés of the devastation of the human and natural environment by rapacious global capitalism. But there is nothing in the content or analysis of these stories that is not already familiar from the mass media, and I have seen only insignificant departures from conventional media forms. Such 'artworks' solicit the same range of interests and the same reading competences that the media assumes in its audiences. Complementing 'documentary' work in the art world are other kinds of work offering spectacle, decoration or scandal. Here again we have not left the discursive space of the media, we have simply turned the page or changed channels. Brecht defined 'criticism' as that which is concerned with what is *critical* in society. My own sense of what is now fundamentally critical to the Western societies in which I live and work is the progressive colonisation of the terrain of languages, beliefs and values by mainstream media contents and forms—imposing an industrial uniformity upon what may be imagined and said, and engendering compliant synchronised subjects of a 'democratic' political process in which the vote changes nothing. The art world is no exception to this process. Artists making 'documentaries' usually encounter their subject matter not at first hand but from the media. The audience for the subsequent artworks will instantly recognise the issues addressed, and easily understand them in terms already established by the media. What is 'documented' in such works therefore is not their ostensible contents but rather the mutating world-view of the media, and they remain irrelevant *as art* if they succeed in doing no more than recycle facts, forms and opinions already familiar from these prior sources. I would emphasise that I am talking about documentary *in the art world*. In 2010, the Iranian film maker Jafar Panahi was imprisoned—primarily, it seems, because he was making a documentary about the mass protests that followed the dubious 2009 elections in Iran. The political value of documentary is conjunctural: context is as important as content. The political value of art primarily bears on neither content nor context but upon *language*. I see no point to 'art' that calls upon the same general knowledge and interpretative capabilities I deploy when I read a newspaper.

HVG: What about the other word in Buchloh's expression, 'realism'? Arguably, your work *Zoo* (1978–79), consisting of eight photo diptychs that quite explicitly address the Cold War situation in Berlin, can be seen as a turning/closing point in your view of realism. I say 'arguably' because in 1987, in an essay entitled "Geometry and Abjection," you launch a plea for a 'realist' artistic project. However, you now define this project in terms of "psychical realism," an expression you take from Sigmund Freud (Burgin 1987: 56).[5] The term already takes a central position in your essay "Diderot, Barthes, Vertigo," where you argue that "*psychical-reality*," "unconscious fantasy structures," constantly exercises "its effects upon perceptions and actions of the subject," such that the world can never be known "as, simply what it *is*" (1986a: 105). To what extent do you still rhyme this notion of psychical realism with your earlier emphasis on art's function as cultural critique? In other words, can you articulate the kind of sociocultural reflection you wish to put forward through your work ever since the concept of psychical realism has become one of its principal motors?

VB: The British philosopher Gilbert Ryle long ago commented on the habitual distinction in which 'reality' is seen as something separate from our 'inner' lives. In terms of this distinction we simultaneously inhabit two parallel worlds—one private and psychological, the other public and material. In this view the expression 'psychical reality' would be an oxymoron. Ryle noted, however, that in this version of our experience of the world there is no way of accounting for the *transactions* that take place between public and private histories, as by definition such transactions belong to neither of the 'two' worlds. There is therefore no account of how individual subjects become inserted into general political processes—except in terms of such now largely redundant categories as 'class consciousness'. What Ryle did not note, but might well have done, is that the distinction between private and public is hierarchical—as when 'subjective fantasy' is subsumed to 'objective reality'. With the idea of 'psychical reality' Freud in effect 'deconstructs' this hierarchy. Anticipating Derrida's critique of the 'logic of the supplement' Freud shows how the 'supplemental' category, that which is considered as superfluous and undesirable, is at the very heart of the category that is upheld as primary and essential. I see no contradiction between a commitment to art as cultural critique and a taking into account of psychical reality. The British cultural and political theorist Stuart Hall said that his attempts to understand the mass appeal of Thatcherism had led him to conclude that the logic of the appeal was not that of a philosophical argument but rather the logic of a dream. To take a more recent example, Michael Moore's film *Sicko*—a damning account of the US health care system and the pharmaceutical and insurance industries that benefit from it—was released in 2007 to enormous acclaim, quickly becoming the third largest grossing documentary film of the past thirty years. Barack Obama was elected US president the following year, and afterwards encountered overwhelming opposition to his proposed health care reforms from the very people who had most to gain from them. As the American expression succinctly puts it: 'Go figure'. If nothing else, this recent history might have prompted a little self-reflection on the part of 'political artists' who see their work as 'consciousness raising'. Not only is there something inevitably patronising in the attitude of artists setting out to raise other consciousnesses to the level of their own, but also the exercise is generally futile—either the mass of the people 'know very well, but nevertheless …', or their consciousnesses are the unique and unassailable product of the populist-tabloid Fox News Channel.

HVG: In your work in the 1970s you often drew directly on codes and conventions of the media, especially advertising, to make ironic comment on various kinds of exploitation and inequality, such as in *UK76*, where in one of the panels you insert an excerpt from a fashion magazine into a photograph of a female Asian factory worker. You now say you conceive differently of "the place of the political in art" (Burgin 2008a: 80). In this regard you cite Jacques Rancière, who says that "aesthetics has its own meta-politics" (Rancière 2004: 60), as a privileged ally in your own attempts to understand how art relates to politics and ideology (Burgin 2008a: 43). You conclude by insisting that "the political meaning of attempts … to give aesthetic form to a phenomenological truth or a psychical reality … may lie precisely in the ways in which they *fail* to conform … to established regimes of intelligibility" (2008a: 85; original emphasis). Could you elaborate on this?

VB: Art, at least in our Western populist liberal democracies, has no direct political agency. When I joined the protest march against the Iraq war in London, when I joined demonstrations against the National Front in Paris, I acted as a citizen, not as an artist. (By the way, it does seem that the days when street protest could have a real political effect have now passed into history.) When I refused to cooperate with 'obligatory' but intellectually ridiculous government research assessment exercises, when I refused to join a 'compulsory' training day for academic staff run by a private management training consultancy, I acted as a university teacher, not an artist. The work of 'political artists' usually harms no-one, and I would defend their right to make it; what I cannot support is their self-serving assumption that it 'somehow' has a political effect in the real world. In a university art department, I would prefer as my colleague the artist who makes watercolours of sunsets but stands up to the administration, to the colleague who makes radical political noises in the gallery but colludes in imposing educationally disastrous government policies on the department. The political agency of artists is not 'on the ground' in everyday life—at this level they must be content to act as citizens and/or, in my example, teachers (I have always considered teaching to be my most important political activity)—their agency is in the sphere of representations. Since the work to which you refer, and up to the present day, I have measured the political and critical dimensions of my work by their relation to the mainstream mass media—as the media is most responsible for the production of subjects for the political process, most instrumental in delivering votes to politicians. You are nevertheless right to note that my position in relation to the media has shifted. My initial position combined Lévi-Strauss's notion of bricolage with Barthes's idea of 'semioclasm'. For example, the panel we have already mentioned from *UK76* juxtaposes fragments from two disparate and 'antagonistic' discursive formations—social documentary photography and fashion journalism—in order to bring out a social contradiction. The problem I see with this now is that it leaves the fragments intact, and what one is able to construct—to 'say'—depends entirely on what it is possible to do with the fragments. No great surprise therefore that what I was able to say with this particular panel of *UK76* was already well known, and that the only 'value-added' element to the source materials was my own irony (albeit there was also a cultural-political significance *at that time*—it was relatively short-lived—in putting such content on the wall of a gallery). As I have already said, I see the critical task of art today as that of offering an alternative to the media. I am opposed to any form of conformity to the contents and codes of the doxa—what Rancière calls 'consensual categories and descriptions'—even when these are deployed with a 'left' agenda, as I believe that, in this particular case, 'one cannot dismantle the master's house with the master's tools'. At the present conjuncture it seems to me that society is most present in an artwork—as a critical project—when the artwork is most absent from society.

HVG: If we can turn then to a more recent work: *Hôtel D* (2009) is a site-specific piece consisting of a digital projection loop inside a box installed in a principal room of the ancient former pilgrims' hospital Hôtel-Dieu Saint-Jacques, in Toulouse, once known as the 'Salle des portraits des bienfaiteurs' (Burgin 2016: 100). Could one understand this 'sequence of images' as a '*sequence-image*', a term you have defined earlier in your writings (Burgin 2004: 27), and more recently in conversation with Alexander Streitberger, where you call it "both the elemental unit from which chains of signifiers are formed and the hinge between movement and stasis, the motionless point of turning between unconscious fantasy and the real" (Streitberger 2009: 268)?

VB: The short answer to that question is 'No', as the 'sequence-image' is a purely theoretical entity. I coined the expression to allow me to talk about an image that is neither still nor moving or, to put it the other way, is *both* still and moving. The fact that such an image is by definition impossible signals its location in psychical space, on the side of the unconscious, where the 'law of excluded middle' does not apply (as when a woman in a dream is both the dreamer's mother *and* sister). I coined the neologism reluctantly but there was no other way of speaking about what for me is an important aspect of the 'psychical reality' I try to represent. The material images projected in the Hôtel-Dieu and the material sound of the '*voix off*' in the adjoining chapel were combined in an attempt to represent the strictly unrepresentable (Burgin 2016: 101). Each new work renews this attempt, making its singular contribution to the generality at which I aim. I think by analogy of an old movie version of H. G. Wells', *The Invisible Man*, where a number of devices are used to signify the invisible man's form—for example, in one scene, some trash whirls into the air on a windy street and sticks to him; in another scene, disembodied footprints advance across a snow-covered field. We would not say that either the trash or the tracks are the invisible man, but they are the more or less contingent conditions of his 'appearance' in the visible world. *Hôtel D*, in common with all of my works in recent years, is an attempt to represent some unrepresentable 'thing'—in this case deriving from my being *there*, in the *Hôtel-Dieu* in Toulouse, and being aware of the lives and deaths of those who were there before me, aware of the past function of the building, and at the same time aware of the forms of the architecture, of the time it takes to cross the room—*everything*, in fact, *at the same time*, including the connotations and fantasies that accompanied my perceptual experience and knowledge of the place.

HVG: *Hôtel D* offers itself as a key case study in order to understand your interest in "perceptual reality," as you name it in your "Note" accompanying the piece (2016: 100). The research component of this interest brings in the 'historical identity' of the place as a space of labour for the *filles de service*—female hospital orderlies. The sequence of images and the spoken text testify to a paradox encountered in your own initial observation of the reality of this room. Among the five large-size portraits of illustrious historical benefactors of this establishment you found an equally monumental picture of a woman identified only as *fille de service*. The image of this woman, named at the bottom of the portrait itself as Marguerite Bonnelasvals (†1785), is exhibited together with the other portraits, which are all of people of a higher social rank. Facing Marguerite Bonnelasvals, as you point out, hangs a tableau of Princess Marie-Thérèse de Bourbon, daughter of Louis XVI and Marie-Antoinette. This striking finding, a result of your scrupulous perception and observation of the place, is a key theme in *Hôtel D*. Can you perhaps clarify how, from a strictly methodological point of view, you decided to focus your work on this quite incredible coincidence?

VB: In the perceptual and associative complex that is my experience of a place there is often a privileged point around which everything else turns. It might be a detail, an anecdote or something else. The juxtaposition of the two portraits in the Hôtel-Dieu became this point of anchorage for everything that made up my awareness of the place. One of the things that interests me is the way 'the political' may be manifest as a mutable aspect of our everyday reality, on the same perceptual basis as the changing light, an aching knee or a regret. The coincidence of the portraits is a trace of the political in the overlooked, and therefore part of what I look for in the everyday. There is no need for the Western political artist, too often a disaster tourist, to 'sail the seven seas' looking for injustices to denounce. Inequality and exploitation saturate the ground on which we stand, they are in the grain of everyday life. This granular-perceptual manifestation of the political is part of what I try to represent in my works.

HVG: I have come to understand *Hôtel D* as a work that brings together all the major themes and preoccupations of your oeuvre. With the concept of psychical realism entering your work, your interest in the representation of women entered the foreground. Many of your pieces, as of the early 1980s, take account of the impact of male desire on female perception and vice versa, and the issue of sexuality and sexual difference in general. You have emphasised the influence that 1970s feminism exercised on your artistic trajectory, for example in the attention in your work to "the construction of gendered identities through identifications with images" (2008a: 50). Now, in *Hôtel D*, the long-lasting key importance you have accorded to this very subject appears to engage in a dialogue with an interest you have had, in an even earlier phase of your work, with regard to the representation of labour. Many contemporary artists have taken on the problematic consequences of currently globalised labour conditions by directly representing people at work. Whereas the atmosphere of *UK76* seems to have something in common with such an approach, you have later come to take the representation of labour in your work in a different direction.

VB: I do not understand how 'directly representing people at work' can be said to 'take on' the issue of the globalisation of the labour force—at most it can only redundantly *illustrate* it. Amongst other things, the issue is fundamentally one of organising collective action across cultural, linguistic and legal international borders. How can adding more pictures to the mountain of images of the labouring classes have any relevance to such questions, let alone any purchase on them? And what about the act of picture-taking itself? As your reference to *UK76* invokes the historical perspective, I would like to quote what I said in an interview from the late 1970s when I was asked how I felt about the power relation between myself and the Asian woman worker whose image appears in this work:

> I'd been commissioned to take photographs by the Coventry workshop, they were working with various other local workers' organisations and they wanted someone to take some pictures in some of the factories around Coventry. It was in that capacity that I took that particular picture: it was not shot as a work of art but as something for their publications and their files. [...] No one was photographed who didn't want to be. Some obviously didn't feel comfortable with the camera on them, so I didn't take photographs of them, but others obviously enjoyed being the centre of attention. I was a source of entertainment for them for the afternoon. Having said all that, the fact remains that I was free to walk out of that place and they weren't—a fundamental distinction. The work I was doing was intended to support them, the same goes for the art piece that some of the images were subsequently used in, but the fact remains that my intervention there, if not actually exploitative, was politically irrelevant; that's how I feel about it now, and that's how I feel about the work of other 'artists' who take their cameras into such situations.
>
> *(Burgin 1986b: 39)*[6]

VB: Under what circumstances is it acceptable for a middle-class photographer to point a camera at a wage-slave? A campaigning journalist, illustrating a news story that might mobilise public opinion and embarrass corporations and politicians into changing their behaviour, is certainly justified, but I find something profoundly distasteful in the spectacle of workers having a last increment of value extracted from them by 'political artists' parading their moral narcissism in pursuit of their careers.

HVG: In your photo-textual work *Office at Night* (1986) the 'psychical' component has already entered the very depiction of labour. The work prominently focuses on male–female power relationships in the work place. Its extremely dense, sexually and power(less)-loaded atmosphere differentiates it from Jeff Wall's more neutral photographic depictions of labour, not least with regard to the so-called "iconography of cleaning up," an issue I would like to come to in a minute (Van Gelder 2007: 76). In *Hôtel D*, the representation of labour is only indirectly present, as this was already the case in your *Performative/Narrative* (1971), a photo-textual piece that shows an empty office of a male employer (as the accompanying text indicates). In *Hôtel D*, it is not so much in the sequence of images itself but instead in the *voix off*—the voice heard in the adjoining chapel—that the humble work of cleaning up is more explicitly addressed. The *voix off* operates 'in parallel' to the images, as Philippe Dubois has argued with regard to other of your works with a similar approach (2007: 77). The sequence of images shows the perfectly neat tiled floors, walls and ceiling of the 'salle des portraits des bienfaiteurs' and a perfectly clean hotel room—although subtle details, such as a playing TV, luggage, gloves on a desk and a bottle of pills besides the bed, reveal it is in use. Yet for a major part of the eight-and-a-half-minutes-long parallel audio sequence a woman's voice slowly describes the repetitive activities of making a bed and cleaning a hotel room. I wonder if this (by definition) 'non-iconographic' soundtrack can be understood as performing a double function in your work. I feel that its descriptive character can be seen as programmatic with regard to your decision, articulated one year after *Office at Night*, in "Geometry and Abjection," that a 'political' art theory should simply 'describe' rather than exhort or admonish, or offer 'solutions' (1987: 56).

VB: Perhaps I should first describe the work, as it is unlikely that anyone reading our exchange will have seen it. *Hôtel D* comprises four components: the two actual spaces in the Hôtel-Dieu, an image-track and a soundtrack. The image sequence assembled from the photographs I made in the Salle des Pèlerins is projected in a continuous loop in a 'viewing box' constructed inside the Salle itself. The room represented in the box is therefore a *mise-en-abyme* of the room that contains the box. The 'work of art' here is in good part a work of the visitor in a coming and going between the experience of the actual rooms and their representations. There is an analogous coming and going between the real and projected images in the Salle des Pèlerins (as you have noted, formerly the 'salle des portraits des bienfaiteurs') and the voice heard in the adjoining space of the chapel. Rather than 'voice-over', the equivalent French expression *voix off* is more appropriate here as the text is heard not over the images, but at a distance from them. *Hôtel D* is the product of a reflection upon the 'perceptual reality' of the Salle des Pèlerins—as I experienced it and as it is refracted through the photographs I made there—and upon the historical identity of the room as a place of care for the sick and dying, a place of work for the *filles de service*. Another axis of my work—prompted by the historical function of the Hôtel-Dieu as a place of rest for the pilgrim—is formed in a coming and going between associations with the meaning of the term *hôtel* in this particular building in Toulouse, and with the more usual meaning of the term in everyday use today. Images of a hotel room in a modern city (in actual fact, in Chicago) therefore come to join my images of the Salle des Pèlerins. Similarly, in the *voix off*, references to the repetitive routine task of bed-making occur in both a hospital and a hotel setting. *Hôtel D* is not 'about' such things in the way that either a documentary or a fiction film might be about them. It is a work best considered not as one might view a film, but rather as one might approach a painting.

HVG: You have in fact said that the spectator should try to view the complex perceptual installation called *Hôtel D* as a painting in which you see "everything and nothing at the same time."[7] Could this statement perhaps help to grasp what you have elsewhere identified as the "*uncinematic* feel" of your video practice (2008a: 90; original emphasis)?[8] Also, in order to better understand this fascinating concept of the dispersed painting or tableau, to be discovered layer by layer in a mode of "*reprise*," as you call it (2008a: 91), would it be helpful to recur to an analogy with the notion Allan Sekula coined for several of his works, namely that they are "disassembled movies" (Buchloh 2003: 25)? Could we say with regard to *Hôtel D* that it is to be considered as a "disassembled tableau"?

VB: In the 1970s I used to speak of my large-scale photo-text works as the remnants of hypothetical films—for example, I described *US77* as "a sort of 'static film' where the individual scenes have collapsed inwards upon themselves so that the narrative connections have become lost" (1986b: 40). However, I also at that time spoke of the viewing conditions of such works as being the "negative of cinema"—for example, in the cinema the spectator is in darkness whereas the gallery is light; the cinematic spectator is still while the images move, whereas the visitor to the gallery moves in front of static images; or again, the sequence and duration of images in the cinema is predetermined, whereas visitors to the gallery determine their own viewing times and sequences. Or again, there is little opportunity for reflection during the course of a film (Barthes says the cinema "does not allow you to close your eyes"), whereas my work in the gallery solicits active reflection on the part of the viewer/reader. To take such differences into account is to pay attention to the *specificity* of the practice—that which distinguishes it from other neighbouring practices. For example, one of my constant technical concerns is with the elaboration of forms of language adapted to the situation of reading or listening in the gallery. In general I aim for texts that condense relatively large amounts of information into small spaces, and that allow readers to bring their own associations to fill out the meanings of the laconic texts. Most of the time this requires little more than an attention to economy of expression. For example, the opening sentence of the voice-over to my work *Dovedale* (2010), first exhibited in Cologne, reads: "The major museums are all close to the station, which is by the cathedral so I cannot get lost" (Burgin 2016: 109). This sentence establishes that the speaker is a stranger to Cologne, there to visit the museums, and it also documents a material fact about the city. So far, I might be writing a short story. However, although I referred to this as the "opening sentence" of my text, it is not necessarily the opening sentence for the visitor to my installation, who is free to come and go at any time during the continuously looping audio-visual material. A specific requirement of the voice-over text, therefore, is that it be written so that any sentence may occupy the position of 'first' sentence. Now, although the words and images that make up my work are necessarily deployed in time, my accommodations to the indeterminacy in their viewing and reading in effect breaks up and spatializes the temporal flow—so your expression "disassembled tableau" may fit my work quite well. There is a further 'disassembling' in the material condition of the work as a number of separate but interrelated 'bits'. In Cologne, my moving projection-sound piece is accompanied by a still photo-text work based on photographs I made in the Peak District in Derbyshire, England, at the place depicted in Joseph Wright's landscape painting *Dovedale by Moonlight* (1785), which is in Cologne's Wallraf-Richartz-Museum. There is a 'scattering' of references to the painting here analogous to that of the scattering of a film in the "cinematic heterotopia" I name and describe in my book *The Remembered Film* (2004). All of this is related to my interest in what I have termed the increasing "exteriorisation" of psychical processes in everyday life—especially the "prosthetic memory," and perhaps even prosthetic unconscious, that the Internet increasingly represents. It was with such things in mind that I was struck by the remark by the painter Pierre Bonnard, who said that he would like the experience of his pictures to have something in common with the experience of first entering an unfamiliar room—one sees everything at once, and yet nothing in particular. What I want to add to Bonnard's purely optical picture is the fleeting concatenation of impromptu thoughts one may have at that moment—which, of course, may include what I have already referred to as the "granular-perceptual" manifestation of the political.

HVG: In your projection work *Occasio* (2014), you appear to consolidate this very tactic. The work is made of one digitally composed projected image sequence in which a virtual camera takes 14 min 18 s to complete a 360° turn around a 3D computer model of the lift cage winding tower of a mine (see Plates 20 and 21). While observing the slow circular movement of this image, the spectator listens to a female *voix off* who brings in scattered, fragmented references to both an old master oil painting and to a movie.[9]

VB: *Occasio* was made in 2014 for a retrospective exhibition of my work at the Museum für Gegenwartskunst, Siegen. The painting to which the voice-over refers is a large allegorical tableau by Peter Paul Rubens entitled *The Victorious Hero Seizes Opportunity in Order to Conclude Peace*—which is in the collection of the Siegerlandmuseum, a short walk from the contemporary art museum where my retrospective took place.[10] I chose the painting as the point of departure for my projection work.[11] The Siegerlandmuseum is housed in the old 'Upper Castle', which is near the site of the house in which Rubens was born. The house was destroyed in the Allied bombing of Siegen during the Second World War, which razed almost 90 per cent of the old town centre, but the Upper Castle survived. From the ground floor of the museum visitors may descend into a replica of mine workings typical of the local ore-mining industry that flourished in the Siegerland up to the 1960s. During the war, such subterranean galleries sheltered works of art, albeit the Rubens 'Occasio' now hanging in an upper gallery of the museum was not amongst these. My mind was on the mining industry and the wartime assault on Siegen as I stood in front of Rubens's allegorical plea for peace. These three things coalesced into the kernel of the work as it evolved in my mind. Freud spoke of the contribution made to the formation of a dream by the "day's residues"—memory traces of events and thoughts from the day preceding the dream that are opportunistically seized by the 'dream-work' for the expression of unconscious desires. *Occasio* is a waking product of such residues structured in accordance with the looping and repetitive movements characteristic of daydreams. Of all my projection works, *Occasio* most perfectly meets the requirements discussed in my description of the *specificity* of my practice—most notably that any image, any sentence, may serve as a beginning. Most of my works, for all they loop seamlessly, nevertheless have a narrative arc more or less implied within them. *Occasio* escapes the gravitational pull of linear narrative completely.

HVG: The Rubens 'Occasio' represents Minerva, goddess of wisdom, softly urging a Perseus-like Hero armoured with a Medusa-headed shield to seize the forelock of naked Opportunity's long blonde hair. Accompanying Occasio in order to present her to her bridegroom are her father, Time, and her mother, Peace. Contrary to more conventional representations of Perseus, Rubens' 'Occasio' diplomatically suggests that the successful hero should not seek to overpower his bride and that the soon-to-wed couple can benefit much from the helping hand of their entourage. This sheds light on the artist's opinions regarding equilibriums of power, both between the sexes and on the level of politics within society in general (Rosenthal 2005: 167–197). Balanced relationships are to be considered fragile at all times, for violence can flare up again at any opportunity. The Rubens 'Occasio' thus reads as a warning sign: if the hero misses out on his 'kairotic moment' to unite with Opportunity, her abundant hair will most likely transform into Gorgon's deadly horns—or even coiling snakes. The female *voix off* of your *Occasio* suggestively brings into play such a wide range of reminiscences to the rich iconography of this painting. In doing so, she also introduces listeners to a scene from Claude Chabrol's film *Alice ou la dernière fugue* (1977). Though she inserts minor narrative variations, the *voix off* in the end always returns to the same motif: a naked woman sitting motionless, staring into a mirror, and the camera capturing this scene. The spectator may happen to remember this part of the Chabrol movie, allowing her own daydreams to muse on it. The moment you have selected is the one in which the film's principal character, a beautiful young woman named Alice Carroll (Sylvia Kristel), receives her death sentence from the invisible, devilish male voice of another personage named Henri Vergennes (Charles Vanel)—operating as a *voix off* within the movie. The film scene before this one, which your *voix off* by no means is explicitly alluding to but which the viewer may recall, shows Alice leaving the luxurious old chateau where she—only seemingly it turns out later—found hospitable refuge for the night. Arriving at her car with the intention to continue her journey she finds Time disguised as a snail slowly inching forward on its front window, leaving behind a trace of slime across the window.[12] Unable to recognise Chronos for who he really is, Alice tragically turns out to be not capable of realising that he is about to guide her towards the wall she should have climbed over in order to find her once-upon-a-lifetime opportunity for true liberty. Chabrol painfully stages how Alice, by stopping short at the threshold of the wall, misses her Kairos for finding a peaceful life. Towards the end of the film, when Alice has worked herself through regret and remorse, and when she positively knows her destiny is sealed, comes an unexpected catharsis. Alice encounters Colas, the castle's servant who so generously received her on the first night when she was seeking refuge from stormy summer rains. He quietly informs her she should have trespassed, that "she should have had confidence in herself and have gone to the end of what she had decided." Alice replies firmly, "I can always start again, you know." When Colas triumphantly sibilates, "Good night, Alissss," after having meanly confirmed that for her this option now is forever closed off, she rather unexpectedly hisses back, "Good night Colassss." Alice accepts her imminent death in a fatal car crash, but she feels strong as she knows *she* is the "immemorial image" (*l'image immémoriale*). She is *Ninfa*, the ageless trope, certain that she will continue to return as "the same image," to borrow Giorgio Agamben's terminology (Agamben 2004: 97–110). Alice knows what Aby Warburg's *Mnemosyne* atlas has demonstrated in the transition from Table 46 to 47: that the '*Lastenträgerin*' (porter of burdens) is capable of transforming into '*Kopfjägerin*' (head huntress; Warnke and Brink 2008: 84–87). Judith, after all, ends up slaying Holofernes. Alice as well may likely seize a later opportunity to strike back. Colas, closing his eyes at the end of this overpowering film scene, even appears to concede that. When taking the time to observe the projected image of your *Occasio* while engaging in this reflective excursion that builds on the 'screen memories' of *Alice ou la dernière fugue*, one could imagine the following coda to the film: the deceased Alice returns as a dominant, powerful Gorgon who casts a spell on the water castle in which she was obliged to spend the last, damned days of her life, completely flooding all its surroundings. The basic allegorical message the spectator of your *Occasio* may then take home, is that every refusal to engage in sincerely welcoming and providing hospitality to stranded strangers could very well at some point later in time explode back in one's own face.

VB: You have just given a wonderful description of the unwinding of a line of association in your own mind. For me, a work of art is precisely an *occasion* for such work by the viewer. A more or less spontaneous and unconscious work of association may take place in the contemplative experience of the loop, as it might also take place in contemplation of the Rubens painting. As you have demonstrated, this associative work may then be continued (no longer spontaneously but '*on occasion*'—in response to a conjuncture) in an intellectual process of "secondary-elaboration," to appropriate Freud's expression, *after* the viewing experience.

HVG: Absolutely, and the image projected as a loop in *Occasio*, on which we should definitely elaborate now, suggests such possibility for "secondary elaboration." In fact, Alice's warning to Colas can also be extrapolated to a collective level, to that of contemporary civil society itself. The visitor encounters a flooded pithead amidst a calm ocean. One imagines it to be either sunrise or sunset—a dynamic moment of transition between states of day and night. Because of its peculiar setting, all on its own surrounded by an endless mass of water, the isolated tower may remind of a watch post or a waiting station —such as, for example, the Maunsell Forts built during the Second World War in the Thames and Mersey estuaries to defend UK territory. Will it turn out to be a reliable beacon, a welcoming lighthouse? Or, on the contrary, could the simple act of approaching it already imply that one may get shot? Will it be a refuge or instead become a prison? Entirely inundated, the tower appears far removed from land. Yet one is aware this may change, for it is not unlikely that the waters may eventually recede. From that perspective, *Occasio* reads as a work that both warns about the frailty of balances and pleads for preserving them, nurturing them. In January 2016, Eurotunnel, a limited liability company (SE), announced—shockingly—it was flooding the marshy pieces of land surrounding the Channel Tunnel entrance to prevent people from approaching the barricades closing off the tracks (Gee 2016). The company's spokesperson did not shy away from perversely assessing that the flooded marshland served to use the "natural environment as a layer of protection." As a concerned citizen, one is tempted to ask: 'protection' for—or rather, *against*—what and whom? How is one to come to terms with what, at this very moment in time, is daily business in a region that only a hundred years ago was perfectly capable of providing adequate housing and food for a mass of war refugees? Seen in this light, *Occasio* reads as a silent work of resistance. Stronger even, one may understand *Occasio* as a resolute encouragement to displaced persons seeking refuge away from home: go and meet Kairos, claim your 'right to be reborn', believe in the decision you make and then live it consequently—all the way to the end. Arguably, *Occasio*, as one single moving 'immemorial image' of pure allegory, is one of the most 'political' works that you have made in a very long time. It is so highly abstracted that it becomes terribly, perturbingly tangible and concrete. This is such a striking paradox that I would like to ask you to elaborate on how you came to the decision to make this type of 'political' work of representation? What do you expect *Occasio* to achieve today, where do you feel lies its 'critical' power?

VB: Godard said that for him a film is "*pour en parler après*." Just as the specificity of spectatorship may differ between films, paintings and projection loops, so there may be different specificities of such discursive 'afterwardness' *in practice*—not least in academic practice. The two of us have previously had conversations about the idea of 'art-as-research' as it entered the discourse of art schools and university art departments over recent decades, and which I myself first encountered on my return to the UK in 2001.[13] Just as we are in an evolutionary/revolutionary period in European political history, so we are undergoing a period of radical mutation in the history of relations between text and image—one that is difficult to see clearly, as we are in the middle of it, but one to which the academy must nevertheless respond. As academics and as artists, the specificity of our politics will be formed in the nature and quality of our response. So I would repeat myself and say that the critical power of an artwork lies in its *language* (rather than in what it overtly 'says') and in the *occasion* it provides for the critical speech of others to emerge—which is why it is important that the artist not simply parade her or his own political convictions, leaving others merely to applaud or deride.

Notes

1 See Burgin and Van Gelder (2010); republished as "Art and Politics: A Reappraisal" in *Eurozine*, available at: www.eurozine.com/art-and-politics-a-reappraisal/</URI> [accessed May 31, 2017]; and, in a slightly shortened version, in Burgin (2011: 207–226).
2 *Amnesty International Report 2016/17. The State of the World's Human Rights*, 160. Available at: www.amnesty.org/en/documents/pol10/4800/2017/en/[accessed May 31, 2017].
3 *Amnesty International Report 2016/17:* 84. Laws voted or new policies implemented during an official state of emergency are lifted when the state of emergency ends. Belgium adopted, among others, a parliament bill broadening police surveillance powers. These counter-terrorist policies are now meant to remain in force for an indefinite period of time. Amnesty deplores that, in this process, "little effort was made to assess the human rights impact of new measures."
4 Sincere thanks to Mark Durden and Jane Tormey for having provided a unique opportunity to reconsider what artistic representation can bring to the dismal political reality of today.
5 Further on the notion of 'psychical realism', see Streitberger (2009), "Questions to Victor Burgin."
6 Interview with Tony Godfrey recorded in 1979, originally published in *Block* 7, 1982.
7 Victor Burgin, "Note on *Hôtel D*," unpublished earlier version, 2009, n.p.
8 See also: Symons and Van Gelder (2017).
9 The full text can be consulted in Schmidt (2014: 14–19) and in Mavridorakis (2016: 141–145).
10 The work was painted ca. 1636, and is attributed to Rubens and his workshop. See: Victor Burgin, 'A note on *Occasio*,' in Schmidt (2014: 3).
11 A reproduction of this work is available online via: https://books.google.be/books?id=tIa0iUVpGbcC&printsec=frontcover&hl=nl&source=gbs_ge_summary_r&cad=0—v=onepage&q&f=false[accessed May 31, 2017].
12 On the motif of the snail as an archetypal, apotropaic visual trope for Time (Chronos), see Baert (2016: 86–88).
13 See the previous publications of this interview, referenced in note 1 and Burgin (2009).

References

Agamben, G. (2004) *Image et mémoire. Écrits sur l'image, la danse et le cinema*, Paris: Desclée de Brouwer.

Baert, B. (2016) Kairos or Occasion as Paradigm in the Visual Medium: Nachleben, Iconography, Hermeneutics, Leuven: Peeters.

Buchloh, B.H.D. (1995) "Allan Sekula: Photography between Discourse and Document," in A. Sekula (author and ed.), *Fish Story. Allan Sekula*, Rotterdam: Witte de With; Düsseldorf: Richter, pp. 189–200.

Buchloh, B.H.D. (2003) "Conversation between Allan Sekula and B.H.D. Buchloh," in S. Breitwieser (ed.), *Allan Sekula. Performance under Working Conditions*, Vienna: Generali Foundation, pp. 20–55.

Burgin, V. (ed.) (1982) *Thinking Photography*, London: Macmillan.

Burgin, V. (1986) *The End of Art Theory: Criticism and Postmodernity*, London, Basingstoke: Macmillan; New Jersey: Humanities Press International.

Burgin, V. (1986a) "Diderot, Barthes, *Vertigo*," in V. Burgin, J. Donald and C. Kaplan (eds.), *Formations of Fantasy*, London; New York: Methuen, pp. 85–108.

Burgin, V. (1986b) *Between*, London: Blackwell; ICA.

Burgin, V. (1987) "Geometry and Abjection," In *In/Different Spaces. Place and Memory in Visual Culture*, Berkeley; Los Angeles: University of California Press, pp. 39–56.

Burgin, V. (2004) "Introduction. The Noise of the Marketplace," in V. Burgin (eds.), *The Remembered Film*, London: Reaktion Books, pp. 7–28.

Burgin, V. (2008) "Modernism in the Work of Art," [1976] in A. Streitberger (ed.), *Photographie Moderne/Modernité photographique*, Brussels: SIC, pp. 101–122.

Burgin, V. (2008a) *Components of a Practice*, Milan: Skira.
Burgin, V. (2009) "Thoughts on 'Research' Degrees in Visual Arts Departments," in J. Elkins (ed.), *Artists with PhDs: On the New Doctoral Degree in Studio Art*, New York: New Academia Press, 85–96.
Burgin, V. (2011) *Parallel Texts. Interviews and Interventions about Art*, London: Reaktion Books.
Burgin, V. (2016) "Note on *Hôtel D* (2009)," in V. Mavridorakis (ed.), *Victor Burgin. Scripts*, Geneva: Mamco, pp. 100–101.
Burgin, V. and Van Gelder, H. (2010) "Artistic Representation and Politics. An Exchange between Victor Burgin and Hilde Van Gelder," *A Prior*, 20: 92–116.
Dubois, P. (2007) "'L'événement et la structure. Le montage de temps hétérogènes dans l'œuvre de Victor Burgin'," in N. Boulouch, V. Mavridorakis and D. Perreau (eds.), *Victor Burgin. Objets Temporels*, Rennes: Presses universitaires de Rennes, pp. 69–83.
Gee, O. (2016) "Eurotunnel Floods Land in Bid to Keep Refugees Out," *The Local* (13 January 2016). Available at www.thelocal.fr/20160113/eurotunnel-adds-moats-to-keep-refugees-away [Accessed May 31, 2017]. Footage can be consulted via this weblink: www.youtube.com/watch?v=WG2NB68LFuA [Accessed May 31, 2017].
Mavridorakis, V. (ed.) (2016) *Victor Burgin. Scripts*, Geneva: Mamco.
Rancière, J. (2004) *The Politics of Aesthetics*, trans. G. Rockhill, London; New York: Continuum.
Rosenthal, L. (2005) *Gender, Politics, and Allegory in the Art of Rubens*, Cambridge: Cambridge University Press.
Schmidt, E. (ed.) (2014) *Victor Burgin. Five Pieces for Projection*, Berlin: Sternberg Press.
Streitberger, A. (2009) "Questions to Victor Burgin," in V. Burgin (eds.), *Situational Aesthetics: Selected Writings by Victor Burgin*, Leuven: Leuven University Press, pp. 267–268.
Symons, S. and Van Gelder, H. (eds.) (2017) *Victor Burgin's Parzival in Leuven. Reflections on the 'Uncinematic'*, Leuven: Leuven University Press.
Van Gelder, H. (2007) "A Matter of Cleaning Up: Treating History in the Work of Allan Sekula and Jeff Wall," *History of Photography*, Vol. 31, No. 1 (Spring): 68–80.
Warnke, M. and C. Brink. (2008) *Aby Warburg. Der Bilderatlas MNEMOSYNE*, Berlin: Akademie Verlag.

25

Decentering the photographer

Authorship and digital photography

Daniel Palmer

A "worldwide network of digital imaging systems is swiftly, silently constituting itself as the decentered subject's reconfigured eye" (Mitchell 1992: 85). So concluded William J. Mitchell in one of the first books on digital photography, *The Reconfigured Eye: Visual Truth in the Post-Photographic Era*, published way back in 1992.[1] If the theoretical language of the "decentered subject" reveals the influence of post-structuralism on Mitchell's thinking, in which the subject is caught in language or ideology, now he proposes that figure is enmeshed within new networks of digital imagery. At the same time, it is not immediately clear whose "reconfigured eye" Mitchell is referring to in this sentence or indeed the title of the book. Mitchell contextualizes digital imaging within a longer history of manipulated photography and suggests that the photographer's traditional role as an eyewitness is under threat. He explores the technical implications of the new pixelated image, allied to the emergence of imaging software such as Photoshop, which was commercially released in February 1990, just prior to the book's release. However, he willfully conflates the photographer's eye and the viewer's eye, presumably because the potential for seamless manipulation and image mutation means that every viewer becomes a potential author of a digital image.

Mitchell clearly sought to contrast the image on a computer screen with the traditional photographic print, which comes to stand for an emerging visual regime in which photography is transformed into "a medium that privileges fragmentation, indeterminacy, and heterogeneity, and that emphasizes process or performance rather than the finished art object" (Mitchell 1992: 8). Notably, for all the comparisons between the malleability of pixels and painting, Mitchell's most consistent opposition is that between the digital image and "the finished art object." Ironically, for Mitchell, the analogue photograph—which Walter Benjamin, in his landmark 1936 essay on art in the age of its technical reproducibility, saw as transforming the notion of art—is now his embodiment of a fixed image and what he calls "an increasingly sclerotic pictorial tradition" (1992: 8). By contrast, Mitchell writes of "the age of electrobricollage" (1992: 7), in language that clearly dates the text in then fashionable language of postmodern social and cultural theory (Lister 2004: 316). Meanwhile, his emphasis on "process and performance" echoes the shift from late-modernist to postmodern art in the 1960s and 1970s in the wake of what Lucy Lippard (1997) described at the time as "the dematerialization of the art object." More recently, the notion that digital photography is akin to a performance of data, only ever temporarily stabilized as an image, has reappeared in the work of philosophers such as Boris Groys and Daniel Rubinstein (2009). For Groys, a digital image can only be "staged or performed," as the image file itself is invisible (Groys 2016: 143). In more practical terms, writers and visual activists such as Fred Ritchin have explored the potential of networked digital media transforming photography into a hypertextual medium, enabling a multiplicity of perspectives and a "more sustained collaboration with the reader" (2009: 131).

I begin this chapter by revisiting Mitchell's work not simply to argue once again against the idea of a clean break between analogue and digital images, which, like the notion of "visual truth," has been rightly criticized (Manovich 1995). With hindsight, we can note that early writers on digital photography were overly preoccupied with an apparently fundamental rupture in the truth regime of photography brought about by the malleability of digital pixels. We now appreciate that the conventions of photography have remained largely intact despite the new technical basis of the medium, and we understand that photography's truth effect has always been highly dependent on its linguistic and cultural context. Nevertheless, digital technologies and software *have* brought about radical changes in how photographs are produced, circulated and received, and Mitchell's analysis was in fact prescient in pointing to the importance of transmission and mutation in the photographic process. Moreover, somewhat surprisingly for a digital media enthusiast, his language is haunted by a sense of uncertainty about the future. His "worldwide network of digital imaging systems" sounds as ominous as anything ever conjured by the famously pessimistic media theorist Paul Virilio. Recall that it is transforming by stealth the very nature of perception itself, "silently constituting itself" (1992: 85). Indeed, although it is hard to disagree with Liz Wells' point that the digital is "completely integrated within photographic procedures," her further claim that "the digital is no longer a matter of theoretical challenge or debate" (2015: xiv) is more questionable. Most recently, for instance, the "machine-readability" of digital images means that they are no longer simply representations of the world, but can actively intervene in it, even in the absence of human viewers (Paglen 2016). Thus, I begin with Mitchell to propose that the photographer's eye—which during modernism was effectively another name for authorship—has been in a constant process of decentering since the birth of the medium. As the history of photography is a series of technical developments, and the medium is a "heterogeneous object ... involved in an ongoing dialogue with other media" (Pirenne and Streitberger 2014: xvii), authorship in photography has always been highly contingent.

The automation of the labor of representation

Photography was born out of a rejection of human labor, or more specifically the skill and effort of the artist's hand. In *The Pencil of Nature* (1969 [1844]), William Henry Fox Talbot famously related how, some years earlier during his honeymoon at Lake Como in Italy, his frustrated attempts to sketch the landscapes had helped to inspire his desire to invent a technique to arrest the fleeting image. Photogenic drawing, as he originally called it, not only made traditional drawing skills unnecessary, it was also far more efficient than the human hand. As Talbot wrote in "Some Account of the Art of Photogenic Drawing" from 1839, photography renders the most elaborate architectural ornamentation as quickly and efficiently as the simplest object, "for the object which would take the most skillful artist days or weeks of labor to trace or copy, is effected by the boundless powers of natural chemistry in the space of a few seconds" (1990 [1839]: 39). Moreover, "groups of figures take no longer time to obtain than single figures ... since the Camera depicts them all at once, however numerous they may be" (Talbot 1969 [1844]: n.p). Photography was thereby presented, aside from anything else, as an "ingenious labor-saving device" (Kelsey 2015: 18) in the vein of contemporaneous contraptions such as the sewing machine (1830). Moreover, the camera, like the sewing machine, promised not only individual efficiency but mass participation, and its popular use quickly become more associated with the domain of leisure than work.

The issue of the absence of skilled labor in the mechanical medium was central to early debates around whether photography could in fact be an art. Charles Baudelaire and Lady Elizabeth Eastlake are only two of the best-known critics to argue emphatically that it could not. The question of whether photography even allowed for authorship was later critical to the issue of copyright as it emerged in the decisive legal case of New York studio photographer Napoleon Sarony's image of the visiting Oscar Wilde in the early 1880s (Gaines 1991). And, just as the idea of photographic authorship was being established, Kodak's industrialization of the printing process democratized photographic authorship in a radical act of deskilling captured in Kodak's brilliant marketing slogan "you press the button we do the rest." In response, the artistically aspirational reacted by transferring skill to the process of laborious print-making, with the Pictorialists arguing that the artistry of photography lay in complex printing techniques that translated an individual response to the world. For all their apparent differences, twentieth-century modernists such as Ansel Adams for the most part simply refined this tradition with their insistence that the photographer should be in complete control of every aspect of the medium, as only this would enable them to "pre-visualise" the resulting image. Henceforth, the intuitive (at times approaching mystical) composition of photographs by 'serious' photographers went hand in hand with darkroom acrobatics, both of which preoccupy American and Western European modernist accounts of photographic labor. In short, dominant accounts concentrate on "the creative eye," a form of authorship thoroughly critiqued by politically motivated documentary-makers and photo-cooperatives in the 1970s, as well as postmodern critics such as Abigail Solomon-Godeau (1983), who—influenced by a more politically radical version of modernism—understood this kind of photography as irredeemably individualistic and formalist in orientation.

Meanwhile, by the late twentieth century, manufactures of cameras, in a race for market share, had successfully made photography more and more automated, and the resulting pictorial outcomes more and more reliable. Thus, by the 1970s, auto-exposure and auto-focus features were becoming common, and, by the 1980s, almost no skilled work was required of a human operator of an instamatic or SLR to produce sharp, correctly exposed negatives. Writing about this development in the mid-1990s, at the precipice of the digital era, Julian Stallabrass (1996) celebrated the erstwhile skilled amateur photographer's activities as a zone of compromised but nevertheless non-alienated activity and bemoaned their demise into instrumentalized gadgetry. That essay, which now reads as a homage to the labor of amateur analogue photography on the cusp of its transformation into digital pixels, serves to remind us that camera technology has always shaped the look and practice of photography (the 35 mm Leica most famously). As I have suggested elsewhere, digital cameras render even more obsolete the traditional skills of the individual photographer (Palmer 2013). Digital software increasingly removes decision-making from the photographer—even, in some cases, making them completely unnecessary. Software is even rising to the task of editing. Google, for instance, recognizing that the time-consuming, decision-making labor of photography now lies primarily in the editing rather than the taking, pioneered automatic editing, promising to privilege photos of people recognized to be in a user's closest Google circles. Increasingly, the task of selecting the 'best' image(s) can be outsourced to software, for blink- and smile-detection features allow cameras to recommend the most 'perfect' shot from a series. The technology of the camera is simply following its own black-box logic. As Vilém Flusser (2000) famously argued, the camera is a programmable apparatus and, contrary to marketing myth, photographers are effectively enslaved to the dictates of its program. We may all be photographers now, yet fewer and fewer of us understand the fundamental craft of photography that an artist such as Adams deemed essential. Nevertheless, techniques to automate the labor of reproduction inevitably produce their own unique forms of artistic authorship.

Pictorialism 2.0

Photography multiplies the world and trades in the repetition of clichés. Nearly two centuries after Talbot, a tourist at Lake Como is unlikely to reflect on their poor drawing skills and is more likely to be frustrated by their own photographs not matching the hyper-real images on promotional websites. Faced with such a photogenic landscape, the photographer must then contend with the dispiriting sight of all the other tourists armed with cameras jostling for the same scene. That the same landscapes are photographed over and over is a fact made increasingly visible by the various archives of geo-tagged images available online. Google's chief technology advocate has claimed that the networking of location-aware cameras is creating a situation in which "the earth itself is like a table of contents for direct exploration of all the photographs ... shared by people around the world, automatically" (Jones 2011). In fact, this universal visual mapping—put to more instrumental use in Google Street View—realizes an old fantasy of comprehensive photographic documentation: as early as 1899, *The British Journal of Photography* called for the formation of an archive "containing the record as complete as can be made ... of the present state of the world" (Mitchell 1992: 238). Nevertheless, tourist landscapes are photographed far more than others, a fact Don DeLillo brilliantly parodied with his well-known example of "the most photographed barn in America" in his 1985 novel *White Noise*.

The relentless photographic duplication of the same subjects has been theorized by figures such as Flusser and Andreas Müller-Pohle. In Flusser's 1983 book *Towards a Philosophy of Photography*, he posits the camera as a programmable apparatus that, paradoxically, programs the photographers who use it (2000). For Flusser, most photographs are "redundant"—that is, they carry no *new information*. The "challenge for the photographer," he argues, is "to oppose the flood of redundancy with informative images" (2000: 65), by which he means those that provide the photographic universe with new information. Flusser allocates "snapshots" to the realm of redundant images, and his critique of so-called "creative photography" is based on the idea that most of what people are doing when they photograph is to reproduce clichés set in place by the apparatus (2000: 26). Similarly, Müller-Pohle's manifesto-like essay "Information Strategies" from 1985, written at the cusp of the emergence of digital photography, offered a stinging critique of creative photography as an "exhausted" strategy.[2] Deeply influenced by Flusser, he wrote of the "impressionistic gestures" of creative photographers that "can only be consistent in so far as they are concentrated into 'a personal way of seeing'" (stylization), which he dubbed "photographism."

Regardless of what we wish to call it, authorial aspirations towards pictorial originality survive in the digital era in a number of distinctive ways. In the art museum, for instance, the past two decades have been marked by large-scale colour prints. Although a small number of artists began to work with large colour prints prior to digital imaging in the late 1970s and 1980s, sometimes in a "directorial" style inspired by cinema or advertising, the widespread popularity of large-scale photography has been fuelled by the technical potentials opened up by new digital printing technologies. Many of the key figures associated with the market boom for art photography in the 1990s and 2000s—auteurs such as Jeff Wall and Andreas Gursky—exhibit in their digital prints a form of exaggerated or melodramatic authorial control. This is somewhat ironic in the case of Gursky, given that his teachers, Bernd and Hilla Becher, were known for their seemingly "authorless" style (which is one of the reasons they were taken up by American minimalists and included in the influential "New Topographics" exhibition of 1975, with its return to the supposed "stylistic anonymity" of nineteenth-century landscape views). The work of Wall, Gursky and others, who make work explicitly for the gallery wall to compete with the scale of painting, can thus be accurately described as "neo-Pictorialist," as its emphasis on authorial intention, skilled post-production techniques and often spectacular imagery serves to clearly distinguish their singular images from the realm of popular photography.

Curator and writer Charlotte Cotton, in a recent survey of contemporary art photography, acknowledges that, to a certain degree, "technologies themselves are 'authoring' the images we see." Noting the "(all too democratically) automated character of 'the digital'," she points out that "the pervasive automation of photographic rendering has made software the dominant photographic medium" (2015: 4). However, Cotton goes on to affirm the traditional logic of the art world, celebrating artists who "subjectify the photographic systems in which they operate" through "an immeasurable quantity of active choices" and concludes that "[w]e can now recognize individual artists' signatures through their repeated navigation and articulation of the dynamic behavior of photographic culture at large" (2015: 10). Like many observers, Cotton points to artists' interest in the past decade in analogue materiality, including the revival of the photogram. Various claims have been made for why artists are making such anachronistic work in the context of the digital era. The photography historian Geoffrey Batchen, for instance, has argued that to make camera-less photographs "returns photography to a unique, hand-made craft and away from an automatic subservience to global capitalism and its vast economies of mass production and exploitation" (2016: 47). Camera-less photographs are, for Batchen, "an art of the real," contrary to their often-abstract appearance, as "photographs made by direct contact with the world" allow the "world to speak for itself as itself" (2016: 46). However, this can only happen through the intermediary of 'skillful hands'. Authorship thus survives here in the embodied form of "the touch of the artist," who handles both a referent and light-sensitive surface (2016: 40). Once again, this attention to the unique photographic object bears the mark of a new form of Pictorialism that operates against the tide of the digital age.

Meanwhile, in popular photography, authorship is marked in various ways within the constraints of software design. In a large-scale study of Instagram photography, Lev Manovich (2016) concludes that popular styles on Instagram are associated with the strategic projection of cultural identities and lifestyle groups, noting the link between minimalist aesthetics in the fashion world and what he calls "designed" photos. Millions of amateur photographers now use filters built into camera phone or image-management software to beautify or otherwise distinguish their subjects. This started with early iPhone apps such as Hipstamatic, which have since been made redundant as their features have been incorporated into the popular social media platform Instagram and also into native camera phone apps. Filters very often function to give the images a nostalgic appeal associated with Polaroids or drugstore prints. Even as camera phones are increasingly used to communicate 'presence' in the moment, such images defamiliarize a scene from the here and now, typically layering the present with a simulated image of the past.

Less commonly, amateurs use software to defamiliarize the world through digital montage. For instance, in 2014, Robert Jahns, known as "nois7" on Instagram, produced an image he entitled *The Whale in Venice*, a digital collage of a remotely possible, if unlikely, scene of a huge whale swimming in the Grand Canal. The perspective of Venice is a familiar one, viewed from the Grand Canal's Rialto Bridge, and the image 'went viral' on social media, supported by a series of media articles. The image relies for its effect on the photograph's conventional rhetoric of realism and its supposed anchoring in time and place. In fact, it is not only unclear if the artist actually visited Venice but precisely irrelevant. The Hamburg-based designer claims to have "a massive image archive" from his travels, such that whenever he needs "a specific image there's a good chance that [he] already shot it" (Designboom 2016). Jahn's Instagram account shows many similar images that tend to resemble spectacular advertising for global tourism campaigns (a colored umbrella among a sea of black umbrellas on Brooklyn Bridge, vertiginous cityscapes and air balloons hovering over impossible sunsets, and so on). As he sees it, he wants "to create surreal images which look realistic so you never know if an image is real or not" (Designboom 2016). More specifically, *The Whale in Venice* is a science fiction, a fantasy that relies for its power on a displacement of expectations (possibly tinged by an understanding of the predicament currently facing the world: namely anthropogenic climate change, the reality of rising sea levels, changing habitats and species destruction). Jahn's advertising-induced imagery simply reminds us that, despite the GPS metadata embedded in digital images, place and fantasy have always been confused in 'creative photography'.

Anxiety about the possibility of 'informative' photography in the age of digital hyperabundance has also recently spawned a "concept camera," *Camera Restricta* (2015), by designer Philipp Schmitt. This speculative camera searches the internet for other images that have been captured from the same place and, if too many are found, prevents the user from taking another "unoriginal" photograph (www.philippschmitt.com/projects/camera-restricta). A brilliant parody, the project makes light of, even as it perhaps continues to invest in, a crisis at the heart of the modern photographic project—that is, the humanist project of depicting the world in an original or unique way. In fact, as American artist Penelope Umbrico has demonstrated in her artwork *Four Photographs of Rays of Sunlight in Grand Central Station* (2013), iconic images online are not always authored once and for all. The work comprises 512 prints based on an iconic photograph of light streaming through the windows and pooling on the main concourse of the Grand Central terminal. However, the 'iconic image' turns out to be taken not by a specific photographer, but by four photographers who took almost identical images between 1913 and 2010. Moreover, these four images appear online in slightly different forms: people have added color or sepia tone, made them grainy, introduced high contrast, enlarged and cropped them, reversed them, added graphic framing, 'watermarks' and so on. In short, the images have been subtly modified over time by multiple end users before being sold as posters, 'vintage' prints, mouse pads, coffee mugs and the like. To add to the confusion, the original four images are attributed online to at least eleven different photographers as well as to 'anonymous' and 'photographer unknown'. For Umbrico, this illustrates that, "recontextualized on the web," an individual picture "goes from being an individual and authored image to a collective anonymous image that regards no author at all" (Umbrico and Zach 2013: np).

Conceptual artists, deskilling and the networked condition

From the mid-1960s, a number of influential conceptual artists took a very different approach to authorship in photography than that of the fine art photographers whose images were, at the same time, finally being granted a certain status in the art world (notably at the Museum of Modern Art in New York). Conceptual artists used photography widely but made no claim to the pictorial originality or autonomy of individual photographs; instead, they were interested in series and typologies, which were typically illustrations of an essay or linguistic idea. Highly functional, even 'bureaucratic' in style, and influenced by pop art and minimalism, conceptual artists also refused conventional signs of photographic authorship by substituting a pose of deskilled amateurism or blank professionalism. The most famous example is Ed Ruscha, with books such as *Twentysix Gasoline Stations* (1963). Individual photographs showed no apparent traces of aesthetic decision-making, as if the artist had merely pointed the camera out the car window in order to fulfill the requirements of the title. Undermining the fetish of 'well-composed' individual photographs, Ruscha claimed that his photographs were closer to "technical data like industrial photography" (Coplans 2002 [1965]: 23), "simply a collection of 'facts' ... a collection of 'readymades'" (2002 [1965]: 26). Furthermore, he said, "it is not important who took the photos" (2002 [1965]: 25), and indeed he employed professionals to take some of his series. Similarly, the artist Douglas Huebler famously claimed of his working method in 1969:

> I use the camera as a 'dumb' copying device that only serves to document whatever phenomena appears before it through the conditions set by a system. No 'aesthetic' choices are possible. Other people often make the photographs. It makes no difference.
> *(Alberro 2003: 77)*

Ruscha and Huebler were among others who were insistent that the photographs were unimportant on their own, implicitly rejecting the fine art tradition of authorship in photography. The fascination of conceptual artists lay with the anthropological or quasi-scientific photograph, and, in 1977, the art historian Rosalind Krauss (1977: 60) praised the "quasi-tautological" condition of a documentary image that liberated artists from authorial mark-making. In other words, photography's erstwhile *lack*, the fact that it simply duplicates the world, was turned into a virtue—much as the Surrealists had previously adopted its quasi-automatic quality.

Today, networked digital photography radically multiplies the duplication of the world, generating large and growing databases of digital images. Responding to this new 'networked condition' has required fresh conceptual approaches that have tended to discount picture making in favor of analytical deconstruction. Implicitly recognizing that single images can barely hope to register an impression in the face of the hyperabundance of photographs in and of the world, many artists have gravitated towards the use of found photography, in which meaning is found through an accumulation and recontextualization of existing visual material. Fred Ritchin (2013: 38) has offered the term "metaphotographers" for those who work with photographs that already exist in the world and make those images visible in a different way by providing them with a new context. Ritchin is particularly interested in documentary photography and photojournalism, but his term can be applied more broadly in relation to work that reflects on the labor of the original photographers and those who feature in them, even to point to cultural repetition and clichés. For instance, Dutch art director Erik Kessels has been publishing *In Almost Every Picture* since 2001, a series of books of anonymous photographs found at flea markets in which a common person or object appears: the same middle-aged woman in different holiday-like settings (a dozen years of vacation photographs taken by a husband of his wife), parked taxis amid alpine settings and a series dedicated to one family's photogenic Dalmatian. Kessels claims to be interested in drawing out narratives in photographs that their original authors are unaware of. However, he has become best known for *24hrs in Photography* (2011), a sprawling room-sized installation comprising printouts of 24 hours' worth of photographs uploaded to Flickr, with no attempt to filter or sort, turning photographic excess into rubbish. This work has come to vividly symbolize the apparent excess of networked photography.

Found photography did not begin in the digital era, of course. Artists have worked with anonymous and found photographs and postcards ever since the Dadaists and Surrealists recognized their potential, as readymade fragments, for poetic estrangement. In a more serial fashion, British artist Susan Hiller collected several hundred postcards of the visually seductive cliché of 'rough seas' in her seminal, *Dedicated to the Unknown Artists* (1972–76). However, interest in archives of found photographs has reached a kind of frenzy since the late 1990s, producing a rapid trade in other people's 'obsolete' slide collections and family albums, which now takes place largely online rather than in junk stores or flea markets. It is clearly no coincidence that so many artists and collectors have been drawn to found analogue materials at a time of photography's digital recoding. As photographs are now viewed predominantly on LCD screens, and online sharing has largely replaced traditional modes of archiving and dissemination such as the photo album, the materiality of prints has become newly visible. At the same time, the collecting activity of photographers has been massively enabled by eBay and searchable databases—exemplified by German artist Joachim Schmid's collection of ninety-six books, *Other People's Photographs* (2008: 11), assembled from vast archives of popular photography on sites such as Flickr. The act of photography also now extends to the use of screen grabs, turning the screen interface into a virtual camera (which on an Apple computer turns the cursor into a camera icon).

Artists working with found photographs today are implicitly acknowledging the decentered status of the 'creative photographer'. Moreover, precisely because of the digitally automated drive to create the perfect image, the casual mistakes of twentieth-century photographers are now prized. The Australian artist Patrick Pound, for instance, is one of many who collect photographs *about* photography: decontextualized images of people holding cameras, people holding photographs and, of course, photographs of amateur photographers' shadows—dark figures looming towards or behind the intended subject of the image, hands up, caught in the act of photography (see Plate 23 and Figure 25.1). Pound gives his overall collection of such images the general title *The Photographers* (1990–). In their accumulation, these unintentional self-portraits of photographers offer a collective picture of twentieth-century photographic authorship. His collection of (largely male) shadows can be read as the opposite to the calculated pose of the contemporary (predominantly female) selfie. A subset of his collections, *The Photographer's Hand* (2011), feature the photographer's fingers or thumb in the frame—in a kind of homage to what is perhaps the amateur photographer's most common mistake.[3] Once again, these images can be viewed as accidental portraits of the photographer, in which they are both present and absent. One is also reminded here of a remarkable work by the North American artist Andrew Norman Wilson, *ScanOps* (2011; see Figures 25.2a and 25.2b). The work is comprised of "anomalies" sourced from the massive databases of scanned pages in Google Books, in which software distortions or the hands of the Google employees doing the scanning are visible (overwhelmingly black people's index fingers, wrapped in hot-pink one-finger rubber gloves). In a sense, Pound and Wilson are both collecting photographic evidence of photographic labor, the one as an authorial analogue leisure activity, the other as deskilled digital data entry. Aside from a marker of obscure factory labor, the Google book scanner can also be viewed as a metaphor for the fate of the photographer today.

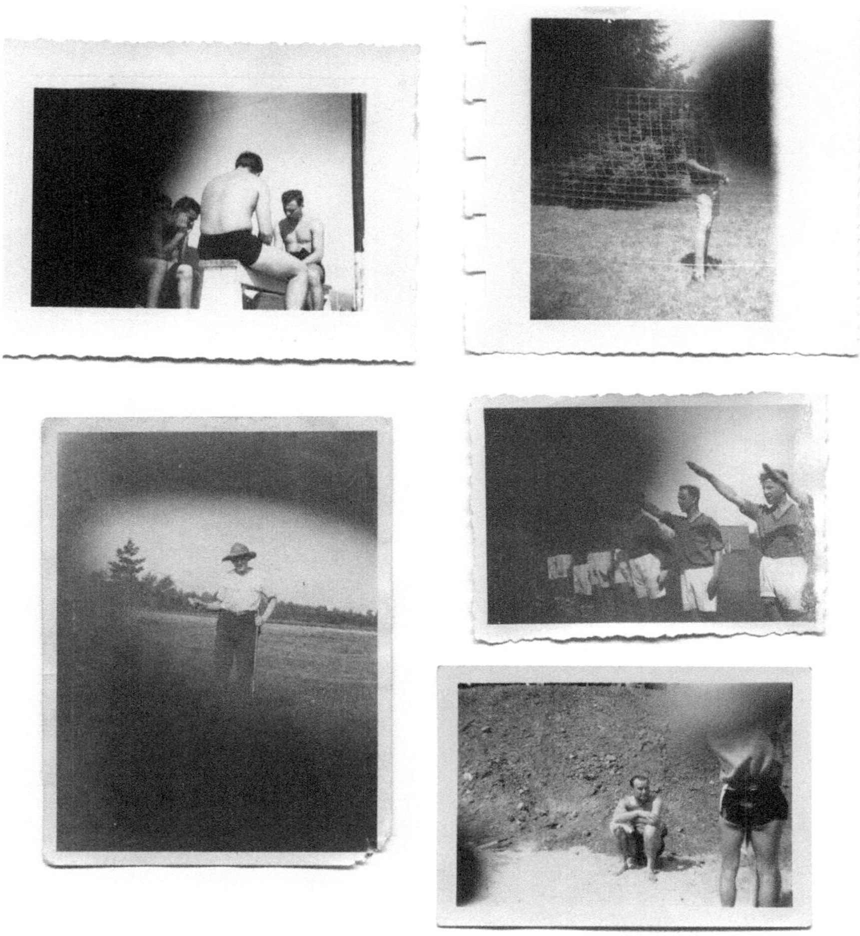

Figure 25.1 Patrick Pound, *The Hand of the Photographer* (2007), detail from an ongoing collection of photographs. Courtesy of Station Gallery, Melbourne; Darren Knight Gallery, Sydney; Hamish McKay Gallery, Wellington; Melanie Roger Gallery, Auckland

Coda: the selfie and authorship in photography

Today, no discussion on digital photography can ignore the selfie, the work of performing and sharing one's self-portrait with a camera phone. So, I want to conclude by reflecting on what has become this most archetypal genre of popular digital photography in relation to the issue of authorship. Everyone is a photographer now, and, as if to underline the difficulty of taking 'original' pictures of the world around us—and perhaps also in response to the uncertainty of our own subjectivity—many of us take pictures of ourselves. Key developments such as the iPhone's front-facing camera (launched in 2010), Instagram and flattering filters all massively accelerated the selfie phenomenon. Oxford Dictionaries famously named the selfie its word of the year in 2013, a moment in which the genre seemed to reach saturation

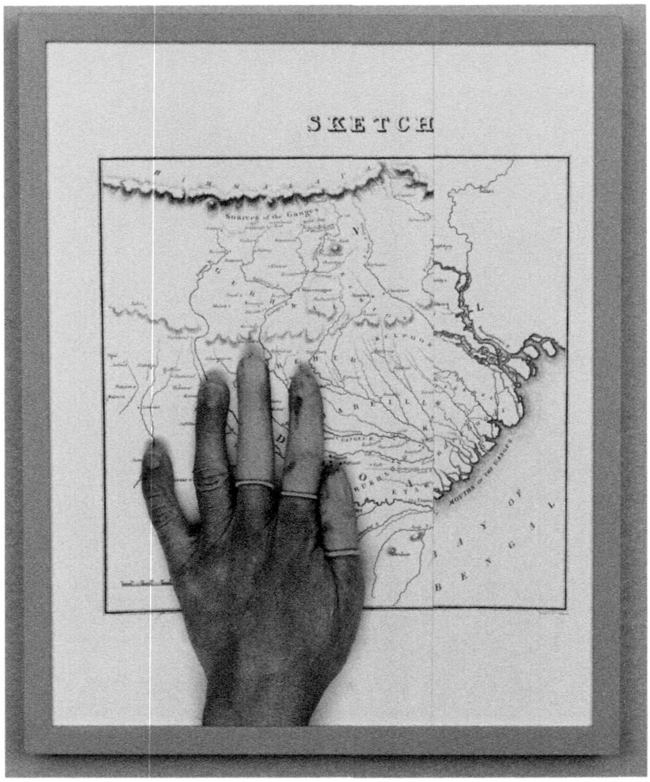

Figure 25.2a Andrew Norman Wilson, *ScanOps* (2011). Courtesy the artist

point, with celebrities and politicians regularly implicated in the practice of turning the camera onto themselves. The act of self-representation must be constantly repeated, and, whatever else we might want to say about selfies, which have now attracted a wide variety of scholarship, their reception clearly belongs in part to photography's long and intimate relationship with narcissism. Such tendencies were already identified in Charles Baudelaire's 1859 essay "The Modern Public and Photography," in which the poet-critic took the daguerreotype's mirrored surface as proof that photography makes narcissists of us all. Baudelaire's critique was based on the rapid success of the daguerreotype as a portrait medium, enabling the mid-nineteenth-century bourgeoisie to look at its own "trivial image" (1980). Every photograph posted on Instagram is a kind of self-promotional portrait. Social media's logic of 'followers' participates in a celebrity model of selfhood, and celebrities make up its most popular participants—most famously, the reality star Kim Kardashian photographs herself obsessively for her Instagram feed, and has compiled a collection of these images in a book, sardonically titled *Selfish* (2014).

What can selfies tell us about photographic authorship? Of the various visual theorists who have sought to salvage the selfie from all-too-easy accusations of narcissism, Nicholas Mirzoeff and Paul Frosh offer some of the most compelling arguments. For Mirzoeff, selfies express a democratic impulse; they are a new form of picturing in which people from

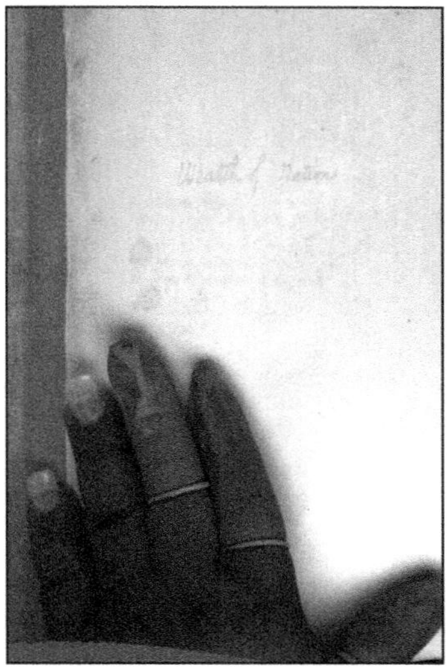

Figure 25.2b Andrew Norman Wilson, *ScanOps* detail (2011). Courtesy the artist

around the world now have access to putting themselves on display as an image for others. They are both an assertion of presence and part of a conversation with others, as "the first visual product of the new networked, urban global youth culture" (2015: 14). Similarly, for Paul Frosh, "accusations of narcissism" common in public discourse about selfies are "unnecessarily reductive" (2015: 1621) and often based on gendered assumptions "linking young women with fickle self-obsession" (2015: 1621). Instead, Frosh argues, selfies are better understood as "a gestural invitation to distant others" (2015: 1621), "a form of relational positioning between the bodies of the viewed and viewers in a culture of individualized mobility" (2015: 1609). Selfies, in short, are "a genre of *personal* reflexivity" (2015: 1621; original emphasis) through which embodied identity is explored, or, in Frosh's words, "a self, enacting itself." As the work of selfies is intertwined with the labor of performing oneself, this often results in images that are self-referential *as* images.

The genre of the selfie has provided a means for several artists to explore the boundaries of authorship in photography. Richard Prince's *New Portraits* (2014), enlarged screen shots of other people's Instagram images, is the most famous example of such an exploration. Well known as an appropriation artist, Prince has attracted considerable media attention for his work's blatant disregard towards both the individuals depicted and the original authors of the photographs, sparking retrograde arguments around copyright and image ownership. Alternatively, the work could be said to represent a tension between the fixities of self-creation and the fluid condition of authorship within photosharing (Palmer 2017: 168). More elaborately, the Australian artist Jackson Eaton has used the selfie to explore the restless quality of the self as an act of mimicry. In his series *Melfies 2* (2014), he photographed various reflections of himself in mirrors (usually in a bathroom or clothing store), then cut up his body into geometric parts in Photoshop and used these to do a reverse Google image search (see Plate 22). Google's image-analyzing algorithm struggle to find an accurate match to these body sections due to their various backgrounds, and generates seemingly random results. Much like the child's misrecognition of its self-image in Lacan's theorization, the results are bizarre collages that replace Eaton's body with commodity fragments. Eaton's "becoming other" thus parodies both the demands for self-representation and the commodification of the self in online networks designed to monetize the expression of desire. At the same time, the photographer's vestigial self-image, no matter how accidentally produced, reads as some kind of resistance to their redundancy in this process.

Simply put, selfies have become the most direct route to experience the world photographically. Selfies speak of a desire to be 'in the picture', in place, in the present. They speak to the personal and personalize digital speech. In their performance of presence, by saying "here I am, now," typically with various body parts in the frame, they aspire not only to capture, but to communicate the embodied experience of being alive. In this respect, they have played a pivotal role in the fundamental and presumably ongoing transformation of photography from being primarily a medium of memory to one of immediate communication. But, although selfies' unique point of view appeals to the most basic human desire to communicate with other humans, the images are perhaps even more importantly scrutinized by machines—by algorithms, for valuable data (Paglen 2016). Moreover, precisely for their anthropocentrism, in their personalization not only of tourist landscapes but of every potential encounter with the world, the selfie seems to render the conventional labor of 'creative photography' largely redundant. Or rather, selfies remove the need to situate oneself in the world photographically, as a 'photographic author', because, as various writers have observed, selfies are an obvious means by which "the photographer's subjectivity is inscribed in the image" (Zappavigna 2016: 283). Once upon a time, that ambition was reserved for modernist art photographers, who insisted on photography as a medium of subjectivity—epitomized by Alfred Stieglitz's cloud studies, *Equivalents* (1922–35). Can we not speculate, then, that the turn towards the self is not merely the substitution of narcissism for reality, not only a refusal of the external world, but a symptom of the near (but obviously not total) impossibility of meaningfully composed individual accounts of the world, that is, of pictorial authorship in photography? Is the often discomfortingly intimate selfie, in which the decentered subject-photographer has internalized the position of the viewer, the actually existing "visual truth" of William J. Mitchell's "reconfigured eye"?

Notes

1 The grandness of such a claim is consistent with Mitchell's previous writings as an urban theorist—and it is worth remembering how unusual it is that one of the first books on digital photography was written by an architect best known as the author of seminal works on the use of computer-aided design tools (his most recent book prior was *The Logic of Architecture: Design, Computation, and Cognition*, from 1990).

2 Müller-Pohle predicted that soon "it will be possible to generate and regenerate literally *every* conceivable—or inconceivable—picture through a computer terminal" (Müller-Pohle 1985).

3 In 2014, the prolific Dutch designer, publisher and artist Erik Kessels devoted Volume 13 of his ongoing series *In Almost Every Picture* to a similar theme of fingers obscuring their subject (www.kesselskramerpublishing.com).

References

Alberro, A. (2003) *Conceptual Art and the Politics of Publicity*, Cambridge, MA: MIT Press.

Batchen, G. (2016) *Emanations: The Art of the Cameraless Photograph*, Munich: Prestel.

Baudelaire, C. (1980) "The Modern Public and Photography," in A. Trachtenberg (ed.) *Classic Essays on Photography*, New Haven: Leete's Island Books, pp. 86–87.

Coplans, J. (2002 [1965]) "Concerning 'Various Small Fires', Edward Ruscha Discusses his Perplexing Publications," in E. Ruscha and A. Schwartz, *Leave Any Information at the Signal: Writings, Interviews, Bits, Pages*, Cambridge, MA: MIT Press, pp. 23–27.
Cotton, C. (2015) *Photography is Magic*, New York: Aperture.
Designboom. (2016) "Robert Jahns' Surreal Scenes Could Only Exist in Our Wildest Dreams," February 15. www.designboom.com/art/robert-jahns-nois7-instagram-digital-art-02-15-2016 [accessed February 20, 2016].
Flusser, V. (2000) *Towards a Philosophy of Photography*, trans. A Matthews, London: Reaktion Books.
Frosh, P. (2015) "The Gestural Image:
The Selfie, Photography Theory, and Kinesthetic Sociability," *International Journal of Communication* 9: pp. 1607–1628.
Gaines, J. M. (1991) *Contested Culture: The Image, the Voice, and the Law*, Chapel Hill: University of North Carolina Press.
Groys, B. (2016) *In the Flow*, London: Verso.
Jones, M. T. (2011) "The Total Archive," unpublished paper presented at *The Photographic Universe* (Parsons), March 2–3, www.youtube.com/watch?v=aG1RMLS5-p0 [accessed August 20, 2011].
Kelsey, R. (2015) *Photography and the Art of Chance*, Cambridge, MA: Harvard University Press.
Krauss, R. (1977) "Notes on the Index: Seventies Art in America," *October* 3: pp. 68–81.
Lippard, L. (1997) *Six Years: The Dematerialization of the Art Object from 1966 to 1972*, Berkeley: University of California Press.
Lister, M. (2004) "Photography in the Age of Electronic Imaging," in L. Wells (ed.) *Photography: A Critical Introduction*, New York: Routledge, pp. 295–336.
Manovich, L. (1995) "The Paradoxes of Digital Photography," in H.V. Amelunxen, S. lgihaut and F. Rotzer (eds.) *Photography after Photography*, Munich: Verlag der Kunst, pp. 57–65.
Manovich, L. (2016) *Instagram and Contemporary Image*, http://manovich.net/index.php/projects/instagram-and-contemporary-image
Mirzoeff, N. (2015) *How to See the World*, London: Pelican.
Mitchell, W. J. (1992) *The Reconfigured Eye: Visual Truth in a Post-Photographic Era*, Cambridge, MA: MIT Press.
Müller-Pohle, A. (1985) "Information Strategies," trans. Jean Säfken, *European Photography 21* (6.1), http://equivalence.com/labor/lab_mp_wri_inf_e.shtml [accessed June 2, 2010].
Paglen, T. (2016) "Invisible Images (Your Pictures Are Looking at You)," *The New Inquiry*, http://thenewinquiry.com/essays/invisible-images-your-pictures-are-looking-at-you
Palmer, D. (2013) "Redundant Photographs: Cameras, Software and Human Obsolescence," in Rubinstein D., Golding J. and Fisher A. (eds.) *On the Verge of Photography: Imaging Beyond Representation*, Birmingham: ARTicle Press, pp. 49–67.
Palmer, D. (2017) *Photography and Collaboration: From Conceptual Art to Crowdsourcing*, London: Bloomsbury Academic.
Pirenne, R. and Streitberger, A. (eds.) (2014) *Heterogeneous Objects: Intermedia and Photography after Modernism*, Leuven: Leuven University Press..
Ritchin, F. (2009) *After Photography*, New York: W.W. Norton.
Ritchin, F. (2013) *Bending the Frame: Photojournalism, Documentary, and the Citizen*, New York: Aperture.
Rubinstein, D. (2009) "Towards Photographic Education," *Photographies*, 2 (2): pp. 135–142.
Solomon-Godeau, A. (1983) "The Armed Vision Disarmed: Radical Formalism from Weapon to Style," *Afterimage* 19: pp. 9–14.
Stallabrass, J. (1996) "Sixty Billion Sunsets," in J. Stallabrass (ed.), *Gargantua: Manufactured Mass Culture*, London: Verso, pp. 13–39.
Talbot, W. H. F. (1969 [1844]) *The Pencil of Nature*, New York: Da Capo Press.
Talbot, W. H. F. (1990 [1839]) "Some Account of the Art of Photogenic Drawing," in V. Goldberg (ed.) *Photography in Print: Writings from 1816 to the Present*, Albuquerque: University of New Mexico, pp. 36–48.
Umbrico, P. and Zach N. (2013) "A Conversation with Penelope Umbrico," *Lavalette*, October 28. www.lavalette.com/a-conversation-with-penelope-umbrico/[accessed July 7, 2015].
Wells, Liz (ed.) (2015) *Photography: A Critical Introduction*, 5th edition, London: Routledge.
Zappavigna, M. (2016) "Social Media Photography: Construing Subjectivity in Instagram Images," *Visual Communication* 15 (3): pp. 271–292

26

Out of language

Photographing as translating

Nancy Ann Roth

Those of us who first approached the work of Vilém Flusser (1920–1991) through *Towards a Philosophy of Photography* (Flusser 2000) may well have found it puzzling. Why did he so rarely refer to actual photographs? Why did his terminology seem so awkward outside the immediate framework in which it was introduced? Why did so few of us—whether photographers, critics, or teachers—absorb memorable phrases, such as "photography is the first technical image," or "the camera is a toy," or "to be free is to play against the apparatus" into our usual ways of thinking and speaking about photography? I found Flusser's terms and structures for *photography* difficult to remember and apply, although there was no such difficulty with his remarks on writing, especially those describing writing and photography as supporting fundamentally different ways of engaging with the world.

Years after that first encounter, with the publication of Andreas Ströhl's anthology of Flusser's *Writings* (Flusser 2002), the issues began to appear in a different light. The texts in *Writings* were selected to provide an overview of Flusser's thought. Within this much more comprehensive outline of a phenomenological approach to all of human communication, photography appeared to play a fairly small part. Eventually I became familiar with the books that expanded and situated the account of photography given in *Towards a Philosophy of Photography* (Flusser 2011a, 2011b, 2014a). Only then did Flusser begin to seem like a writer, rather than a philosopher or a media theorist. This was someone who created a world, or worlds, in language.

Flusser's voice is reliably that of a phenomenologist, someone committed to avoiding preconceptions, 'common sense' associations, or logical assumptions, and relying instead on his own direct observations. Such a writer must trust his reader to recognize something of his or her own experience in the account. Neither Flusser's choices of topic nor his way of locating his own contribution within a field follow the protocols of academic philosophy; nor does he show any particular interest in 'media' as it is widely understood in contemporary discourses, primarily as print and broadcast. In fact, he rarely mentions media at all. Rather, he defines his topic—uniquely, I think—as human communication, in whatever time, place, or form it may occur. In such a framework, it is almost inevitable that communication technologies will assume prominent roles. But, in approaching them as a phenomenologist, always asking about the relationship between them and a consciousness engaging them at any given moment, he opens a framework in which these technologies take on qualities, positions, and interests. He also sometimes speaks of communication technologies as materializations of beliefs or attitudes, ideas that have coalesced into specific material practices. Flusser, that is, effectively endows communication technologies with character and motivation. He envisions them pitted against one another. The most virulent and current such struggle is that between writing and an array of image-making technologies, photography being the first, the oldest of them. Writing, by this account, is committed to defeating images, or, more exactly, to defeating the intolerably woolly thinking and repetitive expression characteristic of people who rely on images to make the world comprehensible. Photography, in its turn, embodies a counter-frustration with writing, a longing to escape the slow, tedious complexity, the difficulty of grasping concepts by means of words lined up on a surface, the effort of acquiring the skill.

Like many writers, Flusser recreates something of the atmosphere of his own life in his books. In his case, it is a climate of anxiety and struggle, early and permanent exile from anything approaching 'home', a radical loss of family, linguistic community, and all hope for a 'normal' career in philosophy. What emerges as the antidote to loss and loneliness in this story is, again and again, invention, creativity, somehow rethinking, finding a new standpoint, a different relationship to the circumstances. The transformation of loss, isolation, despair into a perspective that admits possibilities, even advantages, something like 'fact to fiction', features both in his life and in his writing, always appearing as a movement, always beckoning readers to join in the same transition. Flusser's account of photography follows the same pattern: from a commitment to the philosophy of language over the first 30-plus years of his career, he finds a new standpoint with a vista broad enough to encompass both languages and images. From the earlier standpoint, photographs had appeared to resemble "traditional images" like drawings or paintings. From the new standpoint, the camera becomes a toy, the photograph a 'move' that can be made in either old or new games in an atmosphere of proliferating games. Each game has its own rules and goals—but, more to the point, each sustains crucial features of a given person's consciousness, his or her 'universe'. In short, photography is pivotal both to the story of communication, as Flusser told it, and to the story he lived, in which a language philosopher thinks his way into a future world by projecting contemporary technologies forward in time. Stuck as he was in a universe of writing, sometimes ill at ease with even very commonplace technology (he did not drive an automobile and, despite owning a word processor, never abandoned his manual typewriter), he himself had hardly any experience of this new world. Still, his rather speculative thinking abruptly attracted a readership, an audience. People wanted to listen.

Photography's critical role in Flusser's projected world rests on its having been the first game to require players to plug their eyes, fingers, and brains into a device that produces images automatically. Players, that is, necessarily surrender some measure of control. The rest of Flusser's discussion of photography, in fact his discussion of "technical images" as a whole, including film, video, sound reproduction, digital synthesis—flows logically and imaginatively from this one insight, namely that such devices bind and shape their users' cognitive functions. That makes them something new in history. He seems to have foreseen the spread of mobile devices, the swelling numbers of people completely absorbed in screens and ignoring their bodies, the quick feedback loops between manufacturers and users of devices, the tendency for young people to adapt quickly to technical change and for older people to struggle with it.

Flusser's core concern is whether someone whose consciousness is linked to a partially automated device, playing a game with rules to which other players are similarly committed, can be genuinely free—that is, whether it is still possible to create something new under the circumstances. It is a critical question, because such freedom, he contends, is a prerequisite for any life that can fairly be called 'human'. A truly human player is able to make the camera produce surprises, things the game designers did not anticipate. Flusser eventually came to believe that the game (or "program," a term he often substituted) has exhausted its inherent potential, that as long as it is used as its designers intend, it can only produce redundant information. He pinned his hopes for freedom on efforts to thwart the rules, subvert the design, 'translate' between games, or, best of all, invent a new game altogether.

Flusser's writing spans two continents, three decades, and four languages. He called his topic "communicology," the theory of communication, and it absorbed him all his life (Flusser 2003 [1996], 2009). In addition to books, he wrote reviews and columns, gave lectures and interviews, and delivered conference keynotes. Some of these are on tape in the Flusser archive in Berlin, and some have been transcribed (Flusser 2009). There is also a vast correspondence. Any one such text may have first been written in German, Portuguese, English, or French (in descending order of frequency), depending on many factors, but perhaps above all his own curiosity about what would happen to a given idea when it was translated. Garry Winogrand's famous claim that he photographed "in order to see what something would look like photographed" comes to mind, and in fact Flusser regularly described photography as a means of translating, specifically for translating concepts into images—but more on this below. Flusser, in any case, translated his own work almost obsessively throughout his career, back and forth from one language to another (he wrote for publication in all four) in an effort to, as he put it, "exhaust" its meaning. It is, therefore, not uncommon for one of Flusser's texts to exist in two or more versions in different languages. Conversely, there is no access to the whole of his writing—on photography or on anything else—in any one language.

Photography as such belongs to the later part of Flusser's work—that is, work done after 1972, when he left Brazil, where he had lived for more than 30 years, and returned to Europe. The changes that propelled the shift had been building up for a number of years beforehand, however. An autobiographical essay from 1969, entitled "In Search of Meaning" (Flusser 2002: 197–208), gives some indication of the changes that were underway. The essay tells of a complete loss of meaning in the wake of his flight from Prague in 1938 and, after a brief stay in England, his arrival as a refugee in Brazil in 1940. Shortly after arriving, he learned that the Nazis had murdered his entire family. Between bouts of the severe depression that followed (he admits to a time of persistent suicidal thoughts), he embarked on a series of attempts to find or, better, to generate meaning. He looked first to language, an urgent issue under the circumstances. It became the focus of his reading, writing, and thinking, as well as the subject of his first three books, *Língua e Realidade* (*Language and Reality*; 1963), *A História do Diabo* (*The History of the Devil*; 1965), and *Da Religiosidade: A Literatura e o Senso de Realidade* (*Of Religiosity: Literature and the Sense of Reality*; 1967). Different as they are, all three contend that language creates reality (Osthoff 2007). By 1969, Flusser was earning his living as a writer of Brazilian Portuguese, contributing cultural criticism to journals and newspapers. Based on a growing reputation—although still without academic credentials—he had become a university lecturer as well, often at odds with the academic administration but very popular with students. With the second of the three books written in Brazil, *The History of the Devil* (Flusser 2014b), Flusser had further established his 'signature' writing style, intercutting assertion and argumentation with flights of imagination. He had immersed himself for a time in music and had become something of a force in the administration of the São Paulo Biennale, the state-sponsored art exhibition that effectively represented Brazilian art both within and outside Brazil.

"In Search of Meaning" concludes, in any case, with some thoughts about the new direction his thought was taking at the time. For reasons he himself says he cannot pinpoint, his engagement with language had begun to expand, to encompass other kinds of communication. He was, as he wrote,

> looking for a way out into nonlanguage within the loops of the tissue of language ... The theory of communication implies the theory of decision and the theory of games. And the theory of games implies art in a new sense. This discovery was like a rupture of dams. Suddenly, I saw a whole new field of action extending before me: the field of critique and translation between games; the field of freedom.
>
> *(Flusser 2002: 205)*

There is no specific mention of photography. And yet the juxtaposition of game theory with communication theory, all in connection with images (in the reference to art) lies at the heart of the 'trilogy' of the 1980s that would project a new 'universe' in the future: *Toward a Philosophy of Photography* (1983; Flusser 2002), *Into the Universe of Technical Images* (1985; Flusser 2011b), and *Does Writing Have a Future?* (1987; Flusser 2011a). It was not any slow-burning fascination with either making or looking at photographs, then, that attracted him. In fact, there is scant evidence of any special engagement with any of the technologies he would later group under the term "technical images"—for example, photography, film, video, sound recording, or image synthesis. It was the idea of games that opened "a new field of action" for him, the idea of communication as a rule-bound exchange of information (Flusser 2009: 197–209). It led, in time, to the identification of photography as the turning point, the game that propelled all of us into the universe of technical images: Flusser had sought and found a way *out of language*.

Inasmuch as it drew on the idea of language-games, as introduced in Ludwig Wittgenstein's *Philosophical Investigations* (Wittgenstein 2001), Flusser's interest in games would not have been unusual in the late 1960s. But his drive to get beyond language singles him out, as does his embrace of Wittgenstein's further contention that the meaning of any proposition depends on its use. In 1969, Flusser was still a foreigner without academic portfolio in São Paulo. He did not have the comparative security of a regular academic post, but was obliged to appeal to the wide range of readers constituting the market for cultural commentary. In the newspapers and magazines that published his work, he would have seen an increase in space allocated to images and a corresponding decrease in that devoted to text, suggesting the climate of confrontation between the two that runs through his books from the mid-1980s on.

On the evidence of the quotation given above, in any case, the idea of a language as a game, presumably thinking of words as elements and sentences as "moves," led quickly to the idea of "translating between games." He also began to establish photography as a means of translating from language-games—games that play with concepts—into images. Games further offered a way of integrating his own translation practice into a comprehensive theory of communication. In *Toward a Philosophy of Photography*, in any case, he clearly identified photography as a game: "The camera is not a tool but a plaything," or "a photographer is not a worker but a player" (27), "Apparatuses are playthings that repeat the same movements over and over again. Programs are games that combine the same elements over and over again" (77).

Flusser defined a game as an exchange between people involving elements, or pieces, that can be moved about in meaningful ways according to rules. Chance and repetition often are critical factors. And, although I am not aware that he ever called attention to it, it may have been the idea of games that lent support to the idea of continually moving between established communicative frameworks such as languages or programs without establishing a permanent 'home' in any one of them. For games have limits. There is an outside, a point from which the scope and character of one game becomes perceptible in comparison with another. Flusser does not exactly argue for the wisdom or value of thinking in terms of games, and seems to switch to 'program' without appreciable shift in meaning: like Wittgenstein, he returned again and again to the same two examples of games, namely chess and language. Games provided a flexible designation for structures that make communication possible, in any case, establishing certain essential elements and patterns without restriction to any particular time, place, materials, or goal. Games can be very old or very new, have many rules or very few, and appeal to different players in vastly different ways. It is possible to be completely absorbed in a single game, or to chafe against its limits and long for a new one. Flusser maps his distinction between discourse and dialogue, his two basic kinds of communication, on to such choices. "Discourse" refers to exchanges governed by established rules, building a shared background or history among the players; "dialogue" refers to an exchange that arises from discourse, but that leaves the rules behind. Dialogue is the sole means that human beings have to create genuinely new information. It can occur between different aspects or areas of one consciousness (an example was Isaac Newton, with celestial mechanics firmly in memory, watching an apple fall), between two people, or between a human and an artificial memory—the familiar example of a book or painting or photograph sparking a new thought. But it can also happen between two people playing the same game. In the chapter entitled "To Create," in *Into the Universe of Technical Images*, Flusser gives the helpful example of two players at a chessboard, absorbed in an orderly exchange of information in accordance with time-honoured rules. The possibilities for such an exchange are not infinite, but they are very large, and both players are enjoying the game. The moment of dialogue begins at the moment they become aware that they are in a state of play neither has encountered before. No longer interested in who wins or loses, both come away with something new (Flusser 2011b: 100).

In 1988, Flusser was 67 years old and enjoying a degree of fame for the first time in his life. The stream of publishers' rejection letters that had accompanied him for most of his life had turned into a stream of invitations to speak and requests for interviews. He owed the change of fortune to *Für eine Philosophie der Photographie* (*Towards a Philosophy of Photography*; Flusser 2000), which had been published five years earlier by the Berlin-based press European Photography and which had sold beyond his or anyone else's wildest expectations. When an interviewer asked him for his thoughts about why, after 150 years, there was still so little theory about photography, he answered:

> I don't think I have developed a theory of photography at all, but have relied on Benjamin in my reflections. I have not actually been concerned with the phenomenon of photography, but with the gesture of photographing, which is made available to us by way of the apparatus. I have been interested in that strange interplay that occurs here between a person and the apparatus; an interplay for which we have no past example … the apparatus is a tool. We know just two relationships between people and tools from history: the pre-industrial, in which the tool was a function of the person, and the industrial, in which the person was a function of the machine. But with the photo apparatus comes a completely new relationship, in which person and apparatus mutually complete one another, forming an inextricable whole.
>
> *(Flusser 1996: 35)*

The value of this account rests on an understanding of two critical terms: "gesture" and "apparatus." The term "gesture" in particular, despite its apparently casual use here, refers to a very broad theoretical structure that occupied Flusser throughout his career. For him, gestures are the stuff of communication. Even the most abstract, apparently disembodied message passes between people by means that can be traced back to a "movement of the body, or of a tool attached to the body" (Flusser 2014b: 2).

At the point he was being interviewed here, Flusser had probably already written the essay, "The Gesture of Photographing" (Flusser 2014b: 72–85)—he wrote essays with the set title "The Gesture of …" at various points in his career. The essay is, in any case, Flusser's most detailed account of the state in which "person and apparatus mutually complete one another, forming an inextricable whole" (Flusser 1996: 35). The essay walks its reader patiently through the use of the phenomenological method, framing the topic, specifying the observer's standpoint, systematically rejecting assumptions and "common sense" associations that are likely to come to mind. The opening paragraphs resemble those of Barthes's *Camera Lucida* (Barthes 2000) in the sense that both authors are consciously employing a phenomenological method, and both consider it necessary to clarify the terms of the enquiry at the outset. Yet Barthes and Flusser are examining completely different objects. Barthes enumerates three positions from which photography can be directly observed: the photographer, the photographed, and the viewer of the resulting image. He aligns himself almost entirely with the third standpoint, that of the viewer, so that the object to be analysed becomes his relationship to extant photographs. In "The Gesture of Photographing," Flusser, too, lists three positions, but not the same ones. He describes the photographer, the photographed, and the observer—us—watching, or supposing ourselves to be watching, the *movements* of photographer and photographed. He aligns himself by turns with all three positions and rules Barthes's position—the viewer of the resulting image—out of the enquiry. Flusser is concerned here neither with "photography" nor with "photographs," but with photograph*ing*—not an object, but a movement. The movement starts when the photographer picks up the camera, forming the "inextricable whole," and ends with the decision to release the shutter. It does not include the actual click or the events that follow.

"The Gesture of Photographing" argues for a similarity, almost an identity, between photographing and philosophical reflection. Flusser compares his own working process to a photographer's. In fact, the essay contends that photographing—the active movement, positioning, decision-making—represents philosophy's first alternative to writing. This seems to imply the possibility of displacing or replacing writing, although there is nothing of the atmosphere of contention and struggle between writing and photography that permeates *Towards a Philosophy of Photography*.

It is characteristic of Flusser's writing, as Rodrigo Novaes has pointed out, to expand, to circle out from and eventually back to a particular position (Flusser 2014b: xviii). *Towards a Philosophy of Photography* is a case in point. It steps back from that positive comparison of photographing and writing as meaningful, productive movements and considers associated meaningful gestures, such as looking at photographs, being instructed by them, sustaining a pattern of feedback involving designers and manufacturers of photographic equipment, sellers of photographic products and services, producers of discourse involving forensic and scientific evidence, the work of journalists and artists. Still, the comparison of photography to writing that first appeared as a comparison of gestures never quite disappears.

It may seem obvious, for example, that photographs are images, but, as a phenomenologist examining a potential tool of philosophical thought, Flusser can hardly pass over it lightly. In fact some of his most memorable insights stem from reflections on the differences between reading alphabetic texts and "reading," that is, getting meaning from, images: very briefly, texts must be "decoded" in a fixed, one-directional order, and images cannot be. He gives a telling example of the difference in a passage identifying mathematical language as cognitively visual—like photographs. It is impossible, he writes, for mathematical equations to be integrated smoothly into the flow of a scientific text (Flusser 2011a: 24–25). A reader whose eyes are scanning across the lines and down a page of text will have to stop at the equation, then cognitively shift into a space where the direction of thinking can move equally well in either direction, from one side of the equation to the other. Something similar happens with illustrated texts. The "flow" of thought stops, the eye moves around the image, and usually moves back to the starting point.

This difference underpins two very different, in fact mutually incomprehensible, understandings of time, one logical, linear, and fixed, the other circular, repetitive, and variable. Flusser often describes visually grounded consciousness as "magical," in that it admits the possibility of events repeating themselves or reversing order. The same fundamental difference also forms the basis for the two pivotal points in Flusser's history of communication. The argument is that writing elicits and sustains logical thinking and a linear sense of time. Literate people perceive the past as a chain of events moving toward the present and into the future. He calls this form of consciousness "historical" and locates it between prehistoric, image-based, "magical" consciousness, and post-historical, visually structured, mathematically based consciousness. In keeping with his own firmly historical consciousness, he describes a dramatic story of confrontation and conflict, a chain of events with consequences. First, in pre-history, comes speech, which, Flusser contends, remains close to babble—chaotic, repetitive, ephemeral—until it is subjected to the discipline of writing. Then comes the invention of images, which can be preserved, but which eventually prove to be too vague to register complex evidence and specify obligations. The invention of writing about 5,000 years ago initiates a battle against the power of images. Alphabetic writing successfully and steadily represses images until the 19th century, when texts became so complex as to often be incomprehensible. That, he contends, triggered the invention of photography. The battle between images and texts continued, but writing now began to slowly lose, rather than gain ground. As he describes it, photography—with the other allied "technical images"—has already overcome the power of texts in most important ways.

Flusser registers his own position in this slow, unremitting drama at the end of *Does Writing Have a Future?* By the end of the book he has effectively abandoned hope that he himself could learn the new codes. To learn to think in images rather than in concepts, algorithms rather than sentences—HTML instead of natural language—was simply too much. He would have to start again, like a small child, and he feels sure that those already at ease in the new world would not be interested in teaching him. It is, effectively, another form of exile (Flusser 2011a: 157–161).

If we accept, perhaps heuristically, that images generally support a "magical" form of consciousness, at least in comparison with historical thought, we still need to understand how reading photographs is different from reading paintings or drawings. For it is a fixture of Flusser's thought that, unlike any image that preceded them, photographs are the products of that cognitive mesh called the apparatus. In *Towards a Philosophy of Photography*, he begins to describe the effects of the apparatus spiralling far beyond the immediate gesture of photographing. In fact, the essay examines something like the 'other side' of "The Gesture of Photographing" essay, taking up aspects of this technology that only become conscious when one is *not* actually photographing. It identifies the apparatus-like function of almost any human activity that requires coordinated communicative relationships among human beings and that resists efforts to question it, what it does, why it exists. Apparatuses include disciplines such as science or law or art, institutions such as museums or schools or committees or councils, even nations—perhaps especially nations. "What is the purpose of France?" (Flusser 2014a: 17). The text further touches on the way the photographic apparatus adapts to—or resists—the needs of other apparatuses.

"Apparatus" is the weight-bearing term of Flusser's philosophy of photography. It has a lot to do. Sometimes it seems to simply refer to a camera. Its more significant function, though, is to name the automated aspect of the "interplay," the "inextricable whole" described in the passage above. It is this binding of eyes and fingers, the effective channelling of thought that sets the camera apart from any communications technology that came before, initiating a process of cognitive automation. It is this that can, on the one hand, rob us of essential human freedoms. It can, on the other hand, if fingers and eyes are connected to a different consciousness, be the portal to a new "universe." When one such inextricable union of person and device is connected to many others, the apparatus develops into a vast, substantially automated mesh with enormous power to control people—not so much how they act as what they think—whether they think. Effectively, it controls hearts and minds.

The usage of the term "apparatus" almost inevitably recalls Althusser's famous essay "Ideology and Ideological State Apparatuses," (Althusser 1971 [1970]), and it seems possible that, in reusing the term, Flusser is at once acknowledging an old admiration of Marxism and explaining why he can no longer accept its premises. Like Althusser, Flusser uses "apparatus" to refer to a kind of connective tissue that binds subjects to institutions and institutions to one another, for the most part below the level of consciousness. Flusser's version is different inasmuch as the apparatus is literally a device, and its decisions are substantially automated. This makes human subjects' ideological convictions irrelevant or impossible. It also opens a different space of potential resistance—within consciousness. It is as if he is using two "languages" to describe the same phenomenon. Threaded into the Marxist talk of tools and labour and production are other words, such as information, decisions, probabilities, and play, concepts from game theory. At almost any given point, then, a reader has both sets of terms available, one for thinking of the camera as a tool for work and the other for thinking of it as a toy for play.

Flusser's term for those who sustain and are sustained by the apparatus is "functionary." Particularly in *Towards a Philosophy of Photography*, "functionary" is a negative term, describing someone who is effectively enslaved, without the possibility of acting independently and creatively. What is perhaps not clear at all times is that any one of us, in addition to whatever else he or she may be, is and must be a functionary. By now, the automation of decisions across the vast interlinked apparatuses is so far progressed as to make complete rejection unworkable —literally fatal. The choices we do have lie in developing an awareness of the apparatus, a sense for when it is exerting its claim on us and when the boundaries of that claim come into view, opportunities to exceed or disappoint or deflect expectations. We serve the apparatus most of the time just by, say, fulfilling a contract, showing up to work on time, paying the mortgage, being 'fashionable' as instructed in print or broadcast. But it goes further, to decisions that go against what you want or think is right, internal voices that say "you have to," that you "have no choice" or "it's your job." Flusser is insisting, I think, that we do have a choice. It may be a very subtle one, a shift in attitude, a decision not to accept the 'obvious', not necessarily to always choose the 'cheapest', the 'easiest', the 'safest' option, to recognize the values that are imposed automatically, and judge whether we share them or not. We must choose in awareness of consequences, no doubt—and yet we have a choice. It is possible, he contends, to adopt a new point of view, to rethink one's circumstances, to be surprised and to surprise others. The apparatus tends to disparage such thoughts as 'unrealistic', 'utopian', 'fantastic'. Flusser cautions repeatedly against certainty in general, but in particular against certainty of a clear distinction between fact and invention. Beyond the limits of various apparatuses that demand our conformity in more and more precise detail, in the gaps and malfunctions, lie our spaces of freedom.

In 1985, two years after the publication of *Towards a Philosophy of Photography*, Flusser's publisher invited him to write an introduction to *Herbarium*, a book of new photographs by Joan Fontcuberta (Flusser 1998: 113–116). These witty botanical fictions are now very well known, as is Fontcuberta himself. But Flusser's approach to them is not. In fact, the review represents a relatively unusual instance of Flusser following his own advice, applying the abstract concepts elaborated in his books to the criticism of specific images. The text starts with a question about the concept of "information": could the term mean the same thing in two disciplines as different from one another as biology and photography? Flusser makes a very concise argument—only about three pages long—that the *Herbarium* images successfully address viewers from a point outside or above both biology and photography, a point of view that had not existed in either discipline or anywhere else until now. In other words, the images are presenting new information. The text ends by answering "yes" to the opening question, suggesting that *Herbarium* could in fact shed light on questions surrounding the concept of information itself.

This introduction could well come as a surprise to Anglophone readers of Flusser's writing, for very little of his criticism of photographic books and exhibitions has been translated into English, and, in his theoretical texts, Flusser does not often analyse specific images. Perhaps to accommodate readers who would see his text in a book of photographs rather than a book of philosophy, Flusser reduced the use of his own, then newly minted and relatively unfamiliar, terminology in the review. He does not refer to an "apparatus" specifically. He calls biology and photography "discourses," although elsewhere he quite clearly refers to such rule-bound structures as "programs" or "games." He admires Fontcuberta for recognizing and ultimately breaking the rules of both. He goes on to mention a third discourse, "art," in passing, probably just to note its irrelevance to the discussion at hand. The designation "game" does not appear in this text. But it is clear that Flusser considers the maker of the *Herbarium* images to have successfully escaped the steady, subtle control of the relevant "apparatuses" and established a space for free invention. He has produced genuinely new information. Flusser does not overtly reject or discredit the role photographs usually take in the serious study of plants, nor does he at this point condemn 'straight' photographs' widely accepted relationship to an external 'reality'—that is, a reality external to consciousness. He rather recognizes someone who is aware of both and able to act in a way that does not conform to either. He recognizes someone who has, in other words, grasped conventional discourses as inventions, programs, or games, and found a way to "play" with them using a camera.

In the years following Flusser's death in an automobile accident in 1991, Andreas Müller-Pohle, Flusser's publisher, and the writer's widow, Edith Flusser, assembled a volume of his addresses, interviews, and reviews pertaining to photography. Entitled *Standpunkte: Texte zur Fotografie* (*Standpoints: Texts on Photography*), it contains 48 entries, dating from 1980 to 1991; among them is the introduction to Fontcuberta's *Herbarium* mentioned above (Flusser 1998). The texts vary enormously in length, focus, and level of what might be called playfulness. In one, for example, entitled "Kurzer Abriss Zweier Fototheorien"("Short Sketch of Two Theories of Photography"), a camera is submitted in evidence in a formal debate among angels about whether human beings actually exist or not. In the second sketch, a deep-sea squid, *Vampyrotheutis infernalis*, advocates the development of an undersea photography similar to the photography employed on the surface of the Earth. With such a tool, the squid says, we would be able to fix the light produced in our limbs and so record and communicate our ideas, hopes, and fears.

If any one idea lends these short essays an overall coherence, however, it is a far more serious one, namely a blanket objection to photographic criticism as practised in the mid-1980s. He argues that, because photographic criticism is almost always based on a fundamental misunderstanding of what photographs are and do, there is effectively no criticism of them at all. For, unlike traditional images such as painting or drawing, photography is inherently critical, conceptual, the product of scientific and technical thought. To actually criticize photographs, one must address their conceptual underpinnings. Critical thought must criticize itself. Arguing against the classical criteria for judging images, namely that they should be true, good, and beautiful, Flusser writes "It [photographing] is true inasmuch as science is true; good inasmuch as the camera functions well; and beautiful inasmuch as the media that distribute the photos allow them to model the viewer's experience" (103). The idea is stated in some detail in "Kriterien—Krise—Kritik" ("Criteria—Crisis—Criticism"; 100–109), but may be more readily grasped in reviews of specific photographs.

In "Nancy Burson: Chimären" ("Nancy Burson: Chimera"; 146–148), for example, Flusser, in keeping with his own advice, works back from specific images to underlying concepts. He discusses Burson's *First Beauty Composite* of 1982, a face blending features of five celebrated movie stars, as itself a critical response to the concept of 'perfect' feminine beauty. He goes on to 'read' other composites, such as *Lion/Lamb*, *Human/Chimpanzee*, or *Mankind* (a person who is 57 per cent oriental, 7 per cent black, and 36 per cent white) as a prognosis of genetic combinations synthesizing real animals—and people—that combine features once distinct. The images Burson "computes," as Flusser puts it, introduce something new, something that thereafter cannot be taken apart. Another photograph Flusser reviewed was Boyd Webb's *Trophy* of 1985. "Boyd Webb: vom Inzenieren" ("Boyd Webb: On Staging, 1989"; 173–174): "A naked man," he writes, "floats, weightless, in space and, with the gesture of Michelangelo's Creator, throws some globes acquired in an office supply store toward a simulated heavenly body, where they sink, as if into mud" (173). It is ridiculous, of course. And Flusser reads it as a reminder that it is ridiculous to accept any image of a cosmic "scene":

> All scenes magicians believe in, and all events historians believe in are staged. In these scenes, things are set into relationships with one another. And in the events things are fit into chains of causation. Only magicians and historians "forget" that we ourselves (people like Boyd Webb) have staged these relationships. This image is intended to remind us.
>
> *(Flusser 1998: 174)*

It should probably be noted that the examples mentioned here are art photographs, the framework for Flusser's engagement as a critic at the journal *European Photography*. Elsewhere in his writing he occasionally mentions news photographs or advertising photographs, not in the interests of any aesthetic judgement, but to support his contention that images show states of affairs that resist rational thinking, that effectively deflect attention from real engagement with events, with history. He seems to have had little interest, in any case, in so-called 'straight' photography, in scenes produced when something in the world has triggered the photographer–apparatus mesh to release the shutter.

If a writer develops a world in language, making a concerted effort to establish plausible premises and imagine the way they would play out, and if that world draws aspects of the writer's life experience into play, we may well be justified in calling the writing fiction. But we would then have tacitly accepted a distinction between fiction and 'factual' representation that Flusser was fundamentally unwilling to draw. Meaning, he thought, must be made. The foundations of, say, science, law, or history may be deeply convincing and durable, but all were made by human beings and can be neither absolute nor timeless.

Photographs, too, create reality. He recognizes the feature that sets photography apart from painting or drawing and describes it as effectively reversing the way an image becomes meaningful. The cause of a painting, he writes, lies in the painter's eyes, memory, and fingers. The cause of a photograph lies in the object photographed, in its effect on the mesh of photographer and apparatus. That makes photographs something different from any previous way of projecting meaning, but no less an invention. For Barthes, photographs insist that, "This has been"; for Flusser, they say, "This is possible."

Flusser's account of photography seems like a project in progress, incomplete, rich in digressions, sometimes apparently contradictory. One of the most important of the contradictions, for me, concerns teleology, the idea arguably expressed most fully at the beginning of *Into the Universe*, that the story of communication is moving toward one of two possible endpoints, either "heat death," a world without creativity, or a society creative beyond our current capacity to imagine. But Flusser also insists that "photographs dam up the flow of history" (Flusser 2014a: 126–131), that in the coming universe of technical images there will be no fixed temporal order, that the past could be rewritten in circles or random patterns or no patterns at all. If this is the case, why must we still be moving inexorably forward? Why could not the historical flow of events be pooling up now, provoking strange juxtapositions of old and new with no particular reason to think that new is better? And if writing really is losing its authority, if in time it will become, as he suggests, an esoteric skill, like blacksmithing or hieroglyphics, why does he describe a role for photographic criticism—necessarily *written* criticism—with such energy and precision? Why does the camera's very character seem to morph from one setting to the next? In *Towards a Philosophy of Photography*, the "apparatus" is chilly and fleshless, a forbidding chimera, constantly shifting shape and function. It can be an instrument of automated oppression, yet under the right circumstances a toy, an instrument of joyful creativity. The social function of photography is here deadening, there liberating. It is as if he has his own games, each coherent in itself, but subject to the instincts of an obsessed translator—"games" become "programs." "Apparatus" becomes "toy" or "plaything." He is not penetrating to a core truth about photography, but insisting on photography as a very particular way of being in the world, with its gaps and "moves," its resemblance to stalking prey, its use of its user.

In his recent book *The Philosophy of Perception: Phenomenology and Image Theory*, philosopher Lambert Wiesing raises the question of how a phenomenologist should write, that is, how experience can be shared without discrediting the reader's experience in any way. In his answer, he reintroduces a very old writing practice called *protreptikos* (Wiesing 2014: 60–63). Rather than trying to persuade a reader through arguments, a protreptic writer gives an account based on direct experience, describing the steps he took in getting to the conclusion. The reader then has the necessary information to follow the same path and arrive at his or her own conclusions. Flusser wrote many different kinds of text, from letters to fantastic tales, and "protreptic" would certainly not apply to all of them. But it is helpful to think at least of the books that outline his core ideas, especially the trilogy of the 1980s that is the focus here, as protreptic. The books issue their readers something like an invitation to follow his phenomenological lead in reflecting on their own consciousness as makers or viewers of images, especially photographs, and especially in contrast to writing. Flusser confirmed, for example, my own experience of a profound difference between people whose relationship to the world is mediated primarily by images and those who rely primarily on writing. I suspect that examples will readily occur to those readers who have taught writing-based subjects in higher art and design education. His insights into technologies as materializations of ideas—for example, of photography as the resolution of an old debate about whether the world makes an impression on us, or we make an impression on it (photography confirms that the answer is "both")—remain particularly memorable for me as well (Flusser 2014a: 72).

Flusser wrote his autobiography, entitled *Bodenlos* (Flusser 1992)—meaning 'without foundation' or 'ungrounded'—when he was leaving Brazil and returning to Europe (it was published much later). The move coincided with his conclusion that he would not be able to make a permanent home for himself in Brazil, despite having tried for years to do so. In fact, he would not be able to invent a home for himself at all in the sense of a permanent point of reference, a fixed ground. It would be the nomadic state itself, a state of transition between places and languages and frameworks, that would become permanent. The formal recognition of his own *Bodenlosigkeit* coincided in turn with his embrace of game theory, information theory, then photography, film, video, and computing. It turned a practice of restless translation between languages ("games," programmes, apparatuses) into something positive, creative, free. He turned exile itself into a condition that effectively demanded creativity (Flusser 2002: 104–109). I continue to find his account of photography unfinished, unsatisfying in some respects, but provocative, usually in the very same respects. It is threaded through an account, sober and fantastic by turns, of one man's shaping of his own reality. Because it is a written account, we, its readers, necessarily draw its meaning within whichever language-game it has been published, by way of literate, historical consciousness. We are left to determine whether photography, for us, holds as great a threat or promise as it did for him.

References

Unless otherwise noted translations from German are my own.

Althusser, L. (1971 [1970]) "Ideology and Ideological State Apparatuses (Notes Towards an Investigation)," in *Lenin and Philosophy and Other Essays*, trans. Ben Brewster, New York: Monthly Review, pp. 127–186.

Barthes, R. (2000) [1980] *Camera Lucida*, trans. Richard Howard, London: Vintage.

Flusser, V. (1992) *Bodenlos:einephilosophische Autobiographie*, Bensheim and Düsseldorf: Bollmann.

Flusser, V. (1996) "Interview with Gerhard Johann Lischka 19 March, 1988, in the Kunstmuseum, Bern, 34-40 in," *Zweigesprache: Interviews 1967–1991*, Gottingen: European Photography.

Flusser, V. (1998) *Standpunkte: Texte zur Fotografie*, ed. Andreas Müller-Pohle, Göttingen: European Photography.

Flusser, V. (2000) *Towards a Philosophy of Photography*, trans. Anthony Mathews, London: Reaktion. Originally published as *Für eine Philosophie der Fotografie*, Berlin: European Photography, 1983.

Flusser, V. (2002) *Writings*, ed. Andreas Ströhl, Minneapolis and London: University of Minnesota Press.

Flusser, V. (2003 [1996]) *Kommunikologie*, Mannheim: Bollmann.

Flusser, V. (2009) *Kommunikologie Weiter Denken: Die Bochumer Vorlesungen*, eds. Silvia Wagnermaier and Siegfried Zielinski, Frankfurt am Main: Fischer Taschenbuch. The book is a carefully annotated transcription of Flusser's last lecture series in 1991.

Flusser, V. (2011a) *Does Writing Have a Future?* Minneapolis: University of Minnesota Press.

Flusser, V. (2011b) *Into the Universe of Technical Images*, Minneapolis: University of Minnesota Press.

Flusser, V. (2014a) *Gestures*, Minneapolis: University of Minnesota Press.

Flusser, V. (2014b) *The History of the Devil*, trans. Rodrigo Maltez Novaes, Minneapolis: Univocal. Originally published as *A história do diabo*, São Paulo: Livraria Martins Editoria.

Osthoff, S. (2007) "Philosophizing in Translation: Vilém Flusser's Brazilian Writings of the 1960s," delivered at *re: place2007*: TheSecond International Conference on the Histories of Media, Art, Science, and Technology, available at http://pl02.donauuni.ac.at/jspui/bitstream/10002/444/1/Osthoff.pdf (accessed 8 June 2017).

Wiesing, L. (2014) *The Philosophy of Perception: Phenomenology and Image Theory*, London: Bloomsbury.

Wittgenstein, L. (2001 [1953]) *Philosophical Investigations*, trans. G.E.M. Anscombe,, Oxford: Blackwell.

27

Habitual photography

Time, rhythm, and temporalization in contemporary personal photography

Martin Hand and Ashley Scarlett

Introduction

In this chapter, we consider the ways in which developments in digitized personal photography alter our perceptions, understandings, and experiences of time. We explore several possible connections between the technical complexities of digital mediatization and the variety of practices that now incorporate some aspect of photography. We use the term 'habitual photography' simply, initially, to capture the observable pervasiveness of personal photography in time. Personal, family, or domestic photography has always been bound up with habit of course, in the sense that it has been embedded within habitual ways of seeing, representing, and interpreting the social world (Bourdieu 1990). These tacit knowledges of 'how to' are constituted through historically situated socio-material relations, shaping the possible range of photographic practice and interpretation. More recently, Chun (2016) has argued that 'new' media become embedded in our lives through habit, such that they quickly become elements of an "unreflective spontaneity," when "an action is so free that it anticipates and escapes the will or consciousness" (Chun 2016: 9). This reorientation of the habitual through complex forms of digital mediatization forms the context for our discussions of photographic technology and practice.

Accordingly, we use the term to refer to several aspects of how image production, viewing, and distribution seem to occur habitually through complex, networked, material, and semiotic systems. As contemporary personal photography, particularly via smartphone and social media, takes place (almost) all the time, it intervenes in the rhythms and routines of everyday life in ways that appear unprecedented. Indeed, the most tangible temporal shifts in popular photography are the sheer frequency and pace at which it takes place. This, in turn, has meant that some aspect of photography has become a conventional part of an increasing number of daily activities, altering *their* pace, sequence, and arguably their content. Although such photography often operates as an interface as much as an image-making practice, it often produces visual objects and traces that can be both extended (liked, linked) and reordered to produce endless configurations of the past in the present. In these ways, we go on to suggest that photography is not only 'ubiquitous' in space (Hand 2012) but 'habitual' in terms of the media and practices of temporal experience.

Throughout we emphasize how photography, its associated images, practices, and apparatuses should not be thought of as tangential to the temporal throes of everyday life, but have instead become increasingly central to how we perceive and experience time. Not only are our days frequently 'measured' by the production and consumption of photography, but, as a central means through which we engage with 'the digital', photography also serves as an interface through which the (otherwise imperceptible) times of digital mediation can be experienced. As a result, we argue that, as photography has become increasingly pivotal in shaping our sense of digitally mediated time, it has simultaneously become a tangible means through which to identify, analyze, and critique processes that are proving too fast, too small, and too expansive for people to grasp comprehensively.

The time and temporalization of photography

The potential of the photographic medium is first realized through the timed release of the camera's shutter, linking the medium inextricably to the delineation and punctuation of time. However, the nature of the relationship has provoked significant theoretical examination since the medium's inception. Here, we provide a brief review of selected conceptions of 'photographic time' to provide some grounds for considering points of continuity and novelty in digitization and networked imaging practices, framing photography as both a 'temporalizing device' and the outcome of 'temporal grounds'.

We can think of photography as a temporalizing device in terms of the camera's agency and the temporal nature of the visual markings it produces. In *The Pencil of Nature* (Talbot 1844), a pre-emptive meditation on the grounds of the photographic medium, Henry Fox Talbot identified photography's promise as a technology for record-keeping. Eschewing the typical "injuries of time and weather" (1844: 15), Talbot's camera "make[s] a picture of whatever *it sees*" (1844: 20; original emphasis), unconsciously recording (1844: 40) a durable imprint of "ultimate nature" (1844: 4), of that which has been. Talbot's earliest writings on photography already identify the medium's ability to intervene in the throes of historical recollection as it fixes an image of the present and problematizes linear accounts of present and past.

The camera's unparalleled capacity for exactitude led to much of Baudelaire's vehement critique of the medium. To pose for the camera, Baudelaire relayed, was to experience the 'time of photography'; the subject cannot help but anticipate the moment of capture, dreading its implications for how the present (as past) will be perceived in the future. To this end, the camera is essentially positioned as a 'temporalizing device'; its deployment does not necessarily intervene in the flows of time, but instead *articulates* an explicitly technical relation between time and its subject. For Baudelaire, the passing articulation of photographic time is captured and arrested through the production of a (representational) image, the "cold truth" of which condemns the moment to be potentially reproduced and re-experienced eternally (MacFarlane 2012: 11).

From another perspective, photography has been conceptualized as the iteration of the temporal conditions of its material production. Kracauer claimed that the camera's unprecedented ability to make an image of "time that passes without return" (Kracauer 1993: 424) misled viewers into believing that, "the photograph itself ... is a representation of time" (1993: 424). Rather, it is the spatiotemporal grounds of photographic production that have historically linked the medium to time. When the shutter is deployed, the photographic apparatus necessarily grasps "the spatial configuration of a moment" (1993: 431), transforming it into an image of its likeness. The means of photographic production therefore affix the resulting image to "the moment in time at which it came into existence" (1993: 428), as well as to the spatial continuum within which the camera was physically located. Here, the photograph as such is a matter of "natural necessity" (1993: 427); the grounds of the photographic medium are governed "according to economic laws of nature" (1993: 435) rather than determined by human intention or sociocultural objectives (1993: 428). Although meaning might be attributed to the image, this is not an *essential* component of the photograph. As time passes, "from year to year, the semiotic value [of the photograph] decreases" (1993: 429), until such time as the "image loses its symbolic power" (1993: 434) entirely. What remains at this point is only the 'nature' of the image—its literal appearance and continued connection to a spatiotemporal origin. Here, the time of photography is radically material. Although the photograph presents a still image of a spatial configuration in time, it is ultimately *time* (the time of exposure and the point in time when the image was captured) that constrains and structures the photographic image.

Whereas Kracauer traces a materialist analysis of photographic time such that it escapes the reaches of semantic interpretation, Barthes (1981) identifies the apparent link between time and absence in photography and articulates how the photographic 'aestheticization of time' can potentially affect a viewer. Grounded within the mechanics and presumed indexicality of the medium, Barthes claims that the essence of photography lies in its unequivocal assertion that the thing which it depicts "has been here" (1981: 77), that "it has been absolutely, irrefutably present, and yet already deferred" (1981: 77). By pairing this sense of the referent's contact with the image with a realization of deferred presence, Barthes locates 'absence' as a defining condition of the medium. The photograph materializes a presence that is absent and an absence that is present. While this absence is defined in part by the physical absence of the referent from its original (spatial) configuration (in and out of the image), it also points to the missing *time* of the referent—a past that can "never be repeated existentially," but that is paradoxically made present through the aid of the photographic frame (1981: 4). Although this might appear to reiterate Talbot and Baudelaire's folding of the past into the present, Barthes asserts that this is not the case, as "[t]he photograph does not call up the past ... The effect it produces upon me is not to restore what has been abolished (by time, by distance) but to attest that what I see has indeed existed" (1981: 82).

Although the photograph might not restore the past, for Barthes it instead becomes a punctuating expression *of* time as that which has been and is now abolished. Barthes' famous delineation of 'the punctum' rests upon the viewers sudden and injurious experience of the complex interplay of photographic temporalities as the image simultaneously aestheticizes the terms of presence, past, and loss. Responding in part to perceived shortcomings in Barthes' (1977: 44) earlier consideration of the nature of photography, Thierry de Duve (1978) outlines a fundamentally paradoxical account of the photograph's relation to time. He argues that photographs encompass contradictory modes of temporality simultaneously as they circulate as both image *in* time and *of* time. Looking specifically to the snapshot, he delineates how it is often upheld as an image that captures the 'fluency of time'. Plucked from the temporal flows of everyday life, the snapshot is an instantaneous photograph that exemplifies 'the event' by producing a 'petrified' image of it as it "freez[es] on stage the course of life that goes on outside" (1978: 113). Abstracted from reality, the image captures an impossible posture—a still that attests to the movement of life and time by exposing that which is absent, that moment and movement which are presumed to have preceded and followed the arresting of the image.

Although this formulation positions the snapshot as an image 'in' an aestheticization 'of' time, de Duve reminds the reader that, "reality is not made out of singular events; it is made out of the continuous happening of things ... where the photograph freezes the event in the form of an image, the problem is that is not where the event occurs" (de Duve 1978: 115).

As a result, just as the snapshot appears to capture time as such, it in fact functions to superficially *flatten* time, making the photograph appear "abrupt, aggressive, and artificial, however convinced we might be of its realistic accuracy" (1978: 116). In this sense, the snapshot appears simultaneously as an image participating in the flow of time while paradoxically representing a superficially fixed image of time. Though focusing on a particular genre of photography, de Duve claims that *all* photographs are defined by contradictory and competing modes of temporality.

It is in this latter sense of temporal multiplicity and contradiction that we turn to contemporary photography and time. As the temporal conditions of the social world and the material elements of photography change, the specific ways in which 'photography' remains both a product of time and a temporalizing medium inform what follows.

Temporal mediatization

The temporal conditions in which contemporary photography takes place are significantly, though not wholly, different from those in the 19th and 20th centuries. We want to emphasize two ways of thinking about how time and temporality have become 'deeply mediatized' (Couldry & Hepp 2017) in relation to photography. First, a general intensification of modern, technologically shaped temporalities of which contemporary photography is an increasingly significant 'resource'. The ways in which the digital 'camera' intervenes in reality and the subsequent lives of images are quite different and signal areas in which the temporal implications of photography are changing. Second, although digital photographs, like their analogue predecessors, continue to bear an indexical connection to their spatiotemporal point of origin, digital *images* also operate as performative indices of their 'time critical' mode of technical production (Ernst 2013a). Digital image objects indicate an intersectional layering of temporalities as they function both along the traditional lines of photographic time delineated above, while also materializing a comparatively new mode of photographic temporality hinging upon the execution of digital systems.

First, then, many scholars have argued that the acceleration of time associated with modernity (and concurrently photography) illuminated by Benjamin, Simmel, and others has been *intensified* over recent decades (e.g. Rosa 2013; Wajcman and Dodds 2017). At the broadest level, many of the temporal boundaries characterizing modern society have been reconfigured through extensive digital infrastructures and mobile devices that engender processes of networking, acceleration, and connectivity (cf. Hassan 2007; Sharma 2014; Wajcman 2015). This includes the institutional and infrastructural organization of time through interdependent media and information systems and the changing experience of time in relation to space (through the simultaneous, instantaneous, and almost limitless content of communication).

It has been argued that this turn toward 'synchronization' articulates how "the current prosthetization of consciousness, the systematic industrialization of the entirety of retentional devices, is an obstacle to the very individuation process of which consciousness consists" (Stiegler 2011: 4). But Stiegler's key insights here are that, in the context of "the technological rooting of all relation to time" (1998: 135), technical-temporal objects have the potential to be *both* homogenizing and singularizing. Indeed, it is crucial to stress that current developments do not lead to a standardization of temporal experience (e.g. speed), but rather that:

> We inhabit a social world characterized by the pluralization of temporalities, on the one hand, and the complexification of technological systems for the coordination of temporality, on the other.
>
> *(Couldry & Hepp 2017: 107)*

In this context, and in tandem with the rapid adoption of the densely interconnected smartphone, photography now figures as a *continually available resource* in the conduct of everyday life. As Gómez Cruz argues "[C]amera phones, as an 'always-in-sight' instrument, shapes a practice that becomes part of any other experience, on a daily basis" (Gómez Cruz 2016: 229). The resulting "continuous image-swapping and posting" is but one outcome of "deep mediatization," through which "the texture of everyday life is now largely woven out of media materials, the platforms of externalization and exchange" (Couldry & Hepp 2017: 153). Recently, there has been a multiplication of the kinds of media available, an increasingly complex set of relations between them, plus a greater significance of media-orientated ways of articulating the self 'in time'. While photography has always shaped our sense of time, we suggest that photographic visuality is becoming a more *essential* component of being in media-time.

In relation to our second concern, at the base of contemporary changes to the photographic medium appears to be a fundamental shift in the temporal actualization and orientation of digital media technologies compared with their mechanical predecessors. As Ernst (2013a) has articulated, the foundation of contemporary media technologies rests upon a mode of micro-temporality defined by the 'decisive moment': digital processes are 'time-critical' insofar as they emerge successfully *only* if the exact timing of signals and processes is maintained. Like a metronome, digital devices rely upon a central processing unit to synchronize circuits and 'read' (or clock) the high (1) and low (0) charge signals emitted by hardware. Digital processes take place, shift, and stop only as the clocking mechanism registers a modulated change of state from one interval of time to the next. Not only does this process take place at a rate that is clearly beyond human perception (Parisi 2015; Zielinski 2008), but, as a result, it also establishes a mode of temporality that is born of and particular to digital media devices and the programs that they execute. Unlike film, whose subject is arguably always bound up in some way with humans' perception of time (Ernst 2013a), digital technologies simultaneously rely upon and materialize a machine-specific mode of temporality that necessarily exists outside the field of human perception and cognition.

According to Ernst, "with the digitization (thus mathematization) of photographic matter into information, its temporal essence transforms as well: 'time no longer has physical meaning'" (Ernst 2013b: n.p.). This initial claim is grounded within the historically reified sense that the relation between photography and time hinges upon the image's indexical connection to reality and claim to truth. Countless scholars have argued that the digitization of the medium (chemical to signal) challenged the perceived connection between the photographic image and a seemingly 'causal' reality that lies beyond the camera lens. Whereas some spoke of the 'death of photography' (e.g. Batchen 1994; Mitchell 1994), others argued that digitization had merely denaturalized the privileged status accorded to the photograph's spatio-temporal origin, elevating iconicity as the primary grounds of the medium (Ernst 2013b). What is often overlooked in these debates is that photographs do not only capture a reality that appears external to the photographic apparatus; they also bear the trace of their mode of technical production. Although shaped and realized through an overarching socio-technical apparatus, the instantiated image object indexes the intersection between hardware, software, and code. Though imperceptible, digital processes of instantiation and corresponding indexicalization take place across the execution of every clocked interval, as the digital image is repeatedly sustained, or re-performed and re-established (with potentially different ends). Given the rate at which this occurs, the digital image arguably circulates as a performative index, which, when visualized, aestheticizes and forefronts the time-critical structure and micro-temporal operations of digital systems.

According to Hoelzl and Marie (2015), the performative realization of the digital photograph results in a kind of "photographic now" characterized as a "new kind of representation that is no image, no sign, only the optical illusion caused by the display of a continuous signal" (Hoelzl & Marie 2015: 58). Echoing Manovich (2001), it is their sense that what we see on screens looks like an 'image' as a matter of habit, where rapid scanning produces the illusion of a static image. Although digitally displayed images continue to be conceived of and treated as photographic objects, they argue that contemporary photography theory needs to be reorientated around the signal (rather than sign) as the generative grounds of visual capture and representation. The pixel is advanced as the smallest discernible 'unit' through which the signal is performed and perceived; it is the digital 'immediate in its immediacy' (Hansen 2015b).

Such a conception reveals the digital photograph's alignment with the increasingly 'predictive' orientation of time-critical media. According to Hansen (2015), there is currently a significant shift from deductive and responsive devices founded upon cybernetic feedback mechanisms, towards 'prehensive' modes of algorithmic mediation that (re)act preemptively. Rather than responding to and learning from tangible behavioral inputs, algorithmic systems are increasingly collecting, computing and triangulating vast and diverse sets of "big data" to "detect patterns, rhythms, and regularities" (Ernst 2013b: 55) that might enable the accurate prediction of future scenarios (Parisi 2013). Once determined, these imagined futures are folded back into the present and offered as a set of likely behaviors. As Evans (2016) has succinctly captured, "when the guesses are correct, machine learning operates invisibly, leaving you to experience life as an endless stream of tiny, satisfying surprises" (Evans 2016: 24). But it becomes increasingly difficult to distinguish between a future born out of accident, incident, and chaos, and one that computational systems are choreographing on our behalf (Hansen 2015c).

The predictive orientation of the digital can be recognized within the technical particulates of the digital image. This is evident when considered in relation to the algorithmic correction of photographic file compressions. Compression lowers storage size and improves processing speeds by deleting redundant data (in this case, pixel values). When the file is visualized, these gaps are filled through the application of corrective algorithms (such as the 'dithering' algorithm), which generally work by sampling data from surrounding pixels to calculate what pixel values might correctly recreate the missing bits. Compression correction algorithms are not saved as a part of the file, but are instead activated and applied during the miniscule interval during which the image is called into visual existence. It is for this reason that Ernst (2013b) has called compression "predictive coding," insofar as it identifies and preemptively articulates the future that immediately precedes human cognition.

Photography has always been conceived of as a 'temporalizing' technology, as it intervenes in and shapes our perception and understanding of time. Currently, the ubiquity of photographic technologies and practices results in the intensification of the medium's mediatization of time. This does not take place in a singular fashion, but occurs through a broad socio-technical apparatus comprising diverse times, rhythms, and temporalizing structures realized through practice.

Practices, rhythms, and routines

If we turn our attention to practices, we can consider how the multiple temporalities of digital photography are enacted and subjectively experienced. To speak of photography as a practice here means to think of it in the rather mundane sense of *doing*. This takes many forms, each involving complex relations between material and symbolic elements: bodies, knowledge, technologies, emotional states, ways of seeing, images, and so on (see Couldry 2012; Reckwitz 2002: 249). The precise ways in which these are brought together and 'arranged' in time and space, such that 'photography' is a recognizable mode of meaningful engagement, provides an entry point for thinking about what current practices of photography involve. At the level of practice, personal photography occurring through configurations of smartphones and social media is necessarily indicative of, and implicated within, the temporal changes identified above. Personal photography often takes place in "social media time" (Kaun and Stiernstedt 2014: 1165), facilitated by social media companies and digital networks that favor the 'continual update' (Chun 2016) and the ongoing maintenance of visual 'presence' simply to meet the obligations of *being social* (Couldry & Hepp 2017). In this sense, we can consider Chun's account of 'habitual media' as a sped-up process of machinic habituation:

> Through habits users become their machines: they stream, update, capture, upload, share, grind, link, verify, map, save, trash, and troll. Repetition breeds expertise, even as it breeds boredom.
>
> *(Chun 2016: 1)*

At this level of quotidian experience, contemporary photography is involved in the articulation of *iTime*: the "compressed, elastic time of people who are constantly plugged in" (Agger 2012: 8). Many people appear inescapably tied to *visual* habitual media that challenge existing temporal boundaries as they seek to meet the expectations of the temporality of networked relationships. This now includes myriad activities of photography that constitute the visuality of social media through their embeddedness within so many domains of practice. If having an "unmediated perception of subjective time has become almost impossible" (Rosa & Hassan 2014: 3), we can ask more precisely how the photographic elements of continual mediation figure in shaping temporal experience. For example, does the constant connectivity of smartphones and social media constitute an "eternal present that has no depth" (Agger 2013: 87), composed primarily of visual materials? This is a useful way of thinking about the 'incessant' visual communication of 'moments' (e.g. Snapchat). The platform-specific sharing practices of 'snapping', where photos are used to initiate a conversation composed through caption exchange, privilege the communication of 'backstage moments' rather than considered forms of self-presentation (Best 2016). We might initially ask whether habitual photography occurs in and for the sake of the here and now, recognizing that what counts as the here and now (so-called 'real time') is deeply mediatized such that it can only be perceived through the interface.

However, there may be a tendency to take a temporal category such as 'speed' or 'immediacy' for granted, but "speed only affects us if it requires an adjustment in our practice, and such a requirement is only registered at all if it appears within the matrix of practices in which we are engaged" (Couldry & Hepp 2017: 111). The ways in which different people *articulate* the tendencies and temporal affordances of digital media systems through photography are typically varied (Burstow 2016; Rose 2014). They are varied because they occur as elements within very different practices and broader arrangements—the easy and constant availability of digital 'cameras' means that they become embedded within and shape the daily rhythms and routines that constitute the diverse practices of everyday life. Some reproduce existing conventions of photographic practice (e.g. printing and framing school photographs, ordering them in a linear temporal narrative), where others disrupt and reconfigure practices (e.g. 'seeing' one's environment through the photographic interface, without making any images). To think through how the multiple temporalities of personal photography might be articulated and experienced, we consider two interrelated aspects. First, the ways in which doing photography is framed by expectations around image mobility within conditions of simultaneous networked communication. Second, how this in turn may change the rhythms of other practices with which photography is becoming entangled.

Contemporary photography is often discussed as being 'always on' and 'everywhere', in contrast to the laborious practices intimated earlier, but what does it mean in practice? Photos have always been circulated in time and space—they have complex and unpredictable socio-material lives over time—but this is now radicalized in terms of the pace and reach of circulation in social media, alongside the simultaneity of trajectories and duplication of the 'same' images. Images in social media morph and persist in and over time and across space in ways that seem unprecedented (Ritchin 2009, 2013). Between the smartphone and social media sites such as Flickr, and latterly Instagram, the still photographic image appears in immediate flow and flux as it is tagged and shifted into different contexts (Murray 2013). A collective shift in practice from preservation to communication has been observed as 'streaming' and 'sharing' become *default* 'scripts' in social/networking sites such as Facebook, Tumblr, and Instagram. This has led some to argue that amateur photography has become "a performative practice connected to presence, immediate communication and social networking, as opposed to the storing of memories for eternity" (Larsen & Sandbye 2014: xx). It has also been observed that this facilitates the *multiplication* of image temporalities as experienced:

> a photograph is not necessarily reduced to a mere depiction, and is increasingly inserted into a wider, more complex context, with different temporalities and elements (and this explains many of the current uses of photography in social media)
>
> *(Gómez Cruz 2016: 239)*

To think about this image mobility in any detail, we need to ask how such linkages occur and make sense to those doing photography (we need to remember that not everyone is). These commonly fall under the umbrella of 'networked photography' or 'digital sharing', involving "sharing photographs immediately after capture in real-time, mobile visual communication, using, for example, instant messaging (IM) tools or social media applications ... photo sharing has become a pervasive routine communicative act" (Lobinger 2016: 475). Practices of posting and circulating take many forms. Lobinger (2016) argues that photo sharing has become a pervasive and natural activity, suggesting the alignment of many temporalities enabling the ease of image production, circulation, and viewing to occur in ways that appear seamless to individuals. Far from being an uncritical practice, Lobinger (2016) shows how sharing involves quite different logics—such as posting images to generate talk, to communicate visually, and to engage in phatic communication—related to a range of expectations about the temporalities of communicative practices. Here we might also draw distinctions between those who primarily 'scroll' (e.g. through Instagram feeds), those who 'post' (creating temporal narratives of many kinds), and those who combine several material modes of distribution that include social media platforms. Moreover, the specific practices through which these are being articulated (self-presentation, political activism, fashion, travel) involve their own conventions and logics, not least those mediated by class, gender, ethnicity, and age (see Gómez Cruz & Lehmuskallio 2016).

Whereas personal or domestic photography has always been 'staged' and 'performed', there may be a significant shift here to do with the temporal obligations of immediate capture, simultaneous viewing (often collaboratively and 'in the moment'), posting, 'liking', and commenting within the social media platforms through which visual communication takes place. Although it seems, anecdotally, that people post images for the sake of the platform ('updating my feed'), these obligations are the outcome of the interdependencies of networked media, techniques of image production and distribution, and the visual practices that have become conventional, or even normative, around these. In other words, the 'digital time' of networks (sometimes experienced as 'demands') should be theorized in relation to the communicative practices that co-constitute them. Among some social groups there are precise cultural expectations around message response times; this now includes expectations around image posting, tagging, liking, and commenting.

As such, it would be misleading to understand this 'continuous image swapping and posting' as constituting a straightforwardly continual practice. Photography always takes place in the context of other practices, becoming a momentary element within them and vice versa. If we are to address the question of how new modes of image production, viewing, and distribution might alter the temporal rhythms of daily life, some consideration must also be given here to the temporal structure of other practices. Within the literature, a distinction is often made between the notions that specific practices are situated within socio-temporal order through their 'essential' temporal qualities and, alternatively, that it is the outcome of how multiple practices are patterned and organized as a whole (Shove et al. 2012). We suggest that the 'time(s) of photography' depends as much on its increasing entanglements with other practices in time and space (e.g. Instagram and eating), as it does on anything inherent in photography, whether that be the infrastructural components of the process or the material qualities and subsequent social life of images.

There are several ways in which the insertion of photography into other practices might alter their temporal structure. First, as social media orientated photography makes more social practices 'visible', there are an increasing number of opportunities for image selection—momentarily reflecting upon and deciding what could and should be visually recorded. Second, as there are now established cultural expectations about making oneself visually available, this can lead to the *reenactment* of the practice to produce the 'right' image. Although this is clearly the case in many performances of the selfie, it is not unusual for events that comprise many rhythmic elements (such as the presentation of a child's birthday cake, the blowing out of candles) to be temporally reordered in this way. Third, as social media photography arguably elevates the significance of text in contextualizing images, a novel element in contemporary photographic practice is the circulation of images *through* the mechanisms of following, liking, and commenting, such that "[R]andom 'likes' are interwoven into the rhythms of everyday life" (Hjorth & Hendry 2015: 1). In this way, the ongoing activities of scrolling, glancing, seeing, liking, and commenting become entangled with established practices and their temporal logics (think here of the teenager *needing* to scroll their image feed at dinner, thus configuring several domains of practice through doing 'photography'). Of course, these significant elements of contemporary photographic practice might interrupt, puncture, or maintain the temporal expectation and flow of what people are doing.

It is hard to imagine a practice that does not now involve photography. Much has been made of how this might question prior boundaries between specialized domains of photography (between journalist and amateur, for example), but less has been said about how the temporal structure and rhythm of those new hybrid practices take place and how this might shape the aesthetics of images. The use of Instagram in war reporting presents an illuminating case, where the complex media-making practices of soldiers are mimicked by smartphone-wielding reporters (Alper 2014). This is to do with manufacturing authenticity, partly through the simulation of the embedded temporal realities of conflict. Similar observations have been made about the perceived authenticity of selfies, where critical judgments are made about the *duration* of preparation and staging observable in an image that seeks to imitate rather than communicate a 'true self' (Lobinger & Brantner 2015). Some have argued that this quintessential social media image articulates precisely the anticipation of this future circulation and critique: its value is entirely generated by its future potential. In this way, it is anti-introspective; it is only concerned with fulfilling the requirements of social media and their audiences. From this perspective, the selfie is:

> A repeated gesture of externalization ... not for immediate consumption but for deferred value that will come from its circulation via social media. The selfie integrates the deferred possibility of online circulation perfectly into the present.
>
> *(Couldry & Hepp 2017: 160)*

It is important to note the differences in platforms here; people are often engaged in very different modes of self-presentation for different audiences on Facebook, Flickr, Instagram, and Twitter. But there are also different temporal 'intensities' (frequency, volume, pace) associated with the most commonly used social media through which photography is often articulated. Surveys of US college students find that, in terms of volume, Instagram and Snapchat are used the most and with the most intensity daily (Alhabash & Ma 2017). Beyond the current dominance of photo-based platforms, we need to consider the ways in which the temporal affordances of specific platforms are being 'meshed' with the temporal structures of college life and how they mutually shape one another to produce the contours of phenomenological experience. The significance of different visual 'feeds' in shaping the conduct of other practices (e.g. producing 'likes' while in the classroom) through their temporalities (which are the unfathomably complex outcome of interconnected systems and practices) of flow, interruption, and attention warrants more considered analysis.

The temporal structures of photographic practices are also related to the dynamics of place. Images that communicate one's location, emotions, and appearance are expected to be made and distributed to others in 'real time', often in the context of multiple preparations for other social practices (especially social events) and already implying the nature of viewing (Pargana Mota 2016). The capacity of social media platforms to 'calibrate flows of attention' in a specific environment relies on people's selection and circulation of images in the first instance (Carah & Dobson 2016). The current conjunction between locative technologies and camera-phone practices is producing new "visualities and socialities of place and placemaking" (Hjorth & Pink 2014: 40–57). Crucially, the geotagging features of Instagram and similar apps are becoming the default, folded into everyday routines and repetitions performed by the 'perpetually moving mobile media user'. Habitual photography then involves entanglements and reconfigurations of the temporal rhythms of apps, mobilities, places, and practices. This, in turn, generates vast amounts of visual data that can intentionally and unintentionally produce temporal reorderings.

Digital traces, imaging time

> A tool is, before anything else, memory: if this were not the case, it could never function as a reference of significance.
>
> *(Stiegler 1998: 254)*

As photographic visuality becomes a potentially continuous mode of engagement in practice, it produces visual and other digital traces of life being lived. Photography is just one aspect of the broader phenomenon of digital archiving, whereby almost all our activities are recorded. This is related to the dynamics of habitual photography: making, distributing, and viewing images is a key ingredient component of many social practices both *in* time and simultaneously constituting detailed digital traces *of* the temporality of those practices. Furthermore, these can be viewed later, making 'the past' always available in the present and, crucially, activities in the present be framed by expectations about their future traceability. Visual communicative practice in space (circulation) and in time (archiving) generates unintended consequences at different scales, often at odds with the anticipated effects of social actors. From this perspective, it might be said that:

> [V]iewing photographs is no longer about forging a tenuous connection to the past—or even about memory. It is, rather, an act of repeatedly reconstituting a presence that feels situated in time, resonating between a past and a future that suggest the now, while constantly deferring it. The picture is always present, even before it is fixed.
>
> *(Muellner 2014: 79)*

Similarly, Schwarz (2014) theorizes this fluidity in terms of how the database and algorithm materially intersect, arguing that digital memory objects such as photos 'lose their thing-like quality', as their presence and absence is not stabilized in space but rather is subject to continual reordering (see also Bowker 2005; Hand 2014).

This has significant implications. The always-accessible nature of habitual photography positions it within what has been called the "continuously networked present" (Hoskins 2012: 101). The production and distribution of visual objects as data become part of the unpredictable 'living archive' that can surprise individuals with personal data 'discovered' instantaneously and wholly out of context (e.g. as Facebook timelines are 'refreshed') that they had forgotten (Hoskins 2013: 388). In this sense, Schwarz (2014) argues that our relations with the past are being fundamentally redistributed through digitization. Photography plays a key role here in *habituating* individuals to a 'hyper connected' realm that both accumulates visual potential and makes them subject to the vulnerabilities of instant decay (Hoskins 2013). Individuals now habitually engage in highly affective yet unnoticed parts of the "media everyday" (Grusin 2010), such as the continual viewing of digital photos. Although it has been recognized for some time that the contemporary media environment encourages photographic immediacy of communication over a deliberative recording of the past (Van Dijck 2008), we now must consider the increased complexity of interconnected technologies of immediacy and simultaneity and how these might impact the individual perception of 'what is happening':

> But if multi-tasking is facilitated by intensified communication-at-a-distance, it has a profound impact on our sense of "the present". It imports the time-signals and time-related obligations from multiple activities into a *single time-flow*.
>
> *(Couldry & Hepp 2017: 111 [original emphasis])*

We suggest here that the 'moment' has thus become 'packed' with data from myriad sources requiring simultaneous responses. Sociologically, the resulting difficulty of temporal coordination and synchronization has been identified as a primary source of time-related pressure and anxiety within this context (Southerton 2009). While this is described above almost as a matter of 'keeping up' with the overarching and intervening rhythms of photo-sharing platforms, the micro-temporalities that are specific to digital systems also appear to be creeping up on us in ways that are establishing impossible temporal standards. For example, in the name of 'machine learning,' so-called 'micro-laborers' working within Amazon Mechanical Turk's 'image annotation' division are increasingly encouraged to 'reliably' attribute semantic tags to images at perpetually shrinking fractions of a second (Malevé 2017). Although driven in part by the micro-pay-per-service orientation of the platform, it is becoming evident that the expected rate of human behavior intensifies and demands a shift in the rhythms of practice once it is conflated with the impossible speeds at which algorithmically automated image recognition (machine vision) takes place. As in the heightened visual response time documented in avid gamers (Strobach et al. 2012), it is as though individuals are increasingly expected to embody and therefore act in conjunction with the micro-temporalities of the digital.

At stake in this case is not only how photography has become a habitual part of everyday life, but also how it functions in turn to habituate individuals to the time-critical operation and prehensive orientation of digital media technologies more broadly. Numerous scholars have detailed the intersection between photography, big data, and the mode of 'cognitive capitalism' that underscores much of contemporary digital culture (see Manovich 2013; Paldino et al. 2015; Pasquinelli 2008). The constitution of digital photographs as a constellation of hard and soft data points executed at micro-temporal rates means that networked practices of capturing, sharing, and communicating operate perceptibly at the level of social engagement while simultaneously driving subsidiary 'algorithmic economies' that rely upon the massive accumulation, valuation, and commodification of data (Terranova 2012). We are told that these economies are made technically possible because of the rates at which the digital takes place and, correspondingly, through the speeds at which computers can collect, collate, and algorithmically analyze unprecedented amounts of discretized information. Not only do the data gathered through photographic practices (from the level of pixels to the metadata added through tagging) generate capital within the 'attention economy', but they are also put to predictive ends, as the algorithmic analysis of digital photographs is in turn used to shape and place limits around future behaviors and ways of experiencing the world. This includes the predictive automation of tagging (Chelmis & Prasanna 2013), a process that again generates data input through the identification (and potential reification) of perceived connections, as well as the tailoring of media environments "based on predictions of value generation" (Carah & Dobson 2016: 3).

We have argued that the images and practices associated with digital photography function to make the otherwise imperceptible temporalities of digital processing available to the senses. In doing so, it is not simply that digital platforms are intervening in and affecting the rhythms of practice, but that they are in turn mediatizing and therefore reconstituting humans' experience of time (Stiegler 1998: 27). Through the facilitation of temporal habituation, digital photography might arguably be said to further obfuscate the ideological and market-derived interests that inform computational systems at their deepest levels. From this perspective, not only are we potentially unable to perceive and intervene in the predictive operation of contemporary digital technologies, but, through its habituation, we forget to question the times of digital mediation, simply appropriating them as our own with varying degrees of success.

This being said, it is important to recognize that there is another side to habit and the work of habituation. As Grosz (2013) argues, habit might not simply be:

> that which reduces the human to the order of the mechanical … but rather has a fundamentally creative capacity that produces the possibility of stability in a universe in which change is fundamental.
>
> *(2013: 219)*

From this perspective, to become habituated to media technologies also means to become immune, to a certain extent, to the spectacle of their novelties. In an increasingly privatized world, the habitual rhythms of photography also facilitate a temporal stabilization of community, opening opportunities for 'networked inhabitation' (Chun 2016). What is interesting is how the perceived 'immateriality' and 'ephemerality' of digitally grounded social practices and platforms may in fact be stabilized precisely through modes of temporal habituation. Furthermore, there is a sense in which this kind of habituated stabilization may counterintuitively be generating critical reflexivity, refusal, and rejection of the temporal structures that the digital appears to be mandating (Portwood-Stacer 2012). Recognizing the 'value' and 'loss' of time spent on social media platforms, as well as the technical incompatibility of human and digital time, many users are deactivating and disconnecting as a means of resisting the encroaching implications of 'iTime' (Agger 2012; Light & Cassidy 2014).

Conclusion

In writing about contemporary photography and time, we have necessarily provided a partial account of the many possible histories, connections, and trajectories involved. Our task has been to point toward some of the key issues and trajectories as new entanglements of photography and temporality emerge. We have tried to be attentive to where we think there are continuities—for example, in how efforts to theorize the photographic medium have often returned to similar themes, of temporal construction, mediation, reconstruction, and memory. But our central aim has been to advance the view that there are significant points of difference between earlier and contemporary modes of (personal) photography, and that these are to do with the quite transformative relational shifts in technology, temporality, and practice across society. We have employed the term 'habitual photography' to try and capture the extent to which some of these developments have become adopted. We have used this relatively loosely, but, in this short conclusion, we will reiterate the functions of habituation identified in this chapter and begin to question what is at stake when people become 'habituated to' these new conditions of visual temporalization.

First, the increased pace of image making and viewing is altering the nature of that visual engagement, from looking and glancing to 'scrolling'. For many, this means that "Photography is increasingly being used as an interface, without even involving an image" (Gómez Cruz 2016: 229). Second, the connections between image making/viewing and time are changing because photography, and its rhythm and sequence, has altered, both as a specific visual practice shaped by the dominant configuration of smartphone and social media platform, but crucially as an element within 'complexes of practice' that seem unprecedentedly varied. The entangled rhythms of individual smartphone use coupled with multiple platform dynamics, feeds, algorithms, and so on, are certainly more complex than can be grasped by individuals in the moment. But these entanglements are precisely where disjunctions arise between photography and established daily practices (these might be ethical, political, civil) and where recognition of, and critical self-reflection on, the pervasiveness of mediated visuality and the impossibilities of constructing the self outside of this may occur. It is a question not of 'speed', but of temporal multiplication and contradiction. Third, the multiple temporalities of social media platforms embedded in the contexts of everyday life change how events in time are perceived, how memory is constructed, assembled, and encountered through myriad digital traces. Revisiting is always (re)connecting, always a reconfiguration. The micro-temporal and increasingly predictive grounds of photographic technologies are playing a significant role here in reconstituting the subjective experience of time as it takes shape across these multiple levels of photographic practice. In this latter regard, to be habituated to digital photography is in some ways to be habituated to the temporal registers and orientations that ground its technological realization. Contemporary personal photography pivots troublingly around humans' potential to align and perform in conjunction with the micro-temporal operation of digital systems. However, habituating to the times of photography might also provide solid grounds through which to reflexively engage, critique and resist digital processes that have proven difficult to intervene in precisely because of their phenomenological evasiveness.

References

Agger, B. (2012) *Oversharing: Presentations of Self in the Internet Age*, New York: Routledge.

Agger, B. (2013) *Texting toward Utopia*, Boulder, CO: Paradigm.

Alhabash, S. & Ma, M. (2017) "A tale of four platforms: Motivations and uses of Facebook, Twitter, Instagram, and Snapchat among college students," *Social Media + Society*, 3 (1), pp. 1–13.

Alper, M. (2014) "War on Instagram: Framing conflict photojournalism with mobile photography apps," *New Media & Society*, 16 (8), pp. 1233–1248.

Barthes, R. (1977) "Rhetoric of the Image," in *Image/Music/Text*, trans. Stephen Heath, New York: Hill & Wang, pp. 32–51.

Barthes, R. (1981) *Camera Lucida: Reflections on Photography*, New York: Hill & Wang.

Batchen, G. (1994) "Phantasms: Digital imaging and the death of photography," *Aperture*, 136, pp. 46–51.

Best, C. (2016) "These snaps are made for talking: Visual communication and instant expression on snapchat," paper presented at *AoIR 2016: The 17th Annual Conference of the Association of Internet Researchers*. Berlin, Germany: AoIR. http://spir.aoir.org [accessed June 19, 2017].

Bourdieu, P. (1990) *Photography, A Middle-Brow Art*, Cambridge: Polity Press.

Bowker, G. (2005) *Memory Practices in the Sciences*, Cambridge, MA: MIT Press.

Burstow, S. (2016) "The carte de visite and domestic digital photography," *Photographies*, 9 (3), pp. 287–305.

Carah, N. & Dobson, A. (2016) "Algorithmic hotness: Young women's 'promotion' and 'reconnaissance' work via social media body images," *Social Media + Society*, 2 (4), pp. 1–10.

Chelmis, C. & Prasanna, V. (2013) "Social link prediction in online social tagging system," *ACM Transactions on Information System*, 31 (4), pp. 20–47.

Chun, W.H.K. (2016) *Habitual Media: Updating to Remain the Same*, Cambridge, MA: MIT Press.

Couldry, N. (2012) *Media, Society, World*, Cambridge: Polity Press.

Couldry, N. & Hepp, A. (2017) *The Mediated Construction of Reality*, Cambridge: Polity Press.

de Duve, T. (1978) "Time exposure and snapshot: The photograph as paradox," *October*, 5, pp. 113–125.

Ernst, W. (2013a) *Digital Memory and the Archive*, Minneapolis: University of Minnesota Press

Ernst, W. (2013b) "Translation of photographic archive into algorithmic time," *Either/And*. http://eitherand.org/archiving-line/translation-photographic-archive-algorithmic-time/

Evans, M.S. (2016) "Algorithms: The future that already happened," *Los Angeles Review of Books*, https://lareviewofbooks.org/article/algorithms-future-already-happened/

Gómez Cruz, E. (2016) "Photo-genic assemblages: Photography as a connective interface," in Gómez Cruz, E. & Lehmuskallio, A. (eds.) *Digital Photography and Everyday Life*, London: Routledge, pp. 228–242.

Gómez Cruz, E. & Lehmuskallio, A. (eds.) (2016) *Digital Photography and Everyday Life*, London: Routledge.

Grosz, E. (2013) "Habit today: Ravaisson, Bergson, Deleuze and us," *Body & Society*, 19 (2&3), pp. 217–239.

Grusin, R. (2010) *Premediation: Affect and Mediality after 9/11*, Basingstoke: Palgrave.
Hand, M. (2012) *Ubiquitous Photography*, Cambridge: Polity Press.
Hand, M. (2014) "Persistent traces, potential memories: Smartphones and the negotiation of visual, locative, and textual data in personal life," *Convergence*, 22 (3), pp. 269–286.
Hansen, M. (2015) *Feed-Forward: On the Future of Twenty-First Century Media*, Chicago: University of Chicago Press.
Hansen, M. (2015b) "Speculative protention, or, are 21st century media agents of futurity?" presentation delivered at Society for Cinema and Media Studies, Montreal, March 27, 2015. Retrieved from https://vimeo.com/127347772 [accessed July 6, 2017].
Hansen, M. (2015c) "Our predictive condition; or, prediction in the wild," in Grusin, R. (ed.) *The Nonhuman Turn*, Minneapolis: University of Minnesota Press, pp. 101–138.
Hassan, R. (2007) "Network time," in Hassan, R. & Purser, R.E. (eds.) *24/7: Time and Temporality in the Network Society*, Stanford, CA: Stanford University Press, pp. 37–61.
Hjorth, L. & Hendry, N. (2015) "A snapshot of social media: Camera phone practices," *SocialMedia + Society*, 1 (1), pp. 1–3.
Hjorth, L. & Pink, S. (2014) "New visualities and the digital wayfarer: Reconceptualizing camera phone photography and locative media," *Mobile Media & Communication*, 2 (1), pp.40–57.
Hoelzl, I. & Marie, R. (2015) *Softimage: Towards a New Theory of the Digital Image*, Bristol: Intellect.
Hoskins, A. (2012) "Digital network memory," in Erll, A. & Rigney, A. (eds.) *Mediation, Remediation and the Dynamics of Cultural Memory*, Berlin/Boston: DeGruyter, pp. 91–106.
Hoskins, A. (2013) "The end of decay time," *Memory Studies* 6 (4), pp. 387–389.
Kaun, A. & Stiernstedt, F. (2014) "Facebook time: Technological and institutional affordances for media memories," *New Media & Society*, 16 (7), pp. 1154–1168.
Kracauer, Z. (1993) "Photography," *Critical Inquiry*, 19 (3) pp. 421–436.
Larsen, J. & Sandbye, M. (eds.) (2014) *Digital Snaps*, New York: I.B. Tauris.
Light, B. & Cassidy, E. (2014) "Strategies for the suspension and prevention of connection: Rendering disconnection as socioeconomic lubricant with Facebook," *New Media & Society*, 16 (7), pp. 1169–1184.
Lobinger, K. (2016) "Photographs as things—photographs of things. A texto-material perspective on photo-sharing practices," *Information, Communication & Society*, 19 (4), pp. 475–488.
Lobinger, K. & Brantner, C. (2015) "In the eye of the beholder: Subjective views on the authenticity of selfies," *International Journal of Communication*, 9, pp. 1848–1860.
MacFarlane, D. (2012) "Waiting still: Baudelaire and the temporality of the photographic portrait," *History of Photography*, 36 (1), pp. 3–14.
Malevé, N. (2017) "Variation on a glance," paper presented at the *Ways of Machine Seeing* workshop, University of Cambridge and Anglia Ruskin University, Cambridge, UK, June 26–28, 2017.
Manovich, L. (2001) *New Language for New Media*, Cambridge, MA: MIT Press.
Manovich, L. (2013) *Software Takes Command*, New York: Bloomsbury.
Mitchell, W.J.T. (1994) *The Reconfigured Eye: Visual Truth in the Post-Photographic Era*, Cambridge, MA: MIT Press.
Muellner, N. (2014) "The New Interval," in Moschovi, A., McKay, C., & Plouviez, A. (eds.) *The Versatile Image*, Leuven: Leuven University Press, pp. 75–82.
Murray, S. (2013) "New media and vernacular photography: Revisiting Flickr" in Lister, M. (ed.) *The Photographic Image in Digital Culture*, 2nd edn, New York: Routledge,, pp.155–165182.
Paldino, S. et al. (2015) "Urban magnetism through the lens of geo-tagged photograph," *EPJ Data Science*, 4 (5), pp. 1–17.
Pargana Mota, S. (2016) "'Today I dressed like this': Selling clothes and playing for celebrity: self-presentation and consumption on Facebook" in Gómez Cruz, E. & Lehmuskallio, A. (eds.) *Digital Photography and Everyday Life*, London: Routledge, pp. 35–51.
Parisi, L. (2013) *Contagious Architecture: Computation, Aesthetics, and Space*, Cambridge, MA: MIT Press.
Parisi, L. (2015) "Instrumental Reason, Algorithmic Capitalism, and the Incomputable" in Pasquinelli, M. (ed.) *Alleys of Your Mind: Augmented Intelligence Traumas*, Lüneberg: Meson Press, pp. 125–138.
Pasquinelli, M. (2008) *Animal Spirits: A Bestiary of the Commons*, Rotterdam: NAi.
Portwood-Stacer, L. (2012) "Media refusal and conspicuous non-consumption: The performative and political dimensions of Facebook abstention," *New Media & Society*, 15 (7), pp. 1041–1057.

Reckwitz, A. (2002) "Toward a theory of social practices: A development in culturalist theorizing", *European Journal of Social Theory*, 5 (2), pp. 243–263.
Ritchin, F. (2009) *After Photography*, London: W. W. Norton.
Ritchin, F. (2013) *Bending the Frame: Photojournalism, Documentary, and the Citizen*, New York: Aperture.
Rosa, H. (2013) *Social Acceleration: A New Theory of Modernity*, New York: Columbia.
Rosa, H. & Hassan, R. (2014) "Editorial," *Time & Society*, 2 (1), pp. 3–5.
Rose, G. (2014) "How digital technologies do family snaps, only better," in Larsen, J. & Sandbye, M. (eds.) *Digital Snaps*, New York: I.B. Tauris, pp. 67–86.
Schwarz, O. (2014) "The past next door: Neighbourly relations with digital memory-artefacts," *Memory Studies*, 7 (1), pp. 7–21.
Sharma, S. (2014) *In the Meantime*, Durham, NC: Duke University Press.
Shove, E., Pantzar, M., & Watson, M. (2012) *The Dynamics of Social Practice*, London: Sage.
Southerton, D. (2009) "Re-ordering temporal rhythms," in Shove, E., Trentmann, F., & Wilk, R. (eds.) *Time, Consumption and Everyday Life*, Oxford, UK: Berg, pp. 56–73.
Stiegler, B. (1998) *Technics and Time 1: The Fault of Epimetheus*, trans. Richard Beardsworth & George Collins, Stanford: Stanford University Press.
Stiegler, B. (2011) *Technics and Time 3: Cinematic Time and the Question of Malaise*, trans. S. Barker, Stanford: Stanford University Press.
Strobach, T., Frensch, P.A., & Schubert, T. (2012) "Video game practice optimizes executive control skills in dual-task and task switching situations," *Acta Psychologica*, 140, pp. 13–24.
Talbot, H.F. (1844) *The Pencil of Nature*, London: Longman, Brown, Green & Longmans.
Terranova, T. (2012) "Attention, economy and the brain," *Culture Machine*, 13. Retrieved from www.culturemachine.net/index.php/cm/article/viewArticle/465
Van Dijck, J. (2008) "Digital photography: Communication, identity, memory," *Visual Communication*, 7 (1), pp. 57–76.
Wajcman, J. (2015) *Pressed for Time*, Chicago, IL: Chicago University Press.
Wajcman, J. & Dodds, N. (2017) *The Sociology of Speed*, Oxford: Oxford University Press.
Zielinski, F. (2008) *Deep Time of the Media: Toward an Archaeology of Hearing and Seeing by Technical Means*, Cambridge, MA: MIT Press.

Index